A Wesleyan-Holiness Theology

A
Wesleyan-Holiness Theology

J. Kenneth Grider

Foreword by Thomas C. Oden

Beacon Hill Press of Kansas City
Kansas City, Missouri

10   9   8   7   6   5   4   3   2   1

To my wife, Virginia,
who knew before I did that I should become a scholar
who has always encouraged me in my work
who has helped much on this volume
—and to my students

CONTENTS

ABOUT THE AUTHOR

J. Kenneth Grider brings to this magnum opus of his career a rich background of scholarly inquiry and achievement.

He holds the Ph.D. degree in theology from the University of Glasgow (Scotland); he did postdoctoral studies in theology and literature at Oxford University in England and theological studies at Claremont School of Theology. He holds the M.A. (1950) and M.Div. (1948, summa cum laude) from Drew University; the B.D. (1947) from Nazarene Theological Seminary; and the Th.B. (1944) and A.B. (1945) from Olivet Nazarene University.

Dr. Grider is one of the translators of the *New International Version* of the Bible. He is listed in many "Who's Who" publications, including *Who's Who in America* (43rd-46th biannual editions). He received his alma mater's Clergy Alumnus of the Year award in 1966 and Nazarene Theological Seminary's quinquennial Citation of Merit Award in 1985.

He is the author of *Gibraltars of the Faith* (1983); *Born Again and Growing* (1982); *Entire Sanctification: The Distinctive Doctrine of Wesleyanism* (1980); *Taller My Soul* (1965); and *Repentance unto Life* (1964), all published by Beacon Hill Press of Kansas City.

Dr. Grider has contributed to many reference works: "Commentary on Ezekiel" in *Beacon Bible Commentary* (Beacon Hill Press of Kansas City, 1966); "Commentary on Zechariah" in *Wesleyan Bible Commentary* (Baker Book House, 1969); and the general essay on the 16 prophetic books in *The Biblical Expositor* (Holman, 1960). His reference articles have also appeared in Eerdmans' revision of the *International Standard Bible Encyclopedia* (William B. Eerdmans Publishing Co., 1979—); *Baker's Dictionary of Theology* (Baker Book House, 1960) and its revision; and *Wycliffe Encyclopedia of the Bible* (Zondervan Publishing House, 1975). In addition, he is one of two associate editors of a major reference work, *Beacon Dictionary of Theology* (Beacon Hill Press of Kansas City, 1983), having also written 77 of its articles.

Dr. Grider has written chapters for numerous symposia and is the author of many series of adult Sunday School lessons. Over his byline have appeared dozens of poems in several magazines. Hundreds of his articles have appeared in such publications as *Christiani-*

ty Today, Pulpit, Decision, Action, and *The Wesleyan Theological Journal.*

He has lectured at several colleges and has presented papers at national and sectional meetings of learned societies in the areas of theology and ethics. He is a member of the American Theological Society and the Wesleyan Theological Society and a past member of various learned societies, including the American Academy of Religion.

Dr. Grider holds the distinction of having served as a faculty member at Nazarene Theological Seminary longer than any other professor—38 years. He currently serves as visiting professor of theology at Olivet Nazarene University, Kankakee, Ill.

WHAT OTHERS ARE SAYING

"I have learned from this book. I commend it to both clergy and lay readers as the most thorough systematic theology of the Holiness tradition since the work of H. Orton Wiley. It is significant for all Wesleyans."

> —THOMAS C. ODEN
> Henry Anson Buttz Professor of Theology and Ethics
> Drew University
> Author of *Systematic Theology* (3 vols.)

"A lucid enunciation of the underlying motifs of Wesleyan-holiness theology from a respected theologian in that tradition. The author's readiness to dialogue with other spiritual traditions in the church gives this book added ecumenical significance . . . merits serious consideration."

> —DONALD G. BLOESCH, Professor of Theology
> Dubuque Theological Seminary
> Past President, American Theological Society
> Author of *Essentials of Evangelical Theology* (2 vols.)

"Dr. Grider offers a panoramic view of current Wesleyan-holiness theology, both strengths and weaknesses, as diversity continues to overarch evangelical circles."

> —CARL F. H. HENRY
> Past President, American Theological Society
> and Evangelical Theological Society
> Author of *God, Revelation, and Authority* (6 vols.)

"Dr. Grider has done a good job of expounding Wesleyan holiness for those who are of that particular Christian persuasion."

> —MILLARD J. ERICKSON, Research Professor of Theology
> Southwestern Baptist Theological Seminary
> Past President of American Theological Society
> Author of *Christian Theology* (3 vols.)

"Prof. Grider has endowed us here with the rich and ripe fruits of a half century of scholarly reading, thinking, conversing, teaching, and writing. Reading this work, one constantly and unmistakably tastes, as it were, evangelical fidelity to Christ and to His

11

Church, seasoned by a consistent and persistent commitment to what might be called the conservative or classical tradition in the Wesleyan-Holiness Movement. Seasoning it as well is a consistent and persistent commitment to enabling that tradition to speak understandably and clearly to this era—both to non-Christians and to Christians in other traditions. Here, then, is a legacy that leaves those of us within the Wesleyan-holiness tradition deeply indebted and provides us generous resources for speaking faithfully to the present and the future."

> —PAUL MERRITT BASSETT, Professor of the History of Christianity
> Nazarene Theological Seminary
> Past President, Wesleyan Theological Society
> Former Editor, *Wesleyan Theological Journal*

"Dr. Grider has produced the fruit of his life's work with this comprehensive statement of Wesleyan-holiness theology. This study will be provocative for both Wesleyan-holiness theologians and the general Christian community."

> —THOMAS A. LANGFORD
> Provost, Duke University
> Author of *Doctrine and Theology in the Methodist Church*
> and *Practical Divinity: Theology in the Wesleyan Tradition*

FOREWORD

The Wesleyan-holiness tradition has had a more distinguished theological tradition than is usually recognized. A reputable series of excellent systematic theological works was produced by this tradition throughout the 19th century and into the early 20th century—especially those by Richard Watson, William Burt Pope, Thomas Summers, Randolph Sinks Foster, and John Miley. Samuel Gamertsfelder, A. M. Hills, and H. Orton Wiley are worthy of note.

Although the mid to late 20th century has not shone as brightly as previous generations of this tradition, the vitality of this tradition has been significantly rejuvenated by the appearance of Kenneth Grider's *Wesleyan-Holiness Theology*.

This study astutely accomplishes three objectives: it (1) gathers up the theological wisdom of past writers of the Wesleyan-holiness tradition, (2) places them wisely within the larger stream of classical Christian teaching, and (3) brings the Wesleyan-holiness tradition into a meaningful, cohesive, plausible contemporary systematic formulation.

While this book will undoubtedly be read chiefly by theological students in the Wesleyan-holiness tradition, it will also be read with profit by laypersons both within and without this tradition. It is well written, often engaging, always irenic, and at times even preachable. It is patient enough to explore the intricacies and complexities of theological reasoning within this tradition without being ostentatious or pedantic.

Dr. Grider's magnum opus covers all the main loci of systematic theology. One can get a broad grounding in the field by studying carefully this book alone.

The perspective from which each question is approached is a biblical realism that proceeds with a high view of scriptural authority without being trapped in wooden conceptions of the inspiration of the sacred text.

Grider takes the novice reader gently and gracefully into the perplexing arena of reflection on the revealed God and its relevance for us today. He builds his argument carefully by explaining approachably the nature and sources of theological reasoning, and theology's distinct service to the worshiping and proclaiming community. He then proceeds to work through thicket after thicket of difficult and challenging issues: the existence and nature of God, triune reasoning, creation, providence, theodicy, human existence under the claim of God, yet fallen into sin.

Grider's discussions of the person of Christ as truly divine, truly human, and the work of Christ on the Cross and in the Resurrection are among the most beautiful in the book. This part of the study will for years to come supply preachers of the Wesleyan-holiness tradition with classic arguments on who God the Son is and what He has done for us.

Grider's most distinct and ingenious contributions, however, focus on those themes and questions on which the Wesleyan-holiness tradition of preaching has concentrated its greatest energies and has had its most lasting effects, viz., soteriology and pneumatology. Here Grider shows himself to be a keen analyst of demanding issues and an able apologist for centrist Wesleyan-holiness positions on justification and sanctification.

The heart of this argument is embedded in the three chapters on the second work of grace—entire sanctification, Christ's Spirit baptism, and the patient correcting of misconceptions that have attached to various aspects of the Holiness tradition teaching of perfect love. The discussion is carried out in an irenic spirit with a depth of knowledge of the problematic edges of sanctification issues that is seldom seen.

The work then addresses a host of thorny problems and concerns relating to ecclesiology, sacramental life, the means of grace, and eschatology. Each step brings the reader closer to a plausible and internally consistent account of centrist Wesleyan-holiness teaching on these issues.

I have learned from this book. It stands deservedly alongside the works of Mildred Bangs Wynkoop, H. Ray Dunning, Richard Taylor, W. T. Purkiser, and William Greathouse in an estimable tradition of theological reasoning. I commend it to both clergy and lay readers as the most compehensive and thoroughgoing systematic theology in the Holiness tradition since the work of H. Orton Wiley.

—THOMAS C. ODEN

PREFACE

This is a systematic theology for the clergy and alert laypersons of the many Wesleyan-holiness denominations and parachurch groups and for United Methodism itself—as well as others who wish to know or need to know what the shape of Wesleyan-holiness theology is.

My hope is that the reader will be given joy in a better understanding of our faith and helped toward an authentic worship of God; will see that theology wears overalls and has legs long enough to touch the ground; will, in the reading, hear music once in a while and be gifted with motivation to Christ's servanthood; will hear me out, without at the outset dismissing the visions that seem new or different.

The views are supported basically from Scripture, with corroborative support from John Wesley and the Holiness Movement—and from the entire remembered past of the Church, especially the Eastern and Western fathers, for the water is often sweet when we drink it from near the pristinely apostolic fountain.

It prefers John Wesley (a father of the church birthed later on) to the Holiness Movement on many issues, as on the witness of the Spirit. It prefers the Holiness Movement to Mr. Wesley on two important matters: entire sanctification as instantaneous only and not also gradual (although sanctification as such *is* gradual); and on entire sanctification's being effected by Christ's baptism with the Holy Spirit, which was the unbroken teaching of the Eastern and Western church fathers, as is shown by Paul M. Bassett's careful research published in volume 2 of *Exploring Christian Holiness*. And I add many refinements of holiness understanding that it did not belong to the Holiness Movement to teach, such as the conviction that faith is durative; that the "old man" is not original sin; and that the Roman Catholics do not teach that entire sanctification is delayed until purgatory, as Wesley taught.

The theology here locates closest to that of H. Orton Wiley, my friend and mentor. But it is less philosophical and more biblical than his; it decides theological issues more readily and more vigorously than he did; and it argues with more care than he felt necessary for certain controverted classical teachings, such as

15

Christ's virgin birth and bodily resurrection. It locates precisely with Wiley—and now with H. Ray Dunning's *Grace, Faith, and Holiness*—on the governmental theory of the Atonement, with adaptations and revisions. It is similar to John Wesley, Adam Clarke, and A. M. Hills in arguing for a type of postmillennialism herein called realized millennialism, whereas Wiley was somewhat noncommittal on millennial theory. It advances the viewpoint that predestination is temporal only and does not have to do with eternal destiny, a view never before taken in a systematic theology as far as I know.

This theology locates closer to that of Donald Bloesch than to any other non-Wesleyan-holiness theologian. From such evangelical theologians as Carl F. H. Henry and Millard Erickson, authors of major recent systematic theologies, I have gained, but such is not very observable in these pages. My use of Bloesch is overt at times. At other times he is mentor to me when I do not say so, as in our need of Scripture plus the Holy Spirit, and in his appreciation for the whole span of church tradition, including Martin Luther and other Reformers, and Karl Barth and Peter Forsyth of our century. Bloesch's *Theology of Word and Spirit* (1992), the first of a projected seven-volume systematic theology, is typical of all of this.

The theologian I have most appreciated for some years is Thomas C. Oden, who intends not to be anything but unabashedly classical and evangelical in his three-volume *Systematic Theology* (1987, 1989, 1992), but who is distinctively Wesleyan as in his *Doctrinal Standards in the Wesleyan Tradition* of 1988. His *After Modernity . . . What?* of 1990, a revision and rewrite of his *Agenda for Theology* of 1978, is the strongest opposition I know of to all the modern revisions of classical theology, especially of our century, including the neoorthodox ones. Like Edwin Lewis, he himself earlier drank at the so-called fountains of modernity; but unlike Lewis, who did not come all the way back to classical evangelicalism, Oden did—proudly and persuasively. And Oden is indebted as I am to the late Albert C. Outler, a larger-than-life historical theologian, Wesley scholar and enthusiast, ecumenist, and mentor to Methodism.

ACKNOWLEDGMENTS

Here I must begin with a special thank-you to Prof. Thomas C. Oden of Drew University for this book's Foreword, which is more laudatory than my work deserves.

I also acknowledge my indebtedness to Richard S. Taylor, who read the manuscript carefully and made many suggestions that have been incorporated into it; to my colleague Paul M. Bassett, with whom I have discussed theology more than with anyone else; to William E. McCumber, who edited the whole of it with expertise and made it less unwieldy; to editors at Beacon Hill Press of Kansas City, including Jonathan Wright, who all helped by making corrections and running interference, requiring me to check many sources; to Craig Keen, Roger Hahn, Stephen Gunter, and Max Reams, who read parts of it and gave me valuable suggestions; to librarians William Miller and Mary Jean Johnson; to my student assistants John Wright, Scott Mapes, Steve Brown, and Richard Knox—the last of whom typed much of it, as did Clyde Leigh; and to Janis Srp, Jason Bullock, and James Isabell.

I also thank my distinguished teachers S. S. White, Carl Michaelson, Edwin Lewis, William Barclay, J. G. Riddell, S. L. Greenslade, Henry Chadwick, and Lord David Cecil.

Appreciation is also expressed to the following publishers for permission to reprint excerpts from my materials previously published by them: Christianity Today; Beacon Hill Press of Kansas City; William B. Eerdmans Publishing Company; Holt, Rinehart, and Winston; Baker Book House; and especially to Zondervan Publishing House, which consented to the republishing here of most of my chapter on the Trinity in *Contemporary Wesleyan Theology*. Also, thanks to the many publishers who have granted permission to quote herein from their publications.

1

What Theology Is

Theology is a discipline whose business is to help us reflect on our Christian faith in ways that make a difference in our lives.

When theology is meshed into life as it ought to be, it is not mere verbiage nor ivory-tower speculation. It is as practical as the next breath we are to breathe.

It bites into life, hitting home to people. It helps us make more or less articulate our experience of God's grace. It puts wonder into our worship—and into the work we do within that saved and saving community called the Church.

It serves to make preaching as difficult as it ought to be. Preaching is so difficult that Puritans in Britain often made a distinction in ministers. Some were the "dumb dogs," ordained to do caring, to conduct church services, and to administer the sacraments. Others, being better qualified in theology, were ordained to preach.

Instead of being divorced from the many practical aspects of the church's life, theology is the very commodity that makes all the practical matters practical: church administration, counseling, witnessing, Christian education, evangelism, church growth. It is our theology, our Christian beliefs, in their interrelatedness, in their intermixture, in their overlappings, in their essential and nonessential congruities, that constitute the basis for and the importance of all these so-called practical matters. This is why our century's most distinguished theologian, Karl Barth (1886-1968), called his 8,000-page, 12-volume systematic theology *Church Dogmatics*. It was to be and still is dogmatics, doctrine—for the church, for the church's use, for the church's work.

Theology announces not just what the Bible says but what it means. It announces what it means to sinner folk who, journey-

19

ing from their cities of anywhere to the city of somewhere, are surprised by 10,000 joys and plagued by 1,000 plights.

It puts God into the boundaries where situations rub together, as Paul Tillich (1886-1965) was given to see it; into the center of every situation (family, government, industry), as Dietrich Bonhoeffer (1906-45) described where Christ is; into the humdrum, the stinted fulfillments, the elations, the exigencies. It speaks of a God who can say what He says in those situations because He is God—who did what He did and does what He does. As God, He might not have needed to earn the right to say what He says. Yet He did earn that right by His deeds—in the Exodus, at Bethlehem, at Golgotha, at an emptied tomb.

Theology is a discipline that is for God and for people in these times when there is a fox, a hog, an elephant, and lot of other animals in many people; when an angel has people by the hand and Satan has them by the heart; when people grasp what is worthless and leave unexamined, even untouched, what is priceless; when the more they reach for what they like, the less they like what they reach for; when you sometimes wonder, as you read the morning newspaper, what new form of degeneracy people will next put their hearts to.

Theology admits the enormity of our sin, our colossal wickedness. It also heralds a Christ who more than undoes our rebellious acts and our Adamic racial detriment.

A man, half asleep and glad it was almost noon on Sunday morning, asked his wife, who sat on the pew next to him, "Is the sermon done?" She answered, "No, it's only been said. It is still to be done." As with sermons, so with theology. Thus many of us talk about doing theology.

Theology today seeks to do what it is in libraries and classrooms and out on the front lines where faith confronts unfaith in the world.

Theology helps us see the importance of particularized people—the people who stand tall, yes, but also the little people, the almost *unpeople* whom God made so many of. It helps us see that there are not simply so many souls around us but so many body-soul complexes—persons. It talks about redemption for the whole person, including the body, and about the resurrection of that body—instead of simply about redemption for the soul. It helps us be done with conglomerate conceptions of wall-to-wall humanity, with crowds in services instead of congregations. It helps us count humankind one person at a time.

It helps us be aware of other persons: to reach out and touch them lovingly, to wince at the knowledge of their wounds, to smart when we see beady tears hung on their cheeks. It helps us be sensitive to their bankruptcies, when they hang their harps on the willow trees, unable to sing the Lord's song because of the inviolable mystery of His ways.

It helps us as Christians to choose deliberately to be what we are. It helps us live on the spot, where we are, as Christ had the great facility to do. It helps us be not simply where the action is but where the discriminating action is. It helps us love God recklessly; to live not according to safety but according to sanctity; to enter into that self-naughting experience so necessary for the transfigured life, in which we do not think little of ourselves but in which we think of ourselves little.

Maybe it is "the queen of sciences" if you define *science* loosely. Certainly it is more than a modest pick of the hat among the disciplines, as Karl Barth told us. It is a discipline whose province overlaps just about all the others, so it is a little nosy.

Theology is not a hesitant discipline. It has its cautions, characteristic of all the disciplines: cautions of scholarship. It does not overstate its case. But it does state its case, and it does so with a highborn confidence, sometimes in tears, sometimes merrily. It does not wait to see what is being said in the other disciplines of the university before saying what it must say. It declares that Christ, founded in God and found to be in the flesh, God indeed and Man indeed, was "delivered over to death for our sins and was raised to life for our justification" (Rom. 4:25). Theology is persuaded, and this gives it pluck.

Theology will give us ballast in these times when events make some people question whether the center will hold; when many of us live toothless lives, as one of Jean-Paul Sartre's (1905-80) characters does, never biting into anything; when there is so much knowledge and so little wisdom; when the Ten Commandments are often thought of as the Ten Suggestions.

To people like the young lady who, in her exit interview with her college president, said, "I don't know what I was looking for when I came here, but I didn't find it," theology tells them what it is they are looking for and how to find it. They are looking for God, and they find Him through faith in Jesus Christ.

Theology can nudge us toward integrity, and that is no small help in these times when ethical pygmies are sometimes put into high places. It helps us know that God will hold things together and that He will hold the right things together.

Those who snipe at theology as obtuse and abstract, stultified and impractical, are talking about what it has sometimes been like when its pinnings have been to Platonism—to its metaphysical idealism, to its favoring conceptual reality in contrast to what it thinks of as the shadowy existence of particularized things. The snipers hardly seem to realize that theology in our century has taken some turns that have largely divorced it from the ethereal idealism of Platonism.

Some theology, earlier, did tend to produce preachers who, of all their fellows, were the deepest-down divingest, longest-down stayingest, nothing upbringingest. But that is not theology per se. That is elitist theology of a rationalist brand quite foreign to the kind that proclaim-it and live-it-out theologies of our century have shoved us toward.

Even as "beauty is what beauty does," so with theology: it is what it does. It is what it has impelled and now impels its embracers to be, yes, but also to do and to say.

Jesus said, "Not everyone who says to me, 'Lord, Lord,' will enter the kingdom of heaven, but only he who does the will of my Father who is in heaven" (Matt. 7:21). Similarly He said, "For I tell you that unless your righteousness surpasses that of the Pharisees and the teachers of the law, you will certainly not enter the kingdom of heaven" (5:20). This is congruous with James's insistence on concrete demonstrations of our faith by works (2:14-18), such as giving to the poor and looking after "orphans and widows" (1:27). This is the Bible's call to costly ethical implications of our faith, and theology recognizes its imperative.

Theology, functionally, because of the decent things and costly things it has inclined people to be and do and say, is many things that we can celebrate.

It is the converted Augustine (A.D. 354-430) confessing the greatness and the goodness of God, writing what was perhaps literature's first important autobiography: *Confessions*.

Theology is the monks under Cassiodorus (ca. 490-ca. 585) who copied Bible manuscripts until such tedious work, in poor lighting, caused them to lose their sight.

It is a young monk living the Christic life so well that his teacher, Alexander of Hales, had to say of him, "In Brother Bonaventure, Adam seems not to have sinned." It is Thomas Aquinas (ca. 1225-74) praying all night for illumination on a given issue of the faith.

Theology is a vibrant medieval saint who departs from churchly orthodoxy, whose body is mutilated, but whose right arm is left intact so that he can be a nice boy and write them that statement of conformity. But he will not write it. Not for his life will he write it. They build a huge fire with him tied to the top of it, and he meets his God singing one of the psalms.

Theology is John Huss (ca. 1369-1415) studiedly letting them burn him to death for his faith, with a special regret: that he had had so many exhilarating hours in small board meetings— with chess, that is. Too often he fasted and played!

It is a monk by the name of Martin in the 16th century who stood straight up before the Diet of Worms and announced to all those authorities, Emperor Charles and the others, "Here I stand, so help me God." That was one of our faith's moments of glory.

Theology is Bishops Latimer and Ridley standing in the flames on a street in Oxford (at a now-marked spot that I used to pass twice daily and never got used to), being burned to death for their faith, with the imprisoned Cranmer looking on from his nearby prison cell and Latimer saying, "Play the man, Master Ridley; we shall this day light such a candle by God's grace, in England, as I trust shall never be put out."[1]

Theology is John Bunyan's remaining in England's Bedford jail a second six years because he would not agree to refrain from preaching at meetings that were publicly called. Bunyan was in jail because the law of Anglican England, at that time, prohibited non-Anglican churchmen from preaching at meetings that were publicly announced. And Bunyan felt he had to announce his meetings openly. After six years he was freed. But again he held announced public meetings and was locked up for another six-

---

1. See George P. Fisher, *History of the Christian Church* (New York: Charles Scribner's Sons, 1920), 360.

year limit. Still again he was released, was caught at publicly announced preaching, and was locked up yet again—where he could and did preach to prisoners. But after a few months the law of the land was changed, and Bunyan was freed at age 44. The point here is that his beliefs, his theology, impelled him to do what was costly—and he wrote a little thing called *Pilgrim's Progress* while in the jail.

Theology is things connected with John Wesley (1703-91). It is his holding so loosely to material things. He came to have one of the highest incomes of his time in Britain, but he lived on the amount he had lived on earlier, when his income was meager. His principle was to earn all he could, save all he could, and give all he could. At the time of his death he requested that the money in his pockets and in a certain bureau be divided among four poor preachers. And he requested that no hearse be hired to carry his body to his grave but that instead six poor men be selected to do it and that each be paid an English pound for his labor. Theology is this Oxford fellow they dubbed a Methodist because of his disciplines, who rides those horses all over England, preaching regularly to working people at 5 A.M.—unless all the books are wrong, including his *Journal*, and it was instead at the more decent hour of 5 P.M.

Theology is pawnbroker William Booth (1829-1912) taking the Methodistic faith to London's streets and streetwalkers and sending forth bands of workers who are as terrible as an army with drums and slogans and generals who sit right next to God.

It is Princeton's Walter Lowrie (1868-1959) learning Dutch at the age of 65 and translating much of Søren Kierkegaard (1813-55) into English.

Theology is several things connected with Karl Barth. It is his refusal to preach from the so-called distinguished pulpits of the Chicago area during his only trip to America in 1962—and his preaching instead at Chicago's Cook County jail, deplored for its unlivable conditions. Similarly, it is his preaching God's *yes* in Christ to the prisoners in a Basel jail for many years, riding there by public transportation—and this, continuingly, even after his belated retirement from the university there. It is Mrs. Karl Barth's question to a theologian who had phoned the Barth home to learn if he could visit the distinguished professor. "Are you from the jail?" Mrs. Barth asked, as though anyone released from there might of course see him. It is Barth's writing so much for so long.

Barth shunned vain philosophizing as it belonged to the ancient Tertullian (ca. A.D. 160-ca. 220) to have the wisdom to do. He knew that it does not belong to us humans even to diagnose what our problems are, much less treat them. He knew that we are distanced from the "Wholly Other" to such extent that the seeking, speaking Father of our Lord Jesus Christ must burst into our world with a double disclosure—of what He is like and of what we are like. He knew full well that sinful humans could not discover God by their own discursive reasoning and that instead we are summoned persons—that we look with longing to the Father only after the Father draws us by the Holy Spirit to accept His yes-offer because of Christ.

Theology is Barth's going beyond the interests of his teachers, Wilhelm Herrmann and Adolph Harnack, who simply reconstructed what the Greco-Roman world was like and pretty much left the matter there. Barth was interested in historiography, to be sure, but only as the past throws light upon our own times. He was interested in what the Bible and early Christian theology have to say to Safinwil, the Swiss village where he was a pastor as a young man; and to his own Germany, soon well into the First World War. Not at first was he interested in these life-related matters, for he was at that time too close to the influence of his university teachers. But with the help of his friend Eduard Thurneysen, a pastor in a nearby village, he began to divorce himself from the rationalism and the historicism and the humanism of his university mentors. This divorcement was only enhanced when he found that several of his teachers had signed a statement supportive of Kaiser Wilhelm's war that was enmeshing the whole world.

Theology is Barth at the University of Bonn, being deposed in 1934 from his professorship because he would not say, "Heil Hitler," before his lectures. Instead he prayed.

Theology is a young pastor in America's Motor City, appalled by the depersonalizing of workers in the auto industry as our so-called Christian century was budding. He could have enjoyed the ease a comfortable and comforting pulpit would have yielded him. Schooled in the azure liberalism of the times, when Edens were thought to be just about everywhere, when Walter Rauschenbusch (1861-1918) was saying in 1907 and 1912 books that even with "all our slothfulness" that generation came closer to the ideals Jesus set for human life than any previous generation had, Reinhold Niebuhr (1892-1971) junked the man-is-a-god-writ-small tune he had piped to and disturbed us as a Jeremiah might have because of how difficult it was to be moral in our actions when we were parties to such an immoral society. Theology was concrete, for Niebuhr, because it was interested in workers and their welfare.

It was also concrete because it was interested in our anxieties. It is true that Niebuhr did not want people to resolve their anxieties—their tensions due to the realization that a person is both free, with all sorts of possibilities, and limited, because of the built-in ways in which one is unavoidably finite. He felt that any resolving of the anxieties is unfortunate, since to resolve them, one must artificially disown either one's freedom or one's finitude. If one disowns freedom, owning only finitude, one becomes a sensually dictated person, enjoying "mutable goods" that a life of alcoholism might yield. One who disowns finitude, affirming only freedom, that is, possibility, becomes filled with pride—pride of knowledge or of power or of virtue (ethical) or of spiritual rectitude (pharisaism, the ultimate sin).

This is not idealistic, ethereal theologizing. It is not armchair theologizing in which the well-composed theorist unravels the labyrinthine, innate ideas that supposedly reside in the mind as we come into the world. A really good idealist, after the order of Plato himself, would understand that these innate ideas are located in the mind as we come into the world. This, in great part because we existed previous to this life and brought into this existence, for example, ways of relating one thing to another—which we knew how to do in our previous existence. Niebuhr is informed not by Platonism but by Søren Kierkegaard, the existentially interested mid-19th-century Dutch theologian. Being so mentored, he is interested in our lived experience, in our existence situation. This real existence of ours, with its psychological problems, its anxieties, is concrete—real, close-at-hand, verifiable in the way that data in the field of physics is.

Theology is Dietrich Bonhoeffer, 39 and advanced in academia, not yet wedded to his beloved, sitting alone in one of Hitler's prisons in Berlin, physically unable to lift food to his mouth, asking heaven's forgiveness for hoping that Allied bombs, whose de-

scent and impacts he could hear, would not strike where he sat—
but elsewhere, where their pathos would belong to others. Theology is Bonhoeffer's earlier decision to return to his fatherland to
help, when an antichrist figure whose Christian name was Adolf
had risen to power. It is the studied decision he had finally made
to participate in the plot to kill the führer and thereby extirpate
the cancer that had spread throughout the land and far beyond it.
Theology is his traumatic decision to disciple Jesus Christ in that
kind of way. Finally, it is the theologian dangling from a hang-
man's noose on April 9, 1945, just days before the Second World
War ended in Europe.

Theology, in all the centuries, as it has moored close to the
area of its birthright, has been useful. It has impelled people to be
fairly decent and to do and say decent and costly things, in implementing Christian faith in God's world.

The intent here is to say, on what theology is, that it wears
overalls, and that it has legs long enough to reach all the way to
the ground.

We need now to consider what the nature of theology is, par-
ticularly as we of the Wesleyan-holiness vision reflect upon our
Christian faith—our grandfather being the gargantuan Mr. John
Wesley and our parents the Holiness Movement.

2

The Nature of Theology

Wesleyan-holiness theology, by its very nature, has (1) an experiential interest, (2) an existential element, (3) a large-scoped biblical character, (4) a dynamic quality, (5) a catholicity, (6) a special interest in human freedom, and (7) a homing instinct for the moral.

Its Experiential Interest

John Wesley's theology was intensely experiential, born of the Aldersgate Street experience by which his heart was "strangely warmed." He started the Methodist societies to promote in others the warmed heart—and the kind of Christian life that is its fitting outflow.

At a time when experiential faith was at its lowest ebb in England, Wesley became the most strategic catalyst in a revival that contributed more to social and political freedom than revolution did to France.[1]

Wesley's theology had four main sources, one of them experiential. Important to his theology were the Bible, reason, and tradition. But distinctively, and in some ways dangerously, he stressed the importance of experience as a source for one's theology. George Croft Cell credits Wesley with a theology of personal experience.[2] Harald Lindström says, "In its general structure, Wesley's view of Christianity has been described as a theology of experience: his affirmation of Christian experience is considered his

---

1. J. Wesley Bready, *This Freedom Whence?* (New York: American Tract Society, 1942), 340-41.
2. George Croft Cell, *A Rediscovery of Wesley* (New York: Henry Holt and Co., 1935), 731. See also Robert W. Burtner and Robert E. Chiles, eds., *A Compend of Wesley's Theology* (Nashville: Abingdon Press, 1954), 17.

main characteristic."³ As a "zealous proclaimer of individual, experiential religion,"⁴ Wesley tended at times to give precedence to experience over Scripture, although he states at other times that Scripture has primary authority. Wilbur Mullen has some basis in Wesley's writings for saying that "in practice he judged the validity of biblical and religious claims by experience, not experience by dogma."⁵ In this vein John M. Moore says, "John Wesley received an experience that made him the greatest moral, social, and religious force of his century. . . . Aldersgate Street led out into the fields where men lived, and he took the road and never grew weary of it."⁶

A special aspect of Wesley's emphasis on religious experience is his teaching on the witness of the Spirit. There is a direct witness in which the Holy Spirit inwardly assures us of our acceptance with God in justification and of our entire sanctification; later, and indirectly, the Holy Spirit witnesses to us of such matters by reminding us that the fruits of justification or of entire sanctification are evident in our lives.

Wesley was wise in stressing the importance of Christian experience. The Apostles' Creed does not read, "I believe that," but "I believe in God the Father," etc. Like the early Christians, Wesleyans seek to foster not simply knowledge about God but *the* knowledge of God, including reverence for and obedience to Him.

While the emphasis on experience is proper, if not guarded it can occasion problems. A person in this tradition might believe that a work of grace has been lost because the direct witness of the Spirit to it is at low ebb. The experience of being inwardly assured by the Spirit ebbs and flows, somewhat according to outward circumstances in one's life. Often, a serious physical or psychological illness produces a feeling of depression, at which time we might feel that God has departed from us and does not hear our cries for help. Intense physical pain, especially when it persists, can also produce in a Christian this feeling that God has de-

---

3. Harald Lindström, *Wesley and Sanctification* (Stockholm: Nga bokforlags aktiebolaget, 1946), 2.

4. Wilbur H. Mullen, "John Wesley and Liberal Religion," *Religion in Life* (Autumn 1966), 561.

5. Ibid.

6. John M. Moore, *Methodism in Belief and Action* (New York: Abingdon-Cokesbury Press, 1946), 32.

parted—that one is not God's child after all. Actually, if we have not willfully disobeyed God, He has not cast us off. If we have not sinned willfully, we are still sanctified wholly—assuming that God had earlier granted us this cleansing and empowering grace.

Stressing experience can be hazardous when we concentrate upon ourselves instead of focusing on the objective matters of our faith—God himself, the historic deeds done for us at Bethlehem and at Golgotha, Scripture as the written revelation of God, and our holy Christian tradition, in which we learn about God's faithfulness to His people and the responsive faithfulness of our Christian forebears. Stress on experience must not lead us to deprecate Scripture and Christian tradition, as do modernists.

Its Existential Interest

In distinction from idealism and positivism, Wesleyan-holiness theology is interested in the existing human situation. It is interested in life situations of individual persons. It is interested, therefore, in truth as a way of life lived according to God's will; in love as agapeic, disinterested, caring acts done by one human being on behalf of another; in goodness as consisting of acts that produce a fulfilling life in ourselves and others.

A theology that is properly existential in its interest affirms the reality of both good and evil. Not believing that reasons for anxiety can always be produced, it is content to live with what is rationally muddy. It is content to let God change our anxiety-producing situations or help us live victoriously in the midst of such situations.

Its Wide-Scoped Biblical Interest

Being biblical is important to Wesleyan-holiness theology, as it is for evangelical theologies of varying kinds. Wesleyan-holiness theology is broadly biblical: it intends to be biblical, not merely according to this or that specific scripture passage, but according to the whole tenor of Scripture on each subject explored.

Wesleyan-holiness theology is interested in the Bible's plain and literal sense, understood in light of Scripture's bottom-line teachings, and in light of its meaning for us after allowances are made for differences between those times and ours. Scripture tells us, for example, that our religion is invalid if we do not help the poor right on the spot. We realize that times are different now.

Our taxes and gifts provide for the administration of help to the needy through government agencies and charitable organizations. We think this is an improvement on giving to beggars on the street as was done in century one, for the needy are not then demeaned by public begging.

Slavery is another example. We do some transposing in what the New Testament's teaching on that matter means to us. In New Testament times, slavery was more political than racial, and it was often temporary—not for a person's whole life. Also, some New Testament passages condone that type of slavery; in other places its teachings are ruinous to slavery. One such is Gal. 3:28, where Paul says that the bond and free are all one in Christ. John Wesley himself considered all the scriptural data and opposed slavery vigorously; his very last letter was addressed to Wilberforce, encouraging his opposition to slavery in Britain.

Likewise in America the Wesleyan-Holiness Movement was in the vanguard of opposition to slavery. In 1843 the Wesleyan Methodist church was founded, partly to emphasize the doctrine and experience of entire sanctification, but mostly to promote the abolition of slavery.

The Congregational-Presbyterian wing of America's Holiness Movement also stood for abolitionism. In 1835 Presbyterian Asa Mahan (1800-1889) became president of Oberlin College in Ohio, and Presbyterian-turned-Congregationalist Charles G. Finney (1792-1875) its first systematic theologian. Oberlin was founded as an abolitionist school that admitted black students, harbored runaway slaves, and supported state legislation to make harboring them legal.

The American Holiness Movement, in both its wings, interpreted Scripture in a wide-scoped way and thus opposed the slavery then practiced in America.

Numerous Scripture passages can be adduced by proslavery advocates. The New Testament does exhort Christian slaves to be good slaves and Christian masters to be good masters. The apostles were not revolutionaries but worked within social structures of the time. At the same time, they taught basic principles that would one day be seen, as by Wesley and the American Holiness Movement, as fundamentally opposed to slavery.

The same is true concerning the place of women. Specific passages are cited by fundamentalist evangelicals that suggest that women are not nearly the equals of men (e.g., 1 Cor. 11:3 ff.). Women are to keep silent in church services (14:34-36), they are to obey their husbands (Eph. 5:22), and so forth. Again, this is because the apostles were willing to work within society as it was then structured, until it could be changed in basic ways. Basing their action on apostolic teaching, the Wesleyan-holiness people were the first to ordain women. Antoinette Brown, an Oberlin graduate, was ordained in 1853 by Wesleyan Methodist church cofounder Luther Lee, who used Gal. 3:28 as his text on the occasion. Lee argued, in part, that women are supposed to preach— that whereas Paul exhorts them to be silent in 1 Cor. 14:34-36, in the same Epistle (11:5-6) he exhorts them to keep their heads covered when they prophesy.

Wesleyan-holiness theology is biblical but not narrowly or rigidly so. It views Scripture through a wide-angle lens as it applies its meaning to a given time and culture.

Its Dynamic Quality

Another important aspect of Wesleyan-holiness theology is its dynamic quality. It is indeed rooted in yesterday, which includes, of course, the Bible. This rootage is Arminian and Wesleyan and therefore includes the ancient fathers, so valued by Arminius and Wesley.

With all this said, however, it needs to be underscored that Wesleyan-holiness theology is dynamic. It takes seriously the doctrine of the Holy Spirit as Indweller and Guide, who pours himself into living experience. The Spirit inclined people to write the Scriptures. But the selfsame Spirit continues to reveal the Father's will to specific persons in specific situations. This makes for dynamic in our theological enterprise.

Theology must be dynamic to find its way where scriptural directives on supplementary doctrines are unclear. Examples of these are why Christ was born of a virgin, the extent of biblical inerrancy, the mode of baptism, and upcoming events that will close the present gospel era.

This theology is dynamic, further, because of changes in the milieu in which the church functions. Obviously, it will talk more about hope than in the eras prior to Jürgen Moltmann, more about the church than in eras prior to the ecumenical movement, more about the question of abortion than before abortion was legalized in many countries.

New opposition movements arise, doing battle with the faith, and theology must speak to issues of the day. If the gates of hell construct new bulwarks against the Church, theology moves to where the battle is on and there declares God's counsel.

Moreover, Wesleyan-holiness theology must dynamically relate itself to new discoveries made in archaeology and science. Ancient scripts, scrolls, and libraries, unearthed and deciphered, compel theology to consider what this addendum of knowledge means for such a matter as the canon of Scripture.

Scientific breakthroughs require this theology to be dynamic on such matters as transplant givers and receivers, the ethics of engineering human genes, human cloning for the use of the clone's body parts.

The church growth movement occasions theology's dynamic. For example, is it biblically and theologically sound to maintain local churches as homogeneous units simply because homogeneous ones might grow more rapidly than those that are mixed racially or otherwise?

Is smallness not beautiful as well as bigness? A minister in America's mountainous West wrote to the editor of *Christian Century* to affirm this. He would drive up a treacherous mountain road for many ledgy miles to minister to 12 people and would pass, along the way, a memorial to a predecessor who had lost his life driving up there to minister to that small group. He made his point.

Besides all this, theologians keep discovering new or different understandings, and this makes for dynamic in their theology. Speaking of 20 years of work on his three-volume *Christian Theology*, H. Orton Wiley (1877-1961) said, "I was constantly discovering new truth."[7] So was John Wesley, as is well known.[8] So was James Arminius (1560-1609). He accepted an assignment to oppose two ministers who were diverging from the usual kind of

---

7. H. Orton Wiley, "Preface," in *Christian Theology*, 3 vols. (Kansas City: Beacon Hill Press, 1940-43), 1:3.

8. See John Wesley, "Preface" to sermons, in *The Works of John Wesley* (ed. Thomas Jackson, 3rd ed., 14 vols. [London: Wesleyan Methodist Book Room, 1872; reprint, Kansas City: Beacon Hill Press of Kansas City, 1978]), 5:5, where he writes, "Are you persuaded you see more clearly than me? . . . Then . . . point me out a better way than I have yet known."

Calvinism promoted in Holland at the end of the 16th century; after studying the matter, he diverged even further than they did.

Theology, tucked away in a filing cabinet, neat and static, would be worth little. If theology is for God and for the church, it should be as dynamic as it needs to be.

Its Catholicity

Wesleyan-holiness theology is also characterized by catholicity. Historical data warrants this claim.

James Arminius was "a peace-loving man who taught tolerance in the midst of religious dissension"[9] and shrank from defending his views when they were misrepresented.

John Wesley wrote, "For God's sake, if it be possible to avoid it, let us not provoke one another to wrath."[10] During his open controversy with the Calvinists, he implies that the matter of conditional versus unconditional predestination is "opinion" and not doctrine. In "The Character of a Methodist"[11] he asks, "Who is a Methodist?" He gives more than four pages of answer without mentioning one doctrine as such. Then he adds, "These are the principles and practices of our sect; these are the marks of a true Methodist."[12] On the last page he writes, "Is thy heart right, as my heart is with thine? I ask no farther question. If it be, give me thy hand."[13]

Holiness theologians and exegetes are members of various denominations within the Wesleyan-Holiness Movement, where considerable theological differences exist. Whereas Arminius taught God's foreknowledge of our free acts, some Wesleyan-holiness scholars have taught a Socinian-Brightmanian-influenced view that God chooses not to foreknow our free acts.

By the "old man," Paul probably meant the unregenerate life (characterized by both acts of sin and original sin), whereas most Wesleyan-holiness scholars have used the term as a synonym of original sin.

---

9. Carl Bangs, "James Arminius: Christian Scholar. Three Basic Principles of Arminius," *Herald of Holiness,* Oct. 5, 1960, 7.
10. Wesley, "Preface," in *Works* 5:6.
11. Wesley, "The Character of a Methodist," in *Works* 8:340.
12. Ibid., 346.
13. Ibid., 347.

Some Wesleyan-holiness people agree with John Miley (1813-95) and A. M. Hills (1848-1935) that original sin is transmitted by our parents (genetic mode), whereas Arminius and Wesley and H. Orton Wiley are surely Pauline in saying that we enter the world with original sin because Adam the First (as W. B. Godbey called him) represented us badly by sinning, thus causing a fall in the race.

Even the late and great Wiley was expressly Apollinarian in his *Christian Theology.* He also taught that the Jehovah of the Old Testament was Christ. We discussed these issues and disagreed amiably. On a thousand points, however, Wiley is helpful. Significantly, he helped many of us see that the penal theory of the Atonement fits Calvinism but not Arminianism. Still, the majority of persons in this tradition (judging from recent students) think that Christ paid the penalty for us instead of that He suffered on our behalf.

Its Interest in Human Freedom

Wesleyan-holiness theology is not Pelagian, following Pelagius (ca. A.D. 354-ca. 418); it admits original sin and teaches that the unregenerate are free to do a righteous act only when helped by prevenient grace. Nor is it semi-Pelagian, for that compromise position also denied the need of prevenient grace for our turning to God. Instead, this theology inherits the views of James Arminius on human freedom.

Arminius believed profoundly in original sin. He also believed profoundly in prevenient grace—that God draws to himself the unregenerate who, by reason of original sin, would otherwise be inclined only to evil. John Wesley, who, no doubt, had read Arminius,[14] taught similarly.

In Arminian theology, generally, predestination is taught as conditional. God predetermines each individual's destiny based on His foreknowledge of our free acts.

Arminius was careful to teach that there is no merit in our free response to God's offer of forgiveness, for grace alone enables us to make this free response. Wesley's teaching was similar.

---

14. See Herbert McGonigle, *The Arminianism of John Wesley* (Ilkeston, England: Moonly's Bookshop, 1988).

36 ◁ A WESLEYAN-HOLINESS THEOLOGY

Arminius also taught that after we have been saved, we can reject God and be eternally lost. He admitted that believers cannot lose saving grace; but Christians can freely cease to believe, and then they will suffer the loss of saving grace.

Arminius defined an act of sin in the broad, legal, Calvinistic way: any act that does not measure up to God's perfect will for us. Wesley later saw how the Arminian understanding of freedom should figure in one's definition of an act of sin. A proper act of sin, which is serious, he defined as any willful violation of the known law of God. This has been the usual Wesleyan-holiness teaching.

A Homing Instinct for the Moral

We have also taught, at various points in our theology, doctrines that are peculiarly suited to our homing instinct for the moral. We do not hold that the very words of Scripture were divinely dictated to the human writers. Rather, the Scripture writers were freely left to themselves to explain, according to their backgrounds and their interests, the thoughts with which the Spirit inspired them.

Wesleyan-holiness theologians, such as S. S. White, have argued that Christ could have sinned—but did not because He would not. Many of us, also, as did S. S. White, believe that Christ freely chose the Father's will in going all the way to the Cross for us. Many of us also feel that previous to the Incarnation, the Father freely chose to send His Son to the world—and that He might have chosen not to offer us redemption (as in the case of fallen angels).

Another important element of this Wesleyan-holiness instinct for the moral is our interest in actually and freely implementing God's will in the world. In Wesley's time, Calvinists were advancing antinomian notions: for those under saving grace, the keeping of God's laws is not urgent. It is enough that Christ has kept God's laws and that Christ's righteousness is imputed to us. Wesley's main theologian, John Fletcher (1729-85), wrote his *Checks to Antinomianism* in opposition to that view. Wesley and Fletcher, believing in human freedom, taught that as God helps us, we really can—indeed, we really must—keep His laws. We have had therefore this keen interest in a freely chosen and grace-aided Christian life of discipline.

3

Perspective for Doing Theology: Biblical Realism

The perspective from which one enters into the theological enterprise determines the directions it is to take at countless points.

Alternative Perspectives

Thinking in basic ways about perspective for doing theology, six alternatives have presented themselves: idealism, personalism, dualism, process theology, existential interests, and some sort of realistic perspective. The last of these is the most plausible of the alternatives and will be discussed under a separate heading.

Idealism. Idealism posits ideas as ultimate reality. At the headstream of idealism is Plato (ca. 428-ca. 347 B.C.), that Greek philosopher who so revolutionized philosophy in his day. He was mentor to Christian theology in the early centuries and at least until the 12th and 13th centuries, when the more realistic Aristotle (384-322 B.C.) came to dominance.

Greek philosophers from Thales to Plato had been materialistic in metaphysical perspective. Ultimate reality consisted of water, fire, earth, air, or combinations of these. Some, like Heracleitus (ca. 540-ca. 480 B.C.), thought it is in constant change, so that it consists of fire. Aristotle, Plato's student, said the ultimate, God, is the "Unmoved Mover" who changes everything else but remains unchanged himself.

Plato stops materialism in its tracks and says that materiality has only a shadowy and nonreal existence, an existence loaned to it by ideas that are prototypical of it and productive of it. Ideas or concepts, such as the true and the beautiful and the good, were thought of as located at the apex of a whole pyramid of eternal ideas, with the good located at the pyramid's apex. And Plato

37

might have equated the good with what we have come to mean by God.

Platonic idealism sounded good to many early Christian philosopher-theologians. The Christian faith affirms much that is nonmaterial—God, angels, and virtues such as faith, love, and hope. It was felt that Plato's idealism, although manufactured in pre-Christian times and outside the Hebrew corridor of revealed religion, was a basic perspective useful for Christian theologizing. Origen (ca. A.D. 185-ca. 254), Christianity's first major exegete and theologian, used it. He so deprecated the human body that he mutilated himself to keep from being bothered by sexual desires. Ironically, Origen's bishop refused to ordain him, arguing that he was not sufficiently male—and only males could be ordained!

Origen resorted to the already long-used allegorical method of interpreting Scripture—viewing it as having deep, hidden, nonobvious meanings—as a way of amalgamating Platonic idealism with Christian faith. Origen's philosophical perspective also compelled him to universalism—the belief that all humans will finally be redeemed and join in a kind of hallelujah chorus. Indeed, even Satan would finally be redeemed, he said.

This amalgamating of Platonic idealism with Christian orthodoxy occasioned the denial of the body's natural desires, especially in the sexual sphere. Although the Old Testament prophets and New Testament apostles married, although Paul clearly expects elders and deacons to be married (as the Pastoral Epistles show), platonically mentored Christians deprecated marriage.

Many devout men became hermits. Athanasius (ca. A.D. 293-373) wrote letters to "those who practice a solitary life."[1] Indeed, as a young man he was a kind of attendant to a hermit named Antony.[2]

Later, monasteries were built by such men as Cassiodorus, where celibate men congregated for prayerful, world-denying services to Christ, including that of translating and amending Scripture manuscripts—combined with such down-to-earth matters as agriculture and sheep raising.

---

1. Athanasius, Letters of Athanasius 53, "Second Letter to Monks," in *Select Writings and Letters of Athanasius*, ed. Archibald Thompson, vol. 4 of *A Select Library of Nicene and Post-Nicene Fathers of the Christian Church* (Oxford, England: Parker and Co., 1892).

2. See "Life of Antony," in *Select Writings*, where he says, "I was able to learn from him, for I was his attendant for a long time."

Devout women were also celibate. "Married" to Christ, they served Him and the church in nunneries.

About half of all Christendom still views the celibate life as the more spiritual life. Celibacy is required of Roman Catholic priests.

Idealism, then, with its denial of the glory of the world and of the body, was mentor to Christian philosopher-theologians in early and medieval Roman Catholic faith.

Platonic idealism was not totally thrown overboard by the Reformers. Martin Luther (1483-1546) married at age 42 and felt that the privileges of marriage are the next thing to the privileges of salvation.

Luther also contributed to the weaning of the church from Plato by breaking the stranglehold of the Plato-influenced allegorical method of interpreting Scripture. He also stressed the importance of ordinary family life and of ordinary work.

The most basic way in which Luther accomplished this change was his *sola scriptura* approach. From the early centuries, pagan Greek and Latin philosophers and ethicists had been mentors to Christian theologians, and Scripture was only one of numerous sources for theology. Luther announced (and was guided by) the principle that only Scripture is the proper basis for our Christian faith and practice. Much of the same is true for John Calvin (1509-64) as well. He, too, meant to be a *sola scriptura* man.

Despite the Reformers, Protestantism was influenced in the late 18th and early 19th centuries by Immanuel Kant (1724-1804), Friedrich Schleiermacher (1768-1834), and Georg Friedrich Hegel (1770-1831). Their influence again wedded idealism to Christian theology. This is especially so in the metaphysical idealism of Hegel and in the personalisms of such American theologians as Borden Parker Bowne (1847-1910), Edgar Sheffield Brightman (1884-1953), and Albert C. Knudson (1873-1953). It is certainly so, also, of the absolute idealism of America's William Ernest Hocking (1873-1966) and of the "higher" pantheism of Britain's Andrew Seth Pringle-Pattison (1856-1931).

Personalism. Personalism is a form of idealism, but a distinct perspective in its own right. In it, ultimate reality is conceived of as a society of persons, among whom God is the supreme person. Bowne contributed much to the implementing of this perspective in American philosophical theology—as did Brightman and Knudson, all professors of Methodism's Boston University. A number of Wesleyan-holiness scholars received their Ph.D. degrees in philosophy under these personalists. Influenced by them were Russell V. DeLong, Ross Price, and, to some extent, S. S. White.

Wesleyan-holiness scholars often felt personalism to be a useful perspective for several reasons. One is because it corrected absolute idealism's tendency to be pantheistic by advocating a God who is personal and therefore responsive to us. It suited the Wesleyan-holiness tendency to deprecate the physical world, including our bodily nature, which tendency we had learned from earlier idealisms. Significantly, it emphasized human freedom, and this (except for its tendency to deny original sin) tended to be supportive of the Arminianism of the Wesleyan-holiness scholars.

Dualism. In metaphysical dualism, besides God as an ultimate, there is an adversary of God—not created by God, but another ultimate existent. This is the perspective from which Methodism's Edwin Lewis (1881-1959) chose to do his theologizing, at least from 1948 onward—the year of the publication of his *Creator and the Adversary.* In that book Lewis observes, "Cosmic benevolence stands in contrast to cosmic malevolence."[3] Lewis had earlier been a monist, understanding that God's adversary is not eternal. Later, however, he felt that evil does not make sense unless an eternally existent being, whom God did not create but simply "finds," is its author.[4]

On most doctrines, Lewis locates within classical evangelicalism. He affirmed Christ's virgin birth and bodily resurrection (as will be discussed later), conversion, and even a version of Wesley's doctrine of Christian perfection.

---

3. Edwin Lewis, *The Creator and the Adversary* (New York: Abingdon-Cokesbury Press, 1948), 16. Copyright renewal © 1976 by Faulkner B. Lewis.

4. Perhaps it should be explained that Lewis also posited a third ultimate existence, the amorphic, a formless stuff out of which God creates. But the view is a dualism, when one thinks of the opposition between the personal and creative God and the personal or semipersonal adversary (see Lewis, 141-43). The other significant ultimate dualist among Christian theologians and philosophers is the British philosopher C. E. M. Joad. See his *God and Evil* (New York: Harpers, 1943), 63, 65, 85-86, 101-2. Joad says, "If a metaphysical principle is to be invoked to explain good, an equivalent principle must be evoked to explain the evil; if, to put it theologically, there is a God, there is also a Devil, or there is God plus a principle of inertia which obstructs him" (191).

Process Theology. Process theology has rootage in Henri Bergson's upward-moving *élan vital* and in Alfred North Whitehead's (1861-1947) God as a dynamic principle. The main process theologian is Charles Hartshorne (b. 1897), who was once Whitehead's assistant at Harvard and freely admits Whitehead's influence on his understandings.[5] Hartshorne rejected the view that God is a static being, already absolutely perfect, and advanced the vision that God is unceasingly changing—in fact, that the whole universe is.

Process thought is diametrically opposed to materialism. It views the whole universe as alive and growing. It has helped us see that God is not a static, unchanging being, but one who suffers and struggles. Hartshorne himself believed that God is not absolutely perfect but is ever growing toward such perfection. This view, in itself, is unacceptable. At the same time, the Christian view that God is personal, that He answers prayer, that He struggles, and that He suffers with us, is at least in keeping with the nonstatic view of Hartshorne.

There is a somewhat different kind of process understanding of God in Pierre Teilhard de Chardin (1881-1955), who, like Hartshorne, was influenced significantly by both Bergson and Whitehead. Teilhard, a devout Roman Catholic all his life, applied the view of biological evolution to a whole spectrum of understandings, including God—who exists in a developing process.

Bergson did not identify the thrust toward the higher life in the universe as God, but Whitehead did (although, for Whitehead, God seems to be more of a principle than a person). Both Hartshorne and Teilhard emphasized love in God, but there is a basic kind of pantheism in them both. Even so, they and the other seminal process philosophers and theologians are useful in weaning us from the static view of God promoted traditionally by systematic theologians.

Existential Interests. A further possible perspective for doing theology is the existential. Here, the really important matter is what Rudolf Bultmann (1884-1976) called our "act of existing."

---

5. Two students of Hartshorne who are among America's leading theologians are Schubert Ogden and John B. Cobb, Jr. Two other well-known process theologians are D. D. Williams and W. Norman Pittenger.

Here, theologizing is done from the standpoint of our existing situation as human beings. Here the interest is in the individual self, in distinction from globs of wall-to-wall humanity, and in the individual self's present experience.

This interest is found in many forms, some of which are altogether unacceptable. Jean-Paul Sartre was atheistic as an existentialist, and Martin Heidegger (1889-1976) was only quasi-theistic. But the existential interests of Martin Buber, Paul Tillich, and Rudolf Bultmann have about them aspects that are useful to theology. Earlier, the existential theology of Søren Kierkegaard invited use by experience-interested Wesleyan-holiness theology.

Biblical realism can rope itself into existential interests in experience, in authentic living, in treating others persons as "thous," and so forth.

The Perspective of Biblical Realism

By biblical realism is meant a perspective, supported surely by Scripture, in which we do not deny physicality as largely unreal but instead celebrate it as constituting even a residency of grace. This view owns the world as God's creation and affirms it as the milieu in which God's grace is mediated to us.

Nature as a Locus of Grace. All creation, including our bodily nature, is to be celebrated. Since grace resides in the natural world, we celebrate the Incarnation, physical healings, the sacraments, the hope of the resurrection of the body, and much more of what has thingliness attached to it.

Too long has a pagan by the name of Plato mentored us who are Jesus Christ's. Too long we have deprecated whatever is particularized, whatever our senses can survey, in favor of ethereal ideas that we have said are real, eternal, unchanging, and prototypical of the shadowy and less-than-real touchable world. We were often taught these etherealisms by pastors who themselves had been taught in Wesleyan-holiness schools—where one could sometimes take an entire course on Plato without hearing or reading any questioning of his idealism.

This influence of Platonism has meant several things in our theologizing. For one thing, it has meant that we have deprecated nature—the created world.

Nature does indeed seem to be fallen, as we humans are. It is therefore often "red in tooth and claw." Its woes and its wastes are obvious. Often a senseless tyrant, nature is inadequate as a revelation of God. It is true that "the heavens declare the glory of God" (Ps. 19:1), and we know about God's invisible power and His Godness from the things He has made (Rom. 1:19-20). Yet God is a person; and persons must reveal themselves to us if we are to know about them. A spouse might become reserved, and we might not be able to guess why. We will learn why only after the spouse chooses to disclose what the trouble is. This is because spouses are persons.

God is a person, too, even tripersonal. He tells us only tidbits about himself in the natural world. Yet what we humans as sinners most need to know about God—that He is a God of forgiveness—we cannot find out from nature. That He is all-powerful and ingenious, we can observe. That He forgives, we cannot observe anywhere in the created world.

Furthermore, nature has been polluted in our time by our technology, coupled with our overobeying the divine command to multiply the human species.

With these things admitted, however, we Christians ought not to denigrate nature. For one thing, God pronounced His creation "good" (Gen. 1:10, 12, 18, 21, 25, 31).

Nature is the offspring of God even as we are. Our bodies link us with it. In sovereign and lavish freedom, God created the whole visible sphere. If you were to tell an ancient Hebrew that materiality is evil, he would be dumbfounded by your silly talk.

The body is no doubt included when Scripture states that we were made in God's image. Two words are found in the Hebrew: *selem,* for image; and *demuth,* for likeness. The passage reads, "Let us make man in our image, in our likeness" (Gen. 1:26). Both *selem* (image) and *demuth* (likeness) are also used in Gen. 5:3, where we are told that Adam begat Seth "in his own likeness, in his own image." *Selem* originally meant something cut out—that is, something physical. While it came to be used sometimes of something more shadowy than a body, such as the form that a dream took (Ps. 73:20), yet "a concrete representation clings to the word."[6]

H. Wheeler Robinson contended that the word implies that we humans were literally a copy of God in our physical form. E. C. Rust agrees that "man was created in a bodily form on the

---

6. E. C. Rust, *Nature and Man in Biblical Thought* (London: Lutterworth Press, 1953).

divine pattern."[7] This does not mean, of course, that God has a body. Some writers suggest that our bodies are in God's image because we walk upright, with a dignified bearing, and not as beasts do. The body might be said to be in God's image because of the purpose with which it has been endowed as a total functioning organism. James Arminius felt that our bodies are in God's image because "if man had not sinned, his body would never have died and because it is capable of special incorruptibility and glory."[8]

In keeping with this is the fact that our flesh, our *basar,* could "rest secure" (Ps. 16:9) and long for God (63:1). True, "all flesh is grass" (Isa. 40:6, KJV), and "no flesh shall have peace" (Jer. 12:12, KJV). It is weak, but it is not evil.[9]

The most obvious indication that nature in general, and the body in particular, is not evil is the fact that "the Word became flesh and made his dwelling among us" (John 1:14). In the fullness of time, when our finest hour had come, "the desire of all nations" (Hag. 2:7, KJV) entered into human life, body and all. And while in human form He healed all manner of disease and even raised the dead on a few occasions.

After Christ's return, too, the whole creation is to be renewed, sharing in the glorification that awaits us (Rom. 8:18-21; 1 Cor. 15:42 ff.). Transformed nature is poetically conceived in Scripture as joining with us in worshiping and praising God. Thus we read, "Then I heard every creature in heaven and on earth and under the earth and on the sea, and all that is in them, singing: 'To him who sits on the throne and to the Lamb be praise and honor and glory and power, for ever and ever!'" (Rev. 5:13).

All this means that the Christian doctrine of redemption is as broad as the Christian doctrine of creation. It means that the world itself is Christic, that it is sacramental, that we are to view it eucharistically. It means that in the thingliness of things there is a residency of grace.

Joseph Sittler said that we need to perceive a residency of grace not only in nature per se but in fabricated nature as well.

7. Ibid., 118.
8. James Arminius, "Private Disputations," in *Works of Arminius* (London: Longman, Green, 1828), 2:363.
9. Some think that the use of *flesh* for *sacrifices* implies that it is not degraded. See A. C. Knudson's *Religious Ideas for the Old Testament* (New York: Abingdon Press, 1918), where Knudson suggests this as he discusses *basar,* the Hebrew word for *flesh.*

Our world is becoming increasingly urban. Because of this, what the individual Christian observes more often than not is fabricated nature—roads, buildings, machines, instruments. If we learn to see a residency of grace only in a meadow or a crooked mountain trout stream, we might not be very often reminded of the eucharistic qualities of the world. Why not, then, learn to observe a residency of grace in what people have done as coworkers with God in nature? The ingenuity of our fellows is imbedded in fabricated nature, as well as God's ingenuity. Sometimes human life was given in the construction of a bridge, building, or freeway. Always, human sweat was expended on them. When we use such structures, we enter into all that kind of cost. We use the special skills of people we have never known. Perhaps fabricated nature ought to be celebrated with more delight yet than nature per se. All of it is the theater for the glorification of God.

God the Son did indeed enter into human life. He did not simply think compassionately about us but joined himself with us and journeyed with us all the way to ignominy—"for our sorry case," as the ancient Athanasius said.

Time Is Real and Important. Besides viewing nature as a locus of grace, biblical realism regards time as real and important.

Time is not discounted in Scripture as it is in idealism. This is evidenced, in part, by the frequency of scriptural references to various periods of time: *hēmera*, "day"; *hōra*, "hour"; *chronos*, "time"; *kairos*, "season"; *aiōn*, "age"; *aiōnes*, "ages." The Bible also often uses other words that are closely associated with time and its passage: *nun*, "now"; *arch*, "beginnings"; *telos*, "end"; *plērōma*, "fulfillment"; *aparchē*, "firstfruits"; *arrabōn*, "earnest."

Eternity is not an abstraction in Scripture. As Cullmann says, "Eternity is the endless succession of the ages."[10] Eternity is nothing more than endless time—all of time. It does not start after time "ends," as is often supposed. The New Testament Greek word for *eternity* is the singular *aiōn*, "age," or the plural *aiōnes*, "ages." According to Thayer's *Lexicon*, *aiōn* means "an unbroken age, perpetuity of time, eternity."[11] The cognate word *aiōnios*, for "eternal," according to the same lexicon, means "without begin-

---

10. Oscar Cullmann, *Christ and Time* (Philadelphia: Westminster Press, 1950), 62.

11. *Greek-English Lexicon of the New Testament*, trans., rev., and enl. by Joseph H. Thayer (Grand Rapids: Zondervan Publishg House, n.d.), 19.

ning or end, that which always has been and always will be."[12] It is used of time itself (*chronois*) in Rom. 16:25, as well as in referring to God in verse 26.

God is the One "who is, and who was, and who is to come" (Rev. 1:4)—that is, who is not timeless but is instead linked to all the time periods and thus filled full of time. He is the Alpha and the Omega, the A and the Z, "the beginning and the ending" (v. 8, KJV). All things come forth from Him, and from Him they have their salvific function. Not only that, but He is at present linked to all things and to all people through both creation and incarnation. He is linked to them conjugally, inextricably, ontologically. He is conjoined to them in a sustained way as the ages pass, one into another.

Admittedly, both time and space are relative, as Albert Einstein taught us. Time is relative to various organisms, as Henri Bergson taught us, so that it is stepped up in the case of an ephemeral organism and slowed down in the case of a turtle, which might live 200 years. Even so, time is real. It is actual. It is not simply ideological, not simply in the mind, without any out-there-ness attached to it.

Time is real, whether or not you agree with the usual view that time is of two types in Scripture: simple duration (*chronos*) and special season of opportunity (*kairos*). J. A. T. Robinson says, "Kairos is time considered in relation to personal action, in reference to ends to be achieved in it. Chronos is time abstracted from such a relation, time as it were, that ticks on objectively and impersonally, whether anything is happening or not."[13]

Professor C. B. Caird, however, has pointed out[14] that *kairos* and *chronos* are sometimes used interchangeably in the New Testament, a conclusion confirmed by James Barr's detailed study.[15] (See, for example, Acts 3:19, 21; 1 Pet. 1:5, 20; Jude 18.)

In any case, time is real, even if it is sometimes spoken of as a season of special opportunity. The father who advised his son to attend chapel at college—saying that if you are working at a grindstone, every moment counts alike, but that in building a life, it is the inspired moments that count—was not saying that when we sit in chapel, time is not actual. As a period of simple dura-

12. Ibid., 20.
13. J. A. T. Robinson, *In the End, God* (New York: Harper and Row, 1950), 45 ff.
14. See C. B. Caird, *The Apostolic Age* (London: Gerald Duckworth and Co., 1955), 184.
15. See James Barr, *Biblical Words for Time* (London: SCM Press, 1962), 20 ff.

tion, time functions in an empty chapel at midnight even as it does when 1,000 students are there, buying up their opportunities with eager minds. No dean will tell you that time ceases to exist when the speaker continues past chapel-closing time!

The past, the present, and the future are all important. We cannot get along without any of them as a Platonist can, who holds to a cyclic view of history and says that time is not real to God, so that the Incarnation did not make any change in God's life. Time had a "not yet" period before God's only Son visited us. There was a period when kings and commoners, the classes and the masses, looked toward a day when God would do a new and wondrous thing for us foul and foolish humans. We read about it all in the beforehand time of what J. Barton Payne liked to call the Older Testament. During the times of ancient Israel's ups and downs, its faithings and its murmurings, its wonderings and its wanderings, select persons with stout hearts entered into *Yahweh's* privy council chambers and came forth to announce what God would do through Israel for all people.

When Christ came, at a certain year in the reign of Augustus Caesar, new and wondrous things began to happen that had never before occurred. The epitome of the prophet was here. The epitome of the priest was here. The King of those who are kings walked among us. And He let people hang Him on a cross, after which God raised Him from the dead.

Perhaps some have emphasized the past too much. Historicists, we might call them. They find out what standout people of the past have said and consider that sufficient. They borrow the religion of their forefathers, taking it secondhand without encountering God on their own in primal I-thou ways.

Existentialists such as Sartre and Albert Camus overemphasized the present. The church's stored-up *sophia* is thrown to the winds in favor of what suits people or meets their needs in the present moment. Even Joseph Fletcher's situation ethics, in which he suggests that one should decide what to do at the time each situation arises that calls for a decision, tends in this direction. Fletcher says, "In every 'existential moment' or 'unique' situation . . . one must rely upon the situation itself, *there and then,* to provide the ethical decision."[16]

---

16. Joseph Fletcher, *Situation Ethics* (Philadelphia: Westminster Press, 1966), 22.

Some of the hope theologians tend to discount both the past and the present, putting too many of their eggs into the basket of the future. They might not seem to be doing this, however. Jürgen Moltmann and Wolfhart Pannenberg make much of the historical resurrection of Christ, for example. Yet Carl Braaten and Pannenberg both seem to be saying that God is pulling history to a hope-filled future from a stance out there in the future. Pannenberg, for example, implies that kind of stance on the Father's part when he uses "the Father" and "God's coming Reign" synonymously and when he continues: "Only so was the coming Reign of God—God himself—already present in him [Jesus]."[17] John Cobb seems quite certainly to be saying such as this. In doing so, they all seem to be not altogether different from Thomas Altizer, who has been willing to say that God is dead—although it is only Cobb, and not Braaten nor Pannenberg, who expresses special affinity with Altizer's view.[18] In either case, God's existence is sort of questionable, whether He is said to have died or is not quite existing now.

In the Bible, surely, time is real in all its tenses. The past, present, and future all have their distinct places. A proper realistic, biblical theology will not emphasize any one of them to the deprecating of the others; it will take all of them seriously.

History Is Real and Important. Time is broader than history, if history is thought of as the record we humans have written—that is, as our remembered past. Even so, time and history are closely related. And even as time makes a difference by its passage, so does history.

The Greeks believed that history is cyclical—that we do not really get anywhere by the passing of events. Some of the Gnostics adopted a similar view, found, for example, in the Coptic-language Gospel of Philip.

Only the Hebrews, of all ancient peoples, wrote careful and nonmythopoeic histories of what was happening. Long before Je-

---

17. Wolfhart Pannenberg, "Appearance as the Arrival of the Future," in *New Theology No. 5*, ed. Martin Marty and Dean Peerman (New York: Macmillan Publishing Co., 1968), 120. Pannenberg writes much more as a classically oriented theologian in his *Jesus—God and Man*, trans. Lewis L. Wilkins and Duane A. Priebe (London: SCM Press, 1968).

18. Cobb says, "No theological formulation of our time has surpassed the power of Altizer's. Although I affirm a theistic form of Christian faith, my chastened and deepened appreciation of theism is indebted to Altizer's atheism." John B. Cobb, Jr., *God and the World* (Philadelphia: Westminster Press, 1969), 33.

hoshaphat and other secretaries to kings, histories were being written. It is even probable that they were being written long before the time of Moses. Many scholars believe that the Hebrew lexicons that render a certain word as "generations" should have rendered it "histories." If this is so, "This is the book of the generations of Adam" (KJV and RSV) would read "of the histories of Adam" (Gen. 5:1). The same would be true of the *histories* "of Noah" (6:9) and the *histories* "of the sons of Noah" (10:1, KJV). Indeed, the NIV translates "the written account" (5:1) and "the account" (6:9; 10:1).

Supporting the importance of history, also, are Scripture's numerous genealogies. They are not accurate in the modern sense, since they skip numerous generations. The Hebrew language had no word for grandson; they are simply called "sons," especially if the actual son was not a standout figure.

Also, much attention is given to chronology in the Old Testament. James Barr says:

> The Old Testament contains a complete and carefully worked out chronological system, by which a large number of the important events (and a good many details of less apparent significance) can be dated in relation to one another, and in particular dated from the absolute datum point of the creation of the world. . . . Such figures as the 430 years of the sojourn in Egypt (Exod. 12:40), or the 480 years from the Exodus to the beginning of the construction of Solomon's temple, are cardinal points in the scheme.[19]

When Emil Brunner (1896-1966) and Rudolf Bultmann say that the Incarnation took place without a virgin birth, and when Brunner and others say that Christ was raised but not bodily, they are taking a kind of idealistic, Platonic view of history, which deprecates it.

Special meanings or values, and matters of facticity, do not exist divorced from each other in ordinary life. One does not love a sweetheart or spouse out of the blue, divorced from the times when two people smiled at each other and held hands and communicated with each other in numerous real ways. As love is born and begins to grow on the basis of happenings, so does the Christian faith. It roots in the soil of history, as John S. Whale says.[20]

---

19. Barr, *Biblical Words for Time*, 27.
20. John S. Whale, *Christian Doctrine* (Cambridge: Cambridge University Press, 1941), 17.

Bultmann deprecated much of New Testament history[21]—for example, the various interventions of God and angels from "above" and of Satan and demons from "below," calling such interventions first-century myth that we can dispense with and still have the kerygmatic kernels of truth that Christianity offers. But certain students of his—among them Kasemann and Pannenberg—were correct in breaking off from their mentor on this matter. They view history as significant for Christian faith.

History is not to be deprecated. Instead, it is to be viewed as soil in which the Christian faith took root and in which it has grown until the present time.

Offspring of the Realistic Perspective. We ought, then, to do theology from a realistic perspective instead of an idealistic one. Nature, even fabricated nature, is a locus of grace; and both time and history are real and important. Now let us consider several matters that might be called the offspring of a realistic perspective.

1. This perspective eliminates the invisible Church in favor of *a church that is observable* the way a light is on a dark night.

As Hans Kung says, "External voluntary adherence to the Church and true inner membership are not necessarily synonymous."[22] Not all church members are authentically Christ's disciples. Instead, both tares and wheat grow together in the Church, and the difference between them is not altogether visible. That fact, however, gives us no excuse for taking flight into a Platonic idealism and stating that the real Church is invisible. While Hans Kung is not willing to junk the phrase "invisible Church,"[23] he deplores using the phrase as an idealist does to deprecate the Church in its visible aspects. He says:

The real Church made up of real people cannot possibly be invisible. There is no place here for fantasies . . . about a Platonic idea. The Christian's starting-point . . . is a real Church. The Church he believes is visible as a human fellowship and through its acts. . . . By being visible the Church is being true, not false, to its essential nature. Only

---

21. See Rudolf Bultmann, "New Testament and Mythology," in *Kerygma and Myth*, ed. Hans Bartsch, trans. R. F. Fuller (London: Society for Promoting Christian Knowledge, 1953), 11, 12, 16.
22. Hans Kung, *The Church* (New York: Sheed and Ward, 1967), 264.
23. Ibid., 34.

a visible Church can be a home for human beings, a place where they can join in, give assistance, build.[24]

Twenty times the New Testament refers to the Church as the Body of Christ. That is, it is the kind of embodiment that Jesus Christ now has in the world—"an extension of the Incarnation"[25] that had lasted some 33 years. It is an organism, as a body is, and not simply an organization. It is flesh-and-blood believers who are the Body of Christ, and vibrant, witnessing believers are not invisible by any means. They are lights to lighten this otherwise dark world. They are candles set on candlesticks so that all and sundry can see them plainly.

The invisible Church is usually argued for philosophically, but some say that the word "church" in the singular in Scripture might at times refer to the invisible Church. Thus the "church" in the province of Galatia, where there were local churches at Antioch, Iconium, Lystra, is a reference to the invisible Church. Yet the singular usage of "church" refers to nothing more or less than all the local churches, that is, all the Christians. As Kung says, "There are not two Churches, one visible and one invisible. Nor must we think, with Platonic dualism and spiritualism, of the visible Church (being earthly and 'material') as the reflection of the real part of the Church (being spiritual and heavenly). Nor is the invisible part of the Church its essential nature, and the visible part the external form of the Church."[26]

The word "church" occurs 115 times in the New Testament, and in all except 3 of these instances the reference is simply to faithing and loving and hoping Christians.[27] William Robinson says, "The church is that concrete reality by which Christ becomes manifest to the world, and by which he acts in history."[28] George Laird Hunt's main theme in *Rediscovering the Church* is that the Church is a community—a beloved community; and this, too, is basically correct.[29]

---

24. Ibid., 35.
25. Whale, *Christian Doctrine,* 140.
26. Kung, *The Church,* 38.
27. In Acts 19:32, 39, and 41, "church" refers to an assembly of people who objected to Paul at Ephesus.
28. William Robinson, *The Biblical Doctrine of the Church* (St. Louis: Bethany Press, 1948), 99.
29. See his article on the church in the Amsterdam Assembly Series, *Man's Disorder and God's Design* (New York: Harper and Row, 1948).

The Church is often described in Scripture in ways that suggest its reality as visible. It is the Bride of Christ (Rev. 21:2, 9). It is a "colony of heaven" (see Phil. 3:20; Eph. 2:6; Col. 3:1), which suggests that its relation to heaven is similar to a Roman colony's relation to Rome—very much like Rome but removed geographically. It is the "Israel of God" (Gal. 6:16) and God's own people (1 Pet. 2:9). It is the righteous remnant spoken of by Isaiah (Rom. 9:27). It is the people of the new covenant, spoken of by Jeremiah (2 Cor. 3:5 ff.). It is the saints of the Most High referred to by Daniel (1 Cor. 1:2).

Like her Lord, the Church is both human and divine; both unconquerable and conquering (Matt. 16:18). It is triumphant, since many Christians have died in the faith; and it is militant, since it marches in vibrancy to where sinful people are, and proclaims Christ. The Church is all these things, certainly, but it is invisible neither in Scripture nor in our time.

The Church is characterized by oneness in Scripture. Brethren from Judea interested themselves in the affairs of the church at Antioch, Galatia, Corinth, Rome. Relief was taken from remotely situated churches to the Jerusalem Christians. A council was held at Jerusalem to talk over some matters on which there was dispute. There was one olive tree, God's true Israel, into which Gentiles, being "a wild olive shoot" (Rom. 11:17), were grafted "contrary to nature" (v. 24, KJV). We read that He has made us both (Jew and Gentile) one (see Eph. 2:11, 17-22, RSV). Jesus prays that His followers "may be one" even as He and the Father "are one" (John 17:11, 22). There is "one Lord, one faith, one baptism" (Eph. 4:4 ff.). It is to the one Church that the Lord adds daily the ones who were being saved (Acts 2:46-47). And organismic unity exists in the Church, according to 1 Corinthians 12. Nothing of invisibility is suggested by any of these descriptions.

The same is true when the New Testament Church is said to be a koinonia—a fellowship in which sharing happens. Often, this is a sharing of funds (Rom. 15:26). Paul also speaks of "the fellowship of the ministering to the saints" (2 Cor. 8:4, KJV). Here, the reference is to a kind of love offering that Christians in Macedonia were to send to the Jerusalem Christians.[30]

---

30. See Roy Hoover, unpublished B.D. thesis on *Koinōnia,* Nazarene Theological Seminary, Kansas City, 1956.

Koinōnia is also used of fellowship in a more spiritual way, as when we read of "the fellowship *[koinōnia]* of his Son Jesus Christ our Lord" (1 Cor. 1:9, KJV); of "the fellowship *[koinōnia]* of the Holy Spirit" (2 Cor. 13:14); of "the right hand of fellowship *[koinōnia]*" (Gal. 2:9); and of "the fellowship *[koinōnia]* of His [Christ's] sufferings" (Phil. 3:10, NASB).

Whether *koinōnia* is used of sharing money, or of personal fellowship, in the 13 instances where it is found in Paul's writings, and where it is found elsewhere in the New Testament, it is a sharing of fellowship of real believers with each other and with the Persons of the Trinity. It does not suggest that the Church in its true form is somehow ethereal and invisible.

2. Another offspring of a realistic perspective is *the denial of eternal concepts.* It is Plato, again, who has influenced us incorrectly in our belief in eternal concepts that are prototypical of and creative of particulars.[31] Plato believed that concepts exist prior to particularized expressions of them. Cow as a concept exists prior to cows; truth exists prior to any given instance of what is true. As noted earlier, at the very apex of a pyramid of ideas, for Plato, was the idea of the good.[32]

The Neoplatonism of Plotinus (A.D. 207-70) and others influenced Christian theology in the early centuries. Plotinus taught that the universal soul, a kind of third-ranking member of a divine triad, created everything according to the ideas resident in the second-ranking member it contemplates. John Scotus Erigena (ca. 810-77), a Christian Platonist, taught that there are 10 primordial ideas resident in the Logos, according to which the Logos, Christ, created all things.

Realizing that a Christian is not supposed to teach that numerous ultimates exist in and of themselves and outside of God, as Platonism seems to suggest, Christian Platonists have suggested that these eternal concepts exist in God's nature. In doing this, however, Platonism has still been maintained in a basic way. The concepts are kept, and therefore what is foreign to Scripture is imposed upon the teachings of Scripture. Scripture teaches, surely, that God is personal and sovereign. Scripture knows nothing of

---

31. Plato, *The Republic,* trans. F. M. Cornford (New York: University Press, 1945), 183.
32. Ibid., 212 ff.

54 ◁ A WESLEYAN-HOLINESS THEOLOGY

static concepts dictating to God what He may will, even if one locates those concepts in His nature.

Surely cowness does not exist before cows do. A concept is probably no more than a class or a set to which we ascribe a name because it is composed of certain types of look-alike particulars. But pure nominalism might not be correct, in which concepts are names only and have no existence whatever. Abelardian conceptualism might be correct—in which a concept does exist as a way in which rational minds group particulars but not as what predates and governs particulars. Beauty does not exist as an unchanging concept eternally, prior to particular beautiful things. The saying "Beauty is in the eye of the beholder" is partly correct. It is both in the beholder and in what is beheld—but it does not exist in a prior way as an eternal concept.

The same is true as relates to truth: it is not an eternal, unchanging standard of rightness that we only more or less measure up to in our living—as it is in Platonism. Jesus taught us differently, saying, "I am the way and the truth and the life" (John 14:6). That in itself shows us that truth is not an eternal concept. He said it in the same breath in which He said that He is the Life and the Way, so we should have known that truth means the proper way to live, the proper direction to walk in—the way God wills, that is, instead of the way an impersonal and eternal concept prescribes.

3. A third offspring of a realistic perspective is *opposition to occult mysticism.* Much of the occult mysticism that is gaining such a foothold in the United States (for example, Buddhism) is an idealism that has skipped across the Pacific from the Orient. Some of it—astrology, for example—has Greek and Roman sources. Of a piece with such is New Age thought. None of this has come out of Palestine. It has not issued from the springs of the Hebraic-Christian faith. In such occult mysticism each person's own flights of imagination, tutored from strange and disparate sources, are what guide human life, and not the historic revelation in the Scriptures and Christ.

Even the Christian mysticism of the Quakers, which Wesley opposed so vigorously, is off base due to a kind of idealism. Quakerism's theological classic, Barclay's *Apology,* states: "These divine inward revelations . . . are not to be subjected to the test . . . of outward testimony of the Scripture . . . for this divine revelation and inward illumination is that which is evident and clear of itself."[33] This view deprecates Scripture and the history of the Church with its stored-up Christian wisdom and looks for guidance to an inner light that is assumed to be divine and trustworthy. John S. Whale properly observes that "mysticism often pays a heavy price for its tendency to belittle the historical and the factual."[34]

4. Still another offspring of a realistic perspective is *the rejection of the pagan notion of the immortality of the soul,* an inheritance from Platonism. The soul will indeed survive this life. But in Platonism only the soul, and not the body, is to survive this life. The body is evil, even as all materiality is. It now clothes the soul as a punishment for the soul's wrong decision in a previous noncorporeal existence. The body will be sloughed off utterly as a butterfly sheds its cocoon. And as a butterfly comes forth in new life without its hull, so, in Platonism, the soul will come forth without a body—without a spiritual body.

We Christians believe that the soul of every person will survive death. But it will not become dormant or unconscious. According to Luke 16, it will be fully conscious after death and will not need resurrection. What will need and receive glorification or immortality or resurrection is the body—the body of the Christian, that is.

Paul says that "as in Adam all die, so in Christ all will be made alive" (1 Cor. 15:22). We will die physically, that is, and we will rise physically. The resurrection of the body is one of our special assurances that we will be individuated in the next life and not merged into an oversoul.

Paul makes it clear that "this mortal nature must put on immortality" (1 Cor. 15:53, RSV). The Bible nowhere states that the soul will be given immortality. What is mortal, the body, will put on immortality. The "perishable," the body, "must clothe itself with the imperishable."

Since "flesh and blood cannot inherit the kingdom of God" (1 Cor. 15:50), and since we will have bodies "like his glorious body" (Phil. 3:21), the body, when raised, will be a "spiritual body" (1 Cor. 15:44)—but a body nonetheless.

---

33. Robert Barclay, *An Apology for the True Christian Divinity* (Philadelphia: Friends Society, 1872), Prop. 2.
34. Whale, *Christian Doctrine,* 17.

Immortality, then, is for what is mortal, the body, and not for the soul. And it is a gift for those who are Christians. The bodies of the finally impenitent will be raised in "the resurrection of judgment" (John 5:29, RSV; cf. Rev. 20:6), but Scripture does not tell us that they will be given immortality. This is because immortality is about the same as glorification; it is an aspect of redemption and for Christians.[35]

5. Still another offspring of this realistic perspective is that we look to *a real Christ*. Much recent teaching on Christology, especially concerning Christ's virgin birth and resurrection, is a revival of Docetism. Those who deny the Virgin Birth but believe nonetheless in the Incarnation are expressing a form of idealism. According to the biblical realism being advocated here, we Christians look to a Christ who really was virgin born and who really was raised from the dead.

Emil Brunner denies the virgin birth of Christ but affirms the Incarnation on a kind of ethereal, idealistic, mysterious basis. He says, "The truth that the Eternal Son of God meets us in the Man, Jesus, necessarily leads to the doctrine of the Incarnation of the Son of God."[36] So history's most colossal event has occurred. Yet Brunner would rather "stand amazed before the fact itself" than accept the Virgin Birth as the means to this "great, unthinkable, unimaginable miracle of the Incarnation."[37]

Rudolf Bultmann affirms the Incarnation but wants it to stand there in pure "mystery,"[38] without any legs on it. He denies the Virgin Birth as its means. He opposes all miracles and is frank to say that Matthew and Luke are in error because "they make the other-worldly—Jesus' mysterious origin in God—into a this-worldly thing."[39] John he appreciates, as does Brunner, and he says, "The true mystery is comprised in 'The word became flesh' (1:14), and John either does not know or refuses to know any-

---

35. Excellent treatments similar in tone to the one I have presented here are to be found in Oscar Cullmann's Ingersoll lecture on immortality at Harvard and René Pache's *Future Life* (Chicago: Moody Press, 1962).

36. Emil Brunner, *Dogmatics,* trans. Olive Wyon (Philadelphia: Westminster Press, 1950), 2:350.

37. Ibid., 356.

38. Rudolf Bultmann, *Theology of the New Testament* (New York: Charles Scribner's Sons, 1951), 2:30.

39. Ibid.

thing of an attempt to draw this mystery down into terms of this world by a story of a mythological birth."[40]

Gustav Aulén (1879-1977) talks of the Incarnation but deprecates the Virgin Birth as a "rationalistic explanation"[41] of it.

Nels F. S. Ferré likewise believes in the Incarnation, but he does not like to see it supported by so suitable a doctrine as Christ's conception by the Holy Spirit. He believes the eternal Christ united with Jesus not at the conception but at some time during Jesus' adult life.[42] Jesus himself might have been conceived by a German mercenary soldier stationed at a Nazareth garrison— or by Joseph himself, which is "the simplest thing to believe."[43] It might have happened as Matthew and Luke tell it,[44] for that matter. In any case, the Incarnation occurs much later, and Ferré tends toward the etherealism of idealism when he adds, "Every child of God must have his virgin birth in order to become joint heir with Christ."[45]

All these teachings are docetic and idealistic. While the Docetists spiritualized Christ by saying He was divine and only appeared to be human, these men leap to a conclusion that Christ is divine. Their conclusion does not assure Christ's founding in God the way the doctrine of Christ's conception by the Holy Spirit does, but simply asserts it without support—even as Christian Platonists assert the existence of the eternal ideas. Admittedly, as Barth says, it is the Incarnation that has ontic importance. Yet the Virgin Conception[46] doctrine does have noetic significance: "It advertises what here takes place,"[47] as Barth says. It is connected

---

40. Ibid.
41. Gustav Aulén, *The Faith of the Christian Church* (Philadelphia: Muhlenberg Press, 1948), 221 ff.
42. Nels F. S. Ferré, *The Christian Understanding of God* (New York: Harper and Brothers, 1951), 193.
43. Ibid., 192.
44. Nels F. S. Ferré, *The Christian Faith* (New York: Harper and Brothers, 1942), 109.
45. Ibid., 139.
46. Technically, we ought to refer to this doctrine as that of the Virgin Conception, for it is in the conception that the miracle occurs, and not in the birth nine months later. The term Virgin Birth is now used because it needed to be used in the early centuries. At that time the Gnostic Docetists did not mind admitting the miraculous conception. But they denied the normalcy of the birth, saying instead that Christ was "poured through" Mary's womb and did not become tainted with her humanity.
47. Karl Barth, *Credo* (New York: Charles Scribner's Sons, 1936), 69.

with the Incarnation, as Barth explains, "as sign with thing signified."[48] It is also, as Barth says, the "miracle that is a pointer to the mystery [the Incarnation]."[49] Barth has in mind the faith-without-legs etherealism of such men as Brunner and Bultmann when he warns against "parenthesising the miracle of the *Nativitas* and wanting to cling to the mystery as such."[50]

The resurrection of Christ is treated similarly by many theologians who affirm that it happened on some kind of idealistic, mysterious, spiritual level but not bodily. Brunner delineates with care the Bible's teaching about the significance of Christ's resurrection, yet he says it did not actually happen. He admits that Luke thought it did, since Luke speaks of the resurrected Christ's eating (Luke 24:43; Acts 1:1-5), but denies that Paul believed in the bodily resurrection of our Lord. Brunner says that Christ appeared only to believers (see 1 Cor. 15:5-8) and that only believers could have been aware of His presence since He was raised only spiritually—in a way that must be apprehended by faith.

Barth feels the same way about Christ's bodily resurrection as about His virgin birth. Opposing them both in his earlier writings, by the 1930s he was affirming them both. He finally said, "These two miracles belong together."[51]

All these denials discussed are docetic flights into the ethereal, the idealistic, the philosophical, in which the historical and material roots of our faith are deprecated.

We Christians often tend not to want a flesh-and-blood God-man Savior after we have been given one. We tend to take flight from the historical to the ethereal, the mysterious, the idealistic. Witness the popularity of New Age.

John the apostle was not like this. He has to be about as much of a Hellenist as any of the New Testament writers, with his extensive interest in the Logos, with his kind of dualisms between Church and world and light and darkness. Yet the apostle of love was no Hellenist at all. He packed different meanings into these matters than did the Greeks; he was markedly different from

48. Karl Barth, *Church Dogmatics,* trans. G. T. Thomson (New York: Charles Scribner's Sons, 1955), 2:184.
49. Barth, *Credo,* 70.
50. Karl Barth, *Dogmatics in Outline* (New York: Philosophical Library, 1949), 100.
51. Barth, *Church Dogmatics* 2:182.

them in his Christology. They would not have had God fouling himself with human flesh. They would not have had Him visiting us during the reigns of Augustus and Tiberius Caesar to ransom us from sin by death on a Roman gibbet. John saw that the Son of God, who "was God" (John 1:1; 20:28), did all this and more. And John says, "That which was from the beginning, which we have heard [no ethereal idealism here], which we have seen with our eyes [no ethereal idealism here], which we have looked at and our hands have touched—this we proclaim concerning the Word of life" (1 John 1:1). He goes on to say, "We proclaim to you what we have seen and heard" (v. 3).

6. Biblical realism also inclines one toward a kind of *natural theology*, but not the Thomas Aquinas type of natural theology in which reason supplies the data for theology. If, similarly, we mean by reason what it meant for 18th- and 19th-century Protestantism, it should be rejected and with Martin Luther called "the devil's bride." For persons of this stance, to believe only what reason can lead you to believe is a rationalism that biblical realism must reject. Such use of reason has led to a denial of much that is contained in the historic creeds of the Church. It has denied the forgiveness of sins, the efficacy of the sacraments, the Trinity, the Incarnation, miracles, and original sin, to name only a few ways in which it has impugned the faith.

We are certainly to use reason for the ordering and examining of data, but not to originate or limit that data. Because of the wrong use of reason, Tertullian said that philosophers are the patriarchs of the heretics.

The word *reason* barely occurs in Scripture. In the rare instances where it is found, it is not used in the sense of proving or disproving something by the use of sheer logic. We are to "reason together" (Isa. 1:18) about something that unaided human reason could not arrive at: "Though your sins are like scarlet, they shall be as white as snow."

According to the KJV, we are to "be ready always to give an answer to every man" who asks us for "a reason of the hope that is in" us (1 Pet. 3:15). The word here is *apologian*. It means "verbal defence, speech in defence."[52] The RSV translates it simply

---

52. Thayer's *Lexicon*, 65.

"defense" instead of "reason." A defense can be made on revelational and life-transforming bases and not simply by giving rational supports—and this is probably the kind of basis for our faith that we are to be ready to give.

In Rom. 12:1, the KJV speaks of our "reasonable service." But that service is not reasonable in the usual sense of that word; it is an unreasoned abandoning of oneself to God—an abandon that does not calculate ahead of time benefits that will accrue to us when we lose ourselves in God's will. Instead of "reasonable service," therefore, the RSV renders it "your spiritual worship."

If it be suggested that Paul "reasoned" with his hearers, again it was not reasoning in the philosophical sense of giving logical supports that all intelligent creatures should accept—because it is "from the Scriptures" (Acts 17:2) that he reasoned, "explaining and proving that the Christ had to suffer and rise from the dead" (v. 3). What does reason in the other sense know about the efficacy of Jesus Christ's death and the power of His resurrection? It does not even turn to Scripture for its supports as Paul did. Paul also "reasoned in the synagogue" every Sabbath (18:4), but we may be sure that his approach was revelational and experiential. The RSV says that he "argued" with them. Paul also "reasoned" (KJV) or "argued" (RSV) before Felix (24:25); but it included a discussion of "righteousness" (KJV), or "judgment" (RSV), and philosophical reason cannot net you very much on that kind of subject.

Reason dictates that we will receive a just recompense for our deeds—not forgiveness of sins. If a person cries out with Horatius Bonar, "Ah! mine iniquity crimson hath been, / Infinite, infinite, sin upon sin," reason answers, "Sorry, Scum. You're stuck with it."

So the natural theology that is an offspring of biblical realism is not of the rationalistic sort. Instead, it is the kind of natural theology in which nature, the created world, is a bearer of the holy, a medium through which God speaks. In this understanding nature is not deprecated but instead is celebrated. The world God made was repeatedly said to be good in Genesis 1—2, as mentioned earlier. The land given to Israel was precious, and they longed for it when they could not live in it. The Tabernacle and three successive Temples, constructed according to special specifications, were bearers of special meaning—as was the ark of the covenant. Certain mountains, as Sinai and Horeb, were more than mountains. A rod in Moses' hand was more than a rod.

Ezekiel went way out on a limb to be a realist instead of an idealist. He lay 390 days on his left side and 40 days on his right side to remind the exiles graphically of their earlier troubled destiny (Ezek. 4:5-6). Whether he lay there all day long each day, or struck his pose when Mrs. Ezekiel would see someone coming up the walk and holler, "Zeek," in any case the man knew that people can often latch onto an important insight if they are helped along by a physical image. That is why he portrayed a siege of Jerusalem on a large clay brick (v. 1). That is why this eagle-sighted seer broke open a large hole in the wall of the living room of his home and piled his belongings on the living room floor as a way of demonstrating to the exiles that Jerusalem would fall suddenly and that they would need to escape stealthily with only a few belongings if they escaped at all. "Dig through the wall in their sight," he was told, "and go out through it. In their sight you shall lift the baggage upon your shoulder, and carry it out in the dark" (12:5-6, RSV). And Mrs. Ezekiel was still living when he used their house in that way, although she did not live very long afterward.

Physical things often count for more than themselves in the New Testament also. The sacraments of baptism and the Lord's Supper employ elements. Other concrete, physical things have symbolic significance. That is so in footwashing (John 13:14); in the oil used for anointing the sick (James 5:14); in the "handkerchiefs or aprons" that were "carried away from his [Paul's] body to the sick" (Acts 19:12, RSV) to help incite them to faith. The laying on of hands in receiving the Holy Spirit (v. 6), and in setting apart for special ministry (13:3), is in keeping with this, as is the raising of hands as a benediction (Luke 24:50), and "the right hand of fellowship" (Gal. 2:9).

All this is in keeping with the Aristotelian principle that there is nothing in the mind that is not first in the senses—although that principle is itself far too inclusive, not overtly allowing, for example, for our learning things from the event-and-word-revelation of Scripture. It is foreign to Platonism, which intuits God with the eyes closed; and it is therefore foreign to much of Protestantism, which has often been informed by Platonism's idealism. Yet, what is typically Roman Catholic is also typically biblical at this point because Aristotle, with his regard for physical things, whom the Catholics follow and whom Luther called the blind heathen master, is closer to Scripture than Plato is. Protestantism broke away from Roman Catholicism over other matters—indulgences, penances, prayers to saints, papal authority, and so forth. We thought we needed to break away from their realistic kind of theology, but that is surely the kind that is biblical.

Of the possible perspectives for doing theology that we have discussed, the appropriate one is biblical realism. In treating and promoting this perspective, I have stuck my neck out many times in ways that might be disturbing to people who have previously accepted a lay theology that is platonically oriented. I have stuck my neck out in order that theological progress might be made—much as a turtle does to make its advance. The directions suggested lead away from liberal influences and toward evangelical and biblical directions. If the views are perceived as radical, it is hoped they will be perceived as radically biblical and conservative and evangelical—for this, indeed, is what they are.

We turn now from a consideration of theology's perspective to a treatment of its written source: Scripture.

4

Theology's Written Authority

Since Scripture is the one primary source of written authority for us Wesleyans, as it is for Protestants generally, it must be discussed rather early in any systematic and constructive treatment of theology. We need to consider such matters as its inspiration, the changes in it from the time it was autographs to the time it became the canon of the synagogue-church believing communities, the much-controverted matter of its inerrancy, its authority, its genuineness, the translation of it, the interpretation of it, and the place it should enjoy as the main written source of our theology and our practice of the Christian life.

The Inspiration of Scripture

The Greek word for inspiration, *theopneustos,* literally means "God-breathed." When we say the Scriptures are inspired, this means in part that the breath of God is in them. And since the Hebrew *ruack* and the Greek *pneuma* both mean "spirit," "air," or "wind," the *pneustos* part of *theopneustos* can be thought of as referring to the Holy Spirit and His function in helping the Scripture writers. Thus we might think of *theopneustos*—found in 2 Tim. 3:16, "All Scripture is inspired by God" (NASB), as meaning that the Scriptures are "God-inspired" or "God-breathed."

A number of the Bible's internal evidences suggest that the Scriptures are inspired. Perhaps most significant of these are the numerous, often specific, fulfilled prophecies—especially those fulfilled by persons who had no special interest in fulfilling them.

Numerous prophecy passages of the Old Testament quite evidently are fulfilled in the New Testament. One of them is that Christ was to be born in "Bethlehem" (Mic. 5:2; see Matt. 2:1-6).

Another is that He was to be the product of a virgin (Isa. 7:14; Matt. 1:18-25). Isaiah 53 foretells the crucifixion that Christ would suffer between two transgressors, and a prolonging of His days as happened in the Resurrection—for Acts 8:28-34 states that Isaiah 53 refers to Christ. Zech. 11:12-13 prophesies specifics about Christ's betrayal by Judas and what would be done with the 30 pieces of silver (see Matt. 26:15; 27:3-10). Here we have prophecies being fulfilled by persons with no vested interest in fulfilling them—Judas and the chief priests.

In addition to specific prophecies and their fulfillments, only a few of which are mentioned above, Christ himself—and other New Testament personages—state clearly that in Moses, the prophets, and the Psalms, Christ was foretold. To Cleopas and his friend on the Emmaus roadway Jesus said, "O foolish men and slow of heart to believe in all that the prophets have spoken" (Luke 24:25, NASB). Then Luke adds, "And beginning with Moses and with all the prophets, He explained to them the things concerning Himself in all the Scriptures" (v. 27, NASB). Philip said of Christ, "We have found Him of whom Moses in the Law and also the Prophets wrote, Jesus of Nazareth, the son of Joseph" (John 1:45, NASB). Numerous such passages appear in the New Testament (e.g., Matt. 2:17; 4:14; 13:35; 26:56; John 12:38; Acts 3:18; Rom. 3:21). A classic passage is Acts 28:23-26. Paul was "trying to persuade" his hearers "concerning Jesus, from both the Law of Moses and from the Prophets" (v. 23, NASB). Paul's parting word was, "The Holy Spirit rightly spoke through Isaiah the prophet to your fathers" (v. 25, NASB). This indicates the Spirit's inspiration of Isaiah.

This inspiration has to do mainly, but perhaps not exclusively, with the first writing-down of material that became Holy Scripture. It would perhaps also include the help given by the Holy Spirit when a Scripture writer was guided to incorporate what had previously been written by someone else. Furthermore, in the case of interpolations made by later editors, such as the inclusion of the account of Moses' death at the end of Deuteronomy, who is to say that the later editor was not inspired to write what was added? Sometimes, no doubt, inspired interpolations were made by the same person who had earlier written the document (see Luke 3:22).

Inspiration is a form of revelation—revelation being the broader term. Revelation includes all of God's disclosures made to us humans. He has made disclosures to us in nature itself. Nature reveals something of God's power, of His ingenuity. But that is not inspiration. By inspiration, as a theological term, we refer to God's help given to those who wrote the autographs of Holy Scripture— and to additions made later, between the time of the autographs and the time when the writings became canon.

Degrees of Inspiration. Are there degrees of inspiration in various areas of Scripture? Some evangelicals have been reticent to admit degrees of God-help in the writing of them, lest a limited acceptance be given those we regard as opposing a high degree of inspiration in the writing of the Scripture.

However, there were surely degrees of inspiration in the writing of Scripture. It would not take much help from the Holy Spirit for a king's secretary to record important happenings, or for a writer to decide to include that record in his writings. Nor would it have taken any high degree of help from the Spirit for a historian such as Luke to state that Paul traveled from a given town to a different one. It would take more God-help for such a secretary or a historian to pick out the important from the unimportant and record it than simply to mention something that in itself has no evident bearing upon either beliefs or practices. For example, the apostle Paul would no doubt have received a higher intensity of inspiration to write Phil. 2:5-13—which capsules the Christian doctrine of Christ's incarnation, death, and resurrection—than simply to thank the Philippians for their help given him.

Theories of Inspiration. Modernistic theology tends to be humanistic. It opposes the doctrine of a racial fall through a historical Adam and tends to view human reason as capable of figuring out what God is like and what He expects of us. It does not altogether require special revelation in inspired Scriptures. Modernists respect Holy Scripture in part because it was written by eyewitnesses to the sacred events of Israel's Old Testament history and of New Testament times. Yet they do not usually view Scripture as qualitatively different from early noncanonical writings.

Accordingly, liberal theology has little to say about theories of inspiration. Some theologians teach a "superintendence theory" of inspiration, talking vaguely about God's help in heightening the religious and the natural faculties of the Scripture writers.

This help was not qualitatively different from the help He has given literary figures through the intervening centuries.

Neoorthodox theologians, such as Karl Barth, can hardly be said to teach a given theory of inspiration. Barth preferred to teach the inspiringness of Scripture rather than its inspiredness—they inspire us, now, when we read them. Barth preferred to say that the Scriptures contain revelation for us, instead of that they were inspired revelations to the writers themselves.

Emil Brunner's understanding was similar. He said the Bible is no more accurate than other ancient literature on such matters as astronomy.[1] He spoke of "the word of God in the Bible,"[2] suggesting that it *contains* God's Word, not that it *is* God's Word. He said that Scripture contains both historical and scientific errors and that we should disregard such matters, pursuing its religious truth as the Holy Spirit is our Helper.[3]

It is conservative evangelicals who teach theories of inspirations as such. These can be listed as the dictation (mechanical), the verbal, and the dynamic.

1. *The dictation or mechanical theory.* Some 17th-century Lutherans in France taught that the Holy Spirit had given the holy writings to people with utmost precision. Some of them even taught that the vowel points added to the all-consonant Old Testament Scriptures were inspired. This bordered on heresy, because it moved inspiration to such a late date, centuries after the canon itself had been gradually agreed upon.

A type of dictation theory has also been taught, or at least implied, in some folk theology within fundamentalism.

2. *The verbal theory.* This is the view that each word of all the autographs of Scripture was inspired by the Spirit. It is the view held generally in Calvinistic evangelicalism, whether fundamentalist or not.

Yet distinguished evangelicals who advertise themselves as verbal theory advocates explain their theory in a way that belies word-for-word inspiration. Such scholars often say, for example, that the theory is entirely consistent with the human element in the various writers. The Spirit gave them word-inspiration in

---

1. See Emil Brunner, *The Theology of Crisis* (New York: Charles Scribner's Sons, 1929), 4.
2. Ibid., 20.
3. See his *Reason and Revelation* (Philadelphia: Westminster Press, 1951).

keeping with their personalities and experiences. These scholars also affirm that this verbal theory is consistent with (1) varying reports of a given incident; (2) varying reports of a given statement or sermon (e.g., by Jesus); and (3) other not-absolutely-accurate matters such as round-number mathematics and hyperbolic statements. When careful Calvinistic evangelical scholars finish their explanations of what they mean by verbal inspiration, it is not unlike what is meant by the dynamic theory of inspiration usually espoused by Wesleyan-holiness evangelicals.

3. *The dynamic theory.* According to this view, the Holy Spirit inspired the Scripture writers with thoughts but left to them the choice of the words used to express those thoughts. This is the view of A. M. Hills, who writes:

> There is also the *Dynamical Theory,* which holds that there is a supernatural operation of the Spirit within the consciousness and appropriate faculties of the mediate agent. Through this agency, the true and sufficient authorship of the Scriptures is with the Holy Spirit. . . . This theory avoids *the insuperable difficulties of a plenary and verbal inspiration* throughout all the Scriptures.[4]

H. Orton Wiley also espoused the dynamic theory of inspiration. Of it he says:

> This is a mediating theory and is advanced in an effort to explain and preserve in proper harmony, both the divine and human factors in the inspiration of the Scriptures. It maintains that the sacred writers were given extraordinary aid without any interference with their personal characteristics or activities. It preserves the scriptural truth that God speaks through human agencies, but insists that the agent is not reduced to a mere passive instrument. Against this theory little objection can be urged.[5]

Wiley does not distinguish the verbal theory from the mechanical theory but does treat the mechanical as though it really is held by scholars.[6]

4. A. M. Hills, *Fundamental Christian Theology: A Systematic Theology,* 2 vols. (Pasadena, Calif.: C. J. Kinne, 1931), 1:127. Used by permission of Point Loma Press.
5. Wiley, *Christian Theology* 1:176.
6. Ibid., 172-75.

Almost all the significant Wesleyan-holiness theologians have espoused the dynamic theory, including S. S. White[7] and W. T. Purkiser.[8] Richard S. Taylor teaches this view—although he states, as many of us do, that inspiration extended to "the very words" when such help was needed. He writes, "To whatever extent was necessary, this inspiration extended to the very words, certainly to the ideas, and certainly to the inclusion of this or that bit of history, or this or that viewpoint [as in the incorrect viewpoints of some of Job's 'comforters']."[9] He implies the dynamic theory, as what he holds basically, when he says that inspiration applies "certainly to ideas."

Ralph Earle, probably the most voluminous writer of the Wesleyan-holiness movement since John Wesley himself, has taught the dynamic theory of inspiration. In a presidential address to the Evangelical Theological Society he implies acceptance of this theory. He quotes Adam Clarke as saying, "'I only contend for such an inspiration . . . as will assure us of the truth of what they wrote, . . . but not for such an inspiration as implies that even their words were dictated, or their phrases suggested to them by the Holy Ghost,'" and adds: "This is a good description of plenary dynamic inspiration."[10]

This dynamic view of inspiration is consistent with Arminianism, which teaches that the sovereign God relegates to us many freedoms that are exercised with limitations. God needed to inspire the Scripture writers supernaturally, especially with theological and moral insights. Humans are fallen in all aspects and cannot, unaided, invent correct doctrine and practice. God treats us as humans, not as robots. He likes to persuade us instead of driving us. Because of this, Wesleyan-holiness evangelicals understand that God inspired prophets and apostles and others with thoughts that they were to write down, but He left to them, in

7. S. S. White, *Essential Christian Beliefs* (Kansas City: Nazarene Publishing House, 1940), 92.

8. W. T. Purkiser, ed., *Exploring Our Christian Faith* (Kansas City: Beacon Hill Press, 1960), 72-73.

9. Richard S. Taylor, *Biblical Authority and Christian Faith* (Kansas City: Beacon Hill Press of Kansas City, 1980), 62.

10. Ralph Earle, "Further Thoughts on Biblical Inspiration," lecture given Dec. 27, 1962, at the annual meeting of the Evangelical Theological Society and soon printed in its *Evangelical Theological Journal*, 1963, 13.

their intelligent and redeemed freedom, the choice of words with which to write down the inspired thoughts.

This dynamic view is supportable from our scholarly studies of the canonical writings. We find many instances of what is often called the human element entering into the writings. We find the various authors writing the way we would expect them to, based on other things we know about them. Since Luke was a physician, we should expect him to use the word for a physician's needle in recording Jesus' statement: "For it is easier for a camel to go through the eye of a needle, than for a rich man to enter the kingdom of God" (Luke 18:25, NASB). Other writers who were not physicians used different words for "needle" in recording the statement (Mark 10:25; Matt. 19:24). On the basis of verbal inspiration, word-for-word sovereign guidance, all the writers reporting in Greek what Jesus had said in Aramaic would surely have used the same word for "needle."

Often, perhaps, verbal inspiration occurred. Prophets often seemed to be given messages word for word. Besides, not just any word would convey a given inspired thought. Not just any tense of a verb would convey a given thought. All the while, the Holy Spirit protected the writings from error, especially on doctrine and practice matters.

Sometimes Wesleyan-holiness scholars have tended to deprecate the inspiration of Scripture, suggesting instead that what is important is its sufficiency in guiding us to redemption though Christ, the living Word of God. Its sufficiency for redemption though Christ is of paramount importance, but Scripture would not be characterized by this redemptive sufficiency if it were not God-inspired in the first place. The apostle Peter says, "We did not follow cleverly invented stories when we told you about the power and coming of our Lord Jesus Christ, but we were eyewitnesses of his majesty" (2 Pet. 1:16)—a reference to the transfiguration of Christ (see vv. 17-18). Then, besides being an eyewitness authority, Peter says, "And we have the word of the prophets" (v. 19). Speaking further of Scripture and of God's help in the writing of it, he says, "Above all [as though this God-help is even more important than his having been an eyewitness to God's giving Christ authority at the Transfiguration], you must understand that no prophecy of Scripture came about by the prophet's own interpretation. For prophecy never had its origin in the will of man, but men spoke from God as they were carried along by the Holy Spirit" (vv. 20-21). We read elsewhere of Peter's high respect for Paul's Epistles, though he finds parts of them difficult to understand (2 Pet. 3:15-16).[11] And as mentioned earlier, Paul said, "All Scripture is inspired by God" (2 Tim. 3:16, NASB). Besides, it is well known that Christ respected the Old Testament, quoting it often, as to Satan (Matt. 4:10ff.), and otherwise referring to it frequently. On all these bases, and others not mentioned here, it can be said that the divine inspiration of Scripture, in part, assures its redemptive sufficiency and its authority.

From Autographs to Canon

God's helping us with special revelation did not stop with the initial inspiration help in the writing of Scripture. The Holy Spirit, Guide into all truth, helped in other ways. He helped His people to decide which writings, even which fragments of writings (as in the case of Proverbs and Psalms), should be respected highly and later included in what we call the canon of Scripture.

At first, says Claremont's James Sanders (who has made in-depth study of the matter), the people viewed what came to be the canonical books as containing sacred story. This relates more especially to the Old Testament writings than to those of the New Testament. As centuries passed, he says, the sacred story came to be conceived of as sacred text. Adaptations were then discouraged, and the text was protected. Care in preserving the text was stressed. No doubt the Holy Spirit figured profoundly in all of this.

While Scripture was sacred story, it was changed in various ways according to the interests and the needs of people in different eras. And perhaps the Holy Spirit inspired these changes. That such adaptations were made can be seen in the actual texts, and in allusions to texts, that are available to scholars.

This creates difficult problems for the fundamentalist Christian who believes in verbal inspiration and in total inerrancy—not only in faith and practice matters but also in mathematical, historical, and geographical matters, which often count very little.

---

11. Peter says, "Just as also our beloved brother Paul, according to the wisdom given him, wrote to you, as also in all his letters, speaking in them of these things, in which are some things hard to understand, which the untaught and unstable distort, as they do also the rest of the Scriptures, to their own destruction" (2 Pet. 3:15-16, NASB).

Yet Wesleyan-holiness evangelicals have no problem with inspired writings becoming changed somewhat between the time when they were first written and the time when they became canon. Believing in thought-inspiration in general instead of the word-attached-to-word kind, we are not as anxious about an unaltered text as is the fundamentalist. Understanding that inerrancy relates to doctrine and practice matters, we get less uptight about finding certain Spirit-guided alterations.

Of exceeding importance, nevertheless, is our understanding of the Holy Spirit's continuing protection and preservation of the story-text that became our canon.

Protestants generally have long believed in the Holy Spirit's continued help in guiding the Church into and in all truth. We believe profoundly that the Holy Spirit guided the various changes that occurred between the time when the text was first written and when it became recognized as canon. We believe the Spirit has helped in the translation and the interpretation of the canonical text. Since He ministers by persuasion instead of coercion, He has not always secured exactly what He has wanted. Still, He has guarded orthodoxy, even though the exactness of the originally inspired writings may have been lost to us in part.

Exceedingly important, in all of this, is the fact that when the 66 books of the Christian canon were gradually decided upon, so that nothing else was to be read in the churches as Scripture, it was not the inspired autographs that were so esteemed. At the Council of Carthage in 397, and at other times, the Spirit-guided Church, in establishing the canon, was making decisions, not about the autographs, but about copies that had been altered somewhat, yet protected from significant error, preserved in their basic integrity. While inspiration had to do especially with the writing of the autographs, and probably with decisions to include what was already written, the Holy Spirit continued to guide God's faith-filled people all through the centuries from autographs to canon. And it was the text as it appeared in the early centuries of the Christian era that the Spirit-guided Church viewed as canon. We do not have the autographs, and it is not very likely that we will ever have them. If one of them were ever unearthed, we could hardly be certain that it was indeed an autograph—the inspired writer's original copy.

In Wesleyan-holiness theology we are confident about the inspiration of the original writers. We are also confident about the Holy Spirit's continued protection of the text. Perhaps He inspired additions to the autographs and other changes in them. The Holy Spirit guided the Church, in many ways, to forge a canon gradually. Our confidence therefore is not placed in autographs that we do not have and probably never will have, but in a canon that we do have in more or less its pure form.

We have New Testament manuscripts that date approximately to the time of the formal decisions on the canon, and many papyrus fragments dating to an earlier time—the third century. Sinaiticus and Vaticanus date to the fourth century, and other manuscripts such as Alexandrinus date nearly to that time. It does not overly concern us that these various handwritten manuscripts contain numerous variations. It does not even concern us greatly that, for example, Sinaiticus contains the Shepherd of Hermas, a book not accepted as canonical by the Roman Catholic and Protestant West, but only by Eastern Orthodoxy.

If we were bibliolatrous, we would be deeply troubled over the thousands of variations in the manuscripts we possess. As it is, we steadily, knowingly, and happily worship the God of the Bible—Father, Son, and Holy Spirit—one God, world without end. Scripture points us to them, and it does so with full adequacy.

After all, it was not autographs that Christ and other New Testament personages quoted as Scripture. It was not even the autographs of the Old Testament plus the changes occurring between autographs and canon. It was a Greek translation of texts that had developed from the autographs. It is that kind of writings that the first-century believing communities (synagogue and church) respected as canon and found functionally useful. Likewise, in the case of the New Testament writings, it was not autographs that the Church of the early centuries respected and found useful. It was the autographs plus changes (not nearly as many as in the case of the Old Testament).

Our canon is richer than the autographs had been. It contains what the Holy Spirit had persuaded people to add to the autographs. It might even contain deletions from the autographs, if the original writers did not write precisely what the persuading, not coercing, Spirit had wanted them to write. It contains changes in the writings that the believing communities had found to be functional.

If the writings that the believing community possessed during the Exile, and during the later Diaspora, could hold it together when all other peoples of the Near East lost continuity with their past and ceased to exist, give me that part of the canon! And give me the rest of the Old Testament canon and the New Testament canon. The whole of it, changed somewhat from the autographs, has been found to be survivingly and nurturingly and evangelistically useful by my forebears and my contemporaries.

We do not crave a precanonical text that we can use more wholeheartedly than we can use the canonical text. What is being said here, also, is that we are more interested in dropping from our biblical text whatever postcanonical changes are in it, such as the ending of Mark's Gospel, than we are in dropping from it the precanonical changes made between the time of the autographs and the decisions on what was canon.

Determining the meaning of the canonical text is vastly more important than reconstructing a precanonical text. We need to know about genre and forms and how and why redactors did what they did; therefore, we are not interested in junking the historical-critical sciences. They can help us find out what the meaning of the text was and is. What we are hungry for, what we pursue, is this meaning, this theological meaning, this soteriological meaning, this evangelistic meaning, this meaning that searches us and stretches us and secures us.

O give me that canon! It will point me to Christ, to the lost and the least of this world, to a nurturing ministry, to ethical responsibilities, and to heaven.

The Inerrancy Issue

The issue of the Bible's inerrancy, when expressed carefully, refers to the extent of the inerrancy of the autographs of Scripture—which of course we do not have. Inerrancy could not be affirmed of any copy or translation or version of Scripture. It certainly could not be affirmed of any given manuscript. Multiplied thousands of variations appear in the extant manuscripts of the Old Testament and the New Testament books.

The Total Inerrancy View. Some evangelicals understand that the inerrancy of Scripture is not limited to doctrine and practice matters but includes such matters as geography, science, mathematics, and historical statements. This is not the usual view in the

Wesleyan-holiness tradition, although it is the teaching of Stephen Paine, who figured importantly in a change whereby the Wesleyan Methodist church (now The Wesleyan Church) came to teach it officially.

The total inerrancy view is taught by such widely published Calvinistic evangelicals as Francis Schaeffer (1912-85), Norman Geisler, and Harold Lindsell. Lindsell teaches that the Bible autographs were inerrant on all matters. This view, he believes, has been normative throughout Christian history; and what he calls "believers in errancy"[12] have appeared in any force only during the past 150 years. He even prefers to define *evangelical* on a "total inerrancy" basis,[13] although he is not willing to label so-called errancy people as non-Christians.

Lindsell contends that the early Christian creeds (Apostles', Nicene, Athanasian) have no article on Scripture because their writers assumed a total inerrancy view to be commonly believed, so that no article on the matter was needed. Lindsell also assumed that the later creeds, such as the Westminster Confession, regard the Bible as inerrant, although this is not explicitly stated in these creeds. Lindsell also tends to interpret numerous fathers and medievals and Reformers, even John Wesley, as teaching total inerrancy, when they do not do so expressly—or at least not with consistency, as in the case of Wesley. Lindsell then calls the inerrant-on-doctrine-and-practice view as taught by many evangelicals a departure from the Church's historical stance.

Jack Rogers, in his *Confessions of a Conservative Evangelical,*[14] studied the writings of the seven Englishmen and the four Scotsmen who served on the committee that wrote the article of faith on Scripture for the Westminster Confession, and he found that not one of them in his writings taught that Scripture is inerrant on matters such as science and history. His sleuthing tends to undermine the view of Lindsell and others that the article of faith on Scripture in that confession intends total inerrancy.

The total inerrancy view came to be taught by B. B. Warfield at Princeton at the beginning of the 20th century; and it is es-

---

12. Harold Lindsell, *The Battle for the Bible* (Grand Rapids: Zondervan Publishing House, 1976), 141.

13. Ibid., 139.

14. Jack Rogers, *Confessions of a Conservative Evangelical* (Philadelphia: Westminster Press, 1974).

poused by many evangelicals today. Indeed, national meetings of fundamentalist evangelical scholars have been held in order to promote the total inerrancy view.

Doctrine and Practice Inerrancy. The present writer, not admitting that there were any errors of any kind in the autographs, is noncommittal about any possible nonfaith, nonpractice errors in those nonextant manuscripts. A faith-confidence that cannot be altogether supported is that the autographs would not have contained errors on doctrine and practice matters—if allowance is given to interpret with wide brushstrokes the manuscripts we do possess. Yet the real interest, as noted earlier, should be in the canon and not in the autographs.

Most of us Wesleyan-holiness scholars are hunters after the Bible's soteriological message and do not like to engage ourselves with such matters as whether it errs on nonfaith and nonpractice matters.

God-inspired writers were illuminated with insights into the correct understanding of countless issues. So guided, they did not teach errors on doctrine and practice. A careful student of the Scriptures, however, can only say this if allowed to interpret Scripture with Scripture, often explaining the difficult and seemingly inconsistent passages with those that are more clear in their meaning.

On a number of bases, Wesleyan-holiness evangelicals hold the confidence that Scripture is inerrant on doctrine and practice but that it might contain error on matters relating to mathematics, science, geography, or such like.

1. If God had been interested in wooden accuracy on nondoctrinal and nonethical matters, it is strange He would have chosen Hebrew as the language of about three-quarters of the Bible. Hebrew has no vowels—no letters to express such sounds as *a, e, i, o,* and *u.* Vowels have been supplied to the consonantal text, making for an inexactness not in keeping with total inerrancy interests. The consonants *f* and *r,* for example, can mean numerous words in the English, according to which vowels we add to them. They can mean fur, fir, fire, fair, fare, for, four, fore, and so forth. The context usually helps us be confident about what vowels to add, and most would agree that the Masoretes did very well, several centuries into our era, in adding vowels to the Old Testament Hebrew text. Yet inexactness is introduced. Although many of us understand that the Holy Spirit would have helped in the adding

of vowels, it is not usually understood that they were inspired by the Holy Spirit to add the correct vowels to the postcanonical text. Since the discovery of the Dead Sea Scrolls, we now possess much of the Old Testament in vowelless Hebrew. We are able to start over almost from scratch on the matter of adding vowels to the consonants, but we would not necessarily be more exact than were the Masoretes. We could not be sure that the Holy Spirit had guided us invariably to include the vowels that would convey any intended sense with total accuracy.

2. Also, how could God have used the Greek language of the New Testament Scriptures, as that language was being written in the first century of our era, if He was interested in total accuracy? All the letters were capitals in these manuscripts, which we call the uncials. Which words we capitalize and which we lowercase becomes a decision for editors and translators; and this sometimes makes considerable difference. Take, as a single example, *spirit*. If it is capitalized today in a version, translators thought, from the context, that the Holy Spirit—or perhaps just God—is referred to. If they lowercase it, they suppose the human spirit is being referred to. The context usually makes the choice simple; but occasionally the matter is not altogether clear.

Another thing: Koine Greek had no punctuation marks and did not even leave spaces between the words.

God-inspired thoughts could well be conveyed in Hebrew and Greek. God could have used those languages if He was interested in writings that contain no errors in doctrine and practice matters. But neither Hebrew nor Greek would have been an adequate language if God were anxious about total accuracy in all details.

3. Further, if God were interested in total inerrancy, why are the approximately 300 quotations in the New Testament not from the inspired writings of the Hebrew Old Testament, or from inspired, on-the-spot translations of them, but instead from a Greek translation of the Hebrew—the Septuagint? The Septuagint is a dependable translation, yet something of total accuracy is always lost in a translation. No doubt the Holy Spirit helped the Septuagint translators, but the Church has not regarded them as inspired. People usually spoke Aramaic in Palestine in New Testament times, and many people also spoke and wrote Greek. A fisherman such as Peter probably did not even know Hebrew. If God were interested in total accuracy, perhaps He would have

THEOLOGY'S WRITTEN AUTHORITY ▷ 77

used only writers who knew Hebrew. Then, under inspiration, those persons might have translated the Hebrew Old Testament instead of using the uninspired Septuagint translation.

4. Moreover, if the Holy Spirit were interested in exact accuracy, why would writers couch religious truth in inexact allegories and metaphors? In Revelation, He would surely not have had the writer use Babylon, a white horse, beasts, and so forth, if accuracy were what He was after, for we know only more or less what is meant by those symbols. And perhaps Jesus would not have used metaphors, such as when He called himself "bread," "the door," and especially "the resurrection and the life" (John 11:25), if He had been interested in conveying exactness of meaning.

5. Still further, what great advantage would there have been in totally inerrant Hebrew, Greek, and Aramaic autographs, when the writings would soon need to be translated into other languages and the wooden accuracy would have been lost anyway? In the thousands of extant New Testament manuscripts, we find tens of thousands of minor variations. We find numerous such variations if we collate our few oldest Old Testament manuscripts (and if we compare the Dead Sea Scrolls with our vowels-added Hebrew Old Testament manuscripts). Why should the Holy Spirit guard those original autographs on all minute, nonfaith matters, when the equivalent meaning of what was said had to be translated into all sorts of languages—and fine, precise accuracy was going to be lost anyway? Evidently, what is important is that the meaning be guarded sufficiently so that matters of doctrine and practice are protected. That is one of the continuing works of the Holy Spirit of truth.

6. Significantly supportive of this is the New Testament writers' use of the Old Testament. They do not quote it with exactness. Yet, if a wooden and total inerrancy were a special interest of the Holy Spirit, surely He would have inspired the New Testament writers to quote with precision the so-called totally inerrant Old Testament writings.

7. Another and smaller factor in this is the negative direction in the inerrancy interest. It hunts for reasons why seeming errors are not errors. When our interest is in Scripture's authority, because of its witness to Jesus Christ and redemption offered through Him, a person hunts out what is positive: its authority,

especially its Christic, redemptive, nurturing, and apocalyptic authority.

8. Still another basis for this view lies in the fact that Scripture's inerrancy on doctrine and practice is the important matter.

9. Besides, it might not even make much sense to express confidence in the total inerrancy of the autographs, which we do not possess. How can we know confidently that writings that no living person has ever seen were totally without error? It is the canon that we can express confidence about, and, regarding it, we can be confident about the doctrine and practice taught in it. But even as regards the canon, we do not know enough about it to declare as an article of faith that it contained no tiny errors in unimportant matters. We possess various Old Testament and New Testament manuscripts dating to about the time when the texts became canon, and what we possess shows no special conflicts between the writers on doctrine and practice matters.

10. Besides, an article of faith should have to do with faith—and not with matters of uniform accuracy on nonfaith matters.

11. Of bearing also on the inerrancy issue is the fact that even the four Gospels, which give details of Christ's life, tend to give only such details as relate in some way to the redemption He provided for us. These strange-looking books we call Gospels, which do not seem to conform to any previous literary form, are not simply biographies. They do not give biographical details one by one but give details that relate to redemption. They give accounts of His teachings, His mighty works, and His death and resurrection. Two of them, Matthew and Luke, start with His birth, no doubt because they understand that its supernaturalness and its naturalness related to His ministry. John gives us a different order of events, one that will facilitate his purpose—an account of the redeeming Christ in whom he wants the reader to believe savingly.

12. Moreover, Scripture itself is not interested in total inerrancy. It makes a claim for inspiration but not for total inerrancy. The most express passage of Scripture on inspiration states clearly that inspiration insures or results in doctrine and practice matters: "All Scripture is inspired by God and profitable for teaching, for reproof, for correction, for training in righteousness; that the man of God may be adequate, equipped for every good work" (2 Tim. 3:16-17, NASB).

13. A final observation: to express a total inerrancy view of Scripture might mean that we would be expressing a "higher" view of Scripture than the Church usually expresses in Christ our Godman Savior. We express confidence that Christ was sinless. Paul says this in 2 Cor. 5:21: "He made Him who knew no sin to be sin on our behalf" (NASB). The writer of Hebrews says it in 4:15: "For we do not have a high priest who cannot sympathize with our weaknesses, but one who has been tempted in all things as we are, yet without sin" (NASB).

Christ was without original sin because He was a new Adam, a new representative of the race, and was not represented by the first Adam. And Scripture declares in effect that He did not ever disobey the Father who had sent Him.

Yet Scripture does not declare outright that Christ never erred in any way whatever. Scripture does not tell us any detail of Christ's life between ages 12 and 30; and the Gospels pick out things to tell us about Christ's three years of public ministry that relate to redemption. If Jesus erred, as in looking in the wrong place for someone, it would not matter, even as it would not matter if the autographs of Scripture might have erred in mathematical figures.

What is being said here is that Scripture and the Church have taught unequivocally that Christ was sinless, not that He was totally errorless on unimportant matters. If we were to say that the autographs of Scripture were totally without error, even on inconsequential matters where doctrine and practice are not involved, we would be saying something more select about them than the Scriptures and the Church have usually expressed about Christ himself.

John Wesley's Views. John Wesley can be quoted in support of a total inerrancy view. He can also be quoted as teaching the view here being argued for. Wesley made at least one statement, in his journal, that might imply total inerrancy. He said, "Nay, if there be any mistakes in the Bible, there may as well be a thousand. If there be one falsehood in that book, it did not come from the God of truth."[15] This statement, quoted by Harold Lindsell in *The Bat-*

---

15. John Wesley, *The Journal of the Rev. John Wesley, A.M.*, ed. Nehemiah Curnock, 8 vols. (London: Epworth Press, 1938), 6:117.

tle for the Bible, differs from much that is contrary to it in Wesley. Indeed, even this statement is not a clear teaching of total inerrancy. He has not clearly stated that he is including unimportant matters when he says there are no mistakes in the Bible. Since "falsehoods" is his synonym for "mistake," then "mistake" must have to do with a consequential matter. Besides, since he uses the word "truth" here, implying that the Bible, without any falsehoods in it, comes from "the God of truth," he seems to be talking about its consequential matters instead of its mathematics, geography, genealogical tables—things of that sort.

Many things that Wesley says about Scripture show clearly that he views it in much the same way as is held in the Wesleyan-holiness tradition. For one thing, he allows that the genealogies in Matthew and Luke might be incorrect. In his comment on Matt. 1:1 in the *Notes* he says:

> If there were any difficulties in this genealogy, or that given by Luke, . . . they would rather affect the Jewish tables than the credit of the evangelists: For they act only as historians, setting down these genealogies as they stood in those public . . . records. Therefore they were to take them as they found them. Nor was it needful they should correct the mistakes, if there were any. For these accounts sufficiently answer the end for which they are recited. They unquestionably prove the grand point in view, that Jesus was one of the family from which the promised seed was to come. And they had more weight with the Jews than if alterations had been made by inspiration itself.[16]

Wesley's use of "true," in "infallibly true," also suggests that he understood the Scriptures to be infallible on important matters instead of always correct on such matters as mathematics. In this connection he says, "'All Scripture is given by inspiration of God,' consequently, all Scripture is infallibly true."[17] In this context he also, continuing, says that the things the God-breathed Scripture is profitable for are "doctrine," "reproof," and "correction"—not geography.[18]

16. John Wesley, *Explanatory Notes upon the New Testament* (London: Epworth Press, 1941), 15.
17. Wesley, *Works* 5:193.
18. Ibid.

In another sermon, "The Witness of the Spirit," he also refers to this 2 Tim. 3:16 passage; and he points out the same things as what Scripture is profitable for.[19]

It is also correct that he and other Holy Club members were called "Bible moths,"[20] who fed on the Bible as moths do on cloth. This suggests a high view of Scripture as a means of grace, but it suggests nothing concerning total inerrancy.

Early Methodist Adam Clarke (1760-1832), biblical scholar extraordinaire, said, "I only contend for such an inspiration, or Divine assistance of the sacred writers of the *New Testament*, as will assure us of the truth of what they wrote, . . . but not for such an inspiration as implies that even their words were dictated, or their phrases suggested to them by the *Holy Ghost.*"[21]

That Clarke was interested in faith and practice matters, instead of anything like total inerrancy, is shown when he says, "The Sacred Scriptures . . . are alone sufficient for everything relative to faith and practice of a Christian, and were given by inspiration of God."[22] Along with this, it should be noted that Clarke believed that at times "the Holy Ghost . . . dictated to them . . . what to write."[23] This heightened degree of the Spirit's help in certain parts of Scripture has been properly taught also by many others inside and outside the Wesleyan-holiness tradition.

On inerrancy specifically, Clarke implies that this has to do with matters of salvation when he writes, "The Bible . . . declares his [God's] will relative to the salvation of men . . . Men may err, but the Scriptures cannot."[24] He also says, "The apostles were assisted and preserved from error by the Spirit of God; and therefore were enabled to deliver to us an unerring rule of faith."[25] Again, this is inerrancy on the "rule of faith."

---

19. Ibid., 136.

20. See Richard Green, *John Wesley, Evangelist* (London: Religious Tract Society, 1905), 76-77.

21. Adam Clarke, *The New Testament . . . with Commentary and Critical Notes* (New York: Abingdon-Cokesbury, 1836), 1.

22. See J. B. B. Clarke, ed., *An Account of the Infancy, Religious and Literary Life of Adam Clarke*, 3 vols. (London: T. S. Clarke, 1833), 1:172.

23. Adam Clarke, *Commentary*, comments on 2 Pet. 1:20-21.

24. Adam Clarke, *Miscellaneous Works*, 13 vols. (London: T. Tegg, 1839-45), 12:132.

25. Adam Clarke, *Commentary* 5:11.

H. Orton Wiley's View. Wiley, author of *Christian Theology,* viewed inerrancy similarly.[26] The present writer studied under him, taught a course jointly with him at Pasadena College during the 1952-53 school year and visited with him on theological matters almost daily, and corresponded with him occasionally until near the time of his passing in 1961. We discussed specifically the matter of the Bible's total inerrancy, and he was clear in not taking that position. I remember this clearly because his view was different from mine at that time; I was then taking a total inerrancy stance. Besides, a search of Wiley's *Christian Theology* has indicated that he nowhere takes a total inerrancy view.

Wiley says that the Spirit's "inspiration" means that "the Bible becomes the infallible Word of God, the authoritative rule of faith and practice in the Church."[27] This is not a total inerrancy statement. At one place he gives seven bases for believing that the Scriptures have been kept intact and free from essential error, so that we may be assured of the truth originally given by the inspired authors.[28]

A. M. Hills's View. Hills, perhaps second only to H. Orton Wiley in significance as a theologian of the Wesleyan-holiness tradition, taught that Scripture does contain error on unimportant matters—so that he was farther yet from total inerrancy than were Wesley, Clarke, and Wiley.

Sometimes it seems that Hills means only that the copies of the autographs introduced errors—which all scholars agree on. He writes, "Thus by the negligence or inaccuracy of the copyists, through the many centuries, in hundred of manuscripts, there came to be ten thousand various readings in the Old Testament, and one hundred and fifty thousand in the New Testament, as the eminent scholars tell us."[29]

---

26. Wiley seems to have written the Nazarene article of faith on Scripture, which speaks of it as "inerrantly revealing the will of God concerning us in all things necessary to our salvation" (see *Manual,* 1928, p. 22). This is not a total inerrancy view. A. Elwood Sanner stated in the Wiley Lectures at Pasadena College that Wiley had told him that he, Wiley, had written this article, and that Wiley added, "I wanted to state it so that there would be a little bit of elbow room in there." Stephen S. White stated in the *Herald of Holiness* in 1955: "I had nothing to do with writing this statement, but I am quite sure Dr. Wiley did have" (Nov. 9, 1955, p. 14).
27. Wiley, *Christian Theology* 1:171.
28. Ibid., 212-14.
29. Hills, *Fundamental Christian Theology* 1:106. Used by permission of Point Loma Press.

At other times, though, he simply admits that there are inconsequential errors and discrepancies in our Bible, and he does not seem to be speaking of copying variations. In this connection he says, "But to say that *all of Scripture* was so inspired [verbally], is to put too great a tax upon faith. In view of the discrepancies, and the disagreements and misquotations, or inaccurate quotations, and the manifestly lower moral and spiritual tone in some passages than in others, these strong theories [of 'universal' plenary and 'common' verbal inspiration], if applied to the whole Bible cannot be successfully defended."[30] He goes on to say, "But if the inspiration of the *original text* [the autographs] were absolute and complete [he implies that it was not], and were absolutely proved, no one can maintain that we have that original text in every minute particular."[31] Later he says, "But, in spite of all discrepancies, and disagreements, and errors, and minor inaccuracies, the Bible still remains God's inspired and infallible book."[32] And soon he adds, "The marvel and the miracle is that there are so few discrepancies of any real importance."[33]

Hills might be the only major Wesleyan-holiness theologian to teach that there were unimportant errors in the autographs. The present writer understands that there might have been inconsequential errors, not that there were. It would seem that even such an error as crediting a quotation to the wrong prophet might have been introduced into the text by a copyist. Yet it would be of no special consequence if the autographs did contain occasional errors of that sort. It is interesting, though, that Hills took this kind of view in a 1931 publication, just after evangelicalism generally in America had been pushed in fundamentalist directions.

Richard S. Taylor's View. Taylor's teaching is similar to Wiley's on inerrancy. He says, "Of course, the whole question of 'inconsequential error' remains debatable; this book is not assuming that such error existed in the autographs."[34]

---

30. Ibid., 126.
31. Ibid.
32. Ibid., 134.
33. Ibid.
34. Richard S. Taylor, *Biblical Authority and Christian Faith*, 80.

H. Ray Dunning's View. Dunning argues against even an interest in the "inerrancy"[35] of Scripture, and for its "authority" attested to be "the internal testimony of the Holy Spirit,"[36] which is "a special case of prevenient grace."[37] Like earlier Wesleyans, and like prefundamentalist Calvinists for that matter, he is interested in the Bible's faith and practice matters—and sometimes he simply singles out the Bible's theological teaching as what is important, especially as we are existentially transformed by the Spirit through use of it. Autographs have no special place here; they do not even get you into the court of the Gentiles.

The Authority of Scripture

God only, and not Scripture, is absolutely authoritative. Yet, as a written-down revelation of what the absolutely authoritative God has done and offers to do, and of what God's will is, Scripture is the primary written authority. All other written authorities, such as creeds and confessions and the best insights of the righteous and the wise, are only secondary or tertiary.

Basically, it is the Holy Spirit's inspiration of the Scripture writers that invests Scripture with authority. At the same time, Scripture is authoritative because it prophesies Christ in the Old Testament, narrates His life and works and death and resurrection in the Gospels, and interprets the meaning of the Christ events in the Epistles. In the Christ events themselves, there are revelations to us. For example, in the event of the Cross, God's love is spelled out for us in blood dripping from a thorn-crowned brow. Yet we would not know about the revelatory events without the revelatory Scriptures that narrate them and discourse on their salvific meaning.

Other factors, secondary to those above, figure in the authority of Scripture. One is the fact that Scripture writers were often eyewitnesses of the events. Most of the New Testament writers knew Christ in the flesh. This is somewhat true of Mark and more so of Matthew. It is eminently so of James, the Lord's half brother, and of John and Peter, who were members of the inner circle of

35. H. Ray Dunning, *Grace, Faith, and Holiness* (Kansas City: Beacon Hill Press of Kansas City, 1988), 60.
36. Ibid., 62.
37. Ibid., 63.

the Twelve. And Paul counted Christ's appearance to him on the Damascus road as giving him a belated direct acquaintance with Christ (Acts 9:3-5; 1 Cor. 15:8).

The attestation of the Church, the believing community, also argues for the authority of Scripture. This is somewhat so of the present faithing, loving, and hoping community. It is eminently so of the Early Church. We believe the Holy Spirit guided the Church to select the canonical books and to allow the near misses, such as First Clement and even the Shepherd of Hermas (in the West), to slough off. This reflects a gradual and imperceptible growth in respect for the authority of especially the New Testament books. The Old Testament books had already, even before the Council of Jamnia in A.D. 90, become established as authoritative in the consciousness of God's faithful people. When such councils as that at Carthage in 397 agree that no other books than the 27 (of our New Testament) are to be read in the churches as Scripture, you have an early and official recognition of authority in those canonical books.

The believing community from that time to the present also figures in the authority of the canonical books. The Bible books still, in a living way, are authoritative written sources for our faith. This is in part because we Spirit-guided Christians have become enthusiastic rediscoverers of what the pristinely apostolic early Christians had discovered.

The Genuineness of Scripture

A classically evangelical appreciation of Scripture includes an acceptance of its basic genuineness—that it was written by its declared authors. It is to the Pastoral Epistles that the problem of genuineness perhaps most especially applies. Paul states that he wrote them; yet many scholars have said that he did not. In part, they say this because they feel the Pastorals suggest a more developed organization within the Church than they would expect if they were written in Paul's lifetime.

Yet if these Epistles were not written by Paul, they are labyrinthine fabrications. Timothy would not then be the writer's "true child" (1 Tim. 1:2, NASB), nor his "beloved son" (2 Tim. 1:2, NASB; see 2:1). If it was written by someone else at a much later time, the fabrication includes the writer's acting as if he is Paul in numerous ways. The writer refers to having urged Timo-

thy to "remain on at Ephesus" (1 Tim. 1:3, NASB) and to teach
correct doctrine there when he, Paul, had departed from "Macedonia." He refers to Timothy's "frequent ailments" (5:23, NASB),
to his "grandmother Lois" and his "mother Eunice" (2 Tim. 1:5),
to himself as suffering "hardship even to imprisonment as a criminal" (2:9, NASB), and to Timothy's "childhood," from which time
he had "known the sacred writings" (3:15, NASB).

In the Pastorals the writer refers to himself, alone or with
others, with 94 personal pronouns, an immense sustained fabrication if Paul is not the author.

References made to numerous named persons in these three
Epistles would add to the contrived fabrication if the Pastorals are
not Paul's. These individuals include "Hymenaeus and Alexander," whom the writer had "delivered over to Satan" (1 Tim. 1:20,
NASB); "Phygelus and Hermogenes," Asian Christians who had
"turned away from" the writer (2 Tim. 1:15, NASB); "Onesiphorus," who "often refreshed" the writer (v. 16, NASB); "Hymenaeus
[again] and Philetus," whose "empty chatter . . . spread like gan-
grene" (2:16-17, NASB); unnamed men who, like "Jannes and
Jambres," had opposed "the truth" (3:8); "Demas," who had "deserted" the writer; "Crescens" and "Titus," faithful persons (4:10);
"Luke," who was with the writer (v. 11) and who, according to
Acts, was often with Paul; "Mark," whom Timothy (who would
have been long dead, on the late dating) was to "bring to" the
writer; "Tychicus," whom the writer had "sent" to "Ephesus" (v.
12); "Carpus" of "Troas," from whose home Timothy was to bring
to the writer "books" and "parchments" (v. 13, NASB); "Alexander the coppersmith," who had done the writer "much harm" (v.
14, NASB), whom Timothy was to be on guard against; "Priscilla
and Aquila and the household of Onesiphorus" (v. 19), whom
Timothy was to "greet" for the writer; "Erastus," "Trophimus,"
"Eubulus," "Pudens," "Linus," and "Claudia" (vv. 20-22); and
"Artemas," "Tychicus," and "Zenas" (Titus 3:12-13).

If all these pains are taken to devise a sustained fabrication,
in which the writer states that he is Paul; in which he is writing to
Timothy and Titus, whom we know from other biblical books to
have been Paul's associates; in which he uses 94 pronouns referring to himself after stating his name; in which he names 26 different persons—how are we to trust the other things said in the

three Epistles, especially the many things that have to do with Christian doctrine and practice?

It is interesting that the late maverick Anglican bishop-professor J. A. T. Robinson, who was extremely modernistic in earlier writings, wrote a thorough treatment of the dating of the New Testament books, in which he supports a view that all 27 books were written before A.D. 70—including the Pastorals.[38]

Translations of Scripture

Pentecost is sheer proof that God wants His written Word to be translated into the many languages of the world. At that event, people from 13 language areas heard the Christian message in their own tongues.

Before New Testament times, the Old Testament had been translated from Hebrew (with some Aramaic, as in part of Daniel) into Greek. It was that Greek translation that the New Testament writers quoted some 300 times, as mentioned earlier.

In the 2nd century A.D. the New Testament was translated into the Syriac, a version with few equals in broadness of impact. The Bible was rendered into Old Latin and into Coptic dialects, and then into Latin in the 4th and 5th centuries. Armenians and Georgians received their Bible in the 5th century. By the time of the invention of printing in the 15th century, 33 languages had received parts of the Scriptures, and 71 by 1800. In the next 30 years, in the wake of the Evangelical Revival, 86 more languages had been invaded, this being the era of such missionary translators as Carey in India, Morrison in China, and Judson in Burma. During this time also the British and Foreign Bible Society (1804) and the American Bible Society (1816) were founded, which have been important factors in the increase, by 1988,[39] to some 1,907 languages into which at least one book of Scripture has been translated. Of these, more than 310 include the entire Bible; other hundreds the entire New Testament; and many more hundreds at least a Gospel or some other whole book. In scores of languages lacking a whole book of the Bible, short passages or collections of

---

38. See J. A. T. Robinson, *Redating the New Testament* (Philadelphia: Westminster Press, 1976). Robinson's basic reason for saying all the books were written before A.D. 70 is that the Temple's destruction that year is the most historic event of the first century, and yet it is not alluded to as having already happened.

39. As of 1988. (See *Christian Century*, Feb. 22, 1989, 201.)

passages have been published. In this way Christ the Redeemer marches into more groupings of people with His power to transform utterly.

Many of the Bible's translators are widely known scholars and missionaries, so that a roll call of them sounds like a listing of the Church's greats: Origen and Jerome (ca. A.D. 347-420) in early times, and Caedmon and Bede; Wycliffe (1320-84) later, and Luther, Tyndale, and Coverdale in Reformation times; the missionaries such as Robert Moffat, in the last 200 years of the Church's unparalleled expansion.

Typical of dedicated translators was Edward Steere, described by one of his early parishioners as a "downright shirt-sleeved man and a real Bible parson."[40] He translated the New Testament and part of the Old Testament into the Swahili language.

Another was Bishop Samuel Schereschewsky, who helped immensely in Chinese translations. What a record is his! He was born a Jew and was educated in rabbinic schools but was converted and sent as a Protestant Episcopal missionary to China. He was later appointed bishop after first rejecting the office. He founded St. John's University, Shanghai, often said to be the most important university in China. He was able to speak 13 languages and read 7 others. For 25 of his 75 years he was a paralytic and, chiefly during his paralytic years, he translated the entire Bible into Wenli Chinese and most of it into Mandarin Chinese, Matthew into Mongolian—and did a complete revision of the Mandarin Old Testament and the Wenli New Testament, and reference editions of both entire Bibles. All this he did while often in poor health as well as being financially strapped. The Wenli translation he called the "one-finger Bible" because he tapped out the whole of it with one finger on a typewriter.[41]

Nationals have often helped with translating work. Two learned Buriat Mongols were engaged to translate the New Testament in St. Petersburg from 1817 to 1827 and were converted in the process by the sheer integrity of the message. One missionary quite missed a familiar passage by rendering it, "Jesus took the little children in his

40. Eric North, *The Book of a Thousand Tongues* (New York: Harper, 1938), 4. North is also used considerably otherwise in this discussion of translations. It is a brief and well-written account of them.
41. See J. A. Muller, *Apostle of China: Samuel Issac Joseph Schereschewsky* (New York: Morehouse Publishing Co., 1937), 1-256.

arms and pinched them." Nationals help iron out much that would otherwise fail to communicate what was intended.

From early times the 66 books that comprise our canon of Holy Scripture have been esteemed more highly than all other writings.

Said Dr. Harold A. Moody, founder of the League of Coloured Peoples: "Without this comfort [from the Bible] my people would long since have lain down and died. They could never have survived the crushing experiences of these long years of bondage." It has been the same to others also: healing for our deep sin sore; comfort for our trying times; direction for our quandaries. It is more than what Robert Browning thought it to be, "the best of books"; it is the book that, as John Wesley said, points the way to Christ and to heaven.

One realizes that something of exactness is lost when Scripture is translated. Yet one is confident that the Holy Spirit has helped the translators as they have been opened up to His persuasions. Surely no one translation should be thought of as sacrosanct, as some devout Christians seem to think of the King James Version of 1611.

This present systematic theology, based significantly on the Holy Scriptures as inspired and inerrant on doctrine and practice matters, presupposes that there is no great need for any of the autographs. It presupposes that the Early Church held in high respect an existing canon of nonautographs. It presupposes that the Scriptures are inspired, authoritative, and basically genuine. It presupposes that they are crammed full of God and the economy of His redemption and yield their meaning to persons who come to them prayerfully—as obedient seekers after an understanding of the faith to which we have been borne along by grace.

The Interpretation of Scripture

It is one thing to read what the Scriptures say, and another to know what they mean. All who are literate can read what Scripture says; it takes work, often hard work, to learn what it means.

A number of matters are important in interpreting what Scripture means.[42]

---

42. For an important and thorough Wesleyan-holiness study of the interpretation of Scripture, see Wayne McCown and James Massey, eds., *God's Word for Today*, vol. 2 of *Wesleyan Theological Perspectives* (Anderson, Ind.: Warner Press, 1982).

The Age of the Manuscript. When there are variant readings in Greek New Testament manuscripts, the earlier manuscripts are usually preferred. They are more likely to be similar to the autographs or the writings the Church canonized than are the later manuscripts. This is not very significant for Old Testament manuscripts. The only vowelless Hebrew texts we have are from the Dead Sea caves. They do not vary significantly in the dates of origin; they are finely similar to the later Masoretic text.

The Interpreter's Metaphysics. Another hermeneutical matter has to do with whether or not interpreters consider historicity and facticity matters to be important. If we tend to discount these matters and to view conceptual matters as important, we will try to deduce Scripture's meaning without particular regard for historical and facticity matters, such as Christ's enfleshment through the virgin, His miracles, His bodily resurrection, His intended return.

The Canon Versus the Precanon. Our hermeneutical task is determined in part by whether we are going to interpret the actual canon or seek to establish, through various critical studies, a precanonical text and attempt to interpret it. Brevard Childs and James Sanders have told us that we should try to understand what is the meaning of Scripture at the time the Bible books became accepted as our canon.[43] Sanders feels that the Torah and the Gospels are more important than the remainder of Scripture to the communities of faith that developed the Old Testament and New Testament canons. Childs rejects Sanders' view that there are canons within the canon, saying that no part of the canon should

---

43. See Brevard Childs, *Introduction to the Old Testament as Scripture* (Philadelphia: Fortress Press, 1979); and James A. Sanders, *Torah and Canon* (Philadelphia: Fortress Press, 1972). About the "stabilized" canonical Old Testament text, Childs says, "The term canonical text [which he says the later Masoretic text is very close to] denotes that official Hebrew text of the Jewish Community which had reached a point of stabilization in the first century A.D., thus all but ending its long history of fluidity. From that period on, the one form of the Hebrew text of the Bible became the normative and authoritative expression of Israel's sacred scripture" (p. 100). He goes on to speak of "a pre-stabilization period marked by a wider toleration of divergent text types, and a post-stabilization period characterized by only minor variations of the one official text" (ibid.). He also adds, "There is no extant canonical text" (ibid.). Our earliest manuscript of the Old Testament is a Masoretic text dating to A.D. 1008; but we also have much pre-vowel Old Testament text now from the Dead Sea caves, which predates the Christian era.

Childs deeply respects the Hebrew canon of the first century A.D. He points out on page 668 that the sole passing reference to only one apocryphal book in the New Testament (to Enoch, in Jude 14ff.) suggests the esteem in which Christians of the first century A.D. held the canonical Hebrew Old Testament text.

be held in higher respect or receive more attention by us than the other parts. But both agree that form and redaction and other criticisms tend to atomize the text and to disregard the respect the text had in believing communities when it came to enjoy canonicity. Both focus upon Synagogue and Church, which produced the canon and were also produced, in great part, by the canon. Both scholars also feel we should find what the theology of the canon is and apply it to our lives.

Childs and Sanders nudge biblical scholarship toward the right directions. Even if the inspired autographs had read quite different from our canonical Scriptures, that would not greatly matter. The Holy Spirit guided the development of the text, as discussed earlier. It was a developed text that figured strategically in Israel's survival when whisked into captivity in Babylon.

In the case of the New Testament, the time lapse between autographs and canon was briefer. Besides, the believing community of Christians seems to have come very early, by the end of the first century (see First Clement) and soon afterward (see Papias), to respect the New Testament writings. Yet the Holy Spirit no doubt guided writers to make certain changes in the New Testament text between autograph and canon. Luke himself might have later changed his own Gospel to read that Jesus was Joseph's son "supposedly" (3:23, NASB).

It is the meaning of this text, as Childs insists, that we need to explore. This means that biblical studies should be more constructive than analytical, more theological than critical, more positive than negative, more interested in finding what there is to herald than in finding the extent to which the precanonical text underwent change.

So, in interpreting the meaning of Scripture, it is important to realize that (1) we do not have the autographs; (2) it is the canon we are interpreting; and (3) it is not imperative to interpret it by finding out what stages it went through on its way to becoming canon.

The Importance of the Existential. When we come to Scripture, we are hunting for what will help us individually live out our discipleship to Christ. We who believe in imparted righteousness, who possess hearts that have been evangelically warmed, who seek to promote "Arminianism on fire," read Scripture for what it will mean to us as individuals in our personal bearing before God.

We conceive of it as crammed full of God, and we sit loose and quiet and obedient under the downpour of it and let it drench us. We are not content to study it as mere intellectuals. We study it as persons who are needy and poor, who are fed by it, lighted by it, spurred by it—as persons who find it sufficient for our existential needs.

Such existential help may come from strange passages of Scripture. It might even happen when we are reading a genealogy and come upon a given name. Judah, son of Jacob, for example, is in Jesus' genealogy. Judah is as despicable a character as we find in the Bible. He bought a sexual "privilege" from his disguised daughter-in-law; and when she was to have his baby, he would have, in his "righteousness," put her to death, except that she proved him to be the father because of the three gifts he had given her for the "privilege" (Genesis 38).

He, Judah, in Jesus' lineage? Most of us, if we were tracing our roots, would like to quit if we found such a person in our family tree. But in Jesus' roots, how marvelous it is to have Judah there! It means that Jesus did not come into some sort of antiseptic humanity; He came into real humanity, in a lineage that had awful, flagrant sin in it. And Judah does not by any means exhaust the sinners in Jesus' roots. The harlot Rahab is there, and David, a forgiven adulterer.

The prophet Ezekiel, in a vision, was given words to eat. A voice—it must have been God's—said to him, "Son of man, eat what is offered to you; eat this scroll, and go, speak" (3:1, RSV). And Ezekiel tells us, beautifully, "so I opened my mouth, and he gave me the scroll to eat. . . . Then I ate it; and it was in my mouth as sweet as honey" (vv. 2-3, RSV). This was a scroll, not a roll.

We Wesleyans, with our stress on the experience of God's grace, "eat" Scripture even as Ezekiel did. We use all the means available to us to interpret what it means to us as individuals, in our time, in our quandaries, in our inadequacies, perchance in our sinfulness.

We want to find God and His Christ when we come to Scripture. We see Christ prewitnessed in the Older Testament, when a "not yet" but "someday" is in the air. We see Christ witnessed in the Gospels—a present-tense witness to His virgin birth, His atoning death, His triumphant resurrection. In Acts and the Epistles we see Christ postwitnessed as the propitiation for our sins, who intercedes for us, who is touched by the feeling of a still-common humanity with us, and who is to return—not to be a sin offering again but as King and Judge. We repent and believe, and God forgives us, regenerates us, reconciles us, adopts us into His family as children. We later consecrate our lives to Him and, again by faith, receive the second work of grace—cleansing from Adamic sin, a baptism with the Holy Spirit for witness and service, a sealing with that Holy Spirit promised by Joel (Joel 2:28) and by John the Baptizer (Matt. 3:11-12) and by Jesus (Acts 1:4-5). With John Wesley, our needs are met through use of this Book, which shows us the way to redemption and finally to heaven.

The Bible-Unity Emphasis. Of importance to our interpreting Scripture is its unity. If E. F. Scott was right in his 1943 publication of *Varieties of New Testament Religion,* that there are seven different "religions" in the New Testament; and if the Old Testament is also viewed as fragmented, as some have said, so that, for example, the prophetic and the priestly are antithetical—then one cannot interpret Scripture as though its books are in harmony with each other. But if G. Ernest Wright was correct in what he said about the unity of the Bible in *The Interpreter's Bible,* and if those are correct who say that there are in Scripture connecting threads such as the story of salvation or God's kingdom—then that figures, too, in how Scripture is to be interpreted. Evangelicals, in general, view Scripture as a basic unity, and its differences are viewed as points of emphasis within the same framework of understanding.

The Biblical Theology Movement. The biblical theology movement was a salutary hermeneutical development. Such scholars as Bernard W. Anderson, C. H. Dodd, J. K. S. Reid, H. H. Rowley, H. Wheeler Robinson, and E. C. Rust have contributed to this movement. This movement has been centripetal, welding Scripture into a unified redemptive whole—in contrast to the centrifugal liberal period, when scholars seemed to do more dissecting and splintering and tearing of Scripture into incongruous parts than anything else. Lamentably, however, promoters of the biblical theology movement did not have any special regard for the inspiration of Scripture. This includes the quite-conservative E. C. Rust, for whom the authority of the Bible rests not upon its inspired correctness but upon the Holy Spirit's use of Scripture to point us to Christ the Redeemer.[44]

Archaeology, Especially in Albright. Important for hermeneutics have been many developments in archaeology. William F. Albright, perhaps the foremost archaeologist in the world in the 1950s and 1960s, taught that not a single archaeological find had proved a Scripture writer to be in error, even on factual, historical matters. Instead, he stated that the writers had often been proven correct after being thought by many to be incorrect. As a case in point, archaeology has shown that Daniel really was the third in the kingdom as the Book of Daniel states, instead of the second, because finds have shown that the king over him served under an emperor. James Barr says, "All in all, then, Albright sought to push biblical scholarship into a more conservative orientation, in respect to dates, reliability of narratives, authorship of books and so on."[45] Barr labels the total philosophical, religious, and theological position of Albright as a "broad universal liberal humanism."[46]

He continues, "There is no reason to suppose that doctrines dear to conservative evangelicals, such as the inspiration of scripture or the deity of Christ, had any significant place in his scheme of things."[47] Yet if the data warranted the conservative conclusions, when Albright's basic theology was liberal and humanist, this surely suggests the validity of the conservative conclusions.

The Dead Sea Scrolls have given us Old Testament manuscripts 1,000 years older that the ones we had. The Isaiah scroll is entire. It has been dated prior to the New Testament era, based in part on the dated coins found in the Dead Sea caves. Isaiah was "unified" at least at that time. Evangelicals have usually—but not always—viewed the whole of Isaiah as from the eighth-century prophet.

Discoveries at Ebla in the 1970s should be mentioned—although some scholars question their significance. These finds consist of some 20,000 tablets dating from the fourth millennium to about 1500 B.C. Many of these tablets, admittedly secular (many of them simply receipts of business transactions), predate the patriarchs. We can now check from extrabiblical sources on a very early period. The finds mention several cities, for example,

---

44. See E. C. Rust, "The Authority of Scripture," *Review and Expositor* 57 (1960): 26-57.
45. James Barr, *Fundamentalism* (Philadelphia: Westminster Press, 1977), 150.
46. Ibid., 151.
47. Ibid., 151-52.

referred to in Genesis 14, including Sodom and Gomorrah. We can see that the writer of that chapter was giving us factual history. Although he was using sources some 1,500 years old, where we can check him we find him to be accurate.

Interpretation That Is Wide-Scoped. While we use Scripture to inform our lives, we need to interpret judiciously, and only on the basis of all the information it is feasible to gather together.

We do not universalize from a given biblical passage, applying it to ourselves whether or not. We do not say that Satan causes our illnesses and other untoward experiences just because God permitted him to cause them in Job's case. Many of our unwanted experiences are occasioned by disease germs or by natural "laws," such as gravity or the inertia of motion. Our negligence, our foolhardiness, or our slothfulness is often the occasion of evils that claim us as indiscriminate victims. This means we do not go solely and simply to Job for scriptural light on natural evil but to sundry passages that relate to that matter.

We Wesleyans interpret Scripture with Scripture; we respect the Church tradition in which our sister and brother Christians of the ages have interpreted Scripture; and we ask earnestly and waitingly for the Holy Spirit's guidance as we interpret the meaning of the written Word of God.

Devices Used—Including Allegory. We interpret Scripture according to the historical situation in which the writing appeared and perhaps developed somewhat in content and in usefulness.

This includes interpreting Scripture in relation to the specific literary devices the writers use. They use similes: "As a hart longs for flowing streams, so longs my soul for thee, O God" (Ps. 42:1, RSV). They use metaphors, as when Jesus says of Herod, "Go tell that fox" (Luke 13:32). More subtle than a simile, the metaphor is often exceedingly communicative. They use analogy, in which appeal is made to reason, and which sometimes takes the form of a riddle, as in Ezek. 17:3-21 and Judg. 14:14. Even elements of the fable are found in Scripture: "Once the trees went forth to anoint a king over them, and they said to the olive tree, 'Reign over us!'" (Judg. 9:8, NASB). One characteristic of a fable is a sustained reference in which things or animals are referred to as though they were persons—and we have that here.

Among these forms is the parable, often used by Jesus himself. Here, a fictitious story gathers up a truth, usually in order to teach one important matter.

Typology occurs when there are earlier things, places, and persons that are similar to later ones and are therefore thought of as meaningful anticipations (antetypes) of later ones (types). The Book of Hebrews abounds in these.

It is exceedingly important, in interpreting Scripture, to understand something about the literary device of allegory. The word *allegory* is a combination of *allos,* "other," and *agoreuein,* "to speak," and it means, literally, to speak in a way that is other than what is meant. Allegory, therefore, is a tool whereby a writer conveys hidden, mysterious truths by the use of words that also have a literal meaning. Allegory is also a method of interpreting Scripture (or other literature) in such a way that the interpreter sees mysterious meaning the writer perhaps did not intend. Unlike analogy, which appeals to reason, allegory appeals to the imagination. It is like a metaphor but is sustained. In distinction from typology, no time lapse is necessarily needed before the deeper interpretation can be attempted.

There is some allegory in the Old Testament, especially in the Book of Ezekiel. That prophet was a poet who preferred to say or to act out something that had a deeply spiritual meaning instead of writing down prose that had simply a literal significance.[48]

Many Jewish and Christian scholars have treated the Song of Songs as an allegory depicting, respectively, God's love for Israel and for the Church. This way of interpreting arises out of a Greek-influenced notion that the human body, with its sexual desires, is sinful; the story, therefore, could not mean what it says—that a husband and wife are attracted to each other and describe their love.

The New Testament contains still more allegory than does the Old Testament. Jesus might have used allegory in His own interpretations of some of His parables—for example, of the sower (Mark 4:14-20; Matt. 13:18-23; Luke 8:11-13). Jesus did not interpret the Old Testament allegorically, as Philo did earlier, unless we count as allegory His reference to "the stone which the

---

48. See J. Kenneth Grider, "Ezekiel," in vol. 4 of *Beacon Bible Commentary* (Kansas City: Beacon Hill Press of Kansas City, 1966).

builders rejected," which closes the parable of the wicked husbandman (Mark 12:10; Matt. 21:42; Luke 20:17-18).

The Book of Revelation often employs allegory, where such references as "woman" (12:1) and "beasts" (4:6; 19:4) and a "white horse" (6:2; 19:11) must be interpreted as having a deeper-than-literal meaning. So many allegories, in fact, appear in this book that Martin Luther (who preferred plain teachings to obscure ones) did not include Revelation among first-class books of the canon.

Most notable and explicit in the use of allegory is the apostle Paul. Paul even names as an allegory one of his interpretations of an Old Testament passage. In Galatians he refers to Abraham's "free" wife, Sarah, and his "slave" wife, Hagar, and says, "Now this is an allegory: these women are two covenants. . . . Hagar is Mount Sinai in Arabia" (4:24-25, RSV).

Another definite allegory is Paul's interpretation of the law forbidding the muzzling of an ox. He reads it as teaching that the Christian Church should support its ministers financially. Paul is so extremely allegorical at this point that he denies the literal sense of the Mosaic law. He asks, "Is it for oxen that God is concerned?" He implies "No" by another question: "Does he not speak entirely for our sake?" Then he adds positively, "It was written for our sake" (1 Cor. 9:9-10, RSV).

No one knows just when the interpretation of literature by the allegorical method of discerning hidden meaning first began. It was at least several centuries before the Christian era. Among the earliest known usages of this method are those connected with interpretations of Homer.

A Jew named Aristobulus, who lived during the early half of the second century B.C., was probably the earliest allegorist of the Old Testament. He was confident that Moses had taught what Plato and other Greek philosophers later advocated. Portions of Aristobulus's work have survived in Eusebius, the fourth-century A.D. historian, in which, for example, David's adultery is allegorized so as to make him a model of virtue.

Philo of Alexandria (49 B.C.—A.D. 20) also allegorized the Old Testament, harmonizing it with Plato and other Greek philosophers. He "summoned to his aid, as the solvent of all problems, the system of allegorical interpretation."[49] To Philo, the

---

49. James Drummond, *Philo Judeas* (London: Williams and Norgate, 1888), 18.

literal sense of Scripture is not important. Its spiritual, mystical meaning has far greater significance.

Justin Martyr used the allegorical method of interpretation to make Scripture teach Greek philosophy. Clement of Alexandria (ca. A.D. 150-ca. 215) and his successor, Origen, capitalized on this method in order to baptize Platonic views and Judaistic faith into Christianity.[50]

Until you get to Luther, Origen and his like prevail. The School of Antioch sounded alarms against the allegorical interpretation of Scripture, but such alarms were seldom heeded. Jerome criticized the divorcement from Scripture that such interpretation can get one into, and he said many unkind things about the allegorical method used by Origen and others, yet he himself resorted to this method frequently. Origen allegorized for reasons philosophically important to him. Jerome would allegorize for fanciful and frivolous reasons.[51]

Augustine had sound things to say about rules for interpreting Scripture but often ignored those rules in his actual comments on Scripture. Convinced that nothing in Scripture could possibly oppose his own theology and what he considered Christian orthodoxy, he fitted Scripture into his own schema by mystical interpretations.

For all his theological acumen, Aquinas is like the Scholastics in general, including his teacher, the encyclopedic Albert the Great, in fanciful flights of allegory in Scripture interpretation.

Just after the time of Aquinas, the little-known Nicholas of Lyra (1270-1340) exegeted the Scriptures with real respect for the literal sense. But his teaching was little heeded, and only the Reformation broke the stranglehold of the allegorical interpretation of Scripture.

Martin Luther did far more than anyone up to his time to break down the traditional use of allegory in Scripture interpretation. Luther knew Hebrew and Greek well, held a doctoral degree in the Holy Scriptures, translated the entire Bible into German (New Testament, 1522; Old Testament, 1534), and wrote many

---

50. See Clement's *Stromata* 7:16, in *Ante-Nicene Christian Library* 2 (Edinburgh: T. and T. Clark, 1897); and Origen's *Concerning Principles,* Books 4, 5, *The Ante-Nicene Fathers,* James Donaldson and Alexander Roberts, eds., 10 vols. (Buffalo, N.Y.: Christian Literature Publishing Co., 1886-87), 4:349 ff.

51. For a careful and documented study of this, see Frederic Farrar, *History of Interpretations* (New York: Dutton, 1886), 222 ff.

commentaries. In these he often resorted to allegory, especially to find Christ in the Old Testament. But for the most part, he advanced and supported the method of interpreting Scripture from the standpoint of the grammar and the historical situation in which each passage is set.

John Calvin was more consistent than Luther in avoiding the allegorical method. He helped measurably in establishing a continuing tradition of interpretation that does not rule out the allegorical method but uses it only with care, as does Scripture itself.

The Place of Scripture

Scripture, then, is thought-inspired generally, although it might well be verbally inspired at certain special points. It consists of a canon that is pretty much extant, instead of autographs that we do not possess and probably never will. The inspired canon, changed somewhat from the autographs by Spirit guidance, is our Scripture. It should be regarded as inerrant on matters of doctrine and practice, although inconsequential errors on matters such as geography, mathematics, or history may have existed even in the autographs. This body of writings is authoritative for Protestant Christians. Denominational creeds and confessions, intended to be based on Scripture, are official ways of interpreting Scripture for their adherents. The quality of translations into English and other languages varies. The matter of interpreting the Bible's meaning is most significant.

Wesleyan-holiness people respect other sources, such as the reservoir of wisdom contained in the Church's creeds, confessions, and theologies. But all these must submit to Scripture as the primary written authority.

In Roman Catholicism, the tradition is authoritative on matters clearly not taught in Scripture—such as the celibacy of monks, nuns, and priests. Tradition is authoritative for the "immaculate conception" of Mary in her mother's womb so that she escaped original sin, Mary's perpetual virginity, and the bodily assumption of Mary. The Roman Catholic church understands that baptism and the Lord's Supper are the sacraments instituted by Jesus, but they have—without biblical authority—added five other sacraments.

Not so in Protestantism, and Wesleyanism is certainly Protestant in this regard. We understand that specific aspects of doctrine or practice might be taught only by implication in Scripture—such as a proscription of tobacco use. But support for the prohibition is in Scripture, or else we do not teach it. Where Scripture sometimes leaves us in the dark on a given subject, individuals may theorize, but the Church should not dogmatize.

Wesleyanism has affinity for, and interest in, promoting only those doctrines that are clearly taught in Scripture, where prophets and apostles, and other inspired persons, have left us written legacies. Wesleyanism's theologians are not inventors of doctrines; they are only expounders of teachings found in the canonical Scriptures. Ideally, at least, they do not confirm Scripture but affirm it. They affirm what it teaches on the entire theological spectrum: on God, ourselves, sin, redemption, the Church, last things, Christian practice, whatever.

Scripture contains unsystematized revelation of God. Just as people observe nature and build physical and biological sciences from it, so theologians come to the spread-out revelation of God in Scripture, sort through it, order it, systematize it, and often use its raw material to build theological sciences that are useful to the Church in its worship, its faith, its hope, its love, its evangelism.

All theologians bring certain doctrinal presuppositions and biases to Scripture as they seek to construct from Scripture their theologies. The true Wesleyan admits this and does not make correct doctrine a condition for salvation. We understand that if our sins are forgiven at the time of our death, we will be taken to heaven, even if our theology is off base a thousand miles. We are Christians if God, for Christ's sake, forgives our sins. He is able to do this only because of the death and resurrection of the virgin-born God-man, Jesus Christ. But we do not need to believe in any given theory of the Incarnation or the Atonement in order to be forgiven through Christ.

Martin Luther taught the dictum, still widely held in Protestantism, of *sola scriptura*—Scripture alone. Christian doctrine and practice should be founded only upon what is taught in Scripture; what Scripture does not teach should not be taught by us.

Luther used this principle in re-forming the church in the 16th century. Wesleyanism in general has accepted the use Luther made of the *sola scriptura* principle, espousing it in wide-scoped and often open-ended ways.

Such views as these, relating to Scripture, undergird and give form to this present systematic theology.

5

God's Existence and Nature

A young Anglican curate asked Bishop Stubbs what he should preach about. "Preach about God," said the bishop, "and preach about 20 minutes."

The advice is wise, because God is permanently interesting to people. Other human interests may fluctuate or cease, but God is permanently interesting. This is in part because we cannot fully find out about Him. He does reveal what we most need to know: that He offers redemption to sinners.

Revelation is necessary because we are finite and He is infinite. God exists "in unapproachable light; whom no man has seen or can see" (1 Tim. 6:16, NASB). His thoughts are higher than our thoughts, His ways higher than our ways (Isa. 55:8-9). Because of this difference between God and us, He will need to reveal himself to us if we are to learn about Him.

Revelation is also necessary because God is a person—tripersonal, even. One characteristic of a person is the capacity for privacy. A husband can clam up, and the wife will not know what he is thinking, feeling, or devising. A wife can clam up, and the husband will not know why he is in the doghouse.

God, too, is a person—three Persons. He is an infinite composite of intellect, feeling, and will. As personal, He can choose to hide himself. A desk must yield its contents to us if we decide to search it. God is not an object at our disposal. If we are to know about Him, He will need to reveal himself to us.

The Existence of God

Scripture assumes God's existence. "In the beginning God" are the Bible's first words. To its closing words, none of its many writers, at work over 1,500 years, seek to prove God's existence. Instead, they reveal the kind of God who does exist. God's greatness, for example, is seen from nature in Ps. 8:3-4: "When I consider Thy heavens, the work of Thy fingers, the moon and the stars, which Thou hast ordained; what is man, that Thou dost take thought of him?" (NASB).

God's majesty is splashed around in the heavens, according to the same psalm at verse 1: "O Lord, our Lord, how majestic is Thy name in all the earth, who hast displayed Thy splendor above the heavens!" (NASB).

The glory of God, but not His existence as such, is shown in Ps. 19:1: "The heavens are telling of the glory of God; and their expanse is declaring the work of His hands" (NASB).

Although "the heavens declare His righteousness" (Ps. 50:6, NASB), they are not said to declare His existence.

Psalm 104 cites the created world as evidence of God's greatness: "O Lord my God, Thou art very great; Thou art clothed with splendor and majesty . . . He makes the clouds His chariot; He walks upon the wings of the wind; . . . He established the earth upon its foundations, so that it will not totter forever and ever" (vv. 1, 3, 5, NASB).

Isaiah also argues for God's greatness on the basis of the created world: "It is He who sits above the vault of the earth, and its inhabitants are like grasshoppers, who stretches out the heavens like a curtain and spreads them out like a tent to dwell in" (40:22, NASB).

Isaiah 42 proclaims the caring God who will not break a "bruised reed" (v. 3), but who "will faithfully bring forth justice" (v. 3, NASB). This God "created the heavens and stretched them out" (v. 5), and "spread out the earth" (v. 5). The created world shows that God cares but not simply that He exists. His existence is taken for granted.

Perhaps the main natural theology passage in all the Bible is Rom. 1:18-20. There Paul says that "the wrath of God is revealed . . . against all ungodliness . . . because that which is known about God is evident within them; for God made it evident to them" (vv.

18-19, NASB). And the special way God revealed himself is through nature: "For since the creation of the world His invisible attributes, His eternal power and divine nature, have been clearly seen, being understood through what has been made, so that they are without excuse" (v. 20, NASB). The things that "are made," the created world, gives people everywhere knowledge about what God is like, including what He expects of us; but it is not quite said here that the created world argues for God's existence as such.

Scripture assumes that everyone believes that God exists, but that some simply do not live accordingly. The atheism of which it speaks is practical, not theoretical. "The fool has said in his heart, 'There is no God.' They are corrupt, they have committed abominable deeds" (Ps. 14:1, NASB).

One verse of Scripture implies the possibility of a theoretical atheism: "And without faith it is impossible to please Him, for he who comes to God must believe that He is, and that He is a rewarder of those who seek Him" (Heb. 11:6, NASB). The possibility of not believing in God's existence is implied in saying that a person coming to God "must believe that He is"—as though one might not.

However, though Scripture has no formal argument for God's existence, theology does. The question of God's existence has figured significantly in the history of philosophy and philosophical theology and must be addressed.

The Cosmological Argument. This is the argument that God exists because the world must surely have had a cause—and that cause must be the kind of being who could make the world. It is an argument from effect to cause of that effect. It is understood that anything that is made must be of a lower order than what made it. That being so, a being of inestimable capacities must have made this world in all its extent. Aristotle argued for God on this basis. Muslims have argued in this way, as does Al-Farabi; so have Jews such as Moses Maimonides, and Christians such as Anselm, Bonaventure, Aquinas, and James Arminius.

Another form of the cosmological argument engages itself with motion. Some ancient Greek philosophers had denied motion, or change, saying that a body that seems to be in motion is actually at many fixed points in a brief span of time. Other philosophers, such as Heraclitus, said oppositely that motion or change is what ultimate reality consists of. Heraclitus said that fire, which is in constant flux, comprises ultimate reality.

Aristotle agreed that change is caused by what is changeless: God. Nature per se is the unmoving moved: it does not move of itself but is moved upon by outside forces. We humans are the moving moved: we do some moving in the world of nature, and we are moved upon by God. God is the Unmoved Mover. He said that God moves or changes all besides himself but that He himself is not moved or changed by anything or anyone.

Change is proof that God exists, because all motion or movement implies a cause, and that cause is God.

Another aspect of the cosmological argument relates to graduation within creation, which implies the existence of an infinitely high graduation—God. Within the created universe there are wide variations of quality. The inanimate is a lower form of creation than is the animate. And within the inanimate there is graduation in beauty, utility, and value.

In the animate sphere, graduation also appears. The worm is among the lower forms of life; on an upward scale are dogs and other pets, fine racehorses, whatever.

And finally, there is rational, human existence. Among humans you have those who are highly antisocial, those who are social, those who are highly creative: poets, musicians, artists.

This graduation in the world, from the inanimate to the animate to the rational and to the highly creative among the rational, might point to the existence of God—infinitely higher than the most creative of humans. Where the ascent in graduation stops, there is God.

The Teleological Argument. According to this refinement of the cosmological argument, the purpose observed in creation argues for the existence of a supremely intelligent being—God—who implanted in the world the purpose that is there.

Nature is purposive. What we need in order to sustain fulfilling human life, we have. Air rises when warmed, producing breezes that are good. Water expands when frozen, so that it floats instead of sinking, allowing it to melt more readily and preventing the buildup of ice from the bottom of seas and lakes and rivers. Because of this, too, icebergs are visible to sailors.

Scientists also note that if the earth were either much closer to the sun or much farther from it, earth's temperature would be either too hot or too cold to sustain human life as we know it. Earth's rotation occasions our seasons, which are advantageous to us.

The human body itself contains almost numberless instances of what is purposeful, of what argues for a supremely intelligent purposer. Respiratory, digestive, circulatory, and reproductive systems, working in organismic unity, did not happen by mere chance.

If the moon were 40,000 miles closer to earth, huge tides would inundate large areas of the land. The moon's size as well as its distance from the earth are appropriate for us, for both figure in the amount of tide.

Immanuel Kant and others have countered the teleological argument for God's existence because dysteleology is also present in the universe. Gene transmission sometimes gets mixed up, and you have Down's syndrome, spina bifida, and so forth. Tornadoes and hurricanes occur. Large fish and large land animals eat small ones to survive, and this is sometimes said to be dysteleological.

Yet surely, the dysteleological does not cancel the teleological. The teleological is far more usual than is the dysteleological and is also of more significance.

The Ontological Argument. Another classical argument for God's existence is the ontological: God exists because people find, in their minds, an idea of an infinitely perfect being. Plato laid the foundation for this argument, teaching that ideas of the true and the beautiful and the good are real. Augustine added to the development of the argument by saying that if God is in our thoughts, this indicates that He really does exist.

Anselm (1033-1109) first formally delineated the argument. Much later René Descartes (1596-1650) refined it: God must exist, in order to cause in people's minds the idea of Him. Since we find nothing in our empirical experience that is analogous to God, the idea of His existence must be caused in our minds by God himself.

Kant opposed this argument. He said that he might have an idea of money in his pocket, or of an island in a sea, but this would not mean that the money or the island existed. Yet Kant did not adequately understand the argument. The idea of God is quite different from the idea of money or an island. In the case of God we are talking about an idea of a most-perfect being. Further, proponents argue, perfection includes existence. Also, the existing perfect being causes in our minds the idea of His existence, which, of course, money or an island could not do.

Kant's opposition to the classical arguments for God's existence, in his *Critique of Pure Reason*, has been quite influential in the later history of philosophy and theology. Nevertheless, many significant philosophers and theologians continue to view the classical arguments as validly proving that God exists.

Harvard's William Ernest Hocking, just after the century's turn, argued painstakingly for the significance of the ontological argument in *The Meaning of God in Human Experience.*[1] Andrew Seth Pringle-Pattison later also used the ontological argument significantly.[2]

The Moral Argument. This is the argument for God's existence particularly associated with the views of Kant (although anticipations of it appear in the thought of Peter Abelard [1079-1144] and James Arminius, among others). This argument is that God must exist to cause in the minds of people a certain kind of "categorical imperative": that they should do their duty just because it is their duty ("duty for duty's sake"), and not because of something objective, such as a poor widow's need. Kant argued that if we had been the originators of this moral ought, we would not feel obligated to respect it. He also felt that a supremely moral being must exist in order to assure that, at least finally, the virtuous life will result in happiness.

The moral argument breaks down if one actually believes in the classical Christian doctrine of original sin. People who do not believe in original sin tend to exalt human nature and its capacities. With a Pelagian view of human nature, a person can believe that we have an inner imperative to do the right, which is one's duty. However, if we believe in original sin, we understand that apart from either prevenient or redeeming grace, a person is inclined only and always toward evil. We understand that we are fallen in all aspects of our nature—intellect, will, emotion, even in our bodily nature—and that we have no implanted imperative to do our duty. Besides, evangelical, classical, biblical Christians do

1. William Ernest Hocking, *The Meaning of God in Human Experience* (New Haven, Conn.: Yale University Press, 1912).
2. Andrew Seth Pringle-Pattison, *The Idea of God in the Light of Recent Philosophy*, rev. ed. (Millwood, N.Y.: Kraus, 1920).

not have any particular interest in duty. Our interest is in such matters as the three classical Christian virtues of faith, hope, and love—the Bible's interests. *Strong's Exhaustive Concordance*, based on the KJV, lists only eight appearances of the word "duty," six of which are in the Old Testament—and there are no cognates of the word; but we all know how frequently the other words appear.[3]

The Dialectic of Desire. This is a psychological argument for God's existence originated by E. S. Brightman and found in *A Philosophy of Religion*.[4] It is the argument that God exists because we always keep on desiring what is higher until we desire God, beyond whom there is no desiring. Early, we desire simply pleasure, but our desires progress to physical things, to activity for others, to ideals, finally to God, in whom our highest ideals are located.

God exists because our desires keep on questing to what is higher until our desire is for this supreme, ideal Person—after which there is and can be no desire for what is still higher.

Brightman's argument is invalid because, like the moral argument, it presupposes that human nature is not characterized by original sin but is basically good. Due to original sin, the natural person's desire, apart from prevenient grace, is for sin, not for God. One's inward, basic yen is toward some form of human degeneracy.

Religious Experience. Another argument for God's existence is based on our experience of God. He must surely exist since we and others have experienced, and do now experience, His forgiveness, His sanctifying grace, His comfort, His guidance, whatever. This is not in the full sense an argument at all, for we are not going discursively from one step to another, asking disinterested people to believe in God because of a process of reasoning. While it is the most convincing proof of God's existence to a believer, it is not a proof of God's existence to a person who has not received this real and transforming experience of God.

Conclusion. With the exception of the argument from the experience of God, which is not actually an argument, the various

---

3. Approximately 600 times we find the word "faith" (or "faithful," "faithfully," "faithfulness," "faithless"). "Hope" (with "hoped," "hope's," "hopeth," "hoping") appears 125 times. "Love" (with "loved," "lovedst," "lover," "lovers," "love's," "loves," "lovest," "loveth," "loving," "lovingkindness," and "lovingkindnesses") appears about 560 times.

4. Edgar Sheffield Brightman, *A Philosophy of Religion* (New York: Prentice-Hall, 1940), chap. 8, sec. 7.

so-called proofs for God's existence are inadequate, on a number of bases.

For one thing, they are inadequate because their basic direction is from ourselves and our world to God. In tower of Babel fashion, we are building structures by which we will climb up to heaven; and we suppose that we find God just because we set for ourselves that kind of project.

Scripture portrays God as seeking us. God is the Hound of Heaven, as Francis Thompson experienced Him, searching for us rebels who avoid or even flee Him.

The proofs are also inadequate because they lead only to the existence of the God of the philosophers, not to the Father of our Lord Jesus Christ who offers redemption to rebels, one and all. What sinners most need to know about God is not merely that He exists or that He exists as a person who makes the universe and invests it with purpose; sinners most need to know that God holds out the offer of forgiveness because of Jesus Christ's substitutionary atonement and His all-victorious resurrection—and this is not revealed in nature.

Another basis for the inadequacy of the arguments is their failure to take into account our total depravity. In our fallenness, and apart from prevenient grace, we are basically inclined to sin. Apart from grace, people do not seek God at all.

There is only one scriptural passage from which some have argued the importance of rational proofs for God's existence: "But sanctify Christ as Lord in your hearts, always being ready to make a defense to everyone who asks you to give an account for the hope that is in you, yet with gentleness and reverence" (1 Pet. 3:15, NASB). After quoting this verse, Norman Geisler wrote, "Most theists believe in God because they have been persuaded by evidence that it is most reasonable to do so."[5] But Peter here speaks of defending our hope, not God's existence. That hope is based on the redemptive work of Christ. The apologia for which Peter calls is a witness to what God has done for us in Christ to produce our hope, hope that triumphs in suffering.

It is true that Paul "reasoned" with his listeners (Acts 17:2; 18:4, 19; 24:25). He seeks to persuade them "from the Scriptures"

---

5. Norman Geisler, *Philosophy of Religion* (Grand Rapid: Zondervan Publishing House, 1974), 94.

that Jesus is the Christ, not from philosophical arguments that God exists.

Reason is mainly a vehicle for taking revealed data and sorting out what it means. It is a vehicle that we humans can use to sort out what is meant by the Word of God lived out in Christ and written out in Scripture.

We believe in God, not because He is the product of our rational processes, but because He has spoken to us in Christ and Scripture, because He still speaks to us by the Holy Spirit, because of the common witness of our sisters and brothers in Christ's Church—militant in life and triumphant in death.

The Nature of God

While Scripture does not argue for God's existence, it tells us much about what God is like. Using Scripture (and nature to some extent), and taking into account what we know about God through the prophesied, incarnated, crucified, resurrected, interceding, returning Lord Jesus Christ, an attempt is here made to suggest some aspects of what God is like.

At the same time, it should be admitted that God is far more than we can know or say. We are enabled, as He becomes to us the speaking God, to know many things about Him; but He in himself exists transcendently above our comprehension of Him.

The medieval mystics such as Meister Eckhart were correct in saying that there are taboo areas of mystery, beyond which we are not admitted. We can learn confidently, through revelation, all we need to know about Him for our redemption and for our servanthood on earth; but we are not permitted to learn all there is to know about Him. Indeed, our very finiteness, besides our fallenness, prevents that kind of understanding. Only God can fully know God.

The Holiness of God. God's holiness is basic to Scripture's disclosure of Him. It is the summation of what He is.[6] He is the Holy

6. Gustav Aulén says that "holiness is the foundation on which the whole conception of God rests" (see Donald S. Metz, *Studies in Biblical Holiness* [Kansas City: Beacon Hill Press of Kansas City, 1971], 34). Olin A. Curtis taught that God's holiness in early usage refers to His being "unapproachable" (*The Christian Faith* [New York: Eaton and Mains, 1905], 261), and that in New Testament times it meant that God "is both absolutely perfect and absolutely moral" (ibid., 263). Among those who simply relate God's holiness to His moral purity is Augustus H. Strong, who defines it as God's "self-affirming purity" (*Systematic Theology* [Philadelphia: Grif-

One often, as in Isaiah; and He is the thrice-holy One in Isa. 6:3 and Rev. 4:8. He and He alone is fully holy: "There is no one holy like the Lord" (1 Sam. 2:2). God's holiness is a synonym of His deity, of himself. That is implied where we read: "'To whom then will you liken Me that I should be his equal?' says the Holy One" (Isa. 40:25, NASB).

God is never called the Loving One, but He is called the Holy One. A similar statement is found in Prov. 30:3: "And I have not learned wisdom, nor have I knowledge of the Holy One." Again, the Holy One is His name (or designation). And the Hebrews understood that God and humans are bound up inextricably with their names.

The Book of Amos clearly shows that holiness is a synonym for God. We read, "The Lord God has sworn by Himself" (6:8, NASB). If to swear by His holiness is the same as to swear by himself, holiness seems to be synonymous with God. It is what God's isness is.

The Hebrew word for holiness, which may be transliterated as *qodesh*, is one of the Old Testament's most frequently used words.[7] Most scholars would agree with Norman Snaith that its basic meaning is to separate.[8] A. C. Knudson suggests that when applied to God, it means that He is separated from us creatures, and that as such its meaning has to do with God's unapproachableness.[9] Donald Metz is probably correct in suggesting that in

---

fith and Rowland Press, 1907], 1:268-74). Similarly, Louis Berkhof says: "It [God's holiness] may be defined as that perfection of God in virtue of which He eternally wills and maintains His own moral excellence, abhors sin, and demands purity in His moral creatures" (*Manual of Christian Doctrine* [Grand Rapids: William B. Eerdmans Publishing Co., 1933], 68). H. Orton Wiley, eclectic as he often is, seems to teach both ways. He says: "Holiness, then, is primarily that disposition which is back of all the attributes" (*Christian Theology* 1:370-71). If it is God's nature, back of all the attributes, it should not be said that God is "holy love" as he does. This makes love the noun, and holiness merely the adjective describing love and therefore even less basic than love. But basically, it suggests that holiness is related only to the so-called moral attributes and not to what might be called His metaphysical attributes.

7. George Allen Turner says *qodesh* appears 830 times in the Old Testament (see his *Vision Which Transforms: Is Christian Perfection Scriptural?* [Kansas City: Beacon Hill Press, 1964], 18). I count quite fewer than that, and yet it is used most frequently. Turner might be counting also some of its synonyms, such as *kabod* for glory or radiance and *cherem* for devoted. Yet their usage is infrequent.

8. Norman H. Snaith, *The Distinctive Ideas of the Old Testament* (New York: Schocken Books, 1964), 21.

9. A. C. Knudson, *The Religious Teaching of the Old Testament* (New York: Abingdon Press, 1918).

reference to God the word denotes "both ontological and moral transcendence."[10] My own study of *qodesh* suggests that it means basically separation or perhaps similarly elevation. Applied to God, it means that He is separated from and elevated above all other so-called deities. Applied other than to God, it often designates what is separated from common or profane use to God's use. Thus, the Sabbath is often said to be holy (e.g., Exod. 16:23); Israel as a nation is holy (19:6); garments are holy (28:2); as are anointing oil (30:25), the congregation (Num. 16:3), the people (Deut. 7:6), vessels (1 Kings 8:4), Jerusalem (Neh. 11:1), and the Temple (Ps. 5:7)—to list several of the numerous references.

Whether or not the word carried moral content in its earliest usage is moot. We do know that temple prostitutes for the Canaanite deities were called holy, not because they were morally holy, but because they were separated to the use of the so-called deities.[11] By the time of Isaiah, a clear connection is in evidence. When that prophet glimpsed God's holiness he became aware of his own unholiness. After seeing the Lord exalted in holiness, Isaiah says, "Woe is me, for . . . I am a man of unclean lips" (6:5, NASB). Later, during the Exile, a tie-up between God's holiness and our moral purity is positively stated. We read, "And the house of Israel will not again defile My holy name, neither they nor their kings, by their harlotry" (Ezek. 43:7, NASB).

The Personality of God. Scripture never states that God is a person or that He is tripersonal, as we Christians understand that He is. The word *person* is not found in Old Testament Hebrew or New Testament Greek. We get the word from the Latin *persona.* Yet the Holy Book still presents God as personal—even as tripersonal.

If we define *person* as Aristotle did, as a locus of intellect, feeling, and will, then God is a person. If we define *person* as Bowne did, as characterized by "selfhood, self-consciousness, self-control, and the power to know," then God is a person—or tripersonal.

It is important that God be understood as personal. The highest kind of existence we know of is personal, so that a less-than-personal God might not be a worthy object of our worship.

---

10. Metz, *Studies in Biblical Holiness,* 38.
11. Of them we read in the ISBE: "The temple prostitute was invested with sanctity as a member of the religious caste, as she is in India today. . . . The Canaanite sanctuaries were gigantic brothels" (George B. Eager, "Harlot," *International Standard Bible Encyclopedia* [Chicago: Howard-Severance Co., 1915], 2:1339).

Scripture portrays God as personal. We find in Scripture physical anthropomorphisms, and they imply that God is personal. God walks in the Garden of Eden (Gen. 3:8) and comes down to see how people are deporting themselves as they begin to build the tower of Babel (11:1-5). God is said to have eyes and eyelids (Pss. 11:4; 34:15; Hab. 1:13), hands (Pss. 95:4; 139:5), fingers (8:3), feet (Exod. 24:9-11; Isa. 66:1), a nose (Exod. 15:8; 2 Sam. 22:9), ears (Pss. 17:6; 31:2), and so forth. He is said to be a white-haired man in Dan. 7:9.

Psychological anthropomorphisms abound, in which God is said to have humanlike passions and motives. He has joy (Isa. 65:19: Zeph. 3:17), anger (Deut. 1:37; Jer. 7:18-20), hatred (Ps. 5:5-6; Prov. 6:16), wrath (Exod. 32:10; Ps. 2:5, 12; Rev. 15:7), and, of course, love (Jer. 31:3; John 3:16; 1 John 3:1; 4:16).

God is also said in Scripture to do, or to be, what humans do and are, and this, a kind of anthropomorphism, also suggests that He is personal. He is called a shepherd (Ps. 23:1; cf. John 10:11), a judge (Gen. 18:25; Isa. 33:22), a husband (Isa. 54:5; Jer. 31:32), and a physician (Exod. 15:26; Ps. 103:3).

Besides anthropomorphisms, the name Yahweh suggests that God is personal. While Elohim is a generic name for God as the powerful Creator, Yahweh, often translated "Lord," is a personal name. It is almost like a given name for humans, such as John, while Elohim is like the generic term "mankind."

Something else in Scripture that suggests that God is personal is what A. C. Knudson (in *The Religious Teaching of the Old Testament*) calls His free relation to both nature and history.[12] As to nature itself, God freely creates it out of nothing—by origination, which is probably what *bara*, used three times in Genesis 1, means. When God works miracles in the sphere of nature, as by making a borrowed axhead "swim" so that it can be found, this, too, suggests a free relation to nature (see 2 Kings 6:5). God's free relation to history is indicated by His fulfilling His promises (as giving Israel the land of Palestine) and by His not being pressured into doing for Israel simply what Israel wanted Him to do. In this connection Otto Baab says that Yahweh is "the supreme obstacle

---

12. Knudson, *The Religious Teaching of the Old Testament,* 61 ff.

in the nation's self-chosen path."[13] As sovereign Lord over history, leading His people toward His own somewheres and His own somewhens, God is portrayed as personal.

The Living God. Scripture affirms God as the Living One. While "holy" is what God most basically is, Otto Baab is correct in suggesting that "living" is the most typical word for identifying God in the Old Testament—and it also appears at times in the New Testament.

Plato pictured the Deity as a thinker; Scripture portrays Him as one who acts.[14] It is the living God who can and does act on our behalf. It is the living God who delivers, who evidences His power. It is the living God who is pitted against idols—as in Jer. 10:10: "But the Lord is the true God; He is the living God and the everlasting King. At His wrath the earth quakes, and the nations cannot endure His indignation" (NASB).

It is the living God who disposes of Israel's enemies (Josh. 3:10), who can assuage spiritual thirst (Ps. 42:2; 84:1-2), who renews one's strength (1 Sam. 17:26, 36). The oath formula, "As Yahweh lives," occurs at least 60 times in the Old Testament (as in Judg. 8:19).

The understanding of God as the Living One is quite frequent in the New Testament. Jesus is "the Christ, the Son of the living God" (Matt. 16:16). Believers are "sons of the living God" (Rom. 9:26). Paul can speak of "the Spirit of the living God" (2 Cor. 3:3) and suggest that "we are the temple of the living God" (6:16). We find such expressions as "the church of the living God" (1 Tim. 3:15), and we "have put our hope in the living God" (4:10). People "serve the living God" (Heb. 9:14).

The Fatherhood of God

The "Fatherhood of God," along with "the brotherhood of man," is one of the two basic tenets in the unwritten liberal creed.

---

13. Otto Baab, *Theology of the Old Testament* (New York: Abingdon-Cokesbury, 1949), 30. As an example of this, Jeremiah says to Shallum, a king of Judah (son of Josiah), "But your eyes and your heart are set only on dishonest gain, on shedding innocent blood and on oppression and extortion" (Jer. 22:17).

14. See George Ernest Wright, *God Who Acts* (Chicago: H. Regnery, 1952). It should be noted that Wright has felt in more recent years that he might have overdrawn the picture in that book.

Evangelicals usually understand that God is not the Father of everyone, but only of those who are responsive to Him.

In the Old Testament, God's Fatherhood of Israel is implied when Israel is called His child. We read, for example, "When Israel was a child, I loved him, and out of Egypt I called my son" (Hos. 11:1). And in Isa. 1:2 we read, "I reared children and brought them up, but they have rebelled against me." And Jer. 31:20 asks, "Is not Ephraim [the Northern Kingdom] my dear son, the child in whom I delight?" These passages imply that God is a Father to His special people, but perhaps not to everyone.

God is not addressed in prayer as "Father" in the Old Testament, not even in the prayer intimacies of the Psalms. One passage in Jeremiah does imply such address: "Have you not just called to me: 'My Father, my friend from my youth'?" (3:4). And two passages in Isaiah refer to God as Father (63:16; 64:8).

In the New Testament, however, "Father" is an oft-used way of addressing God. Jesus often spoke of God as His Father, and He wanted the disciples to glorify the "Father" (Matt. 5:16). He also wanted them to pray for their persecutors "that you may be sons of your Father" (v. 45). Paul referred to God as Father in the opening of all his Epistles.

Neither in the Old Testament nor in the New Testament is God spoken of as the Father of everyone—not even in Mal. 2:10, where we read, "Have we not all one father? Has not one God created us?" (RSV). The "we" and the "us" in the passage refer to Israel, not to all people, as the context makes clear. God's Fatherhood seems to express a special kind of relationship He has with Israel and with redeemed persons in the New Testament. Of God's Fatherhood Terry says, "The highest and most endearing concept of God, whether in the Old Testament or in the New, or among the nations anywhere, is that of Father."[15]

Donald Bloesch believes that God's Fatherhood expresses His relationship with Christ first of all, and then with us; and he opposes recent feminism's opting to call God "Mother." Bloesch says:

> Against this position I maintain that "Father" in the believing community is not a metaphor based on cultural experience but an ontological symbol describing the relation of the first person of the Trinity to the Son and then to

15. Milton Spenser Terry, Biblical Dogmatics (New York: Eaton and Mains; Cincinnati: Jennings and Graham, 1907), 549.

the Spirit. It is God's designation of himself in relationship to Jesus Christ first of all and then to the members of Christ's body.[16]

The Righteousness of God

Many systematic theologies include God's righteousness as one of His attributes. It is not so treated here. If an attribute is an aspect of God's nature, then righteousness might not be one of them. Perhaps Scripture declares God to be righteous because He makes us righteous and treats us justly. If He is only "naturing" when He makes us righteous, that is, doing what His nature dictates, we would not wonder at being made righteous. Likewise, if He treats us justly simply because it is His nature to do so, without a free and personal decision to do so, being so treated would not incite wonder in us.

If this understanding is correct, it means that to some extent God is what He is because He does what He does. It means that static, metaphysical, Platonic categories or concepts or principles are not actual in themselves but are postact, built upon the basis of concrete function. It means that we declare God to be righteous because He makes us righteous and treats us justly.

This fundamental meaning of righteousness is why Scripture speaks as it does on the subject. True, the Lord is the righteous one (Exod. 9:27; 2 Chron. 12:6). And we read, "You are righteous" (Ezra 9:15; Neh. 9:8); and learn of the "righteous God" (Ps. 7:9). Of the 317 instances of "righteous" in the NASB, many of them simply state, as these do, that God is righteous. If we had only those passages, we might think that righteousness is an attribute of God's nature. But we have numerous other references that suggest a functional meaning of "righteous." Scripture speaks of "the righteous acts of the Lord" (Judg. 5:11), and of "your righteous laws" (Ps. 119:7, 62, 106). Many passages connect the state of righteousness with His acting righteously, as when we read, "The Lord is righteous in all his ways" (145:17).

Other Scripture uses of "righteous" suggest this also. We read of "righteous lips" (Prov. 16:13, KJV), which surely does not mean that our lips are of a righteous nature, but that they speak what is right, or just, or honoring of God.

A study of the 315 instances of "righteousness" in the NASB suggests a similar conclusion. We read, "I will ascribe righteousness to my Maker" (Job 36:3, NASB). If we ascribe it to Him, it must be on the basis of what He does that is just and gracious. And if we ascribe it to Him, perhaps righteousness is not one of the attributes of His nature; and since a Psalmist pleads, "Lead me in Thy righteousness" (Ps. 5:8, NASB), perhaps God's righteousness is a way of life, a way of acting kindly, instead of an aspect of His nature—which, by all means, is holy.

The Love of God

As with righteousness, so with love: it, too, is usually treated as one of God's attributes in systematic theologies. But if love is an attribute of God, then He is only "attributing," only "naturing," when He loves us. If love is an attribute of God, then when God loves us, He is only doing what is His nature to do and not what is His free decision to do in spite of what His nature is like—which is holy.

God's basic nature is characterized by holiness, as noted earlier. As infinitely holy, His basic nature is to love only creatures who have similar natures. His nature, as holy, is to withhold from fellowship with himself creatures who are sinful and erring. Yet contrary to His nature, He loves the rebels all, and those who become redeemed but are still erring creatures.

Since Scripture twice states, "God is love" (1 John 4:8, 16), we have tended to understand that God's love is an aspect of His nature—an attribute. Yet it might be that John twice says this because God is loving. Perhaps John does not mean that God's nature is love or that love is an attribute of God. Perhaps John thinks of the concrete ways in which God reveals himself as loving toward us, and says, "God is love," because he has found God to be loving toward us. It is no doubt the same John who said, "For God so loved the world, that He gave His only begotten Son" (John 3:16, NASB). It is the same John who said so many other things about God's love being extended toward us, such as, "See how great a love the Father has bestowed upon us, that we should be called children of God" (1 John 3:1, NASB). Perhaps John had become overwhelmed by the many ways in which God reveals His love for people and, on the basis of those instances of love, says, "God is love."

This interpretation would bring the Bible's two verses that might be interpreted as suggesting that love is in God's nature into line with the numerous times when Scripture states that God loves us. Actually, the two instances when John says that "God is love" appear in a context where the writer says many things about God's being loving toward us.

This understanding is supported in the numerous instances where Scripture writers extol God for the manifestations of His love for us. For example, Hosea says for Yahweh: "I will heal their apostasy, I will love them freely" (Hos. 14:4, NASB).

The "freely" here suggests that love is not simply natural with God but is decisional. Jesus says, "He who loves Me shall be loved by My Father, and I will love him, and will disclose Myself to him" (John 14:21, NASB). Again we see that God is loving in His actions, and not merely that love is an attribute of His nature. Paul says, "But when the kindness of God our Savior and His love for mankind appeared, He saved us" (Titus 3:4-5, NASB). Here God is said to express love for us by sending His Son to redeem us. God's love is again bound up with an action, nothing being said about love as an attribute out of which a gracious action arose.

The Attributes of God

It can be seen, then, that God's righteousness and love might not be attributes of His nature, but instead what we ascribe to God based on concrete instances of what He does in acting justly and lovingly toward us.

Truth and Justice Not Attributes. Although often treated in systematic theologies as moral attributes, truth might be what we ascribe to God based on His being true and faithful to us. The same is true of justice. God's justice is integrally tied up with His righteousness and does not require separate discussion.

Too Many Attributes Advocated. God's attributes have often been multiplied beyond the need for them. One instance of this is the so-called attribute of aseity—God's self-causedness. Indeed, God is self-caused, but this is not necessarily an attribute of His nature. Likewise, God is eternal, but to say, as Olin A. Curtis does, that eternity is an attribute is to multiply terms beyond the need for them. God has existed eternally, but eternity is not an attribute; it is not one of the ways in which He has existed.

Immutability Not an Attribute. Something else customarily treated as an attribute in countless systematic theologies is God's so-called immutability. The immutability of God was taught by Aristotle but is not taught by Scripture.

Aristotle taught that both the worlds of nature and of humankind change but that God does not change. Therefore, he said, there is no need to pray to God. Aristotle is at the headstream, historically, of the deists, who have always taught that God will not change His operation of the universe in response to prayer.

Aristotle, of course, was guessing. He did not have the help of scriptural revelation. He even preceded by a few centuries that special event that divides all history—the Incarnation.

We Bible-believing, Christ-believing Christians think differently. We believe God created the world out of nothing, and in time; by His will, and not by His nature. It would be almost silly to believe that He did not change in any way after He had a world to relate to, from what He had been like previously.

God also chose a people, Israel, to demonstrate through them what He would do for any nation that would serve Him. He called Abraham at a given time, promised to bless the whole world through him, and promised him the land of Canaan. Later God changed plenty, as personal, delivering His chosen people from Egypt, the Red Sea, and the peoples of Canaan. He fought Israel's battles for them, fed them with manna, and promised them a day of classic redemption through the Messiah.

Yahweh, the personally named Deity, was, and is, anything but changeless. There came the time when His eternal Son became enfleshed as a human, changing forever the very nature of the Deity. If the Incarnation left Him unchanged in His nature, then the Christian faith has been sacrificed to the man Martin Luther called the "blind heathen master," Aristotle.

If the language here is strong, it is because the matter is felt strongly. Immutability is one of the most fantastically incorrect understandings ever introduced into the Christian faith. Since God is personal, He is not immutable. Since He is taking history to a somewhere and to a somewhen, He is not immutable.

The two so-called immutable passages of the Bible teach that God is dependable, that He is faithful, not that He is immutable.

The writer to the Hebrews is exhorting Christians to maintain their faith in Christ and not to take up with new and strange doctrines about Him. In 13:7 he says, "Remember those who led you, who spoke the word of God to you; . . . imitate their faith" (NASB). The next words are, "Jesus Christ is the same yesterday and today, yes and forever" (v. 8, NASB). His next words are, "Do not be carried away by varied and strange teachings" (v. 9, NASB). This has nothing to do with the Deity's being immutable or with Christ's being immutable. The writer is saying that the correct teachings about Christ and the redemption He provided for are unchanging, so that the readers should not take up with new and strange teachings.

The other so-called immutability passage reads, "For I, the Lord, do not change" (Mal. 3:6, NASB). Yahweh declares that He is going to send His "messenger" to "clear the way" (3:1, NASB) before Christ; and that he intends to "purify the sons of Levi and refine them like gold" (v. 3, NASB), a probable reference to Pentecost. Then he says that God will judge "sorcerers" and "adulterers" and "those who oppress the wage earner in his wages, the widow and the orphan," and others (v. 5, NASB). Then he says that the readers can expect both this coming redemption and this judgment because "I, the Lord, do not change." This statement has nothing to do with God's being immutable in His nature or impersonal in His relationship with His people. It means that He will not change His intention to redeem people and to judge those who will not allow themselves to be redeemed.

Hendrikus Berkhof properly speaks of "the unchangeableness of God's faithfulness."[17] Yet he believes that God changes. He writes, "From the time of creation God was changed."[18] He soon adds, "And when he created man he changed again."[19] And he says, "In Christ he again experienced a profound change when the Word became flesh."[20] All the while, though, God is unchangeable in His faithfulness. Berkhof writes, "Not in spite of but precisely in his change God follows a straight line."[21]

---

17. Hendrikus Berkhof, *Christian Faith* (Grand Rapids: William B. Eerdmans Publishing Co., 1979), 140.
18. Ibid., 141.
19. Ibid.
20. Ibid.
21. Ibid.

Although some so-called attributes are perhaps not actually attributes (righteousness, love, truth, justice), and although some "attributes" are not needed as attributes (aseity, eternity), and although one so-called attribute is foreign to our faith (immutability)—there are some attributes of God that require our attention: omnipotence, omnipresence, omniscience.

Omnipotence as an Attribute. God's omnipotence means that He has all power. It is an aspect of God's very nature, a way in which He exists. So it is properly an attribute—a metaphysical attribute, as all God's attributes are.

It is understood that God does not have certain kinds of unimportant power. He cannot make a being greater than or equal with himself. He cannot do what is rationally inconsistent, such as to make a muley cow to have horns, or make a thing both exist and not exist, or to be both square and round.

What God's omnipotence really means is that God has unlimited power to implement what His infinite goodness and His infinite wisdom see to be desirable.

Scripture surely supports this understanding of God. Numerous passages in both the Old Testament and the New Testament teach God's unlimited power and suggest that no one can prevent Him from doing what He wants to do (for example, Isa. 50:2; Jer. 10:6; Dan. 4:35). Some rare passages, however, bear specifically upon what is meant by God's possessing all power. We read that "with God all things are possible" (Matt. 19:26; cf. Mark 10:27; Luke 18:27). Jesus said, "Abba! Father! All things are possible for Thee" (Mark 14:36, NASB). An angel said to Mary, "For nothing will be impossible with God" (Luke 1:37, NASB).

Many philosophers have opposed God's omnipotence. All dualism does this, for if there is one ultimate evil being, then he would limit God's power. William James's pluralism denies God's omnipotence, for in that view God is only one of a whole multitude of ultimate existences. E. S. Brightman's finitism, in which God is limited by that eternal evil quality in His nature, the Given, denies God's omnipotence. Yet Scripture is so clear in teaching that God has all power that the view has always been taught by Christians far and wide.

Omnipresence as an Attribute. This is usually thought of as God's everywhereness. But God's everywhereness might be a pantheistic understanding—in agreement with Spinoza's *Ethics,* which teaches that God is the sum total of all thinking and extended substance. God would be everywhere, because thinking and extended substance is everywhere. According to this view, God's omnipresence means, for example, that He is in everything that exists. It is preferable to understand that God's omnipresence means His anywhereness instead of His everywhereness. God is not inside all physical things, for example. He is a personal being—tripersonal—and exists objective of physical things, all of which He made. Surely it is more scriptural and more experientially meaningful to teach God's anywhereness instead of His everywhereness. God is anywhere He needs to be, anywhere we might need His help. Thus a Psalmist writes: "Where can I go from Thy Spirit? Or where can I flee from Thy presence? If I ascend to heaven, Thou art there; if I make my bed in Sheol, behold, Thou art there. If I take the wings of the dawn, if I dwell in the remotest part of the sea, even there Thy hand will lead me, and Thy right hand will lay hold of me" (139:7-10, NASB).

In Jer. 23:24 we read: "Can a man hide himself in hiding places, so I do not see him?" (NASB). Jonah found that he could not. He fled God, but God pursued him. We read, "But Jonah rose up to flee to Tarshish from the presence of the Lord. So he went down to Joppa, found a ship which was going to Tarshish . . . from the presence of the Lord" (Jonah 1:3, NASB). The next words are "And the Lord" (v. 4), and there follows an account of what God does in tracking down this prophet who sought to escape His presence.

Omniscience as an Attribute. God has all knowledge. This is an actual attribute of God because it is of His very nature to be all-knowing. He does not elect to be, as He elects to act justly or lovingly. He simply is all-knowing. That is the kind of being He is.

The medievals were correct in saying that God knows not only all things that were, are, and will be but also all things that never were but might have been, that are not but might be, and that never will be but could possibly be. God's knowledge in these contingency areas provides infinite wisdom in guiding the destiny of people and nations.

A special theological problem has to do with whether God foreknows our free acts. Some people deny that God knows our acts until they occur. Others say that if He knew our free acts ahead of time, they would not be free, but necessitated by His foreknowledge of them. Yet James Arminius said correctly that God does indeed foreknow our free acts but that His foreknowing them does not cause or necessitate them. Followers of Arminius have refined his understandings and have supported his view with care by suggesting that divine foreknowledge does not cause our acts but rather that our freely acting in a certain way is what causes God to know the action. God might be like a 20th-century historian who knows the free acts of the 18th century but who does not cause the earlier people to act as they did. It is not easy to comprehend a being like this, but then it is not at all necessary that we comprehend God.

The Socinians denied God's foreknowledge of our free acts, as did the Bostonian personalists, including E. S. Brightman. But both the Arminians and the Calvinists have traditionally taught divine foreknowledge.

Perhaps the strongest support for the view that God foreknows our free acts is fulfilled biblical prophecy—especially when prophecy is fulfilled by people like Judas, who evidently did not set about to fulfill it.

Scripture makes it clear that God is all-knowing. We read, "I know their intent which they are developing today, before I have brought them into the land which I swore" (Deut. 31:21, NASB). Also, "But He knows the way I take" (Job 23:10, NASB); "One who is perfect in knowledge is with you" (Job 36:4, NASB; cf. 37:16); and "For all my ways are before Thee" (Ps. 119:168, NASB). More specifically related to foreknowledge, we read: "I am God, and there is no other; I am God, and there is no one like Me, declaring the end from the beginning and from ancient times things which have not been done" (Isa. 46:9-10, NASB). A similar passage in Isaiah reads: "Therefore I declared them to you long ago, before they took place I proclaimed them to you" (48:5, NASB).

With this study of God's existence and nature completed, it is fitting that the Christian doctrine of the Trinity should be studied. This doctrine is so basic to the Christian faith, so ramified in its involvement in other doctrines, and so historically significant in controversies and in creeds, that it will be treated in a somewhat sustained way in a separate chapter.

6

The Tripersonal God

The audacious Christian view of God is that He is three Persons existing eternally in one nature or essence. He is three centers of self-consciousness existing in one underlying nature. The oneness is so real that it flows into the three Persons, interpenetrating them, so that, while they are distinct as Persons, they are one in substance—in the fundamental nature the three possess.

Explanation of the Doctrine

This oneness is not arithmetical. It is the kind of oneness that obtains in an organism when all its "systems" interpenetrate each other and work together. This oneness is intensified, not sacrificed, by the three personal distinctions in God.

This understanding of the Trinity is the "central doctrine of our faith."[1] This doctrine of

> The Immortals of the eternal ring,
> The Utterer, the Uttered, Uttering,

to quote from a poem by Gerard Manley Hopkins, is "at once the ultimate mystery and the supreme glory of the Christian faith."[2] As Lowry further says, "The doctrine of the Trinity is the most comprehensive and most nearly all-inclusive formulation of the truth of Christianity . . . not inadequate summation of the principal teaching of the Christian religion."[3]

All explanations of the Trinity are inadequate. We are talking about a revealed mystery, something that by its very nature, and by our very nature, cannot be figured out by our rational processes.

---

1. G. A. F. Knight, *A Biblical Approach to the Doctrine of the Trinity* (Edinburgh: Oliver and Boyd, 1953), 1.
2. Charles W. Lowry, *The Trinity and Christian Devotion* (New York: Harper and Brothers, 1946), xi.
3. Ibid., 79.

Since Scripture clearly teaches that the Father and the Son and the Holy Spirit are all divine, and that there is but one God, it evidently teaches what the Church later put into its creedal formularies: that God is both one and three.

Some, confronted with this "bad arithmetic," have discounted and even slurred this Christian teaching. Thomas Jefferson labeled it "incomprehensible jargon." Matthew Arnold slighted the doctrine as "the fairy tale of the three Lord Shaftesburys." But Christians, from the early centuries until now, have thankfully received the doctrine as a revealed mystery.

Thomas Aquinas talked about the liberating effect of accepting by faith such doctrines as that of the Trinity, which cannot be attained to by reason. Mere reason, he said, chains us down to what is merely logical—to what our own mental capacities can deduce. Aquinas was correct. We have the capacity for "opticality" as well as for logicality, as the Old Testament prophets such as Ezekiel had. We, too, are seers. When we see the truth of the Trinity, we are "in possession of a prize of rare and marvelous beauty."[4] Scripture does not specifically seek to support the doctrine of the Trinity any more than it does God's existence. It simply states, over and over, that there is but one God; nonetheless, it often speaks of the Father and the Son and the Holy Spirit. The ingredients of the doctrine, therefore, are in Scripture, but construction of the Trinity doctrine was left to the Church during the early centuries of our era.

Tertullian was the earliest of the church fathers to attempt a careful explanation of the doctrine. Tertullian might or might not have been the first to use the term *trinitas,* or "trinity." Yet he was certainly the first to describe God as one in substance and three in Persons. He was probably the first to use *persona* for "person" and *substantia* for "substance"—the terms later appearing in the creeds that officially explain the orthodox Trinity doctrine.

In his important treatise *Against Praxeas,* which is the earliest extant treatment of the Trinity, Tertullian explains: "This . . . [is] unity in trinity, . . . Father, Son and Spirit—three . . . but one nature and of one reality and of one power, because there is one God."[5]

---

4. Ibid., 54.
5. See Tertullian, *Against Praxeas,* trans. A. Souter (New York: Macmillan, 1920), 30.

Emphasizing God's threeness but maintaining at the same time His oneness, Tertullian says that "unity, deriving trinity from itself, is not destroyed by it, but made serviceable."[6]

The most influential of the church fathers, Augustine, contributed significantly to the doctrine of the Trinity. He said that "no one" should "wonder and think it absurd that we should call the Father God, the Son God, and the Holy Spirit God, and that nevertheless we should say that there are not three Gods in that Trinity, but one God and one substance."[7]

Speaking of "the Trinity, one God, of whom are all things,"[8] he explains, "Thus, the Father and the Son and the Holy Spirit, and each of these by himself, is God, and at the same time they are all one God; and each of them by himself is a complete substance, and yet they are all one substance."[9]

Augustine also said, "To all three belong the same eternity, the same unchangeableness [a questionable matter as noted in the last chapter], the same majesty, the same power"[10]—which is the usual Christian view.

Others attempted to explain the Trinity doctrine. Henry Thiessen (b. 1885) says, "In Christian theology, the term 'trinity' means that there are three eternal distinctions in the one divine essence, known respectively as Father, Son, and Holy Spirit."[11] Thiessen further explains, "These three distinctions are three persons, and one may speak of the tripersonality of God."[12]

A number of analogies have been offered in attempting to explain the doctrine of the Trinity. In his treatise *On Christian Doctrine*, Augustine used a tree, with its root and trunk and branches, as an analogy. He writes:

> But in the case of that Trinity, we have affirmed it to be impossible that the Father should be sometime the Son, and sometime the Holy Spirit: just as, in a tree, the root is nothing else than the root, and the trunk (*robur*) is nothing

---

6. Ibid., 31.

7. Augustine, *On Christian Doctrine* (Edinburgh: T. and T. Clark, 1892), 359-60.

8. Ibid., 10.

9. Ibid.

10. Ibid.

11. Henry C. Thiessen, *Lectures in Systematic Theology* (Grand Rapids: William B. Eerdmans Publishing Co., 1979), 90.

12. Ibid.

else than the trunk and we cannot call the branches anything else than branches; for what is called the root cannot be called trunk and branches; and the wood which belongs to the root cannot by any sort of transference be now in the root, and again in the trunk, and yet again in the branches, but only in the root; since this rule of designation stands fast, so that the root is wood and the trunk is wood, and the branches are wood, while nevertheless it is not three woods that are spoken of, but only one.[13]

Augustine seems to temper his use of this and other physical analogies by saying that they tend to depict the oneness of God more adequately than they do His threeness. In this connection he explains:

But these examples in things material (*corporalia exempla*) have been adduced not in virtue of their likeness to that divine Nature, but in reference to the oneness which subsists even in things visible, so that it may be understood to be quite a possibility for three objects of some sort, not only severally, but also all together, to obtain one single name.[14]

Numerous other analogies have been used to illustrate the Christian doctrine of God as both three and one. A family composed of a father and a mother and a child has often been cited. The shamrock, with its three petals extending from one petiole, has sometimes been used. The triangle has served as an analogy, there being one triangle with three sides. Also, the sun has been said to be analogous to the Father; the sun's light to the Son; and the warmth, to the Holy Spirit. Some have used the prism, in which there is a oneness, along with three kinds of light. Water has been used as well; it possess a oneness as water but is found in three states: ice, liquid, and vapor.

Physical analogies cannot adequately explain God, who is not physical in nature. There is nothing in the physical world that is actually analogous to the threeness-in-oneness, the oneness-in-threeness, of the Trinity.

A Revealed Mystery

The doctrine of the Trinity is of necessity a revealed mystery. Here the ground Christians stand on is holy (Exod. 3:5). Moses

---

13. Augustine, *On Christian Doctrine*, 359. Reprinted with permission of Macmillan College Publishing Company. Trans. D. W. Robertson, Jr. Copyright © 1958 by Macmillan College Publishing Company, Inc.
14. Ibid., 359-60.

could not explain how a bush could burn without being consumed, but still he witnessed what was happening; so too we cannot explain the doctrine of the Trinity, but we affirm it audaciously. As Paul "heard things that cannot be told, which man may not utter" (2 Cor. 12:2-4, RSV), so it is with us in regard to this doctrine.

As we look and listen, we learn what God is like. He elects to disclose himself to those who are opened up to Him, and He discloses to us that He is three Persons in one underlying nature.

It has been said that while we may be in danger of losing our souls by denying the doctrine of the Trinity, we are in equal danger of losing our wits if we try to understand it. Thus John Miley said that this doctrine "is exclusively a question of revelation."[15] Similarly Thomas Aquinas said that the "truth that God is three and one is altogether a matter of faith."[16] Thus Karl Rahner speaks of "the revelation of the Trinity,"[17] and calls it a "mystery."[18] He even says, "The dogma of the Trinity is an *absolute mystery* which we do not understand even after it has been revealed."[19]

Thiessen calls this doctrine "the greatest mystery of all revealed truth."[20] He suggests, however, that even though it is a mystery, this "should offer no objection to a doctrine [such as this] based on revelation."[21] He says it is altogether understandable, if the nature of God, the Infinite One, should "present mysteries to the finite mind."[22]

Augustine insists that the pure in heart alone can "see God" in this way. He says: "For these things cannot be seen except by the heart made pure; and (even) he who in this life sees them 'in part,' as it has been said, and 'in an enigma,' cannot secure it that the person to whom he speaks shall also see them, if he is hampered by impurities of heart. 'Blessed,' however, 'are they of a pure heart, for they shall see God.'"[23]

---

15. John Miley, *Systematic Theology* (New York: Methodist Book Concern, 1892), 1:272.

16. Thomas Aquinas, *The Trinity and the Unicity of the Intellect,* trans. Sister Rose Emmanuell Brennan (St. Louis: Herder Book Co., 1946), 42.

17. Karl Rahner, *The Trinity* (New York: Seabury, 1974), 7.

18. Ibid.

19. Ibid., 50.

20. Thiessen, *Lectures in Systematic Theology,* 273.

21. Ibid.

22. Ibid.

23. Augustine, *On Christian Doctrine,* 365.

Augustine goes on to say that although "it is our duty to enjoy the truth . . . the soul must be purified that it may have the power to perceive that light, and to rest in it when it is perceived."[24]

Granting that the doctrine is a mystery, we regard it as above reason, not contrary to reason. Thiessen says: "Revelation concerning a trinity of Persons related in one Essence contradicts no absolute truth. It is evident that as to wholly separated and individually identified subjects, one is not three, nor are three one. Such is a contradiction. The doctrine of the Trinity asserts no such inconsistency."[25]

But why is this doctrine a mystery? Why has God seemed to reveal himself as a triunity, three in one and one in three? And why is it so difficult for us to understand what the existence of this tripersonal God is like? Why can we not figure it out, to our greater satisfaction? On this, Augustine had some devout things to say. Referring in part to the revealed doctrine of the Trinity and the difficulty we have in trying to understand it, he wrote: "And I do not doubt that all this was divinely arranged for the purpose of subduing pride by toil, and of preventing a feeling of satiety in the intellect, which generally holds in small esteem what is discovered without difficulty."[26]

By reason and observation we exist. By revelation we live. In order to our living, as creatures under God, He has revealed himself to us as one God who is at the same time Father and Son and Holy Spirit.

The Teaching of Scripture

Scripture does not teach the doctrine of the Trinity as such. It speaks of the Father and the Son and the Holy Spirit, with varying names for the three, and the three seem to be in a unique relationship. Several passages mention the three within a brief compass— sometimes in a single verse. But Scripture never states that the three are one.

In the King James Version both the threeness and the oneness are mentioned: "For there are three that bear record in heav-

---

24. Ibid., 13.
25. Thiessen, *Lectures in Systematic Theology*, 274.
26. Augustine, *On Christian Doctrine*, 37.

en, the Father, the Word, and the Holy Ghost: and these three are one" (1 John 5:7). But this verse is not in any of the older extant New Testament Greek manuscripts, nor is it in any of the early Latin codices. It is never quoted by any orthodox Greek or Latin father. Tertullian's teaching, however, is so similar to it that some scholars think his teachings presuppose his knowledge of the passage. Most scholars assume that this verse was added by a later editor of 1 John, an editor familiar with the doctrine of the Trinity that had developed among Christians. The addition did, strangely, get into the Latin Vulgate version. Erasmus included it in his third edition of the Greek New Testament. It is thus in the Textus Receptus, the received text, used by the translators of the 1611 King James Version. Erasmus seems to have been pressured into including it by persons with vested interest in the Latin version. They seem to have exacted a promise from him that he would insert the "Trinity" passage if he were shown even one Greek manuscript in which the passage was found. A very late manuscript was shown him, and he inserted the questionable passage.

With all this said about 1 John 5:7, the doctrine of the Trinity is taught in Scripture clearly enough for Christians to have affirmed it since the early centuries as perhaps our most fundamental doctrine.

The Unity in Scripture. The unity of God—His oneness—is an emphasis of Scripture in both of the Testaments. A central Old Testament unity text is Deut. 6:4: "Hear, O Israel: The Lord our God, the Lord is one." According to Isaiah, God says, "I am the Lord, and there is no other" (45:18); and again He says, "Turn to me and be saved, all you ends of the earth; for I am God, and there is no other" (v. 22). God's unity was exceedingly important to the Jewish mind. Jews were especially enjoined to teach this to their children.

1. *Reasons for the Old Testament emphasis on God's unity.* To combat Canaanite polytheism, it was of paramount importance that the new settlers, the Israelites, be taught God's oneness. Other gods are not really gods and cannot hear the supplicator's request. Yahweh alone, the living God, is the one and only God.

A second important reason was Israel's nationalism. This was so even after the division of the kingdom in 933 B.C. at Solomon's death. A. C. Knudson says, "The pronounced nationalism of their religion made it impossible that there should at any time have been any serious peril from poly-yahwism."[27] One nation, so one God!

2. *Evidences of the unity in the Old Testament.* As there are two basic reasons why Israel emphasized God's unity, there are at least two basic evidences of that emphasis. One is the centralization of worship in the Temple at Jerusalem. Unity of sanctuary helped the popular mind to conceive of the unity of God.

The other special evidence of God's oneness in Old Testament times lies in the fact that there was no sexual distinction in the Hebrew understanding of God. Yahweh had no feminine counterpart, as did some of the baals. C. H. Cornhill says, "Israel is the only nation we know of that never had a mythology, the only people who never differentiated the Deity sexually."[28] The Hebrew language did not even contain a word for *goddess*. This oneness of the Deity, with no sexual distinction, contributed to the high moral tone of Jewish life—in contrast to the Greeks, who taught that the gods loved each other and even cohabited with humans.

3. *The New Testament emphasis.* The New Testament also teaches that there is but one God. Unitarians base their teaching of God's oneness on three particular passages: John 17:3; 1 Cor. 8:6; and Eph. 4:6. Trinitarians, no less than Unitarians, support the doctrine of God's oneness, in part on the basis of these passages.

John 17:3 is part of Jesus' priestly prayer, in which He says, "And this is eternal life, that they may know Thee, the only true God, and Jesus Christ whom Thou hast sent" (NASB). When Jesus speaks of the Father as "the only true God," He is not denying that He and the Holy Spirit are divine Persons of the Godhead. He is distinguishing God from the so-called gods that are idols made with human hands. Other words of Jesus show that He and the Father are one: "Anyone who has seen me has seen the Father" (14:9); "I and the Father are one" (10:30); "And the glory which Thou hast given Me I have given to them; that they may be one, just as We are one" (17:22, NASB). When He said that "the Father is greater than I" (14:28), He was not denying His substantial oneness with the Father; He was instead speaking of a certain pri-

---

27. Knudson, *The Religious Teaching of the Old Testament,* 73.
28. C. H. Cornhill, *The Prophets of Israel* (Chicago: Open Court, 1895), 23.

ority that the Father has in authority and other functions, which will be discussed later.

In 1 Cor. 8:6 Paul says, "Yet for us there is but one God, the Father, from whom are all things, and we exist for Him; and one Lord, Jesus Christ, by whom are all things, and we exist through Him" (NASB). Trinitarians believe this as heartily as Unitarians do. The New Testament usually means the "Father" when it speaks of "God." And God is one, although Christ is divine. Besides, this very passage implies Christ's deity. Other passages also clearly state His deity.

Paul speaks similarly in Eph. 4:4-6: "There is . . . one Lord, one faith, one baptism; one God and Father of all, who is over all and through all and in all." Again, the clear statements elsewhere that Jesus is divine help us see that Paul means to say here only that the Father is the Person of priority in the Godhead.

The unity of God is also taught when Paul says, "Now to the King eternal, immortal, invisible, the only God, be honor and glory for ever and ever" (1 Tim. 1:17).

4. *The significance of God's oneness.* When we are thinking theologically about the meaning of unity, unity means more than mere oneness. Karl Rahner makes a helpful distinction between unicity (a word he seems to have coined) and unity. By God's unicity he refers to the oneness of essence of the three Persons of the Trinity. And by unity he means the agreement, the "teamwork," the organismic working together of the three Persons.[29]

It is difficult for Jews, Muslims, and Unitarians to understand what Christians mean by God's oneness. They think we sacrifice God's oneness when we teach that the Son and the Spirit are Deity even as God the Father is. They think we are talking mumbo jumbo when we say that there are three divine Persons but only one divine Being. They cannot conceive of three divine Persons except in terms of three Gods. But Christians are as zealous for teaching God's oneness as they are for teaching the threeness. As James Denney says: "The apostles were all Jews—men, as it has been said, with monotheism as a passion in their blood. They did not cease to be monotheists when they became preachers of Christ,

---

29. See Rahner, *The Trinity,* 45-46.

but they instinctively conceived God in a way in which the old revelation had not taught them to conceive him."[30]

Actually, Christians with a Trinitarian view of God emphasize God's oneness more than do Jews or Muslims or Unitarians. We teach not only the numerical oneness of essence, of nature, of substance, of kind of being, but also that the three are one as an organism is one. And that is more of oneness than mere numerical oneness is. A stick is not one to the extent that an organism is—whose respiratory and digestive and reproductive systems work together in organic unity. Three divine Persons who share one nature and who work together in complete harmony are more one than a unipersonal being would be. Thus Chafer writes, "To acknowledge the triune mode of existence does not impair, diminish, or complicate the doctrine of the *one God,* or lessen the obligation to uphold it."[31] Chafer also calls God's oneness "a fundamental theme which he [the Christian] is appointed to exhibit and defend."[32]

Threeness in Scripture. Even as God is absolutely one, He is absolutely three. Even as He is one in nature, He is tripersonal—three infinite and eternally existing centers of self-consciousness.

1. *Threeness in the Old Testament.* Admittedly, God's threeness is not as clearly taught in the Old Testament as it is in the New Testament. Yet the Old Testament contains indications of the threeness of God found in the New Testament. For example, the name for God as the God of power is Elohim—found hundreds of times in the Old Testament in this plural form (not simply in the singular El). While it regularly appears with a singular verb, and while it might indicate only a plurality in God's powers, it is taken by many Christians as a foregleam of the later revelation of God as tripersonal.

Somewhat more significant than the plural name Elohim are the Old Testament references to God in the clearly plural form. This appears in Gen. 1:26: "Then God said, 'Let us make man in our image, in our likeness.'" The "us" and the "our" imply plurality. Gen. 3:22 likewise contains a plurality reference: "Then the

---

30. James Denney, *Studies in Theology* (Grand Rapids: Baker Book House, 1976), 70.

31. Lewis Sperry Chafer, *Systematic Theology* (Dallas: Dallas Theological Seminary, 1947), 1:287.

32. Ibid.

Lord God said, 'Behold, the man has become like one of Us, knowing good and evil'" (NASB). This implied plurality also appears in Gen. 11:5-7: "And the Lord came down to see the city and the tower which the sons of men had built. And the Lord said, '. . . Come, let Us go down and there confuse their language, that they may not understand one another's speech'" (NASB). Another reference to plurality is in Isa. 6:8: "Then I heard the voice of the Lord, saying, 'Whom shall I send, and who will go for Us?'" (NASB).

Still more significant are the threefold distinctions in God in certain Old Testament passages. Ps. 33:6 refers to the "word of the Lord" and thus also to "the Lord" and also to "the breath [Spirit] of His mouth." It reads, "By the word of the Lord the heavens were made, and by the breath of His mouth all their host" (NASB). This vague reference to threeness, used in connection with creation, is in agreement with other references to the Persons of the Trinity as participants in creation. God the Father creates. He is at least included in the plural Elohim in Gen. 1:1: "In the beginning God created the heavens and the earth." If the word of the Lord in Ps. 33:6 is a reference to Christ, often called the Word in the New Testament, this would agree with John's Gospel, where creation is attributed to Christ, the Word: "All things came into being by Him ["the Word," v. 1], and apart from Him nothing came into being" (1:3, NASB). In that Gospel we also read that "the world was made through Him [the Word]" (v. 10). Ps. 33:6 is also in agreement with Col. 1:16, where Paul says, "For by him [Christ] all things were created." Since the Ps. 33:6 passage refers to "the breath" or the "[Spirit] of his [God's] mouth," it might be in agreement with the vague reference to the Spirit's figuring in creation, according to the Genesis account: "And the earth was formless and void, and darkness was over the surface of the deep; and the Spirit of God was moving over the surface of the waters" (1:2, NASB). There is a possible indirect reference to threeness in Isa. 61:1: "The Spirit of the Sovereign Lord is on me, because the Lord has anointed me." Here the "Spirit of the Sovereign Lord" might be the Holy Spirit, the "Sovereign Lord" might be the Father, and the "me" who is anointed does evidently refer to Christ. Such a passage, also, is Isa. 63:9-12. There the "Holy Spirit" is twice mentioned (vv. 10, 11), the Father is clearly referred to in the passage, and Christ might appear in verse 9 in the reference to "the angel [messenger] of his presence."

There is a possible anticipation of the Trinity doctrine in Isaiah's reference to God as thrice holy in 6:3: "Holy, holy, holy, is the Lord Almighty."[33]

Besides the plural form of Elohim, the references to God in plural pronouns, and the "threeness" references to God, there is some support for the doctrine of the Trinity in the Old Testament references to the Spirit or to the Holy Spirit, and in its possible references to Christ.

The Old Testament uses the designation "Holy Spirit" only three times, but numerous references are made to the "Spirit of God" or the "Spirit of the Lord" (for example, Gen. 1:2; Judg. 3:10; 6:34; 14:6; 15:14; 1 Sam. 11:6; Job 26:13; 27:3; 32:8; 33:4; Pss. 33:6; 104:30; 139:7; Isa. 40:7, 13; 59:19, all KJV). God's Spirit, in these and other passages, is the Source of blessings, gifts, courage, bodily strength, etc.

The Old Testament probably refers to Christ many times. Some theologians, such as H. Orton Wiley, think that each reference to Yahweh in the Old Testament is a reference to Christ. Wiley says, "Christ was the Jehovah [Yahweh] of the Old Testament."[34] The view of Augustine, however, seems preferable: that Yahweh might be any one of the Persons of the Trinity, or all three conceived of as God, according to indications in the context.[35]

Even if the many occurrences of Yahweh are not special references to Christ, many other Old Testament passages probably refer to Him. Christ is possibly referred to when, many times, God is said to have created the world through the word—the word being more of a power than a mere voice would be (see Gen. 1:1 ff.; Pss. 147:18; 148:8; Joel 2:11, all KJV).

In addition, the Old Testament's personification of Wisdom might constitute vague references to Christ. The most vivid such personification is in Prov. 8:12ff. There, Wisdom is an "I," who dwells together "with prudence" (v. 12). This "I" possesses

---

33. It is unlikely that the three angels who appeared to Abraham, according to Genesis 18, were the three Members of the Trinity, as some have suggested.

34. H. Orton Wiley, *Christian Theology* 2:173.

35. The present writer discussed this with Wiley considerably and corresponded with him on it. In a letter he indicated that Augustine's view would be entirely acceptable to him. He was working on a revision of his *Christian Theology* at the time of his death and was considering this and scores of other changes.

"knowledge and discretion" (v. 12). By him "kings reign" and "rulers decree justice" (v. 15, NASB). Of this Wisdom we read, "The Lord possessed me at the beginning of His way, before His works of old" (v. 22, NASB). Of Wisdom we also read, "I was there when he set the heavens in place" (v. 2). Some scholars of Platonic leanings, who believe that concepts such as wisdom are eternal, interpret this hymn about wisdom as referring to an eternal "wisdom" concept or idea that God followed when He created the world. Those of us who do not believe that beauty, goodness, and so forth, are eternally existing concepts and who believe that Scripture does not teach such tend to interpret this lengthy "wisdom" passage in Proverbs as a reference to Christ. It fits in with many things we read elsewhere about Christ, such as His figuring so significantly in creation and His being with God "in the beginning" (see also John 1:1)—that is, eternally.

A similar reference to wisdom as figuring in creation and possibly referring to Christ is in Prov. 3:19: "The Lord by wisdom founded the earth" (NASB). Another such possible reference is in Jeremiah: "It is He who made the earth by His power, who established the world by His wisdom" (10:12; 51:15, NASB).

As wisdom might refer to Christ in certain places in the Old Testament, the angel of Yahweh, the angel of Elohim, or the messenger of the covenant might also in certain places refer to Him. The phrase often refers simply to an angel (for example, 1 Kings 19:5-7; Dan. 3:25, 28; 6:23; 10:13). But certain other instances of the phrase might refer to Christ. Mal. 3:1 surely does: "'And the Lord, whom you seek, will suddenly come to His temple; and the messenger of the covenant, in whom you delight, behold, He is coming,' says the Lord of hosts" (NASB). Of the many instances of "the angel of Yahweh," Herman Bavinck says that "though distinct from Jehovah [a different way of transliterating the Hebrew for Yahweh] this Angel of Jehovah bears the same name, has the same power, effects the same deliverance, dispenses the same blessings, and is the object of the same adoration."[36] Such men-

---

36. Herman Bavinck, *The Doctrine of God,* trans. William Hendricksen (1895-99; reprint ed., Grand Rapids: Baker Book House, 1951), 257. This book is a reprint of a large section of Bavinck's magnum opus, *Gereformeerde Dogmatiek.* Although I found an occasional incorrect Scripture reference in it, it was the most helpful of all my sources on the doctrine of the Trinity in Scripture.

tions of the angel of Yahweh are found in numerous Old Testament passages, including Job 33:23; Ps. 34:7; and Zech. 1:8-14.

2. *Threeness in the New Testament.* Augustine's observation that what is concealed in the Old Testament is revealed in the New Testament would certainly include the doctrine of the Trinity. God's threeness in the Old Testament—concealed by being only germinally indicated—is made plain in the New Testament.

The baptismal formula, coming from Jesus himself, found in the Great Commission, is a most significant aspect of this New Testament revelation: "Go therefore and make disciples of all the nations, baptizing them in the name of the Father and the Son and the Holy Spirit" (Matt. 28:19, NASB).

Paul's benediction, found at the close of 2 Corinthians, and used widely in closing worship services, is another significant "threeness" passage: "May the grace of the Lord Jesus Christ, and the love of God, and the fellowship of the Holy Spirit be with you all" (13:14). Here the apostle links the Son and the Spirit with the Father as though they are of equal status with Him—as though they share fully in His divine nature.

The three are mentioned in Eph. 4:4-6 as though, again, the Spirit and the Son are in the same class with the Father: "There is one body and one Spirit, just as also you were called in one hope of your calling; one Lord, one faith, one baptism, one God and Father of all who is over all and through all and in all" (NASB). While Arians view this as saying that Christ and the Spirit are not divine, Trinitarians read it as teaching that they are divine, but indicating a priority in the Trinity that belongs to the Father.

The three are mentioned again in 2 Thess. 2:13: "But we should always give thanks to God [the Father] for you, brethren beloved by the Lord [Christ], because God has chosen you from the beginning for salvation through sanctification by the Spirit and faith in the truth" (NASB). Again, the passage could be read with an Arian or Unitarian frame of mind as teaching that only the Father is divine, since the Son and the Spirit are not called God. But the Father is the One normally called God in the New Testament. He is the One we are to pray to, and prayer to Him is mentioned in this verse. He does enjoy a status of priority over the others within the Godhead. At the same time, the Son and the Spirit are mentioned along with God the Father with the implication that they too are divine. And if it is not clear from this and other passages that they are also divine, there are certain other passages that declare outright that the Son is divine (for example, John 1:1; 20:28) and imply that the Holy Spirit is also (Heb. 9:14)—as we shall see.

The apostle Peter spoke of the Father, the Son, and the Spirit in one verse, as though the Son and the Spirit are of the same nature with the Father. Writing to Christians generally, he says that you have been "chosen according to the foreknowledge of God the Father, by the sanctifying work of the Spirit, that you may obey Jesus Christ and be sprinkled with His blood" (1 Pet. 1:1-2, NASB).

The apostle John likewise links together the three Persons of the Trinity in 1 John 5:4-7. In that passage he refers to the Father in the phrase "born of God"; he speaks of "Jesus" as "the Son of God . . . who came by water and blood"; and he refers to the Holy Spirit, saying, "And it is the Spirit who bears witness, because the Spirit is the truth" (NASB). Again the three are not here declared to be Deity. Such specific declaration, regarding all three, is not found in Scripture but only in creeds. But this linking of the three, taken together with such passages as John 1:1 and 20:28, where Christ is referred to as "God," indicate the sameness of nature of the three as expressly stated and restated, as, for example, in the Athanasian Creed.

The Deity of Christ. The New Testament's clear teaching of the deity of Christ, along with its implied teaching of the deity of the Holy Spirit, is the strongest biblical support of all for the doctrine of the Trinity. It is especially the New Testament's teaching of Christ's deity that nudged the early Christians to yield their unipersonal view of God and to begin the long process whereby they came to teach officially the threeness as well as the oneness.

It was not especially Christ's miraculous works that "declared" Him to be divine. Some early fathers did feel that Christ's works were proof of His deity, and many theologians and church leaders have felt the same way, including John Wesley. But Christ prayed to the Father to raise Lazarus and to do other such stupendous works. And Christ declared that He could not do them of himself—evidently because of His taking on human nature and holding in reserve His divine attributes. So the miracles as such were not proof of His deity; they were only indicators of it.

More significant than Christ's miraculous works as indicators of His deity are certain names given Him. Names such as Jesus and Christ are not particularly significant here. His being called

Lord so frequently is indeed significant, for that word translates especially two frequently used Hebrew words designating God: Yahweh and Adonai. Jesus is referred to in prophecy as "Immanuel," which means "God with us," and this name is certainly supportive of His deity (see Isa. 7:14; Matt. 1:22-23). Some scholars feel that when Peter and others called Christ "the Son of God," they indicated His deity, and this might be so; yet this should not be rated as highly as "Lord" and "Immanuel," since the New Testament also called believers sons of God (for example, John 1:12; 1 John 3:1-2, all KJV).

It is when the New Testament actually calls Jesus "God" (*theos*) that we have its most important support of Christ's deity and of the doctrine of the Trinity. There are two passages that might or might not do this, depending on how they are translated and interpreted. One of them is Titus 1:3, where Paul speaks of "God our Savior," but it might refer to God the Father. The other is Heb. 1:8: "But about the Son he says, 'Your throne, O God, will last for ever and ever.'" This is part of a more lengthy quote from Ps. 45:6-7, and the writer of Hebrews seems to be saying that that passage in the Psalms refers to God's Son, Jesus Christ.

A few other passages also refer to Jesus Christ in such a way that His deity is indicated. One is Col. 1:13-20. There the "Son" (v. 13) is declared to be "the image of the invisible God" (v. 15)— the One who as enfleshed was the very image of God. This is a closer "image" than that in which we were made, for Paul also here says, "For it was the Father's good pleasure for all the fulness to dwell in Him" (v. 19, NASB). Besides, we were "made," according to Gen. 1:26-27, whereas Christ was "begotten," even the "only begotten" (John 1:18; 3:16; 1 John 4:9ff., all KJV). Origen viewed the *monogenēs* (only begotten) passages as meaning "eternally begotten," and the Church has in general accepted the interpretation.

One of the strongest supports of the deity of Christ in all of Scripture, and therefore one of the Bible's strongest supports of the later-developed doctrine of the Trinity, is John 1:1: "In the beginning was the Word, and the Word was with God, and the Word was God." John says that the Word, Jesus Christ, existed "in the beginning." This probably denotes the Word's eternality. Chafer suggests, "The phrase *in the beginning,* as used here by John, could hardly be a reference to aught else than the eternity

THE TRIPERSONAL GOD ▷ 139

past which was prior to the event mentioned in the next verse, namely, 'All things were made by him.'"[37] Besides, this "Word," Christ, as God's message to us, simply "was"—that is, He existed eternally. And He was "with God," the word here (*pros*) meaning near to, in the vicinity of, God. Not only that, but this Word "was God" (John 1:1). There it is! That is one of the most anti-Arian statements in the Bible. It does not say that Christ was like God. It states that He indeed "was God." It matters not that the definite article does not appear before *theos* here. In abstract nouns such as God, love, etc., the definite article might or might not appear in the Greek. The Jehovah's Witnesses, who do not believe in Christ's deity or in the Trinity, translate it as saying Christ was "a god." This is about all they can do when such a strong declaration of Christ's deity appears in Scripture.

Another similarly strong support of the deity of Christ—and finally of the doctrine of the Trinity—is also in John's Gospel (20:28). There Thomas, the one who had been most prone to doubt Christ's resurrection, exclaims, "My Lord and my God!" Actually, this declaration of Christ's deity is the earliest such statement in Scripture. It was made shortly after the resurrection of Christ, perhaps some 60 years before the John 1:1 statement was written, and earlier than those in Hebrews, Colossians, and elsewhere. The one most prone to doubt became the first person we know of to express the highest, most profound faith in Christ—that He is *theos*, God.

Christ is also called God in Rom. 9:5, where Paul says of the Jews, "Theirs are the patriarchs, and from them is traced the human ancestry of Christ, who is God over all, forever praised!"

In two other passages it seems that Christ is called God. In 1 John 5:20 we read, "And we know that the Son of God has come, and has given us understanding, in order that we might know Him who is true, and we are in Him who is true, in His Son Jesus Christ. This is the true God and eternal life" (NASB). This seems to say that Christ is the "true God." The other passage is Rev. 1:8, 17. In verse 8 we read, "'I am the Alpha and the Omega,' says the Lord God, 'who is and who was and who is to come, the Almighty'" (NASB). This is in a context that is clearly speaking of

37. Chafer, *Systematic Theology* 1:297.

Christ, who "released us from our sins by His blood" (v. 5, NASB), and who "is coming with the clouds, and every eye will see Him, even those who pierced Him" (v. 7, NASB). Besides, in verse 17 of this chapter "the first and the last" (NASB) who would be "the Alpha and the Omega" of verse 8, is clearly Christ, for of this "living One" we read, "I was dead, and behold, I am alive forevermore" (v. 18, NASB).

It is also probable that Christ is called God in two other places. One of them is 2 Pet. 1:1, NASB: "Simon Peter, a bond-servant and apostle of Jesus Christ, to those who have received a faith of the same kind as ours, by the righteousness of our God and Savior, Jesus Christ." "God," here, does not seem to mean the Father, but Christ. Another text is Titus 2:13, where Paul speaks of "the glory of our great God and Savior, Christ Jesus" (NASB).

Besides all these scriptural supports of Christ's deity, which admittedly depend on how we translate and on how we weigh manuscript variations, there are many others, although some of them are not quite as clear and direct as these.

Some of the others cluster around Christ's eternality. He is "the firstborn over all creation" (Col. 1:15), meaning that He was not made, but eternally begotten. Jesus himself said, "Before Abraham was born, I am!" (John 8:58), suggesting His eternality. Christ also prayed, "And now, glorify Thou Me together with Thyself, Father, with the glory which I had with Thee before the world was" (17:5, NASB). Later in the same prayer Jesus speaks of "the glory you have given me because you loved me before the creation of the world" (v. 24). If some of these passages could be taken as teaching only Christ's preexistence, they may be interpreted as teaching His eternal preexistence, because they are passages, as shown, that teach that the preexistence was eternal.

One other "deity of Christ" passage is Phil. 2:6, where the KJV reads, "Who, being in the form of God"; the NASB has "Who, although He existed in the form of God"; and the NIV reads, "Who, being in very nature God." This not only declares Christ's deity but also is a scriptural support of the view later developed that the Son (and the Spirit too) is of the same nature or substance with the Father.

Still other suggestions of Christ's deity are His statements "Just as the Father knows me and I know the Father" (John 10:15); and "No one knows the Son, except the Father; nor does anyone know the Father, except the Son, and anyone to whom the Son wills to reveal Him" (Matt. 11:27, NASB). Jesus declares that He knows the Father as intimately as the Father knows Him, and this can be true only if Jesus is divine.[38]

The Deity of the Holy Spirit. Along with the dawning realization that Christ is divine came the apostolic and Early Church's understanding that the Holy Spirit is also divine. The phrase "Holy Spirit" occurs once in what is probably a Davidic psalm, Psalm 51, written after the king's sin with Bathsheba. David pleads for "mercy" (v. 1) and for cleansing (vv. 2, 7) and prays, "Do not cast me from your presence or take your Holy Spirit from me" (v. 11). The KJV does not capitalize "holy spirit" here, but some versions, such as the NASB and the NIV, do—indicating that the translators understood the reference to be to the One we have come to call the Third Person of the Trinity.

The other two instances of "Holy Spirit" in the Old Testament are in Isa. 63:10-11. Here the KJV capitalizes "Spirit" only, but the NASB and NIV capitalize "Holy" also. Isaiah would hardly have been intending to speak of a divine person distinct from the One we have come to call God the Father. But we are given here a fore-gleam of what our New Testament Scriptures make much more clear. Isaiah says the people "rebelled and grieved his Holy Spirit" (63:10), a concept in keeping with the New Testament teaching about Him, because Paul urges the Ephesians, "And do not grieve the Holy Spirit of God" (4:30). "Of God" here probably means "who proceeds eternally from the Father" (see John 15:26).

The designation "Holy Spirit" in Isa. 63:11 seems to refer to a being distinct from God the Father—although, again, Isaiah was probably saying more than he realized. He asks, "Where is He [God] who put His Holy Spirit in the midst of them . . . ?" (NASB).

The Old Testament also indicates the Holy Spirit's deity by speaking of "The Spirit of the Lord [Yahweh]" (Isa. 11:2) and "the Spirit of God [Elohim]" (Exod. 31:3). Without the New Testament revelation, we would say these passages are speaking of Yahweh's Spirit or Elohim's Spirit—meaning simply the spiritual being sometimes called Yahweh and sometimes called Elohim. But passages such as Rom. 8:9, where Paul speaks of "the Spirit of

---

38. For the same view on the impact of these passages see ibid., 296.

God," which we take to mean the Holy Spirit who proceeds eternally from God, interpret for us the Isaiah and Exodus passages as perhaps referring to the Holy Spirit.[39]

Another such passage is Isa. 6:5-9, compared with Acts 28:25. In Isa. 6:9 it is "the Lord," Yahweh, who says to Isaiah, "Go, and tell this people: 'Keep on listening, but do not perceive . . .'" (NASB). In Acts 28:26 this is quoted, prefaced by the statement, "The Holy Spirit rightly spoke through Isaiah the prophet to your fathers" (v. 25, NASB).

Also, in Exod. 17:7 we read that "they tested the Lord [Yahweh]," and Heb. 3:7-9 implies that it was "the Holy Spirit" whom they had tested.

Further, in Jer. 31:31-35 we read, "'Behold, days are coming,' declares the Lord [Yahweh], 'when I will make a new covenant with the house of Israel and with the house of Judah'" (v. 31, NASB); and Heb. 10:15-18 attributes these words to the Holy Spirit: "The Holy Spirit also bears witness to us; . . . saying, 'This is the covenant that I will make with them after those days'" (vv. 15-16, NASB). Yahweh sometimes seems to be the same as the Holy Spirit. Passages such as these, and those that equate Christ with Yahweh, occasioned Augustine's correct view referred to earlier, that Yahweh is sometimes a reference to the entire Trinity and at other times a reference to any one of these three Persons of the Trinity. Even so, it seems that both Yahweh and Elohim, used so often in the Old Testament, ordinarily refer to God the Father.

In denying the deity of the Holy Spirit, liberals also denied His personality, saying more or less that He is an influence. Therefore, before we discuss the "deity" passages, let us note that the New Testament portrays the Holy Spirit as a person. Although in Greek *pneuma* ("Spirit") is neuter in gender, personal pronouns are used with reference to the Holy Spirit. Thus Jesus says, "He [the Holy Spirit] will bear witness of Me" (John 15:26, NASB). Thus Jesus also says: "But when he, the Spirit of truth, comes, he will guide you into all truth. He will not speak on his own; he

---

39. The Son is also sometimes called "God" (El) in the Old Testament, as in Isa. 9:6, where it is said that the "child" to be born will be called "Wonderful Counselor, Mighty God," and in Ps. 68:18: "When you [Christ] ascended on high [after the Resurrection], you led captives in your train; you received gifts from men, even from the rebellious—that you, O Lord God, might dwell there."

will speak only what he hears, and he will tell you what is yet to come. He will bring glory to me by taking from what is mine and making it known to you" (16:13-14).

Besides, His personality is implied when He is called a "Counselor" (John 15:26) and "another Counselor" (14:16-17).

The Holy Spirit is mentioned with the Father and the Son in the formula for baptism in Matt. 28:19, and this is an important biblical suggestion of His deity. The very first Christians, soon after Pentecost, baptized only in the name of Jesus, according to the Book of Acts (2:38; 8:16; 19:5), seeming not to have remembered Jesus' statement that baptism should be in the name of all three Persons. But after the Gospel of Matthew was written and disseminated, probably in the A.D. 60s, the baptismal formula in the Great Commission became a kind of first creed for Christians. It helped them toward the consciousness that the Holy Spirit is divine.

Much early Christian teaching is supportive of the Spirit's deity. The earliest Church discipline, the *Didache,* written somewhat before or after A.D. 100, and purporting to teach what the apostles did, calls attention to this baptismal formula.[40] Clement of Rome implies the Spirit's deity,[41] as does Ignatius.[42] Justin Martyr refers to the Trinity,[43] as does Theophilus.[44] Tertullian taught it, as discussed earlier, in his "Against Praxeas," as did Origen.[45] Later, Cyprian (d. 258) mentions the baptismal formula and says "the Three are one."[46] Athanasius taught the deity of the Holy Spirit, although his emphasis was on the Son's deity. He said there is "one Godhead in Trinity."[47] Augustine often taught the Spirit's deity expressly, as when he wrote, "The Holy Spirit, who is not of a nature inferior to the Father and the Son, but, so to say, consub-

40. "Didache or Teaching of the Twelve Apostles," in *The Fathers of the Church* (New York: Cima Publishing Co., 1947), 1:177.

41. Clement of Rome, "The Letter to the Corinthians," in *Fathers of the Church* 1:54.

42. Ignatius of Antioch, "Letter to the Smyrnaeans," in *Fathers of the Church* 1:119.

43. Justin Martyr, "First Apology," in *Ante-Nicene Fathers* 1:164, 185.

44. Theophilus, "The Autolycus," in *Ante-Nicene Fathers* 2:101.

45. Tertullian, "Against Praxeas," in *Ante-Nicene Fathers* 4:598.

46. Cyprian, "To Jubarian," in *The Fathers of the Church,* ed. Roy Deferrari, 69 vols. (Washington, D.C.: Catholic University of America Press, 1946), 51:271, 275.

47. Athanasius, "Discourse I Against the Arians," in *A Library of Fathers of the Holy Catholic Church,* 41 vols. (London: Rivingtons, 1844), 18:205-6.

stantial and coeternal."[48] In general, the fathers of the East and the West taught the Spirit's deity and the doctrine of the Trinity, such as Gregory Nazianzen,[49] Gregory of Nyssa,[50] and Basil,[51] to mention a few. However, there were denials of the Spirit's deity (and of that of the Son) on the part of some often-devout persons, as we will see when we trace heretical views.

The Nicene Creed of 325 mentions the Holy Spirit as though He is divine—along with its clear teaching of Christ's deity. At Constantinople in 381, the Holy Spirit's deity was expressly stated, because the Pneumatomachians had begun to deny it. The Athanasian Creed, which seems to be of the late fifth century (subsequent to the Council of Chalcedon of 451), states and restates the Holy Spirit's deity.

But this discussion of the deity of the Holy Spirit in the early centuries of the church's history gravitates us toward the creeds of the church; and the creeds need to be discussed from the wider standpoint of their declarations regarding the doctrine of the Trinity as such.

As mentioned, the baptismal formula was a kind of early creed and implied the threeness of the Godhead without actually stating that the Son and the Spirit are divine. Also, it says nothing about the oneness of the three. In this connection Emil Brunner says, "Very early the Christian Church had fixed the main content of its faith in a threefold 'triadic' baptismal formula as a kind of creed."[52]

The Trinity in the Creeds

The Apostles' Creed. The earliest of the creeds is the Apostles' Creed, so named because it purports to teach, in brief compass, what the 12 apostles taught. It dates in most of its clauses to about the middle of the second century A.D.[53] No copy exists from that time, but historians are quite confident about which clauses were present then and which were added later.

---

48. Augustine, *On Christian Doctrine,* 357.
49. Gregory Nazianzen, "Funeral Oration," in *Fathers of the Church,* ed. Deferrari, 22:86.
50. Gregory of Nyssa, "On Perfection," in *Fathers of the Church,* ed. Deferrari, 58:106.
51. Basil, "To Meletius, Bishop of Antioch," in *Fathers of the Church,* ed. Deferrari, 13:267.
52. Emil Brunner, *The Christian Doctrine of God,* vol. 1 in *Dogmatics,* 220.
53. See Wiley, *Christian Theology* 1:40.

The creed seems to have been divided roughly into three parts—relating to the Father, the Son, and the Holy Spirit.

While it lists the Persons of the Trinity and is a kind of extension of the baptismal formula of Matt. 28:19, it is not an adequate Trinitarian statement. Only the Father is called "God." "I believe in God the Father Almighty," we say. Christ is named as God's "only Son," but that does not necessarily affirm the Son's deity. Still less is said of the Holy Spirit that might imply His deity. Besides saying, "I believe in the Holy Spirit," this creed states only one other thing about Him, something merely functional—that Christ was "conceived by the Holy Spirit."

The Apostles' Creed says nothing whatever about the oneness of the Father and the Son and the Spirit.

Still, the Apostles' Creed is about as Trinitarian as we could expect, dating as it does to so early an era. At that time the Church had not been confronted with the heresies that later creeds were intended to combat. The writer or writers of the early form of the Apostles' Creed were unaware of a need to express Christian faith in a way that would obviate these later heretical understandings.

The Nicene Creed. Historically the second of ancient Christian creeds, it is based on the decision of an ecumenical council that met at Nicea, in Bithynia, during May or June of A.D. 325. Over 300 bishops from both Greek-speaking (East) and Latin-speaking (West) areas were called together by Emperor Constantine, who presided. Present also were presbyters and deacons, none of whom had a vote. Among the deacons was the young Athanasius, who had already written *Concerning the Incarnation of the Word of God,* to this day one of the most significant books ever written on the Incarnation. Athanasius helped his bishop (from Alexandria) and defended the teaching of Christ's deity, so crucial for the Trinitarian understanding. Some 20 bishops were either Arians (very few in number), who stressed Christ's nature as unlike that of the Father, or Eusebians, who believed that Christ's nature was like *(homoiousia)* that of the Father.

The Athanasian view won out. The council declared that Christ is of the same substance *(homoousia)* with the Father: "of one substance with the Father," "very God of very God." He is the "only begotten Son of God," "not made" as the world was made.

The Niceno-Constantinopolitan Creed. The deity of the Holy Spirit was not controverted at the Council at Nicea, so His status was not defined. The Pneumatomachians latched onto this and began to teach a kind of binitarianism, in which the Father and the Son were divine but not the Holy Spirit. Their teaching occasioned the next ecumenical council, which met in 381 at Constantinople and made the Holy Spirit's deity quite express, adding to the Nicene Creed that, "with the Father and the Son," He "is to be worshiped." It also added that He is "the Lord and Giver-of-Life, who proceeds from the Father." The Nicene Creed, with these additions, came to be known as the Nicene-Constantinopolitan Creed.

The Athanasian Creed. This creed, named for the fourth-century defender of orthodoxy, Athanasius, was written by an unknown person or persons some time after the Council of Chalcedon of A.D. 451. Over and over, it teaches that Father, Son, and Holy Spirit are all divine, sharing one nature and constituting one God. It reads that "we worship one God in Trinity, and Trinity in Unity; neither confounding the Persons: nor dividing the Substance." It further reads, "So likewise the Father is Almighty, the Son Almighty: and the Holy Ghost Almighty. And yet there are not three Almighties: but one Almighty." It affirms the double procession of the Spirit: "The Holy Ghost is of the Father and of the Son." It further states that "the Trinity in Unity is to be worshipped." Interestingly, it declares that one must believe precisely what it stated in order to be saved: "He, therefore, who will be saved must thus think of the Trinity."[54]

The Augsburg Confession (1530). This early Lutheran confession expresses full agreement with "the decree of the Nicene Synod concerning the unity of the divine essence and of the three persons . . . : to wit, that there is one divine essence which is called and is God . . . ; and that yet there are three persons of the same essence and power, who are also coeternal, the Father, the Son, and the Holy Ghost."[55]

---

54. Paul T. Fuhrmann, *An Introduction to the Great Creeds of the Church* (Philadelphia: Westminster Press, 1966), 49-50.

55. Philip Schaff, *Creeds of Christendom,* 3 vols. (1878; reprint, Grand Rapids: Baker Book House, 1977), 3:7.

The Formula of Concord (1577). This late Lutheran confession expresses full agreement with "the Apostles', the Nicene, and the Athanasian Creeds," stating, "We publically confess that we embrace them, and reject all heresies and all dogmas which ever have been brought into the Church of God contrary to their decision."[56]

The Thirty-nine Articles (1562). This official statement of the Church of England (and Episcopalianism generally) is classical on the doctrine of the Trinity: "There is but one living and true God, everlasting, without body, parts, or passions; of infinite power, wisdom, and goodness; the Maker, and Preserver of all things both visible and invisible. And in unity of this Godhead there be three Persons, of one substance, power, and eternity: the Father, the Son, and the Holy Ghost."[57]

The Belgic Confession (1561). One of the important confessions official for Reformed branches of Christianity, the Belgic Confession reads: "According to . . . this Word of God, we believe in one only God, who is one single essence, in which are three persons, really, truly, and eternally distinct, . . . the Father, and the Son, and the Holy Ghost."[58]

The Westminster Confession of Faith (1647). This creed, official for Presbyterian denominations of various types, likewise affirms the doctrine of the Trinity in its classical purity. On the Trinity it states: "In the unity of the Godhead there be three persons, of one substance, power, and eternity: God the Father, God the Son, and God the Holy Ghost. The Father is of none, neither begotten nor proceeding; the Son is eternally begotten of the Father; the Holy Ghost eternally proceeding from the Father and the Son."[59]

Here again the deity of all three and the Spirit's double procession are affirmed.

We shift now to a study of the principal problem of the centuries among believers in the Trinity.

---

56. Ibid., 93-95.
57. John Leith, *Creeds of the Churches* (Richmond, Va.: John Knox Press, 1973), 487-88.
58. Schaff, *Creeds of Christendom* 3:389.
59. Leith, *Creeds of the Churches,* 197. Quoted from the 1801 American revision, which is identical to the 1562 original on the doctrine of the Trinity but which updates the English.

The Procession of the Holy Spirit

While the Son is generated eternally (from the Father), the Holy Spirit eternally proceeds—either from the Father only or from both the Father and the Son (see John 15:26; Rom. 8:9; etc.).

The Nicene Creed stated simply, "And [we believe] in the Holy Spirit."

The Second Ecumenical Council (Constantinople, A.D. 381) had expanded this to include: "And in the Holy Spirit, the Lord and the Giver-of-Life, who proceeds from the Father." This Niceno-Constantinopolitan Creed was received in the West as well as the East as the official Christian creed.

The Third Ecumenical Council (Ephesus, A.D. 431) prohibited any creed that differed from the Nicene Creed, but the Fourth Ecumenical Council (Chalcedon, A.D. 451) refers to the Niceno-Constantinopolitan Creed as official. So it was permitted, even in the East, to change the Nicene Creed by adding that the Holy Spirit "proceeds from the Father."

Augustine, before the third and fourth ecumenical councils had met, in *Concerning the Trinity* and elsewhere in his writings, had taught that the Holy Spirit proceeds from the Son as well as from the Father. Augustine had added a four-syllable Latin word to what the official Niceno-Constantinopolitan Creed taught: *filioque*, meaning "and the Son."

His teaching was promulgated by various Western theologians of the next few centuries.

Eastern theologians, however, rejected the *filioque,* and lengthy controversy ensued. Papal acceptance led finally to creedal endorsement in the West, while Eastern Orthodoxy continued to regard the *filioque* as heretical. Since the Reformation was a breakaway from the Roman Catholic church, the Reformers never made the *filioque* an issue. It has been generally received by Protestants and is affirmed in Lutheran, Calvinist, and Anglican confessions of faith.

The Priority of the Father

Within the Trinity there is a certain priority that belongs to the Father. When the three are named in Scripture, as in the baptismal formula (Matt. 28:19), the Father is usually named first. An exception occurs in the benediction that closes 2 Corinthians:

"May the grace of the Lord Jesus Christ, and the love of God, and the fellowship of the Holy Spirit be with you all."

All three Members of the Trinity are Deity. All possess divine attributes. For example, all have existed eternally: The Father: "The eternal God is your refuge" (Deut. 33:27); the Son: "But of the Son He says, 'Thy throne, O God, is forever and ever'" (Heb. 1:8, NASB); and the Holy Spirit: "Who through the eternal Spirit offered Himself without blemish to God" (Heb. 9:14, NASB). Yet Scripture describes the Godhead in a way that clearly gives the Father a place of priority.

Paul indicates the Father's priority in 1 Tim. 6:15-16. The Father is "the blessed and only Sovereign . . . who alone possesses immortality and dwells in unapproachable light; whom no man has seen or can see" (NASB). There has been no incarnation of the Father; therefore no one has actually seen Him. He dwells transcendently in "unapproachable light." This cannot be said of the Son; and it would not be said of the self-effacing Holy Spirit.

Paul teaches the Father's priority more clearly in other passages. One is 1 Cor. 11:3: "But I want you to understand that Christ is the head of every man, and the man is the head of a woman, and God is the head of Christ" (NASB). This is a teaching Paul wants the Corinthians to hold onto, for the previous verse reads, "I praise you for remembering me in everything and for holding to the teachings."

Paul seems to suggest a priority of the Father in 1 Cor. 8:6, saying, "Yet for us there is but one God, the Father, from whom are all things, and we exist for Him; and one Lord, Jesus Christ, by whom are all things, and we exist through Him" (NASB). Here the word *theos* (God) refers expressly to the Father, as is usual in the New Testament as a whole. And the Father, here, has a priority, for it is from Him that all things came. This includes the eternal origination of Christ, as Jesus says: "For just as the Father has life in Himself, even so He gave to the Son also to have life in Himself; and He gave Him authority to execute judgment, because He is the Son of Man" (John 5:26-27, NASB).

The first-named Person of the Trinity is "the God and Father of our Lord Jesus Christ" (Eph. 1:3), another Pauline suggestion of the Father's priority. This is logical and originative priority, not chronological priority.

In Paul's writings the Father has priority as the One who plans the future. Paul says we were chosen to be in Christ "according to the plan of him [the Father] who works out everything in conformity with the purpose of his will, in order that we, who were the first to hope in Christ, might be for the praise of his glory" (Eph. 1:11-12). This is in keeping with Christ's oft-used statement that the Father had sent Him and that He had come to do the Father's will.

Paul reveals a priority of the Father when he asserts, as do other New Testament preachers and writers, that the Father raised Jesus from the dead. Thus Paul speaks of God's "mighty strength, which he exerted in Christ when he raised him from the dead and seated him at his right hand in the heavenly realms" (Eph. 1:19-20). And "God [the Father] placed all things under his [Christ's] feet and appointed him to be head over everything for the church" (v. 22). And clear priority is shown when Paul speaks of "one Lord [Christ], one faith, one baptism; one God and Father of all, who is over all and through all and in all" (4:5-6).

And although Christ had been "in the form of God" and on a plane of "equality with God" (Phil. 2:6, NASB), it is God the Father who, by Christ's resurrection, "highly exalted Him, and bestowed on Him the name which is above every name" (v. 9, NASB).

The Father's priority in the Godhead is so often implied and stated in the New Testament generally and in Paul's writings particularly that it scarcely needs elucidation. Yet it does need to be pointed out, because much of evangelicalism has tended to give Christ the first position in the Trinity. Paul and other writers would have us keep in mind that Christians are not "Unitarians of the Son," that we are not "Jesus only" people. Scripture makes the Father's priority clear. That the priority of the Father will obtain eternally Paul affirms in 1 Cor. 15:27-28: "For he 'has put everything under his feet.' Now when it says that 'everything' has been put under him, it is clear that this does not include God himself, who put everything under Christ. When he has done this, then the Son himself will be made subject to him who put everything under him, so that God may be all in all." Everything is put under Christ, but Christ is somehow "under" God the Father, that the Father might be "all in all."

And subsequent to the years of Christ's enfleshment, Paul says, "But I want you to understand that Christ is the head of every man, and the man is the head of a woman, and God is the head of Christ" (1 Cor. 11:3, NASB). Christ is coeternal with the Father, but in the Godhead He is the Christian's Blessed Number Two.

While recent fundamentalism has been prone to make the Son the number one Member of the Trinity, the Church historically has not done this. From the earliest centuries it has understood that there is in the Godhead a priority of the Father. In the earliest extant treatise on the Trinity, *Against Praxeas,* Tertullian taught the Father's priority in several ways. In his use of the terms *"trinitas," person,* and *substance,* he taught the Father's priority. Tertullian used three analogies to illustrate this, and in one passage he groups these analogies together and speaks of them in one rounded discussion:

> Therefore according to the pattern of these examples I declare that I speak of two, God and His Word, the Father and His Son. The root and the shrub are also two things, but joined together; the source and the river are two forms, but undivided; the sun and the ray are two forms, but they cleave together. Everything that proceeds from something, must be second to that from which it proceeds, but it is not therefore separated. Where, however, there is a second, there are two, and where there is a third, there are three. The Spirit is third with respect to God and the Son, even as the fruit from the shrub is third from the root, and the channel from the river is third from the source, and the point where the ray strikes something is third from the sun.[60]

Tertullian also writes, "So also the Father is other than the Son, since He is greater than the Son, since it is one that begets, another that is begotten; since it is one that sends, another that is sent; since it is one that acts, another through whom action takes place."[61]

Tertullian goes on to speak of "The Holy Spirit," the third name of Divinity and the third stage of majesty.[62] He saw things scripturally, even at so early a time.

Augustine, who wrote the next really influential work on the Trinity, likewise clearly taught the Father's priority. He quoted and elucidated this biblical passage: "All things are yours . . . and ye are Christ's; and Christ is God's" (1 Cor. 3:21, 23, KJV). Augus-

---

60. Tertullian, *Against Praxeas,* 45.
61. Ibid., 46-47.
62. Ibid., 116.

tine also refers to other priority-of-the-Father Scripture passages: "'For the Father is greater than I'; and, 'The head of the woman is the man, the Head of the man is Christ, and the Head of Christ is God'; and, 'Then shall He himself be subject unto Him that put all things under Him'; and, 'I go to my Father and your Father, my God and your God'; together with some others of like tenor."[63] Then, about these, he comments:

> Now all these have had a place given them, (certainly) not with the object of signifying an inequality of nature and substance; for to take them so would be to falsify a different class of statement, such as, "I and my Father are one" (*unum*); and, "He that hath seen me hath seen my Father also"; and, "The Word was God,"—for He was not made, inasmuch as "all things were made by Him"; and, "He thought it not robbery to be equal with God"; together with all the other passages of a similar order.[64]

One can readily see that Augustine understands that the Scriptures teach the Father's priority.

Throughout our Christian era, the Church has taught the Father's priority. The Apostles' Creed implies it by beginning with the father and by referring only to Him as "God." The other creeds both imply it and assert it. In general, too, the fathers, the Scholastics, and the Reformers have viewed the Trinity in this way.

In our time Karl Rahner has taught this imaginatively. He does so by calling the Father "the simply unoriginate God."[65] He implies that Christ and the Holy Spirit originated from the Father, but that the Father had His origination from no one. Similarly, he speaks of "the unoriginatedness of the Father."[66] He explains: "The bond between the original self-communicator and the one who is uttered and received, a bond which implies a distinction, must be understood as 'relative' (relational). This follows simply from the sameness of the 'essence.'"[67]

---

63. Augustine, *On Christian Doctrine*, 361.
64. Ibid.
65. Rahner, *The Trinity*, 84.
66. Ibid., 78.
67. Ibid., 102-3.

To see the priority of the Father, with its ramifications in such matters as redemption and prayer, will help the student greatly in understanding this doctrine.

The Question of Person

In recent times, the principal problem within the doctrine of the Trinity has to do with whether or not the Father and the Son and the Spirit should be called Persons. Karl Barth, for example, who is profoundly Trinitarian, believes that it is a bit misleading to call them persons. He uses the term *Persons* for the three, occasionally, as when he says that "the Father, the Son, and the Holy Spirit in the Bible's witness to revelation are the one God in the unity of their essence, and the one God in the variety of His Persons: the Father, the Son, and the Holy Spirit."[68] Yet Barth does not like to call them Persons, for he thinks the term suggests tritheism to people. Barth prefers to call them "Modes"; but he avoids the ancient heresy of Modalism by saying that the three Modes exist simultaneously, not successively.

Karl Rahner defends "person," saying, "The word 'person' has been consecrated by the use of more than 1,500 years, and there is not really a better word, which can be understood by all and would give rise to fewer misunderstandings."[69] However, Rahner prefers to speak of "three distinct manners of subsisting." He says that "the Father, Son, and Spirit are the one God each in a different manner of subsisting and in this sense we may count 'Three' in God."[70]

Rahner also says, "But even so there are advantages in speaking of the 'distinct manner of subsisting' or of God in three distinct manners of subsisting, rather than of persons. 'Three persons' says nothing about the unity of these three persons so that this unity must be brought from outside to the word by which we designate the three persons."[71]

One of the reasons for urging some other term than *persons* is to avoid tritheism, and another is to make more clear what we

68. Karl Barth, *Church Dogmatics,* ed. G. W. Bromiley and T. F. Torrance (Edinburgh: T. and T. Clark, 1936-69), 353.
69. Rahner, *The Trinity,* 44.
70. Ibid., 114.
71. Ibid., 111.

mean when we refer to God's threeness. Paul Tillich supplies another reason: since humans are persons, to talk about the Ground of our existence in terms of our own human existence is an affront to the greatness of God. Tillich's motive for reticence is good, but Scripture does not reflect the same concern. Scripture writers often speak of God as being like humans, using psychological anthropomorphisms such as jealousy; and physical ones, such as hands, feet, back, face, and so forth.

A further reason why some scholars urge a change is that the literal meaning of "person" does not apply to God. "Person," not found either in the Hebrew Old Testament or the Greek New Testament, is from the Latin *persona*, which means "mask (especially one worn by an actor), actor, role, character, person."[72] However, since "role" is close to the "modes" Barth likes, and since "person" is certainly one of the meanings of *persona*, the term does not really miss the mark of what we mean when we refer to the three as Persons. Each of the three does have a role in creation and in redemption; and each is a Person in the ancient Aristotelian meaning of *person* as characterized by intellect, feeling, and will. By the Persons of the Godhead we do not mean three beings, such as three human beings are. There are in God, as stated earlier, three centers of self-consciousness;[73] but these so interpenetrate each other that a oneness of being obtains that does not obtain in the case of three human individuals.

The use of "Person" in referring to Father, Son, and Spirit has a long history in Christianity—and this augurs for its continued use. Tertullian spoke of God's "Triune Personality."[74] Yet he may have gone too far when he said of Christ that "a wholly different 'self' has stepped into the scene with *his* own validity."[75] The

---

72. *Webster's Third New International Dictionary, Unabridged*, s.v. "person."

73. Some scholars, such as Karl Rahner, teach differently. Others teach this profoundly; for example, Lowry in *Trinity and Christian Devotion*, 79 ff.

74. Tertullian, *Against Praxeas*, 256.

75. Ibid. Karl Rahner disagrees with this. He says, "Thus . . . when nowadays we hear of 'three persons,' we connect, almost necessarily, with this expression the idea of three centers of consciousness and activity, which leads to a heretical misunderstanding of the dogma" (*Trinity*, 56-67). Rahner also says, "But there are not three consciousnesses; rather, the one consciousness in God, which is shared by the Father, Son, and Spirit, by each in his own proper way. Hence the threefold subsistence is not qualified by three consciousnesses" (ibid., 10). Many scholars disagree with Rahner on this matter. One of them is Lowry, in *Trinity and Christian De-*

phrase "wholly different" is perhaps too much, since the three are one in nature. The three-Person language was used in early creedal statements. It is the language of the centuries, and the word *Person*, it seems, best describes the distinctions in the God-head indicated in Scripture.

Opposition to the Trinity Doctrine

The doctrine of the Trinity has had numerous opposers as the centuries have passed. Any doctrine this significant would inevitably be conceived of in certain aberrant ways that, after the church had declared itself in official councils, were stamped as heretical. Those offering aberrant interpretations were often bishops who were devout and well-intentioned.

Praxeas was a kind of Monarchian, conceiving that the Father and the Son and the Spirit are actually one and the same. Tertullian says, "So Praxeas managed two pieces of the devil's business at Rome: he drove out prophecy and brought in heresy, he put the Paraclete to flight and crucified the Father."[76] Also, "Crudely expressed," Praxeas held that "the Father alone was God, and all the experiences undergone by Jesus in His earthly life were undergone by the Father."[77]

Sabellius taught that the Father, Son, and Spirit are one God, one Person, manifested in three successive modes or fashions. His teaching was called Modalism because the three were conceived of as three modes instead of three Persons; or Monarchianism, because God consisted of only one, and not three, and so was like a monarch who is a sole ruler.

The chief heresy was Arianism. It posed the greatest threat of them all. The Council of Nicea was called in A.D. 325 to decide whether or not Arius was right, and it was decided that he was not. The council stated that Christ was *homoousia*, of the same substance with the Father, not *homoiousia*, of like substance. The

---

votion. Another is John Lawson, who writes about "person": "In usage it has become enriched since then, and one might say that as used in the trinitarian formula it includes the conception of self-consciousness, but not that of exclusiveness. We may symbolize the Three as 'knowing' one another, but not as 'shutting one another out.' The divine persons are not exclusive, like human personalities, but are inclusive" (John Lawson, *Introduction to Christian Doctrine* [Wilmore, Ky.: Asbury College Press, 1980], 123).

76. Tertullian, *Against Praxeas,* 27.
77. Ibid., xvii.

position of Athanasius carried in the council but not in the whole Church. In ensuing years, Athanasius, then bishop, was exiled several times during political attempts to cement the empire by capitulating to the Arians. In A.D. 336 Arius, who had been excommunicated, was to be reinstated but died the night before this was to happen. He had many followers for centuries.

As a leading presbyter at Alexandria, Arius taught that Christ, the Son, was a created being, made "out of nothing"; that He was the greatest of the creatures and that through Him the rest of the universe was made; that He was not eternal, but only preexistent; that He was not of divine nature or substance, and that He was not able to comprehend the Father.[78] Whereas Origen had taught that there never was a time when the Son was not, Arius said, "There was when he was not." And Arius taught that the Holy Spirit is a still less-exalted creature than Christ, and that He was created by the Son even as the rest of creation was.

In medieval times most theologians accepted the doctrine of the Trinity as described in the Niceno-Constantinopolitan Creed and in the Athanasian Creed. During these centuries the Monarchian-Sabellian heresies were squelched, and Arianism was altogether unofficial. The Reformers had no special differences with the Scholastics on the matter of the Trinity. Servetus (d. 1553) was executed for teaching pretty much what came to be unitarianism. Faustus Socinus (d. 1604) taught a kind of anti-Trinitarianism, which came to be known as Socinianism and which also was a precursor of unitarianism. In important ways, too, Socinianism-unitarianism is a revival of Arianism.

Also opposed to the doctrine of Trinity were the English deists such as Lord Herbert and John Locke, whose views spread to Germany where we know it as the Enlightenment, represented by such men as Leibnitz and Wolff. The great triumvirate of German philosophical theology—Immanuel Kant, Friedrich Schleiermacher, and Friedrich Hegel—all denied the doctrine of the Trinity, although Schleiermacher and Hegel taught threeness of a sort in the Deity. In fact, rationalists and modernists in general have denied the doctrine, usually teaching that Christ was only a man, albeit a good and great man, and that the Holy Spirit is an influ-

---

78. James Orr, *The Progress of Dogma* (London: Hodder and Stoughton, 1897), 113.

ence and not a divine person. One of them, William Adams Brown, a liberal theologian of America, figured that the threeness is simply the way we think about God, not the way He exists.[79]

Recent opposition to the doctrine of the Trinity has come from Cyril C. Richardson in his *Doctrine of the Trinity*. Richardson likes to speak of the three as "symbols,"[80] not Persons. Frequently he calls them "terms."[81] He supposes that the doctrine of the Trinity "often beclouds . . . the vital concerns of the Christian faith."[82] To him, the doctrine is "an artificial threefoldness."[83]

Oxford's Leonard Hodgson has given us an excellent recent study of Trinitarian doctrine. While Hodgson affirms three centers of consciousness in God that make for a more intensive unity, Richardson asks, Why stop with three centers of consciousness? Richardson says, "The logic of this should perhaps have driven Hodgson to posit an *infinite* number of persons in the Trinity." The reason, of course, why Hodgson posits only three—and this might sound strange to Richardson—is that both the Bible and the creeds stop at three.

Another important recent denial of the doctrine of the Trinity has come from Hendrikus Berkhof. Berkhof speaks of "God's external triune being."[84] He refers often to the Father, the Christ, and the Spirit. Yet he denies the doctrine of the Trinity in a sustained way (see pp. 330-39), even labeling it "dangerous to the faith."[85] He advocates an economic trinity of the functions of God, but not an ontological trinity in which all three exist eternally.

Significance of the Doctrine

The doctrine of the Trinity in the Christian faith holds a place of primal importance among the doctrines.

---

79. William Adams Brown, *Christian Theology in Outline* (New York: Charles Scribner's Sons, 1907), 156.

80. Cyril C. Richardson, *The Doctrine of the Trinity* (New York: Abingdon Press, 1958), 111.

81. See ibid., 98.

82. Ibid., 114.

83. Ibid., 15.

84. Berkhof, *Christian Faith*, 324.

85. Ibid. Berkhof is somewhat of an enigma among theologians. He often teaches what is classical and what has gospel in it; yet he denies other classical Christian teachings. He has a sustained denial of eternal punishment.

It Presupposes Various Beliefs. The doctrine of the Trinity presupposes the existence of God and the doctrines of creation, God's sovereignty, providence, as well as others that relate more particularly to God the Father than to the other two Persons of the Trinity.

It presupposes the deity of Christ and the virgin birth of Christ—since conception by the Spirit instead of by a human male is what founds Jesus in Deity. It presupposes the Incarnation, since that is Deity's becoming enfleshed.

Likewise, the doctrine of the Trinity presupposes the Spirit's deity and His being a person. It presupposes His work as the Executive of the Godhead, who implements the Father's grace—prevenient, justifying, sanctifying, and sustaining. It presupposes His work in the inspiration of Scripture.

This doctrine of the Trinity, so fundamental and elemental to Christian faith, is more basic than any other Christian doctrine.

It Helps Our Worship. One of the most important reasons why we Christians should hold a correct view of the doctrine of the Trinity is that we may worship God more correctly and more fulfillingly than would otherwise be possible.

For example, since the Father has priority among the Persons of the Trinity, and since the Father actually answers our prayers, it is to Him that we ought to address our prayers. All the actual prayers of Scripture are addressed to the Father. Only one is addressed to God the Son, Stephen's one-sentence prayer in Acts 7:59: "Lord Jesus, receive my spirit." Not even a sentence prayer is ever addressed to God the Holy Spirit. The Son and the Spirit are divine, so they could hear and answer our prayers; but we do not normally address them because we are taught in Scripture to address the Father instead. According to Scripture, the Son intercedes for us and the Spirit helps us pray, but it is to the Father that our prayers are addressed.

A correct understanding of the doctrine of the Trinity will also help us in praising God in our worship. We will direct our praise of all three to the Father, since He is the One we address. It will help us articulate what we praise the Son and Spirit for. We will tell the Father we are thankful for His sending Christ the Son into the world, for the Son's permitting people to hang Him on a Roman crossbar, for the Father's great power by which Christ was raised bodily from among the dead.

Worshiping more or less correctly, we will express gratitude to the Father for the Holy Spirit's special and gracious ministries to us. We will become filled with praise for the Holy Spirit's ministries of conviction, of guidance, of illumination; for His function in the conception of Jesus Christ in Mary's womb; for His function in inspiring the many and diverse writers of Holy Scripture. We will praise the Father for the Holy Spirit's using specific persons, events, and circumstances to urge us toward justifying and sanctifying grace.

The fact that correct theology is important for correct worship is pointed up by the root meaning of the word *orthodoxy. Ortho* means "straight," as in *orthodontist.* The *doxy* part of the word is from a Greek word meaning "glory," our *doxology* being from it. The combined word, therefore, means something like "straight glorifying," or "straight worship." Straight doctrine is called straight worship because correct doctrine has correct worship as its chief purpose.

It Helps in Evangelism. A more-or-less correct understanding of the doctrine of the Trinity will help us in our winning people to Christ. It will help people understand the offices of the three Persons of the Godhead if we say that it is the Father who sent the Son and who actually does the forgiving of us; if we say that the Father is enabled to forgive us and still himself remain just (Rom. 3:23-26) because of Christ's function of dying on our behalf and being raised from the dead; and if we tell people that the Holy Spirit's special function is to apply what is said to specific persons in specific ways, to convict individuals of sin, and to help those who are forgiven of their acts of sin to yield themselves up to God in order, by faith, to receive both cleansing from Adamic depravity and empowerment.

7

The Christian Doctrine of Creation

Having discussed God's existence and nature, and the doctrine of the Trinity, it is needful now to discuss several matters that may be subsumed under the creation of God.

Essentials of the Christian View

In the Christian view only God is eternal. He created all that exists besides himself—out of nothing but through His word and from His will (not His nature).

Creation Is Not Eternal. Aristotle viewed matter as eternal. In that view, God finds matter and uses it to form the world and ourselves. God is thus an architect, not an outright creator.

It is the Christian view, however, that only God has existed eternally and that, at a given point in past time, He began to create the universe. This is implied in Scripture's opening statement, "In the beginning God created the heavens and the earth" (Gen. 1:1). The beginning, here, is not the beginning of eternity; it is the beginning of the creation.

It is after this "beginning" that the first "day" is mentioned. This also suggests that creation is not eternal—that it began to happen at a given point in the past.

Creation Is out of Nothing. It is also the Christian view that the creation was out of nothing. The Hebrew word *bara* often seems to refer to this kind of creation—origination instead of mere formation. This word is used of the creation of "the heavens and the earth" in Gen. 1:1; of "the great sea monsters, and every living creature that moves, with which the waters swarmed . . . and every winged bird" in verse 21 (NASB); and of Adam and Eve's creation

160

in verse 27: "So God created man in his own image, in the image of God he created him; male and female he created them."

In Genesis 1, then, *bara* is used of the creation of water as such, then of animal creation, and finally of ourselves. It is not used of the other things that God made. Some scholars understand that this word, being used in the case of three special step-ups in the creative process, suggests outright, originative, out-of-nothing creation. It is used 5 other times in Genesis (2:2, 4; 5:1, 2; 6:7), 20 times in Isaiah, and about 9 times in the remainder of the Old Testament.

In the New Testament, *ktidzō* appears frequently, which also seems in several contexts to suggest creation out of nothing. It is quite often used of the creation of the world or of ourselves (e.g., Mark 13:19; Eph. 3:9; Col. 1:16). It is also used of spiritual life being created or formed in us (see Eph. 2:10; 4:24).

Even in places where this particular word is not used, the New Testament sometimes quite clearly teaches that the world was created *ex nihilo*. We read of "God, who gives life to the dead and calls into being that which does not exist" (Rom. 4:17, NASB). We also read, "By faith we understand that the worlds were prepared by the word of God, so that what is seen was not made out of things which are visible" (Heb. 11:3, NASB). The clarity of these two passages has given continuing support to the Christian view of *ex nihilo* creation.

It is also of interest that the most widely held theory among scientists today, the big bang theory, is that the entire universe seems to have originated from almost nothing: original matter was perhaps the size of a human fist.

It Is from God's Will. Creation is from God's will, and not from His nature. The eternal generation of the Logos, Christ, is from God's nature, in the way that light comes from the sun. Had the world and humans originated from God's nature, they would be eternal. As long as God has existed, He would have been originating the universe. Since it is from His will, creation was His special, voluntary choice.

Creation Is Through God's Word. This is important to the Christian understanding of creation. The creative power does not reside magically in the words themselves, as the pagan ancients often supposed. According to Scripture, the power is in the source of the words: God. When we say that creation is out of nothing, we mean that it is not made out of previously existent material. Yet, in a sense, creation is indeed out of something—God's word. Genesis 1 states, "And God said," several times. There we read: "And God said, 'Let there be light,' and there was light" (v. 3). "And God said, 'Let there be an expanse . . .'" (v. 6). "And God said, 'Let the water . . .'" (v. 9). The phrase "Then God said," or "And God said," appears also in verses 11, 14, 20, 24, 26, and 29. It seems that God needed to say that a given aspect of creation would be made, and then it would appear.

What God's word made it also sustains: "And He . . . upholds all things by the word of His power" (Heb. 1:3, NASB).

According to Peter, the world was made, and is continued in existence, by God's word: "By the word of God the heavens existed long ago and the earth was formed out of water" (2 Pet. 3:5, NASB). He goes on to say, "But the present heavens and earth by His word are being reserved for fire, kept for the day of judgment and destruction of ungodly men" (v. 7, NASB).

Deuteronomy ascribes even our natural existence to God's word: "Man does not live by bread alone, but man lives by everything that proceeds out of the mouth of the Lord" (8:3, NASB).

A Psalmist says, "By the word of the Lord the heavens were made" (33:6); and he soon adds: "For He spoke, and it was done; He commanded, and it stood fast" (v. 9, both NASB). We also read: "Let them praise the name of the Lord, for He commanded and they were created" (148:5, NASB).

In keeping with this understanding, the writer of Hebrews says, "By faith we understand that the worlds were prepared by the word of God" (11:3, NASB).

Advantages of the Christian View. Understanding creation from nothing by the will and word of God makes possible our desacralizing of the world, our Christian secularization. Pagans have often spiritualized the physical world and worshiped many parts of it. Animism primitively conceived of rocks, etc., as somehow alive. Fearing what nature could do to them, animists have sought to placate it.

In the Christian view, however, the world is mere world. Distinct from God, it is not sacred but is the secular part of God's own creation. Thus we own a secularity; we have desacralized nature and do not view it as having magical powers over us.

The Christian view of creation allows us to teach and emphasize a number of important doctrines. One of them is that the created world is good and to be appreciated. It prevents us from understanding, as did Plato, that all physicality including the body is evil. It helps us acknowledge that human sexuality, properly disciplined and implemented, is a gift from God for which we praise Him, not a drag upon human nature that prevents us from being spiritually minded. This kind of view would have prevented Origen from castrating himself. It would have prevented the Early Church—and the present Roman Catholic church—from extolling celibacy above marriage. This kind of view can help us celebrate the created world and see a residency of grace in many aspects of creation.

This view also helps us receive thankfully the Incarnation. Deity could enflesh himself, and that is what actually happened at the first Christmas.

This view helps us see why Jesus instituted two sacraments, the Lord's Supper and baptism, both of which are administered with physical elements. It helps us see that, lo, our very bodies really are to be resurrected.[1]

This view should help us respect our physical well-being. It should help us Christians exercise religiously, seeing that our bodies are given us by the kindliness of the Creator. It should prevent us from making light of large abdomens. Fortunately, many evangelicals do not smoke nor drink. Yet we have not always seen that commitment to Christ should include commitment to diet and exercise regimens that better assure health and longevity for our bodies, which are the very temples of the Holy Spirit.

This view also helps us see our responsibility for maintaining a degree of ecological balance between ourselves and other organisms and our environment. This is so important a matter that it needs to be discussed as one of the major topics of this chapter.

The Ecological Imperative

The created world has issued from God's will and word. It is not evil per se but is often a bearer of the holy. In these days,

---

1. Some of these matters were mentioned at an earlier time, but they need to be restated in this context.

therefore, when advanced technology tends to upset the world's ecological balance, it is imperative that Christian theology address this matter.

Our Ecological Problem. It has been said that the only command of God that we humans have overobeyed is the command to multiply ourselves. At that, we have done so well that birth control has become an important imperative in our world.

Rapid urbanization, even in the third- and fourth-world countries, has created megalopolises and strip cities, concentrating large populations in small areas. In those areas, industries that pollute the environment have developed. The omnipresent automobile continuously pollutes the air. The small percentage of the population who still live on farms often operate large agribusinesses and pollute the soil with weed killers. This pollution drains into our waterways and underground water and pollutes the water we drink and use otherwise, as for swimming.

Already in 1830 Samuel Taylor Coleridge was concerned about water pollution. He wrote:

> The river Rhine, it is well known,
> Doth wash your city of Cologne;
> But tell me, Nymphs, what power divine
> Shall henceforth wash the river Rhine?

It is fancied that one caveman said to another, after drinking from a chemical-saturated river, "It tastes like progress."

A river in Ohio was so full of pollution that it caught on fire. Some streams are too polluted to sustain animal life. Many signs on America's coasts forbid swimming because of pollutants in the water.

Chemicals pollute the land, and many chemicals are spewed into the air. What is in the air and the soil finally gets into streams, flowing at last into the oceans, thus threatening a significant source of food for the future.

Pointers Toward Solution. Our problem is obvious, the solution less so. A few suggestions are herewith tendered.

1. *Realize the significance of the problem.* We are on the way to a possible remedy for the ecological imbalance when we view that imbalance as an utterly serious problem. To know that much of the air pollution comes from cars is a help—cars so close together on our freeways that, as one person joked, a motorist can run out of gas and not know it for 35 miles. To realize that in New York

City the pollution one breathes is roughly equal to that received by smoking 38 cigarettes a day is important information.

2. *Read Genesis correctly.* Some writers blame the ecological imbalance on a Judeo-Christian exploitation of Gen. 1:28, where God commands, "Be fruitful, and multiply, and replenish the earth, and subdue it: and have dominion over the fish of the sea, and over the fowl of the air, and over every living thing that moveth upon the earth" (KJV). "Subdue" is a good translation, used in such versions as the RSV and the NIV. But Gen. 2:15 states that Adam is to "till" and "keep" the Garden of Eden (RSV). This, taken seriously, would mean that we are not to rape the earth by taking coal out of strip mines and leaving the heaped-up dirt. It would mean that we are not to harness the earth's resources and then uncaringly leave air, land, and water polluted by poisonous chemicals. In Shinto Japan, where Genesis has not shaped the culture, pollution is so serious that I have seen people going about their daily routines wearing masks to filter out the carbon monoxide and other gasses and chemicals in the air. Genesis cannot be blamed for the spoiling and polluting of our world.

3. *Adopt an ethic of love.* Such an ethic would prompt us to give other persons a wholesome environment in which to live. Henlee Barnette, in one of the best books available on the church's responsibility in our ecological crisis, urges such a love ethic. He says, "Love constrains us not only to will the welfare of our neighbor, but also to preserve and promote the kind of environment that maximizes the possibility of full selfhood for each."[2] He feels that "the world is a bearer of the holy"[3] and that to "ruthlessly rape and degrade it violates God's creative love."[4]

4. *Revive the appreciation of nature.* Such appreciation was surely the mind-set of many of the Psalm writers—in Ps. 19:1, for example. If we view nature as the lavish splendor of God's creative ingenuity, we will likely promote a wholesome and nonrapacious use of our natural environment. Ecological balance between the environment and all us creatures who share its use and enjoyment will become an aspect of our stewardship.

---

2. Henlee Barnette, *The Church and the Ecological Crisis* (Grand Rapids: William B. Eerdmans Publishing Co., 1972), 36.

3. Ibid., 37.

4. Ibid.

5. *Adopt a life-style of ecological discipline.* We can use less energy by turning lights off, by setting furnaces lower and air conditioners higher, and by taking care not to buy items that will measurably increase our trash. It might mean driving smaller cars that use less gasoline.

Surely the God whose wisdom created such balance between living organisms and the nonliving aspects of the world, and who visited us for our salvation 2,000 years ago, wants us to do for the whole world what Adam was to do for Eden—"dress it and . . . keep it" (Gen. 2:15, KJV).

Angels: Their Origin and Function

Their Origin. The creation accounts in Genesis do not mention the creation of angels. On several bases, however, Scripture elsewhere implies that they were created prior to the world and us. Job 38:6-7 tells us that the "sons of God" (angels) "sang together" before God even laid the other creation's "cornerstone" (NASB). Also, in Ps. 148:1-6, God is praised for various aspects of His creation, and angels are listed, prior in order to the sun and moon: "Praise him, all his angels . . . Praise him, sun and moon . . . For he commanded and they were created" (vv. 2-5).

Besides this, Adam and Eve were confronted by a tempting serpent sent by Satan who, according to various passages of Scripture, seems to have been a fallen high-ranked angel (see Genesis 3; Luke 10:18; 2 Pet. 2:4; Jude; Rev. 12:1ff.).

Further, Scripture implies that they must have been created at some point in time, since it implies that only God existed "in the beginning."

The Form of Their Ministry. Scripture assigns the following roles to angels:

1. *Angels make announcements for God.* An angel announced to Abraham and Sarah that a son would be born to them in their old age (Gen. 18:9-10). An angel announced the birth of John the Baptist and Jesus (Luke 1:5-38). An angel announced to shepherds the event of Jesus' birth, and a choir of angels joined in (2:8-15).

2. *They forewarn of impending judgments.* Angels forewarned Abraham and Lot of the coming destruction of Sodom and Gomorrah (Gen. 18:16—19:22). An angel warned Joseph to take Baby Jesus and His mother and flee to Egypt to protect the Child

THE CHRISTIAN DOCTRINE OF CREATION ▷ 167

from Herod (Matt. 2:13). An angel was used to communicate to John, on Patmos, upcoming things. Thus the last book of the Bible opens: "The Revelation of Jesus Christ, which God gave Him . . . and He sent and communicated it by His angel to His bond-servant John" (Rev. 1:1, NASB).

3. *They guide and guard.* Abraham, and later persons in Old Testament times, were often guided and guarded by angels. An angel prevented Abraham from sacrificing Isaac (Gen. 22:11-12). This was "the angel of the Lord," which some interpreters understand to be the preincarnate Christ. An angel guarded Daniel and his friends (Dan. 3:28; 6:22).

Jesus says that children are helped by guardian angels: "See that you do not despise one of these little ones, for I say to you, that their angels in heaven continually behold the face of My Father who is in heaven" (Matt. 18:10, NASB).

Jesus said He could have asked for help from angels to protect Him from those who were soon to crucify Him: "Or do you think that I cannot appeal to My Father, and He will at once put at My disposal more than twelve legions of angels?" (Matt. 26:53, NASB).

4. *They help in miscellaneous needs.* An angel assured Moses that God's people would be delivered from the afflictions of the Egyptians (Exod. 3:2, 7 ff.). Angels ministered to Jesus when He was weak after a 40-day fast (Mark 1:13). An angel appeared to Jesus in Gethsemane and strengthened Him during His agony (Luke 22:43). It was an angel who rolled the stone from Jesus' tomb (Matt. 28:2).

5. *They assist in judgment.* An angel struck Herod Agrippa, for we read, "And immediately an angel of the Lord struck him because he did not give God the glory, and he was eaten by worms and died" (Acts 12:23, NASB).

Angels will accompany Jesus at His second coming, when He will sit on His throne and judge the nations (Matt. 25:31; Luke 9:26; Matt. 24:31).

Some Special Considerations. We are told several special things about angels in Scripture.

1. *Only two are named.* One of these is Michael, called an archangel by Jude (v. 9) and in Daniel "one of the chief princes" (10:13) and "the great prince" (12:1). He seems to be the commander of the army of good angels, according to Rev. 12:7-8. The

other angel mentioned by name is Gabriel. He announced to Zacharias the birth of John the Baptist (Luke 1:5-20). He also announced the miraculous conception of Christ (vv. 26-38). This is the angel who interpreted a dream (see Dan. 8:15 ff.; 9:21 ff.).

2. *The angel of the Lord.* Bible interpreters differ on whether or not the "angel of the Lord" in the Old Testament refers to Christ; also, on whether the phrase is used with a consistent meaning. Sometimes, it seems to be used of any given angel, for all of them are "of the Lord." Thus, 1 Kings 19:5 says an angel touched the discouraged Elijah under a juniper tree, and further on in the narrative the angel of the Lord spoke to him (see something similar in 2 Samuel 24). However, there are numerous times when the "angel of the Lord" seems to be the proper name of a specific angel, and many interpreters believe that these might be references to Christ in His preincarnation doings.

3. *The angels of the Asia Minor churches.* In Revelation 2 and 3 a message is sent to "the angel" of each of the seven churches of Asia Minor. Since the words for "angel" in Greek and Hebrew mean "messenger," many interpret these angels as the pastors of these churches. This might be the case, for the writer of this book often does not use a literal word when he figures a symbolical one will do. Even so, it would not be exegetically incorrect to understand that angels minister in special ways to local churches as well as to individual Christians.

4. *Angels were not offered redemption.* It is widely understood by Bible students that among the angels, prior to our creation, there was an uprising, and one-third of them were cast out of heaven and not offered any possibility of redemption. The little Epistle of Jude speaks of this uprising; and Rev. 12:1 ff. speaks of one-third of the "stars," who seem to be angels, being cast out of heaven along with Satan the dragon.

Careful Bible students do not call Satan "Lucifer" because it is not certain that the Bible's one mention of Lucifer, in Isaiah 14, is anything but a reference to a pride-filled earthly monarch or to a nation. Methodist commentator Adam Clarke was quite sure that Lucifer is not a reference to Satan.

In any case, Satan and the angels who sided with him were not offered any redemption. This is basically because they were not on probation, the way we humans are. Some interpreters believe that, without physical bodies, which often occasion sin in us humans, it was more "unthinkable" that some of the angels should have disobeyed God as they did.

5. *The demons are the fallen angels.* The angels who sided with Satan (perhaps as Satan got lifted up with pride and tried to occupy the place Christ held in heaven) became the demons, so often referred to in the New Testament. Evangelical Christians in general believe in the existence of these demons, who are now spirit emissaries of Satan and who implement his evil will.

Since only one-third of the angels fell, according to the usual interpretation of Rev. 12:1ff., we Christians may take courage in the fact that there are still two angels on the side of God's people for every demon arrayed against us.

We Protestants have often ignored the ministry of angels, overreacting perhaps to Roman Catholics, who have made so much of angel helps. They teach each child, for example, that he or she has a special guardian angel. Mainly, however, we Protestants have minimized the ministry of angels because of our profound confidence in the ministry of the Holy Spirit—especially since Pentecost.

However, there are several bases for our understanding that God still uses angels to administer His government over the world. An angel helped Peter and John escape from jail, shortly after Pentecost (Acts 5:19-20). Later, when Peter was in prison again, an angel helped him walk out, right past the guards (Acts 12:7-10). Still much later, John's visions of things to come were "communicated" to him by an angel (Rev. 1:1).

Nothing is said in Scripture about any cessation of the ministry of angels.

So while many of us believe in the gracious ministry of the Holy Spirit, we also believe profoundly in the continued ministry of those spiritual beings whom Scripture so often refers to as the angels.

Satan: Adversary Number One

One angel of high rank seems to have tried to usurp the place Christ had in heaven, and he fell from heaven in the process.

Modernism has simply denied Satan outright. Liberalism is positive, upbeat, rational, humanistic. It stresses God's love and says little about God's holiness. It denies original sin and stresses free will and human responsibility. It tends to regard Satan as a mere concept invented to account for our irresponsible behavior as humans. Modernism denies the utter sinfulness of sin, tending to regard it as a mere lack of righteousness, something we will slough off as we continue our moral becoming. It denies demons as well as angels and denies eternal hell.

The polar opposite of the liberals are the fundamentalists. They tend to overteach most of the doctrines denied by the liberals. They present apologias against the "hell-bound" modernists. Stressing teachings about Satan seems to be their special calling.

One popular fundamentalist treatment of Satan is that of Hal Lindsey in *Satan Is Alive and Well on Planet Earth*—a book that has enjoyed sales in the millions of copies.[5] This book teaches what is usual in fundamentalism, a too-extreme view of Satan.

Its thesis, that Satan is "alive and well," is extreme and incorrect. Instead of teaching that Satan is alive and well, Scripture portrays Satan as a limping sovereign, at best, seriously wounded by the resurrection of Jesus Christ. It is correct, as Edwin Lewis taught in *The Creator and the Adversary*,[6] that Satan and Christ engaged in significant battle, dramatized by Jesus' death on the Cross. But Jesus Christ was raised from the dead, and this leaves Satan maimed, anything but alive and well.

Fundamentalists also tend to imply, hardly realizing it, that Satan is another deity—albeit an evil one. They tend to suggest that his attributes are infinite—that his power, knowledge, and presence are unlimited. If Satan does what he is purported by many fundamentalists to do, he would personally tempt multiplied millions of Christians at the same instant. He would have charge over an unrestricted number of diseases and would dole them out according to his nefarious whims. A miracle a day will likely keep him away, but something like that is called for, if this evidently infinite being is to be warded off—being so "alive and well."

Let it be noted that Scripture does paint vivid pictures about Satan. For one thing, he is a personal being. For Paul Tillich and other such theologians, Satan is not personal. He is simply the demonic, the abstract drag upon what is of God. They feel that the

---

5. Hal Lindsey, *Satan Is Alive and Well on Planet Earth* (New York: Bantam Books, 1974).
6. Lewis, *Creator and the Adversary*.

demonic is as real as a personal Satan would be, but that there simply is no personal Satan.

Edwin Lewis is ambivalent on whether or not Satan is personal. Although Lewis shed his early liberalism, he did not clearly present Satan as a personal being in *The Creator and the Adversary.* Lewis strangely taught that Satan is an eternal adversary of God, whom God "found" but did not create. Wherever and whenever God creates anything, Satan, God's eternal adversary, moves in to discreate it. Lewis declares that this adversary is semipersonal. He does say that Satan moves to whatever place is necessary to thwart God's people. If this malignant maneuvering means that Satan is personal, Lewis will grant the ascription.

Evangelicals have no problem with viewing Satan as personal. He is portrayed in Scripture as more than an abstract demonic thwarting power, more than merely semipersonal. He is personal enough to send an emissary to personally and individually tempt the first human pair. He is personal enough to do all those things ascribed to him in the Book of Job. He is personal enough to tempt Jesus Christ and others, according to Scripture.

Satan is personal, then, and he is superhuman—a high-ranking angelic being who sinned and was cast out of heaven. He is not infinite, but he often seems so, since he is served by many demons and humans. He is called the father of sinners: "You belong to your father, the devil" (John 8:44). He seems to head up a whole kingdom of evil. The demons who were cast out of heaven with him do his bidding, tempting humans. Also, human beings under Satan's sway often occasion our being tempted. It is not entirely incorrect, when we are tempted, or in any way hindered from doing God's will, to say that Satan tempted or hindered us, even if he accomplished it, as head of the kingdom of evil, through a demon or a sinful person (see 1 Thess. 2:18, KJV). Nevertheless, Satan is not another infinite being besides God, an evil second deity. The God who is in us Christians is far greater than Satan, who is in the world (1 John 4:4).

The Age of the Earth

Some fiat creationists believe the earth to be something like 6,000 to 15,000 years old. These young-earth theorists are often called creation science people—partly because a given organization of evangelicals who are also scientists have called their view creation science. They have promoted their views through newsletters and books, including textbooks for public schools intended to give educators alternative sources to evolutionary textbooks.

Extremely opposite in view to scientists generally, these creation scientists tend to make news, leaving the impression that theirs is the one major alternative to evolutionary theory. In 1982, when the Arkansas state law requiring both creationism and evolution to be taught in public schools was tested in court, it was the young-earth creation science type of creationism that was represented as the alternative to evolutionary theory.

However, creationism is also being represented and promoted by scientists who are evangelical but who are not obscurantists, as the creation science people tend to be at certain points. One such evangelical creationist is Pattle P. T. Pun, who in 1982 wrote *Evolution: Nature and Scripture in Conflict?*[7] perhaps the single most significant recent book on creationism and evolution.

Pun is a specialist who discusses the pros and cons of recent developments in such areas as fossil finds and scientific methods of dating. At the same time he is most respecting of what Scripture actually teaches.

Pun believes that the earth is exceedingly old and that Scripture teaches nothing contrary to this scientifically-arrived-at conclusion. He included in an appendix a superb support for the view of the creation days as ages, found in a study made by conservative-evangelical theologian J. Oliver Buswell, Jr.

Davis A. Young's *Christianity and the Age of the Earth* is also a significant evangelical study. Young particularly treats Genesis 1—the length of its days, the age of the earth, and evolution-creationism. This credentialed scientist who believes in the infallibility of Scripture denies that the earth is young and that the days of creation were literal 24-hour days. Young shows that neither of these views is taught in Scripture and that the best in recent geological science is not discordant with Scripture.

The method of carbon 14 dating itself can establish with reasonable assurance the age of organic materials up to some 100,000 years. The various radioactivity methods, testing the degree of the loss of radioactivity in, for example, rocks, establishes their ages in

7. Pattle P. T. Pun, *Evolution: Nature and Scripture in Conflict?* (Grand Rapids: Zondervan Publishing House, 1982).

billions of years. To say as some do that elements such as rocks were created with various degrees of radioactivity in them seems to be a bending of facts to suit a preconceived notion. Also, the view that certain environmental conditions might have occasioned a wide variance in the loss of radioactivity seems to be the same kind of selective use of scientific fact.

Particularly, the many millions of light-years required for light from distant stars to reach us is positive proof that our universe is exceedingly old. The creation science view that the universe is young and that God also created the light between those admittedly far-off stars and us savors of obscurantism. Such views do a disservice to evangelicalism. Many people would laugh evangelicalism out of court on such matters and then be loath to accept what is significantly redemptive in its message of Christ.

It is true that many earlier Christian scholars taught the young-earth theory. Martin Luther completely rejected Augustine's more-or-less day-age view of Genesis 1, instead insisting on six literal days of creation. Luther also said that the earth was not yet 6,000 years old. Philipp Melanchthon (1497-1560) agreed with Luther on these matters. John Calvin likewise taught a 6,000-year-old earth. Archbishop James Ussher (1581-1656) taught specifically that the creation of the world occurred in 4004 B.C. Bishop Lightfoot of Cambridge University (1828-89) said that it occurred October 22, 4004 B.C., at 9 A.M. Actually, the usual view "in the Christian world until the eighteenth century was that the Earth was only a few thousand years old."[8]

Those who advocate the young-earth view do so on two or three principal bases. One is a naively literal interpretation of Genesis. Another is the interpretation of the Hebrew word *yom* as a 24-hour day, an interpretation that does not allow for vast time spans within each of the creation days or ages of creation. Still another basis for this view is the reckoning of time elapsed by working back through the various genealogies in Genesis, assigning a certain number of years to each generation.

The old-earth view, with which I identify, interprets the Hebrew *yom* as an age of indefinite duration, not a 24-hour day. This is likely the meaning of the Hebrew *yom*, as J. Oliver Buswell, Jr.,

---

8. Davis A. Young, *Christianity and the Age of the Earth* (Grand Rapids: Zondervan Publishing House, 1982), 25.

suggests.[9] For one thing, all six days are called a single day in Gen., 2:4, where we read, "In the day that the Lord God made earth and heaven" (NASB). Also, a Psalmist says that "a thousand years in thy sight are but as yesterday when it is past, or as a watch in the night" (90:4, RSV).

The sun, which occasions the 24-hour day, was not created until the fourth "day" (Gen. 1:14-19, NASB). Augustine, who taught the day-age view, noticed this (*City of God,* bk. 11, chaps. 6, 7).

Some have argued for a 24-hour day on the basis of the Sabbath. Since our day of rest is a 24-hour one, God's must have been. Yet Buswell observes, "There is no more reason to conclude that God's creative days are as short as man's days of the week, than there is to conclude from the same Scripture that God himself is no greater than we are."[10] Buswell adds, "Man must work six days and rest one because God in His greatness has chosen to observe a similar practice."[11]

Further, many outstanding geologists have taught the day-age view. These have included four of the best-known geologists of the 19th century: Benjamin Stillman (1779-1864) of Yale, James Dwight Danal (1813-95) of Yale, Arnold Guyot (1807-84) of Princeton, and J. William Dawson (1820-84) of McGill. A significant support of the day-age view was presented by the Scottish geologist and churchman, Hugh Miller (1802-56), in *The Testimony of the Rocks* (1857).

Outstanding Christian scholars and churchmen of the 19th century have also espoused this view. German Bible commentators Franz Delitzsch (1813-90)[12] and John Peter Lange (1802-84)[13] did. Scotland's Alexander MacLaren (1826-1920)[14] did also, as did systematic theologians Charles Hodge (1797-1878)[15] and

9. Buswell has good insights on this. He is quoted by Pun, *Evolution,* 305.

10. Ibid.

11. Ibid.

12. See Delitzsch, *A New Commentary on Genesis* (Edinburgh: T. and T. Clark, 1899).

13. John Peter Lange, *Commentary on Holy Scripture: Genesis, Exodus, Leviticus, and Numbers* (Grand Rapids: Zondervan Publishing House, n.d.).

14. Alexander MacLaren, *Exposition of Holy Scripture: Genesis et al.* (Grand Rapids: William B. Eerdmans Publishing Co., 1944).

15. Charles Hodge, *Systematic Theology* (Grand Rapids: William B. Eerdmans Publishing Co., n.d.).

W. G. T. Shedd (1820-94),[16] Presbyterian James Orr (1844-1913)[17] of the Scottish Free Church, Baptist A. H. Strong (1836-1921),[18] Methodist John Miley,[19] and even the total-inerrancy fundamentalist of Princeton, B. B. Warfield (1851-1921).[20]

In our century, the day-age view has been espoused by physicist-theologian Bernard Ramm (b. 1916),[21] Herman Bavinck (1854-1921),[22] E. J. Young (1907-63),[23] H. Orton Wiley,[24] and J. Oliver Buswell, Jr. (b. 1895)[25]

This brings us to where the matter of creationism needs to be discussed in relation to evolution—organic evolution.

Creationism Versus Evolution

The seeds of evolutionary thought were in some ancient philosophies. Heracleitus taught that ultimate reality is in continual flux and that it therefore consists basically of fire. With that understanding, he taught an evolutionary metaphysic. Even Aristotle's metaphysics is evolutionary. Although he taught that God does not change, he taught that all else does change.

When evolution is broadly viewed as the philosophy of a universe where change obtains, in distinction from a purely static universe, no evangelical would necessarily object to it.

Inorganic evolution is surely factual. The Colorado River might have dug out the Grand Canyon; if it did, that was inorganic evolution. The Niagara River, flowing from what we call Niagara Falls, probably dug out a deep channel in pure rock, and that would be in-

---

16. W. G. T. Shedd, *Dogmatic Theology*, 2nd ed., 3 vols. (New York: Charles Scribner's Sons, 1899).

17. James Orr, *The Bible Under Trial* (London: Marshall, 1907).

18. Strong, *Systematic Theology*.

19. John Miley, *Systematic Theology* (New York: Eaton and Mains, 1892).

20. B. B. Warfield, "On the Antiquity and the Unity of the Human Race," in *Biblical and Theological Studies* (Philadelphia: Presbyterian and Reformed Publishing Co., reprinted 1952).

21. Bernard Ramm, *The Christian View of Science and Scripture* (Grand Rapids: William B. Eerdmans Publishing Co., 1955).

22. Herman Bavinck, *Our Reasonable Faith* (Grand Rapids: William B. Eerdmans Publishing Co., reprinted 1956).

23. E. J. Young, *Studies in Genesis* (Philadelphia: Presbyterian and Reformed Publishing Co., 1964).

24. Wiley, *Christian Theology*.

25. J. Oliver Buswell, Jr., *A Systematic Theology of the Christian Religion*, vol. 1 (Grand Rapids: Zondervan Publishing House, 1962). It should perhaps be noted that Louis Berkhof (1879-1950) took the 24-hour view in his *Systematic Theology* (Grand Rapids: William B. Eerdmans Publishing Co., 1930).

organic evolution. No doubt inorganic evolution took place, through which the Mississippi River deposited silt in the Gulf of Mexico and built up a large flatland area around New Orleans.

Nor would evangelicals necessarily object to an organic or biological evolution that takes place within species. We know that a Luther Burbank, by breeding roses, can produce a better variety—the American Beauty rose, for example. We know that, by careful breeding, varieties of cattle, or hogs, or horses, or whatever, can be bred up to desired levels of usefulness to us humans.

It is not correct, as some evolutionists have said, that theirs is the view of a changing universe, whereas creationism is the view of a static universe.

Sometimes, admittedly, we creationists have not properly understood evolutionists. William Jennings Bryan, arguing the case of creationism against the evolutionary theory of Clarence Darrow at the Scopes trial in Tennessee in the mid-1920s, did not properly understand evolutionary theory. Bryan and others seemed to think, for example, that evolutionists say that humans evolved from apes or monkeys—and humor has flowed from us creationists about that development. Yet evolutionists have never taught that humans descended from apes or monkeys. They have taught only that such animals, and humans, have a common ancestry—that they are something like cousins.

Likewise, evolutionists have not always understood creationists. For one thing, they have often accused creationists of adhering to a static universe per se. Also, they have often opposed creationists as though we were all believers in a young earth and in a mere 6,000 years of history. Yet many creationists believe the earth is millions or even billions of years old and that organic life has existed on it for a very long time. The special difference between the creationist and the evolutionist is that the creationist does not believe that the various species evolved, through natural processes, from lower complexity to higher complexity. They do not believe that *Homo sapiens*—vertebrates combining physical systems with rational, moral, and emotional capacities—developed naturally from some unicellular form of life. And they do not believe that unicellular life developed naturally from nonliving existence. Creationists believe that God created the species, and they do not necessarily limit the eternal God to any particular time schedule in what He has accomplished.

Various arguments present themselves for and against the theory of organic evolution and will now be discussed.

Arguments for Organic Evolution. It is widely believed today by evolutionists that the development of organisms has occurred because of two important factors: the survival of the fittest organisms; coupled with rare beneficial mutations, which spread through plants and animals, occasioning new species.

The survival of the fittest, as an explanation of evolution, is what Charles Darwin taught in *The Origin of Species* of 1859. It is believed by some that no book had been published on the basis of as much research as this one. Darwin, who had seriously considered the Christian ministry as a vocation, was an invalid and found it desirable to live and work in tropical climates, where he studied the various species of animals he found in his travels.

One link in Darwin's chain of reasoning was that plants tend to reproduce themselves according to the arithmetic ratio (1, 2, 3, 4, 5, 6), whereas animals tend to reproduce themselves according to the geometric ratio (2, 4, 8, 16). For basic insights on this, he was indebted to the somewhat earlier work on population theory by Thomas Malthus. Though Darwin predated by a long time the development of hybrids that produced better crops of wheat and corn than had been obtained in his time, he was basically correct about animals tending to reproduce at a faster pace than plants do. A sow, for example, can produce large litters of pigs within a few month's gestation time.

Another link in Darwin's chain of reasoning is that plants that supply food for the more prolific animals tend to be in short supply.

A third step in his reasoning is that conflict occurs among the animals over this food supply.

A fourth step is that in this conflict, the fittest of the animals survive and reproduce their better kind—thus occasioning, naturally, an evolution of biological organisms.

Right away, Darwin's theory of evolution, based on the processes of nature themselves, became widely acclaimed in the scientific community. Modernistic theology largely espoused the view but usually changed it somewhat to say that God stepped in at certain points, as for the origin of life itself, and also for the appearance of rational organisms. This is called theistic evolution. God is introduced, as Darwin had not done; but in agreement with Darwin, much of the evolvement occurred through natural processes themselves. On this view, evolution did take place—development from lower types of species to more complex types.

Some Protestant theologians who were not modernists also espoused theistic evolution, one of whom was Methodism's Olin Alfred Curtis, who took this position in his *Christian Faith* of 1905.

To combat a growing acceptance of modernistic understandings in Roman Catholicism, partly stemming from the influence of Darwin's evolutionary theory, papal encyclicals ordered priests and students for the priesthood to study especially the writings of the 13th-century Thomas Aquinas.

Evangelical Protestant theologians in general were not convinced by Darwin.

Darwin's theory became widely questioned in the present century by the main body of the scientific community. This was partly because it seemed to imply that acquired characteristics are passed on to offspring, and partly because scientists had found that members of a given species, both human and subhuman, sometimes cooperate together and thus allow the weak members of a species to survive. It was still believed that evolution had occurred, but no single theory could be agreed upon as to how it had occurred.

At this time Darwin's view was modified by the concept of mutations. Not only did the fittest organisms survive and pass on their better characteristics, but also rare and beneficial mutations occur and pass on their characteristics to offspring. This view is often called neo-Darwinism and is today the most fashionable theory in the scientific community—notwithstanding the fact that mutations are known to be almost always degenerative instead of evolutionary.

Besides those two basic arguments for evolution, the survival of the fittest (often called natural selection) and mutations, several other matters are thought by evolutionists to argue for the view—all of them coming from various subsciences of biology. One of them is from embryology—that the development of the individual recapitulates the development of the race. It is said, for example, that there is a time when a human fetus has gill slits—as exist now in fish and as existed when, in our prehuman history, we lived in the sea. Another argument is from serology, the science of blood, which is that blood similarities run roughly parallel to physical similarities. Still another argument is from morphology, or taxonomy, in which it is said that those animals with similar physical forms, such as hinge and ball-and-socket joints, have a common ancestry—although it might of course only point to a common creator. Another argument for evolution is based on geographical distribution. Many species are unique to certain areas, suggesting that evolution happened there independently of what was happening in other environments.

Some of the strongest supports for evolution come from paleontology, the science of extinct life. Here we are dealing with the distribution of organisms in time. Here it is felt that hard-and-fast evolution supports exist in the form of various kinds of fossil remains.

Arguments Against Evolution. Evolution began as a hypothesis and continued as a theory. Some evolutionists contend that we should talk about the law of evolution. They compare opposition to the view with opposition in the church, centuries ago, to the sphericity of the earth and the heliocentric view of our solar system. It is lamentably correct that these advancements in human knowledge were widely opposed in the church. The church "imprisoned" Galileo for teaching this, convinced that such views made the earth and humans of too little significance in the whole of creation.

It is also correct that the church was slow to accept other discoveries of science, such as that of gravity, because Christians wanted to understand that whatever happens is directly ordered by God. When Scotland's James Y. Simpson discovered an anesthetic, many Christians were loath to have it used in surgeries, saying that pain is quite evidently God's will.

Yet the matter of evolution is surely a different type of issue. It is not opposed by evangelicals because it is unbiblical. Give it a God-dimension, and you would be hard put to show that the view would be necessarily opposed to the teaching of Scripture. The chief bases for opposition to evolution among evangelicals are more or less scientific ones—those taken from the observable, provable world of science itself.

1. *The origin of life is not explained.* Evolution does not explain the origin of life itself. Darwin's theories about life's origin are only educated guesses, not based on what is observably prov-

able from experimentation. We can have all the ingredients for life and have them in the exactly correct proportions, yet we do not necessarily have life. However, if scientists are ever able to produce life, as their present capabilities suggest they might be able to do at some time in the future, creation will not at all be disproved—they will only have found out how the Creator did it.

2. *Entropy opposes evolution.* Entropy suggests that everything tends to run down, to lose steam, instead of gaining momentum, heat, or anything else. This is a scientific law that surely militates against evolution. According to the second law of thermodynamics, heat tends to be lost. The stars tend to cool off, as does the sun. Motion cannot perpetuate itself without outside help.

Applying this to plants and animals, instead of evolving, they tend toward devolvement when left to themselves and, say, the sun, with its impersonal powers. Most long-term homeowners have observed that roses tend toward devolvement when unattended. Also, tulips become smaller and less beautiful if left to themselves and not separated and replanted. And of course, they would, as far as we have been able to observe, always be roses and tulips. We can breed only to the state of homozygosity, of the purity of genes, and not to a new species—although some say that in rare forms of life, such as certain fruit flies, development to a new species might have been observed. It is understood by evolutionists that the origin of a new species is so slow a process that we cannot expect to keep records over such a long period of time and scientifically prove that a new species has originated.

3. *Mutation unlikely as occasioning humans.* The most fashionable theory of how evolution occurred is the neo-Darwinian view that it was through rare mutations, which then spread out through offspring into new species. Yet surely the best in biological science does not actually support the theory that new species, including humans, originated in this way. It is correct that each cell's genes in reproduction get mixed half and half with the coding characteristics of other cells, the offspring of each cell inheriting the mixture. It is also correct that mistakes are made in this process, and that you then have mutations, most of which are degenerative, producing weakened offspring. Neo-Darwinians know all this but insist that an occasional mutation is beneficial and occasions new species—and that this accounts for the human species.

In 1966 Murray Eden, then a professor in electrical engineering at Massachusetts Institute of Technology, stated that human chance emergence as a mutation was as likely as "typing at random a meaningful library of thousands of volumes using the following procedure: Begin with a meaningful phrase, retype it with a few mistakes, make it longer by adding letters; then examine the result to see if the new phrase is meaningful. Repeat this process until the library is complete."[26] In order for sight to occur, for example, some 130 million light-sensitive rods and cones cause photochemical reactions and transform the light into electrical impulses. Thousands of lucky mutations would have to happen coincidentally so that the eye's lens and its retina (which cannot work without each other) evolved in synchrony.

4. *The problem of the fossil gaps.* A most significant fact that militates against the theory of evolution, especially as advocated by Darwin himself, is the gaps in the fossils that we have found. The fossil record in general does not show progression from one species to another.

The six living forms Darwin felt evolved from one to another are bacteria and slime, sponges and jellyfish, fish with backbones, amphibians (living partly on land), reptiles (including the dinosaur), and birds and mammals. If these did develop, slowly, from one to another, as Darwin taught and as evolutionists generally teach, why are there almost always, if not always, fossil gaps? Some feel that some intermediary fossils have been found, but even this is debatable. If they developed gradually from one to another, with the intermediate creatures existing for perhaps millions of years, why do we not have the intermediary fossils?

Hitching, in the above-quoted article, says, "But there is a consistency in the fossil gaps: *the fossils are missing at many of the most important places.* Links between some major groups of animals simply aren't there." Museums hold thousands of invertebrate sea creatures and thousands of vertebrate sea creatures, but no intermediaries whatever from the approximate 100 million years that elapsed between the two kinds of sea creatures. No intermediary fossil has been found between the bat with wings and

---

26. Cited by Francis Hitching, "Where Darwin Went Wrong," *Reader's Digest,* Far East Edition, October 1982.

its wingless ancestor. No fossil has been found that suggests any slow development from a limb for walking to a wing for flying.

It is assumed that whales developed from an amphibious mammal with hoofs that moved from land to sea. Yet we have no fossils of such a creature.

It is also a problem for Darwinism that we have one-celled and many-celled fossil creatures, but no two-celled creatures.

5. *Other fossil problems besides gaps.* Fossil evidence, especially in human fossil "history," is scanty. Of *Pithecanthropus erectus,* the Java ape man, we have only a molar tooth, a skull top, and a thighbone. Yet the public is often misled on this matter because artists take these small, disconnected parts and imaginatively draw them into a humanlike being with flesh and bones, according to evolutionary theory.

Although tools are sometimes found near prehuman fossils, it is only assumed that the creatures were intelligent enough to have made and used the tools. The tools might have been made and used by a real human and simply got deposited near a prehuman creature's fossil.

In South Africa Dr. Richard E. Leakey found human fossils in rock strata far lower than where other prehuman fossils have been found, producing inconsistency in the fossil record. In Leakey's much older fossils, the human is quite like us in the shape of his skull; he measured 3½ to 4½ feet in height, "made tools, and quite probably had the gift of speech."[27]

A still further problem with fossil evidence is that upheavals in the earth's surface, produced by cooling and earthquakes, might have rearranged the rock strata and their depth and therefore the "age" of the strata where fossils are found.

One has some hesitancy in pointing out another problem in human fossil "history," since it is so flagrant a fault. Piltdown man, which had a respected place in the human fossil pedigree from 1912 until the early 1950s, is now known to be a mere hoax. Charles Dawson had found an ape's jaw, had ground and flattened the teeth in it, then stained it carefully and passed it off as a prehuman creature, apelike and yet humanlike.

---

27. S. Maxwell Coder and G. Howe, *The Bible, Science, and Creation* (Chicago: Moody Press, 1965), 81.

Science is a voyage in which new discoveries replace earlier understandings. *Time* magazine's February 22, 1993, issue says that science's new fad, on how life and the whole universe originated, is the complexity theory: that large amounts of what is chaotic tend to organize themselves into complex structures. Surely, on the matter of evolution, the wiser course for evangelicals is to understand that the eternal God created the species and that the time involved was exceedingly immense.

This, then, finishes the topics to be discussed in this chapter on creation. It remains now to discuss natural evil—the abysmal problem of why the created world is often red with blood in tooth and claw, of why the righteous and innocent suffer involuntarily if indeed a wise and benevolent God is in charge of the world He has created.

This subject of natural evil could be subsumed under the Christian doctrine of creation. However, because of its importance to all theology, and because of this writer's career-long interest in the subject, a special chapter will be devoted to it.

8

The Mystery of Evil

God's creation is earmarked with evil. Its "woes and wastes"[1] do not predominate, but they are formidable. C. S. Lewis speaks of evil's "rough, male taste of reality, not made by us, or indeed, for us, but hitting us in the face."[2]

Evil's name is legion, even in these technostructured times. In its myriad dread shapes, its path and its pathos rebuke our genius.

We still find as Job did, that "man is born to trouble as surely as sparks fly upward" (Job 5:7). We still taste things that are as "bitter as a broth of blood."[3]

Still a part of the human pageant is the "thousand natural shocks that flesh is heir to,"[4] spoken of by Shakespeare. Still "a plaint of guiltless hurt doth pierce the sky."[5]

In James Cozzens' novel *By Love Possessed,* Helen perceived "the dreadful eyeless face of our existence."[6] This requires many of us to keep our thumbs on our thoughts, especially if we believe in God and feel that we are not orphaned to providing our own providence.[7]

---

1. H. Wheeler Robinson, *Suffering: Human and Divine* (New York: Macmillan Publishing Co., 1939), 5.
2. C. S. Lewis, *The Problem of Pain* (New York: Macmillan Publishing Co., 1945), 13.
3. Archibald MacLeish, *J. B.* (Boston: Houghton Mifflin Co., 1946), 19.
4. William Shakespeare's *Hamlet,* act 3, sc. 1.
5. Quoted without reference in Lewis's *Problem of Pain,* 117.
6. James Cozzens, *By Love Possessed* (New York: Harcourt, Brace and Co., 1957).
7. See Roger Hazelton, *God's Way with Man* (New York: Abingdon Press, 1956), 5.

Evil denotes both moral and nonmoral meanings.[8] In itself, it consists of whatever frustrates the ideal fulfillment of human life—especially the lives of innocent and righteous persons who are obviously not deserving of its visits—assuming that the world is ordered by an all-good, all-wise, and all-powerful God. As all-good, He would want only the best for innocent and righteous persons. As all-wise, He would know what is the best for them. As all-powerful, He would be able to thwart all hindrances and implement what is best. Because of this understanding of God, James Bryden has the prone-to-be skeptical Mark ask, "Why does God let people suffer? My religious beliefs—tentative as they are—are all jumbled together in my mental basket and this question is a hole in the bottom of it; through this hole my beliefs keep slipping away."[9] The problem is so great, for Bryden, that we soon find him saying, "If the Church has nothing to say on this problem, I doubt if it has anything to say about anything—except, perhaps, to give us some practical advice on how to make the best of a bad mess."[10]

When the wicked flourish and the righteous are stunted, people begin to wonder if Ultimatus might be eyeless, or at least insensitive. Thus C. S. Lewis speaks of "the universal feeling that bad men ought to suffer."[11] And he adds, "It is no use turning up our noses at this feeling, as if it were wholly base. On its mildest level it appeals to everyone's sense of justice."[12]

Instrumental evils, both moral and natural, consist of whatever is a means to the frustration. An instrumental moral evil would be a gun used in murder. An instrumental natural evil would be the microbe that produces human misery.

---

8. For a discussion of the moral and nonmoral uses of words such as *trouble, bad,* and *evil,* see C. Ryder Smith, *The Bible Doctrine of Sin and the Ways of God with Sinners* (London: Epworth Press, 1953). He discusses the Hebrew word *ra,* found some 800 times in the Old Testament, which means "bad," basically—or evil. There are "bad" figs (Jer. 24:8), bad herbs (2 Kings 4:39-40), as well as bad (evil) deeds of men (Gen. 38:7; Deut. 4:25; Ps. 51:4). The Greek word *kakos,* found 78 times in the New Testament, similarly might mean either moral or nonmoral evil or badness—but usually refers to moral evil. See further discussion of these terms in chapter 10.

9. James Davenport Bryden, *Letters to Mark* (New York: Harper and Brothers Publishers, 1953), 19.

10. Ibid., 27.

11. Lewis, *The Problem of Pain,* 81.

12. Ibid.

Intrinsic evils, both moral and natural, consist of whatever is frustrating in and of itself. An intrinsic moral evil would be a murder. An intrinsic natural evil would be death from a hurricane.

Of all these distinctions, that between moral evil and natural evil is the most important for our purposes here.

Moral Evil and Natural Evil Distinguished

Moral Evil. This is Pearl Harbor, Siberia, Auschwitz, and a host of other foul places. It is foul faces too: those of Hitler and Hess and Eichmann. It is Al Capone. It is Watergate—its entry and its intrigues.

Moral evil is the strut of sin in the early Nero, and in many another person less infamous but no less a pompous island of sovereignty in God's domain. It is one Seigneur, who, on returning from the hunt, could "kill not more than two serfs, and refresh his feet in their warm blood and bowels."[13] It is what Carlyle Marney says you have "on most any twenty feet of street the world around."[14]

It is much more. It is Goethe's Faust, whose deliberate sin is what troubles him. Hamlet's problem, too, is moral evil: the sins of the high and mighty pain him, even those of his mother, including her complicity in the murder of his father and her incest. The anguish that pierced Lady Macbeth through was from her own performance.

Moral evil is the first man lifting puny fists against the Almighty and cowering behind a bush when Yahweh-Elohim walks by. It is King Saul of Israel, who stood so tall, but whose rebel within stood taller still and sentenced him to a suicide's end. It is King Herod, who massacred all infants around Bethlehem for fear that one of them would someday be given his throne. It is denial of Jesus by the Galilean fisherman who most shouldn't have done so—and was most sure he would not.

According to John Hick, moral evil reaches its "ultimate maximum" in the execution of Jesus. He writes:

> And the climax of this biblical history of evil was the execution of Jesus of Nazareth. Here were pain and violent destruction, gross injustice, the apparent defeat of the righ-

---

13. Thomas Carlyle, *The French Revolution* (New York: Random House, 1934), 11.
14. Carlyle Marney, *Faith in Conflict* (New York: Abingdon Press, 1957), 50.

teous, and the premature death of a still-young man. But further, for Christian faith, this death was the slaying of God's Messiah, the one in whom mankind was to see the mind and heart of God made flesh. Here, then, the problem of evil rises to its ultimate maximum; for in its quality this was an evil than which no greater can be conceived.[15]

Moral evil obtains when angels have people by the hand while the evil one has them by the heart;[16] when we grasp what is worthless but leave unsniffed what is priceless; when we reach for what we like—and like less and less what we reach for.

It is more than a soft infirmity of blood, or a lack of learning as for the ancient Greeks, or mere illusion as in Spinoza, or a false subordination of reason to sense as in Kant.[17] It is more than "the temporary power man has to resist God [as a] consequence of the irrationality that he has brought up with him from the animal world."[18]

In the record we have written, treachery is there, wantonness, crookedness, trespassings, stubbornness, lawlessness, profanity, folly, to mention only a few members of moral evil's family.

Theologians give it the name of "sin," and the Church seeks to foster a life of righteousness as the alternative to it. But in this chapter we are talking about evil with a different trademark.

Natural Evil. This is a quake that rocks San Francisco in 1906—or in 1989—and spills out a guiltless hurt on a whole urban area. It is a London plagued by a germ that beats the best of people. It is the dark, changeless quiet that was Helen Keller's, the wheelchair of baseball's Campanella. It is the torrents of water that rush down California hillsides and take with them roads and bridges and houses and people.

To some extent, it is the auto accidents that kill and mangle so indiscriminately. About half of America's auto fatalities are alcohol-caused; but the deaths occur among both the drinkers and the nonsippers. A church family might rise one morning, pray together for God's help on a vacation trip, and all get killed by a

---

15. John Hick, *Evil and the God of Love* (New York: Harper and Row, 1966).
16. Marney, *Faith in Conflict,* 48.
17. For a summary on this topic, see F. R. Tennant, *The Origin and Propagation of Sin* (Cambridge: Cambridge University Press, 1902), 51-67.
18. George A. Gordon, *Immortality and the New Theodicy,* 82, quoted in E. W. Cook, *Origin of Sin* (New York: Funk and Wagnalls Co., 1899), 34.

drunk or a fleeing bank robber as they are backing out of their driveway.

We can fly over the Gulf of Mexico, locate a hurricane's eye and determine its direction, and use radio and television to warn people in coastal cities of its latent havoc. But it rides on toward our cities as though the Stoics were right—that a law of necessity is written into the nature of existence, and we are powerless to do much about it.

The hurricane is as indiscriminate in destruction as it is savage in force. Of this indiscriminateness in evil's intrusions John Hick writes, "The problem consists . . . in the fact that instead of serving a constructive purpose pain and misery seem to be distributed in random and meaningless ways, with the results that suffering is often undeserved and often falls upon men in amounts exceeding anything that could be rationally intended."[19]

Natural evil is the moans and groans of the sick and dying in our hospitals. It is those in our mental hospitals who do their best to recontact reality, and those who do not even know that they ought to try. It is those who lie upon white beds, sick in both mind and body, yet stuck in this world, unable to enjoy life on earth, but not released to enjoy life in paradise.

We are not always accomplices in the evils that confront us. They simply strike us whether we would have it so or not. That is what makes them so rough and so rude. What if we do serve God? What if we are of innocent years, too small to serve God?

People who know God and are seeking to mature in Christian graces get sucked in by evil just as others do. They do not dissipate as others might, so on the average they might have better resistance to the microbes, for example, that communicate disease. And miracles might happen in their case. Yet it is about the same with them as with others. Rain falls on the crops of the just and the unjust, and so do natural frustrations. In its dread shapes evil seems to lie in wait to pounce upon us.[20]

That is why evil causes such consternation for the person who believes in God. It has ever been so. Hear the believing Psalmist complain, "Evils beyond number have surrounded me" (40:12, NASB). Such persons "expected good, then evil came"

19. Hick, *Evil and the God of Love*, 369.
20. Davie Napier, "The Problem of the Dark," *The Pulpit*, November 1958, 18.

(Job 30:26, NASB). If God is God, they think, why do the wicked often flourish like the green bay tree while many of the righteous salt their bread with tears?

Besides the specific evils that intrude into our lives, we suffer from a generalized dread. John Hick explains, "Because we are finite, mortal, and insecure we not only from time to time fear this and that specific danger but we also (according to existentialists from Soren Kierkegaard onwards) suffer chronically from *Angst*, a generalized anxiety or dread, which cannot be appeased by guarding against particular concrete perils."[21]

Natural evil is a more serious theoretical problem than is moral evil. This is because the responsible agent of moral evil is more easily located than is the agent of natural evil. Moral evil, just because of its volitional character, is quite readily seen to arise from our prostituted use of freedom. We ourselves, even if we are dizzy with such frames of mind as despair or dread, bring it upon ourselves. Why is a bank robbed? Why is a person murdered? Many are the contributing factors, of course, but such evils are perpetrated volitionally. In natural evil, however, our volition is not involved at all, or it is not importantly involved.

In natural evil, frustrations of our ideal existence visit us quite apart from our own choosing. We want good health and a long life, so we avoid smoking and keep down our cholesterol count; yet we contract an incurable cancer or might be struck dead by lightning.

Perhaps no problem has loomed so large in the minds of philosophers and theologians as has that caused by natural evil—with its indiscriminateness and its seriousness. Leslie Weatherhead says, "The subject of pain has haunted my thinking ever since I began to think for myself at all."[22] John S. Whale refers to it as "this notorious problem which has vexed thought and tried faith in every age of human history."[23] Another writer calls it "man's overwhelming problem."[24] Of it Alfred Hoernle says, "It is

---

21. Hick, *Evil and the God of Love*, 189.
22. Leslie D. Weatherhead, *Why Do Men Suffer?* (New York: Abingdon-Cokesbury Press, 1936), 9.
23. J. S. Whale, *The Christian Answer to the Problem of Evil* (London: Student Christian Movement Press, 1936), 13.
24. Radoslav A. Tsanoff, *The Nature of Evil* (New York: Macmillan Publishing Co., 1931), viii.

undoubtedly one of the gravest problems which the philosophy of religion has to face."[25] Oxford's John Hick says, "The fact of evil constitutes the most serious objection there is to the Christian belief in a God of Love."[26]

Three major kinds of response have been made to the problem of natural evil—pessimistic, optimistic, and melioristic.

The writer's own persuasion falls within the melioristic response, located somewhere between the denial of natural good in pessimism and the denial of natural evil in optimism. Meliorism admits the reality of both good and evil and urges a willingness to work toward the promotion of the good and a lessening of the evil.

Within this melioristic persuasion, it has occurred to the writer that the Christian doctrine of the Incarnation contains important pointers toward our learning to live with nature's seamy side.

Eastern Orthodox Christianity saw in the Incarnation a pointer in the midst of natural frustrations. Irenaeus taught that "the Word, having been firmly united to flesh, . . . has reclaimed the savage earth."[27] Athanasius declared of Christ that "even while present in a body and himself quickening it, He was, without inconsistency, quickening the universe as well, and was in every process of nature."[28]

While the West from Augustine onward (especially after Anselm) stressed the death of Christ and its provision for our sin, the East continued to talk in terms of an entire cosmic redemption by reason of the Incarnation. Recapitulation, re-creation, renewal, deification—you hear about all this from them. Father Sergius Bulgakov carried forward this kind of thinking in our own century. He wrote, "The Lord is not only Saviour of souls, but of bodies also, and consequently of the entire world."[29] In another work he said, "God created the world only that he might deify it and himself become all in all to it."[30]

25. R. F. Alfred Hoernle, *Matters, Life, Mind, and God* (New York: Harcourt, Brace and Co., 1922).

26. Hick, *Evil and the God of Love,* 273.

27. Irenaeus, *Against Heresies,* vols. 1-5, trans. Alexander Roberts and W. H. Rambaut, as well as some other writings (Edinburgh: T. and T. Clark, 1919), 4, chap. 34, par 4.

28. Athanasius, *Select Writings, De Incarn,* 17, 2.

29. Sergius Bulgakov, *The Orthodox Church,* trans. Elizabeth S. Cram, ed. Donald A. Lowrie (London: Century Press, 1935), 159.

30. Sergius Bulgakov, *The Wisdom of God* (London: William and Norgate, 1937), 203.

Bulgakov and other Eastern Orthodox theologians, such as Father George Florovsky, have helped many of us of the West to rethink the significance of the Incarnation in relation to suffering.

We have had a George McLeod and an Iona community, for example, where Christians have sought to live according to a heightened view of the natural world made possible by an adequate understanding of the Incarnation. D. M. Baillie saw that the Incarnation is a key to natural evil.[31] His brother, John Baillie, says that the solution to the problems of sin and natural evil lies in the story of the life and suffering and death and resurrection of Jesus Christ. T. F. Torrance is quite "Eastern" in saying that through the Incarnation the Eternal Son of God has embodied himself within the creation and has assumed it into union with himself. Missionary Bishop Leslie Newbigin reflected the influence of recent Scottish thought when he said that in Scripture salvation is concerned with the whole created order.

That the Son really took a body suggests that the natural world is not evil per se. While enfleshed, God the Son healed diseased and maimed persons and even raised some from the dead—which suggests that God the Father does not necessarily will each instance of disease, incapacity, and death; if He does, Christ would have been opposing the Father's will by alleviating those heaps of human hurt He gave attention to.

Perhaps, then, Christ is the Answer to both problems, that of moral evil and that of natural evil. Perhaps we are redeemed from moral evil peculiarly through His death on the Cross and redeemed from natural evil peculiarly by His incarnation. And whereas we are redeemed from moral evil by faith, perhaps we are redeemed from natural evil by a proper assessment of the import of the Incarnation and by works that, in light of that assessment, alleviate natural evil in all possible ways. Christ's resurrection might be the event that validates that whole moral and cosmic redemption scheme. This event, through which Christ comes forth Victor over death, symbolizes the redemption from moral evil by conquering death, a punishment for moral evil. And the Resurrection also symbolized redemption from natural evil because it takes the worst that natural evil can do to us—death—and conquers it.

---

31. See D. M. Baillie, *The Theology of the Sacraments* (New York: Charles Scribner's Sons, 1957), 44.

What, then, if evil's name is legion? What if, in its myriad dread shapes, its path and its pathos rebuke our genius even in these technostructured times? When our world seems to tumble in on us from nature's indiscriminate and sometimes whimsical intrusions, we *are* Christians, so we have on our side an Incarnation—an Incarnation that was real—whose savory effects were all validated by the Resurrection, which makes the whole world sport a halo. It is toward such directions and conclusions that the present writer's research and existential predicaments have inclined him. And it is toward such directions as these that this chapter's study leans, at least finally.

First, however, the reader is asked to consider the three major kinds of response to natural evil that other researchers and sufferers have made—the pessimistic, the optimistic, and the melioristic.

Following this, a historical study of the Incarnation and its bearing on natural evil will be given as a theological foundation for the writer's views.

The Pessimistic Embitterment

Pessimism is the view of despairists who believe that evil is "rooted and dominant in the very heart of ultimate reality."[32] It may be called a position of "pandiabolism,"[33] in which a metaphorical devil, instead of God, is everything.

For them, the world is a headache we are born with and die with. "Born, suffered, died" sum up human life, and the sooner it is summed up the better—at least theoretically. While this obtains for all life on our planet, the worst trick has been played on us humans, because we are the only ones who can complain, and yet there is no one to complain to. Real pessimists feel they are orphans in the universe.

Like the wind, which seems to come from nowhere and go nowhere, the usual pessimist feels that we humans have not come from anyone, such as Creator Ultimatus, and that we do not go anywhere from here. Purely natural forces have conspired to produce us and the non-self-conscious animals. Even if we clothe ourselves with culture for a time, we die shortly, even as they die,

---

32. Tsanoff, *The Nature of Evil*, 7.
33. Ibid.

to exist no more. Pessimists talk about "this look of loathing"[34] that life wears. Theirs is a pale cast of thought. They sour to evil's shapes and feel lost in the labyrinth of things as they are but ought not to be as they are.

Hamlet's soliloquy contains a practical statement of pessimism, where Shakespeare has the prince say:

> To die: to sleep:
> . . . and by a sleep to say we end
> The heart-ache and the thousand natural shocks
> That flesh is heir to, 'tis a consummation
> Devoutly to be wish'd.[35]

Othello also stated what pessimists believe when, after striking deceptive Iago with the sword, he exclaims:

> I'ld have thee live;
> For, in my sense, 'tis happiness to die.[36]

The view of pessimism is expressed in Archibald MacLeish's J. B., a play in verse where we read of "this reeling, reeking earth."[37]

James Thomson[38] states it with approximate blasphemy in City of Dreadful Night (1874):

> Who is most wretched in this dolorous place?
> I think myself; yet I would rather be
> My miserable self than He, than He
> Who formed such creatures to His own disgrace.
>
> The vilest thing must be less vile than Thou
> From whom it had its being, God and Lord!
> Creator of all woe and sin! abhorred,
> Malignant and implacable! I vow
>
> That not for all Thy power furled and unfurled,
> For all the temples to Thy glory built,
> Would I assume the ignominious guilt
> Of having made such men in such a world.

---

34. Ibid., 20.
35. Shakespeare's Hamlet, act 3, sc. 1.
36. Shakespeare's Othello, act 5, sc. 2.
37. MacLeish, J.B., 143.
38. Thomson often wrote under the pseudonym "Bysshe Vanolis."

Pessimism is found in many forms, four of which deserve treatment here.

Religious Pessimism. This is an embittered despair arising out of frustrated ultimate-concern strivings. The most conspicuous instance of this type of pessimism is Buddhism, in its various historic forms. Gautama, founder of Buddhism, became troubled by the evils of nature that seemed to be so sovereign and so indiscriminate. In his Indian village he was awed by the human plight of the aged, the lame, the sick, the dying. The "why" of all such plagued him. At 29 he left his wife and son in search for a religious answer.

Gautama propounded "Four Noble Truths" in a sermon preached at Benares to the five companions of his hermit life.[39] Burnouf sees them as "sorrow, the production of sorrow, the extinction of sorrow, the path which conducts to the extinction of sorrow."[40] A fair listing is given by A. S. Geden: "All existence involves suffering; suffering is caused by desire, especially desire for continuance of existence; the suppression of desire therefore will lead to the extinction of suffering; this deliverance can only be effected by the Noble Eight-fold Path."[41]

Boiled down, the terms that gather up the essence of the four truths are pain, cause (of the pain), suppression (of the pain), and path (to the extinction of pain). One authority suggests, "Howev-

---

39. The following paragraphs are from this sermon and enlarge upon the Four Noble Truths: "Now this, O recluses, is the noble truth concerning suffering. Birth is painful, and so is old age; disease is painful, and so is death. Union with the unpleasant is painful, painful is separation from the pleasant; and any craving that is unsatisfied, that, too, is painful . . .

"Now this, O recluses, is the noble truth concerning the origin of suffering. Verily it originates in that craving thirst which causes the renewal of becomings, is accompanied by sensual delight, and seeks satisfaction now here, there—that is to say, the craving for the gratification of the passions, or the craving for a future life, or the craving for success in this present life.

"Now this, O recluses, is the noble truth concerning the destruction of suffering. Verily it is the destruction in which no craving remains over, of this very thirst; the laying aside of, the getting rid of, the being free from, the harbouring no longer of, this thirst.

"Now this, O recluses, is the noble truth concerning the way which leads to the destruction of suffering. Verily it is this Eight-fold noble path; that is to say: Right Views, Right Aspirations, Right Speech, Right Conduct, Right Livelihood, Right Effort, Right Mindfulness, Right Rapture" (from Prof. Rhys David's translation and quoted in Annie H. Small's *Buddhism* [London: J. M. Dent and Co., 1905], 24-25).

40. *Introduction to Buddhism*, 629, quoted by Marcus Dods, in *Mohammed, Buddha, and Christ* (London: Hodder and Stoughton, 1877), 165.

41. A. S. Geden, "Buddha," in *Encyclopaedia of Religion and Ethics*, ed. James Hastings, vol. 2 (Edinburgh: T. and T. Clark, 1909).

er much Buddhists differ on other points, they are agreed on these."[42]

For the Buddhist, "Birth is painful, disease is painful, death is painful, contact with the unpleasant is painful."[43] These are painful for all of us, but they seem to loom larger than life, larger than love, for Buddhists. Since Buddhists feel that pain arises from desires, they seek to free themselves from desires—not having to return to this world after death if they succeed.

Buddhists are often charged with teaching transmigration of souls, but H. H. Rowley correctly points out that for Buddhism, "Man is never the same for two consecutive moments, and is without any abiding principle. Neither in this life, nor beyond it, has he any enduring soul."[44] Rowley thinks that what you have is a transmigration not of the soul, but of character, of personality without a person—if such can be conceived. Misery exists continuingly, but no miserable one. This is the extent of Buddhism's despair.

Philosophical Pessimism. Embittered despair sometimes arises from an exaggerated dependence on reason in "explaining" the evils of life. Arthur Schopenhauer, the 18th-century German philosopher, is probably the most noted example of this type of pessimism.

He was an "antirationalist, pessimist, atheist; 'tough' as opposed to 'tender' minded, a wild ass in the desert of philosophy."[45]

One of his editors says that for Schopenhauer, evil is "no accidental or incidental fact in the world, but inescapable, essential. It is our central illusion, he tells us, to suppose that we are destined to be happy."[46] Tsanoff observes that "from Schopenhauer's point of view pleasure is the exception; pain, the rule in human life."[47]

42. Alfred W. Martin, *Great Religious Teachers of the East* (New York: Macmillan Publishing Co., 1911), 60.
43. Ibid.
44. H. H. Rowley, *Submission in Suffering* (Cardiff, Wales: University of Wales Press, 1951), 24.
45. Dewitt H. Parker, ed., *Schopenhauer Selections* (New York: Charles Scribner's Sons, 1928).
46. Ibid., xii.
47. Tsanoff, *The Nature of Evil*, 286.

To Schopenhauer, "The innermost kernel of Christianity is the truth that suffering—the Cross—is the real end and object of life."[48] He denied even the utility of religion, including Christianity, calling it a "pack of lies."[49] As proof of this he writes, "The fruits of Christianity were religious wars, butcheries, crusades, inquisitions, extermination of the natives in America, and the introduction of African slaves in their place."[50]

In Schopenhauer you have a despair that knows no hope.

Scientific Pessimism. Here there is disparagement of human existence resulting from an overdependence on the data derived from observation and experimentation in the sphere of the physical world.

Joseph Wood Krutch, author of *The Modern Temper,* was a leading representative of this type of pessimism. The "temper" he describes is his own—atheism, despair, pessimism—stemming out of the problem of natural evil and based on an exclusive dependence on sense data. He calls his "temper" "modern" because it is scientific, as opposed to traditional and emotional, and thus "up to date."

In Krutch's view, nature has no purpose. He says, "The universe . . . was not designed to suit man's needs."[51] He further asserts, "Nature's purpose, if purpose she can be said to have, is no purpose of his [man's] and is not understandable in his terms."[52] He refers to nature's "ruthless indifference to his [man's] values, and the blindness of her irresistible will, which strike terror to his soul."[53] Nature "has no ends which the human mind has been able to discover or comprehend."[54]

In Krutch's world, devoid of purpose and Purposer, humans have no more importance than insects. He writes, "Nature, in her blind thirst for life, has filled every possible cranny on the rotting earth with some sort of fantastic creature, and among them man

---

48. Arthur Schopenhauer, "On Suicide," in *The Works of Schopenhauer,* ed. Will Durant (New York: Simon and Schuster, 1928), 435.
49. Ibid., 483.
50. Ibid., 490.
51. Joseph Wood Krutch, *The Modern Temper* (New York: Harcourt, Brace and Co., 1929), 7.
52. Ibid., 8.
53. Ibid.
54. Ibid., 39.

is but one—perhaps the most miserable of all, because he is the only one in whom the instinct of life falters long enough to enable it to ask the question, 'Why?'"[55] Of our unimportance Krutch also says, "There is no reason to suppose that his own life has any more meaning than the life of the humblest insect that crawls from one annihilation to the next."[56] Edwin Lewis once said, "The best criticism of Comte is exposition."[57] That is how one might react to Krutch's pessimism. Suffice it therefore to say this: Krutch's keen intellectual delineation of man's worthlessness, plus the very fact that he gives any time at all to writing a book for people to read, argue against the worthlessness and futility of our existence.

Naturalistic Pessimism. In Archibald MacLeish's *J. B.*, the play in verse that won the 1959 Pulitzer prize for drama, you have pessimistic gripes about the Deity, engendered by natural suffering and resolved naturalistically by J. B., the main character, who decides to renew the love he and his wife had known earlier.

J. B. is a 20th-century Job, who wrestles with the natural disvalues humans are heir to—as E. S. Brightman referred to them. These debits on life's ledger give rise to the proposition, stated early:

If God is God He is not good,
If God is good he is not God.[58]

It seems for a while that J. B. will maintain his confidence in God's justice. Actually, Nickles, who plays Satan, even congratulates Mr. Zuss, who plays God, that J. B. has not succumbed, although Nickles says it is because the "proud, contemptible" J. B. simply has not "the spunk to spit on Christmas!"[59]

But J. B. does succumb finally. He agrees with his wife that God is unjust[60] and says of Him, "He does not love."[61] J. B.'s wife, who had left him because his loss was proof that God is unjust, has now returned and rejoins, "But we do. That's the wonder."[62]

---

55. Ibid., 9.
56. Ibid.
57. Lecture by Edwin Lewis, "Philosophical Theism," Drew Seminary, 1949-50.
58. MacLeish, *J. B.*, 14.
59. Ibid., 136.
60. Ibid., 151.
61. Ibid., 152.
62. Ibid.

Although there is no justice in the world, there *is* love[63]—not the love of God for people or of people for God, but the love of a woman for a man and of a man for a woman. Since the only thing really wholesome is this love, J. B.'s wife urges:

> Blow on the coal of the heart.
> The candles in churches are out.
> The lights have gone out in the sky.
> Blow on the coal of the heart
> And we'll see by and by.[64]

The subtle ending of the play implies that J. B. agrees to fan their love that had once burned hot.

This play depicts pessimism, treated here as naturalistic pessimism, because the one thing J. B. and his wife hesitatingly decide to turn to is an earthly, natural love for each other. Along with Buddhism, Schopenhauer's philosophy, and Krutch's scientism, it is a major form of this type of response to natural evil.

We turn now to optimistic views of natural evil.

The Optimistic Denial

Pessimism's opposite, its "antonym superlative,"[65] is optimism, and many more people have opted to read life in this way. Robert Browning gives a classic statement of optimism in his dramatic poem "Pippa Passes By." Pippa is a poor working girl with only one day off during the year. On that day, despite her hardships, she flitted down the street singing:

> The year's at the spring
> And day's at the morn;
> Morning's at seven;
> The hill-side's dew-pearled;
> The lark's on the wing;
> The snail's on the thorn:
> God's in his heaven—
> All's right with the world![66]

---

63. Ibid., 151.
64. Ibid., 153.
65. Tsanoff, *The Nature of Evil*, 1.
66. Robert A. Browning, *Pippa Passes By and Other Poems,* in The Temple Classics (London: Dent and Co., 1846), 25.

Alexander Pope's *Essay on Man* is an optimistic affirmation in view of natural evil. The affirmation reaches a climatic point when Pope declares:

> *All nature is but art, unknown to thee;*
> *All chance, direction, which thou canst not see;*
> *All discord, harmony not understood;*
> *All partial evil, universal good;*
> *And, spite of pride, in erring reason's spite,*
> *One truth is clear, "Whatever is, is right."*[67]

At least three major types of optimism have been espoused: the religious, the philosophical, and the theological.

Religious Optimism. Christian Science is probably the truest and most prevalent expression of religious optimism.

Since Christian Science was founded by Mary Baker Eddy, and since her teachings are authoritative wherever the religion functions, this form of religious optimism may be studied with reference to Mrs. Eddy's principal work, *Science and Health with Key to the Scriptures*—probably ghostwritten by a Mr. Quimby, who had a divinity education, but at least attributed to her.

Mrs. Eddy defines God as "The great I Am; the all-knowing, all-seeing, all-acting, all-wise, all-loving, and eternal; Principle; Mind; Soul; Spirit; Life; Truth; Love; all substance; intelligent."[68]

The optimistic Mrs. Eddy denied the reality of evil. "If God, or good, is real, then evil, the unlikeness of God, is unreal. And evil can only seem real by giving reality to the unreal."[69] Mrs. Eddy also remarks, "We bury the sense of infinitude, when we admit that, although God is infinite, evil has a place in his infinity, for it could have no place, where all space is filled with God."[70] "Hence, evil is but an illusion," she insists, "a false belief."[71]

Mrs. Eddy affirms that error, also, is unreal. "Error is unreal because untrue. It is that which seemeth to be and is not. If error were true, its truth would be error."[72]

---

67. Alexander Pope, *Essay on Man*, ed. Mark Pattison (Oxford: Clarendon Press, 1904), 36.

68. Mary Baker Eddy, *Science and Health with Key to the Scriptures* (Boston: Joseph Armstrong, 1934), 587.

69. Ibid., 470.

70. Ibid., 469.

71. Ibid., 480.

72. Ibid., 472.

Mrs. Eddy often discusses three unrealities in the same sentence: sin, sickness, and death. She explains: "That which He creates is good, and He makes all that is made. Therefore the only reality of sin, sickness, or death is the awful fact that unrealities seem real to human, erring belief, until God strips off their disguise. They are not true, because they are not of God."[73]

Many just criticisms have been leveled against Christian Science. One of the most forceful was written by the late E. Stanley Jones. He says of Christian Science:

> The movement has been plagued within itself with charges and countercharges of fraud and deception. I do not believe that this fraud has been deliberate; rather, it is the inevitable result of trying to make life square with an impossible religious position. For it is an impossible position to waive all sickness, all suffering, all sin, all death out of existence as unrealities. If there is no such thing as suffering, the cross of Christ is a travesty. We suspect any solution of the problem of suffering that leaves us with that result. No, the answer of Christian Science is a surface answer, and its steps are dogged by the inevitable nemesis of superficiality. It is not strange that it has its greatest vogue among the past-middle-age-comfortably-well-off, where optimism is easy, and yet at the same time where men and women are in need of assurances against the approaching disillusionment of old age and death. In it there are no Wounds which will heal our wounds, no Death which will heal our deaths.[74]

Christian Science has come to its error by two related processes: first, it has employed subterfuge; it has evaded what appears to common sense and intelligence to be real—pain, suffering, death. Second, it has exaggerated the good aspects of life. They exist in abundance, it is true, but beside them are the evils. And as the 20th century nears its close, this non-Christian "Christian" religion is in decline.

Philosophical Optimism. This is a negative view of evil arising from a predominant dependence on human reason in offering a solution to the "apparent" irrationality of life and existence.

---

73. Ibid.

74. From *Christ and Human Suffering* by E. Stanley Jones (New York: Abingdon Press, 1933), 65-66. Copyright renewal © 1961 by E. Stanley Jones. Adapted by permission of the publisher.

This type of optimism was germinated in the thought of Plato, who applied his reasoning powers to "apparent" evil and came to consider it as mere nonbeing—a negation of the good, but not positively opposed to it.

Origen, for all his attention to Scripture, was Platonic in basic ways. Evil is not really real: it is cathartic, contributing toward a redemption that even includes Satan.

Neoplatonism may certainly be regarded as an example of philosophical optimism. Concluding that evil is purely negative, it affirmed that all human souls will finally receive their fulfillment by completing the cycle and reuniting with *to hen,* which is Greek for The One, his name for God—from whence they have come forth—through the Principle of Intellection.

Philosophical optimism is generally pantheistic. Benedict de Spinoza, the arch-pantheist of all time, is representative of the view.

For Spinoza everything is God. He writes, "Besides God no substance can be granted or conceived . . . If any substance besides God were granted it would have to be explained by some attribute of God, and thus two substances with the same attribute would exist, which is absurd; therefore, besides God no substance can be granted, or consequently, be conceived."[75]

All is God, and this God is all-powerful. Spinoza joins these concepts in the following statement: "From the sole necessity of the essence of God it follows that he is the cause of himself and of all things. Wherefore the power of God, by which he and all things are and act, is identical with his essence."[76]

Optimism is the logic of belief in pantheistic absolutism. Therefore he can say that "since whatsoever exists expresses God's nature or essence,"[77] whatever exists would have to be good. No evil can exist, because "whatsoever exists expresses God's power, which is the cause of all things."[78]

Evil, for Spinoza, is not positive but negative. It is imperfection. He declares, "Now pain is the transition to the lesser perfection, and therefore cannot be understood through man's nature."[79]

75. Benedict de Spinoza, *Philosophy of Benedict de Spinoza,* trans. R. H. M. Elwes (New York: Tudor Publishing Co., 1933), 49.
76. Ibid., 70.
77. Ibid.
78. Ibid.
79. Ibid., 236.

Evil consists only in our thinking of a thing or condition as such. He says, "If the human mind possessed only adequate ideas, it would form no conception of evil."[80]

Most optimists advocate submission and resignation to the evils of nature, because they look upon its every manifestation as the result of divine decree. Spinoza, on the other hand, presented an active method of dealing with what is apparently evil. He said, "Whatsoever in nature we deem to be evil, or to be capable of injuring our faculty for existing and enjoying the rational life, we may endeavor to remove in whatever way seems safest to us."[81]

In taking this position, however, Spinoza compromised his optimism. If all is good or instrumental to good, why endeavor to avoid or remove any apparent evils?

Theological Optimism. By this is meant the negative conception of natural evil as resulting from a primary concern for the doctrines of the Christian faith.

Many influential theologians have been optimists. Augustine, John Scotus Erigena, and John Calvin were all optimistic, however much they disagreed on other points. Calvin will be treated in detail as a representative of them.

Calvin holds that God never faces any condition in the universe that His will did not directly create or immediately cause. To Calvin, God is the direct cause of everything. He writes, "For Augustine, in expounding this passage, where power is connected with patience, justly observes, that God's power is not permissive, but influential."[82] He also says, "How exceedingly presumptuous it is only to inquire into the causes of the Divine will; which is in fact, and is justly entitled to be, the cause of everything that exists."[83] He continues, "For the will of God is the highest rule of justice; so that what he wills must be considered just, for this very reason, because he wills it."[84]

For Calvin, therefore, everything that exists is good because God even "influentially" wills it. He feels it presumptuous to question the goodness of what comes to people. He writes:

---

80. Ibid.
81. Ibid., 243.
82. John Calvin, *The Institutes of the Christian Religion,* trans. John Allen (Philadelphia: Presbyterian Board of Publication and Sabbath-School Work, 1813), 2:165.
83. Ibid.
84. Ibid., 169.

Do you seek a reason? I will tremble at the depth. Do you reason? I will wonder. Do you dispute? I will believe. I see the depth, I reach not the bottom. Paul rested, because he found admiration. He calls the judgments of God unsearchable; and are you come to scrutinize them? He says, his ways are past finding out; and are you come to investigate them? We shall do no good by proceeding further.[85]

Also, in defense of his theory that we should not question the goodness of what befalls us, he declares, "When it is inquired, therefore, why the Lord did so, the answer must be, because he would."[86] He concludes, "Faithful ignorance is better than presumptuous knowledge."[87]

Calvin's entire system rests on his emphasis upon the sovereignty of God. He understands that God will have His way regardless of what we humans do. God's will is supreme, and we are not free to thwart it. That will has even predestined some to eternal life and others to eternal death; and no matter what we do, we cannot alter this predestined fate. Calvin asserts: "To say that others obtain by chance, or acquire by their own efforts, that which election alone confers on a few, will be worse than absurd. Whom God passes by, therefore, he reprobates, and from no other cause than his determination to exclude them from the inheritance which he predestinates for his children."[88] He also writes, "Hardening proceeds from the Divine power and will, as much as mercy."[89] And he says, "God knows what he has determined to do with us: if he has decreed our salvation, he will bring it about in his own time; if he has destined us to death, it will be in vain for us to strive against it."[90]

How does Calvin explain the suffering that comes to those who are predestined to eternal life? From the following quotations it will be noted that in his opinion all natural evil is disciplinary and therefore good. He says that suffering comes in order that the righteous might sin less: "But believers, admonished by the Divine corrections, immediately descend to the consideration

85. Ibid., 165.
86. Ibid., 168.
87. Ibid.
88. Ibid., 162.
89. Ibid., 174.
90. Ibid.

of their sins, and, stricken with fear and dread, resort to a suppliant depreciation of punishment. If God did not mitigate these sorrows, with which wretched souls torment themselves, they would be continually fainting, even under slight tokens of his wrath."[91]

Natural evils visit the elect to teach them to rely on God. He writes of the arrogant view of questioning God in relation to what He is advocating:

> This [the arrogant view] inflates us with a foolish, vain, carnal confidence; relying on which, we become contumacious and proud, in opposition to God himself, just as though our own powers were sufficient for us without His grace. This arrogance He cannot better repress, than by proving to us from experience, not only our great imbecility, but also our extreme frailty. Therefore He inflicts us with ignominy, or poverty, or loss of relatives, or disease, or other calamities.[92]

Natural evils also visit the predestined in order to increase their patience: "The Lord has also another end in afflicting his children: to try their patience, and teach them obedience."[93] He adds, "For the scripture applauds the saints for their patience, when they are afflicted with severe calamities, but not broken and overcome by them."[94]

The optimistic Calvin makes some summarizing statements about the discipline of natural evil. He says, "The Lord repeatedly chastises his servants, yet does not deliver them over to death; wherefore they confess that the strokes of his rod were highly beneficial and instructive to them."[95] He admits: "Poverty, considered in itself, is misery; and the same may be said of exile, contempt, imprisonment, ignominy; finally death is of all calamities the last and worst. But with the favor of our God, they are conducive to our happiness."[96] Of ignominy and calamities he says: "We are chargeable with extreme ingratitude if we do not receive them from the hand of the Lord with cheerful resignation."[97]

---

91. Ibid. 1:594.
92. Ibid., 630-31.
93. Ibid., 632.
94. Ibid., 636.
95. Ibid., 592.
96. Ibid., 634.
97. Ibid., 635.

It is plain from all this that Calvin was a true optimist. No trace of pessimism can be found, nor any symptom of meliorism. Evil is not real, which teaching would be denied by both pessimists and meliorists. And not being actual, it is not a thing that needs to be removed, as the meliorist attempts to do. Calvin does what all consistent optimists do: he meets natural evil with resignation and argues for this way of receiving (not dealing with) suffering by stating that "the saints bore these corrections with resignation of soul."[98]

Appraisal of Optimism. Tsanoff says that optimism "is a virtual rejection of the clear point with which we start, and . . . leads not to the solution but to the abandonment of the problem of evil."[99] The problem is abandoned when the optimist asks, "Who are we that we should try to comprehend the ways of God's omnipotence?"[100] It is also abandoned when the optimist states, "God's ways are mysterious and the faithful will be content to leave the mystery unresolved, knowing that God acts for the best."[101]

E. Stanley Jones writes, "Any system that takes your attention off the grim facts of life and creates a shallow optimism by calling attention to butterflies only, is doomed to be sent into an inevitable pessimism as the blows of life fall."[102] This probably does not occur in the case of every optimist who experiences misfortune, but undoubtedly it often happens.

To hold the theory, one must overlook reasonable facts and maintain a forced mental state that reiterates, "I know all is good. I know all is good." Christian Scientists attempt this.

Henry Van Dyke opposes the view of optimism. He writes, "If evil is a nothing, it is a strangely active, positive, and potent nothing with all the qualities of a something."[103]

Evil is often denied because, "When most people, whether theologians or ordinary citizens, ask for a solution of the problem of evil, what they want is some argument to convince them that

---

98. Ibid., 592.
99. Tsanoff, *The Nature of Evil*, 388.
100. Joad, *God and Evil*, 37.
101. Ibid.
102. Jones, *Christ and Human Suffering*, 66-67.
103. Henry Van Dyke, *The Gospel for a World of Sin* (New York: Macmillan Publishing Co., 1899), 22.

206 ◁ A WESLEYAN-HOLINESS THEOLOGY

all evil is really good, either intrinsically or instrumentally."[104] Optimism is seldom if ever arrived at by investigation. Its adherents have already posited a perfectly good universe, one that is the handiwork of God and the object of His immediate direction.

Van Dyke says, "The theories which attempt to account for its [evil's] origin by tracing it to a mere negation or absence of good, raise a larger question than that which they attempt to answer."[105] This more difficult question may be phrased this way: "Since all is good, why does so much of existence appear to be evil? Since imbecility, for example, appears to be evil, why and how is it actually good?"

Tsanoff rightly asks, "If the evils of life are but illusion, is this illusion aught but evil?"[106] Why should a good God desire to put the objects of His affection under such an illusion? Since evil is apparently real, it is hardly our fault if we think it is real. Thus, if evil is only apparent, it is perhaps the fault of God that we labor under the illusion that it is real; and, if this is so, can God be said to be perfectly good?

One of Voltaire's "undoubted joys, during the latter part of his life, was flaying optimists to disclose their unsound substance."[107] Voltaire was a gifted reasoner. He showed their arguments to be unsound indeed. Yet a person of very little reasoning ability can prove optimism to be unsound. But this must be said: it is more plausible than pessimism.

While theological optimism is more plausible than the religious or the philosophical, all forms of optimism fail to understand properly the Christian doctrine of the Incarnation as it relates to the problem caused by the evil aspects of nature.

Melioristic Activism

Meliorism is not simply a view, but a way of life. It does not curse the darkness as does pessimism, nor deny it as does optimism, but it lights at least one small candle to dispel it. Meliorism is the persuasion that "in some sense both good and evil are real,

---

104. Brightman, *A Philosophy of Religion*, 278.
105. Van Dyke, *The Gospel for a World of Sin*, 22.
106. Tsanoff, *The Nature of Evil*, 373.
107. Ibid., 150.

but good is dominant in that the state of affairs in the universe is always susceptible of improvement."[108]

The out-and-out pessimist takes the attitude at the outset that we are defeated, that nature's evils are dominant, that they alone are real, that effort—even technological effort—will not measurably improve existing conditions.

Optimists look lightly upon what "appears" to be evil, avow that only the desirable operations of the natural world are real, and sit back leisurely to meditate on the good and to keep themselves in the state of mind necessary for this view. In one sense they thwart evil: they improve conditions subjectively. For this they deserve higher marks than the pessimists, who grit their teeth and bear their load—or perhaps react with hostility. But consistent optimists, not believing in the real existence of evil, do nothing objectively to improve conditions. Christian Science, for example, discourages vaccinations.

The meliorists, holding that evil as well as good is real, set out to rid a desirable world of its undesirable intruders. Methodism's Harris Franklin Rall reveals a melioristic attitude when he says, "The floods may destroy, but we can halt forest destruction, impound waters, and change the process from destruction to service."[109]

Clarence Beckwith is hoping as extreme meliorists do when he says that "scientific men, working in different fields of research, are confident that all accidents and diseases, and, by wiser economic and sanitary administration, all famines and pestilences will be replaced by healthy, wholesome human life."[110]

John Fiske put Darwin's biological evolution to work theologically, offering the kind of meliorism one often saw before the First World War. Fiske suggested: "From the general analogies furnished in the process of evolution, we are entitled to hope that, as it approaches its goal and man comes nearer to God, the fact of evil will lapse into a mere memory, in which the shadowed past shall serve as a background for the realized glory of the present."[111]

---

108. Brightman, *A Philosophy of Religion*, 276-77.

109. Harris Franklin Rall, *Christianity* (New York: Charles Scribner's Sons, 1944), 334.

110. Clarence Beckwith, *The Idea of God* (New York: Macmillan Publishing Co., 1922), 183.

111. John Fiske, *Through Nature to God* (Boston: Houghton Mifflin and Co., 1990), 55.

Meliorists differ widely in their conception of ultimate reality. This difference is what most distinguishes them. They will be differentiated, therefore, according to their metaphysics. Among meliorists, four principal types of metaphysics have been in play: pluralism, finitism, dualism, and absolutism.

Pluralistic Meliorism contains at least three elements: that both good and evil are actual, that we can and should set ourselves to the task of exterminating the evil, and that there are many qualitatively different[112] ultimate realities. This view suits the philosophy of pragmatism, whose principal exponent was William James.

James says that the alternative between pluralism and monism constitutes "the most pregnant of all the dilemmas of philosophy."[113] The question, he says, is this: "Does reality exist distributively? or collectively?—in the shape of *eaches, everys, anys, eithers?* or only in the shape of an *all* or *whole?*"[114] That reality exists as a whole is monism, or absolutism. James rejects this view, convinced that reality is of many kinds.

His pluralism is derived from his idea of the nature of reality. Whereas absolutists usually hold that reality is static, he says, "The full nature . . . of reality we now believe to be given only in the perpetual flux."[115] This flux, he says, is "continuous from next to next," but "nonadjacent portions of it are separated by parts that intervene, and such separation seems in a variety of cases to work a positive disconnection."[116] Because of the fact that in the continual flux, which is characteristic of reality, there are elements that are "unrelated or related only remotely,"[117] he says that

---

112. Personalistic idealism, popularized in America by Borden Parker Bowne, E. S. Brightman, and A. C. Knudson, and still a view of some significance, is pluralistic quantitatively: it affirms that ultimate reality is composed of a society of persons. Yet it is qualitatively monistic: ultimate reality is only one in kind—personality. It is readily seen that there is a significant difference between this type of pluralism and what we are treating just now, which is the view that ultimate reality is many in kind. It is an inadequacy of Pringle-Pattison's treatment of pluralism, in the last chapter of his *Idea of God,* that he does not sufficiently distinguish between these two types of pluralism.

113. William James, *Some Problems of Philosophy* (London: Longmans, Green and Co., 1924), 114.

114. Ibid.

115. Ibid., 113.

116. Ibid.

117. Ibid.

reality itself is many in kind and not one. It is pulverized, rather than unified.

What place does God have in this pluralistic system? He is only one of the many ultimate realities, one of the ontological eaches.

This God, who is only one of the eaches, is somewhat similar to the other eaches; He is not absolute. James explains: "Yet because God is not the absolute, but is himself a part when the system is conceived pluralistically, his functions can be taken as not wholly dissimilar to those of the other smaller parts—as similar to our functions consequently."[118]

James observes of God that He "works in an external environment, has limits, and has enemies."[119] He explains:

> The finite God whom I contrast with it [absolutism] may conceivably have *almost* nothing outside of himself; he may already have triumphed over and absorbed all but the minutest fraction of the universe; but that fraction, however small, reduces him to the status of a relative being, and in principle the universe is saved from all the irrationalities incidental to absolutism.[120]

In his finitism, James espouses the view that evil as well as good is real. He assumes the reality of good, which, of course, caused no problem in his understanding of existence. But he also faces up to the unwholesome aspects of existence. He speaks of "all those tremendous irrationalities"[121] of the universe. And he says that absolutism, or the traditional belief that God is the Author of all phases of creation, "leaves us wondering why the perfection of the absolute should require such particular hideous forms of life as darken the day for our human imaginations."[122] He also writes of the "tremendous imperfection of all finite experience."[123]

Evil as well as the good, therefore, is a fact of existence. This is the situation. And what is to be our reaction? For James it should not be despair, nor should it be optimistic acquiescence.

---

118. William James, *A Pluralistic Universe* (London: Longmans, Green and Co., 1909), 318.
119. Ibid., 124.
120. Ibid., 125-26.
121. Ibid., 116.
122. Ibid., 117.
123. Ibid.

He holds that we can and should oppose evil. He explains, "Not why evil should exist at all, but how we can lessen the actual amount of it, is the sole question we need to consider."[124]

James's pluralism makes God only one of the many "eaches" of which reality is composed. But in order to be consistent, James should leave God in that minor role. Instead, he brings God back into his scheme to play a quite important role. His God is finite, to be sure, but James is a little cautious in affirming this when he says that "he is finite, either in power or in knowledge, or in both at once."[125] Of course God is finite in pluralism! He is much more finite than in dualism. He is not one of two ultimates, but one among countless qualitatively different ultimate realities. If James, therefore, is going to follow through with the pluralism he sets up, and he thinks to single God out for discussion at all, he should not say that He is finite either in power or in knowledge or in both, but should have no reticence in admitting a distinct finiteness in every respect.

Finitistic Meliorism is a type held by persons who say that natural evil originates in an aspect of God's very nature; God is hence a limited, finite being. Radoslav Tsanoff and E. S. Brightman—especially the latter—figure importantly among finitistic meliorists.

Tsanoff calls his theory "The Gradational View" of the nature of good and evil. He explains, "In this gradational view of things, evil is literally *degradation,* the surrender of the higher to the lower in the scale of being, the effective down-pulling incursion of the lower against the higher."[126]

Although he defines evil as "degradation" or as negative value,[127] he still holds that it, as well as good, is actual. Of good and evil he writes, "We have them both on our hands, both actual."[128] And he explains, "Evil is not 'somehow good,' anymore than sinking is somehow rising. Evil is evil and the opposite of good, contrary in course and direction."[129]

124. Ibid., 124.
125. Ibid., 311.
126. Tsanoff, *The Nature of Evil,* 392.
127. Ibid., 387.
128. Ibid., 388.
129. Ibid., 397.

Although good and evil are opposites and both actual, they are nevertheless gradational and interdependent. Tsanoff hastens to say, "Good and evil are not distinct realities and have no status in isolation; they are always relative to each other." And he adds, "Evil is that ever-present side or factor in the actual world, by resistance to which a possible worthier side or nature affirms itself and gains reality through attainment."[130]

But what view of God accompanies his gradational view of the nature of good and evil? It is a theistic finitism, with evil in the very nature of God. Speaking of the rivalry between good and evil, he says, "This contest is at the heart of things."[131] He makes it more plain when he writes, "Value positive and negative is not to be located in certain areas of existence but in a fundamental and ultimate character of all existence."[132] More precisely still, he observes that "the evil tug is not outside of God or alien to the divine nature, but just as in finite beings so in the cosmic system of them, in God, it is the negative moment, the obverse of positive enhancement and ideal activity."[133]

This finite God is working toward the improvement of the world, for Tsanoff writes: "In God is no stagnant plentitude but plentitude of ideal activity, no dull placidity but ever-heroic redemption of the world from the hazard of settling back. 'My Father worketh hitherto, and I work.' Not less than myself but more is God thus resistant to the evil tug of the down pulling and the inert and the complacent."[134]

Though God is doing more to redeem the world than we can, Tsanoff still leaves much for us to do. In Platonic spirit he writes, "Evil and the perception of it are conditions for heroic recognition and pursuit of value, be it truth, beauty, goodness."[135] He also remarks, "In applying science to the demands of modern industry, man may use the forces of nature as levers for the upbuilding of the higher values."[136]

---

130. Ibid., 104.
131. Ibid.
132. Ibid., 389.
133. Ibid., 400.
134. Ibid., 399-400.
135. Ibid., 400.
136. Ibid., 395.

Speaking now of the part of both God and ourselves in the redemption of the world, he writes in typically melioristic fashion, "The best we have a right to hope, is that the struggle, real and hard enough, is yet not futile, that possibly and in ways at present unknown to us this half-wild and half-saved universe is ever more truly being redeemed."[137]

Perhaps the most articulate finitistic meliorist of the present century is E. S. Brightman. Theistic finitism is the distinguishing feature of his philosophy and theology. He defines theistic finitism as the view "that the will of God does face conditions within divine experience which that will neither created nor approves."[138]

For Brightman, God is finite because in His nature there is an uncreated, eternal, recalcitrant surd, which obstructs God's plans. He explains:

> The present writer began in *The Problem of God* (1930) the development of the idea of a personal God whose finiteness consists in his own internal structure; an eternal unitary personal consciousness whose creative will is limited both by eternal necessities of reason and by eternal experiences of brute fact. These limits he called *The Given*— an aspect of God's consciousness which eternally enters into every moment of the divine experience and into everything that is.[139]

When we study Brightman's theory of value, we find meliorism coupled with finitism. Both good and evil are actual, as we note when he writes, "Some, among them the present writer, think that a rational definition of the evil of evil and of the good of good and of their relations to purpose in the universe would be a genuine solution of the problem."[140] Of evil itself he writes, "So real are the evils of life, that man's first gods were puny, local creatures, sources of highly precarious goods in a world of hostile powers."[141]

137. Ibid., 368.
138. Brightman, *A Philosophy of Religion,* 282.
139. Edgar Sheffield Brightman, *The Finding of God* (New York: Abingdon Press, 1931), 119.
140. Brightman, *A Philosophy of Religion,* 282.
141. Ibid., 248.

His *Philosophy of Religion* contains a section called "Perfection or Perfectibility," in which he takes the position that neither God nor the universe are perfect but that both are perfectible.

From what has been quoted, it can readily be understood that he would write:

> The objection to optimism is that it is not fair to the experience of intrinsic surd evil. The objection to pessimism is that it is not fair to the experience of intrinsic good. The objection often urged against meliorism is that it states the problem and takes a practical attitude toward it, but does not solve it in principle. Yet if any solution is to be found, it must, in view of the fatal objections to other alternatives, be found in some form of meliorism.[142]

Dualistic Meliorism is the view that nature as both good and evil are real, that evil can and should be thwarted, and that evil originates in a discreative power pitted against God. A brief treatment of three dualistic positions will focus this type of theory.

Zoroastrianism, an ancient but now nearly abandoned religion, illustrates dualistic meliorism. Zoroaster, believed to have been born about 600 B.C., held that the universe is under the control of two opposing principles or powers, the one good and other evil. Ahura Mazda, or Ormuzd, is the good power who created the beautiful in us and nature; and Angro Mainyus, or Ahriman, the evil power who matched every good thing with countercreation of something evil.

The good, however, is gradually overcoming the evil and will finally completely triumph over it. The good is now triumphing both by the activity of Ormuzd against the obstructive work of Ahriman and by the active work of the faithful as they join forces with Ormuzd. The gradual victory will result in the final victory of Ormuzd over the power that hampers him. About it Tsanoff writes, "If a grim sense of the moral struggle dictated a dualistic theology to the Zoroastrian, a confident meliorism enabled him to look forward to a monistic[143] finale."[144]

---

142. Ibid., 277.

143. Most authorities, such as Tsanoff and Andrew Seth Pringle-Pattison, do not consider Zoroastrianism as an ultimate dualism. They are correct if its metaphysics is considered in the light of its hope of the triumph of Ormuzd; but as regards existence as it has been and is, and as it is to be for a long while yet, the dualism may be understood as ultimate. Thus the present study of it is as a dualism.

144. Tsanoff, *The Nature of Evil,* 367.

The "Vendidad," which is one of the four parts of their authoritarian book called the *Avesta,* urges a routing of evil:

> Contend constantly against evil, strive in every way to diminish the power of evil; strive to keep pure in the body and mind and so prevent the entrance of evil spirits who are always striving to gain possession of men. Cultivate the soil, drain marshes, destroy dangerous creatures. He who sows the ground with diligence acquires more religious merit than he could gain by a thousand prayers in idleness . . . The man who has constantly contended against evil may fearlessly meet death.[145]

Dualistic meliorism is also advocated by British philosopher-theologian C. E. M. Joad in *God and Evil.* His position is not easily understood, because his view has changed much, as he admits, and because his view was in process as he wrote.

It was not Joad's view of God that led to his theory of good and evil. Rather, his view of good and evil led him to postulate a certain type of God. He writes, "There is good in the world, and there is also evil";[146] both are real. Evil is the aspect of existence that led Joad to reopen the question of whether or not God exists. He says, "Now, paradoxically, it is this fact of one's conviction of the objective reality of evil, that imparts to the mind the disposition to search for God and to turn toward Him when He is found."[147] And he gives it as his own experience: "I do not doubt that in my own case it is the conviction of the pervasiveness and reality of evil that has led me . . . to examine again the arguments which seem to me to tell finally and convincibly against the theistic hypothesis some thirty years ago, in the hope that what seemed convincing then may now seem convincing no longer."[148]

Joad looks upon both good and evil as real and posits two different ultimates that cause these opposites. He says:

> The religious hypothesis, if it were to be accepted at all must be accepted not in its usual form, but in a form which has always been regarded as heresy. This consists in accepting good and evil as two equal and independent principles, the expression of two equally real and conceivably

---

145. Martin, *Great Religious Teachers of the East,* 88.

146. Joad, *God and Evil,* 101. The author and publisher made every effort to locate the owner or the owner's agent for permission to use the material from this source. Appropriate recognition of the copyright holder, if known, will be included in any reprintings.

147. Ibid., 63.

148. Ibid., 101.

equally powerful antagonists, God who is good but limited, and God's adversary who is evil, between whom the perpetual battle is fought in the hearts of men for the governance of the world.[149]

He also writes, "If a metaphysical principle is to be invoked to explain good, an equivalent principle must be invoked to explain the evil; if, to put it theologically, there is God, there is also the Devil, or there is God plus a principle of inertia which obstructs him."[150] He further elucidates, "If we are to go beyond simple agnosticism, then what must be surmised is that there are two Gods, a good one and a bad; or, since the notion of a bad God is revolting and not absolutely necessary, there must be a good God and an obstructive hampering principle in and through and in spite of which He seeks to work."[151] This hampering principle is not something within God's own nature against which He must labor; it is outside of God. Thus his dualism.

It has been shown that for Joad both good and evil are real, and that God and His opposite are the respective sources of each. It remains to substantiate his meliorism. In this connection he elaborates:

> It follows that either one must supinely acquiesce in the evil one cannot resolve, or else—there are two alternatives.
>
> The first, since the world is evil, is to escape from it and to find, first in withdrawal, and, as an ultimate hope, in Nirvana, the true way of life. The second is to face evil and seek to overcome it, even to take it up and absorb it into one's own life, transcending it and enlarging one's own personality with what one has transcended. The first is the way of the East, the second of Christianity. My temperament and disposition incline me to the second, but I know it to be impossible unless I am assisted from without. By the grace of God we are assured, such assistance may be obtained and evil may be overcome.[152]

Yet another type of dualism is that espoused in his last years by the American Methodist theologian Edwin Lewis. His theory is

---

149. Ibid., 85-86.
150. Ibid., 191.
151. Ibid., 101.
152. Ibid., 104.

set out in *The Creator and the Adversary,* much of which deals
with natural evil.

Lewis is not a pessimist: he would be among the last to deny
the desirable features of the world. Nor is he an optimist, for he is
profoundly aware of nature's seamy side. Lewis conceives of both
good and evil as real. He writes, "The presence of good and evil,
both in the world itself and in human life and experience, is too
self-evident to be denied."[153]

Lewis perceives vividly the conflict between good and evil.
He observes, "Cosmic benevolence stands in contrast with cosmic
malevolence."[154] He also says, "On any showing, life is a conflict
and the world is a battlefield."[155] Again he writes, "Something
good is forever coming to be, and something is forever seeking to
prevent it."[156] This conflict is waged by God the Creator and His
adversary, the discreator.

In Lewis's understanding, the conflict is real, and the two opponents are eternally and intrinsically and structurally opposed.
It is not that the Creator sets up His adversary in order to oppose
him; the Creator eternally finds His adversary.

Lewis's position is classed as dualistic, because the battle between two absolutes is eternal. However, his is an ultimate tri-
adology rather than an ultimate dualism. Besides the Creator and
His adversary there is a third ultimate existent. This he calls the
"residue" or the "residual constant." By it he means "the permanent possibility of empiric actualities."[157] That is, it is the eternal
formless stuff out of which the Creator creates. It is "constant"
because it "never increases or diminishes in its total quantity."[158]

Back of these three ultimate and prime existents is prime existence. This "existence," or "pure existence," "is under a necessary law of self-differentiation."[159] It functions in the three primal
forms as explained above. He writes, "There is one eternal existence, but it exists as three eternal existents."[160] Lewis admits that

---

153. Lewis, *The Creator and the Adversary,* 15. Adapted by permission of Abingdon Press.
154. Ibid.
155. Ibid.
156. Ibid., 52.
157. Ibid., 143.
158. Ibid.
159. Ibid., 141.
160. Ibid., 142.

this is highly speculative but believes it necessary if one is to give an adequate account of existence as we know it.

How should we humans react to this type of existence? Lewis holds that we should not despair, since there is always the good. Nor would he say that we should call the evil a result of God's direct will and acquiesce to it. His is an aggressive meliorism. Chapter 11 of the book is captioned, "The Challenge to Moral Combat." In it he writes, "The will of God in respect of famine is that the hungry shall still be fed, and that means shall be devised whereby famine, like wars, shall be made to cease to the ends of the earth."[161] He also says, "The surgeon who makes an incision in quivering human flesh to remove a malignant growth, lessen suffering, and perchance save a life, is not seeking to frustrate the will of God, as men at one time actually thought and said."[162] Again he writes:

> A speaker who called upon the American people to cease believing in God because seventeen million persons now living would die of cancer would have made a much better and a much wiser use of his time had he called upon the American people to join with God in the fight against cancer by the use of the means which God is seeking to put into their hands for his purpose, *because the only way in which God can use the means is through human minds and hands.* "We are laborers together with God."[163]

In the last chapter, titled "The Church Militant," Lewis says that "there is nothing the Church more manifestly exists to do than to fight the enemy of human good."[164] Lewis gives Jesus as an example to be followed in combating natural evil. Of the "mighty works" of our Lord he says, "They were directed against pain, against disease, against maimed bodies, against hunger, against the griefs that are born of these evils, and even, on occasion, against death itself."[165] And he adds, "For Jesus these were not the evidences of the will of God but the denial of his will."[166]

---

161. Ibid.
162. Ibid.
163. Ibid., 149-50.
164. Ibid., 259.
165. Ibid., 266.
166. Ibid.

Lewis advocates an active confrontation of evil in the faith that one day, God and man working together, righteousness will so prevail that God's children will be granted a state of existence—eternal life—which the adversary will not be able to touch. The promise of the Creator's ultimate victory is in the Cross, in which the Creator and the adversary came to a death grapple and in which the Creator was victorious, since the "defeat" of the Cross was succeeded by the resurrection of the adversary's Victim.

This dualistic meliorism of Lewis has the merit of being a frank facing of the problem of natural evil, and it is one of the most vigorous calls of recent times for an all-out campaign for the extermination of evil. Its chief inadequacies are that it conceives of matter as eternal and views Satan as God's eternally existent adversary.

Absolutistic Meliorism. Pluralism, finitism, and dualism have at least one element in common: they all affirm that God is limited. One of them, finitism, locates the limitation within God's nature, and the other two postulate it as external to God; but all agree that He is limited.

Opposed to this "limited God" theory is the view of absolutism. This is the view that God is unlimited in such attributes as goodness, wisdom, and power. Absolutistic meliorism is the theory that although God is unlimited, we can and should engage ourselves as coworkers with Him to alleviate or even exterminate the evils in nature.

Some might question connecting absolutism with meliorism. It might be thought that belief in an unlimited God precludes belief in the radical reality of evil and in our obligation to thwart it as we are able to. It is hoped, however, that as the treatment progresses, the compatibility of the terms will become evident.

An outstanding representative of absolutistic meliorism is Andrew Seth Pringle-Pattison. Since he constructed his own views by the criticism of the positions of others,[167] the task of ex-

---

167. Of this methodology he writes, "This method of construction through criticism is the one which I have instinctively followed in everything I have written [this was in 1916]. I do not claim that it is the best method; I simply desire that its nature be recognized" (Pringle-Pattison, *The Idea of God in the Light of Recent Philosophy* [New York: Oxford University Press, 1920], preface, vii). It will henceforth be called simply *The Idea of God.*

tracting his own views is tedious but possible. Especially helpful are his Gifford Lectures, *The Idea of God in the Light of Recent Philosophy.*

Pringle-Pattison is not pluralistic, nor finitistic, nor dualistic; he is absolutistic. But he is not an absolutist of the Aristotelian sort; his God is not an Eternal Thinker,[168] contemplatively detached from the world. Nor is he an absolutist typified by Philo, whose absolute was inaccessible and unknowable. Pringle-Pattison writes, "Hence when Philo came, as a philosopher, to consider the relation of God to the world, the fact most present to his mind was the gulf between the two. God was so great as to be beyond the reach of our thought, exalted beyond any categories we could frame."[169] He conceives of the Absolute as closely related to us and the world.

Pringle-Pattison is an absolutist of the pantheistic type. He emphasizes the immanence of God with us and nature. He even affirms that the relationship is so close that neither exists nor can exist without the other. He writes:

But as soon as we begin to treat God and man as two independent facts, we lose our hold upon the experienced fact, which is the existence of the one in the other and through the other. Most people would probably be willing to admit this mediated existence in the case of man, but they might feel it akin to a sacrilege to make the same assertion of God. And yet, if our metaphysic is, as it professes to be, an analysis of experience, the implication is strictly reciprocal.[170]

This is pantheism, but of a higher type than that of Spinoza and others. Pringle-Pattison calls it higher pantheism or higher naturalism.[171]

Yet God is not so closely related to the world that His identity is lost. He does exist, and He is infinite in power, wisdom, and goodness.

---

168. He writes, "And the purely intellectual character of Aristotle's ideal gives it the same aloofness we have noted from the world's life. It is the ideal of the scholar and thinker who retires into his own thoughts, and finds there his highest happiness" (*The Idea of God,* 408).
169. Brightman, *A Philosophy of Religion,* 197.
170. Pringle-Pattison, *The Idea of God,* 254.
171. Ibid., chapter 5 in particular.

Toward a View of Natural Evil

A proper view of the problem of natural evil, of why the righteous and innocent suffer, has several elements in it.

Absolutistic Meliorism is one element. God should be viewed as absolute—as long as this does not mean that He is removed from us and untouched by our troubles. God is infinite in His nature, and in the wisdom and goodness and power that are outworkings of that nature. He is not finite in any of the senses studied in this chapter, nor is He beset by an eternal and uncreated evil opposite, nor by many eternal opposites, as in James's pluralism.

At the same time, creation's desirable aspects, as well as its undesirable ones, are both actual. It is ours to work with the God of infinite resources in promoting the good and in thwarting, or at least hindering, the evil.

The Light from Arminianism. A proper view of righteous and innocent suffering should also be in keeping with the Arminian tradition in theology—close to Arminius himself, and not to the overly tolerant and liberal wing of Arminianism. This Arminian orientation means that we do not believe (as Calvin did) that God is the absolutely sovereign One who directly orders whatever happens. We understand that He works often through secondary causes, mediately, instead of by direct fiat. He works through what we popularly call natural laws: instances of natural evil occur because of the laws of nature—as in tornadoes, hurricanes, floods, and earthquakes, for examples.

God, as all-powerful, can work miracles whereby natural laws are set aside; and in graciousness, He sometimes does work miracles on behalf of His people. Yet the righteous and innocent often get sucked into natural laws and their devastation, even as the wicked do. In those cases, God does not directly order the frustration in the lives of righteous and innocent persons. He permits them only in a remotely removed sense: by establishing natural laws, which usually work for our good, and which are better for us than a topsy-turvy world without them would be—in which, say, there would not be any way of predicting the direction in which a leaning tree would fall when cut.

Scripture suggests that God usually works mediately, through secondary causes, instead of by direct fiat. He created Eve in that way, using Adam's side, not creating her outright. And once He had the first pair, He created other humans through the human reproductive process.

Leading His people through judges and speaking to them through called prophets are instances of God working with people through intermediaries.

Besides this, and even as part of all this, God orders His world through human beings who are free either to do His will or to oppose His will. This is basic to an Arminian type of theology. We humans really can and often do thwart God's will. Though God is absolutely sovereign, this does not mean that He directly orders whatever happens on the earth. He persuades rather than drives, and He gets only more or less the ideal of what He had in mind. This is so in the moral sphere, and it is so also in the natural sphere. An Arminian does not talk about lightning or tornadoes or floods or other instances of natural evil as "acts of God" —as Calvinism does.

With this kind of understanding, an Arminian does not say to bereaved parents that for some strange and inscrutable reason God took their small girl who was run over when she fell through a hole in the floor of a pickup truck. The Arminian understands that God is not the one who does what we humans are too good to do, but instead He is on the sufferer's side as a refuge and source of strength in the midst of the sorrysome circumstance— which God did not want to happen any more than we did.

Light from Natural Laws. Many of the involuntary frustrations of the ideal existence of innocent and righteous persons arise from the operation of what we often call natural laws—although natural laws as such have been somewhat brought into question by the theory of relativity and by quantum physics. No matter what our metaphysics, and regardless of our type of religion, we must, since we are living in these times rather than in ancient or medieval times, recognize the regularly established procedures of nature.

We cannot, therefore, ascribe the results of every accident to the direct will of God. We realize, for example, that automobile accidents cause suffering and untimely death because the law of the inertia of motion usually remains in effect even when innocent and twice-born persons are involved.

No longer can we ascribe the results of every fire to the direct will of God. We know that when the kindling point of combustible materials is reached, a fire will likely begin, even though it will cause suffering to persons who do not particularly deserve it.

No longer can we attribute every fall from a precipice to the direct will of God. We know that if a child or a twice-born person steps on a loose rock, stumbles, and falls into a mountain gorge, the likelihood is that he or she will be killed. The law of gravity, be that law conceived in theory as Newton stated it or as Einstein has put it more recently, will probably remain in effect, the type of person notwithstanding.

No longer do we ascribe tornadoes and tidal waves to the direct will of God. We know they occur because heat from the sun, intensified at times by natural causes, expands the gases that make up our air. The warmed air rises, and cold air replaces it, causing a wind, sometimes so violent that we call it a tornado and occasionally so strong that it produces devastating tidal waves we call hurricanes. Nor can we look upon floods as the direct will of God. Several natural laws operate in causing them and, consequently, the tragic evil they precipitate.

This "natural laws" phase of what is being called a proper response to natural evil accords with the view that involuntary evil is radically actual, because these natural laws really occasion what obstructs the ideal fulfillment of the lives of innocent and righteous persons. It also accords with the view that God is absolute: His infinite power and wisdom are seen in the extensive orderliness the natural laws make possible; and His infinite goodness, if not seen directly in each operation of these laws, is seen in their total function, since they make possible an orderly world rather than a chaotic one, and one that most people would surely think of as the more desirable.

Light from the Fall. A fall in the natural world, to suit the environment to the now-fallen Adam and his posterity, occasions natural evil that is organic—the kind that visits us through organisms such as germs and viruses, poisonous reptiles, ferocious beasts, and mosquitoes. These appear to have originated through a fall in organic creation.

Such organic media of frustration do not appear to be a part of creation as we read of it in chapter 1 of Genesis. After each creative day, in that account, it is declared that what was made was good; and of the aggregate of creation, at the close of the account of it, it was affirmed: "And God saw all that He had made, and behold, it was very good" (Gen. 1:31, NASB).

But what does not appear to be included in the geological ages of creation prior to our creation and our initial sin is evidently introduced as a result of human disobedience. To Eve, Yahweh says: "I will greatly multiply your pain in childbirth, in pain you shall bring forth children" (Gen. 3:16, NASB). And to Adam He says, "Because you have listened to the voice of your wife, and have eaten from the tree about which I commanded you, saying, 'You shall not eat from it'; cursed is the ground because of you; in toil you shall eat of it all the days of your life. Both thorns and thistles it shall grow for you" (vv. 17-18, NASB).

Evils resulting from natural laws and evils consequent upon the Fall are both consistent with absolutism.

Light from the Incarnation. Though the Incarnation is not of direct bearing on why natural evils occur, it is nevertheless of indirect bearing on that matter. With the doctrine of the Incarnation as a presupposition, our answer to the theoretical problem of natural evil will not be pessimistic. Through the Incarnation, we have unveiled to us the very God whom some did not find and have consequently espoused views of despair. The Incarnation also precludes optimism, because what God did through the Incarnation in the natural realm, such as healing diseased and maimed persons, is evidence that involuntary evils are not of God's will. And the God revealed to us by the Word made flesh does not appear to be limited in any of the ways claimed by the finitists; He is one for whom "all things are possible" (Matt. 19:26, NASB).

Some of the optimists and meliorists we studied believed in the Incarnation but did not give it the significance it deserves in the solution of the problem of natural evil. John Calvin certainly affirmed the Incarnation in its Chalcedon formulation; but for him it was important mainly as a means to the death of Christ, which made expiation for the moral evil. Calvin looked upon every natural phenomenon as the direct will of God. There is no radical evil in nature, according to this view; nothing has gone wrong, and nothing will ever go wrong. All apparent natural evil is the will of God, and if we cannot understand why He wills certain aspects of it, we should not question His wisdom in directing phenomena in that manner. With this prior, optimistic attitude toward the apparent evils of nature, the Incarnation could not be understood as a significant agent in the solution of the problem caused by natural evils, but at the most as a condition of the divine plan for the moral redemption of that segment of mankind who is predestined to life everlasting.

Meliorist Edwin Lewis affirmed the Incarnation in its traditional, radical character. He said that "God does not stay in his heaven, as one 'sitting apart, contemplating all,' but enters the arena of conflict as a personal participant."[172] He also wrote, "God becomes man."[173] And he said, "For by the Incarnation, God the Father in the person of God the Son . . . receives to himself the worst that evil can do."[174] He speaks of "his [God's] actual participation in the creative strife by means of the incarnation of the Word, known among us as Jesus Christ the only-begotten Son of God."[175]

And the Incarnation, in its traditional, radical character, is for Edwin Lewis of a certain significance in the solution of the problem of natural evil: it is through becoming flesh that God is able to "match His Adversary"[176] in the arena where that discreator has brought about natural evil.

But in the view of Lewis, it is not primarily the Incarnation itself that is the instrument whereby God seeks to alleviate the world of such evil; the prime method whereby God combats it is through the death of Christ, which death assured the gradual redemption of natural evil because it was succeeded by the Resurrection.

Andrew Seth Pringle-Pattison believes that the doctrine of the Incarnation should be understood as pointing toward an answer to the problem of suffering. As we read through his theodicy, we find that the Incarnation is given a prominent place in the solution of the difficulty arising from natural evil. For example, by emphasis upon the doctrine of the Incarnation, Pringle-Pattison is able to give a Christian tone to his "higher naturalism."[177] Also, because God is understood as having entered our sphere in order

---

172. Lewis, *The Creator and the Adversary*, 153.
173. Ibid., 154.
174. Ibid.
175. Ibid., 176.
176. Ibid., 174.
177. Pringle-Pattison, *The Idea of God*, 209.

to fight with us, Pringle-Pattison is able to affirm that God is interested in us, suffers with us, and leads us into a type of life in which suffering is overcome.[178]

Yet Pringle-Pattison's view of the Incarnation is inadequate. According to him, God is already, by metaphysical status, linked organically to humanity. It is not that God the Father, through the person of God the Son, enters the arena of conflict; it is that God, only one in person, is always here, in the conflict, not by any sacrifice, but by His permanent, ontological mode of existence. He speaks of the error of "dividing the functions of deity between the Father and the Son, conceived practically as two distinct personalities or centers of consciousness, the Father perpetuating the old monarchical ideal and the incarnation of the Son being limited to a single historical individual."[179] This reveals his denial of the distinction of personalities in the Godhead, a denial that makes impossible both the Trinity and the Incarnation.

Another group of theologians, whose views have not been studied earlier, give too much significance to the Incarnation in the solutions they offer to the problem of natural evil, because they all say the Incarnation has already abolished natural evil.

One of these is the ancient Irenaeus (ca. A.D. 130-ca. 202). Nature's ills, according to him, were corrected by the One who came for the express purpose of recapitulating—or re-creating, re-making—both fallen humanity and the fallen world. This is something that has already been accomplished: all of creation, both human and natural, has been remade. Restored to its prefallen condition, it is supposedly perfect in all its aspects. The empirical fact of continuing natural evil makes it impossible for us to accept Irenaeus' view. We simply do not experience a perfected world.

Athanasius is another ancient theologian who placed the same kind of overemphasis on the Incarnation. He would rather use "re-creation" or "renewal" than "recapitulation," but by these terms he meant to denote virtually the same idea. All aspects of nature have already been quickened. He says that "straightway [because of the Incarnation] all things were set right and perfect."[180]

---

178. Ibid., 409-17.
179. Ibid., 409.
180. *On Luke 10:20*, sec. 2.

But again, the ills are still here. The cobra is still a menace to missionaries and their children. There is still an abundance of microbes to bring misery to the innocent and the twice-born the world over.

Certain rather recent theologians have likewise presented an overemphasis upon the Incarnation in relation to natural evil. One of them is Sergius Bulgakov (1871-1943). Bulgakov is an Orthodox theologian in the tradition of Irenaeus and Athanasius. Although he did not give them prominent mention as sources of his theology of natural evil, he quite evidently used them in his oft-treated idea of deification, which is a degree of godlikeness found, through the merits of the Incarnation, in both humans and nature. This "deification," as it applies to nature, is a complete redemption of it from its fallen state.

Again, as in Irenaeus and Athanasius, but with more detailed statement than can be found in their writings, it is a redemption that has already been accomplished. The principal criticism, therefore, of this system, as with the earlier ones, is that the Incarnation is supposed to have already redeemed creation.

In still more elaborate detail, Lionel Thornton taught that nature has been already redeemed by the Incarnation. In spite of his philosophical optimism, and regardless of his detailed teaching that the re-creation of nature has already taken place, Thornton does maintain a quite healthy meliorism, in which he urges us to work with God in effecting the redemption of nature. Because of this view, his position, in comparison with that of the other three incarnationalists just discussed, more nearly approximates the incarnational answer that the writer will now present.

The Incarnation might be thought of as the event whereby redemption is made for natural evil; the Crucifixion, as the event whereby redemption is made for moral evil; and the Resurrection, as the event whereby the worth of both the Incarnation and the Crucifixion is validated (as Karl Barth would say). By these events, as Allan Galloway says, "Christ restored all evil to a place within the intrinsic meaning of the world."[181]

But surely our redemption from moral evil, through the death of Christ, is only provisional. Not all people everywhere, re-

---

181. Allan D. Galloway, *The Cosmic Christ* (New York: Harper and Brothers Publishers, 1951), 259.

gardless of their attitude toward Christ, are redeemed from sin; only those who by faith personally appropriate to themselves the redemption provided are redeemed.

Similarly, our redemption from natural evil is only provisional. The Incarnation does no more than make it a possibility; it only points out, particularly to those who come to be redeemed from moral evil, the way of redemption from natural frustration. We must, on our own part, as the condescended God assists us, make actual what is by that event only made provisional. This redemption becomes actual only as we take advantage of the fact that God is metaphysically one-with-us, thus near us; and experientially one-with-us, thus understanding of our predicaments; and as we see that He is consequently able and willing to assist us in preventing natural frustrations and in transforming them into creativity if the prevention measures fail and such evils still intrude themselves into our lives.

Through the Incarnation, God has become metaphysically one-with-us. The metaphysical wall of partition, because of this event, has been abolished, so that there is no longer a chasm between us, as finite existents in the universe, and God as the supreme, infinite Existent. It is not that we have become gods, or deified, as Irenaeus, Athanasius, and others have maintained; it is that God, although still existing as the Transcendent One, has become what we are and has in this way bridged the metaphysical chasm between himself and us. The writer of John's Gospel says that "the Word became flesh, and dwelt among us" (1:14, NASB). And Paul wrote of Christ, "Who, although He existed in the form of God, did not regard equality with God a thing to be grasped, but emptied Himself, taking the form of a bond-servant" (Phil. 2:6-7, NASB).

Through the Incarnation, also, God has become experientially one-with-us. The writer of John and the author of the Epistle to the Hebrews have a more profound conception of this experiential oneness than do the other New Testament writers. But if the others did not stress it as much, and even if some of the others did not mention it at all, none of the New Testament writers denied this corollary truth of the Incarnation. This means that those of us today who walk with God and whose ideal lives tend to become frustrated by involuntary evil can be assured that the God who, in Christ, came down to be metaphysically one-with-us went through frustrating experiences when He was in this sphere and therefore knows our experiences on the basis of like ones that came to Him.

Since God, therefore, through the Incarnation is both metaphysically and experientially one-with-us, and since we know that natural evils are not in each instance His direct will but occur through natural laws and the Fall in the natural world, we can be certain that He will assist us in our efforts to prevent involuntary frustrations. Because of His metaphysical oneness with us, we can know that God is not the Wholly There, the Wholly Then, but the Wholly Here, the Wholly Now; and since He is this, we can be assured that we will have His help in preventing involuntary frustrations. Further, because of His experiential oneness with us, we know He understands both the strain of the task and what the impending evil will be like if the prevention measures do not succeed. God thus rides in our machines when we build dams and levees. He is in our heaving when we make a levee of sandbags to prevent a flood's devastation. God rides with pilots out into the hurricane eyes hundreds of miles off the coast of Florida as they seek an early knowledge of a coming wind so that preparations for it can be made.

God is predisposed to be with us whenever we seek to prevent natural evils. Sometimes He is present to give us guidance as when, through prayer, a person seeks to learn which of alternative prevention measures should be employed. Occasionally direct revelational assistance may be given, as for the research scientist who needs but one key for unlocking a door that, when opened, will permit exploring new territory and finally learning ways of preventing some means of human frustration such as a disease. But whether God is with us for guidance, special revelational assistance, or other helps, a proper conception of the Incarnation assures us that He is always near and always humanly sympathetic.

In like manner, since God is metaphysically and experientially one-with-us, and since natural evils are not His direct will, He assists us when they have not been prevented and they flood in upon us. At such times, the God of natural laws and the Fall in organic creation becomes, because of the still-in-effect Incarnation, the God who knows something about their frustrating effects and who is therefore able and willing to assist righteous persons in transforming such frustrations into what is creative.

The Christian doctrine of the Incarnation, then, has only an indirect bearing on the theoretical problem of why natural evil exists, but it has a most direct bearing on the solution of the life-situation problem of preventing natural evil and of reacting to it creatively when it comes calling.

This view of the Incarnation, coupled with the absolutism espoused earlier in this chapter, makes conceivable the hope of most people of every age, that righteousness will finally triumph over all evil. John the Revelator expressed this hope when he wrote:

> And I saw a new heaven and a new earth; for the first heaven and the first earth passed away, and there is no longer any sea. And I saw the holy city, new Jerusalem, coming down out of heaven from God, made ready as a bride adorned for her husband. And I heard a loud voice from the throne, saying, "Behold, the tabernacle of God is among men, and He shall dwell among them . . . and He shall wipe away every tear from their eyes; and there shall no longer be any death; there shall no longer be any mourning, or crying, or pain; the first things have passed away" (Rev. 21:1-4, NASB).

Having treated the doctrine of creation in the previous chapter, and in this chapter the corollary problem of natural evil, we are prepared to study the doctrine of ourselves.

9

The Doctrine of Ourselves

The doctrine of ourselves will be treated in this order: our origin, the problem of abortion, God's image in us, conscience, the elements of our nature, human freedom, and predestination.

Our Origin

Our creation was treated in chapter 7. There support was presented for the classical Christian view that we were created by God, as opposed to the view that we have evolved by the natural process of mutation as organisms that have spread out and survived by being peculiarly fit and environmentally adaptable.

The Origin of the Soul. This is an aspect of our origin not treated in that earlier chapter. Several views have competed.

1. *Preexistence* is the view that our souls existed in an earlier life and are now embodied. Plato taught that our souls existed previously; in that existence we freely transgressed the laws of heaven and are now in evil physical bodies as a way of winning our redemption from the earlier disobedience. Only Origen, among significant Christian theologians, taught the soul's preexistence—a theologian far too much influenced by Platonic philosophy.

2. *Creationism* used in this connection is the view that God now creates all souls individually to accompany the bodies that originate from their parents. Reformed theology, with its teachings about God's absolute sovereignty, has tended to favor this view.

3. *Traducianism* is the view that the soul as well as the body originates through the parents. This is the usual view among Arminians. It suits Arminianism's understanding that God often works mediately, instead of immediately. It is in keeping with the biblical teaching that God created Adam outright but used Adam's

rib or side to create Eve—creating her mediately. And it is in keeping with the biblical teaching that whereas God created the pair, the race has been continued and extended by human reproduction. Scripture never differentiates between how the body and the soul arise; they seem therefore to arise in the same way.

Traducianism also has at least four other special advantages. (1) God is not directly involved in the conception of a child outside of marriage. (2) God does not directly create a soul tainted by original sin. (3) Traducianism does not bifurcate a human being into body or soul, with different origins for these two aspects of our nature. (4) Traducianism does not imply that the body is unimportant, coming from the parents, and that the soul is important, originating from God's creation power. Scripture unifies human nature and does not teach that the body has a less divine origin than does the soul.

Our Unitary Origin. Many areas of evidence figure in Christian theology's usual understanding that we humans have a common origin, a common parentage, a common stock. Gen. 1:27 seems to suggest this: "So God created man in his own image . . . male and female he created them." And Gen. 3:20 says, "Adam named his wife Eve, because she would become the mother of all the living." Soon we are reading in Genesis that from Adam and Eve came Cain (4:1) and Abel (4:2) and Seth (5:3). Then Adam is said to have lived 800 more years after Seth's birth and to have "had other sons and daughters." This seems to suggest that all humans came from Adam and Eve, as does the passage in Acts 17:26, where we read, "From one man he made every nation of men, that they should inhabit the whole earth."

Several scientific facts also suggest this common origin: the commonality in humans of length of pregnancy, vertebrate formation, body temperature, life expectancy, and blood types (interchangeable in all three races); and the fact that whatever the type of racial intermarriage, no hybrids are produced (demonstrating that humans are all of one species). Less certainly supportable as evidences of the common origin of all humans is the suggestion of many philologists that there seems to have been a common origin of the world's 3,000 or so languages. There are also certain evidences of a common religiosity.

The Matter of Abortion

Discussion of human origin requires that the matter of abortion should be treated here, especially because it has become so widespread, so legal, and often so trivial.

Varying Reasons for Aborting. Factors that tend to encourage abortion are numerous and vary in their intensity. Among the less significant ones are (1) lack of financial means to rear a child, or an extra child beyond the planned number; (2) it would threaten the mother's career to birth and rear a child; (3) a marriage would be threatened if one or both marriage partners had not wished a child; (4) the mother (and/or father) is too young for the responsibility; and (5) the mother is not married.

More serious factors also tend to encourage abortion. The fetus might be a product of incest, adultery, or rape. Or the mother might have had German measles during the first part of the gestation period. Or drugs might have been ingested that multiply the chances that the child would be deformed—or tests revealed that the fetus is indeed deformed.

No doubt the most serious single factor that indicates abortion is that continuance of the pregnancy is a threat to the very life of the mother. Many Protestants, who might be ever so pro-life in their views, believe that the fetus should be aborted in this circumstance—although recent medical finds suggest that the situation is more rare than was previously thought, and that there is perhaps never a case in which it would be known that the mother would certainly die.

When Human Life Begins. This is the all-important question. If the fetus is not an individual human being when it is intentionally aborted, its destruction is less serious. The proabortion advocates tend to deny that it is a human being. Often it is said that the fetus is simply tissue, "a tiny piece" of the mother's body. Marya Mannes says, "Suddenly, the expulsion of a tiny piece of a woman's body is called criminal because long ago, after learned discussions, men determined that this tiny piece was Life, and its expulsion murder."[1]

---

1. Marya Mannes, "A Woman Views Abortion," in Allan F. Guttmacher, ed., *The Case for Legalized Abortion Now* (Berkeley, Calif.: Diablo Press, 1967), 7.

There are numerous bases for viewing the fetus as a human individual from conception onward. As far as we know, nothing happens between conception and birth that essentially alters the fetus's life. Since the chromosomes are already present at conception, the later changes are only more or less quantitative and not qualitative.[2] Even birth produces no qualitative step-up. At that time, respiration and nutrition occur by direct contact with the environment, instead of by an indirect contact with it, but that is about all.

The new specialty of fetology is being replaced by the still-newer specialty of perinatology, because an individual just keeps on developing before and after birth. Birth makes the doctor's patient much more accessible, of course, but it is not the beginning of the patient's individual existence.

The fact of the possibility of a united ovum and sperm dividing, up to 14 days from conception, forming identical twins, presents a certain problem to the view that the whole person, including whatever survives death, is begun at conception. But since twins result from genetic patterning already set up, perhaps two persons are present, or potentially present, at such a conception, even as two biological organisms are present or potentially present.

Actually, civil laws for many decades have recognized the fetus's individuality. In 1795 an English court included an unborn child in the womb as one who shared in a will, and American courts have adopted that interpretation.

Scripture seems to teach that the fetus is an individual human being. In Gen. 5:3 we read that Adam "became the father of a son in his own likeness, after his image" (RSV). H. Orton Wiley, referring to the "begat" that appears in the King James Version, interprets the passage to mean that "it is the whole man who begets and is begotten."[3] Furthermore, if the soul as well as the body comes from the parents, as suggested earlier, the soul is probably present as soon as both parents have contributed their ovum and sperm to the formation of a zygote. That is, it is then a human being.

---

2. Cf. Andre E. Hellengers, "Fetal Development," *Theological Studies* 31 (March 1970): 3-9.

3. H. Orton Wiley, *Christian Theology* 2:29.

Scripture often implies that a fetus is a human individual. Isaiah says, "The Lord called me from the womb" (49:1, RSV). Paul says, "He who had set me apart before I was born, and had called me through his grace, was pleased to reveal his Son to me" (Gal. 1:15-16, RSV). An angel tells Zechariah that his son, John the Baptist, would be "filled with the Holy Spirit, even from his mother's womb" (Luke 1:15, RSV). A Psalmist called himself a "me," a self, a human being, when referring to the time of his conception, saying, "In sin did my mother conceive me" (51:5, RSV). In Ps. 139:13 we read, "Thou didst knit me together in my mother's womb" (RSV). That we are persons before birth, in the womb, is implied when Yahweh says to Jeremiah: "Before I formed you in the womb I knew you, before you were born I set you apart; I appointed you as a prophet to the nations" (Jer. 1:5). And Jeremiah says: "For he did not kill me in the womb, with my mother as my grave" (20:17).

The Question of Rights. This is another significant factor in the abortion issue. Spokespersons for "women's rights" often suggest that opposition to abortion is opposition to the rights of women. Howard Moody deplores "unending disputes about embryonic and fetal life in the womb which would prevent us from dealing with a woman's immediate existential question of what to do with *her* life in the world."[4] Moody also asks, "Is it right to force the unwanted on the unwilling?"[5]

Yet surely the right to life itself is more basic than any other right. It is more basic than the woman's right to emotional poise, to privacy, to continue to work outside the home, or to be free of the responsibility of a given child, or to love and be loved by a husband who threatens to abscond if a child is added to the family, or to love and rear only the previous children whom perhaps she had planned for. Assuming that the fetus is a person, his or her right to life is a more basic one and ought to take precedence. If any of the reasons for aborting, short of the protection of the mother's right to life, make abortion permissible, any of them would make infanticide permissible—and yet no one argues for infanticide.

---

4. Howard Moody, "Abortion: Woman's Right and Legal Problem," *Christianity and Crisis* 31 (Mar. 8, 1971): 27.
5. Ibid., 28.

Other Matters That Figure. Several matters need to be discussed that figure only extraneously in the problem of abortion.

One is that abortions might cause more mental problems than they solve. One author says: "There are no known psychiatric diseases which can be cured by abortion. In addition, there are none which can be predictably improved by abortion."[6] An interesting fact is that "the suicide rate in the pregnant woman is extremely rare . . . about 1/6 the rate in nonpregnant women of the same age."[7]

Another thing: instead of proabortionists being progressive, as they often claim, they might be instead retrogressive, because primitive societies have practiced even infanticide, and abortion might be infanticide by extension.

Also, in advanced societies the strong protect the weak. The fetus, surely, is among the very weak and deserves protection.

Further, if the new Malthusianism of Paul Ehrlich and others inclines us toward abortions as a way of controlling population, surely contraception is where that control ought to begin.

And adoption might be more feasible than we have sometimes thought. While statistics vary from year to year, there are always more couples who want to adopt babies than can be supplied with them.[8]

Further, the early development of biological systems in the gestation period suggests that the fetus is an individual human being. The heart starts irregular pulsations at 24 days, which become regular in about a week. By the end of the second month, an embryo looks distinctly human. And since the child and mother do not exchange blood, and since their blood can be of different types, the child's independence is suggested. The child has pain and can cry, as occurred when an air bubble was injected into an eight-month fetus's amniotic sac for X-ray purposes, after which the baby would keep the mother and father awake with its crying.[9]

---

6. Ibid., 39.
7. Ibid., 40.
8. It is estimated that for each available Caucasian baby there are 10 applicants. And in the case of Afro-American children under two years of age, they are all wanted by families hoping for an adoption."
9. Bart T. Hofferman, "The Early Biography of Everyman," 15-16.

It is supposed by many Christians, including evangelical ones, that the Bible condones abortion. The passage they refer to is Exod. 21:22-24: "When men strive together, and hurt a woman with child, so that there is a miscarriage, and yet no harm follows, the one who hurt her shall be fined, according as the woman's husband shall lay upon him; and he shall pay as the judges determine. If any harm follows, then you shall give life for life, eye for eye, tooth for tooth" (RSV).

This passage does not refer to a planned, induced abortion; it refers to a theoretical circumstance in which a miscarriage might occur if a pregnant woman was hit unintentionally while two men were fighting.

Since the passage prescribes a greater punishment for the death of the mother than for the death of her fetus, many people infer that a fetus has much less value, is not a human being, and therefore we do not take a human life when we induce the abortion of a fetus. Yet while the passage contains implications that can be related to induced abortion, it refers to accidental miscarriage.

Abortion is one of the great moral issues of society. If abortion is morally wrong, if it is a legalized form of murder, it is not simply a possible problem but an evil of monstrous proportions that is already occurring.

One important reason not to abort is because the life that has begun is a being who exists in God's image.

The Image of God in Ourselves

Scripture affirms that we were created in God's own image (Gen. 1:27). There has been until recently a nearly unanimous understanding of what this image consists of. The wide context of Scripture and human experience suggests that the image of God in us consists in part of our rational, volitional, and moral capacities. And the larger context of the image of God passages in Genesis implies that the image consists in part of our authority over the earth and its animal life. Yet the immediate Scripture passage where the image of God is mentioned implies that the image of God in us consists of another matter—love.

Main Aspect of the Image: Love. What the image of God basically consists of is implied in Gen. 1:27-28: "So God created man in his own image, in the image of God he created him; male and female he created them. God blessed them." This implies that

God's image in us is our capacity to love—especially love expressed in our maleness and femaleness, including the commitment of love in marriage. Scripture does not equate our maleness and femaleness with marriage. Jesus never married, but He existed fully as a human in God's image. Indeed, He is declared to be God's image expressed perfectly (Col. 1:15).

The way in which we are most like God is in our capacity to care for other persons selflessly. This view, that the image is mainly in our capacity to love, is in agreement with the New Testament, where love is declared to be the highest virtue (1 Corinthians 13).

Subsidiary Aspects of the Image. While love is the chief aspect of the image of God, there are others.

1. *Authority.* This is one subsidiary aspect, mentioned within the creation story. The divine decision to make us in God's image is followed by the words "and let them rule over the fish . . . and the birds . . . the livestock, over all the earth" (Gen. 1:26). Then God made humans "male and female" (v. 27) and told them to "fill the earth and subdue it" (v. 28). His next words show what this subduing of the earth consists of: "Rule over the fish . . . and the birds . . . and over every living creature" (ibid.). Ruling the earth includes taking care of it (2:15), not ravaging or polluting it.

2. *Reason.* Most theology books have suggested that our reasoning capacity is an aspect of the image of God. Animals, while clever, are stimulus-and-response creatures. They learn to do reasonable things, but they do not discursively and self-consciously reason their way to their reasonable acts. Only humans can do this. We reason discursively, through a process, whereas God reasons intuitively without process—yet we are like God in possessing reasoning powers. It is no doubt an aspect of God's image in us.

3. *Moral volition.* Animals may seem to make decisions at times, but they are acting only on the basis of stimulus-response programming. They make decisions, but not moral ones. They make decisions, but not costly ones.

Human history shows that moral decision is a capacity of ours. Many of these decisions were costly, involving loss of possessions, careers, or even life. Martyrdom is a human capacity that expresses dramatically the image of God in persons.

The authority and the rational and volitional capacity of male and female persons are surely aspects of the image of God in us. But they are subsidiary to the capacity to express love in our maleness and femaleness—including marriage, but not at all confined to marriage. They are supportable somewhat from the immediate context of the Genesis creation narratives. They are more supportable from the wider context of Scripture as a whole. And they are surely supportable from history and from the present we are now passing through. So it is not inappropriate that the theologians of the centuries have said that this is what the image of God in us consists of. Yet it is appropriate that Karl Barth and others, such as Paul Jewett in his *Man as Male and Female*,[10] are helping us see that the image of God in us most basically is in our capacity to love as males and females.

Some theologians understand conscience to be an aspect of the image of God in us. It is not understood in that way here, so it will be discussed separately.

A Study of Conscience

Conscience may be understood as an urge to do the right and leave undone the wrong. A person might be badly informed about what the right and the wrong are; yet conscience is an urge to do the one and to avoid the other.

Edwin Lewis taught that this urge to do the right and leave undone the wrong is an aspect of our natural equipment—a built-in monitor of our thoughts and deeds, giving us a sense of having done well when it is heeded and a sense of shame and guilt when we disregard it. In *The Creator and the Adversary*, Lewis has a chapter on conscience titled "The Leash and the Lash."[11] Conscience has the leash function of giving us a certain freedom within a restricted area, and as long as we respect the boundaries it sets for us, it praises us. If we disregard that function of conscience and transgress the boundary it sets for us, it lashes us with blame and guilt.

Lewis's teaching on conscience is flawed by his rejection of the classical doctrine of original sin. He admits a "radical defect" in human nature, but he does not believe in the historicity of Adam and Eve, nor that humanity suffered a detriment—original sin—due to Adam's sin.

---

10. See figures in H. W. Robinson, *The Christian Doctrine of Man* (Edinburgh: T. and T. Clark, 1911), 16.

11. Edwin Lewis, *The Creator and the Adversary*, 52-62.

The classical doctrine of original sin includes the understanding that fallen persons are naturally inclined continually to evil (see Genesis 6; Rom. 7:14). If this classical view is correct, conscience could not be a built-in natural endowment through which we are urged to do the right, because original sin constitutes an inclination only to do evil acts.

John Wesley understood conscience to be the Holy Spirit's prompting, experienced even by the unregenerate because of prevenient grace. Scripture does not make this matter clear. It usually speaks of conscience without connecting it with the Holy Spirit, precisely so connecting it only one time, where Paul says that he speaks "the truth in Christ" and that his "conscience confirms it in the Holy Spirit" (Rom. 9:1).

Although the Holy Spirit is connected with conscience only once, God is connected with it often, and such connecting of the two might well substantiate Wesley's kind of understanding. Paul said to the Sanhedrin, "My brothers, I have fulfilled my duty to God in all good conscience" (Acts 23:1). To Governor Felix he said, "So I strive always to keep my conscience clear before God and man" (24:16). Paul also writes, "Our conscience testifies that we have conducted ourselves . . . in the holiness and sincerity that are from God" (2 Cor. 1:12). And to the same Corinthian people he says that "by setting forth the truth plainly we commend ourselves to every man's conscience in the sight of God" (4:2). Thus their consciences are connected with what God is pointing out to them. So John Wesley, whom Albert Outler calls a folk theologian, was expert enough in teaching theology to plain folk to make conscience consistent with original sin, connecting conscience in the unregenerate with prevenient grace.

The Elements of Human Nature

Historically, in systematic theologies, only two views have been prominent: dichotomy and trichotomy. After discussing them, the writer's own view—which might be called the poly-partite unitary view—will be discussed.

The Dichotomy View. According to this understanding, humans are of two basic elements: (1) body and (2) soul or spirit. Here, perhaps under the influence of Greek dualism, soul and spirit are understood to be the same and to be immaterial. Besides this immaterial element is the body, the material aspect of human nature. Dichotomists argue for their view in part because one particular Christological heresy, Apollinarianism, is based on trichotomy—the heresy being that Christ had a human body and soul but not a human spirit or person or ego.

The Trichotomy View. This view asserts that human nature is of three basic elements: (1) body, (2) soul, and (3) spirit. All aspects of human nature mentioned in Scripture or supported by science are subsumed under these three elements.

Trichotomists distinguish the soul and the spirit. Both are nonmaterial, but the soul is more closely related to the body than is the spirit. All three are mentioned in Gen. 2:7 where we read, "The Lord God formed the man from the dust of the ground and breathed into his nostrils the breath of life, and the man became a living being." Here the "dust" of the ground is the *basar,* somewhat akin to the Greek New Testament *sōma* and the English "body"; "living being" is from *nephesh,* the Hebrew word for "soul"; and the "breath" of life is *ruach,* the Hebrew word for "spirit." The spirit and soul seem to be different, since God is said to be a spirit ("God is a Spirit" [John 4:24, KJV]), but is never said to be or to have a soul. The Hebrew *nephesh* for soul and the Greek *psuchē* are never used of God.

The Poly-Partite Unitary View. Here, a human is viewed in a unity, not as broken up into actual parts or elements. Here a person is a person: a woman is a woman, a man is a man. In 223 of 754 instances in which the King James Version translates *nephesh* as soul, the context shows that soul is not an aspect of a person but simply the person. *Nephesh* is so used, for example, when we read in KJV that a "soul shall be cut off" (Gen. 17:14); "my soul shall live" (19:20); "if a soul sin" (Lev. 5:1); "one soul of five hundred" (Num. 31:28); "the soul that sinneth, it shall die" (Ezek. 18:4); and "he that winneth souls is wise" (Prov. 11:30).

Since Scripture does not portray the body as evil, there is no need to view ourselves in a bifurcated way as constituted by two opposites: materiality and immateriality.

Not only are the spirit and soul distinguished in Gen. 2:7, but also they seem to be distinguished in Heb. 4:12: "The word of God is living and active. Sharper than any double-edged sword, it penetrates even to dividing soul and spirit, joints and marrow." It is possible that the writer was using only a common understanding inherited from Plato, that the spirit and the soul are distinguishable. Yet it is surely preferable to interpret this passage in keeping with others (e.g., Gen. 2:7 and 1 Thess. 5:23) where the two are indeed distinguishable. Admittedly, they are more similar to each other than they are to the body, and this is why the writer illustrates as he does. He is saying that God's written Word is often so specifically targeted that it distinguishes between matters as much alike as are the soul and the spirit.

Another passage that suggests trichotomy is 1 Thess. 5:23, where Paul prays, "May God himself, the God of peace, sanctify you through and through. May your whole spirit, soul and body be kept blameless at the coming of our Lord Jesus Christ." Some interpreters who tend toward a dichotomy view suggest that Paul is here simply using the common view that spirit and soul are distinct in order to speak of a matter unrelated to that question—the thoroughness of the cleansing God offers to people. Such an interpretation disregards the obvious in the passage, that the soul and the spirit are distinguishable.

Although trichotomy is preferable to dichotomy, the polypartite view is to be preferred to both. Scripture suggests that our basically unitary being has many aspects.

Besides body, soul, and spirit, numerous other aspects of our nature are mentioned. One of them is the heart. The Hebrew *leb,* or *lebab,* for heart, appears hundreds of times; and the counterpart New Testament word, *kardia,* appears with considerable frequency. These words refer to a number of aspects of human nature: our capacities for thinking, for moral decision, for emotional reactions. They are also used with reference to physical life (e.g., Acts 14:17; James 5:5, KJV).

Without presenting a detailed study of them, a number of other words describe our nature in the New Testament—for example, *sōma* for body, *nous* or *dianoia* for mind, and *dzōē* for life.

These and other biblical terms suggest that we humans, certainly unitary as beings, are many-sided in our nature.

Having considered nature and human origin, we turn now to two other matters related to the doctrine of ourselves: human freedom and predestination.

Human Freedom

When James Arminius, John Wesley, and H. Orton Wiley emphasized their non-Pelagian view of human freedom, they understood that they were teaching what was customarily taught by the Greek and Latin fathers.

Human Freedom Before Arminius. Much evidence justifies this understanding that the pre-Augustinians were freedomists.

There were exceptions to this "Arminianism" in the earliest centuries. The greatest theologian before Augustine, Origen, must be thought of as an exception of a sort. Origen seemed to emphasize human freedom, but he did not believe in it as Arminius and Wesley later taught it. He believed that we are so free that we can choose our road back to God and the length of time it will take to get back to God, but that we are not free to choose never to be redeemed.

Yet most pre-Augustinian fathers were freedomists of some sort. They did not give apologies for such a view, since it was not a controverted issue. Tertullian, Cyprian, Chrysostom, and others pretty much assume human freedom. Arnobius, the only annihilationist of the pre-Augustinian period, certainly suggests it. The annihilation of the wicked, after they are resurrected and punished for their sins, will be justly deserved because of their free decision to rebel against God.

Human freedom was not an issue to Irenaeus and Athanasius; they seem to assume it. Pelagius, Coelestius, and others denied original sin resulting from Adam's fall, and the need of prevenient grace, so the human freedom they asserted was of a humanistic type.

The Second Council of Orange (A.D. 529) made an official decision for the Catholic church of the ensuing centuries. It taught that we lost our freedom through the Fall, but that it is restored to us when we are baptized.

Closer to the time of Arminius, the erudite Erasmus was a freedomist and wrote supporting free will only to be opposed by Martin Luther in *The Bondage of the Will.* Erasmus, though, was a humanist and not the kind of freedomist that the later Arminius was. Melanchthon, closely associated with Luther, might have gravitated toward human freedom and conditional predestination in his last years;[12] but if so, his views would not have closely resembled those of Arminius.

---

12. Caspar Brandt, *The Life of James Arminius,* trans. John Guthrie (London: Ward and Co., 1858), 30 ff.

Anabaptists, some of whom later became known as Mennonites, taught the universal provision for redemption in Christ's atonement and that we humans cast the deciding vote on whether we will be damned or redeemed.

At Zurich, also just before Arminius's time, Bullinger questioned at least for a time the denial of human freedom implied in Calvin's unconditional predestination teaching. Jerome Bolsec and Charles Perrot, of Geneva, both opposed Calvin's view and were freedomists of sorts.

After Holland became Protestant, and a few decades before the Synod of Dort (1618-19), most ministers tended to be freedomists. At the newly founded university at Leiden in Holland, most of the teachers were "Arminian" during the six years Arminius studied there (1575-81).

In England, William Barrett was denied his B.D. degree at Cambridge in 1595 because he rejected the freedom-opposed views of Cambridge's distinguished supralapsarian, Williams Perkins. About this same time Peter Baro was deposed from his position at Cambridge for his "Arminian" views.[13] John Playfere, Baro's successor, lectured and published on free will without special trouble, because by then it was becoming increasingly acceptable in England. The Thirty-nine Articles of 1563 (and 1571) of the Church of England took no position on the matter of human freedom—allowing, in the future, either Calvinism or Arminianism among its adherents.[14]

Arminius's View of Human Freedom. James Arminius taught and even emphasized human freedom in various treatises written during his 15-year pastorate at Amsterdam (1588-1603) and in his writings during his tenure as a professor at the University of Leiden (1603-9). He was a pastor and professor of the Reformed church, and he felt, somewhat incorrectly, that his views on free will were not discordant with his group's Belgic Confession (1561) and Heidelberg Catechism (1563).

Human freedom is a distinctive emphasis of Arminius, who permitted accusations of Pelagianism to circulate for two years before responding to them in his *Apology Against Thirty-one*

13. See Carl Bangs, "Arminius and the Reformation," *Church History,* June 1961, 7.
14. See Schaff, *Creeds of Christendom,* 3:486-516.

Defamatory Articles.[15] He was not Pelagian, for he believed profoundly in original sin. He believed therefore that we are fallen and that we thus cannot, unaided by prevenient grace, exercise our capacity of free will in choosing righteousness. He said, "In this state [of original sin], the freewill of man towards the true good is not only wounded, maimed . . . but it is also imprisoned, destroyed, and lost."[16] He also writes, "The mind, in this state, is dark, destitute of the saving knowledge of God, and, according to the Apostle, incapable of those things which belong to the Spirit of God. For 'the animal man has no perception of the things of the spirit of God' (1 Cor. 2:14)."[17] Further, he writes: "Exactly correspondent to this darkness of the mind, and perverseness of the heart, is the utter weakness of all the powers to perform that which is truly good, and to omit the perpetration of that which is evil."[18] Commenting on John 8:36, Arminius wrote, "It follows that our will is not free from the first fall; that is, it is not free to good, unless it be made free by the Son through his spirit."[19]

John Wesley's Teaching on Free Will. Between the time of Arminius and that of Wesley, Arminianism gained much ground. John Goodwin taught Arminianism in England in the middle of the 17th century and directly influenced John Wesley in that direction.[20]

On free will John Wesley wrote, "Indeed, if man were not free, he could not be accountable either for his thoughts, words, or actions. If he were not free, he would not be capable either of reward or punishment; he would be incapable either of virtue or vice, of being either morally good or bad."[21] Wesley also wrote, "Natural free-will, in the present state of mankind [in original sin], I do not understand: I only assert, that there is a measure of free-will supernaturally restored to every man."[22] In another trea-

---

15. See James Arminius, *Writings,* ed. and trans. James Nichols and W. R. Bagnall (Grand Rapids: Baker Book House, 1956 reprint), 1:276-380. He permitted 14 of these misrepresentations to be circulated for some two years, and he opposed them only when 17 others became attached to them.

16. Ibid., 526.

17. Ibid.

18. Ibid., 572.

19. Ibid., 528.

20. See William Strickland's Ph.D. dissertation submitted to Vanderbilt University in 1967.

21. John Wesley, "On Predestination," Sermon 58 in *Works* 6:227.

22. Ibid., "Predestination Calmly Considered," 10:229-30.

tise Wesley says, "I believe that Adam, before his fall, has such freedom of will, that he might choose either good or evil; but that, since the fall, no child of man has a natural power to choose anything that is truly good."[23] Wesley always denied the natural free will to do good since the Fall, but he always taught that prevenient grace is given everyone, so that choices of the good are possible even before regeneration.

It is proper to say that the Arminian-Wesleyan tradition teaches human freedom in the context of prevenient grace. We can either accept Christ or reject Him—and our eternal destiny depends upon our free response to God's offer of salvation.

Freedom as Possibility. This is what Christ teaches in John 8:31-36. To Jews "who had believed him," He portrayed the freedom He offers as the opposite of slavery and as knowing and living by His truth. To disciples who hold to His teachings, He promises, "Then you will know the truth, and the truth will set you free" (v. 32). This freedom comes after slavery to sin has passed. This is what Paul calls "the glorious freedom of the children of God" (Rom. 8:21), and "the freedom we have in Christ Jesus" (Gal. 2:4).

These teachings of Christ and Paul show that freedom is freedom from slavery to sin (see also Rom. 6:18, 20, 22; 8:2), and freedom from legalism. They are part of a wider conception of freedom as simply possibility, which Søren Kierkegaard elucidated to such extent.

For Kierkegaard, reacting against Georg Friedrich Hegel (for whom freedom is simply our liberty to follow what reason dictates), freedom is possibility. In Kierkegaard's *Fear and Trembling,* freedom is the capacity we have to make transitions in life from one stage to another—from simply seeking pleasure to religious decision, where God is figured in. In Kierkegaard's *Concept of Dread,* freedom is the transition we make from the sin-fall to the God-relation, through the dizziness of dread and despair to the willingness to suffer as God's obedient child.[24]

---

23. Ibid., "Remarks on 'A Defence of . . . Aspasio Vindicated,'" 350.

24. Søren Kierkegaard, *Fear and Trembling,* trans. Walter Lowrie (Princeton, N.J.: Princeton University Press, 1941); idem, *Either/Or: A Fragment of Life,* trans. David F. Swenson and Lillian Marvin Swenson (Princeton, N.J.: Princeton University Press; London: Oxford University Press, 1944); and idem, *The Concept of Dread,* trans. Walter Lowrie (Princeton, N.J.: Princeton University Press, 1944).

Freedom as possibility is more than the power given us fallen persons to turn to Christ. It is the freedom to flower in servanthood to Christ.

Freedom and Necessity. We humans have our freedom through prevenient grace, but also in the context of many factors of necessity—which we do not choose. Limits we do not set, and often would not set, condition all that we do. The genes we have no control over determine whether we may become a basketball center, an opera singer, or a select musician. We play the game of life as females or males, gender being already decided for us. We play it as persons being born without choice into a certain kind of family economically, educationally, and religiously, in a certain nation, at a certain time in history.

The fact of our destiny is from a necessitated heritage; the form of it, only, is from our choice, in the context of grace. As Loyd Morgan said, we are consequents (of necessity), but also emergents, with freedom. The present moment, as Alfred North Whitehead suggested, is charged with the promise of all moments yet to be. We are determined in many ways; but in that given context, we are determinants. We are both the summation of many necessity factors and also the locus of novelty.

It is determined that we think with a human mind. It is not determined what we think. As Pascal said, we are often frail reeds (as he was), but we are thinking reeds. And as Henri Bergson taught, the being in whom the greatest risk is involved is the being in whom the greatest gain is possible.

God risked much in creating us humans with the freedom, now, to unleash horrendous nuclear disaster or to love our fellows across all boundaries.

What the Arminian View Means. It means that we Arminian-Wesleyans are not Pelagians, since we believe in original sin and since we believe that prevenient grace is necessary to enable us to use our freedom for taking savory directions in our lives.

This view means that we will use evangelistic methods, such as prayer, to secure an intensifying of the prevenient grace given the person we are seeking to win to Christ.

This view means that we will not say to a congregation in an evangelistic service, "You do your part and God will do His part." Unregenerate persons cannot do any such thing until God first does His part of extending prevenient grace to them.

This view also means that the Arminian-Wesleyan will not say, "God will meet you halfway." We cannot initiate our own salvation. Being fallen creatures, inclined to evil and that continually, God must come all the way to where we are and initiate in us our "first faint desire" to turn to Christ—as John Wesley said.

What Predestination Consists Of

Closely connected with human freedom is the matter of God's predestining us.

The Four Views Historically. Predestination of some sort is taught in Scripture, so all Bible-respecting Christians believe in some sort of predestination doctrine. At least four views of it have arisen historically—three of them major views.

1. *Sublapsarianism* is the view that Adam was free in his crucial sin but that once he sinned freely, the eternal destiny of all other persons in human history was decided by the completely sovereign God. The view should have been called postlapsarianism, because it means that after the Fall, or the lapse, the destiny of each person was decided upon by God. This is the view of Augustine, the first theologian to teach unconditional predestination—that it is not conditioned upon any human response, such as that of repenting and believing on Christ.

James Arminius believed that Augustine got his idea from the Stoics. They taught that there is a law of necessity by which the whole universe and everyone in it functions, and that even God is subject to it. It is possible also that Augustine was borrowing from the Gnostics, for they taught that almost all individuals are born either with a certain divine spark of *gnōsis*, knowledge, or that they are simply animal souls born without that knowledge. Some Gnostics believed that some people are psychics who can change their eternal destiny; but for the most part, the Gnostics believed that each of us is unconditionally predestinated to have salvation or not to have it.

Augustine felt, of course, that he was teaching at this point what Scripture does. Yet it will be shown later that Scripture teaches very differently.

Besides Augustine, Martin Luther taught sublapsarian predestination. Luther even said that he did not know which eternal destiny he himself was predestinated to. He said it would undermine our being justified by faith if we could know, or have knowledge of, our predestinated destiny.

2. *Supralapsarianism* is the view that Adam was not free in his sin and that even his eternal destiny, along with everyone else's, was determined by God before creation. John Calvin seems to have taught supralapsarianism. In his *Institutes of the Christian Religion*, he says, "The decree, I admit, is dreadful; and yet it is impossible to deny that God foreknew what the end of man was to be before he made him, and foreknew, because he had so ordained by his decree."[25] He also says, "Nor ought it to seem absurd when I say, that God not only foresaw the fall of the first man, and in him the ruin of his posterity; but also at his own pleasure arranged it."[26]

Calvin's son-in-law, Theodore Beza (1519-1605), who taught so long at Calvin's school in Geneva and was one of James Arminius's professors, definitely taught supralapsarian unconditional predestination. Likewise, it was taught and promoted in Holland at Leiden University by Arminius's colleague there, Francis Gomarus (1563-1641).

3. *Modified supralapsarianism* appeared in the late 16th and early 17th centuries. Here, the view is modified so that there is no positive decree to reprobation. There is only a single decree, through which God elects some individuals to be saved eternally, and those passed over go to eternal hell—because that is their just deserts, since they sinned in a real way when Adam sinned. This was thought by some to be a bit softer and somewhat protective of God's goodness.

4. *Conditional predestination* is the view of Arminius. God does predestinate each individual to an eternal destiny, but it is based on His foreknowledge of their free response to, or rejection of, the gospel. This is sometimes called class predestination: that God predetermines that the whole class of those who freely believe are predestinated to go to heaven, and that it is predetermined that those who, despite prevenient grace, reject Christ will go into eternal punishment.

---

25. John Calvin, *Institutes of the Christian Religion*, trans. Henry Beveridge, 8th ed. (Grand Rapids: William B. Eerdmans Publishing Co., 1954), 2:232.
26. Ibid.

After Calvin and others had made so much of God's decrees, Arminius taught decrees but changed the order of them.

Whereas the supralapsarians taught that the decree to save and damn certain individuals was followed by a later decree to create them, Arminius taught that God's first decree was to send Christ to redeem sinful people. He said that God's second decree was to receive into favor those who repent and believe. The third decree is that of prevenient grace, enabling everyone to repent and believe. The fourth decree, for Arminius, was to save and damn individuals according to God's foreknowledge of the way in which they would freely respond to His offer of grace.

It is interesting that Arminius felt that eternal decrees, which are never spoken of in Scripture, should be part of one's theological system. They probably are not properly part of an Arminian kind of theology. H. Orton Wiley felt that Arminianism does indeed need decrees. Mildred Wynkoop suggests that decrees are inappropriate for Arminianism. Carl Bangs shows, in his important study of Arminius, that in a number of ways Arminius tried to be as conciliating as possible to the Calvinists of his time, since he ministered in a Reformed denomination. This might partly account for his use of eternal decrees in his theology.

Temporal Predestination. This is the present writer's own view, which seems to be altogether Arminian and truly biblical. It is the understanding that predestination does not have to do with a pre-decision of God regarding the eternal destiny of people, but that it has to do with what God graciously decides for believers temporally—only having to do with Christians.

1. *A study of the six Greek instances.* One of the most interesting theological finds I have made is that divine predestination does not have to do with eternal destiny.

God does indeed predestinate us in certain ways. Six times the word for "to predestinate" is used in the New Testament. Cognates of that word, *prooridzō*, and other "pro" words found in both Testaments, show that God makes predecisions on various matters. But my recent finding is that they never have to do with our eternal destiny.

As mentioned, *prooridzō* occurs six times in the New Testament, in Rom. 8:29, 30; Eph. 1:5, 11; Acts 4:28; and 1 Cor. 2:7. The KJV translates it as "predestinate" in the first four of these instances, and as "determined before" and "ordained" respectively

250 <A WESLEYAN-HOLINESS THEOLOGY

in the other two. The ASV has "foreordained" in all six instances. The NASB changes this to "predestined" in all six instances. The RSV has "predestined" in Acts 4:28; Rom. 8:29, 30; "decreed" in 1 Cor. 2:7; and "destined" in Eph. 1:5, 12 (sic). The NIV uses "predestined" in Rom. 8:29, 30, and Eph 1:5, 11; "decided beforehand" in Acts 4:28; and "destined" in 1 Cor. 2:7.

This means that the Greek word for "to predestinate" is relatively rare in Scripture. Yet there are numerous words with the prefix *pro* in them that have to do with divine or human predecisions to do something at a later time, and they at least relate to the idea of predetermination. Words having to do with prediction of later events, as in the case of Old Testament prophets, also somewhat relate to the idea of predestination. The prefix pro for "before" is used often in the New Testament to refer to what God did or promised or planned before the world was created (see John 17:5; 1 Cor. 2:7; Eph. 1:4; 2 Tim. 1:9; Titus 1:2; 1 Pet. 1:20; Jude 25).[27]

Contrary to what has been understood by Christians in general since Augustine's time, predestination in Scripture does not relate to eternal destiny. In none of the six uses of *prooridzō* has God predestinated anyone or any group of persons (believers, unbelievers) to eternal bliss or to eternal damnation.

Take the Rom. 8:29-30 instances of *proōrisen*. There we read, "For those God foreknew he also predestined to be conformed to the likeness of his Son, that he might be the firstborn among many brothers. And those he predestined, he also called; those he called, he also justified; those he justified, he also glorified." Significantly, "predestined" here is not used with reference to eternal destiny. This passage states that "those God foreknew," meaning surely those He foreknew would believe, "he also predestined to be conformed to the likeness of his Son." That is, He predetermined that believers would be conformed to Christ's likeness. "Conformed," *symmorphous*, is an adjective, from *syn* (with) and *morphē* (form)—and the *morphē* probably refers to the essence of something.[28] The likeness to Christ that the Father predestinates

---

27. For an excellent word study of these matters, see I. Howard Marshall, "Predestination in the New Testament," in *Grace Unlimited,* ed. Clark H. Pinnock (Minneapolis: Bethany Fellowship, 1975), 127 ff. See also William M. Arnett, "Predestination," in *Beacon Dictionary of Theology,* ed. Richard S. Taylor (Kansas City: Beacon Hill Press of Kansas City, 1983).

28. See Ralph Earle, *Romans,* vol. 3 in *Word Meanings in the New Testament* (Kansas City: Beacon Hill Press of Kansas City, 1974), 166-67.

for believers is an approximate one, the kind that relates to what is possible for us as humans with our erring finiteness. The point here, however, is that eternal destiny does not enter into the picture at all—except as an ultimate consequence of the success or failure of this predestination.

In the next verse the same kind of nondestiny meaning obtains. There, "those he predestined, he also called," and the ones He called, He "justified," and the ones He justified, He "glorified." Here the writer does get around, finally, to a word that has to do with destiny: glorification. So it could be interpreted that the predestination has to do with destiny—and it does, finally, as shown above. But having predestined or predetermined various things for believers, through His foreknowledge (v. 29) that they would freely believe, He called them and justified them and, with His intention, as though it had already happened, glorified them.[29]

Arminius and authentic Arminians taught God's foreknowledge of our free acts—even as Calvinists always have because Scripture surely does. So, in Rom. 8:30, God foresees that individuals will believe; and in due time He calls them to himself in various ways, as through preaching and by the Spirit's summons. And as they respond favorably to this call, He justifies them. Then, still based on His foreknowledge (see v. 29) that individuals will keep on believing, He glorifies them. Here Paul enlists a number of his grand theological concepts in a sweeping statement of predestination.

That this is not an Augustinian-Calvinistic teaching of predestination of some—the elect for whom Christ died—to glorification is shown by other teachings in this very chapter of Romans and in other Pauline writings. Paul opens what we have marked as chapter 8 by declaring that those who are "in Christ Jesus" have "no condemnation." These "in Christ Jesus" people are not simply predestinated whether or not, but God has "condemned sin" in them "in order that the righteous requirements of the law might be fully met" in those "who do not live according to the sinful nature but according to the Spirit" (v. 4). That believers are not predestinated in the sense of eternal security is shown by what he asks late in the chapter (after making the two references

---

29. Ibid., 167-68.

to predestination in vv. 29-30): "Who shall separate us from the love of Christ?" (v. 35). Nothing will. It is to be noted, though, that nothing will be able to separate us from Christ's "love." A person might, in persecution or whatever, fall from saving grace as did Simon Magus (Acts 8:9-24); but even if one does fall from regenerating grace, that person is not separated from Christ's love. Christ still loves even the apostate person who crucifies Him afresh (see Heb. 6:4-6).

The two cognates of *prooridzō* in Eph. 1:5, 11 (*proorisas*, v. 5, and *prooristhentes*, v. 11) do not relate to eternal destiny. In Ephesians we have one of the Bible's richest areas of predestination teaching. While only two actual words for predestination appear in the Epistle, the idea of God's having made certain predecisions is prominent.

Paul says in 1:4 that God "chose us in him [Christ] before the creation ["foundation," NASB] of the world to be holy and blameless in his sight." Thus, before creating the world, God decided that all who would freely believe would be chosen, and that they would be "holy" and "blameless." Nothing is here said that has to do with our eternal destiny. Paul goes on to a stronger word than "chosen." He says in verse 5 that God "predestined" the believers to be "adopted as his sons through Jesus Christ, in accordance with his pleasure and will." And in verses 11-12 he says, "In him we were also chosen, having been predestined according to the plan of him who works out everything in conformity with the purpose of his will, in order that we, who were the first to hope in Christ, might be for the praise of his glory."

Several things are to be noted here. In verse 5 the predestination is not to heaven or hell, but to adoption as sons of God. In verses 11-12, the predestination is again not to destiny, but "in order that we . . . might be for the praise of his glory." The "we" here is probably a reference to Paul himself, for his next words seem, in distinction, to refer to his readers, as he says, "And you also were included in Christ." Again, it is to be noted that they were not included willy-nilly according to an unconditioned election. Paul says, "And you also were included in Christ when you heard the word of truth, the gospel of your salvation. Having believed, you . . ." (v. 13). They were included in actual fact after they had "heard the word of truth" and after they had "believed."

The other two predestination passages need to be considered. The Acts 4:28 one reads in the NIV, "They did what your power and will had decided beforehand should happen."

Proōrisen here has nothing whatever to do with a predestination to eternal destiny. The believers are affirming that the persecuting authorities are unwittingly doing what God had long before purposed.

In 1 Cor. 2:7, where *proōrisen* is also used, the NIV reads, "No, we speak of God's secret wisdom, a wisdom that has been hidden and that God destined for our glory before time began." Again, it does not at all relate to either of the eternal destinies. Paul is simply saying that he and others "speak a message of wisdom among the mature [perfect ones]" (v. 6) "that has been hidden" and that "God destined," or predestined, "for our glory before time began" (v. 7). The passage shows that God planned to offer the gospel even before He created us, just as Arminius taught in what he called God's first decree, which was to send Christ. It implies God's foreknowledge that we humans would sin and would need redemption. It has nothing to do with a predecision to give heaven to some individuals and hell to others.

Besides these six instances of cognates of *prooridzō* in the New Testament (there being no counterpart Hebrew Old Testament word), there are numerous Hebrew and Greek words with the prefix *pro* in them that relate to what either God or humans decide ahead of time to do.[30] Yet not one of them indicates that God predecides individual destiny.

2. *What temporal predestination is not.* For one thing, temporal predestination does not refer to either of the two destinies, as shown above.

Further, temporal predestination does not have to do with what are called unalterable decrees of destiny. While Scripture speaks frequently of temporal "decrees" and "edicts" made by human rulers, and of some as being unalterable—as in the case of the Medes and Persians (cf. Ezra 6:11; Esther 8:8; Dan. 6:8)[31]—it

---

30. A study of many of these is contained in Marshall, "Predestination in the New Testament," in *Grace Unlimited.* (See also David J. A. Clines, "Predestination in the Old Testament" therein.)

31. See N. J. O., "Decree," in *The International Standard Bible Encyclopedia,* ed. Geoffrey Bromily (Grand Rapids: William B. Eerdmans Publishing Co., 1979), 1:909.

only rarely speaks of God making decrees of any kind. And when it does, they are not decrees to destiny; they simply have to do with His rulings. Thus we read, "There the Lord made a decree and a law for them, and there he tested them" (Exod. 15:25). Here God's decree is simply a law such as kings often made. Thus we read that a decree is the same as a covenant: "He remembers his covenant forever, the word he commanded, for a thousand generations, the covenant he made with Abraham, the oath he swore to Isaac. He confirmed it to Jacob as a decree" (1 Chron. 16:15-17).

Another rare instance of a divine decree occurs in Rom. 1:32: "Although they know God's righteous decree that those who do such things deserve death, they not only continue to do these very things but also approve of those who practice them." Here the ruling is not an arbitrary, inscrutable, and mysterious decree, through which eternal destiny is decided without regard to the individual's actions. It regards the punishment of those who knowingly commit the sins mentioned in verses 29-31.

God decrees a "disaster" (1 Kings 22:23; 2 Chron. 18:22; Jer. 40:2), a "famine" (2 Kings 8:1), and other such matters, but the decrees are simply His rulings, or His agreements; and they regularly announce what will happen on earth according to whether the people are obedient or disobedient.

3. *What temporal predestination is.* First, temporal predestination is a view that attempts to account for the entire biblical data on the matter of predestination. For example, it does not allow any decree to reprobate individuals, for several good reasons. (1) Many passages state clearly that the Atonement was for everyone (e.g., 2 Cor. 5:15). (2) God loves the whole "world" (John 3:16). (3) God's clear wish is that all will repent: "This is good, and pleases God our Savior, who wants all men to be saved and to come to the knowledge of the truth" (1 Tim. 2:3-4). We also read, "He is patient with you, not wanting anyone to perish, but everyone to come to repentance" (2 Pet. 3:9). Also, Jesus says, "In the same way your Father in heaven is not willing that any of these little ones [children] should be lost" (Matt. 18:14). And (4) the call of God is to everyone, as many scriptures show, such as Rev. 22:17: "The Spirit and the bride [the Church] say, 'Come!'" This view attempts to study all the passages related to predestination in context, without bringing theological baggage to them, and to

take into account the many clear passages that teach temporal and not eternal predestination.

Second, temporal predestination relates only to this life and to the ones who believe. It has to do with God's predecision to bless Christians in various ways.

Third, temporal predestination affirms many other aspects of Christian doctrine: that the Atonement is unlimited, as is the altogether-serious call to repent; that God acts personally as a person, is altogether just, and is unstintingly gracious; that real evil, and a thwarting of God's will, actually obtain; that those who believe can fall from regenerating grace.

This view admits that predestination is a biblical concept. It modifies the concept, however, so that it does not relate to eternal destiny; so that God has foreknowledge of our acts, but that they are still freely chosen; so that predestination is affirmed along with a kind of total depravity (all aspects of our nature being partially depraved); so that the Atonement and call to repentance are universal; so that God's offer of saving grace is resistible; so that believers may cease to believe, as Arminius said, and be eternally lost (see, for falling from grace, 2 Pet. 2:20; Heb. 4:6-11; 10:29; Rev. 22:19; etc.).

These, then, are important aspects of the Christian doctrine of ourselves: our origin, whether abortion is permissible, God's image in us, conscience, the elements of our nature, human freedom, and predestination. This study prepares the way for us to consider the Christian doctrine of sin.

10

The Doctrine of Sin

Our discussion of sin will consider its importance, its origin, the fact of sin, Adamic depravity, the nature and definition of sin as an act, and problem areas—such as sins of ignorance, the difference between the Roman Catholic venial/mortal distinction and the Wesleyan sin/mistake understanding, sin as the opposite of righteousness, sinless perfection, and the unpardonable sin.

Importance of the Doctrine

Some have viewed the doctrine of sin as the central Christian doctrine. Others have viewed it more correctly as simply a most significant area of Christian theology.

Richard S. Taylor writes, "The doctrines relating to sin form the center around which we build our entire theological system."[1] He quotes approvingly, "The sin question is the pivotal question."[2] Of sin as the starting point in Christian theology, Taylor says, "If we are to end right we must begin right, and to begin right we must grapple with the question of sin in its doctrinal significance."[3] Taylor further speaks of this doctrine as the "common denominator"[4] of the others. In his view, this doctrine is the one by which all the others can be reduced to their simplest significance.

Taylor, as a Wesleyan-holiness theologian, is opposing Calvinistic doctrine, which he calls "rectangular." Calvinism begins with predestination (and therefore with God); moves on to

---

1. Richard S. Taylor, *A Right Conception of Sin* (Kansas City: Beacon Hill Press, 1939), 9. This book was published early in Taylor's scholarly career, and recent correspondence with him suggests that he might not take this position now.
2. Ibid., 11, quoting H. V. Miller, *The Sin Problem* (Kansas City: Nazarene Publishing House, n.d.), 28.
3. Taylor, *Right Conception of Sin,* 9-10.
4. Ibid., 9.

sovereign grace (denying human free will in order to sustain unconditional predestination); then affirms, as a natural outgrowth of the first two, that once we are saved we will always be saved; and finally, to sustain particularly this third, it moves to the fourth side, imputed righteousness, for if we do not act "saved," and evidently are not actually righteous, Christ's real righteousness is imputed to us.

While Calvinism is incorrect in beginning with God as absolute Sovereign, who unconditionally predestinates each person's eternal destiny, it surely is not incorrect in beginning with God.

If we start theologizing with the doctrine of sin, how will we know what sin is? How will we see how serious it is? It is because God is a being of transcendent holiness that sin is what it is. When Isaiah glimpsed God as the thrice-holy One, he realized, in contrast, how utterly sinful he himself was and cried, "Woe to me!" (6:1-5).

A fiery coal touched his lips to cleanse away his sin. It was God's holiness that awakened Isaiah to his own colossal sinfulness.

In Hosea, it is an understanding of God that makes the sin of Gomer and Israel so great. There, when the loving prophet buys back his adulterous wife, Gomer, her sinfulness is defined in bold relief. This is illustrative of how sinful is Israel's sin, since it is against a God who is even more loving than was Hosea toward Gomer.

King David's sin was serious because of what God is like. David says, "Against you, you only, have I sinned and done what is evil in your sight" (Ps. 51:4). As king, he possessed the power to do as he pleased with Bathsheba, her husband, or anyone else. But David acknowledged his "transgressions" (v. 3) and pled for "mercy" (v. 1), because he knew God demanded much better things of him—the God who is or has a "Holy Spirit" (v. 11).

Several passages in Ezekiel show that sin is sinful because God is holy. There, as the "house of Israel" serves "idols," the matter is serious because they thereby "profane" God's "holy name" (20:39). The "prostitution" of Israel and her kings before pagan altars was sin because it defiled God's "holy name" (43:7).

The New Testament also shows that sin is what it is because of who God is. A single passage will suffice to sustain the point. Peter urges, "As obedient children, do not conform to the evil desires you had when you lived in ignorance" (1 Pet. 1:14). Life must change because God is holy. Thus the next verses read, "But just as he who called you is holy, so be holy in all you do; for it is written: 'Be holy, because I am holy'" (vv. 15-16).

Some who do not make sin the central doctrine do make it the starting place in theology. Such theologies begin with ourselves instead of with God. Schleiermacher, the founder of modern theology, did this. Tending toward a pantheistic view, he did not see humanity as utterly sinful. Looking inward instead of upward (to God), he saw God within himself. And seeing God there prohibited him from viewing himself or humans generally as being utterly sinful.

Paul Tillich began his theologizing with us and our situation in the world and proceeded to what is beyond.

Beginning with us and not with God, Tillich still views "man" as sinful—"radically estranged from his essential being."[5] This estrangement is coincident with the very beginning of our existence. It "underlies all human history and makes history what it is."[6] Tillich speaks of sin as "disbelief, the state of estrangement from God, the flight from him, the rebellion against him, the elevation of preliminary concerns to the rank of ultimate concern."[7] Tillich also says, "Man is bound to sin in all parts of his being, because he is estranged from God in his personal center. Neither his emotion, his will, nor his intellect is excepted from sin."[8] Although sin is inevitable, we are nonetheless responsible, and worthy of judgment: "Jesus and the New Testament writers . . . are keenly aware of the universal and inescapable dominion of sin over this world," but they call "sinners sinners. Understanding does not replace judging."[9]

Yet if the doctrine of sin is not properly the central doctrine or the starting point, it is a most significant Christian doctrine. Christian theology in its classical form has taken sin seriously. Luther viewed sin as enslaving of everyone who is not a Christian. Calvinism and Arminianism have not differed on the significance of sin as a Christian doctrine. The various other theological and denomi-

---

5. Paul Tillich, *Biblical Religion and the Search for Ultimate Reality* (Chicago: University of Chicago Press, 1955), 55.

6. Paul Tillich, *The Protestant Era,* trans. James Luther Adams (Chicago: University of Chicago Press, 1948), 166.

7. Tillich, *Ultimate Reality,* 55.

8. Ibid.

9. Paul Tillich, *The New Being* (New York: Charles Scribner's Sons, 1955), 5.

national groupings of Christians have viewed sin as a most significant doctrine, vigorously opposing those who make light of it.

Benedict de Spinoza (1632-77) made light of sin, holding that it is "unreality or illusion." This is how Mary Baker Eddy viewed sin in her *Science and Health with Key to the Scriptures.*

Immanuel Kant's view of sin was somewhat similar. Sin obtains whenever we do not act rationally—specifically, when we act according to our sensuous nature instead of our rational powers. His view incorrectly deprecates our bodily nature; suggests that doing what is rational, instead of doing God's will, is our proper goal; ignores our bondage to sin, as Romans 7 suggests; and overlooks original sin as the state that enslaved us to acts of sin.

Hegel's pantheistic view of sin is also far too light: Sin is only a lack of righteousness. It is a privation of what we ought ideally to be like. It is godlikeness on the way to being realized; it is not the opposite of godlikeness, not wickedness.

The classical view of sin also differs from the neoorthodox view.

Sin is significant for Søren Kierkegaard. Kierkegaard had known the sin-fall experience with its dread, its guilt, its despair, its sense of finitude—and pretty much only that. No redemption that one can be exuberant about is ever found by the melancholy Danish psychologist-theologian.

Emil Brunner, whose *Man in Revolt* is one of the more important 20th-century works on sin, views sin as significant—but never seems to enjoy any victory over it. Brunner says that he himself had always lived in the seventh chapter of Romans.

Wesleyan theology not only agrees that sin is serious and powerful but also teaches that through the Father's kindliness we can become redeemed from "all sin" (1 John 1:7, NASB).

The Origin of Sin

At least seven non-Arminian-Wesleyan theories obtain as to how sin originated.

The Ignorance Theory. This view is that sin is the result of human ignorance. It was the simplification of Socrates[10] and the

---

10. In the "Introduction" to *Socrates' Discourses,* A. D. Lindsay says that "Socrates' principal doctrine was the identification of knowledge and virtue . . . This means . . . that he could give no explanation of the fact that men may know what is right without doing it" ([New York: E. P. Dutton, 1933], xiii).

Greeks in general. They believed that, from the start, if people had known what was the right course of action, they would have chosen it. Knowledge, in this view, would equal virtue; but people lack knowledge, so they choose to do evil acts. Modern Pelagian theories such as that of A. C. Knudson,[11] with their denial of depravity and their too great reliance on education, are outgrowths of this theory.

The Law of Necessity Theory. This is the view that sin entered human life by a law of necessity written into the very nature of things. The Stoics taught this fatalistic view,[12] denying autonomy to God and humans. The evil in the world is the outworking of these laws of necessity.

The Finitude Theory. This is the theory that sin originated because of human finitude. Paul Tillich advocated this view. For him, our "creation and the fall coincide."[13]

The Anxiety Theory. This is Reinhold Niebuhr's teaching that sin originated initially, even as it does in each of us, in anxiety.[14] This anxiety is born out of our realization that both finitude (limitation) and freedom (possibility) belong to us. The anxiety can be useful, but it becomes sinful if the tension between limitation and possibility is resolved by letting either of the two have free rein. When our finitude is asserted, we go into sensuality, attempting to escape from our "unlimited possibilities of freedom . . . by immersing" ourselves into a "'mutable good.'"[15] When our freedom is asserted, sinful pride results, as we seek to raise our "contingent existence to unconditional significance."[16] This may be pride of power, pride of knowledge, pride of virtue, or spiritual pride—the ultimate sin: pharisaism.

---

11. See A. C. Knudson, *Principles of Christian Ethics* (New York: Abingdon-Cokesbury, 1943), 90-95.

12. See Kenneth S. Kantzer, "Stoics," in *Baker's Dictionary of Theology,* ed. E. F. Harrison (Grand Rapids: Baker Book House, 1960), 503.

13. Paul Tillich, *Systematic Theology,* 3 vols. (Chicago: University of Chicago Press, 1951-63), 1:256.

14. That our sinfulness is not coterminous with our creation, as it is in Tillich, is shown when Niebuhr says, "No man, however deeply involved in sin, is able to regard the misery of sin as normal. Some memory of a previous condition of blessedness seems to linger in the soul" (Reinhold Niebuhr, *The Nature and Destiny of Man* [New York: Charles Scribner's Sons, 1941-43], 1:281).

15. Ibid., 186.

16. Ibid.

The Sensuous Nature Theory. This is the view that sin originated in our sensuous nature. According to this view, which grew out of Platonic and Gnostic teaching, we are sinful because materiality in general is sinful, and we share in materiality by possessing a body with its passions.[17] This view has made monastics of many.

The Lack of Moral Evolution Theory. Here, sin entered because of our lack of moral evolution.[18] This was the view of the earlier Walter Rauschenbusch, influenced by Charles Darwin's theory of biological evolution. Rauschenbusch believed that humans had evolved to such extent by 1912 that most of our task of overcoming sin and evil was finished. He wrote, "The largest and hardest part of the work of Christianizing the social order has been done."[19]

The Divine Determinism Theory. This view is Stoic-influenced.[20] It was held by Theodore Beza and Francis Gomarus in Arminius's time and probably by John Calvin himself.[21] Adam's fall was decreed by the absolutely sovereign God who determines all events, large and small, in the course of human history. Arminius opposed this view with vigor—in one instance giving 20 arguments against it, insisting that the view makes God the author of sin.[22]

The Arminian-Wesleyan Teaching. This is surely the biblical one: that both angels and humans were constituted with an option to throw off God's restraints and go their own chosen way; and that Satan and one-third of the other angels first did this, being followed in this rebellion by the first human pair.

---

17. Julius Muller speaks of those who say that in man's sensuous nature "lie hid the springs of sin; to wit, in the power of man's sensuous nature over his spiritual" (*The Christian Doctrine of Sin* [Edinburgh: T. and T. Clark, 1885], 296).

18. For a discussion of the evolutionary theory of sin's origin see N. W. Stroup, "Evolution," in *The Fact of Sin* (New York: Eaton and Mains, 1908), 71-103. Stroup writes of the evolutionary view, "Sin is made an essential in the upward progress of man" (p. 72).

19. Walter Rauschenbusch, *Christianity and the Social Order* (New York: Macmillan Publishing Co., 1907), 416.

20. Emil Brunner says, "Determinism, through Augustine having found its way into Reformation theology, has a Stoic and not a Biblical origin" (*The Divine-Human Encounter* [Philadelphia: Westminster Press, 1943], 53). And James Arminius says approvingly, "But Philip Melanchthon believed that this doctrine [unconditional predestination] did not differ greatly from the Fate of the Stoics" (Arminius, "Declaration of Sentiments," in *Writings* 1:239).

21. See John Calvin, *Institutes of the Christian Religion*, ed. John T. McNeill, trans. F. L. Battles (Philadelphia: Westminster Press, 1960), 2:920 ff.

22. See Arminius, *Writings* 1:215 ff.

1. *Disobedience is an option.* God made the angels free moral agents, as we say; He made them in such a way that sin was a possibility. Nevertheless, sin is blameworthy, for it was a possibility, not a necessity.

2. *Restraints are set up.* Moral government, as opposed to anarchy, requires restraint upon free beings. Therefore, when God created the angels and humans, being himself the infinitely free Agent, He set up the restraint that their freedom would function legitimately only within His will.

3. *Satan and other angels throw off restraint.* Previous to the creation of Adam, God created numerous angels. A superior angel, who came to be known as Satan, or the devil, chose not to function within the sphere of God's will. He became proud and seems to have attempted to usurp at least some of the function that belonged to the preincarnate Christ.

Multitudes of angelic free agents took sides in this celestial war—one-third of them siding with Satan and being cast out of heaven along with him. This one-third figure is gained by interpreting the "stars" of heaven in Rev. 12:1ff. to mean the angels. These fallen angels became known as demons and continue to serve the interests of Satan and to oppose Christ.

4. *Adam and Eve throw off restraint.* Adam and Eve elected to walk with God for a time (Gen. 2:15-24), but Satan appeared to them in the guise of a serpent and tempted them to jump the traces of God's restraint and strike out on their own (3:1-5). Under Satan's influence, yet freely and therefore in a blameworthy act, they knowingly disobeyed a law God had given them (v. 6). Eve did so first, but Adam's act was the crucial one, since he, and not Eve, represented all humans unborn as yet (Rom. 5:12-21; 1 Cor. 15:21-22, 45 ff.). In this connection Wesley calls Adam "a public person,"[23] and he also calls Adam "the representative man."[24]

Arminius was probably right in saying that there are two kinds of law, natural and symbolical, and that Adam in the garden broke the latter kind. A natural law, says Arminius, is "imprinted on the mind of man," so that we can see it to be needful: for ex-

---

23. John Wesley, *The Doctrine of Original Sin* (New York: J. Soule and T. Mason, 1817), 97.
24. Ibid., 313. Harald Lindström has an excellent discussion of Wesley's views at this point (*Wesley and Sanctification* [London: Epworth Press, 1946], 35).

ample, that he is to love God and other persons. A symbolical law is "one that prescribes or forbids an act which, in itself, is neither agreeable nor disagreeable to God . . . which serves for the purpose that God may try whether man is willing to yield obedience to him, solely . . . because it has been the pleasure of God to require such obedience."[25]

Whatever one believes about the type of law in this case, Adam knowingly disobeyed the one special prohibition God had given him. His attention was drawn to what was forbidden, desire for it arose in him, he felt an impulse to eat the fruit, and though his judgment no doubt flashed a red light, he proceeded and disobeyed God. The proud rebel, having sinned as did Satan, fell into the same condemnation (1 Tim. 3:6).

The Arminian-Wesleyan teaching gives adequate reason why human sin deserves God's wrath instead of simply His pity, no attempt being made to minimize its gravity. It does not charge God foolishly, as authoring sin. And it views sin in us as starting in the same garden of which Genesis speaks, where two real people are persuaded to sin by a real adversary and where they freely choose to act in disobedience. But sin did more than just originate in angels and humans. In humans, it spread out to the entire species.

The Fact of Sin

Since sin is disobedience to God, it is not an objectively verifiable fact as are scientific and historical facts. Yet in some senses, to the believing, sin is a fact of the human past and of our present.

Scripture on the Fact of Sin. Scripture is unsparing in its record of sin. It portrays the sin of kings and commoners alike—vividly.

Scripture depicts the first human pair as disobeying God and hiding in the garden when the Lord God walks by, calling their names, seeking out the sinners (Gen. 3:8). It depicts Esau's sale of his birthright for the temporary satisfaction of food (25:28-34). It depicts Achan's theft of forbidden loot and his effort to hide his guilt by burying his treasures in the floor of his tent (Joshua 7). Scripture depicts Jonah fleeing God (Jonah 1) as Francis Thompson did and as he described it in the poem "The Hound of Heav-

---

25. Arminius, "Private Disputations," in *Writings* 2:71-72.

en." Scripture depicts even the apostle Peter's cowardly denial of acquaintance with Jesus (John 18:15-18, 25-27). It tells of Judas's betrayal of Jesus for a sum of money (Matt. 26:14-16).

Sin in Our Remembered Past. The record we humans have written outside Scripture, in all our "remembered past,"[26] contains the sordid as well as the stately. Rome's Nero holds a place of infamy in such a list, as do Hitler and Hess and their cohorts, including Eichmann.

The human story includes those who steal away "magnificent in sin," as Robert Browning sees the clandestine lovers in "Pippa Passes By." It is the two young people in an automobile where the girl's dreams have tumbled and lie with her garters on the car's floor—deplored in *J. B.,* the late Archibald MacLeish's drama in verse. It includes the "twisted things" T. S. Eliot speaks of who show themselves on city streets between midnight and 4 A.M. It is the deeds done in the darkness that the media shines its light upon each morning as the world eats breakfast.

Adamic Depravity

Some have spoken of the many evil things people do before they get to be evil persons. The truth is, there is a "radical defect" in people from the start, which inclines them to sinful acts. There is a fox in them—and a hog and an elephant and a lot of other animals, as Carl Sandburg saw it. Even if an angel has them by the hand, the serpent has them by the heart. Inmost in them is a condition that is "sin-most."

Since Adam (not Eve) had been sovereignly chosen by God to be the representative of the whole human family, Scripture teaches clearly that the whole human family suffered a detriment due to his disobedience. So clear is Scripture on this that all major segments of Christianity teach the doctrine of original sin—also referred to as Adamic sin (and by many other terms as well).

Adamic depravity will be treated here from the standpoint of (1) scriptural passages on it, (2) scriptural terms for it, (3) historical support for it, (4) theological terms for it, (5) its transmission, and (6) problems in the view of Adamic depravity.

---

26. One of the definitions of history.

Scriptural Passages on Adamic Depravity

That "the bent is in the birth" is often taught in Scripture. The Old Testament does not throw much light on sin's racial effects, as Paul does later in Romans 5 and 1 Corinthians 15, yet it does describe some of these effects.

To the disobedient Eve God said: "I will greatly increase your pains in childbearing; with pain you will give birth to children" (Gen. 3:16).

To the disobedient Adam, God said, "Cursed is the ground because of you; through painful toil you will eat of it all the days of your life. It will produce thorns and thistles for you, and you will eat the plants of the field. By the sweat of your brow you will eat your food until you return to the ground" (vv. 17-19).

Gen. 5:1-2 reads, "When God created man, he made him in the likeness of God. He created them male and female." The next verse states that Adam had a son, Seth, "in his own likeness, in his own image." This suggests that Adam's son was begotten in Adam's fallen image. Cain, Adam and Eve's first child, had already murdered the second child, Abel (4:8). This might be why it is said when Seth comes along that he is born in Adam's fallen likeness and image.

Soon we are reading that "every inclination of his [man's] heart is evil from childhood" (Gen. 8:21). That the sinfulness is universal, and that human "wickedness" stems from an "inclination" to it, is suggested when we read, "The Lord saw how great man's wickedness on the earth had become, and that every inclination of the thoughts of his heart was only evil all the time" (6:5). Sin as a bias or propensity or inclination has a scriptural basis here.[27] The Thirty-nine Articles of Anglicanism (Latin, 1563; American revision, 1801) describe Adam's "offspring" as "very far gone from original righteousness, and . . . inclined to evil."[28]

Job implies this sinfulness at the outset of life. Of "man born of woman" he asks, "Who can bring what is pure from the impure?" (14:1, 4).

---

27. The doctrinal statements of many denominations refer to this inclination to sin. That of the Church of the Nazarene *Manual* (Kansas City: Nazarene Publishing House, 1989), 31, states that due to original sin "everyone is . . . inclined to evil, and that continually."

28. Schaff, *Creeds of Christendom* 3:493.

Two Psalms passages also suggest this racial sinfulness. In one we read: "Even from birth the wicked go astray; from the womb they are wayward and speak lies. Their venom is like the venom of a snake" (58:3-4). The other is where the writer, probably David, says: "Surely I was sinful at birth, sinful from the time my mother conceived me" (51:5).

Some of the prophets teach this also. Jeremiah seems to as he says: "The heart is deceitful above all things and beyond cure. Who can understand it?" (17:9). Isaiah's complaints about human sinfulness seem to suggest that the condition is in the heart before it is in acts. He says: "Ah, sinful nation . . . children given to corruption! . . . Your whole head is injured, your whole heart afflicted. From the sole of your foot to the top of your head there is no soundness" (1:4-6).

As noted, then, the Old Testament describes Adam's first sin and some of its moral and natural effects; and it contains numerous suggestions that sinfulness belongs to us at the outset and constitutes an inclination to sin.

The New Testament, however, expressly teaches that all of Adam's descendants are inclined to acts of sin from the outset of their existence.

The clearest of all the New Testament writers on this is the apostle Paul. He teaches it the most expressly in Rom. 5:12-21. Referring to Adam, he says that "sin entered the world through one man" (v. 12). He adds that "in this way death came to all men, because all sinned"—that is, when Adam sinned, since the word for "sinned" is the aorist *hēmarton* and denotes what happened in a completed way when Adam sinned. Thus "death" in us is a result of Adam's sin, and of our sinning in our representative. This "death" means physical death, from what Paul says in 1 Cor. 15:21-22, where we read, "For since death came through a man, the resurrection of the dead comes also through a man. For as in Adam all die, so in Christ all will be made alive." Evidently, we would not have died physically, except for Adam's sin, but would have perhaps been translated as were Enoch (Gen. 5:24) and Elijah (2 Kings 2:11). In Romans, Paul goes on to say, "If the many died by the trespass of the one man, how much more did God's grace . . . by . . . Jesus Christ, overflow to the many!" (5:15). Adam and Christ are contrasted in several ways in this chapter, and Paul repeatedly says almost the same thing: that as we suffered a racewide detriment due to Adam's sin, Christ provides for even more than the undoing of the Adamic detriment.

The next chapter of Romans relates to this matter of the Adamic racial detriment. It refers 15 times to "sin" with the singular noun form—and in Scripture this often, as here, refers to the state or law or principle of sin in distinction from acts of sin.

Eph. 2:1-5 contains a suggestion that a state of sin exists in us at the very time of our birth. There Paul speaks of "sins" as acts "gratifying the cravings of our sinful nature and following its desires and thoughts" (v. 3). Then he continues, "Like the rest, we were by nature objects of wrath" (v. 3). The word here for "nature" is *phusei*, from *phusis*, which means "native condition" or "birth." Paul uses this term in Gal. 2:15, where he speaks of himself and others who are "Jews by birth." He also uses it twice in Rom. 11:24 as a reference to the way in which we are born, saying, "After all, if you [Gentiles] were cut out of an olive tree that is wild by nature, and contrary to nature were grafted into a cultivated olive tree, how much more readily will these, the natural branches, be grafted into their own olive tree!" Paul is saying that by nature, by birth, Gentiles are not of the proper "olive tree" stock, but that God has graciously grafted them into that stock, "contrary to nature"—contrary to the way they were born, as Gentiles. These and other uses of cognates of *phusis* show that it refers to our "native condition" or to our birth state. And as stated earlier, in Eph. 2:3 he says that the Ephesians (and perhaps other nearby churches being addressed) were "by nature objects of wrath." They were *by birth* objects of God's holy wrath, due to the state of original sin (which must be somehow cleansed away before we can enter into heaven).[29]

Jesus himself taught by implication the doctrine of original sin. He did this most clearly in words recorded in Mark 7:21-23: "For from within, out of the heart of men, proceed the evil thoughts, fornications, thefts, murders, adulteries, deeds of coveting and wickedness, as well as deceit, sensuality, envy, slander, pride and foolishness. All these evil things proceed from within and defile the man" (NASB).[30] He seems to be saying that a deep-

---

29. This cleansing is sovereign and gracious in infants who die, and also in justified persons who die while they are walking in the light (but have not been sanctified wholly). Christ's righteousness is imputed to them.

30. See His teaching on this in a parallel passage in Matt. 15:1-20.

down state of sinfulness now accompanies human nature, which inclines us humans to various acts of sin.

First Corinthians 15 teaches an Adamic racial detriment in the form of physical death. There Paul says, "But Christ has indeed been raised from the dead, the firstfruits of those who have fallen asleep" (v. 20). The apostle is talking here about Christ's bodily resurrection. Paul in the next verses infers that the detriment from Adam is physical death, not sinfulness. The two are closely connected, however, since the physical death detriment referred to here agrees with the "death" detriment referred to in Rom. 5:12—where the context speaks mostly of sinfulness as the content of Adamic racial detriment.

Scriptural Terms for Adamic Depravity

A number of terms are used in Scripture for what is often called original sin.

Indwelling Sin. This is found only twice, both times in Romans 7. Paul says, "As it is, it is no longer I myself who do it, but it is sin living in me" (v. 17). He also says, "Now if I do what I do not want to do, it is no longer I who do it, but it is sin living in me that does it" (v. 20). In the first of these passages the word for "living in" is *enoikousa*. The whole passage is *hē enoikousa en emoi hamartia*—literally translated, "the living-in-me sin." It may be translated as "sin that dwelleth in me" (KJV), or "sin which dwells within me" (RSV), or "sin which indwells me" (NASB). The word is a participle, from *oikos,* for "house." It refers to a state of sin (not an act) that had its abode in the Romans writer. In verse 20 the word is *oikousa,* with *en* occurring separately as a preposition rather than a prefix.

Paul personifies this state of sin in Romans 7. He says it "deceived" him: "For sin, seizing the opportunity afforded by the commandment, deceived me, and through the commandment put me to death" (v. 11). He also calls it a "law at work" that "is right there with me" (v. 21) and that prevents him from doing "the good" that he wants to do (v. 19).

In this treatment, Paul helps us see something of what original sin, here referred to as "indwelling sin," is like. It is deceptive (v. 11). It occasions coveting, for Paul says, "But sin, seizing the opportunity afforded by the commandment ["Do not covet"], produced in me every kind of covetous desire" (v. 8). It is parasitical, similar to a dead body tied to a person, for Paul asks, "Who will rescue me from this body of death?" (v. 24). It is enslaving, for Paul says, "For I have the desire to do what is good, but I cannot carry it out" (v. 18)—due to this state of sin.

The Law of Sin. This is discussed in Rom. 7:21, 23, 25, and also in Romans 8. In chapter 8 we read that "the law of the Spirit of life set me free from the law of sin and death" (v. 2). It is called a law, meaning that it is a principle or state or condition. This law is no doubt the same as the indwelling sin of the previous chapter. And Paul says that he has been freed from it.[31]

The Sinful Nature. This term is also used for Adamic depravity in Romans 8 in the NIV. We read of the "sinful nature" that weakens God's law (v. 3), and of those "who live according to the sinful nature" (v. 5). And Paul says, "Those controlled by the sinful nature cannot please God" (v. 8). But he then states that victory over it is possible: "You, however, are controlled not by the sinful nature but by the Spirit, if the Spirit of God lives in you" (v. 9). This "sinful nature" is the same as the "sinful mind" referred to elsewhere in this same chapter. Paul says that the "sinful mind is hostile to God. It does not submit to God's law, nor can it do so" (v. 7). The KJV calls this the "carnal mind," and the RSV renders it "the mind that is set on the flesh"; and the NASB, similarly, has "the mind set on the flesh." The important matter is that the law of sin, the sinful nature, and so forth, all seem to be references to the indwelling sin of Romans 7, and this condition seems to come from Adam's sin, according to Rom. 5:12-21. We can be free from it, according to Rom. 8:2, 9, and 6:11, 18, 22.

A "Worldly" Condition. Original sin is referred to as a "worldly" condition in the NIV of 1 Corinthians 3; as a state of being "carnal" in the KJV;[32] of being "of the flesh" in the RSV; and of be-

---

31. There is variation in the way the old Greek New Testament manuscripts read on the "me" of Rom. 8:2. The two very oldest ones read "you" (i.e., the Sinaiticus and the Vaticanus). But the Alexandrinus and the Codex Bezae, not quite as old, read "me." The RSV and NIV read "me," while the NASB reads "you." William Sanday and A. C. Headlam and James Denney and others prefer the *me* reading because he has just been talking about himself, and not his readers, in what we have marked off as chapter 7. In any case, either Paul or his readers are declared to be free from this law of sin—original sin. Sin is not merely suppressed; it can be cleansed away.

32. Those who wonder what the carnal nature consists of, in distinction from the human nature, should note its characteristics mentioned here in 1 Cor. 3:1 ff. and in Rom. 7:11-25 (much of which describes the outworkings of the indwelling sin mentioned in vv. 17 and 20).

ing "fleshly" in the NASB. It is the opposite of being "spiritual" (v. 1, KJV, RSV, NASB, NIV). People so characterized are "mere infants in Christ" (v. 1) who must be fed with "milk" (v. 2). Its outworkings are "jealousy and quarreling" (v. 3) and divisiveness (vv. 4-5).

The Flesh. This is from the Greek *sarx,* which is actually one of the several biblical terms discussed just above (the "sinful nature," the "sinful mind," the "worldly" condition). In the New Testament, the Greek word *sarx* is used in several different senses—even by the same writer. In John 1:14 it seems to mean "of human nature": "And the Word became flesh *[sarx],* and dwelt among us" (NASB). Paul often used it in this wholesome sense. He used it to mean simply "the sphere of man"[33] in Rom. 9:3, where he speaks of the Israelites as "my brethren, my kinsmen according to the flesh" (NASB). When Paul said, in Gal. 1:16, that he had not gone to Jerusalem to "consult with flesh and blood" (NASB), he used "flesh" of "man as such"[34]—so that Eduard Schweizer can say, "The nuance of that which is sinful is completely absent."[35]

Yet Paul does, in a number of places, use *sarx* as a synonym of what is sinful, as one of the names for the state of Adamic depravity or original sin. And when *sarx* is so used, it is often antithetical to the Spirit (as in Rom. 8:4-9 and especially in Gal. 5:17). In Rom. 8:4-9 Paul contrasts the flesh and the Spirit, writing, "For those who are according to the flesh set their minds on the things of the flesh, but those who are according to the Spirit, the things of the Spirit" (v. 5, NASB). Then he adds, "For the mind set on the flesh is death, but the mind set on the Spirit is life and peace, because the mind set on the flesh is hostile toward God; for it does not subject itself to the law of God, for it is not even able to do so" (vv. 6-7, NASB). Further, to all this he adds that "those who are in the flesh cannot please God" (v. 8, NASB).

---

33. See Eduard Schweizer, *Theological Dictionary of the New Testament,* ed. Gerhard Friedrich Kittel, trans. Geoffrey W. Bromiley (Grand Rapids: William B. Eerdmans Publishg Co., 1971), 7:127 (TDNT). This article by Schweizer treats in great detail the many ways in which *sarx* is used in Scripture and in other ancient literature (see 7:98-151). See also the unpublished Ph.D. dissertation of the late Willard H. Taylor, in the Nazarene Theological Seminary's Broadhurst Library, on the contrast of the flesh and Spirit in Paul's writings.

34. Schweizer, TDNT 7:128.

35. Ibid.

THE DOCTRINE OF SIN ▷ 271

So to be in the flesh is often bad. Yet the flesh can be vanquished, not at death, but during this life. Paul teaches this twice in Romans 8. In verse 4 he speaks of "us, who do not walk according to the flesh" (NASB). And in verse 9 he says, "However, you are not in the flesh but in the Spirit, if indeed the Spirit of God dwells in you" (NASB).

A similar discussion of the flesh and Spirit as contrasted, and of the flesh being vanquished, appears in Gal. 5:17, 24. In verse 17 Paul says, "For the flesh sets its desire against the Spirit, and the Spirit against the flesh; for these are in opposition to one another, so that you may not do the things that you please" (NASB). The person described is regenerate, since the Holy Spirit indwells him or her (see John 3:5-8). The person described is not sanctified wholly, however, since he or she is still indwelt by the *sarx*, which is surely used here as a synonym of original sin and its personified power.

After listing the "deeds" of this "flesh" condition (vv. 19-21, NASB), Paul shows that, already in this life, while we are still in the flesh in the sense of our earthly and faltering humanity, this "flesh" can be crucified. He says, "Now those who belong to Christ Jesus [he seems to mean those who belong most truly, after the *sarx* has been cleansed away through the second work of grace] have crucified the flesh with its passions and desires" (v. 24, NASB).[36]

Sin, or the Sin. Often it has been said, simply, that in Scripture *hamartia*, when in the noun form and in the singular, refers to original sin. This is taught by George A. Turner, W. T. Purkiser, Richard E. Howard, and the present writer.[37] This widespread understanding, especially disseminated in the Holiness Movement (which has a special interest in the matter of original sin, since its main emphasis is that original sin can be cleansed away in this present life), must be challenged.

---

36. This "belong," interpreted here as referring to the second work of grace, might well refer to belonging in the sense of ownership and approval, which H. Orton Wiley, S. S. White, and many others say is what sealing (as of a letter or college degree) consists of. Paul refers to this sealing in Eph. 1:13-14.

37. See George Allen Turner, *The Vision Which Transforms*, 99; J. Kenneth Grider, *Entire Sanctification: The Distinctive Doctrine of Wesleyanism* (Kansas City: Beacon Hill Press of Kansas City, 1980), 21-24; W. T. Purkiser, *The Biblical Foundations,* vol. 1 of *Exploring Christian Holiness* (Kansas City: Beacon Hill Press of Kansas City, 1983), 131-32; and Richard E. Howard, *Newness of Life: A Study in the Thought of Paul* (Kansas City: Beacon Hill Press of Kansas City, 1975), 39-40.

There are indeed many times when *hamartia,* in the noun form and in the singular, does refer to original sin, and that will be shown presently. But there are in Scripture many appearances of the singular noun *hamartia* that do not refer to original sin.

John, for example, seems to have used the singular noun *hamartia* in several ways. In 1 John 1:7, the word *hamartia* seems not to refer to original sin but to the state of sinfulness that results from nonwillful breaches of God's will. The passage reads: "But if we walk in the light, as he is in the light, we have fellowship with one another, and the blood of Jesus, his Son, purifies us from all sin" (1984 ed.; "every sin," 1973). The word for "sin" here is the singular genitive case noun *hamartias.*

We are cleansed "all at once," at what H. Orton Wiley calls a "single stroke," from original sin by Christ's baptism with the Holy Spirit. The aorist "completed" tense is used for that cleansing, as in Acts 15:8-9 and in 1 Thess. 5:23. But the blood of Christ cleanses us moment by moment from the state of acquired sinfulness that results from involuntary transgressions committed while we are walking in the light as Christians—a moment-by-moment cleansing. So, in 1 John 1:7, the singular noun (in the genitive case) *hamartias* refers not to original sin but to the state of sinfulness that results from nonwillful breaches of God's will. The *hamartias,* here, cannot refer to original sin (1) because its cleansing is gradual, since the word for cleansing, *katharidzei,* is in the present tense and not in the aorist tense; and (2) because this is a cleansing that happens not by faith (see Acts 15:8-9; 26:18) but simply as the believer is walking "in the light."

In 1 John 1:8 we also have an instance of the singular noun *hamartia,* in the accusative case, *hamartian,* which does not refer either to the state of original sin or to acquired sinfulness. It refers simply to what might be called the fact of sin. The passage reads, "If we claim to be without sin, we deceive ourselves." This seems to refer to the fact of sin, including acts of sin and original sin, since the next words speak about both the first and the second works of grace. There we read, "If we confess our sins, he is faithful and just and will forgive us our sins and purify us from all unrighteousness" (v. 9). It is to be noted, again, that this passage states that we are forgiven for the acts and purified from the state of sin. Since we are cleansed from all unrighteousness, John seems to be referring here to the cleansing of the second work of grace—in which case the unrighteousness would be a reference to the Adamic state of sin.

Another passage where the singular noun *hamartia* refers to the fact of sin or the fact of sinfulness, and not to original sin, is John 1:29. There John the Baptist says, "Look, the Lamb of God, who takes away the sin *[hamartian]* of the world!" This is surely "sin" in all its ramifications—sin simply as a fact.

The singular *hamartia* (in the dative) seems also to refer to the universal fact of sinfulness, and not specifically to original sin, in John 8:21, where Jesus says, "I am going away, and you will look for me, and you will die in your sin." Here "sin" surely means their total distancing from God, perhaps in both willful act and Adamic state.

An interesting similar use of the singular noun *hamartia(n)* appears twice in John 9:41, where Jesus says, "If you were blind, you would not be guilty of sin *[hamartian]*; but now that you claim you can see, your guilt *[hamartia]* remains." This NIV rendering has "guilt" instead of "sin" in the second instance here of this singular noun. The RSV has "guilt" in both instances, but the usually-more-literal NASB has "sin" both times. The importance of these appearances of *hamartian* and *hamartia,* for the present discussion, is that the singular noun is twice used when it quite evidently does not refer to Adamic sin. It refers to their own acts of sin, for which, if they had been blind, they would not have been guilty—but for which they are guilty, since they were not blind but sinned willfully.

Hamartian also refers to an act or to acts of sin in John 19:11, where "the greater sin" (NASB) is a reference to the betrayal of Jesus by Judas.

Jesus, more than anyone else, uses this singular noun of acts of sin—as the Gospel writers report His teaching. He uses it this way when He says, "If I had not done among them what no one else did, they would not be guilty of sin *[hamartian]*" (John 15:24). Immediately before this, He had twice used this singular noun of a condition that resulted from their acts. He had said, "If I had not come and spoken to them, they would not be guilty of sin *[hamartian]*. Now, however, they have no excuse for their sin *[hamartias]*" (v. 22).

Numerous other instances of *hamartia* as a singular noun not referring to original sin can be cited, including 1 Pet. 2:22; 1 John 3:4-6; and 5:16.

Yet the singular noun *hamartia* does often refer to the state of original sin. It does so numerous times in Romans 5—8. Quite evidently from the context there and elsewhere the state or principle of sin—original sin—is being referred to.

In Rom. 5:12 the "sin" that entered the world through Adam is *hē hamartia*—and the "sin" in "death through sin" is from that same singular noun. But in "all sinned" a verbal form, the aorist *hēmarton*, is used. It states that people unborn as yet participated in Adam's sin, since he was God's chosen representative of them.

In Romans 6 numerous instances of the singular noun *hamartia* appear, quite evidently referring to the state of sin discussed in chapter 5, a racial detriment stemming from Adam's transgression. The NIV has "Shall we go on sinning . . . ?" in verse 1. But the Greek has *hē hamartia,* a noun and not a verb, so that "in sin," evidently referring to the state of sin, is the translation in KJV, RSV, and NASB. The word "sin" in "We died to sin" (v. 2) is the noun *hē hamartia.*[38] In verse 6, "sin" in "the body of sin," which is "destroyed," according to the KJV and RSV, and "done away with" in the NASB and NIV, is this singular noun—not a verb.[39] In the remainder of this chapter this singular noun appears 12 times (in vv. 7, 10, 11, 12, 13, 14, 16, 17, 18, 20, 22, 23). All of them, from the context, refer to the state of sin—there being only one verbal, *hamartēsōmen,* "Shall we sin . . . ?" (v. 15, NIV, NASB), which is a reference to acts of sin. Interestingly, and excitingly, the people Paul was writing to had already become "freed" from this principle of sin, according to verses 18 and 22, where we read, "You have been set free from [the] sin." "Free from" means more than the suppression of sins (Calvinism) and more than the counteraction of sin (Keswickism). It means that we are cleansed from it so that it is destroyed, as is taught in Wesleyan-holiness circles.

---

38. This is one of the scriptural bases for the widespread holiness movement reference to "dying to sin" or "dying out," as what is preparatory to faith for receiving entire sanctification.

39. The NIV until 1984 rendered it too lightly: "so that the body of sin might be rendered powerless." The Greek word here, *katargēthē,* warrants a stronger translation, and the NIV has been changed to say that this "body of sin" is "done away with."

It is clear that often, especially in Paul's writings, *hamartia* as a singular noun does indeed refer to original sin.

The terms we have surveyed are not the only ones occurring in Scripture. They are the most obvious ones. Others are found in both Testaments, but these must suffice in this limited discussion.

Besides scriptural support of the doctrine of original sin, there is much historical support of it—to which we now turn.

Historical Support for Adamic Depravity

The doctrine of Adamic depravity or original sin has a long and strong support in the history of Christianity. Most of the fathers, East and West, taught it more or less, including the influential Augustine, as did all the Reformers. The rationalists and modernists have denied it, but the neoorthodox have set forth some form of the doctrine. And, of course, evangelicals have advocated the doctrine in its classical form.

In general, the early fathers understood that physical death results from Adam's sin. Tatian seems to have been the first to see that the natural world also suffers effects due to Adam's sin. Theophilus of Antioch taught that animals were not at first ferocious nor venomous. He wrote, "But the sin in which man was concerned brought evil upon them [the animals]."[40] Irenaeus gave considerable treatment to the doctrine of original sin, but Clement of Alexandria did not seem to be aware of it. Origen, following Plato, sometimes taught that we are born in a kind of sinfulness due to our own sins prior to this life—for he agreed with Plato on each individual soul's existence before this life. However, in Origen's commentary on Romans, he clearly espouses the doctrine of the racial fall in Adam.

Athanasius sometimes taught that the race fell due to Adam's transgression, but he was not nearly as clear in the teaching as some, such as the second-century Irenaeus.

It was certainly taught by Cyril of Jerusalem and John Chrysostom. And Augustine, of course, taught and elucidated it more than any other father East or West—partly because of what Daniel Steele called his "collision" with Pelagius (who denied it, along with Coelestius).

---

40. See F. R. Tennant, *The Sources of the Doctrines of the Fall and Original Sin* (New York: Schocken Books, 1968), 281.

Peter Abelard denied original sin, as he did certain other received doctrines (such as the Trinity). Yet in general the doctrine was taught in medieval times.

The Reformers all taught and emphasized original sin. In his Ninety-five Theses Martin Luther said that since the fall of Adam we humans will, taking our natural way, fall inevitably into sin. He thus sided with Augustine that original sin enslaves us. His doctrine of original sin and its enslaving results was basic to his view that justification is necessarily by grace alone through faith alone.

James Arminius also emphasized the doctrine of original sin. He said that the whole race fell when Adam sinned, and that due to that Fall we lost the knowledge of God, the knowledge of things pertaining to eternal salvation, the rectitude and holiness of the will, and the immortality of the body.[41]

Significantly, Arminius taught that "the power of willing" was not lost in the Fall, but that the power to will any good thing was lost. Thus, if we will any good thing before our regeneration, such as to turn to Christ, we must be assisted by prevenient grace.

Even more so, John Wesley emphasized the doctrine of original sin. Besides sermons on the subject, such as "Sin in Believers," and discussion of it in his *Explanatory Notes upon the New Testament,* he wrote his most sustained treatise on "The Doctrine of Original Sin." He considered anyone who did not believe in original sin to be "a heathen still."

Interestingly, on the very first page of his treatise on original sin, he refers to it as a "state" five times. Some relationists, who prefer to say that original sin constitutes a deprivation but not so much depravation, and that it is not so much a state or condition but an alienated relationship to God, do not follow Wesley in this regard.[42] For Wesley, correctly, original sin is a state or condition that is, of course, relational—and that inclines us to acts of sin. He

---

41. See Arminius, "Private Disputations," in *Writings* 2:71.

42. Mildred Wynkoop is such a theologian. Of sin she says, "It is a relational term" (*A Theology of Love: The Dynamic of Wesleyanism* [Kansas City: Beacon Hill Press of Kansas City, 1972], 1949). She also says, "Holiness and sin are, thus, two kinds of relationship to God" (ibid., 177). She prefers not to refer to either sin or holiness as states. Of holiness she says, "It is dynamic—a 'way,' not a state; a life, not a static goodness" (ibid., 360). On its consisting of deprivation, and thus a lack of a correct relationship to God, she says, "Sin is simply the absence of this relationship [of "personal fellowship with God"] because man has repudiated it" (Ibid., 154).

takes great pains in his treatise on the subject to support it from Scripture and from human history. He says that due to original sin there is in us no "mixture of good,"[43] and that "every imagination" of the heart and "every thought" is "only evil continually."[44]

The confessions and articles of faith of many Protestant denominations teach similarly.

Theological Terms for Adamic Depravity

Besides terms for original sin found in Scripture, there are numerous theological terms for the doctrine that have been developed.

Original Sin. This is no doubt the most widely used theological designation for Adamic depravity.

The wide use of this term for referring to the racial detriment stemming from Adam gives the doctrine recognition. Yet both words in the phrase "original sin" are in themselves misleading as to what is intended. To the altogether uninitiated, the word "original," coupled with the word "sin," would suggest the first act of sin—Adam's act of rebellion in the Garden of Eden. However, "original sin" refers to a state of sin in us due to that original act of sin on Adam's part.

The word "sin" also tends to be misleading. In this phrase it refers to a state, but it is commonly used of an act of disobedience. And we think of being guilty for sin, whereas for this original sin we are not now guilty (because of Christ), and it therefore does not make us culpable (so that, as John Wesley said, no one will ever go into eternal hell for this sin alone).

Inherited Depravity. This term also has both advantages and disadvantages. To call this racewide state "depravity" is less ambiguous than to call it sin—for it is indeed a state of being inclined toward, or biased in favor of, acts of sin. That is its advantage.

Unfortunately, however, the word "inherited" suggests what is biologically inherited; yet Scripture does not locate sin in our genes but in our solidarity with Adam, who represented us badly (Rom. 5:12-21; 1 Cor. 15:21-22). Scripture nowhere teaches that this racial detriment is ours because of our parents.

---

43. John Wesley, "The Doctrine of Original Sin," in *Works* 9:197.
44. Ibid.

Adamic Sin and Racial Sin. These are similar theological terms. They are advantageous as referring to original sin's historical origin in the first man and in referring to the extent of the Adamic detriment as racewide. The disadvantage is that calling it "sin" would no doubt mean to many people that we are now guilty for it. And the term "sin" does not state what it particularly consists of—a bias toward acts of sin.

Inherent Depravity. This certainly has advantages. The word "depravity" is not misleading at all, for this Adamic detriment consists of an inclination to acts of sin.

But the disadvantage of the word "inherent" is that the word suggests what is part and parcel of the human nature—what we cannot expect to be redeemed from.

Inbred Sin. This is quite misleading. It sounds as if we are talking about something located in the genes that is passed on from one human generation to the next. Besides, if this condition is "bred" into humans, we cannot get rid of it, even as we cannot get rid of traits bred into us through our genes and chromosomes.

Racial Depravity. This is one of the best of the theological terms for the detriment being treated here. The word "depravity," as mentioned, is better than the word "sin" in referring to this condition as a tendency to acts of sin. The word "racial" has the advantage of pointing to the extent of this detriment—as widespread in humans as the human race itself.

Adamic Depravity. This would not be felicitous to anyone who believes in biological evolution and denies the historicity of Adam and Eve, and who therefore does not agree with the apostle Paul that there was indeed an Adam the First, even as there was a Second Adam, Christ.

Evangelicals, however, have no problem with the reference to Adam in this term. And the term "Adamic" has the special advantage of indicating the source of this detriment. It also has the advantage of distinguishing this type of depravity from acquired depravity, the inclination to acts of sin that builds up in us as we repeatedly do certain acts of sin such as stealing or lying. The word "depravity," furthermore, is felicitous, for reasons mentioned earlier.

All these matters considered, "Adamic depravity" is probably the most serviceable of the theological terms.

The Transmission of Adamic Depravity

Two major theories and one minor view have developed on the matter of how the racial detriment got from Adam to us.

The Realistic Theory. According to this view, also called the Natural Headship theory, we were somehow racially bound up with and in Adam to such extent that we actually sinned when he did. This is the theory of Augustine and of many theologians in the Augustinian-Calvinistic theological tradition.

On the basis of the Realistic view, God predestinates the eternal destiny of each of us before we are ever born. The unconditional reprobation of those not elected to salvation is their just desert, since they stand guilty before God for having really and actually sinned when Adam did. Those unconditionally elected to heavenly bliss also sinned in that way and are thereby deserving of eternal damnation; but God in His sovereign kindness elects unconditionally that they will instead enjoy His presence forever.

The Representative Theory. This is the view that each person in the whole human race comes into the world in a state of sinfulness because Adam had been chosen as our representative and because our representative sinned against God. This is sometimes called the Federal Headship theory. Adam is like the head of a federation of individuals; and when our federal head, our representative, sinned, we all suffered. Indeed, we all sinned, in a sense.

This is probably the theory of James Arminius, who says: "The whole of this sin [Adam's sin], however, is not peculiar to our first parents, but is common to the entire race and to all their posterity, who, at the time when this sin was committed, were in their loins."[45] It is strange that he includes Eve, with Adam, as occasioning the racial detriment. Paul refers to Eve's sin (1 Tim. 2:13-14), but he speaks only of Adam's sin as racially significant (Rom. 5:12-21; 1 Cor. 15:21-22).

In Arminius's time, the Realistic and the Representative theories had not been differentiated clearly; yet he likely taught what would now be called the Representative theory, since he does not view us as being guilty at present due to Adam's sin as in the Realistic theory, and therefore deserving of eternal damnation.

---

45. Arminius, "Public Disputations," in *Writings* 1:486.

This is more clearly the theory of John Wesley, who writes: "Sin is entailed upon me, not by immediate generation, but by my first parent. In Adam all died; by the disobedience of one, all men were made sinners; all men without exception, who were in his loins when he ate the forbidden fruit."[46] The phrase "not by immediate generation" shows that Wesley does not accept anything like the Genetic theory, developed later. He states clearly that the detriment is not transmitted by our parents, but only through Adam. Like Arminius, Wesley taught that no one will suffer eternal punishment for Adam's sin alone, and that no one is deserving at birth (or later, unconditionally) of eternal damnation. Obviously, he did not hold to the Realistic view.

Likewise, the Representative theory is held by H. Orton Wiley, who explains: "The Federal Theory accounts for it [guilt and depravity] on the purely legal ground of a covenant, in which Adam became the divinely appointed representative of the race. Hence his obedience was reckoned or imputed to his posterity as their obedience, and his transgression as their transgression."[47] Here Wiley even uses the word "representative" of his understanding. We shall soon see, however, that Wiley also adheres to the Genetic Mode view.

The Representative theory accords with Scripture. According to the apostle Paul, Adam's sin had dire consequences for all of us. He says, "The judgment followed one sin [Adam's] and brought condemnation" (Rom. 5:16). Paul also says that "the result of one trespass was condemnation for all men" (v. 18).

In this view, as in the Realistic theory, it is understood that we sinned, in some sense, when Adam sinned. This is in part because of the word *hēmarton* in Rom. 5:12. As aorist in tense, this word requires us to translate Paul as saying "all sinned" when Adam sinned. The KJV's "all have sinned" would require a perfect tense in the Greek. Colonial American children learned the rhyme "In Adam's fall, we sinned all," and the rhyme taught correctly, since Paul uses this aorist-tense word and says "all sinned." In the Representative theory understanding, we all sinned because our

---

46. John Wesley, *A Plain Account of Christian Perfection* (Kansas City: Beacon Hill Press, 1950), 21.
47. Wiley, *Christian Theology* 2:114.

representative did—the federal head of our species, chosen as such by God.

The Genetic Theory. This was first taught by John Miley in his systematic theology of 1892. Miley says, "There is an entirely sufficient account in the law of genetic transmission. The corruption of the progenitors of the race is thus transmitted to their offspring."[48] He also explains, "As the law of genetic transmission rules in all forms of propagated life and determines the likeness of the offspring to the parentage, and as it was sufficient for the transmission of the primitive holiness to all the race, it must be a sufficient account of the common native depravity."[49]

In this Genetic theory, Miley probably did not mean to say that original sin is simply passed on through the genes and is something biological as are human traits. Yet he did want to teach that original sin is a depravity passed on to us by our parents, even as physical characteristics are ours due to their genes.

Theologians have not generally espoused the Genetic theory. H. Orton Wiley did, who also taught the Representative theory. He thinks the Genetic Mode theory is taught in both the Realistic and the Representative Mode views. After defining the Genetic Mode view as "simply the natural law of heredity,"[50] Wiley says: "The Augustinian anthropology with its realistic mode of accounting for original sin, is based upon this law of genetic transmission."[51] Then he says, "The Federal theory of imputation regarded Adam as the representative of the race, solely on the ground of his natural headship."[52] And he continues: "Arminianism has made much of this genetic law in its explanation of native depravity."[53] His next words are a lengthy and sometimes vague quote from John Miley, which ends up with a clear statement of Miley's Genetic Mode theory.

Richard S. Taylor views the transmission of original sin in the same way as Wiley. He, too, accepts the Representative Mode theory but couples with it the Genetic Mode view. The place where Tay-

---

48. John Miley, *Systematic Theology,* 505.
49. Ibid., 506.
50. Wiley, *Christian Theology* 2:118.
51. Ibid.
52. Ibid.
53. Ibid.

lor most clearly takes this combination view is in his article on "Geneticism" in *Beacon Dictionary of Theology*. There he says of the Genetic Mode theory, which he calls "Geneticism": "This is the view that original sin, in the sense of moral depravity, is transmitted from Adam to his posterity by natural generation."[54] Of this view he says, "Wesleyan-Arminianism and Augustinianism presuppose geneticism."[55] Taylor continues, "Some suppose that if one is a realist or federalist ([that is, a] representative theory adherent), he cannot be a geneticist. This is an error. Wesley was a geneticist, but also a federalist."[56] Soon, then, Taylor gives another clear and correct definition of the Genetic Mode theory. He says, "A geneticist is simply one who believes that each generation inherits a sinful bias from the previous generation, and so on back to Adam."[57]

Taylor defines the Genetic Mode view correctly. Yet Wiley and Taylor seem not to understand what the Realistic and the Representative view are, or else they would not teach that either of them can be combined with the Genetic Mode view.

Take the Realistic Mode view. As explained earlier, it is the view that each person is now born with original sin due to actual participation with Adam in that first disobedience in the Garden of Eden.

And take the Representative Mode view. Again, as explained earlier, it is the understanding that we are all born with original sin because Adam had been appointed by God as the representative of us all, and our representative failed by disobeying God.

In neither of these two classical views is anything said about our inheriting original sin from our parents. No single passage of Scripture suggests that it comes from our parents. Paul, who is the only Scripture writer who speaks of its source, says only that Adam's sin is the occasion of it. Paul make it clear, even, that the cause of it is not Eve's sin, but Adam's only—which makes one wonder why Arminius and Wiley both say, as quoted above, that it comes from both of our "first parents."

If we understand what Paul is saying, we do not need to add anything to it.

---

54. Richard S. Taylor, "Geneticism," in *Beacon Dictionary of Theology*, 231. See also his *Theological Formulation*, vol. 3 of *Exploring Christian Holiness* (Kansas City: Beacon Hill Press of Kansas City, 1985), 96-98, for his most complete discussion of this.

55. Taylor, "Geneticism," 231.

56. Ibid., 232.

57. Ibid.

Hitler badly represented many Germans unborn as yet when he led the Third Reich during the 1930s and 1940s. Germans who have had no physical contact with Hitler, and who might utterly scorn what he did, were represented badly by him—and consequently suffer a detriment.

In contrast to Adam, Christ, the Second Adam, was also chosen by God to be the Representative of the race (see Rom. 5:12-21; 1 Cor. 15:21ff.). Christ, in His perfect obedience to the Father, represented us well and provided for the undoing of the detriment caused by the first Adam. Christ was made the new Head of the race, and there does not need to be any physical or genetic connection between Christ and us for us to have been represented favorably by this Second Adam.

Everything that Wiley and Taylor say about the laws of genetics and the natural laws of heredity as the way original sin is transmitted to us, through our parents, not only adds to what Paul says but indeed conflicts with what he says. Wiley and Taylor know what Paul teaches, and they teach it, but they also add what is foreign to what Paul says. Evidently, Wiley and Taylor speak of both Adam and Eve as occasioning original sin in us in part because they believe it is transmitted genetically through both parents.

Wesley knew nothing of the Genetic theory. This is clearly shown in what was quoted earlier, where he says, "Sin is entailed upon me, not by immediate generation [meaning not by my parents], but by my first parent."[58] He even avoids the error of Arminius and Wiley, who said the detriment is due to our "first parents," and singled it down to Adam only, as Paul did. Yet Wesley taught not only the negative deprivation due to the Holy Spirit's withdrawal because of Adam's sin but also the utter depravation of human nature. Paul did not say we got it from our parents, through genes, but only through Adam; and yet it is a state or condition that is so utterly real for Paul that he often personifies it, speaking of it as though it is an entity, saying that it "deceived" him (Rom. 7:11), dwelt in him (vv. 17, 20, KJV), and wrought in him "all manner of coveting" (v. 8, ASV).

The word *transmission,* long associated with this matter of how the Adamic detriment gets from Adam to us, is somewhat

---

58. Wesley, *A Plain Account,* 21.

misleading. The word might suggest something physical, something biological, but that does not obtain.

Interest in the Genetic theory, on the part of theologians such as Richard Taylor, is appropriate because it is intended to guard our being born with a corrupt nature. Original sin does constitute more than a deprivation—a lack of certain ministries of the Holy Spirit, a withdrawal of those ministries after Adam disobeyed God. It constitutes, in great part due to that negative deprivation, a positive depravation—a real, actual bent or propensity or inclination to acts of sin. Yet this kind of understanding can be entirely and vigorously incorporated into the Representative theory of the so-called transmission.

Problems in the View of Adamic Depravity

Although the doctrine of Adamic depravity or original sin is clearly taught in Scripture, so clearly taught that it is almost a universal teaching of Christian denominations, several theological problems gather around the doctrine.

It Seems to Be Unfair. Many people feel this way. Charles G. Finney, who located sin only in the will, felt that it would be unfair for the whole race to suffer a detriment due to Adam's sin. He wrote, "Moral depravity can only be predicated of violations of moral law."[59] He is obliquely saying that it does not stem from Adam's sin, but from our own acts of sin. He defines sin as "the violation of moral law," which "must consist of choice."[60] Of moral depravity he further says, "It cannot consist of anything back of choice . . . What is back of choice is without a pale of legislation."[61] Finney certainly believed in depravity, but not in Adamic or racial depravity. That is why his favorite term for it is "moral depravity"—by which he means a depravity resulting solely from our disobedient acts.

Those who feel that the doctrine suggests unfairness should realize that it would be unfair only without the place Christ has as the Undoer of the Adamic detriment. In Romans 5, Paul twice affirms the "much more" of saving grace. "But the gift [of Christ]

---

59. Charles G. Finney, *Finney's Systematic Theology,* ed. J. H. Fairchild (1846; Minneapolis: Bethany Fellowship, 1976 reprint), 166.

60. Ibid.

61. Ibid., 167.

is not like the trespass [of Adam]. For if the many died by the trespass of the one man, how much more did God's grace and the gift that came by the grace of the one man, Jesus Christ, overflow to the many!" (v. 15). Again, "For if, by the trespass of the one man, death reigned through that one man, how much more will those who receive God's abundant provision of grace and of the gift of righteousness reign in life through the one man, Jesus Christ" (v. 17). These passages show that we are much farther ahead, because of Christ, than we would have been had we not had the Adamic detriment. Understood in this way, the charge of unfairness is dissipated.

Unavoidable Guilt Is Wrong. Many people are sensitive about our being guilty, as well as inclined to sin, due to our representative's transgression. Methodism's Edwin Lewis used to pound his lectern and oppose original sin doctrine by saying, "No one can be guilty for another person's sin."

Both Calvinists and Arminians (and others) teach that guilt, as well as depravity, was passed on the race because of the sin of Adam the representative. Yet James Arminius, John Wesley, H. Orton Wiley, and Arminians generally understand that a racewide "free gift" occurred through Christ by which the guilt (but not the depravity) was done away with. The guilt did indeed obtain, because we did all sin through our representative, Adam. Paul says that we were under some kind of blanket "condemnation" (Rom. 5:16), from which Christ absolved us all.

So the objection to original sin doctrine (because it means that we are guilty for Adam's sin) evaporates. Original sin doctrine can be held, as in Arminianism, without holding that we are now guilty for Adam's transgression.

It Seems Substantival. This objection comes from those who might be called relationalists—such as Mildred Wynkoop. She does not like to speak of original sin as a state or condition. She thinks that it is basically an estranged relationship to God, and not also a state or condition that occasions such an estrangement.

As a relationalist, she distinguishes between "the substantival versus [the] relational concept of sin."[62] She says of both sin and holiness that they are "not things that can be weighed"[63]—

62. Wynkoop, *A Theology of Love*, 50. She also says, "Sin is not a substance," 49.
63. Ibid., 51.

strangely implying that some people think we can weigh them. She says, "Man's problem is not . . . some alien substance clinging to this soul but his own alienation from God."[64]

Several responses can be made to this kind of objection. One is that the usual and proper understanding of original sin is that it is a state or condition, and not what is substantival. Another is that no theologian or even layperson means to suggest that sin can be weighed or otherwise measured physically. Another is that Wynkoop does not seem to say nearly as much as Paul does about our existing in original sin due to Adam. If sin in the sense of original sin is "basically self-separation from God,"[65] it seems that we ourselves might be responsible for its origin, instead of Adam. Sin and holiness as states that are relational, also, is to be preferred to the view that they are only "personal relationships." If original sin is a state, then cleansing from it is called for—its purging.

From this study of original sin, perhaps ideally referred to as Adamic depravity, we turn now to a study of the other type of sin: acts of sin.

The Nature of Sin as an Act

A study of biblical terms for sin as an act will contribute to a definition of an act of sin. Also, such a study will help the Christian communicator to be specific in exposing the nature of sin acts.[66]

Sin as an Act in the Old Testament. In the Old Testament, as in the New Testament, there are generic terms for sin acts, metaphors, and concrete terms, such as theft.

1. *Generic terms.* One generic term is ra', found some 800 times and meaning "bad," the opposite of tob, "good." It is often translated "evil"; but like the English word "bad," it means whatever is harmful, and does not necessarily refer to what is morally bad. Figs can be "bad" (Jer. 24:8, NASB); but the term is used of Er's being "wicked in the Lord's sight" (Gen. 38:7). Another generic term is rasha', used about 350 times, best rendered

---

64. Ibid., 164.
65. Ibid., 51.
66. In this study of words for sin, the writer has received much help from C. Ryder Smith's *Bible Doctrine of Sin.*

"wicked," and always used in a moral sense (as in Exod. 2:13; Ps. 3:7). A third such term is *'asham,* appearing about 100 times and denoting the idea of guilt (see Hos. 4:15; Ps. 68:21).

2. *Metaphors.* Besides these generic terms, there are in the Old Testament numerous metaphors that describe acts of sin. The most common of these is *chattath,* the Old Testament counterpart of the New Testament *hamartia,* appearing some 600 times and denoting a missing of a mark. It is usually translated "sin" but often "sin offering." Its literal meaning of "missing the mark" is suggested by a few contexts where it is used. In Judg. 20:16 we read, "Among all these soldiers there were seven hundred chosen men who were left-handed, each of whom could sling a stone at a hair and not miss." Here it is used of missing a mark. It is used of missing one's path in Prov. 19:2: "It is not good to have zeal without knowledge, nor to be hasty and miss the way."

Well over 500 times it occurs of an act that is opposed to God's will, as in Exod. 10:16: "I [Pharaoh] have sinned against the Lord your God." Some 30 times it occurs in reference to an act that is directed against other human beings, as in 5:16: "Your servants [the Israelites] are being beaten, but the fault [or sin] is with your own people."

Another metaphor is *'aven,* literally meaning to "miss the way," appearing 220 times and usually translated "iniquity." The NIV renders it "sin" in 1 Sam. 3:13, where God says, "For I told him [Eli] that I would judge his family forever because of the sin he knew about." Eli's sin was not restraining his sons in their "contemptible" deportment.

Another metaphor is *'abar,* found some 600 times and literally meaning to "pass over." Usually it appears in a nonmoral sense. Yet it occasionally denotes a moral transgression, as in Hos. 8:1, where God says that "the people have broken ["transgressed," KJV] my covenant."

An interesting usage of the metaphor *shagag* is connected with the cities of refuge account in Num. 35:6-34. This word has to do with an "error"; and a distinction is made between culpable and nonculpable errors in this account. A murderer could not take sanctuary in one of the cities of refuge, for we read, "But if a man schemes and kills another man deliberately, take him away from my altar and put him to death" (Exod. 21:14). Even if a person hit someone with a stone or a piece of iron, killing him or her unintentionally, refuge was not available. Anyone should know that such an instrument could kill a person.

Similar to *shagag* and *shagah* is *ta'ah,* appearing 47 times, and meaning to "wander away." It is used in Isa. 28:7 of the responsible irresponsibility of the drunkard who would "stagger from wine and reel from beer." Ezekiel praises the sons of Zadok, "who were faithful in serving" the Lord and who "did not go astray as the Levites did when the Israelites went astray" (48:11).

Besides these various metaphors, which have negative literal meanings but which are often positively serious, there are exceedingly strong metaphors for acts of sin in the Old Testament that signify rebellion and treachery. Rebellion is denoted by four Hebrew words, the most commonly occurring (171 times) being the noun *pesha'* and its verb, *pasha'.* Usually translated "transgression," it denotes rebellion. *Marah* (48 times) denotes refractoriness. It is chiefly used of rebellion against earthly rulers but sometimes relates to revolt against God, as in 1 Sam. 12:15. Again, *marad* (29 times) is usually rendered "rebel," as where we read, "How could you . . . build yourselves an altar in rebellion against him [the "God of Israel"] now?" (Josh. 22:16). And there is *sarar* (20 times), which denotes stubbornness, as when the "forefathers" are called "a stubborn . . . generation" (Ps. 78:8).

Another metaphor for sin is *chanaph* (20 times), which literally means "to lean away from," and is translated "renegade" or "apostate" or "godless."

This does not exhaust the Old Testament metaphors for acts of sin. Enough of them have been discussed, however, to show that, in the Old Testament, sin as an act is described in many ways. It is missing the mark, missing the way, culpable error, wandering away, rebellion, stubbornness, apostasy, treachery, etc.

This kind of study can help us toward a language, for speaking and writing, in which we do not simply and always speak about sin, but in which we speak of it with the exactness of these numerous terms.

3. *Concrete acts.* Besides the generic terms and the metaphors, there are concrete acts of sin such as murder, adultery, theft, lying, coveting, etc. The Ten Commandments prohibitions have to do with sins of this sort.

Sin as an Act in the New Testament. The New Testament, too, is richly diverse in its language about acts of sin.

1. *Generic terms.* One generic term is *kakos* (78 times), denoting evil in a general way, moral and natural. Another is *ponēros* (82 times), usually referring to moral evil or wickedness (see Matt. 7:17-18 and Rev. 16:2 for rare natural evil meanings). *Asēbes* (17 times with cognates) is another, literally meaning godless or ungodly, or irreverence or impiety (see Jude 15, etc.). *Enochos*, for guilty, appears 9 times. It is significant that *plēmmeleia*, found in the Greek Old Testament, the regular rendering for the Hebrew *'asham* and meaning "ritual guilt," never appears in the New Testament. This means that no guilt attaches to ritual breaches in the New Testament. A person characterized by *enochos* in the New Testament has usually committed a crime that demands death as penalty (cf. Mark 14:64).

2. *Metaphors.* A number of metaphors for sin appear in the New Testament. The most frequent of these is *hamartia* (174 times), which, with its cognate words, appears 270 times—making it the New Testament's most frequently used word for sin. Like *chattath* in the Old Testament, it literally means a missing of the mark. But while its literal meaning has to do with what is negative, a lack, its actual meaning is positive.

Although a few passages might seem to suggest that one can sin simply against one's brother or one's body, it needs to be noted that sin is always against God.

Ordinarily, it is against God the Father that one sins. But there is a rare instance of sin being against Christ, where we read, "When you sin against your brothers in this way and wound their weak conscience, you sin against Christ" (1 Cor. 8:12). This speaks of sinning against humans, "brothers," but it is expressly said to be a sin against them because it is a sin against Deity. But the Deity here is Christ, unusually. Perhaps to sin against the One who died for us is to sin against the Father.[67]

Another of the New Testament metaphors is *adikia*, appearing 26 times—there being 42 appearances of other forms of this word. The stem of all of these is *dikē*, which originally referred to the justice of a lawcourt. It quite often refers to an injustice done by one person against another, but it, too, is also at the same time

---

67. It might be that the reason it is the Father, and not Christ, who forgives us, is that it is almost universally stated in Scripture that it is God, or the Father, whom we sin against.

something done against God. A well-known biblical definition of sin uses this word, where we read: "All wrongdoing is sin" (1 John 5:17, also RSV). The word for "wrongdoing" is *adikia,* and the word for sin is *hamartia.* The NASB has the literal "unrighteousness" instead of "wrongdoing," as does the KJV.

Still another of these New Testament metaphors is *anomos.* From *nomos,* for "law," with the beginning *a* to negate the word, it literally means "lawlessness." It appears 8 times in the New Testament, and the cognate *anomia* appears 14 times (with *anomos,* once). It usually refers to a breach of God's law widely conceived, instead of simply a breaking of the Jewish law.

The word for "transgression," *parabasis,* appears seven times, and *parabatēs,* for "transgressor," five times. These terms always imply the concept of law, and they are sometimes used of the transgression of a particular law (as with Adam and Eve in Rom. 5:14 and 1 Tim 2:14). Paul makes it clear that "where there is no law there is no transgression" (Rom. 4:15). This is one basis for the Wesleyan insistence that it makes worlds of difference whether or not an act breaches "a known law" of God. Whereas *anomia* usually refers to the breaking of God's law in a wide sense, *parabasis* and *parabatēs* are usually connected with the breaking of the Jewish law (see Rom. 2:23, 25, 27; Gal. 3:19; Heb. 2:2; 9:15).

The word *agnoein* appears 21 times in the New Testament—*agnoia* 4 times, *agnōsia* twice, and *agnoēma* once. These words are from *gnōsis,* for "knowledge," with the *a* to negate it; so *agnoein* literally means "not to know"; and it (with its cognates) is usually translated with some form of the word "ignorance." Often, the ignorance referred to is obviously not culpable. Thus Paul says, "I do not want you to be unaware ["ignorant," KJV], brothers" (Rom. 1:13; cf. 2 Cor. 6:9; Gal. 1:22). And thus we read, "But they did not understand what he [Jesus] meant and were afraid to ask him about it" (Mark 9:32). And Paul writes, "For we are not ignorant of his [Satan's] devices" (2 Cor. 2:11, KJV). And in Heb. 5:2 we read of the high priest, who "is able to deal gently with those who are ignorant and are going astray, since he himself is subject to weakness." Other such examples could also be mentioned, for they seem to be preponderant, among the 21 instances of *agnoein* and the 7 instances of its cognate words.

At times, however, some sort of culpability is attached to the word. Such seems to be implied in Rom. 10:3: "Since they [the Israelites] did not know the righteousness that comes from God and sought to establish their own, they did not submit to God's righteousness." Their ignorance figures positively in establishing their own righteousness, and it receives Paul's scorn. The ignorance is culpable also where we read, "If he ignores this, he himself will be ignored" (1 Cor. 14:38). The culpability of the ignorance is indicated in the previous verse where we read, "If anybody thinks he is a prophet or spiritually gifted, let him acknowledge that what I am writing to you is the Lord's command."

A strange introduction of ignorance into one of Paul's testimonies seems on the surface to be an ignorance that is nonculpable; but the matter referred to is utterly serious, and forgiveness was evidently needed. This is where Paul says, "Even though I was once a blasphemer and a persecutor and a violent man, I was shown mercy because I acted in ignorance and unbelief" (1 Tim. 1:13). It is possible, as some scholars suggest, that the introduction of "because I did it ignorantly" (KJV) might have been an early editorial addition to Paul's statement made by a person friendly toward Paul who wanted him to be seen in a good light. At least, it would be strange for Paul to imply that God's forgiveness is not forthcoming if we repent after sinning intentionally and not in ignorance.

Besides all these Old Testament and New Testament generic terms and metaphors for sin acts, Scripture refers to numerous concrete acts of sin, such as stealing, lying, adultery, coveting, and so forth The Ten Commandments speak of such sin acts, as do many other passages of Scripture. These concrete sin acts are not as difficult to understand as are the generic terms and the metaphors, so they have not been treated here. Yet they are part of the whole picture of what the nature of sin as an act is (in distinction from the Adamic state of original sin).

From this study of generic terms and metaphors in Scripture, and this mention of concrete sins, a few observations about a definition of sin are in order. One is that it makes very much difference, in Scripture, whether or not an act is willful disobedience to God. Scripture sometimes uses words for sin, including cognates of *chattath* in the Old Testament and *hamartia* in the New Testament, in a wider sense than of willful disobedience to God. Yet, surely sin acts that are serious, utterly serious, and that need to be forgiven upon request of the transgressor are, as John Wesley suggested, "voluntary transgression[s] of a known law of God."[68]

Other Matters Related to Sin

Before finishing this chapter on the doctrine of sin, it is appropriate to discuss briefly a few other matters: sins of ignorance, venial and mortal sins in relation to mistakes and sins, sin as the opposite of righteousness, sinless perfection, and the unpardonable sin.

Sins of Ignorance. Both Testaments refer to nonwillful sins. Should we call them sins? Scripture does: "When anyone sins unintentionally and does what is forbidden in any of the Lord's commands" (Lev. 4:2). We also read, "If the whole Israelite community sins unintentionally and does what is forbidden in any of the Lord's commands, even though the community is unaware of the matter, they are guilty" (v. 13). Also: "If a person sins because he does not speak up when he hears a public charge to testify regarding something he has seen or learned about, he will be held responsible" (5:1). Even unintentional ceremonial breaches are called sin (vv. 2-6).

Certain New Testament passages have a bearing on this matter. One of them is Heb. 10:26. There we read, "For if we sin deliberately" (RSV); "For if we go on sinning willfully" (NASB); "For if we sin wilfully" (KJV); and "If we deliberately keep on sinning" (NIV). This passage implies that we can sin without its being willful or deliberate. Of bearing also is Rom. 5:13, where we read that "before the law was given, sin was in the world. But sin is not taken into account when there is no law." Before Moses' law, then, human breaches of God's law are called sin; but since the people had not as yet received God's law, the "sin [was] not taken into account."

The Leviticus 4—5 discussions, therefore, as well as certain New Testament ones, show that in Scripture breaches of God's will are called sin even if they are not deliberate acts of disobedience. John Wesley evidently realized this, because he said that sin "properly so-called" is a willful violation of the known law of God—as though he knew that Scripture refers also to nonwillful acts as sin.

---

68. Wesley, *Works* 12:394.

Wesley felt, however, and Wesleyans have also, that there is a vast difference between unintentional and intentional sins—the latter being utterly serious, dislodging us from our redeemed relationship with God. Wesley was often wise to call the unintentional sins mistakes or blunders or infirmities. If we today call them all by the same name, sin, which Scripture might allow us to do, we are liable to discount the difference between the two kinds of sin.

It should be noted that Scripture teaches that even unintentional sins need to be atoned for—or cleansed moment by moment—by Christ. Leviticus 4—5 teaches that such sins need to be atoned for. When a person "sins unintentionally . . . he is guilty" (4:27), and "When he is made aware of the sin . . . he must bring . . . his offering for the sin he committed" (v. 28). Likewise in the New Testament, such sins need to be cleansed away. In 1 John 1:7 we read, "But if we walk in the light, as he is in the light, we have fellowship with one another, and the blood of Jesus, his Son, purifies us from all sin." Here, as the believer is "walk[ing] in the light," some things done are called "sin." They are so serious that the blood of Jesus Christ needs to cleanse them away. It is to be noted, though, that the word for "purifies" is the present tense in the Greek. This means that such a believer is cleansed right as the sin occurs, so that the person does not stand guilty between the time of the sin and a later time of recognizing its seriousness.

Some Wesleyan-holiness people ask for forgiveness as they later realize that they have breached God's will. Others of us understand (1) that since the act was not willful, perhaps we do not require forgiveness, but only cleansing (according to 1 John 1:7); and (2) that since we receive Christ's cleansing at the time, we do not later pray for either cleansing or forgiveness. We understand that, at the time, as we were walking in the light, Christ's blood cleansed us (and that it keeps cleansing us). This way, we understand that we do not stand guilty before God between the time of the unintentional breach and a request for its cleansing or its forgiveness. In any event, we praise God then for the cleansing that has occurred, telling Him how regretful we are for doing the act, and asking His help that it does not recur.

Venial/Mortal and Mistake/Sin. The Roman Catholic distinction between venial and mortal sins and the Wesleyan distinction between mistakes and sins are in some ways similar, but in one respect quite different.

They are similar in at least these ways. Venial sins are less serious than mortal sins, even as mistakes are less serious than sins as such for Wesleyans. Even venial sins need to receive God's mercy, however, just as mistakes do in Wesleyanism. Further, Roman Catholics say that an act is a mortal sin if it is thought to be such a sin, even if as an act it is only a venial sin. The Wesleyan view would also suggest that if we understand that we are disobeying God, we are, even if God does not actually prohibit the act. In both the Roman Catholic view and the Wesleyan view, then, conscious disobedience is crucial in determining culpability. The two views are similar, further, in that neither venial sins nor mistakes would occasion eternal punishment.

There is one particularly important difference, however, between the Roman Catholic venial/mortal distinction and that of the Wesleyan mistake/sin. In the Roman Catholic view, sin is only venial—even if it is entirely willful, against a known law of God —if it is not very grave. The willful theft of money is often interpreted as venial if the amount is less than a day's wages in the area—but mortal, however small the amount, if it is taken from a destitute person. In Wesleyanism, an act would be sin in the most serious sense, though it had to do with a small matter, if the act was in willful disobedience to the known will of God.

Sin as the Opposite of Righteousness. In Hegelian philosophy, an act can be less than it ought to be, but it is never simply the opposite of what it ought to be. An unrighteous act is not a wicked act, but one which is lacking in righteousness and is on its way to becoming a righteous one.

In Scripture, however, human acts are presented as opposites. This can be seen in both Testaments, but the present study of opposites works only with the Old Testament.

1. *Purity and filthiness are contrasted.*[69] An example is Ezek. 36:25, 29: "I will sprinkle clean water on you, and you will be clean; I will cleanse you from all your impurities and from all your idols. . . . I will save you from all your uncleanness."

2. *Wisdom and folly are also contrasted.* In the Wisdom literature, the "beginning of wisdom" is to "fear the Lord"—in the

---

69. Much use is being made in this study of opposites, as in other areas of the nature of sin, of the late C. Ryder Smith's *Bible Doctrine of Sin.*

sense of reverencing Him (Ps. 111:10, NASB). The person who lives according to wisdom trusts God and lives according to His ways (Prov. 3:5-8). The opposite of wisdom is folly; contrasted to the wise person is "the fool." Common Hebrew words for "fool" often, but not always, denote a person who is morally unwise.

3. *Likewise, glory and shame are contrasted.* The righteous person should glory in God, and the wicked person should be ashamed in God's presence. Shame is sometimes the proper garment for a wicked person to wear, as in Ps. 35:26. An innocent person might be ashamed, but this is rare (as in 2 Kings 2:17; Prov. 17:2, KJV). Shame is the feeling we should have when we have sinned against God.

4. *Holiness and profanity are also opposites.* Sometimes "holy" and "profane" are contrasted in single texts (as in Lev. 10:10; Ezek. 22:26, both NASB). The word for "profanity," *chalel,* appears 13 times in the Code of Holiness in Leviticus 19. Although it occurs here and elsewhere, it also denotes what is moral here and elsewhere.

The Question of Sinless Perfection. John Wesley believed basically in sinless perfection, but he tried to avoid using the term, since it is so easily misunderstood.[70] Today, in the Holiness Movement, there is perhaps an even greater aversion to its use than Wesley felt.

In a sense, and technically, to be sinless pretty much describes what Wesley taught and what is taught in Wesleyan-holiness circles. Believers who do not willfully disobey God are sinless. However, as noted earlier, since Scripture also refers to nonwillful breaches of God's will as sin (as in Leviticus 4—5; Heb. 10:26; Rom. 5:13-14; Luke 11:4), using "sinless" of the justified state is questionable. Since we mean that God helps the believer not to disobey Him willfully, it is better to say just that.

The term "sinless" might also refer to the experience of having had Adamic depravity, the racial sin, cleansed away through the second work of grace. It is correct that the believer is then sinless in a certain sense. Yet, as noted earlier, depravity is proba-

---

70. In a letter to Mrs. Maitland (May 12, 1763) Wesley says, "As to the word 'perfection,' it is scriptural: Therefore neither you nor I can in conscience object to it, unless we would send the Holy Ghost to school, and teach Him to speak who made the tongue" (Wesley, *Works* 12:257).

bly a better term for describing the Adamic detriment than is the word "sin." Thus, the awkward "depravity-less" perfection would be preferable to "sinless" perfection. Moreover, Scripture speaks of "sin" even in the life of entire sanctification, right while we are walking in the light, as we saw in our study of 1 John 1:7.

Thus, on several bases, "sinless perfection" is not quite appropriate to describe the life that God's grace makes possible for us.

The Unpardonable Sin. This has been widely misunderstood, partly because of incorrect interpretation of a few isolated passages of Scripture, and partly because of an excessive zeal to secure an immediate response to the gospel in evangelistic services.

This sin no doubt consists of a repeated and willful attributing of the work of the Holy Spirit to demons. This is what Mark 3:28-30 suggests: "'I tell you the truth, all the sins and blasphemies of men will be forgiven them. But whoever blasphemes against the Holy Spirit will never be forgiven; he is guilty of an eternal sin.' He said this because they were saying, 'He has an evil spirit.'" Attributing the Holy Spirit's work to an evil spirit is blasphemy (cf. Matt. 12:31-32). It is unpardonable because the person sets himself or herself into this kind of stance and will not let God transform the mind and forgive. It is therefore unpardonable more from our standpoint than from God's—for we read elsewhere in Scripture that God will graciously forgive anyone at all who asks for pardon (see Hos. 14:4; Eph. 4:32; Rom. 8:32; Col. 2:13; Heb. 10:17; Luke 15:11-32).

Some people use Isa. 63:10 to teach that God will refuse to forgive some people. There we read: "Yet they rebelled and grieved his Holy Spirit. So he turned and became their enemy and he himself fought against them." Adam Clarke is no doubt correct when he suggests that this turning to become their enemy, on God's part, is a reference to the Last Judgment—when probation is past.

Some people feel that 1 John 5:16 refers to the "unpardonable sin": "There is a sin that leads to death. I am not saying that he should pray about that." This more likely refers to a sin that carries the death penalty in civil law. We are not necessarily to pray that the civil law's penalty will be alleviated, although God will, of course, forgive the repentant sinner.

The most important thing to remember about the unpardonable sin is that all who fear that they have committed it, and are concerned about the matter, have not.

11

The Person of Christ

At this point in this treatment of interrelated Christian doctrine, it is appropriate that the person of Christ be discussed. The anticipation of Christ will first be treated, then the Incarnation, the Church's understanding of Christ (the Christological heresies and the orthodox teaching), and Christ's virgin conception.[1]

Old Testament Anticipation

In the Old Testament, Christ is anticipated in many ways by the writing prophets and other writers.

Anticipation in the Prophets. The Old Testament prophets, whose important work was to tell of Christ's coming, were stouthearted, hard-hitting persons who spoke to people in Yahweh's stead.[2]

Sinful people then, as now, wanted an undisturbing gospel, but that is not what the prophets delivered.

These men exhibited themselves to the people: to the masses and the classes. Not all heeded, but the prophets stood before them and declared what they had been told in Yahweh's council chambers. Know-it-alls, sufficient to themselves, heady and haughty, the Israelites often "turned their backs," "stopped up their ears," and "made their hearts as hard as flint" (Zech. 7:11-12).

The prophets seldom earned money at prophesying. Their lives were frequently endangered. Yet, with the ruggedness of the deserts that often produced them, they dispensed God's Word as responsibly as has any group of people the world has known.

---

1. The next two chapters will treat the Atonement and Christ's resurrection. Christ's second coming will be treated among eschatological matters in the final chapter.

2. The prefix *pro* in *prophet* indicates especially "instead of" as in *pronoun* and not so much "before," as in *processional.*

A motley group, actually, the prophets were: no tears for Amos, but floods of them for Hosea and Jeremiah. Isaiah was likely of a royal family, whereas Amos was from the farm. Malachi had a lot of steel in him, while Jonah sulked "in proud isolation"[3] outside Nineveh, jealous that heathen as well as Hebrews had a place in Yahweh's love.

Andrew Blackwood is right: as a whole, these men were greater than kings.[4] In their day, too, they were consorts to kings, advisers on policy. Whether the king was a saint like Hezekiah or a sinner like Ahab, the prophets were God's preachers at the palaces.

And while some, like Ezekiel and Zechariah, were priests as well, the prophets were nearer to God than the priests. The priests sought to present the people to God, and the prophets presented God to the people. To do that, the prophets had to be in closer converse with Him. This is what enabled them to see to the center of things present and to the distant future that had Christ enfleshed in it. This is why they were able to give "an inspired glimpse into the eternal present of the divine mind."[5] This is why they could "look at temporal things under eternal points of view."[6] This is why they could foretell Israel's doom, herald her dawn, and announce the coming of Jesus Christ, her Dayspring from on high.

Prophets were numerous. The schools of the true prophets produced many who claimed to divine for Yahweh. Four hundred false prophets gathered about King Ahab (1 Kings 22:6). Only a few, among the entire number, are known to us by name. And some of them were captivated by the hope of Christ's coming— Isaiah, for example.

In connection with Christ, two kinds of prophets stood up and stood out for Yahweh: those who made only vague reference to coming redemption, and those who spoke of Christ in more

3. John Paterson, *The Godly Fellowship of the Prophets* (New York: Charles Scribner's Sons, 1948), 279.

4. See Andrew Blackwood, *The Prophets: Elijah to Christ* (New York: Fleming H. Revell Co., 1917), 11-12.

5. A. F. Kirkpatrick, *The Doctrine of the Prophets* (New York: Macmillan Publishing Co., 1907), 520.

6. Carl Heinrich Cornill, *The Prophets of Israel,* trans. S. F. Corkran (Chicago: Open Court Publishing Co., 1895), 36.

explicit terms. Especially is this so for us, on this side of Bethlehem and Golgotha and the emptied tomb—as those events, with their apostolic New Testament interpretations, help us discern what was meant at the earlier time by the statements of the Spirit-inspired prophets.

1. *The vague prophetic anticipations.* As we on this side of the Christ events read the Old Testament through Christ-baptized lenses, we see at least vague Christ legacies wherever we see that Yahweh's mercy is roomy.

The legacy of the prophets often included Gentiles in Yahweh's loving care. The prophets knew even then, as Peter said later, that Yahweh is "not wanting anyone to perish, but everyone to come to repentance" (2 Pet. 3:9). The Book of Jonah, for example, exhibits a wide-hearted outlook on God's readiness to spare even Gentile Nineveh if its people would repent. Even back there, as F. W. Faber expressed it much later,

> There's a wideness in God's mercy
> Like the wideness of the sea;
> There's a kindness in His justice
> Which is more than liberty.

Isaiah spoke at times in only vague notes about the wideness in Yahweh's mercy. He saw that the One high and lifted up has a map of the whole world in His hands. It did not matter to Him whose sins were as scarlet: the scarlet in the hearts of people in all nations could be erased (1:18). The redemption offered by the thrice-holy Lord of Hosts included Egypt and Assyria—whose threat to Israel was imminent.

Zechariah, that prophet of the placid who dreamed his dreams during the rebuilding days, told a people full of hope that "ten men from nations of every language shall seize the skirt of a single Jew, saying, 'We will go with you, for we have heard that God is with you'" (8:23, Moffatt).

Malachi, God's messenger on world mission, went so far as to admit that Gentiles were rendering a more acceptable worship to Yahweh than were the Jews themselves (1:10-14, cf. trans.). There is something of the apostle Paul in these bighearted Hebrew prophets, something even of Jesus himself.

The mercy of Yahweh is there, inclusive of Gentiles. But the prophets are often vague about how Yahweh offers the redemption. In much of this, the reader does not know that the redemption is offered through a Christ who is to visit earth and die and become resurrected for our redemption.

2. *The clear prophetic anticipations.* There are anticipations of Christ in the writing prophets that are more clearly Christological—although this clarity is often much greater after we read the Old Testament anticipation in the light the New Testament throws upon it. Malachi, for example, sees that Messiah's coming is to be heralded by a forerunner (3:1), and Jesus himself states that the prediction was fulfilled by John the Baptist (Matt. 11:10).

Kirkpatrick says that, summed up, it was "the function of prophecy to prepare for Him."[7] Andrew Blackwood says that these prophets rose to their loftiest heights "when they pointed men's weary eyes to the Redeemer"; and he sees the prophets in their distilled essence when he says: "The great reason, after all, why we should study the prophets is because they prepared the way for the coming of Christ."[8] Even A. C. Knudson, who as a liberal wanted to cut down on prediction as much as possible, says of the preexilic prophets: "These men were not merely preachers of repentance. They were heralds of the coming kingdom of God."[9] In the New Testament itself we read, "All the prophets testify about him that everyone who believes in him receives forgiveness of sins through his name" (Acts 10:43). And Jesus knew they had talked of Him, for "beginning with Moses and all the Prophets, he explained to them what was said in all the Scriptures concerning himself" (Luke 24:27). But not just Christ and Christians think the prophets are shot through with the messianic. Many Jews do also. Their Talmud states that "all the prophets have only prophesied concerning the days of the Messiah."[10]

More than broad outlines of Christ's coming were seen by the prophets. "A righteous Branch" would appear in the lineage of David (Jer. 23:5). The time of this appearance is told by Daniel (9:24-26), and the place by Micah (5:2). That the birth was to be by a virgin mother was seen by Isaiah (7:14), who saw more perhaps than any of those who lived beforehand (see chaps. 7, 9, 11, and 53). Isaiah also reported details of Christ's death (cf. Acts

---

7. Kirkpatrick, *The Doctrine of the Prophets,* 521.
8. Blackwood, *The Prophets: Elijah to Christ,* 35, 46.
9. A. C. Knudson, *The Beacon Lights of Prophecy* (New York: Eaton and Mains, 1914), vii.
10. "Sanhedrin," xxxiv, col. 2.

8:32-35); for example, that He would be "numbered with the transgressors" (53:12).

Zechariah saw Christ ahead of time in a concreteness not given to many of his fellows. He entered into Jesus' high triumph when he exclaimed, "Rejoice greatly, O Daughter of Zion! . . . See, your king comes to you, righteous and having salvation, gentle and riding on a donkey, on a colt, the foal of a donkey" (9:9; cf. Matt. 21:5-9). In a reference to Judas' betrayal of Christ he writes, "So they paid me thirty pieces of silver. . . . So I took the thirty pieces of silver and threw them into the house of the Lord to the potter" (11:12-13; cf. Matt. 26:15; 27:5).

It never dies—that dream of the prophets about the coming Deliverer. It never even fades. Malachi, the last of them, is as full of hope as any. He looks for a Refiner (3:2) who with fire would purify presumptuous people, a Fuller (v. 2) who would clothe people with garments washed in His own blood.

And finally He appeared, He "of whom Moses in the law, and the prophets, did write, Jesus of Nazareth" (John 1:45, KJV). The prophets had foretold Him—sometimes vaguely, sometimes more clearly. Their characters had foreshadowed His; and their teachings, learned by "mouth-to-mouth" converse with the speaking God, had prepared the way for what He would say and do.

Anticipation Outside of the Prophets. Christ is anticipated among the Old Testament writers who were not prophets as such. Usually this occurs in passages that have become clear only after we have come to know "the rest of the story."

Beginning especially with the protevangelium (as it is called) of Gen. 3:15, the Old Testament is replete with the promise of redemption through a Coming One who, when He came, was named Jesus because He would save His people from their sins. In this first glimmer of Scripture's good news, the usual Christian interpretation is that the woman's offspring, Christ, would be pitted against Satan (here spoken of as the serpent) and his offspring (sinners who follow him); and that especially by Christ's resurrection Satan's very head would be crushed. Admittedly, this reads into the meaning of this passage what we Christians now know to have happened; but such interpretation is legitimate.

Besides the protevangelium, there are other Christological foregleams in Genesis. One is the promise that "all nations on earth will be blessed through him [Abraham]" (18:18). Jesus, of

Abraham's seed, occasions the Father's blessing "all peoples on earth" (Acts 3:25).

The Book of Psalms contains a number of Christological foregleams, according to the New Testament itself. Pss. 69:25 and 109:8 foretold what would happen to Judas. Citing these passages, Peter said, "The Holy Spirit spoke long ago through the mouth of David concerning Judas" (Acts 1:15-20). Ps. 110:4 reads: "You are a priest forever, in the order of Melchizedek"— and Heb. 6:20 states of Jesus, "He has become a high priest forever, in the order of Melchizedek" (see also Heb. 5:5-6; 7:15-21).

The Incarnation

The Incarnation, the enfleshment of the Deity, is important in many ways. For one, it means that the God who had been speaking to us now visited us. The God who had spoken to us at different times in various ways by prophets spoke to us in the Incarnation by visiting us in His Son (see Heb. 1:1-3). In what was our finest hour, God came calling.

The Incarnation means that God is conjoined to us more closely than men and women are conjoined in marriage. In marriage, the partners do not take on each other's nature as God did ours in the Incarnation. Furthermore, marriage is only for earth; the Incarnation is forever. The Incarnation was not terminated when Christ ascended. He is forever the "Godman"—better spelled without the hyphen so as to indicate the completeness of the joining of God and ourselves that occurred at Bethlehem. Christ, in heaven, is still touched by the ecstasy and the agony of our human experience (Heb. 4:15). He remembers what it was like to be a human being on earth—birthed, growing, hungering, dying. Something was added to His divine nature at the Incarnation that will never be subtracted from it. This enriches, dignifies, enables, and enhances human nature without in any way diminishing the divine nature.

The Incarnation means that we joy to a Christian mystery. God and ourselves conjoined in a human person, Jesus of Nazareth— this is high mystery. Hearing and believing this mystery, we are transformed from rebels against God to servants of God.

The church has theologized about the Incarnation for centuries, seeking to better understand it; and that theologizing needs to be discussed here. Indeed, the seven ecumenical councils of the early centuries were called to discuss theories of the person of Christ—which basically means theories of what the Incarnation actually consists of.

The Christological Heresies and Chalcedon Orthodoxy

In order to understand Christ's person as correctly as possible, it is important to understand what the various ancient Christological heresies were. They may be studied from the standpoint of (1) those that overstressed Christ's humanity, (2) those that overstressed His deity, and (3) others.

Overstress on Christ's Humanity

1. *Ebionism* is the view that Christ was human only, not divine, and that He was empowered in a special way at His baptism. The name comes from a Hebrew word meaning "poor," and it describes this early heresy because, in this view, Christ is a "poor" human being devoid of deity. It is not essentially different from the Jewish appraisal of Jesus. It sought to protect the Judaistic conception of monotheism.

2. *Adoptionism* is the view that Christ has not existed eternally as the Father's Son or in any other way, but that He was human only and that He was adopted (especially at the time of His baptism) as the Father's Son.

Overstress on Christ's Deity

1. *Docetism* is the view that Christ was fully divine, but not fully human. It is the view of the Christian Gnostics, whose teachings are mentioned with some frequency in the New Testament by Paul and John and who gained considerable following during the second century. In this view Christ only seemed or appeared to have had a human body. He could not have possessed a human body because all matter is evil, and a human body participates in materiality.

The Christian Gnostics, perhaps influenced by the body-spirit dualism of Plato and a similar type of dualism in Zoroastrianism, understood that Christ was only "poured through" Mary's womb, so that He did not partake of her humanity. They had no problem with the Virgin Conception doctrine, believing as they did in Christ's deity. Saying that Christ did not undergo the nine-month gestation period and that He was "poured through" Mary, they denied His birth. This occasioned the need for Christians to speak of the birth—of the Virgin Birth, that is.

First John 1:1-3, with its emphasis on seeing, hearing, and touching, is a sustained statement against the Gnostic denial of Christ's humanity.

The apostle Paul probably had the Gnostics in mind when he wrote: "See to it that no one takes you captive through hollow and deceptive philosophy, which depends on human tradition and the basic principles of this world rather than on Christ. For in Christ all the fullness of the Deity lives in bodily form" (Col. 2:8-9).

The Gnostics pretty much died out during the fourth century. Until recently, Gnosticism, with its docetic view of Christ, had been known to us only through the writings of its enemies. Discovery and study of their own writings reveals that their enemies, the Christians, had not greatly misrepresented them.

2. *Apollinarianism* is the heresy advanced in the latter part of the fourth century by Apollinaris—that Christ possessed a human body and soul, but not a human spirit (or ego or person), and that His spirit was the eternal Logos who joined himself to a human body and soul. It is here classified as a Christological heresy that overstressed Christ's deity because, at the crucial point—the ego or the person or the spirit, the highest aspect of human nature—Christ did not become human, or take on humanity, at all. Christ was simply the eternal Logos strangely amalgamated with what was conceived of as the two lower of three aspects of human nature. Thus, Christ did not think or make decisions from within human nature, as a human being who was also divine. He did not possess a human psyche.

If some Christological heresies are somewhat more acceptable than others, this might be one of them. In this view, both the deity and the humanity of Christ are affirmed in a sense. The main inadequacy of the view, however, is that Christ did not become fully human, since He did not become human at the main point: the human ego, person, psyche, spirit.

H. Orton Wiley, in his *Christian Theology*, discusses Apollinarianism as one of the heresies, and yet he himself teaches the view. Wiley says, "The union of the divine and human natures in Christ is a personal one—that is, the union lies in their abiding

305 THE PERSON OF CHRIST ▷

possession of a common Ego or inner Self, that of the eternal Logos." This is precisely what Wiley, just earlier, had explained as Apollinaris's view. Wiley further explains, "The possession of the two natures does not involve a double personality, for the ground of the person is the eternal Logos and not the human nature."[11] Wiley seemed unable to see that the Incarnation consisted of a mystical and real amalgam of the eternal Logos with humanity, including a human ego or mind or spirit or psyche. Without that, there would have been no mysterious union of the divine with humanity, for at the point of what is highest in humanity, the ego, there would have been no humanity in this Incarnation. As a young theology teacher, I exchanged lengthy letters with him on this issue, and Wiley simply said in his letters that this is the appropriate view as he saw the matter.

3. *Eutychianism* is the view that, after the Incarnation, Christ had only one nature and that it was divine. It was the view of Eutyches (of Constantinople) and many others, and occasioned a sustained and intense controversy in the fifth century.

Eutyches was deposed at a synod in Constantinople in A.D. 448 because he would not state that in Christ there were two natures after the Incarnation and for refusing to confess that Christ was of one substance with us after the flesh. Dioscorus of Alexandria responded by receiving Eutyches into communion with Alexandria, and the two called for an ecumenical council. Emperor Theodosius II hastily decreed one to meet in 449 at Ephesus. It was presided over by Dioscorus, who was opposed by Pope Leo, who urged the condemnation of Eutyches. Leo regarded Eutyches as one of the "masters of error" for denying that Christ was of the same substance with humanity. Leo insisted that even after the Incarnation, the union of God the Son with humanity, both the divine and the human natures still existed, and that the divine nature did not swallow up the human nature.

These views in Leo's *Tome* were sent to Flavian of Constantinople; and at Ephesus in 449 Dioscorus deposed and imprisoned Flavian—who died four days after imprisonment.

But the decision of this hastily called council at Ephesus, dubbed by Leo "the robber synod," did not stand. Emperor Theo-

---

11. Wiley, *Christian Theology* 2:180, 181.

dosius II died suddenly, and a change of political leadership occasioned the calling of another ecumenical council in 451. It opened at Nicea and then changed to Chalcedon.

En route to Chalcedon, Dioscorus excommunicated Leo. But at Chalcedon, Dioscorus was condemned, deposed, and banished, and died in exile—venerated by the Monophysites but widely regarded by Catholic Christianity as a fanatic who used power that had been given him to promote an errant teaching.

Two later heresies, based on the one divine nature of Eutychianism, were developed: Monophysitism, that Christ had only one nature, it being divine; and Monothelitism, the view that Christ had only one will, arising from His one nature.

Eutychianism, Monophysitism, and Monothelitism are similar heresies. All of them basically teach the one-divine-nature view of Christ. The ecumenical councils condemned all of them in favor of the view that Christ consisted of two natures (divine and human, with a will in each nature) and one person.

Theological modernism has been similar to the Ebionites and Adoptionists. Evangelicalism at least tends in the direction of Docetism or Eutychianism. In opposing the human-only view of Christ in liberalism, many evangelicals, especially those who are fundamentalists, tend toward viewing Him as wholly divine but not wholly human. Bending over backward to defend Christ's deity against modernism's attack, they do not admit His full humanity. Some of them oppose the classical Christian understanding that Christ is eternally begotten of the Father. They say that John's four uses of *monogenēs*, "only born," "only begotten," as in John 1:18, refer not to Christ's being eternally begotten by the Father, but to His being born of Mary to the incarnate state. They tend to put Christ on a par with the Father even origination-wise, whereas Christ's eternal origination is from the Father.

Other Christological Heresies. Other heresies were also developed in the Early Church that were opposed to what came to be orthodox Christology.

1. *Nestorianism* was one of them. Nestorius, deposed from office in 431, taught that Christ was fully human and fully divine. But he so stressed both the deity and the humanity that he was understood to be saying that Christ possessed two persons as well as two natures. This view, whether or not Nestorius actually taught it, neglects to emphasize the union of the two natures of

Christ in one Person. In this view, no real Incarnation took place. It is as though, in Christ, God and humanity are Siamese twins— not that in Christ the deity and the humanity are interpenetratingly unified in one Person.

2. *Arianism* is the view that Christ was neither divine nor human, but a third type of being (a tertium quid)—the first and highest being God created.

Arius, of Alexandria, began to teach this in about A.D. 318 and gained sufficient following for this issue to occasion the calling of the first of the seven ecumenical councils—the one that met at Nicea in 325.

This council, presided over by Emperor Constantine, decided against Arianism. It decided that Christ's nature was of the same substance as that of the Father.

Athanasius, then a deacon without voting privilege, was present. He had already written his significant work on Christ, *De Incarnationes* (Concerning the Incarnation), no doubt the most significant on this subject prior to Anselm's *Cur Deus Homo?* (Why the God-Man?) of the late 11th century. He advised his bishop, Alexander of Alexandria, and their view is the one the council decided upon.

Arianism was a serious and continuing threat for a long time. Athanasius was himself exiled several times when the emperor thought Arianism gave more promise than Athanasianism of cementing together the empire. The Goths, Visigoths, and other barbarians to whom Rome fell in 476 were Arian "Christians"— whose Arianism did not succeed as well as their attempts at political conquest.

The Council of Chalcedon more or less fixed the Christology of Christianity generally, stating that Christ possessed two natures (divine and human) and one Person. The natures should not be "confused" into one, and the Person should not be divided.

Christ's Virgin Conception

Christ's entrance into the world was sheerly miraculous—He was conceived by a virgin through the power of the Holy Spirit.

Usually, the Virgin Conception has been called the Virgin Birth because of an accident of history. Christian Gnostics taught that Christ was not really born of a woman, but that He was "poured through" Mary's womb. Thus, when the early Christians affirmed the Virgin Birth, they meant to affirm the reality of the birth of Christ, since that was being denied by the heretical Gnostics.

Its Biblical Support. The miraculous conception of Christ in Mary's womb is clearly taught in Scripture. James Orr, after much research for a book on the Virgin Birth, was convinced of the "integrity" of the Virgin Birth narratives.[12] So was J. Gresham Machen a generation later, who also wrote an entire book on this doctrine.[13] And Karl Barth said, "No one can dispute the existence of a biblical testimony to the Virgin Birth."[14]

It is expressly taught in Matt. 1:18-25. This passage is too extensive and detailed to be explained away as a later editorial interpolation. The passage states several things: (1) Jesus was conceived without a human father: "His mother Mary was pledged to be married to Joseph, but before they came together, she was found to be with child through the Holy Spirit" (v. 18). (2) Instead of a human father, the Holy Spirit figured in His conception: "An angel of the Lord appeared to him in a dream and said, 'Joseph son of David, do not be afraid to take Mary home as your wife, because what is conceived in her is from the Holy Spirit'" (v. 20). (3) This conception fulfills the Isa. 7:14 prophecy: "All this took place to fulfill what the Lord had said through the prophet: 'The virgin will be with child and will give birth to a son, and they will call him Immanuel'—which means, 'God with us'" (vv. 22-23). (4) Joseph took Mary home with him but "had no union with her until she gave birth to a son" (v. 25).

Besides Matt. 1:18-25, the Virgin Conception is taught clearly in Luke 1:5—2:52 and in 3:23. Luke 1—2 is an extensive, typically Palestinian narrative that again teaches several things: (1) Mary is a "virgin pledged to be married to a man named Joseph" (1:27); (2) Mary is "highly favored" (v. 28); (3) although she is a "virgin" (v. 34), "The Holy Spirit will come upon" her, and "the power of the Most High will overshadow" her, so that "the holy one to be born will be called the Son of God" (v. 35); and (4) Mary responds with humility and obedience (v. 38) and sings a hymn of praise to God (vv. 46-55).

---

12. James Orr, *The Virgin Birth of Christ* (New York: Charles Scribner's Sons, 1907), 227.

13. J. Gresham Machen, *The Virgin Birth of Christ* (London: J. Clarke, 1958).

14. Barth, *Church Dogmatics* 2:176.

And Luke 3:23 reads, "Now Jesus himself was about thirty years old when he began his ministry. He was the son, so it was thought ["as was supposed," KJV], of Joseph." The "so it was thought" or "as was supposed" might have been an interpolation added by a later editor. Yet it is in agreement with Matt. 1:18-25, and no manuscript exists in which this does not appear. Vincent Taylor regarded it as an interpolation made by Luke himself as an afterthought.[15]

The Luke 1:5—2:52 passage is included in the second-century *Diatessaron*, Tatian's Gospel harmony, and in all the Greek manuscripts of Luke and in all the versions. But because Marcion, the Gnostic, omitted it from the Lucan Gospel that he used, and because Luke does not later in the Gospel refer to the birth-narrative section, some have surmised that the Gospel did not at first contain the birth account. A pedantic attempt has even been made to exclude the Lucan birth narrative because the "former treatise" referred to in Acts 1:1, KJV, is said to have treated what Jesus "began to do and to teach," no mention being made of the birth section. So brief a summary of Luke's Gospel, however, would not likely include the birth narrative.

Paul may have meant to imply the Virgin Conception doctrine in Gal. 4:4 when he wrote, "But when the time had fully come, God sent his Son, born of a woman, born under law, to redeem those under law." Scripture much more often speaks of the father of a person than of a person's mother, yet Paul here mentions only that Christ was "born of a woman." However, William Barclay says that "born of a woman" is "the regular phrase for mortal man,"[16] citing Job 14:1 and 25:4. He concludes, "The phrase 'born of a woman' has nothing to do with the Virgin Birth."[17]

History of the Doctrine. In the early centuries the virgin birth of Christ was generally accepted and supported. Ignatius called it a "mystery of loud proclamation." Irenaeus affirms that the Church "scattered over the whole world" had received from the apostles faith in Christ's "birth of the Virgin." In the same century, the early form of the Apostles' Creed spelled it out plainly. The

---

15. Vincent Taylor, *The Historical Evidence for the Virgin Birth* (Oxford: Clarendon Press, 1920).

16. William Barclay, *Crucified and Crowned* (London: SCM Press, 1961), 189.

17. Ibid.

Greek and Latin fathers in general affirmed it, as did the Scholastics and the Reformers. J. Gresham Machen called it "a universal belief of the historic Christian Church."[18]

Recent Status of the Doctrine. In this résumé evangelicals will not be treated, because they all teach the doctrine and because it should be of more special interest to see what others of recent times have taught.

1. *On the Continent.* In Europe it has been denied by some. Emil Brunner, for instance, continued the opposition presented in an earlier era by such men as Schleiermacher (*The Christian Faith*) and Strauss (*The Life of Jesus*). Unlike them, however, he admitted the full deity of Christ. He was like many others in affirming the Incarnation while denying birth from the virgin as its means. He wrote, "The truth that the Eternal Son of God meets us in the Man, Jesus, necessarily leads to the doctrine of the Incarnation of the Son of God."[19] Yet Brunner would rather stand "amazed before the Fact itself" than accept the Virgin Birth as the means to the "great, unthinkable, unimaginable miracle of the Incarnation."[20]

Brunner considered the Virgin Birth doctrine unnecessary in supporting the deity of Christ and harmful to the full humanity. Of course, he had to reckon with the plain teaching of Matthew and Luke. He offers the unsupported statement, "There are indications that . . . even these early passages of Matthew and Luke once read very differently."[21] He also wrote, "Although we cannot say absolutely that the narrative of both Synoptists is evidently non-historical, yet we must admit that the historical basis is uncertain."[22] Yet James Orr said that "the texts of these narratives have come down to us in their integrity."[23] W. E. Orchard, after considering the Codex Sinaiticus' mere variation on Matt. 1:16, 25, and the lone Latin manuscript that omits reference to the Virgin Birth in Luke 1:34, concluded: "As far as textual testimony is

18. Machen, *The Virgin Birth of Christ,* 1.

19. Brunner, *Dogmatics* 2:350.

20. Ibid., 356.

21. Emil Brunner, *The Mediator: A Study of the Central Doctrine of the Christian Faith,* trans. Olive Wyon (Philadelphia: Westminster Press, 1947), 324.

22. Brunner, *Dogmatics* 2:355.

23. Orr, *The Virgin Birth of Christ,* 227.

concerned, the Gospel record is overwhelming and unshakable."[24] And Karl Barth, as noted above, says that no one can "dispute" the fact of "a biblical testimony" to the Virgin Birth doctrine.[25]

Rudolph Bultmann denied the Virgin Birth partly because of its miraculous character. He liked "mystery" but not miracle.[26] He was frank to say that the Jews are in error because "they make the other-worldly—Jesus' mysterious origin in God—into a this-worldly thing." John he appreciates, as does Brunner. Bultmann wrote, "The true mystery is comprised in 'The word became flesh' (1:14), and John either does not know or refuses to know anything of an attempt to draw this mystery down into terms of this world by a story of a mythological Birth."[27]

One might have looked for support of the doctrine of the Virgin Birth in Lutheran bishop Gustav Aulén. Yet Aulén throws off on it as (of all things) a "rationalistic explanation" of the Incarnation.[28]

Wolfhart Pannenberg also opposes the "legend" (as he refers to it 16 times in one nine-page treatment) of the Virgin Birth, although he thinks one can still repeat the Apostles' Creed in worship because it has a function of opposing both Docetism and Adoptionism.

Pannenberg discusses the Virgin Birth in a somewhat sustained way in his *Jesus—God and Man* under the heading "Virgin Birth and Incarnation."[29] He writes:

> In its content, the legend of Jesus' virgin birth stands in an irreconcilable contradiction to the Christology of the incarnation of the preexistent Son of God found in Paul and John. For, according to this legend, Jesus first *became* God's Son through Mary's conception. According to Paul and John, on the contrary, the Son of God was already pre-existent and then as a preexistent being God bound himself to the man Jesus.[30]

24. William Edwin Orchard, *Foundations of Faith* (New York: George H. Doran Co., 1924), 2:119.

25. Barth, *Church Dogmatics* 2:176.

26. Rudolph Bultmann, *Theology of the New Testament* (London: SCM Press, 1955), 2:30.

27. Ibid.

28. Aulén, *Faith of the Christian Church*, 221 ff.

29. Pannenberg, *Jesus—God and Man*, 141-50.

30. Ibid., 143.

The only passage of Scripture he gives immediately, as support of all this, is Paul's Gal. 4:4 statement that carries no such weight.

Pannenberg strangely says that the "legend" of the Virgin Birth is "irreconcilable" with the doctrine of "the divine Sonship" of Jesus.[31] He says, "Sonship cannot at the same time consist in preexistence and still have its origin only in the divine procreation of Jesus in Mary."[32] The opposite is surely more correct: a normal birth would not indicate preexistence, whereas a virgin conception by the Holy Spirit would. The Spirit's part in the birth would indicate that Jesus is, as Barth says, "founded in God"—that a preexistent being is hereby fully humanized.

Significant continentals who supported the doctrine of the Virgin Birth until their deaths in the 1940s include Sergius Bulgakov, Nicholas Berdyaev, and Martin Dibelius. Karl Barth lent to it a weighty voice. Of these, only Barth will be treated here. On the whole, Barth's teaching on the Virgin Birth is quite simply that of Scripture, the Apostles' Creed, and the historic church in general.

With men like Brunner and Bultmann evidently in mind, he warns against "parenthesizing the miracle of the *Nativitas* and wanting to cling to the mystery as such."[33] To him, the Virgin Birth is the "miracle that is a pointer to the mystery [the Incarnation]."[34] It has not ontic, but noetic, significance. "It advertises what here takes place."[35] It is connected with the Incarnation "as sign with thing signified."[36] While some accept the Resurrection and assail the Virgin Birth, Barth says: "These two miracles belong together."[37]

Barth has some pertinent reminders for those who have regarded the Virgin Birth as simply the pagan idea of the gods cohabitating with humans. "This has nothing to do," he says, "with myths narrated elsewhere in the history of religion, myths of the procreation of men by gods. We have not to do with such a procreation here. God himself takes the stage as the Creator and not

---

31. Ibid.
32. Ibid.
33. Barth, *Dogmatics in Outline,* 100.
34. Barth, *Credo,* 70.
35. Ibid., 69.
36. Barth, *Church Dogmatics* 2:184.
37. Ibid., 182.

as a partner to this Virgin."[38] It was no sexual event, but a procreation realized "rather by way of the ear of Mary,"[39] as Christian art has frequently portrayed it.

He has little patience with those who want to maintain a high view of God's free grace through the Incarnation and yet deny the Virgin Birth. Barth says, "One thing may be definitely said, that every time people want to fly from this miracle, a theology is at work, which has ceased to understand and honour the mystery as well, and has rather essayed to conjure away the mystery of God's free grace."[40]

The Basel professor calls the maintenance of this doctrine "a watch at the door."

2. *The belief in Britain.* W. R. Inge was not a man for the miraculous at all. He wrote, "We should not now [in our scientific age] expect, *a priori*, that the Incarnate Logos would be born without a human father."[41] And he added: "An Incarnation which needs to be helped out by supernatural intervention is not a complete Incarnation."[42]

John Baillie was on the side of the new theology at this point as at others. He would have none of a Virgin Birth, which would have made Christ "an unrelated historical prodigy."[43] He suggests, "To believe in the interruption of ordinary history by the appearance of one prodigious and miraculous event may indeed have a salutary effect upon our dronish minds. . . . But the advantage is bought at too big a price, because we call 'ordinary' history as being, by contrast, even more ordinary than before."[44] This book was written early in his career, but his later writings imply a similar position.

William Barclay, one of the present writer's professors at Glasgow University, opposed the Virgin Birth doctrine with the vehemence of an evangelist. His exegetical and theological writings

38. Barth, *Dogmatics in Outline,* 100.
39. Ibid.
40. Ibid.
41. W. R. Inge et al., "The Person of Christ," in *Contentio Veritatis* (London: J. Murray, 1902), 88.
42. Ibid.
43. John Baillie, *The Place of Jesus Christ in Modern Christianity* (New York: Charles Scribner's Sons, 1929), 119.
44. Ibid., 119-20.

contain few denials of classical Christian belief, but they occur openly in his autobiography. In his book *Crucified and Crowned*,[45] he does oppose the Virgin Birth, giving pretty much the same arguments he presented to the present writer and others in a New Testament course at Glasgow University.

One of his arguments was based on the silence of most New Testament writers; only two of them (Matthew and Luke) mention the Virgin Birth. Barclay then admits what he evidently wished he did not have to: "In spite of all this the idea of the Virgin Birth appears in all the early Fathers and is lodged immovably in the earliest of the creeds."[46]

Barclay's second argument was that Matthew and Luke must have thought Joseph to be the actual father, since they trace Jesus' lineage to Joseph. One must admit that there is, here, at least an indication that Joseph was significant in Jesus' life. But Matthew, in particular, could not have here meant to teach that Joseph was the real father, since, immediately after he had finished the genealogy, he makes it amply plain in the birth narrative that Joseph was not the father.

Nevertheless, Barclay writes, "Both genealogies of Jesus (Matthew 1:1-17, Luke 3:23-38) trace the lineage of Jesus through Joseph and not through Mary. It is quite clear that the compilers of these genealogies were seeking to prove that Jesus was the son of David because he was the son of Joseph."[47]

Barclay's third argument was based on Mary's reference to Joseph as Jesus' father in Luke 2:48: "Son, why have you treated us like this? Your father and I have been anxiously searching for you." But this is surely an accommodated use of the term "father." First, "Father" is the natural term by which she would refer to Joseph. Surely she would not say "your foster father" or "your stepfather." Would she say "my husband," or "this carpenter with whom we live"? Surely not. Second, perhaps Jesus knew that Joseph was not His actual father, yet He noticed that Joseph had been so designated, as was no doubt usual. For He immediately switches the object of reference and, in the next verse of the account, calls God His Father. "Didn't you know I had to be in my

---

45. Barclay, *Crucified and Crowned*, 186-92.
46. Ibid., 192.
47. Ibid., 187.

Father's house?" (v. 49). Third, if Joseph was the actual father, why is he not given a significant place in the records of Christ's life, since the father, and not the mother, was the important person in the Jewish mind? Mary, however, receives prominence in those accounts, and Joseph is never referred to after this incident.

Barclay's fourth argument was based on the fact that Mary did not stop the brothers of Jesus in their attempt to alter the course of His ministry. This incident is recorded in John 7:2-9, and only there. The "Jewish Feast of Tabernacles was near" (v. 2), and Jesus' brothers, who actually "did not believe in him" (v. 5), wanted Him to go to Jerusalem and there perform miracles openly so that He could show himself to the world (v. 4). Jesus refused to comply with their wishes, saying, "The right time for me has not yet come" (v. 6). This account does not say that Mary was present during the discussion between Jesus and His brothers. The professor, however, assumes that she was, and that if she had known Him to be of miraculous birth, she would have known that He knew best, and she would have dissuaded her other children from trying to influence His ministry. Perhaps if Mary was present, she did not try to keep His brothers from influencing Him for the very reason that she knew He was of miraculous conception and special destiny.

The professor's fifth argument against the doctrine of the virgin birth of Christ was based on the fact that the word translated "virgin" in Isa. 7:14 may also be rendered "young woman" or "maiden," and that it should be so rendered in both the prophecy of and the record of Christ's birth. He would therefore translate Isa. 7:14 as does the RSV, "young woman," and not with "virgin," as do the KJV, ASV, NASB, and NIV; and he would render Matt. 1:23 and Luke 1:27 as "young woman" or "maiden." Yet there is much basis for rendering *almah* as *parthenos,* "virgin," as did the Septuagint translators two centuries before the time of Christ—in great part because its 70 translators, at that time, decided on thus translating the word.

Supporting the Christmas miracle in Britain have been several theologians of note, such as H. R. Mackintosh (d. 1936), William Temple (d. 1944), and J. K. Mozley (d. ca. 1951). Of the Virgin Birth, H. R. Mackintosh wrote that "strong grounds can be adduced for accepting the belief as in complete harmony with the Christian thought of Jesus, as dovetailing into the rest of our conviction naturally and simply."[48] He also asserts: "Supernatural conception is a most credible and befitting preface to a life consummated by rising from the dead."[49] He concludes: "If Christ is Son of God in a lonely and unshared sense, free from all taint of sin, and Head of a redeemed race, He is clearly so unexampled a person that we cannot assume Him to have been subject either in birth or death to all normal sequences."[50]

Archbishop William Temple, Platonist-Christian, was one to see God in all occurrences, including such miracles as the Virgin Birth. He wrote, "God is immanent to the Eternal Logos, . . . this Logos is the explanation of all things that occur, whether it be the regular and customary growth of a seed into the plant, or the birth of His own fleshly tabernacle from the Virgin-Mother."[51]

William E. Orchard carefully supported belief in the Virgin Birth even before he became a Roman Catholic in late middle life. The common objections to it are taken up one by one and dismissed convincingly, but without any particularly distinctive contributions.[52]

Anglo-Catholic L. S. Thornton can be fanciful at times, as when he says that "as Adam was formed by his Creator from virgin soil, so Jesus was formed in his human nature from the flesh of a Virgin's womb."[53] And unlike most scholars, he figures that John also teaches the Virgin Birth in his Gospel. Thornton suggests, "Whichever reading be adopted in 1:13 ["Who was born" or, "who were born," "not of the will of man," etc.] the language employed contains an unmistakable reference to the Virgin Birth."[54] Yet this disciple of the late Sergius Bulgakov studies the related scripture with considerable patience and lends a kind of ancient-church support to the belief.

Not to be forgotten is the support of so prominent a theologian as John S. Whale. He speaks of "the Gospels of St. Matthew

---

48. H. R. Mackintosh, *The Doctrine of the Person of Jesus Christ* (New York: Charles Scribner's Sons, 1912), 531.
49. Ibid.
50. Ibid., 532.
51. William Temple, *Nature, Man, and God* (New York: AMS Press, 1979), 299.
52. Orchard, *Foundations of Faith*, 64.
53. Lionel S. Thornton, *Revelation and the Modern World* (London: Dacre Press, 1950), 436.
54. Lionel S. Thornton, *The Common Life in the Body of Christ* (London: Dacre Press, 1942), 436.

and St. Luke, which describe his [Christ's] divine Sonship in terms of his miraculous Birth."[55] Continuing, he writes: "The meaning of the Virgin Birth is ultimately dogmatic: it is one of the many ways in which the New Testament asserts that the Son of God came into history; he did not come out of it."[56]

3. *The miracle in America.* On this side of the Atlantic we have experienced more flaunting of historic Christianity than the European continent and Britain have. An evidence of this is the fact that most of our recent major voices in theology have denied the Virgin Birth.

Take Richard Niebuhr. He says, "Revelation of the person of God through Jesus Christ does not include the communication of the propositions that Jesus was born of a Virgin, that the Scriptures are inerrant, and . . ."[57] He also says that we can be "freed from the necessity of putting our confidence in a natural miracle of birth."[58] The Yale theologian was no friend of biblical miracles such as this.

Reinhold Niebuhr uses myth and symbolization to such extent that his meanings are at times vague. Yet it is clear that he gives no credence to the Virgin Birth. He writes, "The flaw in the logic of the Virgin birth apologetics is amply revealed by the need of the corollary Catholic doctrine of the immaculate conception of the Virgin Mary."[59] And he suggests that "infinite regression of the immaculate conceptions could hardly remove the taint."[60]

Paul Tillich impugns with hearty confidence. Like Reinhold Niebuhr, he teaches that Jesus was a sinner. He writes, "Protestantism . . . demands a Christology of the participation of Christ in sinful existence."[61] In this vein he also says, "Jesus, like every man, is finite freedom. Without that, he would not be equal with mankind and could not be the Christ."[62] It is his belief that the Virgin Birth "story"[63] is one of several rationalizing attempts (even

---

55. John S. Whale, *Christian Doctrine* (Cambridge: Cambridge University Press, 1941), 109.

56. Ibid.

57. Richard Niebuhr, *The Meaning of Revelation* (New York: Macmillan Co., 1941), 73.

58. Ibid., 175.

59. Reinhold Niebuhr, *The Nature and Destiny of Man* (New York: Charles Scribner's Sons, 1941-43), 2:73.

60. Ibid.

61. Tillich, *Systematic Theology* 2:149-50.

62. Ibid., 127.

63. Ibid., 149.

on the part of the Bible writers themselves) to suggest that Jesus was sinless: "As early as in the New Testament, such rationalizations appear in several places, as for example, in some miracle stories—the story of the empty tomb, the virgin birth, the bodily ascendance, etc."[64]

The most widely disseminated opposition to the Virgin Birth in America has come from Nels F. S. Ferré. He views the "stories" in Matthew and Luke as "forced throughout."[65] Ferré thinks a German mercenary soldier might have been Jesus' father, which would account for the tradition in art that Jesus was a blond. Yet that the father was Joseph, he thinks, may be "the simplest thing to believe."[66] Also, for Ferré, it could have been as the accounts narrate it. As a matter of fact, it does not greatly matter, for the eternal Christ united with the human Jesus not then, but later— perhaps during His adult life.[67] This experience of Jesus is spoken of as a virgin birth, one not unlike what should happen to each of us. He writes, "Every child of God must have his virgin birth in order to become joint heir with Christ."[68] When you argue painstakingly that Jesus was a sinner as Ferré does, doctrines like the Virgin Birth simply hinder what you want to say of the Lord Jesus. Yet, in his respect for the Father's omnipotence, Ferré admits it could possibly have happened.[69]

Edwin Lewis, in the 1920s, urged an "open mind" on the Virgin Birth because of "the fact that it has no vital bearing on that one thing, the Incarnation, that gives Jesus His distinction and assures forever His place of supremacy in the regard of men."[70] Later he wrote, "The evidence is overwhelming that when men begin to surrender belief in the Virgin Birth and the Resurrection, they are also getting ready to surrender that belief regarding Christ himself [the Incarnation] which is the vital center of the whole body of faith."[71] The Virgin Birth and the Resurrection, "two veritable stones of offence," are both "vital parts of the organism of Chris-

64. Ibid., 127.
65. Ferré, *The Christian Understanding of God*, 192.
66. Ibid.
67. Ibid., 193.
68. Ibid., 139.
69. Ferré, *The Christian Faith*, 109.
70. Lewis, *Jesus Christ and the Human Quest*, 98.
71. Lewis, *A Philosophy of the Christian Revelation*, 186.

tian faith, or better, of the organism of Christian truth."[72] The Virgin Birth is "sheer miracle"; and if a "parthenogenetic human birth" could ever be proved as having occurred, it would have little bearing upon the "inexplicable divine event" by which God became incarnated.

4. *Impressions from this résumé.* When you report on such scholars as these, some for the Virgin Birth and some against it, you gather a few impressions in the process. For one thing, it is not simply the conservatives who affirm the miracle by which the Incarnation was effected; many others, as well, are of this persuasion—scholars of great prominence in our time.

Also, you figure that Albrecht Ritschl, although gone from us long since (1889), speaks particularly in some of the recent impugners. The distinction he made between facts and values, and his view that theology should concern itself only with the latter, is at least similar to the tendency of some to affirm the Incarnation while rejecting the Virgin Birth as its historical, factual means.

It would seem, too, that all the wide agreement in recent decades on the unity of the Bible would have a bearing on the fact that only two of the New Testament writers spell the doctrine out plainly. If there is such a unity, as G. Ernest Wright insists upon in his article on "The Faith of Israel" in *The Interpreter's Bible,* the Holy Spirit, who kept the books unified in essential thought, and who did not allow any opposition to the Virgin Birth within the canon, did not need to inspire still others to narrate the same event.[73]

This limited report on the Virgin Conception seems to confirm what James Orr was saying at our century's beginning: "It is a fact we cannot ignore—it will appear more clearly as I proceed—that the great bulk of the opposition to the Virgin Birth comes from those who do not recognize a supernatural element in Christ's life at all."[74]

Importance of the Doctrine. The doctrine of Christ's conception in a virgin woman's womb is important on a number of bases.

---

72. Ibid., 183 ff.
73. G. Ernest Wright, "The Faith of Israel," in *The Interpreter's Bible,* ed. George A. Buttrick (Nashville: Abingdon Press, 1952-53), 1:349-89.
74. Orr, *The Virgin Birth of Christ,* 9.

1. For one thing, and perhaps most significantly, it is important as *indicating Christ's deity*. If Christ had been born through the participation of a male, He would have been human only. Born by stupendous miracle as He was, through Mary's conceiving by a special act of "the Holy Spirit" (Matt. 1:20; Luke 1:35), His deity is assured. As Karl Barth has said, the Virgin Conception means that Christ is "founded in God." The angel Gabriel said, "The Holy Spirit will come upon you, and the power of the Most High will overshadow you" (Luke 1:35).

2. The Virgin Conception is also significant in *assuring the Incarnation*. Again, if Christ had been born through the participation of a human father, the enfleshment of the Deity in Jesus of Nazareth would not have occurred. With an ordinary human conception, we would have had only the ordinary and usual wonder of a human-only person being born. God the Father might have conceived another strategy to achieve an Incarnation of the Deity with humanity. Perhaps He was not limited to Spirit conception as the means to the Incarnation. Yet, according to Holy Scripture, that is the method He chose. And if that method is denied, the Incarnation cannot then still be affirmed—although such theologians as Emil Brunner and Rudolph Bultmann have attempted precisely this. Another means to the Incarnation would be simply a human invention—an invention designed to net us Incarnation without the embarrassment of Spirit conception in a virgin's womb.

3. A third importance of the Virgin Conception is that *it assures Christ's humanity*—His full humanity, if you please. Through the Spirit's power, Christ was conceived in and born from Mary's womb. He was not poured though her womb, as the docetic Gnostics said. He was gestated through an entire nine-month period. In this way, He who was above us was made of us—was made one with us. In this way, He was made very flesh with us. In this way, also, He became what He seemed to be: a human being who thirsted, hungered, wept, suffered and died, and was raised bodily.

4. A fourth importance of the Virgin Conception is that *it suits God's usual way of accomplishing things*, not by fiat, but by human participation. He could have had His Eternal Son assume human flesh without the participation of a woman, as angels at times seem to have done (Genesis 18—19). But He did not do this. Instead, from outside and above the human experience, He entered into human form and life and experience. From outside

and above the historical, He entered into the historical. All this is in keeping with His usual way of acting creatively and redemptively on our behalf.

5. A fifth factor in the importance of the doctrine of the virgin conception of Christ is *its harmony with a wide range of supernatural events in our Christian faith*. If respect for science causes us to oppose the Virgin Conception, the door is opened for a wider erosion of faith. Next to go may be Christ's miracles, His physical resurrection, the efficacy of the sacraments, the objective value of prayer, etc. If science cancels the supernatural, Christianity will be reduced to a religious humanism void of redeeming power.

6. A sixth basis for the importance of the Virgin Conception is that *it gives the whole Christmas story a facticity basis*. The actual, factual birth of the virgin-conceived Jesus is what Christmas, the principal holy day of Christianity and of the Western world generally, is all about. The Christmas mother, Mary; the Christmas miracle, Virgin Conception; the Christmas mystery, Incarnation; and the Christmas message, redemption through Jesus—these things are all bound up in this doctrine, this understanding, this confidence, this heady joy.

The Virgin Conception, then, is richly important theologically and is, as a doctrine, in keeping with a historical Resurrection. It also figures significantly in why the Atonement made Christ a Savior instead of a mere martyr.

12

The Meaning of the Atonement

The word "atonement" translates the Hebrew Old Testament word *kippur,* but there is no Greek New Testament word for atonement. *Hilastērion* ("propitiation") is sometimes translated "sacrifice of atonement" (Rom. 3:25). Cognates of *katallagē,* "reconciliation," are also sometimes so rendered. The Old Testament word's basic verbal meaning is "to cover."[1] This basic meaning of the Old Testament word has suggested to many interpreters that our sins are only covered over, without righteousness being imparted to us. But the word probably means that our sins are covered over as a wound is covered when it heals and new flesh takes the place of, say, an infected cut (see Ps. 32:1; Rom. 8:4).

God Planned the Atonement. Some writers have suggested that the Cross was not planned—that it intruded itself into the situation, and then God made use of it. Alan Walker, for example, says that the Father "did not intend" the Crucifixion, but that "once it happened . . . God seized upon the Cross and . . . made it the occasion of salvation."[2]

Yet Scripture teaches that Christ's atoning death was in God's plan all along. It speaks of Christ as the "Lamb that was slain from the creation of the world" (Rev. 13:8). Some seven centuries beforehand, Isaiah had foretold that Christ would suffer death on our behalf (chap. 53). And Jesus said, "For even the Son of Man did not come to be served, but to serve, and to give his life as a

---

1. A popular notion is that "atonement" means "at-one-ment." This is incorrect because "atonement" refers only to the provision for "at-one-ment."
2. Alan Walker, *The Many-Sided Cross of Jesus* (New York: Abingdon Press, 1962), 75.

ransom for many" (Mark 10:45; see Matt. 20:28). Christ came to earth for the purpose of giving His life on our behalf.

Blood, in Atonement. Blood is significant for the Atonement. "Without the shedding of blood there is no forgiveness," we read in Heb. 9:22. But Scripture says that "the life of every creature is its blood" (Lev. 17:14). So we are redeemed through Christ's death because a life was given—not because any given amount of literal blood was poured upon us. In Old Testament times the priest drew blood from animals until no life was left in them— and with that blood made atonement for the sins of the people.[3] That blood represented the life of a perfect animal given for the covering over of sin—in the sense of healing.[4]

Necessity of the Atonement. There are two senses in which the necessity of the Atonement can be discussed. It can be necessary either as the only way in which God could have provided for an atonement, or simply as the one way in which He did indeed provide for it.

If we say that the Atonement provided is the only kind that was open to God, we get into an evangelical rationalism. If we say this, we restrict God, questioning His sovereignty and making Him subject to certain laws of necessity, as the ancient Stoics taught.

We can say only that some kind of atonement was necessary if the holy God was to forgive and cleanse us sinful human beings. We can speak of the appropriateness of the method of atonement that He chose. But God was surely free to choose the method of atonement: a different kind of death, or even a method other than death. God is God. We are the creatures, and the creatures do not tell God that He is required to act in certain ways.

The Propitiatory Element. Liberals, who overemphasize God's love and say little about His holiness, deny that there is a propitiatory element in the Atonement. They oppose the view that

---

3. On that Day of Atonement, blood was also applied to the head of another animal, a scapegoat, which was chased away to symbolize that our sins are carried away. This scapegoat's blood was not taken. It only received the blood from the slain animal and carried it away. This symbol does not counter the point being made here: that the blood is the life given all the way to death, providing for the removal of sin.

4. See Wilfred Winget, "The Significance of Blood in Atonement" (Thesis, Nazarene Theological Seminary Library, 1955).

Christ's death on the Cross assuaged God's holy wrath against us as rebellious sinners. They view His death as expiation, in which we see and are captivated by God's love as shown us by Christ's death on the Cross.[5] They like to quote 2 Cor. 5:18-20 in support of the understanding that the world is reconciled to God through Christ, but that God does not need to be reconciled to us.[6]

Yet while Scripture only says that the world is reconciled to God, and never that God is reconciled to us, there are passages of Scripture that basically teach that God needs to be and is reconciled to us. These passages do not use cognates of *katallagē* for reconciliation, but they nonetheless teach that reconciliation is a two-way street. Various passages about God's wrath imply such as this (see John 3:36; Rom. 1:18; 5:9; 9:22; 12:19; Eph. 5:6; Col. 3:6; Rev. 14:10, 19; 15:1, 7; 16:1; 19:15). Most explicitly, however, this is taught, or at least implied, by the four propitiation passages of the New Testament where cognates of the verb *hilaskomai* are found: the noun *hilastērion*, Rom. 3:25; *hilaskesthai*, Heb. 2:17; and *hilasmos*, 1 John 2:2; 4:10. All four of these passages are translated as "propitiation" in the NASB; but the NIV renders them somewhat less vigorously as "a sacrifice of atonement" (Rom. 3:25), to "make atonement" (Heb. 2:17), and "atoning sacrifice" (1 John 2:2; 4:10).[7]

These words are translated as "expiation" in the RSV in all four of these instances. This version was translated by more or less liberal scholars, and such scholars have seldom wanted to admit that Christ's death propitiates or assuages God's holy wrath.[8]

---

5. Expiation should be thought of as the removal of man's guilt; and propitiation, as assuaging God's holy wrath. Leo G. Cox says, "Actually, God's wrath is propitiated and man's guilt is expiated" ("Propitiation," in *Beacon Dictionary of Theology*, 425).

6. The word for reconciliation, *katallagē*, is also found twice in Romans (5:11; 11:15) and is used somewhat similarly there. Rom. 11:15 speaks of "the reconciliation of the world." Rom. 5:11 speaks of "Christ, through whom we have now received reconciliation," suggesting that we get reconciled to God, not that God becomes reconciled to us.

7. It should not be assumed that this NIV translation is liberal. Even the very conservative Merrill F. Unger defines *hilastērion* as "atoning sacrifice" (see Unger, *The New Unger's Bible Handbook*, rev. Gary N. Larson [Chicago: Moody Press, 1984], 631, 635, in comments on 1 John 2:2 and 4:10). See also Leo G. Cox, "Propitiation," in *Beacon Dictionary of Theology*, 424; and Leon Morris, "Propitiation," in *Evangelical Dictionary of Theology*, ed. Walter Elwell (Grand Rapids: Baker Book House, 1984), 888.

8. Liberals have often admitted God's wrath as such but have preferred to say that it is not personal—that it is automatic, more or less cause and effect. Evangelicals tend to want to hold onto the propitiatory aspect of the Atonement (1 John 4:10).

They view propitiation as placating or appeasing God, a view that obtained among the ancient Greeks, and prefer to translate these as "expiation."

The word "propitiation" means to soften, to assuage, to lessen. Used in connection with what is accomplished by Christ's death, it means that the death assuages God's holy wrath against us as sinners. When that is accomplished, God is reconciled to us. Then He is able to be still just or righteous and to justify us, as Rom. 3:25-26 says: "God presented him as a sacrifice of atonement, through faith in his blood. He did this . . . to demonstrate his justice at the present time, so as to be just and the one who justifies those who have faith in Jesus."

God is not capricious, nor is He one who is easily offended and who needs to be placated. Yet, due to His holiness, He is wrathful toward us when we lift puny fists in His face. He does not and cannot overlook such rebellion in the fashion of a doting grandfather. The death of the sinless Christ, on behalf of us sinful humans, the just for the unjust, assuages the Father's holy wrath against sin, reconciles the Father to us, making it possible for Him to forgive all who repent and believe.[9]

The Subjective and the Objective. The subjective aspect of the Atonement has to do with its appeal to us. The Atonement does reveal God's love for us, as Scripture clearly shows (e.g., John 3:16). If, however, the subjective aspect is understood as the principal accomplishment of the Atonement, then the Atonement is viewed as primarily expiation, not propitiation.

Besides the subjective element in the Atonement, an objective element obtains. Besides evidencing God's love for us, it assuages God's holy wrath toward us as sinners.

One way to think of the subjective and the objective aspects of the Atonement is to understand that the bar to our salvation lies partly in us, but chiefly in God. Thus its chief accomplishment is an objective one. The Atonement occasions the altogether-holy Father's becoming kindly toward us rebels.

---

9. There are a few New Testament instances of the verbal form of *hilastērion, hilaskomai,* and quite a number of Hebrew counterpart words to *hilastērion* in the Old Testament, which are not discussed here. Likewise, it has not been deemed necessary to discuss here the more than 800 Old Testament instances of words denoting God's wrath—which is what is softened by Christ's propitiation.

Theories of the Atonement

Of the five theories of the Atonement now to be discussed, only the Moral Influence view is subjective. The other four theories, the Ransom, Satisfaction, Punishment, and Governmental theories, are objective ones, but they include a subjective aspect.

The Ransom Theory. This view regards the death of Christ as a price paid to Satan for our release from slavery. The Greek *lutron* was a slave's release price. Paul used the term *antilutron* in 1 Tim. 2:6, where he speaks of "Christ Jesus, who gave himself as a ransom for all men." And the writer of Hebrews explains, "For this reason Christ is the mediator of a new covenant, that those who are called may receive the promised eternal inheritance—now that he has died as a ransom to set them free from the sins committed under the first covenant" (9:15). There are six Hebrew Old Testament words for ransom that get translated as "ransom," "ransomed," or "ransoms" in 21 Old Testament passages.[10]

Particularly from the four New Testament ransom passages mentioned above, a vaguely expressed Ransom theory of the Atonement was developed by numerous early Christian fathers. Until Anselm this theory, sometimes called the classical or the dramatic theory, was the only one developed.[11] A chief problem with this theory concerned the one who is paid, usually thought of as Satan. Some of the fathers and most later theologians could not accept the notion that Satan had a right to be paid for the release of his slaves.

The Satisfaction theory solved this problem. Christ's death became a price paid to God the Father so that He could forgive people and still maintain His honor.

The Satisfaction Theory. The first formal theory of Atonement to be developed in the history of Christian theology was the Satisfaction theory, advanced by Anselm in his *Cur Deus Homo.* Based on the feudal system prevalent at the time, Anselm viewed God as similar to a baron, and ourselves as similar to serfs. In those days the serf would be given a small piece of land to till—a field—in

---

10. These are Exod. 30:12; Lev. 19:20; 27:29; Num. 35:31, 32; Job 5:20; 6:22, 23; 33:24; Ps. 49:7, 8; 55:18; Prov. 13:8; 21:18; Isa. 35:10; 43:3; 47:11; 50:2; 51:11; Jer. 31:11; Hos. 13:14.

11. The fathers and later figures concerned themselves much more with the person of Christ than with the work of Christ.

exchange for his promise to protect the baron against enemy troops. The serf often got into debt to the baron. The baron could not simply forgive such debt and still maintain his honor—and honor was highly prized in those feudal times. According to Anselm's theory we, by sinning, got into debt to God, and He could not simply forgive us and maintain His honor. The debt we owed was infinitely great, so a mere human could not pay it, yet it had to be paid by a human being. Christ, as fully human, could pay the debt; and as fully divine, could pay a debt infinitely great. He paid it by undergoing physical death when, as sinless, He did not deserve to die. So Christ's death on the Cross paid the debt we owed to God because of our sin, making it possible for God the Father to forgive us and still maintain His honor.

First Cor. 6:19-20 has sometimes been interpreted as teaching this view: "You are not your own; you were bought at a price." This "price" could be thought of as the payment of a debt we owe God due to our sins. That, however, would preclude real forgiveness on God's part. The passage probably means that we who are already Christians should realize that we were bought, from slavery to Satan, by the price of Christ's suffering on the Cross.

The Moral Influence Theory. This was devised by Peter Abelard, who was not satisfied with Anselm's Atonement theory. It is the theory that emphasizes—overemphasizes—God's love. According to this view, Christ died on the Cross to demonstrate God's love for sinners.

This theory suits theological modernism in several ways. For one thing, it overemphasizes God's love, in relation to His holiness, as liberalism does in general. Not that an emphasis upon God's love is incorrect. God did indeed so love the world that He gave His Son for our salvation (John 3:16). The love of Christ, placarded at Golgotha, does entice us to turn to God for forgiveness. Yet the Moral Influence theory overemphasizes God's love. According to this view, the bar to our salvation lies in us, not in God—not in His holiness. So as the Atonement displays God's love, its chief design is to convince us that He loves us, that He has loved us all along, and that He does not even tend to draw away from us due to His holiness.

This theory also suits modernism because it views sin lightly. Like Abelard, it denies the doctrine of original sin. It tends toward a high view of human nature—toward a view of its basic goodness. Humanistic, it deprecates human sinfulness.

The Moral Influence theory is congruous with modernism's view of Jesus as human only and not divine. Abelard himself did not deny Jesus' deity. He was anti-Trinitarian but not Unitarian. But the modernists as such, who generally adopted the Moral Influence theory, all denied Jesus' deity. And that atonement theory accords with the denial of Jesus' deity because it does not take a divine Christ to show us simply that God loves us; it takes a divine Christ to redeem us.

The Punishment Theory. This is the view of Calvin and Calvinism that Christ, by His death on the Cross, took the punishment for our sins. John Calvin himself taught that Christ took the punishment for the sins of everyone, although this was inconsistent with his understanding that Christ's death is unconditional in its benefits to those God has predestined to be saved. Theodore Beza (Calvin's son-in-law), and later Calvinists generally, "corrected" Calvin at this point, teaching that Christ took the punishment of only the elect, dying only for them, not for everyone.[12]

Whereas in the Satisfaction theory it is God's honor that is satisfied by Christ's death, in the Punishment theory what is satisfied by Christ's death is God's justice. In this view, God's justice will not allow Him to forgive without sin being fully punished, and it was fully punished when the sinless Godman died on the Cross for those whom God had previously predestinated, unconditionally, to be saved eternally.

Several significant problems attend the Punishment theory. One is that, like the Satisfaction theory, it denies actual forgive-

---

12. R. T. Kendall did for Oxford University a Ph.D. dissertation in which he has pretty much proven a new understanding of Calvin: that he taught an unlimited atonement theory, whereas the Calvinists from Beza onward, including the Puritans in general (such as John Owen), taught that the Atonement was limited to the elect in its benefits. See also Kendall's chapter on "The Puritan Modification of Calvin's Theology" in the festschrift, *John Calvin: His Influence in the Western World,* ed. W. Stanford Reid (Grand Rapids: Zondervan Publishing House, 1982). Kendall says, "The decree of election, however, is not rendered effectual by the death of Christ. For if that were true, it follows that (1) Christ obviously did not die for the whole world after all, or (2) since He died for all, all are elected. In other words, those for whom Christ died *must* be saved. Calvin, however, thinks that Christ died for all and yet all are not saved. So to the objection Beza might raise, that if some perish for whom Christ died then God would be demanding double payment, Calvin has this answer: they are 'doubly culpable' (R. T. Kendall, *Calvin and English Calvinism to 1649* [London: Oxford University Press, 1979], 15-16).

ness. If the Father's justice must be and is satisfied by punishment, then no forgiveness is possible. It is either punishment or forgiveness, surely, not punishment and forgiveness. If a father were to punish his son with a whipping, he could not then say, "Now, son, I forgive you." If the father were to say that, the son would see through it right away. He would likely say, "No, you did not forgive me—you punished me."

Another problem with the theory is that it throws God's infinite goodness into question. Surely, if God were able to save some people sovereignly because His justice is satisfied by Christ's punishment, why does He not, if He is infinitely good, save everyone in that sovereign way?

Still another problem with the view is that it denies our free moral agency, stating that our decisions do not really count, that they cannot really count.

A further problem with the view is that it is unfair to the nonelect. If they are given no opportunity at all to be saved, and others, the elect, are given the opportunity, for no reason except the inscrutable will of God, it would seem to be unfair to the nonelect. If they go into eternal hell due to the sin of Adam, and if unelected babies are included in this, who do not themselves disobey God in this life, it would seem to be quite unfair.

The chief problem with the Punishment theory of the Atonement, of course, is that it is unscriptural. For one thing, Scripture does not teach any predestination of eternal destiny at all, as was discussed earlier (see chap. 9, "The Doctrine of Ourselves").

It is unscriptural, also, to teach that Christ did not die for everyone, but only for the elect. When Scripture says, "He died for all" (2 Cor. 5:15), it does not mean "all of the elect," as John Owen and other Calvinists have said, but simply all—all of the all.

The principal reason why the Punishment theory is unscriptural is because its basic claim is unscriptural: which is that Christ was punished on our behalf or instead of us. Scripture never states that He was punished for us or that He paid the penalty for us. Scripture always states instead that He suffered for us. Thus Paul says: "The sufferings of Christ flow over into our lives" (2 Cor. 1:5). In Hebrews we read: "And so Jesus also suffered outside the city gate to make the people holy through his own blood" (13:12). In Luke we read: "Did not the Christ have to suffer these things and then enter his glory?" (24:26).

And as John Miley says in *The Atonement in Christ*,[13] suffering is significantly different from punishment. All punishment is suffering, but not all suffering is punishment. The difference between the two is that punishment presupposes guilt, and suffering does not. Since Christ was sinless, He was guiltless. When He died for us, therefore, He suffered but was not punished. And since there was a substitution of His suffering for the punishment that believers otherwise would have received in hell, the Father could actually forgive us. Punishment would have clearly satisfied God's justice. But since Christ suffered instead of being punished, the Father really could forgive those who repent and believe.

The Governmental Theory. This is the view that Christ suffered for us so that the Holy Father could forgive us and still govern us justly. The seeds of this theory are in the teachings of James Arminius, but it was first taught as an Atonement view by one of his students, Hugo Grotius. Late last century it was explicated quite thoroughly by Methodism's John Miley in his *Atonement in Christ.*

The theory will be discussed first by showing what it cannot incorporate into itself, and then by discussing what it can and does consist of.

1. *What it cannot incorporate.* The Governmental theory cannot incorporate into itself the main elements of two major Atonement theories: the payment of a debt (Satisfaction) and Christ's being punished (Punishment).

Whereas Calvinists teach boldly that Christ paid the penalty for us—that He took our punishment—and believe their view to be biblical, it is altogether opposed to the teaching of Scripture. Neither the Hebrew Old Testament nor the Greek New Testament ever teach this view. The NIV, translated by Calvinists in the main, renders the Hebrew *musar* in Isa. 53:5 with "punishment," which is unusual. The KJV, even though translated by 54 Calvinists, does not once use any form of the English word for "punishment" to describe what happened to Christ. Always the word is "suffering" or certain synonyms of that word. Scripture teaches that Christ suffered for us, not that He was punished for us. Three

---

13. John Miley, *The Atonement in Christ* (New York: Hunt and Eaton, 1889), 167 ff.

versions state 28 times that Christ suffered for us: the KJV,[14] the NASB,[15] and the NIV[16]; and the RSV says it 27 times.[17]

The reason Scripture teaches that Christ suffered for us instead of being punished is in part, as mentioned earlier, because He was sinless and therefore guiltless. It is in part also because God the Father really does forgive us—whereas, if He punished Christ instead of us, He could not then have forgiven us. In Christ's substitutionary punishment, justice would have been satisfied, precluding forgiveness. One cannot both punish and forgive, surely.

The other aspect of Atonement theory that the Governmental theory cannot incorporate into itself is that Christ's death paid a debt for us. Even as one cannot punish and then also forgive, one cannot accept payment for a debt and still forgive the debt. Scripture indeed says, "You are not your own; you were bought at a price" (1 Cor. 6:19-20). This no doubt means that we are bought with the price of Christ's suffering, not the price of a debt being paid for us. Neither a human being nor God, surely, can accept payment for a debt and still forgive the debt. And forgiveness, sheer forgiveness, is unique to Christianity, of all the religions, and must be protected.

2. *What it can incorporate.* It can incorporate into itself all the various teachings of Scripture and the numerous understandings promoted in the other major Atonement theories.

For one thing, it can incorporate into itself Peter Forsyth's emphasis on how the holiness of God figures in the Atonement.

---

14. These are: "suffer" (Matt. 16:21; 17:12; Mark 8:31; 9:12; Luke 9:22; 17:25; 22:15; 24:46; Acts 3:18; 26:23; Rom. 8:17); "suffered" (Luke 24:26; Acts 17:3; Heb. 2:18; 5:8; 9:26; 13:12; 1 Pet. 2:21, 23; 3:18; 4:1); "sufferings" (2 Cor. 1:5; Phil. 3:10; Heb. 2:9, 10; 1 Pet. 1:11; 4:13; 5:1).

15. These are: "suffer" (Matt. 16:21; 17:12; Mark 8:31; 9:12; Luke 9:22; 17:25; 22:15; 24:26, 46; Acts 3:18; 17:3; 26:23; Rom. 8:17; Heb. 9:26); "suffered" (Heb. 2:18; 5:8; 13:12; 1 Pet. 2:21; 4:1); "suffering" (Acts 1:3; Heb. 2:9; 1 Pet. 2:23); "sufferings" (2 Cor. 1:5; Phil. 3:10; Heb. 2:10; 1 Pet. 1:11; 4:13; 5:1).

16. These are: "suffer" (Matt 16:21; 17:12; Mark 8:31; 9:12; Luke 9:22; 17:25; 22:15; 24:26, 46; Acts 3:18; 17:3; 26:23; Heb. 9:26); "suffered" (Heb. 2:9, 18; 5:8; 13:12; 1 Pet. 2:21, 23; 4:1); "suffering" (Acts 1:3; Heb. 2:10); "sufferings" (Rom. 8:17; 2 Cor. 1:5; Phil. 3:10; 1 Pet. 1:11; 4:13; 5:1).

17. These are: "suffer" (Matt. 16:21; 17:12; Mark 8:31; 9:12; Luke 9:22; 17:25; 22:15; 24:26, 46; Acts 3:18; 17:3; 26:23; Rom. 8:17; Heb. 9:26); "suffered" (Heb. 2:18; 5:8; 13:12; 1 Pet. 2:21, 23; 4:1); "suffering" (Heb. 2:9, 10); "sufferings" (2 Cor. 1:5; Phil. 3:10; 1 Pet. 1:11; 4:13; 5:1).

One of the contributions of Forsyth, in his great book on the Atonement titled *The Work of Christ,* is that God himself made the "offering." Forsyth says, "The real objective element in atonement is not that something was offered to God, but that God made the offering."[18] He similarly says, "God made the atonement."[19] This is a profound understanding.

Forsyth also says that the Atonement was "something actually done, and not merely said or shown, by God, something really done from the depth of God who is the action of the World."[20] This understanding, which emphasizes what is concretely historical and actual, in distinction from what is merely ideational and ethereal, or conceptual, can be and should be incorporated into the Governmental theory.

A kindred emphasis in Forsyth, which should also be incorporated into the Governmental theory of the Atonement, is that it is not quite that "Christ and His death reconciled God to man"[21] but that in Christ's death we have "God reconciling himself."[22] He means to say that there was no "third party" who got God and us reconciled, but that God himself did it.

Forsyth also viewed the Atonement as something done for the race, somewhat as Olin Alfred Curtis did in *The Christian Faith*—and this racial concept can also be incorporated into the Governmental theory. Forsyth says, "The first charge upon Christ and His Cross was the reconciliation of the race, and of its individuals by implication."[23] Surely Paul had something like this in mind when he speaks of the racial significance of both Adam and Christ in Rom. 5:12-21 and 1 Corinthians 15.

Perhaps the single most basic aspect of Forsyth's Atonement view is his emphasis on God's holiness. Indeed, that emphasis is part and parcel of these other matters just discussed. Forsyth says, "What is meant by the holiness of God is the holy God."[24] He is thus saying that holiness is more than an attribute but is basically what God is, a position taken earlier, in the chapter on

---

18. P. T. Forsyth, *The Work of Christ* (London: Independent Press, 1910), 99.
19. Ibid.
20. Ibid., 100.
21. Ibid., 103.
22. Ibid.
23. Ibid., 99.
24. Ibid., 131.

God's existence and nature. Because of this, for Forsyth, God had to bring judgment upon sin by Christ's atoning death before being able to forgive sin. Sin defied God as the Holy One, and we would not even respect a God who simply told us that our sins were being overlooked. In the Atonement, the holy God himself became an offering for the whole race, judging sin, making it possible for Him to forgive sin without sin being appraised in a light manner. This is similar to the Governmental theory concept of John Miley and others, but even more profound. Forsyth says that Jesus had to go to the Cross because God could not otherwise forgive us and still be the Holy One.

The Governmental theory can incorporate into itself the emphasis on Christ's ransoming us as in the classical Ransom theory of the Atonement. Christ did indeed ransom us from Satan, as Scripture teaches.

Paul uses the ransom figure the only other time it is found in the New Testament in 1 Tim. 2:6, where he speaks of "the man Christ Jesus, who gave himself as a ransom [antilutron] for all men." Here the preposition "for" translates the Greek huper, "on behalf of." Instead of His doing this for "the many" as in the Matthew and Mark statements, which might suggest a limited provision, Paul says it was done for "all," "indicating that the ransom was provisionally universal."[25]

Moreover, the Governmental theory incorporates into itself the emphasis on God's love, which is the main point in the Abelardian Moral Influence theory. John 3:16 excites us Christians commonly, where we all read, "For God so loved the world that he gave his one and only Son, that whoever believes in him shall not perish but have eternal life." Christ's own love spelled out for us in drops of blood is also common to all Christians, for we all read, "For Christ's love compels us, because we are convinced that one died for all . . . And he died for all, that those who live should no longer live for themselves but for him who died for them and was raised again" (2 Cor. 5:14-15). Christ's love, displayed so vividly on the Cross—when He did not need to die but did, when He could have called for more than 12 legions of angels

25. W. E. Vine, *Vine's Expository Dictionary of Old and New Testament Words* (Old Tappan, N.J.: Fleming H. Revell Co., 1981), 247.

to deliver Him from His enemies but did not—compels us to turn to the Father for forgiveness. The RSV, instead of "compels," translates "controls us." The Greek word there means "shuts us up to a given course," so that we can do hardly anything else but respond to such a Golgotha deed.

Moreover, the Governmental theory includes the vicarious aspect of the Atonement, the understanding that Christ did something on behalf of us. Here, the preposition is *huper.* It is used in Scripture numerous times of what Christ did.[26] It is translated "on behalf of," and it means that Christ's death was on behalf of us. This is the special basis for our understanding that there is a vicarious element in the Atonement. Not only was it something done as a substitute for something else, but also it was done vicariously for us or on our behalf, so that its benefit can be transferred to us. The use of this word *huper* means that the worth of His substitutionary suffering can be transferred to our account if we repent and believe.

3. *Some wide applications.* Since Christ's suffering on behalf of everyone is provisionally redemptive, our present suffering on behalf of others is also provisionally redemptive. This might be the inmost kernel of truth of the Christian faith: that suffering is provisionally redemptive. And it is wide-scoped in its application. It means that our suffering for others can become a means of their turning to God to receive the benefits of Christ's suffering love on the Cross.

This is why Paul says, "For it has been granted to you on behalf of Christ not only to believe on him, but also to suffer for him, since you are going through the same struggle you saw I

---

26. This is seen several times in the Gospels. Jesus spoke of His blood "poured out for [*huper*] many" (Mark 14:24); of His body "given for [*huper*] you" (Luke 22:19); and of His flesh given "for [*huper*] the life of the world" (John 6:51). He gives His life "for [*huper*] the sheep" (10:11) and "for [*huper*] his friends" (15:13). The apostle Paul frequently uses *huper* in relation to Christ's atonement. "Christ died for [*huper*] the ungodly" (Rom. 5:6). "Christ died for [*huper*] us" (v. 8). "[God] did not spare his own Son, but gave him up for [*huper*] us" (8:32). See also 1 Cor. 15:3; 2 Cor. 5:15, 21; Gal. 1:4; and Eph. 5:1-2. Likewise, the writer of Hebrews says, "But we see Jesus . . . now crowned with glory and honor because he suffered death, so that by the grace of God he might taste death for [*huper*] everyone" (2:9). And Peter says, "For Christ died for sins once for all, the righteous for [*huper*] the unrighteous, to bring you to God" (1 Pet. 3:18).

This plethora of the *huper* usage in the New Testament shows that Scripture frequently teaches that Christ did what He did on Calvary on our behalf.

had, and now hear that I still have" (Phil. 1:29-30). The word for "granted" here is *echaristhē,* from *charidzomai,* meaning "to give . . . graciously as a favor."[27] It means that the Philippians had been gifted with the privilege of suffering on Christ's behalf.

Paul is clear about the redemptive value of our suffering when he says to the Colossians, "Now I rejoice in what was suffered for you, and I fill up in my flesh what is still lacking in regard to Christ's afflictions, for the sake of his body, which is the church" (1:24). It might seem strange that something is lacking in Christ's suffering, which Paul says he makes up for through his own sufferings. Yet that is what he says. And what is lacking in Christ's "sufferings" (KJV) or "afflictions" (NIV) is that they were done a long time ago and a long way off. They are of infinite worth, of course, but there is a vast gap of space and time between His sufferings and the life situation of specific people today. But when we suffer for them, it commands their attention. The suffering of Christians can occasion a straying person's turning to the God of suffering love for the forgiveness He offers.

The Governmental theory is also substitutionary. According to this theory, what Christ did became a substitute for something else that would otherwise occur. There is a substitution of the guiltless Christ's suffering for the punishment that those who repent and believe would have received in eternal hell.

However adequately we understand the Atonement, Christ's crucifixion would not have achieved our redemption except for His resurrection—to which we now turn.

---

27. William F. Arndt and F. Wilbur Gingrich, *A Greek-English Lexicon of the New Testament* (Chicago: University of Chicago Press, 1957), 884.

13

The Emptied Tomb

Floyd Filson is insightful in saying that "the Christian faith is essentially a resurrection faith,"[1] and in adding: "Christian theology is essentially resurrection theology."[2] It is the "miracle of all miracles," as Thomas Kepler says, for the Christ who entered into the world by the miracle of Virgin Conception exited the world by another stupendous miracle—that of resurrection from the dead.

Karl Barth appropriately called Christ's resurrection the "validating" event, for it supports the truth of other events such as His birth of a virgin, His being divine as well as human, His teachings, His atoning death, His present office as the one Mediator between God and us, and His intention of returning in kingly power and glory.

Paul E. Little says, "Both friends and enemies of the Christian faith have recognized the resurrection of Christ as the foundation stone of the faith."[3] Phillip Schaff calls the Resurrection "a test question on which depends the truth or falsehood of the Christian religion. It is either the greatest miracle or the greatest delusion which history records."[4]

C. S. Lewis said that "to preach Christianity [in New Testament times] meant to preach the Resurrection."[5] In Peter's sermon at Pentecost, as Luke records it, 13 verses relate to the resurrection of Christ, and only 2 mention His crucifixion. Other sermons in Acts have this as their theme also (see 3:15; 4:10; 5:30-32;

---

1. Floyd Filson, *Jesus Christ, the Risen Lord* (New York: Abingdon Press, 1956), 49.
2. Ibid.
3. Paul E. Little, *Know Why You Believe* (Downers Grove, Ill.: InterVarsity Press, 1973), 23.
4. Phillip Schaff, *History of the Christian Church* (Grand Rapids: William B. Eerdmans Publishing Co., 1949), 1:173.
5. C. S. Lewis, *Miracles* (New York: Macmillan Publishing Co., 1947), 171.

10:40; 13:30-34; 17; 26:23). Indeed, James Stewart is correct in saying that not a line of the New Testament would have been written had it not been for the faith of the early Christians in Christ's resurrection from the dead.

Reality of the Resurrection

Three major views have been held on the matter of the reality of Christ's resurrection: outright denial, as in modernism; a spiritual resurrection only, as in Emil Brunner; and the physical resurrection view, in the classical and evangelical understanding.

Outright Denial in Modernism. Modernists, including German rationalists, English deists, and American liberal theologians, have simply denied the Resurrection. John Toland (1670-1722), an English deist, spoke for them all in rejecting the Resurrection because it is "contrary to reason."[6]

Friedrich Schleiermacher, sometimes called the father of modern theology, opposed the doctrine of the resurrection of Christ from the dead. Schleiermacher says that the "right impression of Christ can be, and has been, present in its fullness without a knowledge of these facts"[7]—in which "facts" he included the Resurrection.

Such scholars as these have tended to affirm, in the Christian faith, only what is supportable by reason and to deny whatever is miraculous. Rejecting the inspiration and authority of Scripture, they have tended to apply to the Christian faith their views about biological and religious evolution. In our "advanced state" such matters as Christ's resurrection are not believable.

Existentialist Rudolph Bultmann is similar to the modernists in making outright denials of the Resurrection. He viewed it as an unnecessary encrustation on the Christian faith. He bluntly says, "A historical fact which involves a resurrection from the dead is utterly inconceivable."[8] The "Easter faith" of the disciples, for Bultmann, was an attempt to overcome the scandal of the Cross.

---

6. John Toland, *Christianity Not Mysterious* (1696; New York: Garland Publishing, 1978 reprint), 151.

7. Friedrich Schleiermacher, *The Christian Faith*, trans. H. R. Mackintosh and J. S. Stewart (Philadelphia: Fortress Press, 1928), 418.

8. Bultmann, *Kerygma and Myth*, 39.

Therefore Bultmann concludes that the Resurrection "has been obscured in the tradition by legend and is not of basic importance."[9]

It Happened Spiritually Only. The resurrection of Jesus happened in a spiritual sense, according to some scholars, but there was no historical, physical resurrection. With the special exception of Karl Barth, this is the general direction taken by neoorthodox theology. Emil Brunner, as one of them, affirms the Resurrection and its significance in the New Testament but argues that it did not take place historically. He says that Luke believed it was a physical resurrection, since he depicts the resurrected Christ as eating fish, but that Paul (and other New Testament writers) believed in only a spiritual resurrection. In support of his views, he says that Christ appeared only to believers, according to the New Testament accounts, and therefore He rose only spiritually, to faith. For Brunner, the resurrection is real, significant, and foundational to the Christian faith—but it did not happen on that plane of ordinary history.[10]

The Physical Resurrection View. This is the classical understanding that Christ was raised bodily and that it took place on the plane of actual history. This is the view held by Christians in general through the centuries.

Preeminently among modern theologians, Karl Barth taught this view. Early in his publishing career, Barth denied Christ's physical resurrection, but by the mid-1930s he was affirming the doctrine vigorously. Barth wrote a book on 1 Corinthians 15, teaching the physical, historical resurrection of Jesus Christ in a sustained way.[11]

The apostles witnessed to the Resurrection as a fact, not a theory. Peter, in the first Christian sermon ever preached, said, "God has raised this Jesus to life, and we are all witnesses of the fact" (Acts 2:32). "Fact" does not appear in the Greek and in certain English translations, but "fact" is implied. People did not wit-

---

9. Rudolf Bultmann, *Theology of the New Testament* (New York: Charles Scribner's Sons, 1951), 1:45.

10. All this can be found in various books by Emil Brunner, especially including *The Mediator.*

11. See Karl Barth, *The Resurrection of the Dead*, trans. H. J. Stenning (New York: Fleming H. Revell Co., 1933).

ness to an idea or a theory but to what they had seen or heard (cf. 1 John 1:1-3). To spiritualize the Resurrection would have been quite foreign to them. That view is an ethereal, Platonic deprecating of facticity matters.

Supportive also of the bodily Resurrection are various factors connected with the postresurrection appearances of Christ according to Luke's Gospel, especially the fact that Christ ate food. In Luke 24 we read that "the women" found "the stone rolled away from the tomb" (v. 2). A spiritual resurrection would not require an opened exit. Also, "when they entered, they did not find the body of the Lord Jesus" (v. 3). Had it been a spiritual resurrection, the body would have still been there. And, of course, had the enemies of Christ and His early followers found the body at all, they would have used it to disprove the Resurrection. For no one in those days was thinking about a spiritual resurrection to the eyes of faith. The claim that He was raised was a claim that He had been raised bodily, and the opposition knew that very well.

"Two men in clothes that gleamed" (v. 4) told the women, "He is not here; he has risen!" (v. 6). When the two Marys and Joanna (v. 10) told "the Eleven" (v. 9) and others what had happened, Peter "ran to the tomb" (v. 12) and found that it had been a literal resurrection, seeing "the strips of linen lying by themselves" (v. 12).

Paul describes a literal, physical resurrection in Acts 13: "And when they had carried out all that the scriptures said about him, they took him down the gibbet and laid him in a tomb. But God raised him from the dead; and there was a period of many days during which he appeared to those who had come up with him from Galilee to Jerusalem" (vv. 29-31, NEB). The Resurrection was physical. They had "carried out" literal things, including the removal of His body from the Cross and the placing of that body in the tomb. So when "God raised him from the dead," that would have been literal also. When He "appeared" to them, they saw Him with their physical eyes and not, as Brunner says, simply with eyes of faith.

The factuality of Christ's resurrection is also seen in Luke's account of Christ's appearances to the Eleven and those with them (24:36 ff.). To assure this frightened assemblage of His bodily presence, Jesus said, "Touch me and see; a ghost does not have flesh and bones, as you see I have" (v. 39). When they still could not believe, He asked for food; and Luke says, "They gave him a piece of broiled fish, and he took it and ate it in their presence" (vv. 42-43). Brunner found this inconsistent with his notion of a spiritual resurrection and admitted that Luke believed in the bodily resurrection of Christ.

In Luke we also read that "the eleven" apostles and others said, "The Lord is risen indeed" (Luke 24:33-34, KJV). Barth said that the word "indeed" suggests a bodily resurrection. The Greek word is *ontōs*, an adverb meaning "really, certainly, in truth."[12] The NIV renders *ontōs* with "It is true!" The NASB more expressly translates *ontōs* as suggesting a bodily resurrection: "The Lord has really risen." *Ontōs* suggests that the Resurrection did not happen in a spiritual way, but in a real, bodily sense.

To understand that Christ was raised bodily and to understand that the Resurrection was historical are almost the same thing, looked at from different angles. Those who believe in the bodily Resurrection also believe it was a historical event; and those who believe it was a historical event also believe it was a literal, bodily resurrection.

To say it was historical is to say it actually did take place in a certain year of the reign of a given Roman emperor. To say it was historical is to emphasize there were many witnesses to it who saw the empty tomb, who proclaimed it to others, who wrote Gospels rife with the mention of it.

To say the Resurrection was not historical but that it still happened is to spiritualize it, to say something metaphysical. That position deprecates physicality in favor of a noumenal reality. It is a Platonic view in which the ideational and ethereal are real, while physicality and factuality are only shadows of reality.

In Scripture, physicality is not deprecated. Scripture teaches that the one God created the whole universe and that it is good. It teaches that history is real, that God is Lord over history. It teaches that time is real and that God, who is Lord of history, is taking the world and us, in real time, to a "somewhen"—for example, Christ's second coming; and to a somewhere, heaven. Scripture teaches that miracles actually occur in the natural sphere, that the Deity actually became enfleshed as the Godman Jesus Christ at a

---

12. In Arndt and Gingrich, *"Ontōs,"* in *A Greek-English Lexicon.*

specific time in an emperor's reign. It teaches that Christ was physically slain and that He was literally raised from the dead at a given time and place.

The Resurrection, which happened in history and in a literal, bodily way, has important theological meaning for Christology, for redemption, and for eschatology. These matters will now be discussed.

Its Meaning for Christology

Christ's resurrection is significant for Christology—the doctrine of Christ's person.

It Fulfills Old Testament Prophecies. Peter, Stephen, Paul, and others, in their sermons recorded in Acts, often speak of the Old Testament background of the Christian faith, including its prophecies of Christ and their special fulfillment in Jesus of Nazareth, whom God raised from the dead. We read, for example, "We tell you the good news: What God promised our fathers he has fulfilled for us, their children, by raising up Jesus" (Acts 13:32-33). As Ethelbert Stauffer says, "God has fulfilled His Old Testament promises in Jesus Christ, and brought His Messiah through the darkness of night to the light of day."[13] The "darkness of night" here is the suffering including death; and the "light of day" is the Resurrection.

At Pentecost, Peter cited Ps. 16:8-11 as a reference to Christ's resurrection. To his listeners, who respected Scripture, he identified David as a prophet of that event: "Seeing what was ahead, he [David] spoke of the resurrection of the Christ, that he was not abandoned to the grave, nor did his body see decay" (Acts 2:31). Then Peter adds, "God has raised this Jesus to life, and we are all witnesses of the fact" (v. 32).

The Old Testament does not refer to the Messiah's resurrection explicitly, but apostles interpreted certain Old Testament passages as prophecies of it. Isaiah 53 vaguely but surely prophesies the Resurrection, where we read that "he will . . . prolong his days" (v. 10). In the context Isaiah speaks about Christ's sufferings and death. He says that this Suffering Servant was "crushed for our

13. Ethelbert Stauffer, *New Testament Theology* (New York: Macmillan Publishing Co., 1955), 135-36.

iniquities" (v. 5), and that "by his wounds we are healed" (v. 5). He says that "the Lord has laid on him the iniquity of us all" (v. 6) and that "he was cut off from the land of the living" (v. 8) and "was assigned a grave with the wicked" (v. 9). Nevertheless, "though the Lord makes his life a guilt offering, he will see his offspring and prolong his days" (v. 10). In his encounter with the Ethiopian eunuch who was reading this Isaiah 53 passage, Philip applied it to Christ: "Then Philip began with that very passage of Scripture and told him the good news about Jesus" (Acts 8:35).

Liberal scholars often interpret Isaiah simply as referring to Israel as God's suffering servant.[14] Not holding a high view of inspiration, they disregard the fact that Acts 8 states that Isaiah 53 refers to Christ. Evangelicals in general view Isaiah 53 as referring to Christ, and many of them would say that it refers exclusively to Christ.

So the Resurrection fulfills what are at least hazy predictions in the Old Testament.

It Supports Christ's Deity. The Resurrection is exceedingly important in relation to Christ's deity. Not that it *makes* Him divine! He has been divine eternally, God's only Son eternally, the Second Person of the Trinity eternally. But without the Resurrection we would not have believed in Christ's deity. By raising Him from the dead, God declared openly what had obtained eternally: that this was God's own Son. Thus we read that Jesus "was declared with power to be the Son of God by his resurrection from the dead" (Rom. 1:4).

It Supports Christ's Lordship. The Resurrection supports, substantiates, and confirms Christ's Lordship. The earliest Christian creed, many scholars believe, was "Jesus is Lord." This might be suggested when Paul says to "brothers" (believers) that "the word

---

14. John L. McKenzie, for example, wrote: "The first [theory] is the venerable belief in the Christian church that the Servant poems, in particular the fourth, are predictions of Jesus Christ. In this form the opinion is defended by no one today except in a few fundamentalist circles. This type of predictive prophecy does not appear in the Old Testament. It is another question whether the person and mission of Jesus Christ are interpreted in the New Testament in terms of the Servant poems: that is whether Jesus or his disciples or both identified him with the Servant of Yahweh. This problem lies outside the scope of this volume; but it is my personal opinion that Jesus was identified with the Servant in the primitive church, and that this identification goes back to Jesus himself. But this does not imply that the poems are a prediction of Jesus Christ in the literal sense of the term." John L. McKenzie, *Second Isaiah,* in *The Anchor Bible* (Garden City, N.Y.: Doubleday and Co., 1968), xlix.

is near you," "in your mouth and in your heart," the "word of faith we are proclaiming." That word, boiled down, is this: "If you confess with your mouth, 'Jesus is Lord,' and believe in your heart that God raised him from the dead, you will be saved" (Rom. 10:1-9). This seems to refer to a basic creed Christians publicly confessed to believe. This primitive type of "creedal" distillation is connected with Christ's resurrection and the belief in that event. The Resurrection is connected with Christ's Lordship here because, if Christ had not been raised from the dead, Satan would have triumphed over Him, and He would not have been sovereign.

The Resurrection as confirmation of Christ's Lordship is also indicated in Luke's accounts of Paul's conversion. In those accounts, it is after the risen and ascended Jesus appears to Paul that he is turned about face from being the chief persecutor of Christians to becoming the chief promoter of the Christian faith. Paul became a believer because the risen and ascended Jesus appeared to him on the Damascus road and spoke to him clearly: "Saul! Saul! Why do you persecute me?" (Acts 22:7). Dumbfounded, Paul blurts out, "Who are you, Lord?" (v. 8). "I am Jesus of Nazareth, whom you are persecuting," came the answer (v. 8). Paul responds, "What shall I do, Lord?" (v. 10). Here, *kurie* is used in the sense of one who is sovereign, for Paul here commits himself to the resurrected Christ's Rulership.

The Resurrection as confirmation of Christ's Lordship is directly implied in the exclamation of Thomas, "My Lord and my God!" (John 20:28). Thomas had been slow to believe in Christ's resurrection. He had said, "Unless I see the nail marks in his hands and put my finger where the nails were, and put my hand into his side, I will not believe it" (v. 25). But "a week later" Jesus came and said to Thomas, "Put your finger here; see my hands. Reach out your hand and put it into my side. Stop doubting and believe" (vv. 26-27). Then "Thomas said to him, 'My Lord and my God!'" "My Lord" indicates that Thomas was submitting himself to the raised Christ's Rulership—Christ now being referred to as *Theos*, God.

Its Meaning for Redemption

Crucifixion without resurrection would not have accomplished redemption. If Christ had not been raised, He would have been a martyr, not a Savior.

Paul asserts this in 1 Cor. 15:17: "And if Christ has not been raised, your faith is futile; you are still in your sins." Paul also says that if Christ has not been raised, "Then those also who have fallen asleep in Christ are lost" (v. 18)—no resurrection, no salvation.

Its Meaning for Eschatology

Eschatology is part and parcel of redemption. Redemption includes being raised from the dead to dwell with Christ eternally.

Christ, who is our Best Friend, has power over our worst and last enemy—death. Paul says, "For as in Adam all die [he means physically], so in Christ all will be made alive" (1 Cor. 15:22). He continues, "We will not all sleep, but we will all be changed" (v. 51).

Sin and death cannot defeat the believer. "But thanks be to God! He gives us the victory through our Lord Jesus Christ" (v. 57), whose resurrection is the pledge and power of ours (vv. 20-22).

So Christ, who is the *eschaton,* the last one to appear, himself the epitome of prophet and priest and king, spoke the last word about death by being raised from the death.

In 1962 Jürgen Moltmann published his *Theology of Hope* in German. Moltmann felt that what Europeans needed most, after two world wars, was hope. He saw that hope is not a last doctrine tacked on, but the central doctrine around which all the doctrines should consistently revolve. So he offered hope theology, and he said that Jesus Christ's resurrection, a real event in history, is what gives us Christians this enveloping and buoyant hope.[15] Wolfhart Pannenberg has taught quite similarly, also founding a theology built around hope based on Jesus Christ's resurrection.[16] Moltmann and Pannenberg and others have viewed the Resurrection as having meaning for eschatology, but more as the "whole thing" that includes the last things, the aboveness that includes beyondness.

This theology of hope of Moltmann and Pannenberg is a savory development in recent theology. If Paul at Mars Hill preached to the wise Greeks "Jesus and the resurrection" (Acts

15. See Jürgen Moltmann, *The Theology of Hope,* trans. James Leitch (New York: Harper and Row, 1967).

16. Pannenberg, *Jesus—God and Man.*

17:18), and if the Resurrection made all the difference to the early disciples in general, so that they were basically people who believed in the Resurrection, surely it is more than one doctrine among many. The Resurrection is the basis for our ramified hope as Christians.

Its Practical Meanings

What does the Resurrection mean for our daily lives? Two things need to be mentioned here: (1) It gifts us with a daily Easter; and (2) it gifts us with the help that comes from all Christian preaching.

It Gifts Us with a Daily Easter. It is altogether proper that we celebrate Easter once a year. This allows us to make an annual festival of it, when the minds of believers everywhere are begotten again with new and live hopes. It is a day when, in church services, believers expect to hear about it in sermon and song. Life looks up and death looks sullen on Easter morn, when Christianity's gladdest notes of all are expressed in the best prose and poetry the church can reach for and attain to.

> *Christ is risen! Hallelujah!*
> *Rise our victorious head.*
> *Sing His praises! Hallelujah!*
> *Christ is risen from the dead.*
> JOHN S. B. MONSELL, 1811-75

In His crucifixion Christ gave himself for us. Through His resurrection He gives himself to us. We believe this on Easter. We know this on Easter.

But every Sunday, when we worship on the first day of the week instead of on the seventh, we Christians celebrate the Resurrection. This is why the Christians of New Testament times began to worship on the first day of the week—often worshiping on the seventh day also because of their common heritage with Judaism, but later dropping the seventh-day worship.

Although we appropriately celebrate the Resurrection on Easter Day and each Sunday, Easter is actually an everyday celebration. Each time we pray to the Father in the name of the risen, ascended Christ, who intercedes with the Father, we are practicing our faith in the Resurrection. Actually, each day, in whatever way we practice and promote our Christian faith, we observe a daily Easter, since, as Paul says in 1 Cor. 15:17, we would not be

Christians at all, we would still be living in sin—except for the Resurrection.

It Gifts Us with the Help That Comes from Preaching. Some things have already been said about the way in which the Resurrection figured in the preaching of the apostles. Here, let it be noted that the Resurrection was and still is preaching's gladdest note. After all, Christian preaching is not Jewish preaching—and to say that is not anti-Semitic. The present writer has often told seminary students that if a Jewish rabbi could preach the sermon they are thinking about preaching, they should let the rabbi do it; and they should devise a sermon every time that, even if it is Old Testament-based, is baptized into the New Testament and "Christized." And when the sermon is baptized in this way, the Resurrection is part of it, if only by implication.

Early Christian preaching was like an oratorio—like Handel's *Messiah,* actually, with its "Hallelujah Chorus." As with oratorios, there were not many accoutrements. The Christ theme, nakedly, is what the preaching had to do with—Christ prophesied, incarnated, crucified, raised, interceding, returning.

Karl Barth suggests that in 1 Corinthians 15 Paul is not simply discussing the Resurrection as one more point, but as a teaching that draws together and crowns the whole Epistle and indeed the whole Christian message. Barth writes:

> The chapter devoted to the Resurrection . . . does not stand in so isolated a relation to the First Epistle to the Corinthians as at first glance might appear. It forms not only the close and crown of the whole Epistle, but also provides the clue to its meaning, from which place light is shed on the whole, and it becomes intelligible, not outwardly, but inwardly, as a unity.[17]

In 1 Corinthians 15, Paul says some significant things about the meaning of the Resurrection for Christian preaching. He refers to "the gospel I preached to you, which you received and on which you have taken your stand" (v. 1).[18] The core of the gospel was that "Christ died for our sins according to the Scriptures, that he was buried, that he was raised on the third day according to

---

17. Barth, *The Resurrection of the Dead,* 5.
18. The apostle's "Arminianism" creeps in here. He says, "By this gospel you are saved, if you hold firmly to the word I preached to you. Otherwise, you have believed in vain" (1 Cor. 15:2). Evidently it was possible for them to fall from saving grace.

the Scriptures, and that he appeared to Peter, and then to the Twelve" (vv. 3-5).

Referring to "the apostles" and to his own belated entrance into the gospel work, Paul says, "I worked harder than all of them" (v. 10), then adds, "Whether, then, it was I or they, this is what we preach, and this is what you believed" (v. 11). The others, and Paul, all preached the whole Christ message, especially the Resurrection.

When Christians meet together, therefore, and hear the gospel of Christ preached, the resurrection of Christ should be proclaimed far more than on Easter Sunday; it should always be implied at least in Christian preaching.

Before this treatment of the Resurrection is concluded, the important matter of its being spoken of in the passive voice in the New Testament needs to be considered.

The Passive Voice of the Resurrection

The Bible declares that Jesus was raised, not that He rose. God the Father raised Him from the dead. Thus the active voice is seldom used in regard to the Resurrection, especially after it occurred and is being described. The active voice is used several times prior to the event, but only rarely afterward.

Before the Resurrection occurred, Jesus used the active voice, saying, "Destroy this temple [His body], and in three days I will raise it up" (*egerō*, future of *egeirō*) (John 2:19, KJV). It is entirely possible that He said this because He knew the Father would give Him the power to. Once, after being accused of "making himself equal with God," He said, "I tell you the truth, the Son can do nothing by himself" (John 5:18-19). Other instances of the active voice prior to the Resurrection event include these: Mark 10:34—"Three days later he will rise"; Luke 18:32-33—"They will mock him, insult him, spit on him, flog him and kill him. On the third day he will rise again"; and Luke 24:46—"This is what is written: The Christ will suffer and rise from the dead on the third day."

One of the few instances of the use of the active voice in post-Resurrection interpretations of the event occurs in 1 Thess. 4:14: "We believe that Jesus died and rose again and so we believe that God will bring with Jesus those who have fallen asleep in him." The word for "rose again" here is *anestē*, aorist active indicative of *anistēmi*, which is one of the New Testament words used for speaking of the Resurrection, along with *egeirō*. It is indeed an active voice instance, and as such is rare in Acts and the Epistles.

In another instance, 2 Cor. 5:15, some versions translate with the active voice, but the Greek New Testament word involved is in the passive voice. The KJV reads "rose again," as though it was active voice, as does the NASB. But the NIV more accurately renders, "And he died for all, that those who live should no longer live for themselves but for him who died for them and was raised [also RSV] again."

With those exceptions noted, let us consider the use of the passive voice in the New Testament with reference to the Resurrection. Even prior to the event, the passive voice is used by Jesus. In Matt. 17:22-23 we read, "The Son of Man is going to be betrayed . . . They will kill him, and on the third day he will be raised to life." The Greek *egerthēsetai* is in the passive voice.

In post-Resurrection references to the event, in Matt. 28:5-7, an "angel" twice uses the passive voice to describe what had happened. The angel said "to the women," "He is not here; he has risen, just as he said" (v. 6). Then the angel says to the women, "Then go quickly and tell his disciples: 'He has risen from the dead'" (v. 7). The Greek word for "has risen," in both instances, is *egerthē,* which is passive voice.

In Acts and the Epistles, usage of the passive voice is customary. When the active voice is used, it is clearly stated that God the Father raised Him. These passive instances are numerous and preponderant.

Reading the New Testament, we are impressed with the frequency of passive statements that God the Father raised Christ from the dead.

Significance of the Passive-Voice Resurrection. This New Testament teaching that God the Father raised Jesus from the dead is of considerable importance. For one thing, it indicates that God the Father, the eternally unoriginated Member of the Trinity, not eternally begotten as is the Son, nor eternally proceeding as is the Spirit, is the One who is "all and in all," purposing our redemption, structuring its means, and then finally granting it.

This passive-voice Resurrection also means that there is a significant commonality between the Virgin Conception as the way the Christ entered the world, and the Resurrection as the way in which

He left it. In both cases Christ, the Second Person of the Trinity, was acted upon by another Person of the Trinity—in the case of the Virgin Conception, by the Holy Spirit; in the case of the Resurrection, by God the Father. The three Persons of the Trinity work together in harmony to provide and grant our redemption.

The passive-voice Resurrection also means that if Christ himself was this dependent on the Father, surely we merely human creatures are utterly dependent on God the Father.

14

The First Work of Grace

The meaning of "redemption" is "to buy back." Through Christ, God buys us back from our bondage to sin and Satan. He accomplishes this in two major crisis steps:[1] the first work of grace and the second work of grace. These are then maintained and promoted through the various means of grace: prayer and meditation, Scripture reading, the Lord's Supper, worship, Christian fellowship, and Christian service, along with others.

In this chapter, the first work of grace will be discussed. Then, three chapters will be devoted to the second work of grace[2]—the distinctive doctrine of the Wesleyan-holiness tradition. Following that, a chapter will treat the means of grace.

The "first work of grace" nomenclature is perhaps the most theologically appropriate way of referring to what happens in the first crisis in Christian redemptive experience. Justification, regeneration 'or the new birth, initial sanctification, reconciliation, and adoption—each refer to only one aspect of this miracle of redemptive grace. "The first work of grace" includes them all.

The experiences named above occur at the same time but are logically successive. We will discuss them in order, after considering prevenient grace and repentance as preparatory to them. Faith, of course, is the catalyst for them.

---

1. Glorification is a sort of third special moment in redemptive grace, received at Christ's second coming, first by the righteous departed and then by the righteous who are among the living. It is the time when our bodies will be redeemed (Rom. 8:23).

2. If a person dies while in the experience of the first work of grace, eternal bliss will be enjoyed. The second work of grace, entire sanctification, is important in many ways, as will be seen. Significantly, it helps us maintain the state of justification. Yet it does not change our eternal destiny.

Prevenient Grace as Prerequisite

Prevenient grace, in which God initiates in people, as John Wesley said, the first faint desire for Him, is a prerequisite for repentance and the first work of grace. Without it there would be no repentance nor any justifying faith—no first work of grace.

Calvinists and Arminians both teach that God must initiate the process whereby a person repents and believes, although rigid Calvinists believe that God does not call the nonelect with sufficient seriousness for them to be saved.

Prevenient Grace in Arminianism. James Arminius taught that even before conversion we possess the "power of willing"—that is, a capacity for acting either righteously or sinfully. But he believed that our moral nature is fallen and that we cannot of ourselves exercise this capacity in the direction of righteous acts. Of fallen humans before conversion, Arminius writes:

> In this state, the free will of man towards the true good is not only wounded, maimed, infirm, bent, and weakened; but it is also imprisoned, destroyed, and lost. And its powers are not only debilitated and useless unless they be assisted by grace, but it has no powers whatever except such as are excited by divine grace. For Christ has said, "Without me ye can do nothing," . . . The mind, in this state, is dark, destitute of the saving knowledge of God, and, according to the Apostle, incapable of those things which belong to the Spirit of God. . . . Exactly correspondent to this darkness of the mind, and perverseness of the heart, is the utter weakness of all the powers to perform that which is truly good, and to omit the perpetration of that which is evil.[3]

In support, he cites Matt. 7:18; 12:34; John 6:44; and 8:36. After quoting John 8:36, that only those are free whom the Son has made free, he says: "It follows, that our will is not free from the first fall; that is, it is not free to good, unless it be made free by the Son through his Spirit."[4]

Although Arminius was divinity professor in "Reformed" Leiden University, he did not agree with John Calvin, who had

3. *The Writings of Arminius,* ed. and trans. James Nichols and W. R. Bagnall (Grand Rapids: Baker Book House, 1956), 1:526-27.
4. Ibid., 528.

taught two generations earlier that God's grace is absolutely sovereign—irresistibly received by the elect. Arminius believed that, enabled by prevenient grace, an unregenerate person can believe on Christ for pardon. Indeed, a person must believe, else he or she will be eternally lost. But the believing is always due to God's assistance, initiated at the outset by the Spirit's drawing. Arminius denied that in advocating free will, he was teaching that we do something to merit our salvation. The free will to accept Christ could not be exercised apart from God's help, so there is no merit whatever in our acceptance of the first work of grace.

Like Arminius, John Wesley taught that we cast the vote that decides whether we will be saved or damned. However, we do not and cannot, of ourselves, cast an assenting vote, for the fallen will is by nature free only to evil.[5]

To deny original sin, Wesley believed, is to be a heathen. His view of the racial fall is a bit extreme for many of us, for he believed the image of God was lost entirely. He said that through Adam's sin we "lost the moral image of God."[6] He went so far as to say that we have the image of Satan. If that might have been too extreme, the image is at least utterly defaced. This is why Wesley was correct in saying that salvation begins with prevenient grace, "including the first wish to please God, the first dawn of light concerning his will, and the first slight transient conviction of having sinned against him."[7] And he was correct in saying that prevenient grace is "not natural, but a supernatural gift of God, above all his [man's] natural endowments."[8]

Due to our fallenness and God's prevenient grace, Wesley could say: "Of yourselves cometh neither your faith nor your salvation. 'It is the gift of God;' the free, undeserved gift; the faith through which ye are saved, as well as the salvation, which he of his own good pleasure, his mere favour, annexes thereto. That ye believe, is one instance of his grace; that, believing, ye are saved, another. 'Not of works, lest any man should boast.'"[9] One might quibble with him over whether believing faith itself ought to be

5. See Burtner and Chiles, *Compend of Wesley's Theology*, 132-33.
6. Wesley, *Works* 6:223.
7. Ibid., 509.
8. Burtner and Chiles, *Compend of Wesley's Theology*, 151.
9. Wesley, *Works* 5:13.

called a gift. But if he means only that without God's help we cannot believe, he is surely correct.

The gift of faith, for Wesley, does not mean a gift bestowed upon people whether or not they will have it so. In many passages in his writings he teaches that everyone confronted with a moral choice "has in himself the casting voice."[10] This is the way evangelist Bud Robinson saw it, who used to say, "God voted for me, the devil voted against me, and I cast the deciding ballot for myself."

Prevenient Grace in Scripture. According to Scripture, we as fallen persons are enslaved sinners, of our "father, the devil" (John 8:44), enslaved to sin (Rom. 6:16-17), incapable of performing as our intellect indicates (7:15), lost and without hope (Eph. 2:12), and to be "pitied" (1 Cor. 15:19)—unless outside, supernatural help is given.

The Scriptures also convey the good news that we have the kind of help we need.

To the Jew who despises the Gentiles for gross iniquities, Paul offers the reminder that, apart from God's grace, the Jew is just as sinful. He says, "You who pass judgment do the same things" (Rom. 2:1). Then Paul tells this Jew that "God's kindness leads you toward repentance" (v. 4).

To Gentile Cornelius and his household, we read that "God has granted . . . repentance unto life" (Acts 11:18). The word here for "granted" is the usual Greek verb for "to give, bestow, present, . . . grant." A related word is used in 2 Tim. 2:25, where Paul urges Timothy to correct the opposers of the gospel "in the hope that God will grant them repentance leading them to a knowledge of the truth." Another related teaching, in connection with repentance, is found in Acts 5:31, where Peter and the apostles declare: "God exalted him to his own right hand as Prince and Savior that he might give repentance." Repentance is what God gives to people, what He grants to their cooperating hearts.

That God has a part in one's repentance, although not an overriding part, is shown in Hebrews, where the writer says that when people who have known Christ continue to reject Him, it is impossible "if they fall away, to be brought back to repentance"

---

10. Ibid. 6:281.

(6:6). The implication is that God works toward their repentance, but that, if they will not respond, it is not possible for God to force them to do so.

A number of Scripture passages containing the word "turn" show that God turns us to himself. Lest it be thought that God accomplishes this without our cooperation, however, other passages will be given to show that we ourselves are to turn to God.

Ezekiel exhorts, "Repent and live!" (18:32). Again, he says, "But if a wicked man turns away from all the sins he has committed . . . he will surely live; he will not die" (v. 21).

And Hosea, who knew so much about God's love, knew also that love does not simply override all human rebellion. He said, "Return to your God" (12:6).

Joel, too, speaking for God, says, "'Return to me with all your heart, with fasting and weeping and mourning.' Rend your heart and not your garments. Return to the Lord your God, for he is gracious and compassionate" (2:12-13).

Jesus himself called for human response, warning, "Unless you change and become like little children, you will never enter the kingdom of heaven" (Matt. 18:3).

But there are also passages that show that God enables us, else we do no turning to Him. Psalm 80 is rich in this regard. In verse 3 we read: "Restore us, O God; make your face shine upon us, that we may be saved."

The phrase "restore us" also appears in verses 7 and 19. In Ps. 85:4 is a similar prayer: "Restore us again, O God our Savior."

Most vivid on God's inducement of our repentant turning is Jer. 31:18-19, where Ephraim prays, "Restore me, and I will return, because you are the Lord my God. After I strayed, I repented."

Sinful people do not repent just because evidence is stacked up to show them that they ought to. Dives wanted someone to return to earth and preach to his five brothers, and Abraham said, "If they do not listen to Moses and the Prophets, they will not be convinced even if someone rises from the dead" (Luke 16:27-31). Paul failed to convince King Agrippa sufficiently (Acts 26:28). And even Jesus, the Son of God, failed to persuade the monied young ruler (Luke 18:18-25). Jesus had this to say to the Jews: "If you believed Moses, you would believe me, for he wrote about me. But since you do not believe what he wrote, how are you going to believe what I say?" (John 5:46-47). The drawing of the Holy Spirit—the arresting, tugging, wooing, convincing, enabling—is necessary before people repent and turn utterly to God.

If we love Him, it is because He first loved us (1 John 4:19). If we draw near to Him, it is because He has been at work with us (John 6:44). His "Spirit will not contend with man forever" (Gen. 6:3), but He contends sufficiently—if the sinner will only respond.

In theologies, creeds, and Scripture, the truth is of deep impress that sinners need to repent and that God as Redeemer is after them to that very end.

Repentance as Preparatory

Repentance, a change of mind about sin that includes a willingness to obey and serve God, prepares a person for the first work of grace. It is like the plowing and disking of a field, into which, when the field is thus readied, the seed can then be planted.

Steps in Repentance. Repentance may be said to have at least three steps in it: conviction of sin, regret or remorse, and an actual change of mind in which we turn from sin to God.

1. The Holy Spirit makes us uneasy in our disobedience to God. *Convicted,* we see the "enormity of sin," its "colossal wickedness," to use A. M. Hills's phraseology. We begin to take God's attitude toward sin. We see sin for what it is as we are awakened by conviction.

Of the person under conviction of sin, John Wesley says, "His joy now vanishes as a cloud; pleasures, once loved, delight no more. They pall upon the taste: he loathes the nauseous sweet; he is weary to bear them."[11] With Charles Wesley such a person might say:

> Guilty I stand before Thy face;
> On me I feel Thy wrath abide.
> 'Tis just the sentence should take place;
> 'Tis just—but O Thy Son hath died!

Accompanying the conviction of sin is often a "foretaste" thought, if only faint, that relief is possible.

Martin Luther says that "the proud have no taste for grace, because their sins do not yet taste bitter to them."[12] When a per-

---

11. Burtner and Chiles, *Compend of Wesley's Theology,* 152.
12. Jaroslav Pelikan, ed., *Luther's Works* (St. Louis: Concordia Publishing House, 1958), 14:166.

son's sins taste bitter, through conviction, the Spirit has been at His work of discomforting the comfortable person, arresting the rebel.

2. A second step in repentance is *regret, or even remorse.* Job expressed a deep regret for what he had been and was. On glimpsing God in a firsthand way, he abhorred himself. He said, "My ears had heard of you but now my eyes have seen you. Therefore I despise myself and repent in dust and ashes" (42:5-6).

Utter regret for sin was expressed by Ezra, the priest-scribe. Deeply disturbed by the sins of Israel, he fell to his knees before the Lord and prayed, "O my God, I am too ashamed and disgraced to lift up my face to you, my God, because our sins are higher than our heads and our guilt has reached to the heavens" (Ezra 9:5-6). Ezra's deep regret was occasioned by the sins of others and not his own, but it is the kind of regret that obtains when a rebel turns from sin to serve God.

However, while regret or remorse is a step in repentance, it is not identical with it. In this connection, Ralph Earle writes, "Often the term 'repentance' is used today for an emotional display of sorrow. But real repentance goes deeper than that, involving a reversal of one's inner attitude toward life, an abhorrence of his sins and a deliberate turning away from them."[13]

That repentance is more than mere regret or godly sorrow or remorse for sin is shown by what Paul says: "Now I am happy, not because you were made sorry, but because your sorrow led you to repentance" (2 Cor. 7:9). Evidently, one can be sorry for sinning without repenting. Paul goes on to say, "Godly sorrow brings repentance . . . but worldly sorrow brings death" (v. 10). "Worldly sorrow" is regret at sin's consequence, because society will require payment or because one's health is impaired. "Godly sorrow" is regret for sin because God has been disobeyed and is displeased. This kind of sorrow for sin leads to repentance, in which one purposes to forsake sin and serve God.

The regret and remorse of Judas were of the "worldly" sort. When he saw that Christ was condemned, he "was seized with remorse and returned the thirty silver coins to the chief priests and the elders. 'I have sinned,' he said, 'for I have betrayed innocent blood'" (Matt. 27:3-4). He experienced "remorse," but he did not

13. Ralph Earle, "Mark," in *Evangelical Commentary* (Grand Rapids: Zondervan Publishing House, 1957), 29.

turn to God and seek forgiveness. Instead, he sought escape from his anguish through suicide. His "worldly sorrow" brought only death.

Regret and remorse of the "godly" sort lead to repentance; hence they may be called steps or elements in the overall process of repentance. O. A. Curtis might not be too extreme in saying that "contrition of heart," when "the Holy Spirit" is able to "break the man's hard heart," is "the very marrow of Christian repentance."[14]

3. A third important step in repentance is *turning from sin with resolve to obey and serve God*. This is repentance in its true essence, and it will need to be discussed by treating the two Old Testament and the three New Testament words for repentance.

Bible Words for Repentance. In the Old Testament, there are two words for "repentance." One of them, *nahum*, expresses its emotional aspect. This Hebrew word basically implies difficulty in breathing; hence it originally meant "to pant," "to sigh," "to groan." It naturally came to mean "to lament," "to grieve," or "to repent." In the KJV it is translated "repent" about 40 times and usually refers to what God does. God often repents, being regretful over our sin.

The other Old Testament word for "repentance" is *shubh*, which is generally used to express the idea of true repentance. The prophets called for it frequently. It has to do with "a radical change in one's attitude toward sin and God."[15] Often it is used of people turning from sin to righteousness (Deut. 4:30; Neh. 1:9; Ps. 7:12; and Jer. 3:14). Rather often, it refers to God's disappointment with humans (Exod. 32:12 and Josh. 7:26). Sometimes it is translated by "return," as in 1 Sam. 7:3; Ps. 90:13; and Isa. 21:12; 55:7 (all KJV), whether it has reference to God or to ourselves.

In the New Testament there are three words for repentance. One of them, *metamelomai*, literally means "to care," "to regret." Like *nahum*, it expresses the emotional element in repentance. This care, concern, or regret might issue in genuine repentance or merely in remorse (Matt. 21:29, 32; 27:3).

14. Curtis, *The Christian Faith*, 354.
15. Byron H. DeMent, "Repentance," in *International Standard Bible Encyclopaedia* (ISBE), ed. James Orr (Grand Rapids: William B. Eerdmans Publishing Co., 1955), 4:2558.

A second word, *epistrephō,* means "to turn over," or "upon," or "unto." In Acts 9:35 and 1 Thess. 1:9 it has to do with the spiritual transition from sin to God.

The Latin Vulgate version, used so widely by Roman Catholics, renders this word "exercise penitence." Commenting on this rendering, Byron DeMent says, "But 'penitence' . . . signifies pain, grief, distress, rather than a change of thought and purpose. Thus Latin Christianity has been corrupted by the pernicious error of presenting grief over sin rather than abandonment of sin as the primary idea of New Testament repentance."[16]

A third New Testament word is *metanoeō.* It is used in such places as Matt. 3:2; Mark 1:15; and Acts 2:38. Equivalent to the Hebrew *shubh,* it has to do with genuine repentance, a change of mind about sin. It is from two Greek words, *meta* and *nous* ("mind"). Sometimes when *meta* is a prefix to a word, it means "after." But often, *meta* as a prefix means "change." When a doctor checks us over, our *metabolism* is inspected. In this word, *meta* means "change"—"the chemical changes in living cells by which energy is provided for the vital processes and activities and new material is assimilated to repair the waste," to quote Webster's dictionary.[17] When prefixed to *noia,* from *nous,* which means "mind," the whole means, literally, "change of mind."

It is for this reason that Scripture often speaks of God repenting. He changes His mind, in a sense. His promises (e.g., 2 Chron. 7:14) and His punishments (as in Jonah 3:9 and 4:2) are conditioned on our response to His will. If people submit, God "repents"—changes His mind or intention toward them.[18]

Usually when people repent, they undergo an utter change of life. But at times, when used of ourselves, the simple root meaning of a change of mind, without any soul agony, is intended. One instance is in Matt. 21:29, where a young man, asked to work in a vineyard, at first said he would not, "but afterward he repented, and went" (KJV)—the NIV translates "changed his mind and went."

---

16. Ibid.
17. *Webster's New International Dictionary,* 3rd ed., s.v. "metabolism."
18. The immutability of God, biblically understood, means not that God turns no corners; but that although He turns many of them, He is unchanging in His love for sinners, in His desiring "everyone to come to repentance" (2 Pet. 3:9).

Basically, then, the word "repent," whether used of God of or people, has to do with a change of mind. However, when used of people, it usually means such a change of mind that sin is forsaken and God's ways are followed.

Toward a Definition. If the blueprint for a bridge is changed, the bridge being built will be changed. Repentance is changing the blueprint by which one is ordering his or her life. With the new blueprint, the life itself will be utterly different. Ambitions, ideals, aspirations, desires, sets of values—all get transfigured.

In all this changing, our free will is crucially involved. If it is not, then repentance means simply the falling into place of a pre-determined, absolutely sovereign plan of God. After discussing several biblical terms for "repent" and "repentance," DeMent says, "The words employed in the Hebrew and Greek place chief emphasis on the will, the change of mind, or of purpose, because a complete and sincere turning to God involves both the apprehension of the nature of sin and the consciousness of personal guilt (Jer. 25:5; Mk. 1:15; Acts 2:38; 2 Cor. 7:9-10). The demand for repentance implies free will and individual responsibility."[19]

With these three elements of repentance before us, repentance might be defined as a change of mind in which a person turns from sin to God, purposing to obey and to serve Him.

Its Relation to Regeneration. Scripture is ambiguous about the relationship of repentance to regeneration. For instance, John's Gospel speaks of the new birth, but "repent" and "repentance" do not appear therein. The Synoptic Gospels, in contrast, speak of repentance at least 25 times but never refer to being born again.

Some theologians identify repentance and regeneration. James Denney (1856-1917) writes, "It is called repentance when we think of it from the side of the sinner, and of his responsibility and initiative in it; it is called regeneration when we think of it from the side of God, as something in which a gracious initiative belongs to Him."[20] One finds himself agreeing with Denney's concept of repentance when he writes, "It means that we enter into the mind of Christ in relation to sin, that we see it in its truth as He saw it, that we sorrow over it as He sorrowed, that we repel it

19. DeMent, "Repentance," ISBE 4:2559.
20. James Denney, *The Christian Doctrine of Reconciliation* (New York: Hodder and Stoughton, 1917), 313.

henceforth as He repelled it; all of which is part at least of what is meant by repentance."[21] But Denney adds that it is not preliminary to salvation. He asserts, "We do not first repent of our sins and then come to Jesus."[22]

John Calvin himself identified repentance with regeneration. In his main theological work, which he carefully revised nine times, Calvin says, "Therefore, in a word, I interpret repentance as regeneration."[23]

However, even though a comparison of John's Gospel with the Synoptics might suggest that repentance and regeneration are identical, a study of the entire biblical data suggests otherwise: that repentance is preparatory to regeneration. James Arminius taught that repentance is prior to believing faith. According to his view, the order for conversion is (1) the confidence that God is willing to receive the person if he repents, (2) repentance, and (3) faith in Christ, in which one penitently acknowledges his sins and trusts God for pardon and a new heart.

John Wesley was of the same persuasion. He said that we need to repent before we can believe the gospel.

H. Orton Wiley took the same view, saying, "Repentance leads immediately to saving faith, which is at once the condition and the instrument of justification."[24]

Some individual passages seem to indicate that repentance is all that is needed in order to right a person with God. In Matt. 3:11 John the Baptist says, "I baptize you with water for repentance." Here repentance might be understood as a culmination, not as preparatory to something else, such as regeneration. Another such passage is in Luke 13:3, 5, where Jesus exhorts, "Unless you repent, you too will all perish." Again, nothing is said about repentance being preparatory to something else.

Second Pet. 3:9 declares that God does not wish "anyone to perish, but everyone to come to repentance." Here again repentance seems to be the saving experience itself, not a preparation for it. It seems in itself to be what will prevent perishing.

---

21. Ibid., 324-25.
22. Ibid., 16.
23. John Calvin, *Institutes of the Christian Religion*, ed. J. T. McNeill, trans. F. L. Battles (Philadelphia: Westminster Press, 1960), 3:iii, 9.
24. Wiley, *Christian Theology* 2:364.

Nevertheless, other Bible passages differentiate between repentance and regeneration, or forgiveness. One is Mark 1:4, where a distinction is made between "repentance" and "forgiveness of sins," the former leading to the latter: "John came, baptizing in the desert region and preaching a baptism of repentance for the forgiveness of sins." Luke 3:3 is a parallel passage also containing the distinction.

A clear distinction between repentance and forgiveness is contained in Luke 24:46-47: "This is what is written: The Christ will suffer and rise from the dead . . . and repentance and forgiveness of sins will be preached in his name to all nations." Repentance and forgiveness of sins, here, are to be preached. The *New English Bible* has "repentance bringing the forgiveness of sins," which also makes clear that forgiveness is subsequent to and dependent on repentance.

Elsewhere in the New Testament there is further teaching that repentance is prior to and distinct from forgiveness and regeneration. In Acts 5:31, "Peter and the other apostles" explain, "God exalted him to his own right hand as Prince and Savior that he might give repentance and forgiveness of sins to Israel." Here again, forgiveness is beyond repentance.

When Simon the sorcerer offered money in order to possess "the gift of God" whereby the Holy Spirit might fall on whomsoever he laid hands, Peter rebuked him and said, "Repent of this wickedness and pray to the Lord. Perhaps he will forgive you for having such a thought in your heart" (Acts 8:20, 22). Repentance would prepare the way for pardon.

Another such passage is 2 Cor. 7:10: "Godly sorrow brings repentance that leads to salvation." The process is: godly sorrow, repentance, salvation—each succeeding the other.

When Peter described his evangelism of Cornelius and his household, the listening Jews exclaimed, "So then, God has granted even the Gentiles repentance unto life" (Acts 11:18). The "life" followed the repentance. It was something more.

In summary, then, those biblical arguments for equating repentance and regeneration are properly to be respected. But when one takes into account the entire biblical data, it seems appropriate and more truly biblical to understand that repentance is preparatory for the first work of grace. The five concomitants of that first work of grace will now be discussed: justification, regeneration, initial sanctification, reconciliation, and adoption.

Justification

This is a legal term, used often in Scripture for what God does as a judge in forgiving us. When He forgives us, He acquits us. He absolves us of the guilt that our acts of sin have caused. He declares us to be guiltless. This is not a legal fiction; He declares us to be without guilt because He really has made us guiltless by extending to us a full pardon for our sins.

Calvinists have tended to interpret the meaning of verbals of *dikaiosunē* as "declare you righteous." Arminians, who believe profoundly not only in imputed righteousness but also in imparted righteousness, have tended to understand that these words mean "make you righteous."[25]

We Arminians understand that God as Judge, when He forgives us, really does make us righteous by imparting righteousness to us, and we feel that many passages of Scripture support this understanding. In Rom. 8:4 we read, "In order that the requirement of the Law might be fulfilled in us, who do not walk according to the flesh, but according to the Spirit" (NASB). This teaches that a righteousness is in a real way imparted to us, so that "the requirement of the Law might be fulfilled in us."

Calvinists in general teach that only Christ fulfills the law, and that we are Christ's, so that His righteousness is imputed to us, and we are reckoned as righteous when we are not actually so. They like to quote Rom. 3:10-12, where we read:

There is none righteous, not even one;
There is none who understands,
There is none who seeks for God;

---

25. The NIV New Testament simply uses "justify," as in the KJV, for example, in Galatians. Merrill C. Tenney headed a small NIV translating committee that had rendered verbals of *dikaiosunē* regularly as "declare you righteous." Sitting on a seven-member intermediary committee, the present writer argued for something stronger, suggesting that Arminian-Wesleyans believe the meaning to be "make you righteous." Even Fuller Theological Seminary's George Eldon Ladd had argued in his New Testament theology that God does not declare a fiction—so that "declare you righteous" more or less means "make you righteous." Edwin Palmer, chair of the committee, asked the present writer to study the matter and suggest translations on which we might agree, and "absolve" or "acquit" were suggested after special study. But the central translating committee would not accept either of them. Result: the NIV simply renders as "justify," and readers are required to decide on their own what the word means.

All have turned aside, together they have become useless;
There is none who does good,
There is not even one *(NASB)*.

The first part of this passage is a description of the *nabal*, the empty fellow, the fool, who lives life as though there is no God. The passage describes people who need God's justifying grace; it does not describe justified persons. Arminians understand that we could not fulfill God's expectations in and of ourselves, by some sort of "stock" of righteousness that God gives us. Yet we understand that as Christ continues to indwell us and to keep us, we actually are righteous. As Paul says, "Therefore having been justified by faith, we have peace with God through our Lord Jesus Christ" (Rom. 5:1, NASB).

Regeneration

This is the act of God's grace through which, logically following our forgiveness, we are remade, reborn, born again. Literally, John 3:7 reads, "You must be born from above," *anōthen*.

This is what Jesus tells Nicodemus, a member of the Jewish Sanhedrin. To be born of the flesh (physically) is one thing, but to be "born of the Spirit" (John 3:6, NASB) is another. If this does not happen, Jesus says, a person "cannot see the kingdom of God" (v. 3, NASB).

Paul speaks of this in Ephesians. He tells Christians, "And you were dead in your trespasses and sins" (2:1, NASB). Including himself with them, he goes on to exult, "But God, being rich in mercy, because of His great love with which He loved us, even when we were dead in our transgressions, made us alive together with Christ" (vv. 4-5, NASB).

Regeneration is also what Paul is talking about when he writes, "Therefore if any man is in Christ, he is a new creature; the old things passed away; behold, new things have come" (2 Cor. 5:17, NASB).

Initial Sanctification

This is a sanctification, in the sense of a cleansing, that happens as a concomitant of the first work of grace. It constitutes a cleansing away of acquired depravity—a propensity to acts of sin that builds up in us because of the acts of sin we have committed.

When an act of sin is done over and over, a momentum is built up. We find it easier and easier to do that act of sin, and we become more and more unconscionable about it.

It is for this reason, in part, that we seek to win the young to Christ. Studies a few years ago showed that the optimum age for conversion was 13. As one gets older, acquired depravity so intensifies that the sinner is less and less likely to yield to God's saving grace.

While not all theological orientations teach initial sanctification, Scripture surely does. For example, in Titus, we read of the laver, or the washing, of regeneration. Paul says, "But when the kindness of God our Savior and His love for mankind appeared, He saved us, not on the basis of deeds which we have done in righteousness, but according to His mercy, by the washing of regeneration" (3:4-5, NASB). Scripture also teaches it in Eph. 5:25-26: "Husbands, love your wives, just as Christ also loved the church and gave Himself up for her; that He might sanctify her, having cleansed her by the washing of water with the word" (NASB). This refers to a sanctification subsequent to an earlier cleansing that happens at regeneration—a cleansing "by the washing of water." This is the cleansing properly called initial sanctification.

Initial sanctification is not a partial cleansing as some say, while the later cleansing of entire sanctification is a full cleansing. It is a full, complete, entire cleansing of the acquired (not inherited) depravity resulting from our acts of sin. This enables us to break away from the previous life of sin. Were it not for initial sanctification, we would still have such a propensity to past sinful acts that we could not live a justified life, free from disobedience. When we are justified, but not sanctified wholly, we are inclined to acts of sin both by our bodily nature and by our indwelling original sin. But the slavery to Adamic depravity is broken, and the acquired depravity is cleansed away. So, by God's continued help, it is possible for us to live a Christian life. We are not established in that life as long as original sin inclines us to sin; but according to Gal. 5:17, we are enabled not to sin against God. There Paul says: "The desires of the Spirit are against the flesh . . . But if you are led by the Spirit you are not under the law" (RSV).

The initial sanctification, happening as it does at conversion, is the basis for Christians being regularly called "holy ones," the *hagioi,* in the New Testament. As Alan Richardson suggests, the *hagioi* are synonymous with Christians.[26] And George A. Turner writes, *"Agioi* applies to all believers."[27] This is why the Corinthians are called "holy ones" (NASB margin) and are included among the "sanctified" in 1 Cor. 1:2.

Some have said that initial sanctification has only to do with a Christian being separated to God's use and has no moral significance. Clarence Tucker Craig, for example, says that "sanctified" in 1 Cor. 1:2 has no "specifically moral significance."[28] Yet surely it has such a significance, being a cleansing of acquired depravity and thus giving a believer a fresh start. As Wilbur T. Dayton says, "There is a sense in which initial sanctification can be treated under the terms regeneration and conversion as a fresh, clean start with new life and purpose."[29] The perfect participle in this passage, *hēgiasmenois,* "indicates a condition which has been called into being and which consequently exists."[30]

Reconciliation

Sin estranges, as is well known. It alienates people from each other, and it alienates from God. Paul Tillich viewed sin as essentially estrangement, and he was not necessarily incorrect.[31] When we hurt other people, we often get alienated from them both from our standpoint and from theirs. We need to make amends, to ask for their forgiveness, before the broken relationship is healed.

The same is true with the holy God. By disobedience to His known will, in choosing to go our own way, lifting our fists of rebellion, we alienate ourselves from Him. Likewise, because of His holiness, He becomes alienated from us, and His righteous wrath rests upon us as rebels.

---

26. Alan Richardson, *An Introduction to the Theology of the New Testament* (New York: Harper and Row, 1958), 289.

27. George A. Turner, *The Vision Which Transforms,* 116.

28. Clarence Tucker Craig, "The First Epistle to the Corinthians, Introduction and Exegesis," in *Interpreter's Bible* 10:16.

29. Wilbur T. Dayton, "Initial Sanctification and Its Concomitants," in *The Word and the Doctrine,* comp. Kenneth E. Geiger (Kansas City: Beacon Hill Press, 1965), 208.

30. F. W. Grosheide, "Commentary on the First Epistle to the Corinthians" in *New International Commentary on the New Testament* (Grand Rapids: William B. Eerdmans Publishing Co., 1953), 23 fn.

31. I do think Tillich is incorrect in saying that this estrangement happened early, primitively, when we were created, since we were created finite and therefore fallen—estranged from the Creator by the way we were made, the jig being up as soon as we were cast out into history.

But when He forgives us, absolving our guilt, and giving us life from above in Christ, the situation changes. His holiness is no longer offended. His righteous wrath is propitiated when Christ's atonement is applied to us personally.

Jesus Christ is the "one mediator between God and men" (1 Tim. 2:5), and He has broken down the wall that partitioned us from the Holy Father by saving grace—not from His love. That is why Paul wrote in Eph. 2:13-16 (RSV):

> But now in Christ Jesus you who once were far off have been brought near in the blood of Christ. For he is our peace, who has made us both one, and has broken down the dividing wall of hostility, by abolishing in his flesh the law of commandments and ordinances, that he might create in himself one new man in place of the two, so making peace, and might reconcile us both [Jew and Gentile] to God in one body through the cross, thereby bringing the hostility to an end.

Adoption

Still another concomitant of the first work of grace, conversion, is adoption. Forgiven, newborn, cleansed of acquired depravity, the hostility healed, we are adopted into God's family as a child. Thus Paul says, "For you have not received a spirit of slavery leading to fear again, but you have received a spirit of adoption as sons by which we cry out, 'Abba! Father!' The Spirit Himself bears witness with our spirit that we are children of God" (Rom. 8:15-16, NASB). The "Abba" is from the Aramaic, no doubt the language Christ himself spoke regularly. It means something endearing, like the English "Daddy." We are so reconciled to the Holy Father that we feel close enough to Him to call Him "Daddy."

John also has some beautiful things to say about our adoption into God's family as His children. He says, "But as many as received Him, to them He gave the right [or privilege] to become children of God, even to those who believe in His name" (John 1:12, NASB).

Elsewhere John writes, "See how great a love the Father has bestowed upon us, that we should be called children of God" (1 John 3:1, NASB).

We turn now to a study of the second work of grace.

15

The Second Work of Grace: Entire Sanctification

In the next three chapters the second work of grace will be discussed in some detail, because this is the distinctive doctrine of the Wesleyan-holiness orientation. This second work of grace is obtained by faith, is subsequent to regeneration, is occasioned by the baptism with the Holy Spirit, and constitutes a cleansing away of Adamic depravity and an empowerment for witnessing and for the holy life.

This first chapter on entire sanctification will treat (1) nomenclature, (2) bases for two works of grace, (3) components of the experience, (4) its instantaneousness, (5) receiving and retaining the experience, (6) the witness of the Spirit, (7) carnality and humanity, and (8) its difference from tongues-speaking.

Nomenclature

A variety of terms have been used for the second work of grace, and they are partly appropriate, partly inappropriate.

Perfection or Christian Perfection. Perfection is a biblical word, certainly. We are to go on to "perfection" (Heb. 6:1, KJV). We are urged by Jesus to be "perfect" (Matt. 5:48) as our Heavenly Father is, perhaps by loving our enemies (v. 44). There are other references to our being perfect (Phil. 3:15; 1 Cor. 2:6, both KJV).

Aside from a contextual meaning, as in Matt. 5:43-48, to be perfect is to have attained the maturity[1] of Christian adulthood by

---

1. Note RSV's translation as "mature," e.g., in Phil. 3:15. And note that H. Orton Wiley, in his *Epistle to the Hebrews* (Kansas City: Beacon Hill Press, 1959), 203, suggests that the *hoi teleioi,* the perfect ones, are mature persons—not in the sense of spiritual richness that comes with growth, but in the sense that at age 21 a person is mature by reason of attaining to full adulthood.

being cleansed of Adamic sin. As unalloyed metal is perfect, so we believers are "perfect" when our human nature has been cleansed from the infection known as the carnal nature (see Rom. 8:1; 1 Corinthians 3; Gal. 5:17, 24).

Conduct springing from purified human nature may still be incongruent with God's highest will for us. We are not made errorless or faultless. As Mr. Wesley was forced to explain often, this kind of perfection is consistent with "infirmities" of varying kinds.

While "perfection," then, is appropriate, being often used in Scripture, it is inappropriate because it suggests to outsiders a life perfect in the fullest possible sense.

Perfect Love. This term comes most particularly from 1 John. There we read, "If anyone acknowledges that Jesus is the Son of God, God lives in him and he in God" (4:15). This might be a reference to the first work of grace—conversion. John might then refer to entire sanctification when he adds, "And [Something beyond conversion?] so we know and rely on the love God has for us. God is love. Whoever lives in love lives in God, and God in him. In this way, love is made complete among us so that we will have confidence on the day of judgment, because in this world we are like him" (vv. 16-17). Then John straight out calls this special kind of love "perfect love." He writes, "There is no fear in love. But perfect love drives out fear, because fear has to do with punishment. The one who fears is not made perfect in love" (v. 18).

However, the phrase "perfect love" is misleading to many people and therefore has a degree of inappropriateness about it. They seem to think that it means that our expressions of love to God and others are perfect—whereas we only mean that such love is not mixed with carnal motivations, is not self-seeking.

The Second Blessing. This is another appropriate-inappropriate term. It is appropriate, since entire sanctification is indeed received subsequent to the time of our conversion. It is appropriate as referring to a special kind of "blessing." Yet it is inappropriate because two special problems have been associated with the term. One is the attempt, often made, to support the designation by use of 2 Cor. 1:15, where Paul speaks of a second blessing or a "second benefit" (KJV). J. A. Wood, in the second edition of his *Perfect Love,* wrote,

The apostle also teaches this "second grace" in 2 Corinthians 1:15: "And in this confidence I was minded to come unto you before, that ye might have a second benefit," (margin, "second grace"). The original word, here translated "benefit," is translated grace one hundred and thirty-one times in the New Testament, and is never rendered "benefit," only in this single instance, and then is corrected by inserting "grace" in the margin.[2]

In the same era of the Holiness Movement, Beverly Carradine adopted this understanding of *charin* here. He even suggested that the KJV translators erred because they were in ignorance of this "tender, holy heart experience."[3]

While it is correct that *charis* is almost always translated "grace," such a translation would not fit this context. Paul is clearly talking about a second benefit to be derived from a second visit to the Corinthians. Paul had been pastor of the church there for 18 months; he would already have explained to them the second work of grace. The NIV rendering is sound: "Because I was confident of this [of their appreciation of him], I planned to visit you first so that you might benefit twice. I planned to visit you on my way to Macedonia and to come back to you from Macedonia, and then to have you send me on my way [with a good offering] to Judea" (vv. 15-16).

The paragraph that follows this allusion to a second benefit suggests that, at least largely, the people were already in the experience of entire sanctification: "Now He who establishes us with you in Christ and anointed us is God" (2 Cor. 1:21, NASB). Entire sanctification is properly called the establishing grace, based especially on 1 Thess. 3:13 (see KJV, NASB), and this reference to Paul and his readers having been established might be a reference to the second work of grace. His next words seem to confirm this view: "Who also sealed us and gave us the Spirit in our hearts as a pledge" (2 Cor. 1:22, NASB). Sealing is surely a concomitant of the second work of grace, for Paul says to the Ephesians, "Having also believed [conversion], you were sealed in Him with the Holy Spirit of promise" (1:13, NASB). When Paul says that God "put

---

2. J. A. Wood, *Perfect Love*, rev. ed. (Pasadena, Calif.: John A. Wood, 1880), 197.
3. Beverly Carradine, *The Second Blessing in Symbol* (Louisville, Ky.: Picket Publishing Co., 1896), 21.

his Spirit in our hearts as a deposit" (2 Cor. 1:22), he no doubt refers to the second work of grace received through the Pentecostal baptism with the Holy Spirit. This experience is a "pledge" (Eph. 1:14, NASB), a foretaste of heaven—a little bit of heaven to go to heaven in.

Because some, then, have obtained Holiness mileage out of the "second benefit" reference in 2 Cor. 1:15, the term "second blessing" has had about it a special problem—outsiders have had fun with the term, saying that they have had a second blessing and a third and numerous other blessings. Outsiders have enjoyed attacking that nomenclature itself as a way of attacking the doctrine.

The Second Work of Grace. This is somewhat similar to the "second blessing" but much more preferable. It is one of the more appropriate terms for referring to this Wesleyan distinctive. This designation has the advantage of being general and can include all the concomitants of this experience. The baptism with the Holy Spirit, cleansing from original sin, empowerment, sealing—concomitants of this work of grace—are all included, since no one of them is singled out in the nomenclature.

Some disadvantages, however, attend even this designation. For one, it is so general that it lacks specific content as to what this second work of grace accomplishes. Another disadvantage is that Pentecostals in general also believe in a second work of grace in which they, as believers, are "baptized in the Holy Spirit" and speak in tongues. In this connection Frederick Dale Bruner writes, "From the point of view of the history of doctrine it appears that out of the Methodist-holiness quest for an instantaneous experience of sanctification, of a 'second work of grace' after justification, came Pentecostalism's centering of its aspiration in an instantaneously experienced baptism in the Holy Spirit subsequent to conversion."[4]

Since, then, Pentecostalism also teaches a second work of grace, the content of which is different, especially in not including cleansing from original sin but including tongues-speaking, some disadvantage obtains in referring to the Wesleyan distinctive as the second work of grace.

---

4. Frederick Dale Bruner, *A Theology of the Holy Spirit* (Grand Rapids: William B. Eerdmans Publishing Co., 1970), 37.

Love. Still another appropriate-inappropriate name for entire sanctification is "love," preferred to all others by Mildred Wynkoop, who titled her main writing *A Theology of Love.* In the preface she says, "This is a book about love."[5] Feeling that Wesley "equated holiness and love,"[6] as he indeed sometimes did, Wynkoop suggests that Wesley's basic interest is in "love to God and man"; and with this she agrees.[7] Her thesis in the book is that "love is the dynamic of Wesleyanism."[8] She goes on to say, "Rather than Wesley representing a theology of holiness it would be more faithful to his major emphasis to call it a theology of love."[9]

Yet "love" has some disadvantages as a name for this experience. As Wynkoop has pointed out, "Love is a weasel word."[10] She also says, "Love is a 'hollow word,' drained of its promise of fulfillment by those who have betrayed it by unfulfilled promises."[11] "Love," surely, has many meanings to people, one of which is the very opposite of holiness—referring to sexual experience outside of marriage.

Christian Holiness. This is a particularly appropriate name for entire sanctification if we wish to appeal to outsiders with an inoffensive name for it. Who would not believe in the significance of Christian holiness?

The name does not turn people off, but it is peculiarly inappropriate, because it lacks parameters as does "love." It is a ballpark the size of the Pacific Ocean.

Holiness. This is also both fitting and not fitting. Wesleyans for well over 100 years have been known as the Holiness people. The Wesleyan denominations have been known as Holiness churches, their preachers as Holiness clergy. The ongoing life and work of these churches has been known as the Holiness Movement.

With all this in its favor, however, the term is not altogether appropriate. A minor factor in its inappropriateness is the fact

5. Wynkoop, *A Theology of Love,* 9.
6. Ibid., 10.
7. Ibid., 16.
8. Ibid., 21.
9. Ibid. So much does Wynkoop feel that she is in agreement with John Wesley that I came away from a recent rereading of her book with the impression that perhaps she does not in this book once fault the founder of Methodism on any one aspect of doctrine.
10. Ibid., 9.
11. Ibid.

that all Christian groups believe in holiness in some sense. A major factor is the fact that, technically, we Wesleyans often mean something much broader by "holiness" than we do by entire sanctification. In popular usage, they are synonyms. But when you are being technical, holiness is begun in the first work of grace as Wesley properly said (or even in prevenient grace); and it continues, as growth in grace, after entire sanctification.

Scriptural Holiness. This term is subject to the same criticism as "holiness." The meaning of "holiness," when coupled with "scriptural," is the same as when it stands alone. To include "scriptural" with the word simply emphasizes the principal source for the doctrine.

Second-Blessing Holiness. Of all the terms with "holiness" in them, this is perhaps the most preferable. It suggests that this work of grace is received subsequent to the first work of grace, and it defines "holiness" in such a way that it could only describe the Wesleyan tradition.

In the Holiness Movement, it has been widely associated with those Wesleyans who are not very scholarly in their approach, and this is its chief disadvantage. It is a "true believer" designation, suggesting "I'm loyal," "I'm superorthodox." This kind of overt indication of loyalty and orthodoxy is only sometimes appropriate.

Canaan. Our "Canaan" (or the Canaan Land experience, with Beulah or Beulah Land as synonyms) is still another of these apt and not-so-apt designations for entire sanctification. "Canaan" makes poetic use of an event mentioned often in Scripture. According to this metaphor, the deliverance of the Israelites from their Egyptian slavery typifies our deliverance from bondage to sin and Satan at our conversion; and crossing over the Jordan River and entering into the land of Canaan typifies not death, but entering into the experience of entire sanctification. The analogies have about them a certain plausibility. Deliverance from a cruel taskmaster is true of conversion, and inheritance of positive assets is true of entire sanctification.

However, the designation has nothing exegetically compelling about it. This kind of analogy would not be convincing to someone not yet confident about two works of grace. Indeed, many interpret Israel's entrance into Canaan much differently.

Calvinistic evangelicals view Israel's crossing over the Jordan River as a type of our physical death, and to them Canaan is heaven.

Hebrews 2—4, which speaks of Canaan, is used to support the "holiness" interpretation. To people outside the Holiness Movement, however, the passages would not be compelling. Careful exegesis and exposition of other passages, such as 1 Thessalonians, would be much more convincing.

The Second Rest. Taken also from Hebrews 2—4, this term is more exegetically convincing of entire sanctification teaching than the Canaan analogy. The second rest nomenclature is quite apt because Hebrews 2—4 is clear in calling believers to this rest. The rest is a "second" one, being subsequent to conversion. The writer to Hebrews says, "There remains, then, a Sabbath-rest for the people of God; for anyone who enters God's rest also rests from his own work, just as God did from his. Let us, therefore, make every effort to enter that rest, so that no one will fall by following their example of disobedience" (4:9-11). This is for believers evidently, and it is in keeping with entire sanctification's being an establishing experience.

At the same time, the "second rest" has disadvantages. It would not be as convincing to outsiders as, say, Acts 8 or 1 Thess. 3:10 (studied with 3:13; 4:3; 5:23) would be.

Wesleyanism. This, too, has both advantages and disadvantages. In using it, we thereby associate ourselves with the most distinctive emphasis of a widely recognized person from the faith's past. And a person need not agree with Wesley in all respects in order to be associated with him. We in the Holiness Movement may properly call ourselves Wesleyans, even though we agree with the early fathers, East and West, that entire sanctification is wrought by the baptism with the Holy Spirit—in disagreement with Wesley.

A disadvantage in calling entire sanctification "Wesleyanism" is that some people might think you would then have to mean by it precisely what he did. Another disadvantage is that some people would hear you as saying you are a follower of this standout figure instead of being a follower of Christ, and of viewing this figure's writings, instead of Scripture, as authoritative.

Baptism with the Holy Spirit. This is a term used for the second work of grace by John Fletcher and Joseph Benson in Wesley's time, and in the American Holiness Movement, but not by John Wesley himself.

To use the term has the advantage of identifying the means by which entire sanctification occurs. That passages such as Matt. 3:11-12 make this term almost precisely the wording of Scripture is also advantageous. Still another advantage is its long association with the doctrine of entire sanctification in the Holiness Movement, lending it the advantage of familiarity.

One disadvantage, however, is that Pentecostalism uses a phrase only slightly different—"the baptism in the Holy Spirit"— to refer to something quite different. Its adherents in general do not believe that this baptism cleanses from original sin, and they teach that one either has an initial evidence in tongues-speaking or is given a special tongues-speaking gift for exercising later.

Heart Purity. This is not as widely used as some of the other designations. It is appropriate, for in entire sanctification what Wesley liked to call "inward sin" is cleansed away—the sin of the heart, out of which, as Jesus said, acts of sin come forth (see Mark 7:23). Holiness people have been fond of pointing to one of the Beatitudes as grounding the teaching in Scripture: "Blessed are the pure in heart, for they will see God" (Matt. 5:8). Søren Kierkegaard said that "purity of heart is to will one thing."[12] Paul seems to have been experiencing purity of heart when he wrote, "Brothers, I do not consider myself yet to have taken hold of it. But one thing I do: Forgetting what is behind and straining toward what is ahead, I press on toward the goal to win the prize for which God has called me heavenward in Christ Jesus" (Phil. 3:13-14).

The term, however, might seem to claim too much for the experience; and we might use belief in our heart's being pure as an excuse for less than Christlike attitudes or actions.

The Fullness of the Blessing. This suggests a positive note and is inoffensive to outsiders.

It is somewhat inappropriate, however. To some, it might suggest that the first work of grace is only partial. Donald Metz is a bit misleading in calling initial sanctification "partial sanctification" in distinction from entire or full sanctification, which believers may later receive.[13] Justification, regeneration, initial sanc-

---

12. See Søren Kierkegaard, *Purity of Heart Is to Will One Thing: Spiritual Preparation for the Feast of Confession,* trans. Douglas V. Steere (New York: Harper and Brothers, 1958).
13. See Metz, *Studies in Biblical Holiness,* 112.

tification, etc., are all complete in themselves. The acquired tendency to acts of sin that builds up due to those acts is cleansed in initial sanctification to such extent that we are enabled to break with the life of sin.

To call entire sanctification "the fullness of the blessing" might also associate this Holiness emphasis with some of the tongues-speaking people, because Full Gospel is what a large and influential tongues-speaking association of businessmen calls itself—stemming out of Aimee Semple McPherson's Foursquare Gospel denomination, in which a "full gospel" is promoted by four emphases: salvation, the baptism in the Spirit, healing, and Christ's second coming.

Sanctification. This has the advantage of being a word that most people would at least somewhat understand. Most Christians believe in a sanctification of some sort, usually as occurring gradually. "Sanctification" also has the advantage of being a biblical term frequently used. But the term needs refinement, as by the word "entire," since Scripture uses sanctification of tithes, the Sabbath, the Temple, as well as of persons; and even of persons it is used sometimes in the sense of being set apart to a special office or in marriage, and at other times in the sense of being purified from sin—and purification from sin, even, is sometimes gradual and sometimes instantaneous.

Among Holiness people, "sanctification" is a popular synonym of "entire sanctification." Wesley himself, who sometimes cautioned people to say "entire sanctification" instead of "sanctification" if they were talking about the "second blessing," did not himself always hold to his rule. He often spoke of "sanctification" when, as you can tell from the context, he meant "entire sanctification."

Entire Sanctification. All things considered, this might be preferable to all other designations for Wesleyanism's distinctive emphasis. It might be preferable to all the terms discussed above—and to others not discussed such as "the higher life,"[14] "the deeper life," "Scriptural freedom from sin,"[15] or whatever.[16]

---

14. See W. E. Boardman's *The Higher Christian Life* (Boston: Henry Hoyt, 1871).

15. See Henry Brockett's *Scriptural Freedom from Sin* (Kansas City: Nazarene Publishing House, 1941).

16. See Hannah Whitall Smith, *The Christian's Secret of a Happy Life* (Westwood, N.J.: Fleming H. Revell Co., n.d.). This classic, the most widely used of all Holiness books, has to be carefully read to discover that the "secret" is the experience of entire sanctification.

"Entire sanctification" has several points in its favor. It is perhaps the most widely used designation within the Holiness Movement. John Wesley himself used it quite frequently and urged its use, establishing thereby a tradition within Methodism and the Holiness Movement generally. Calling this work of grace "entire sanctification" also has the advantage of suggesting its most significant aspect: the cleansing away of original sin.

Further, since "sanctification" is a noun, calling this work of grace "entire sanctification" also allows us to indicate that it is a state. As a state, it has about it the condition of a constant relationship with God, within which one is enabled to grow spiritually. As a state, it is more than a series of similar kinds of actions—actions, say, with moral integrity in them. And as a noun, "sanctification" is not also a verb the way "love" is. This specific fact allows one to emphasize its being a state or condition. At the same time, one would not want to de-emphasize love, which Paul called the greatest of all the Christian virtues (1 Cor. 13:13). Love as a virtue, including loving acts, is the highest way we have of expressing the state of entire sanctification.

This designation is scriptural. It occurs in 1 Thess. 5:23. Paul there addresses Christian believers, having already told them he wants to supply what is lacking in their faith (3:10): "May God himself, the God of peace, sanctify you through and through. May your whole spirit, soul and body be kept blameless." The word for "sanctify" is in the aorist tense, suggesting that when this wish, or prayer, is fulfilled, it will happen without reference to time, in a completed way, and not gradually—else the present tense would have been used. The word for "through and through" ("entirely" in NASB; "wholly" in KJV), *holoteleis*, is found only here in Scripture. It is a compound word, from *holos* and *telos*, and literally means "wholly-completely." Martin Luther translated it into German in a way that, in English, would read "through and through." The entire through-and-through sanctification, by which these believers are to be "preserved complete, without blame" (NASB), is to be so pervasive in its purging efficacy that it will include their "spirit and soul and body" (NASB)—which is just about all there is of us.

First Thess. 5:23 refers to a through-and-through cleansing from original sin, because this prayer is clearly for believers (see chap. 1), who have already been cleansed of their acquired depravity through the first work of grace. It teaches that the cleansing for these believers is more than the suppression or counteraction of original sin as taught generally in Reformed circles and in Keswickism.[17]

At this most strategic single verse in the entire New Testament, the NIV, quoted above, reads as satisfactorily to people of the Holiness Movement as does any version—perhaps the most satisfactorily. It is indeed "God himself" who sanctifies us, not we ourselves. We consecrate, and God sanctifies. And this version has in it this happy "Lutherism"—"through and through."

But while the NIV rendering of 1 Thess. 5:23 is excellent, the NASB at 1 Thess. 3:13 is preferable. It there reads, "So that He may establish your hearts unblamable in holiness before our God and Father at the coming of our Lord Jesus with all His saints." This is similar to the KJV and the RSV renderings.

The word "establish" (KJV and NASB) is preferable to the NIV's more vague "strengthen." This word for "establish" is aorist in tense and not present, suggesting that a gradual maturation is not intended.

The NASB's "unblamable in holiness before our God" is also preferable to the NIV's "blameless and holy in the presence of our God." "Unblamable in holiness before our God" suggests that holiness is a state—"in holiness"; and "before God" better suggests that this state can obtain in this life than does the NIV's "in the presence of our God . . . when our Lord Jesus comes."[18]

Yet even "entire sanctification" has disadvantages. (1) It refers specifically to only one of at least five concomitants of the second work of grace—that of cleansing from original sin. (2) It

---

17. This is distinctively a British outgrowth of America's Holiness Movement beginning late last century, often under non-Methodistic and Reformed auspices. Frederick Bruner says that "when brought to birth in America through the activity of Finney, Asa Mahan, the Walter Palmers . . . and others, the holiness movement spread to England where in 1875 the Keswick Convention was born." Bruner, *A Theology of the Holy Spirit,* 44.

18. An initial translating committee led by Merrill C. Tenney had translated *amemptōs* as "faultless" in 1 Thess. 5:23, and the present writer used lexical treatments and the next-life context of Jude 24 to secure the committee's vote to change "faultless" to "blameless." The "faultless" of the KJV, "without fault" of the NIV, in Jude 24, is from *amōmous* (instead of the *amemptous* of 1 Thess. 3:13). It, too, could be translated "blameless," as indeed the NASB renders it. But the next-life context of the Jude passage particularly argues for translating it as "faultless." We can be blameless in this life, but "faultless" only in the next.

is abstract, and not concrete—the way, for example, "baptism" is, when the second work of grace is called the baptism with the Holy Spirit. (3) "Entire" might suggest, especially to outsiders, that God does not still need to give us countless helps toward our maturity. Purity is indeed not maturity. (4) Nor does the phrase make obvious that entire sanctification is not simply a state, but a state that is relational—"love" or "perfect love" being much better terms for expressing its relational aspect.

While there is both appropriateness and inappropriateness in all the terms used to designate Wesleyanism's distinctive emphasis, the term "entire sanctification," all things considered, is perhaps the most advantageous.

Bases for Two Works of Grace

Roman Catholicism and Pentecostalism (with neo-Pentecostalism, beginning at about 1958) teach two works of grace, as do those in the Wesleyan-holiness tradition. All three of these groups of Christians teach that there are two special moments in a person's life when crisis experiences are received on the road to redemption.

For Roman Catholicism, there is regeneration at the time of water baptism (infant or later), and confirmation, when a bishop lays hands on a believer and the person receives a purification from sin as the bishop says, "Receive ye the Holy Spirit." Paul M. Bassett has supported this clearly by much research, especially in the writings of the early Eastern and Western fathers.[19]

Richard Quebedeaux, in *The New Charismatics* (1976), and Frederick Dale Bruner, in *A Theology of the Holy Spirit* (1970), have both shown that the Pentecostals teach two works of grace. For Pentecostals, only people who are already believers may receive the baptism "in" the Holy Spirit. Some Calvinists teach this way also, including the late Harold John Ockenga. Presbyterian Lloyd Ogilvie says that after conversion believers need to receive the Holy Spirit as the early Christians did according to the Book of Acts.

The bases of support for the doctrine of two works of grace differ somewhat among the groups of Christians who support it,

19. Paul M. Bassett and William M. Greathouse, *The Historical Development,* vol. 2 in *Exploring Christian Holiness* (Kansas City: Beacon Hill Press of Kansas City, 1985).

but the bases are somewhat similar. Let us discuss what the main bases are in the Wesleyan-holiness tradition.

The Psychological Basis. One's psychological frame of mind differs so greatly in appropriating the two works of grace that the two experiences could hardly be received at the same time.

The psychological frame of mind needful for receiving the first work of grace is that of a repentant rebel who approaches God, pleading for forgiveness. This person is a disobedient sinner, not a child of God, but is asking to become one; not a Christian, but asking to be made one. When approached in this way, the Father transforms the rebel into a child—because the Just One, Christ, died for the unjust and was raised from the dead.

When we are believers, Christians, already-forgiven persons, asking God for entire sanctification, our psychological frame of mind is quite different. We do not repent of our sins and turn from them, since that has already been done. We yield ourselves to God as His children, willing to be altogether donated to God's cause. We are open to God for His use. Already born again, we want Adamic depravity to be cleansed away by Christ's baptism with the Holy Spirit so that we can serve God in an established relationship and be used of Him in service to other persons. Our frame of mind is vastly different from that of an unbeliever seeking forgiveness; and surely it would be at least next to impossible to have at the same time the two states of mind that are appropriate for receiving the two works of grace. Both works of grace might be received during the same prayer time; but this would be more likely for a person who has fallen from justifying and sanctifying grace and is coming back to God. Yet the works of grace would be chronologically distinct.

Most of us would differ with Melvin Dieter of Asbury Theological Seminary, who says, "The critical point of this purifying experience need not be chronologically distinct from justification and the new birth, but logically it is distinct from them in the continuum of salvation."[20] Dieter's view is like that of Mildred Wynkoop, who writes (as what she incorrectly thinks was also Wesley's view): "One does not believe for justification and then,

---

20. Melvin Dieter et al., *Five Views on Sanctification* (Grand Rapids: Zondervan Publishing House, 1987), 18.

later, believe for sanctification."[21] And she also incorrectly says, "Wesley saw that justification and sanctification were two aspects of one truth, not separated by time or experience."[22] This is incorrect because Wesley does teach that they are "separated" by both "time" and "experience." Wesley did suggest that they might conceivably not be separated in time, but he said he knew of no instance of simultaneity.

Scripture teaches that justification and entire sanctification are "chronologically distinct." This is the official teaching of the Christian Holiness Association and all the denominations that are part of the CHA. Indeed, until Wynkoop, the entire Holiness Movement taught that there are two distinct works of grace in redemption. And even Wynkoop often teaches it clearly, as in *A Theology of Love*. So does Dieter, even in the same symposium chapter from which the quotation above is taken.

The Theological Basis. The principal theological basis for the doctrine is found in the two types of sin from which the two works of grace deliver us—acts of sin and Adamic depravity.

The acts of sin, acts of disobedience against God's known will, are forgiven in the first work of grace—justification. God as Judge pardons us.

But besides having committed acts of sin, every person enters the world with the detriment of Adamic depravity—also called Adamic sin, original sin, racial sin, or depravity. This sin does not require forgiveness, for we were born with it (see Rom. 5:12-21; 1 Cor. 15:21-22). It does not make us culpable; we would never enter into eternal perdition due to it alone, as Wesley said. But as a state it needs to be cleansed away, to be "expelled" as Wesley liked to say, to be "destroyed" (Rom. 6:6, KJV), to be "done away with" (NASB; NIV, a 1984 change). And this occurs in the second work of grace, when believers are granted freedom from sin (Rom. 6:18; 8:1-2); when the body of sin, the state of sin, is destroyed; when the Adamic depravity, which Paul often refers to as the *sarx*, is "crucified" (Gal. 5:24); when believers are "circumcised, in the putting off of the sinful nature, not with a circumcision done by the hands of men but with the circumcision done by Christ" (Col. 2:11).

---

21. Wynkoop, *A Theology of Love,* 20.
22. Ibid.

The Scriptural Basis. This basis is a huge umbrella: it encompasses all aspects of the doctrine. For our purpose, however, we will consider just a few representative scriptural supports.

1. *Two-works passages.* A number of Scripture passages teach both works of grace in one breath, and these are in general the more unanswerably supportive passages.

a. Matt. 3:11. There John the Baptist says, "I baptize you with water for repentance. But after me will come one who is more powerful than I, whose sandals I am not fit to carry. He will baptize you with the Holy Spirit and with fire." In this passage, found also in Mark 1:7-8, Luke 3:16-17, and John 1:26-27, both works of grace are mentioned in a brief compass. John's baptism in water, to symbolize repentance, is the first work of grace; and Christ's later baptism with the Holy Spirit effects the second work of grace. "Repentance" in the Synoptics is the same as "believing" in John's Gospel, as shown in chapter 14. In Christ's baptism, according to John, a radical cleansing would occur—surely the cleansing from original sin. The phrase "and with fire" in verse 11, and the promise in verse 12 of "burning up the chaff with unquenchable fire," speak of this cleansing.[23]

This cleansing is in keeping with numerous other references to cleansing at Pentecost. Ezekiel had said, "I will sprinkle clean water on you, and you will be clean; I will cleanse you from all your impurities and from all your idols. And I will put my Spirit in you and move you to follow my decrees and be careful to keep my laws" (36:25, 27). No doubt Malachi also prophesied of Pentecost's cleansing when he said of "the Lord," "the messenger" who "will come": "He will sit as a refiner and purifier of silver; he will purify the Levites and refine them like gold and silver. Then the Lord will have men who will bring offerings in righteousness" (3:1, 3).

Jesus spoke of the cleansing at Pentecost at different times. Once, on the last day of the Feast of Tabernacles, He said, "Whoever believes in me, as the Scripture has said, streams of living water will flow from within him." John explains, "By this he meant the Spirit, whom those who believed in him [having re-

---

23. Fire is sometimes a scriptural symbol of cleansing, instead of judgment. For a detailed support of this view see Willard Taylor, "The Baptism with the Holy Spirit: Promise of Grace or Judgment?" *Wesleyan Theological Journal* 12 (Spring 1977): 16-25 (hereafter cited as WTJ).

ceived the first work of grace] were later to receive. Up to that time the Spirit had not been given, since Jesus had not yet been glorified" (John 7:38-39). Jesus also used the symbol of baptism, which itself implies cleansing, when He told His disciples, shortly before Pentecost, "In a few days you will be baptized with the Holy Spirit" (Acts 1:5). And when Jesus prayed, "Sanctify them" (John 17:17), a prayer that was surely answered at Pentecost, the meaning of "sanctify" was "cleanse," or "purify from sin," because those disciples had already been sanctified in the sense of being set apart to God's use as ministers.

Further, in describing what happened first to the disciples at Pentecost and later to the household of Cornelius, Peter said that God "made no distinction between us and them, for he purified [*katharisas,* having cleansed] their hearts by faith" (Acts 15:9).

b. Rom. 5:1-5. This passage also teaches both works of redemptive grace. Verse 1 speaks of justification, received "through faith," resulting in "peace with God," and provided "through our Lord Jesus Christ."

Verses 2-5 speak of the second work of grace. Paul continues, "Through whom [an extra "also" is in the NASB, but not in some old manuscripts and therefore not in the NIV or RSV] we have gained access by faith [again the extra "by faith" is not in some of the old manuscripts, so it is not in the RSV, but is in the NIV as well as the NASB] into this grace in which we now stand" (v. 2). On several bases, verses 2-5 seem to be a reference to the second work of grace: (1) the extra "also" of verse 2 suggests that this is beyond justification; (2) the extra "by faith" of verse 2 suggests something beyond justification received also by faith as entire sanctification is (see Acts 15:8-9; 26:18); (3) it is called the grace "in which we now stand" (v. 2), linking it with entire sanctification as the establishing grace (see 1 Thess. 3:13); and (4) it goes on to say that this is received through the Pentecostal baptism with the Spirit: "God has poured out his love into our hearts by the Holy Spirit, whom he has given us" (v. 5).

c. Rom. 6:6. Again, both works of grace are mentioned here. Paul says, "For we know that our old self was crucified with him so that the body of sin might be done away with, that we should no longer be slaves to sin." Paul is saying that we receive the first work of grace in order to go further and receive the second work of grace. The phrase "our old self" is a good rendering of *ho palaios hēmōn anthrōpos*. It refers to the earlier self, prior to regeneration. That self was "crucified," Paul says, in order that (*hina*) "the body of sin," the state of sin, original sin, "might be done away with," or "destroyed" as in RSV.

d. Eph. 1:13. Here Paul says, "In Him, you also, after listening to the message of truth, the gospel of your salvation—having also believed, you were sealed in Him with the Holy Spirit of promise" (NASB). The persons addressed had heard the gospel and had believed—the first work of grace. After this hearing and believing they were "sealed in Him with the Holy Spirit of promise." The "Spirit of promise" is the Spirit promised by Ezekiel (36:25-27), Joel (2:28), John the Baptist (Matt. 3:11), and Jesus (Acts 1:4-5)—passages noted earlier. The sealing means that by this second work of grace they were (1) established in Christ, with original sin being cleansed away; (2) approved of God, since Adamic depravity was destroyed; and (3) owned of God in a deeper sense than obtains at justification—the ancient seal signifying approval (as it does now on a degree), and ownership (as it does now on a letter).

e. Eph. 5:25-27. In this passage, Paul again speaks clearly of two works, if it is read in the Greek or in almost any of the recent versions—instead of the KJV. Here Paul says, "Christ also loved the church and gave Himself up for her; that He might sanctify her, having cleansed her by the washing of water with the word, that He might present to Himself the church in all her glory, having no spot or wrinkle or any such thing; but that she should be holy and blameless" (NASB). We have here an aorist participle, *katharisas*. Aorist participles ordinarily express action that is prior in time to the action of the main verb of a sentence. Thus Paul is saying that, "having cleansed" the church in initial sanctification, or regeneration, Christ later sanctifies [the main verb] her to present her to himself as holy. The KJV rendered the passage without regard to the aorist participle—"sanctify and cleanse"—which obscured the two works of grace. The NASB and RSV, however, render it "having cleansed," making regeneration earlier than this sanctification. The NIV renders without regard to the usual meaning of an aorist participle, reading that Christ gave himself up "to make her holy, cleansing her by the washing with water through the word."

f. James 4:8. This passage might refer to both works of grace: "Wash your hands, you sinners, and purify your hearts, you double-minded." The "hands" have to do with acts, due to which people are "sinners," and need to be cleansed in the "washing of regeneration" (Titus 3:5, KJV). And the heart, out of which Jesus said acts of sin flow (Mark 7:21-23), needs to be cleansed, as were the hearts of the 120 at Pentecost (Acts 15:8-9).

It is not easy to be sure that James is speaking of two works of grace. He does describe original sin as a condition of his readers. They are charged with "friendship with the world" (4:4). They are "envious" (4:2, NASB), and they "quarrel and fight" (v. 2; cf. 1 Corinthians 3). For all this there is a remedy: "But [God] gives us more grace"—perhaps a reference to entire sanctification (4:6). Then he exhorts, "Submit yourselves, then, to God" (v. 7), which might be an exhortation to consecration. Consecration, as preparation for entire sanctification, might be the meaning of his words "Come near to God and he will come near to you," after which he adds the passage under study: "Wash your hands, you sinners, and purify your hearts, you double-minded." The regenerate person, indeed, is double-minded, being indwelt not only by the Spirit but also by the sinful nature (Gal. 5:17). And the cleansed heart, the second work of grace, is the answer to the double-mindedness.

2. *Other passages.* There are numerous other Scripture passages of larger compass in which two works of grace are taught. Only a few of them need to be referred to here, since this study of entire sanctification as a whole is largely a study of them.

a. Acts passages. Several passages in Acts are of this type and will also be discussed in detail in a subsequent chapter. Under the preaching of Philip at Samaria, people "believed" and were baptized in water. Still later, when Peter and John arrived, they "prayed for them that they might receive the Holy Spirit . . . Then Peter and John placed their hands on them, and they received the Holy Spirit" (8:12-17).

Several other such Acts passages teach two works of grace; for example, chapters 9; 10—11; and 18:27—19:6. The last of these needs to be discussed briefly here. Certain disciples had "believed" and had been "baptized" (in water). John the Baptist had done the baptizing. According to Paul, John had told the people to "believe in the one coming after him, that is, in Jesus"

(19:4). Verse 5 reads: "On hearing this, they were baptized into the name of the Lord Jesus" (19:5). This refers to their hearing the Baptist; not to their hearing what Paul had just said. This is not a record of rebaptism. Paul laid hands upon them and "the Holy Spirit came on them" in Pentecostal fullness.

> b. 1 Thessalonians. Two works of grace are surely taught in this Epistle. Paul is here writing to believers. He calls them "brothers" 14 times in the five chapters. He gives special thanks to God for them, continually remembering their "work produced by faith, . . . labor prompted by love, and . . . endurance inspired by hope in our Lord Jesus Christ" (1:2-3). And he says that they had "welcomed" the gospel (v. 6) and were witnessing (v. 8) and waiting for "his Son from heaven" (v. 10).

Yet something is lacking in their faith (3:10)—especially their entire sanctification. In 3:13 Paul writes, "May he strengthen ["establish," NASB] your hearts so that you will be blameless and holy in the presence of our God and Father." He soon adds in 4:3, "It is God's will that you should be sanctified." And before long he is saying, "May God himself, the God of peace, sanctify you through and through" (5:23).

What is lacking is to be supplied, not gradually, since the present tense is not used, but in a completed way and without regard to time and sequence. The Greek word in 3:10, translated "perfect" in the KJV, "supply" in the RSV and NIV, and "complete" in the NASB, is aorist in tense, denoting completed, decisive action, if not instantaneous. And the word for "establish" in 3:13 (NASB), "strengthen" (NIV), is also aorist, suggesting that to be established "unblameable in holiness before God" (KJV) will happen in a completed experience of God's favor. Likewise, in 5:23, "sanctify" is aorist. There the "entirely," in "sanctify you entirely" (NASB) or "through and through" as in the NIV, is from *holoteleis*, a compound Greek word meaning "wholly-completely." This refers to a complete cleansing from sin instead of a complete setting apart—the other meaning, in some other contexts (e.g., 1 Cor. 7:14), of "sanctify."

Components of the Experience

The doctrine and experience of entire sanctification can be viewed from various perspectives.

A Separation to God's Use. This is a component that needs early attention. The Hebrew root, *kdsh,* for holiness, occurs some 830 times in the Old Testament. The word seems to mean to "cut off," "separate," perhaps "elevate."

Perhaps this word for "holiness," which basically seems to mean "separation," "originally had no ethical associations."[24] The fact that temple prostitutes in pagan cultures were called "holy ones" would indicate this.

In Israel's own usage, some argue for an ethical content from very early times in the application of *kdsh* to persons and to animals used as sacrifices (see 2 Chron. 29:5, 15-19; also Lev. 22:21-25; Deut. 15:21; Mal. 1:8).

Turner concludes, "In every one of the more than 800 places where this sort of root is used in the Old Testament the meaning of separation is permissible; in many instances it is demanded."[25]

The counterpart verbal New Testament word for "holiness," *hagiadzō,* "to make holy," includes in its meaning "to separate," while its 28 instances frequently mean, instead, to cleanse from sin.

Separation to God's use is evidently the meaning in John 17:19, where Jesus says, "For their sakes I sanctify Myself" (NASB), for He was without sin (2 Cor. 5:21). He needed no sanctification in the sense of purification from sin. As human, though, He did need to set himself apart to be used by God the Father, especially by going to the Cross for us.

A similar use of a cognate word appears in the Lord's Prayer: "Hallowed be Thy name" (Matt. 6:9, NASB). We are telling God that we want Him to be set apart from and above everything else that touches our lives. As E. F. Walker puts it, "When Peter enjoins to 'sanctify Christ as Lord in your hearts' (1 Pet. 3:15), the meaning is that we are to give the Lord Jesus the supreme place in the throne of our being—'that all may honor the Son, even as they honor the Father' (John 5:23)."[26]

---

24. See George Allen Turner, *The More Excellent Way,* 22. Turner quotes Rudolph Otto, *The Idea of the Holy* (London: Oxford University Press, 1923), 6, 25. A. C. Knudson, in his *Religious Teaching of the Old Testament,* gives considerable support for this understanding, although he and others do need to be studied by evangelicals with the realization that they work according to the Documentary Hypothesis view.

25. Turner, *The More Excellent Way,* 22.

26. Edward F. Walker, *Sanctify Them,* rev. J. Kenneth Grider (Kansas City: Beacon Hill Press of Kansas City, 1968), 20-21. In this book, in this connection, we also read: "The Bible uses

Cognates of "sanctify" with the meaning of separation are found also in John 10:36 and 1 Cor. 7:14.

A Cleansing Away of Original Sin. This is perhaps the most basic component of the second work of grace.

John Wesley taught a radical cleansing away of original sin at entire sanctification, and this has been standard teaching in the Holiness Movement. Wesley spoke of "love filling the heart, expelling [not just suppressing] pride, anger, desire, self-will."[27] Wesley also wrote much about the body of sin being destroyed.

J. A. Wood, in his now classic *Perfect Love,* taught clearly the radical cleansing from Adamic sin through entire sanctification. In the revised edition he wrote:

> In the grace of justification sins, as acts of transgression, are *pardoned.* In the grace of [entire] sanctification, sin, as a malady, is *removed,* so that the heart is pure. In the nature of the case, the eradication of sin in principle from the human heart completes the Christian character. When guilt is forgiven in justification, and all pollution is removed in entire sanctification, so that grace possesses the heart and nothing contrary to grace, then the moral condition is reached to which the Scriptures give the name of perfection, or entire sanctification.[28]

Wood often uses "eradicate" and "exterminate" and "extirpate" as expressions of how God's grace radically deals with original sin.

The witness of many later Holiness writers could be added, such as George Allen Turner, J. Glenn Gould, W. T. Purkiser, Richard S. Taylor, and S. S. White, all of whom have clearly taught that one component of the second work of grace is a real and radical cleansing from original sin.[29]

The Baptism with the Holy Spirit. As this will be discussed presently in an entire chapter, it is only briefly mentioned here. It

---

sanctify in the sense of *hallowing, honoring, glorifying,* but such is not the meaning in the passage under study in this little book (John 17:17)." Passages where hallowing or reverencing is intended include Isa. 5:16; 29:23; and Ezek. 36:23.

27. Wesley, *Plain Account,* 84.

28. Wood, *Perfect Love,* rev. ed., 34.

29. Turner, *The Vision Which Transforms,* 238; J. Glenn Gould, *The Whole Counsel of God* (Kansas City: Beacon Hill Press, 1945), 56; W. T. Purkiser, *Sanctification and Its Synonyms: Studies in the Biblical Theology of Holiness* (Kansas City: Beacon Hill Press, 1961), 43; Richard S. Taylor, *Exploring Christian Holiness,* vol. 3, 161-63; and S. S. White, *Eradication Defined, Explained, Authenticated* (Kansas City: Beacon Hill Press, 1954).

is this baptism with the Holy Spirit that occasions, or effects, entire sanctification. In this baptism the Holy Spirit is poured out upon the believer. The Spirit then indwells the believer pervasively.

An Empowerment. While the Holiness Movement has stressed the cleansing away of original sin, we have also known that power, as well as purity, is associated with the baptism with the Holy Spirit. Acts 1:8 makes this clear: "You shall receive power when the Holy Spirit has come upon you; and you shall be My witnesses both in Jerusalem, and in all Judea and Samaria, and even to the remotest part of the earth" (NASB).

The Holiness Movement could well emphasize this aspect of our Pentecost more than it does. And it could well admit that the power means power for witnessing for Christ. It is more than just the power to live a holy life.

Jesus Christ sits on the edge of our lips, waiting to be talked about. He will give us the power to tell people, in more or less winsome ways, whose we are, and He will help us as we seek to lead them to Him.

A Sealing. Entire sanctification is also described in Scripture as a sealing—somewhat in 2 Cor. 1:21-22 and Eph. 4:30, but clearly in Eph. 1:13-14.

In the first of these, Paul connects establishment and sealing with the giving of the Holy Spirit: "He who establishes us with you in Christ and anointed us is God, who also sealed us and gave us the Spirit in our hearts as a pledge" (2 Cor. 1:21-22, NASB).

While Paul refers to sealing in Eph. 4:30, he does so more explicitly in Eph. 1:13-14: "And you also were included in Christ when you heard the word of truth, the gospel of your salvation. Having believed, you were marked in him with a seal, the promised Holy Spirit, who is a deposit guaranteeing our inheritance."

Some Holiness scholars, such as George A. Turner, associate sealing with the first work of grace, but most (such as H. Orton Wiley and S. S. White) have associated it with entire sanctification. It is to be noted that the Christians being addressed in Ephesians had listened to the "gospel of . . . salvation," had also "believed," and after that had been "sealed in Him with the Holy Spirit of promise" (NASB).

As noted earlier, sealing as a symbol suggests ownership—that the believer is truly owned by God as a sealed letter is owned by its addressee. Sealing also suggests approval, as does a school's seal placed on a graduate's degree. Once we believers are completely yielded to God (Rom. 12:1-2), we are truly owned by God (see Gal. 5:24); and once original sin is expelled, we are approved of God in a deeper sense than obtains when our acts of sin are forgiven at justification.

A Growing State of Right Relationship. The relational theologians such as Mildred Wynkoop rightly hold that original sin and its counterpart, holiness, are relational matters. Original sin constitutes a bias toward acts of sin, due to an estrangement from God. And holiness, too, is relational, in part a correcting of original sin's alienation.

Some have suggested that it is misleading to consider original sin and the holiness experience as states. These critics wish to avoid the implication that original sin and holiness are substantive in nature—that is, weighable, measurable, phenomenal substances. To call them states, however, does not at all imply that they are static or substantive. Concerning original sin, we can use such terms for its cleansing as "removal" or "destruction" without suggesting that the original sin is physical or quantitative in nature.

Numerous statements of various Holiness writers could be marshaled to support the view that entire sanctification is a state as well as a relationship, and that it is, by all means, a growing state. It is only when the recalcitrant original sin is expelled that Christian growth toward a rich and fruitful maturity can best take place.

A Perfection. Another component of entire sanctification is perfection, but only in a certain sense. We are not perfect in our judgment or in ethical conduct. We are perfect in the sense that a metal is perfect when extraneous substances are separated from it so that the metal is all of one kind. When the carnal nature is cleansed away, we are perfect in the sense of having a pure human nature—a human nature no longer infected by carnality. Christians are urged in Scripture to go on to perfection (Heb. 6:1) and to be perfect as our Heavenly Father is (Matt. 5:48).

Perfection sometimes designates the resurrected state (Phil. 3:11-12). It seems to be used as a synonym of the *pneumatikoi*, the spiritual ones, in distinction from the carnal Christians (1 Cor. 3:1 ff.). Paul seems to have had special meetings with the *hoi teleioi*, the "perfect ones," according to the Corinthian correspondence (1 Cor. 2:6, 12; 14:16, 23). These are Christians who have received cleansing from Adamic sin through Christ's Spirit baptism.

Insofar as words for "perfection" can be translated "maturity," as the RSV does at Phil. 3:15, H. Orton Wiley is correct in saying that it means maturity, not in the sense of ripeness of Christian character, but in the sense of adulthood—the way a young person attains maturity or majority or full adulthood at age 21.[30]

There are occasions when the New Testament uses "perfection" to mean "perfect conduct," as in James 3:2. This perfection is not possible in this life.

In the Holiness Movement, when we speak of "perfection," we refer to those whose carnal nature has been expelled, so that the nature is not a mixture of the human and the carnal. In this sense Paul includes himself, and at least some to whom he is writing, as among the perfect, in Phil. 3:15 (see also 1 John 4:16-18).

An Establishing Experience. Often entire sanctification has been called "the establishing grace," based significantly on 1 Thess. 3:13, "So that He may establish your hearts unblamable in holiness before our God and Father at the coming of our Lord Jesus with all His saints" (NASB). It is based in part on Rom. 5:1-2, where Paul refers to a grace, received subsequently to justification, in which a person is enabled to "stand" (KJV, NIV, NASB)—that is, to stand fast in faith.

The Christian who has been sanctified wholly can fall completely from saving grace. But just as surely, such a person is enabled *not* to fall from grace.

The Component of Love. Still another constituent of entire sanctification is love. The second work of grace makes it possible for us to love God and others with all our heart and mind and soul and strength (see Deut. 30:6; Matt. 22:36-39). Wesley emphasized this aspect of entire sanctification experience, often calling the second blessing "perfect love." He appreciated 1 John very much, quoting from it frequently because of its emphasis on love and perfect love (1 John 4:8). Mildred Wynkoop has elucidated this understanding.

The Social Component. John Wesley engaged himself with many helping ministries. He started a credit union. He practiced

---

30. See H. Orton Wiley, *The Epistle to the Hebrews* (Kansas City: Beacon Hill Press, 1959), 203.

medicine. He published Christian literature at low cost with the poor in mind. His last letter was an encouragement to Wilberforce to keep up the fight against legalized slavery in England.

George A. Turner writes, in what might be somewhat of an extreme statement, that "historically, Methodism has been as distinctive for its social service as it has for spreading Scriptural holiness." Again, "It was quite natural that Methodism's first child, the Salvation Army, immediately began to dispense 'soup, soap, and salvation,' but they still found time for the weekly 'Holiness Meeting.'"[31]

Before the middle of the 19th century and somewhat later, according to research by Timothy L. Smith,[32] Donald Dayton,[33] and others, persons in the Methodistic-holiness tradition were in the vanguard of the abolitionist, feminist, and temperance-abstinence movements. At that time at Oberlin College, Holiness giants Charles G. Finney and Asa Mahan and others agitated for freeing slaves and for women's rights. Oberlin was probably the first American college to admit women; and it also admitted Blacks, protected runaway slaves, and sought a change in an Ohio law that required that runaway slaves be returned.

Phineas F. Bresee left Methodism in the late 19th century in order to work in a kind of rescue mission. After a year he left that mission to found the West's Church of the Nazarene—among the familied poor. It was Bresee's social interests that caused him to yearn, most of all, to start holiness work in the great American cities. He was even more keenly interested in doing this than in fostering world missions.

Evidence abounds that the Holiness people have not gone to sleep on social issues. Holiness denominations have made official declarations on such matters as race relations, abortion, and drug use. Numerous inner-city ministries are promoted under Holiness auspices—as of late 1992, 50 in the largest of the Holiness denominations, the Church of the Nazarene.

---

31. Turner, The Vision Which Transforms, 312-13, 259.
32. See Timothy L. Smith, Revivalism and Social Reform in Mid-Nineteenth Century America (New York: Abingdon Press, 1957).
33. See Donald W. Dayton, Discovering an Evangelical Heritage (New York: Harper and Row, 1976).

The Wesleyan-holiness Christians were liberationists of a sort, long before Ruben Alves, a liberal Protestant, founded the radical kind of liberation theology as such with a decisive article in 1964, joined in it after 1968 by such Roman Catholic theologians as Gustavo Gutierrez and Leonardo Boff. But in our tradition we have never promoted violence (often described as counterviolence) or revolution, whereas the radical liberationists have promoted both, even opposing the Bible with its supernaturalism, promoting the slogan, "Put down your Bibles, take up your rifles, and join the revolution."

The World Mission Interest. A world mission interest is also a component of entire sanctification emphasis. The various Holiness denominations have maintained large and sometimes top-heavy world mission ministries—some of them top-heavy because their world mission work could hardly be supported, and they were thrust toward merger with or absorption by another Holiness denomination in part because of it.[34]

The utter consecration to God's use, in order to receive and maintain entire sanctification, figures in both the willingness for missionary service and sacrificial giving for its support.

Its Otherworldliness. A last component of entire sanctification doctrine and experience that should be discussed is its otherworldliness. Like the reform Montanist movement of the second and third centuries, and somewhat like monastic movements in Roman Catholicism, Holiness people have promoted an otherworldly life-style. The Holy Club at Oxford University, begun by Charles Wesley and later led by his brother John, promoted such holy-life procedures that its members were dubbed "methodists," for they methodically lived out a life of spiritual discipline and Christian service.

In America there has been a long and sometimes unenviable history of otherworldliness in the Holiness Movement. Alcohol as

---

34. The International Holiness Mission of Britain was such a group. The present writer, studying and teaching in Scotland (1950-52), was asked by the Nazarene general superintendent in jurisdiction, Dr. Hardy C. Powers, to check on why that denomination was seeking merger with the Church of the Nazarene—and a top-heavy world mission program seemed to figure significantly. This also figured somewhat in the Nazarene absorption of the Pentecostal Mission in 1915 and the Calvary Holiness Church of Britain in 1955.

a beverage and tobacco use have usually been banned, as has much in the theater, in films, in music, and in dance. People were to be Holiness "in life and look"—the "look" having to do with dress. Donald W. Dayton's research shows that simplicity of dress was encouraged to free more money for evangelism and for helping the destitute.

We now look at another major aspect of the doctrine of entire sanctification: its instantaneousness.

Its Instantaneousness

Both John and Charles Wesley and the Holiness Movement writers taught, and the present Holiness writers teach, that entire sanctification in instantaneous. Wesley himself also taught gradual sanctification, by which he seems to have meant a gradual cleansing of original sin. And George A. Turner and Mildred Wynkoop likewise teach that, besides instantaneous entire sanctification, there is a gradual sanctification in which original sin is cleansed away piecemeal.

Almost all the Holiness Movement writers, however, have followed Adam Clarke—who at least sometimes taught that entire sanctification, like regeneration, is instantaneous and not gradual—although many of them have used the phrase "gradual sanctification" or "progressive sanctification" to mean only our gradual preparation. Daniel Steele, H. Orton Wiley, S. S. White, W. T. Purkiser, Richard S. Taylor, and numerous other Holiness writers have taken this kind of view.

Entire sanctification is received instantaneously because (1) "instantaneous" symbols (baptism, sealing, circumcision) are used in Scripture to describe how it is received; (2) it is received by faith; (3) aorist tenses are used; and (4) receiving it is analogous to receiving regeneration.

The Instantaneous Symbols. At least three instantaneous symbols are used in Scripture to describe the receiving of entire sanctification: baptism, sealing, and circumcision.

1. *Baptism.* This is the most significant of these symbols and is used in connection with Christ's baptism with the Holy Spirit. The 120 believers mentioned in Acts 1 were to be "baptized with the Holy Spirit" (v. 5), and this happened on Pentecost Day. The

very symbol of baptism suggests instantaneousness. A person is not gradually baptized.

2. *Sealing*. The three specially related uses of the figure of sealing (2 Cor. 1:22; Eph. 1:13; 4:30), referred to earlier, seem to refer to entire sanctification; and sealing was done instantaneously.[35]

In 2 Cor. 1:21-22 Paul says, "Now He who establishes us with you in Christ and anointed us is God, who also sealed us and gave us the Spirit in our hearts as a pledge" (NASB). "Gave us the Spirit" is a reference to being baptized with the Spirit as at Pentecost. And since this is connected with being established (see 1 Thess. 3:13), it seems to be a description of the second work of grace. God establishes us by giving us the Spirit.

3. ¹*Circumcision*. In Colossians, Paul uses circumcision as analogous to entire sanctification. He says, "And in Him you were also circumcised with a circumcision made without hands, in the removal of the body of the flesh by the circumcision of Christ" (2:11, NASB). The KJV has "the body *of the sins* of the flesh," introducing three words not in the oldest Greek manuscripts, which serve to obscure Paul's meaning. Here Paul is saying that the state or condition or principle of the flesh is circumcised. He is saying that Adamic sin, original sin, is dealt with decisively—excised—as is the male foreskin in circumcision. One moment it is intact; the next moment it is not.

Paul uses the same figure in Rom. 2:29. He says, "No, a man is a Jew if he is one inwardly; and circumcision is circumcision of the heart, by the Spirit, not by the written code." This inner, heart circumcision is "by the Spirit," a reference to the Spirit given at Pentecost (see 5:1-5).

These references to circumcision are in keeping with the heart circumcision promised in Deut. 30:6, which results in wholehearted love for God. One is not gradually circumcised. It is something accomplished instantaneously, in a moment, in a decisive act.

Other symbols and terms used of the second blessing that suggest its instantaneousness include "anointed" (2 Cor. 1:21), "fell" (Acts 10:44), and possibly "crucified" (Gal. 5:24) and "filled" (Acts 2:4). The "pour forth" of verse 17 and the "poured

---

35. Several New Testament uses of "seals" are not related to entire sanctification. Sixteen of these are in Revelation. Others are in 1 Cor. 9:2 and 2 Tim. 2:19.

out" of 10:45 (all NASB) should probably be taken as instantaneous acts, because "baptism" is sometimes a synonym of them (as in Matt. 3:11 and Acts 1:4-5).

Faith as the Means. Entire sanctification is received by faith; hence it is instantaneous. If by works, then it would be gradual— and gradual only, never instantaneous. If by works, it would never be complete. In Reformed theology, which teaches gradual sanctification by devout disciplines, it is understood that sanctification is never completed while we are here in this life.

Wesley was correct in teaching that entire sanctification is received by faith and not by works. Even as we are justified by faith alone, we are sanctified wholly by faith alone. Luther had taught that we are justified by faith alone; but he also had taught that we are sanctified gradually by pious disciplines. This caused Wesley to say that hardly anyone had taught better than Luther on justification or more poorly than Luther on sanctification.

The New Testament clearly teaches that entire sanctification is received by faith. In Acts 15:8-9 Peter says, "And God . . . made no distinction between us [at Pentecost] and them [Cornelius and his household], cleansing their hearts by faith" (NASB). Summed up, Pentecost was a cleansing of their hearts from Adamic sin "by faith." That entire sanctification is received by faith is also stated in the report of Paul's call to preach (26:18). He was sent to the Gentiles "that they may receive forgiveness of sins and an inheritance among those who have been sanctified by faith in Me" (NASB). Sanctification is not received at death, but during this life, not gradually, but instantaneously—by faith.

The Aorist Tense. This New Testament Greek tense, with all the reservations regarding it that the most careful Greek grammarians include in their studies, is also in some contexts supportive of entire sanctification's instantaneousness.

In whatever the mood, the aorist tense denotes what is punctiliar. J. H. Moulton, in his *Grammar of New Testament Greek*, gives an excellent summary of the meaning of the aorist tense as punctiliar. He says it denotes punctiliar action, which "represents the point of entrance (Ingressive, as *balein* "let fly," *basileusai* "come to the throne"), or that of completion (Effective, as *balein* "hit"), or it looks at a whole action simply as having occurred, without distinguishing any steps in its progress (Constantive, as *basileusai* "reign," or as when a sculptor says of his statue, *"epoiesen ho deina"* "X. made it")."[36]

That is, whether the aorist is ingressive (often also called inceptive), or effective, or constantive, it is punctiliar. As punctiliar, it is in itself without any special reference to time. As Robertson puts it, a writer uses the aorist if "duration is not the point about which he is concerned."[37] Yet Robertson adds, "If one desires to emphasize the notion of linear action on the one hand or the state of completion on the other, it [the aorist] is not the tense to use."[38] For this reason, in connection with verbs for "sanctify," and other New Testament Greek verbs relating to entire sanctification (for example, "supply" in 1 Thess. 3:10 and "establish" in v. 13 [NASB]), whether an aorist is inceptive (ingressive) or effective or causative must be decided on the basis of the context.

Since that is so, people who do not believe in a second work of grace are likely to say that the action denoted by an aorist participle takes place at the same time as the action of the main verb of a sentence. In that case, Acts 11:17 is translated "So if God gave them [at Cornelius's house] the same gift as he gave us, who believed in the Lord Jesus Christ, who was I to think that I could oppose God?" (NIV). This translation makes Pentecost the time when the 120 who had already been designated as "brethren" (in Acts 1:15) were justified. The aorist participle, *pisteusasin*, is translated as though its action takes place at the same time as the action of the main verb—"gave."

But the NASB (translated mostly by scholars who did not believe in two works of grace) reads as though the 120 had believed *prior* to Pentecost and that their Pentecost was a second work of grace. "If God therefore gave to them the same gift as He gave to us also after believing in the Lord Jesus Christ, who was I that I could stand in God's way?" The NASB translators here, as at other places, render *pisteusasin* as though its action takes place prior in time to the action of the main verb—no doubt they believed this to be the translation warranted by the context.

---

36. J. H. Moulton, *A Grammar of the New Testament* Greek, vol. 1: *Prolegomena* (Edinburgh: T. and T. Clark, 1906), 109.
37. A. T. Robertson and W. H. Davis, *A New Short Grammar of the Greek New Testament* (New York: Richard S. Smith, 1931), 295.
38. Ibid.

The aorist tense is sometimes used in the New Testament to refer to what, in itself, involved duration. We read that the Temple was "built" (aorist) according to John 2:20, and we know that its building took 46 years. It was viewed by the writer simply as built, without considering the time it took, so the aorist was used.

The aorist tense has been at times somewhat loosely used among Holiness writers to support entire sanctification's instantaneousness. Daniel Steele was perhaps the first to use the aorist tense as supportive of the instantaneousness of entire sanctification. He talked of it as the "lightning tense," and he was almost correct in that expression. It does not indicate duration; it is punctiliar, and it is properly illustrated by a dot, as A. T. Robertson said. Yet Steele did not treat the aorist with sufficient care and led the way to a careless use of the aorist tense as an argument supportive of entire sanctification's instantaneousness.

At the same time, even when all due allowances are made for other possible significations of the aorist tense, it is still an exegetical support of the instantaneousness of entire sanctification in various contexts.[39]

Analogous to Regeneration. Even as the first work of grace is instantaneous, so is the second work of grace.

A long tradition of arguing from this analogy was started by Adam Clarke, Methodism's primary scholar in Wesley's time. It is more or less a support from logic. It would be better used among insiders than as a way of convincing outsiders to the Holiness Movement.

Wesley and Clarke Contrasted. John Wesley taught that prior to entire sanctification there is a gradual sanctification that is preparatory. By this gradual sanctification, he sometimes seemed to mean a gradual lessening of original sin. He spoke of "a gradual mortification of sin."[40] In the same work, *A Plain Account*, which he revised rather late in his life, so that we may understand it to be his mature thought, he suggests that entire sanctification

---

39. Sources helpful in tempering this writer's position previously taken in *Entire Sanctification*, on the aorist tense's significance in the instantaneousness of entire sanctification, are (1) Randy Maddox, "The Use of the Aorist Tense in Holiness Exegesis," WTJ 16 (Fall 1981): 106-8; and (2) a term paper of June 1988, "The Instantaneousness of Entire Sanctification . . . ," by Andy Johnson, one of my students.

40. Wesley, *A Plain Account*, 61.

is analogous to a slow physical death; and this might mean that original sin is gradually lessened. He says, "A man may be dying for some time; yet he does not, properly speaking, die, till the soul is separated from the body . . . In like manner, he may be dying to sin for some time; yet he is not dead to sin, till sin is separated from his soul."[41]

A bit farther on in *A Plain Account* he writes, "It need not, therefore, be affirmed over and over . . . either that most men are perfected in love at last, that there is a gradual work of God in the soul, or that, generally speaking, it is a long time, even many years, before sin is destroyed."[42] He further states that faith "is both the condition and instrument of it. When we begin to believe, then sanctification begins. And as faith increases, holiness increases, till we are created anew."[43] If sanctification can "begin," and if it can increase as faith increases, we seem to be talking about a process of gradual sanctification. Wynkoop thinks so. Commenting on these words of Wesley, she says, "In this passage the process aspect of sanctification is clearly indicated."[44] George Allen Turner also interprets Wesley in this way. He says:

> In Wesleyan teaching regeneration is the positive side of justification and is instantaneous, while sanctification is the gradual work of the Spirit in inner transformation, although there is a time when this process may be consummated instantly in response to faith. If "regeneration" is taken to mean a new beginning and "sanctification" a process of making holy, then the two may be said to be distinct.[45]

Of bearing on the matter, at least, is the fact that Wesley wrote to his brother Charles urging him to "press the *instantaneous* blessings," adding, "then I shall have more time for my peculiar calling, enforcing the *gradual* work."[46]

Adam Clarke, younger contemporary of Wesley, viewed the matter differently. He writes, "In no part of the Scriptures are we directed to seek holiness *gradatim*. We are to come to God as well for an instantaneous and complete purification from all sin as for

41. Ibid., 62.
42. Ibid., 90.
43. Wesley, *Works* 8:279.
44. Wynkoop, *A Theology of Love,* 109.
45. Turner, *The Vision Which Transforms,* 156.
46. Wesley, *Works* 12:130, italics added.

an instantaneous pardon. Neither the *gradatim pardon* nor the *seriatim* purification exists in the Bible."[47] Clarke would evidently admit that much growth in grace can be expected after entire sanctification, but he would not call that gradual sanctification. His next words are, "It is when the soul is purified from all sin that it can properly grow in grace, and in the knowledge of our Lord Jesus Christ."[48]

Holiness Movement Follows Clarke. On this issue of gradual sanctification, the Holiness Movement understood Clarke's view to be scriptural, instead of Wesley's.[49]

1. *J. A. Wood,* for example, a Methodist who seems to have believed, incorrectly, that he was simply teaching Wesley's doctrine, taught, with Clarke, only instantaneous sanctification—not gradual. In the 1861 edition of his *Perfect Love* he writes, "The beautiful analogy in the conditions and experience of regeneration and entire sanctification, favors the idea of an *instantaneous* sanctification similar to regeneration."[50] Since they are both received by faith, an instantaneousness applies to entire sanctification as obviously as to regeneration. Wood illustrates by saying that, even as "the soul does not leave the body by *parts*,"[51] so original sin does not become expelled in parts. In the same edition Wood says, "He who seeks the gradual attainment of entire sanctification seeks necessarily something *less* than entire sanctification *now*; that is, he does not seek entire sanctification at all."[52] Wood continues, "To seek a *gradual* purity renders the attainment

47. Adam Clarke, *Entire Sanctification* (Louisville, Ky.: Pentecostal Publishing Co., n.d.), 38.

48. Ibid.

49. The principal exception to this is Mildred Wynkoop. She understands that a crisis is involved. She writes, "The second 'moment' is a crucial, midpoint correction which 'locks' the compass to the Morning Star" (*A Theology of Love,* 347). She also says, "Whatever sin might be, salvation—to be worthy of God—would be the destruction of the seed of sin, here and now, where it is a reality" (153). She also writes, "Wesleyanism has been convinced that it is proper in some way to speak of second crisis in relation to sanctification" (338). Of sanctification she says, "It has in it elements of crisis and process" (306). Yet Wynkoop teaches, with Wesley, that sanctification is also a gradual process. She says, "Sanctification is the bringing into total integration about the will of God every element of the personality" (201). She also views sanctification as both "a cleansing and a discipleship" (306). This kind of sanctification would of necessity be gradual. She makes it really clear that it is gradual when she says, "Sanctification is the 'growing edge' of justification" (201).

50. J. A. Wood, *Perfect Love* (New York: Office of the Methodist Home Journal, 1861), 75.

51. Ibid., 76.

52. Ibid., 55.

of entire sanctification impossible. It does so because it excludes the conditions of entire sanctification. The faith which is the proximate condition of entire sanctification can only be exercised in connection with the *renunciation of all sin,* and *complete submission to God.*"[53]

In the 1880 revision of *Perfect Love,* he says, "The fact that inborn sin is a *unit,* an evil *principle* or taint infecting our nature, *and cannot be removed by parts,* any more than its antagonism, the principle of life in Christ can be imparted gradually in our regeneration, is evidence that sanctification is instantaneous."[54]

2. *Daniel Steele* supported the instantaneousness of entire sanctification, especially on the basis of the aorist tense, which he understood as denoting instantaneousness instead of completed action without regard to time. He writes:

> But when we come to consider the *work of purification* in the believer's soul, by the power of the Holy Spirit, both in the new birth and in entire sanctification, we find that *the aorist is almost uniformly used.* This tense, according to the best New Testament grammarians, never indicates a continuous, habitual, or repeated act, but one which is momentary, and done once for all.[55]

3. *C. W. Ruth* argued against gradual sanctification. He says, "To teach that the divine work of sanctification in the purifying and cleansing of the heart from all sin is a gradual work would be to admit that a heart might be a little holy, more holy and most holy, so that it might become exceedingly difficult to know just in what degree of holiness the individual experience might be located."[56]

4. *E. F. Walker.* Walker is as clear as any of the others about there being growth, but no gradual sanctification. He exegetes Jesus' prayer, "Sanctify them," as teaching that entire sanctification is instantaneous and not gradual.

> The word *sanctify* in the Greek text of John 17:17 is in the aorist tense and the imperative mood. This fact is conclusive that the work of sanctification for which Jesus prayed cannot be gradual, but must be instantaneous and

---

53. Ibid.
54. Wood, *Perfect Love,* rev. ed., 92.
55. Daniel Steele, *Milestone Papers* (New York: Eaton and Mains, 1878), 65-66.
56. C. W. Ruth, *Entire Sanctification* (Kansas City: Nazarene Publishing House, 1939), 17-18.

complete . . . The imperative mood with the aorist tense exhorts to do something or be something, at once and completely. The word *sanctify* is in the imperative mood and the aorist tense and signifies "instantly and completely sanctify." Jesus did not ask the Father to sanctify His disciples by a gradual process, but by an instantaneous act. If that prayer was ever answered, and we believe it was answered on the Day of Pentecost, the disciples were at once made holy. They could grow in grace before and after their sanctification, and no doubt they did. But suddenly, in the Upper Room, the sanctifying Spirit accomplished this work in them. And this is still the law of the Spirit of life in Christ Jesus: growth in holiness, but instant sanctification.[57]

He argues against gradual sanctification in an ingenious way by saying that it would make growth a necessary condition for the experience. He writes:

Is *growth* a condition? If it is, our sanctification would be dependent on the measure of our maturity in the Christian life. The Bible nowhere teaches that we are to attain this experience by gradual development. Certainly Christians must grow in holy stature, but they cannot grow out of nor outgrow sin. Sanctification is the work of God's free grace.[58]

5. *Thomas Cook,* in Britain, was also teaching against gradual sanctification and using arguments and analogies similar to those being used in the American Holiness Movement. Although he says, a bit misleadingly, "Holiness is both a *crisis* and a *process*,"[59] and quotes Bishop Moule as saying, "It is a crisis with a view to a process,"[60] he opposes gradual sanctification. He distinguishes between "purity" and "growth," noting that the one is negative and the other positive. He explains, "The soul can no more grow pure than the growth of a plant can kill or destroy the worm at its root."[61]

Even as there are no degrees in regeneration, there are none, for Cook, in entire sanctification. He writes, "There are no degrees of pardon: it is full, perfect, and complete." He continues, "In like manner, while the negative aspect of holiness is the purging of the heart from all that is carnal—and this is a full, complete

---

57. Walker, *Sanctify Them*, 55.
58. Ibid., 56.
59. Thomas Cook, *New Testament Holiness* (Salem, Ohio: Schmul Publishers, 1978), 43.
60. Ibid.
61. Ibid., 42.

and entire work, without degrees and gradualism—there is also a positive aspect of holiness."[62]

6. *S. S. White* emphasized entire sanctification's instantaneousness and opposed gradual sanctification. Since he treats it so thoroughly, his various supports for its punctiliar nature will be given.

a. He supports it from his own experience. He says, "The writer received this blessing at once. It took me time to meet the conditions; but when I did, God did the work immediately."[63]

b. The "growth theory as to entire sanctification," he says, "really means naturalism."[64] He feels that since it "is done directly by God himself,"[65] no gradualism is needed.

c. Since regeneration is instantaneous, as nearly all would agree, and both are "spiritual miracles," then the second work of grace is instantaneous even as the first is.[66]

d. The aorist tense is also significant for White. He says, "This tense would not have been used by the writer [he is especially thinking of John 17:17, "Sanctify them"] if his purpose had been to emphasize process or growth."[67]

e. He argues that since "inbred sin is a physical unit," it "cannot be removed in parts."[68] And he continues, "If removed at all, it must be removed all at once."[69]

f. One cannot grow "into grace," he says, "either the grace of regeneration or the grace of entire sanctification."[70] Yet he makes it clear that "there is growth leading up to and following each of these crisis experiences."[71]

In his *Eradication,* in which he supported even the use of this term as well as what it means, he writes, "Entire sanctification re-

---

62. Ibid., 46. Some things Cook says do not locate him necessarily in opposition to gradual sanctification. For example, he writes, "We do not mean instantaneous in the same sense as a flash of lightning, or an explosion of gunpowder, but in the sense in which death is instantaneous. 'A man may be a long time in dying, but there is a moment when he dies'" (ibid., 40).

63. Stephen S. White, *Five Cardinal Elements in the Doctrine of Entire Sanctification* (Kansas City: Beacon Hill Press, 1948), 29.

64. Ibid.
65. Ibid., 90.
66. Ibid.
67. Ibid., 27-28.
68. Ibid., 28.
69. Ibid.
70. Ibid., 31.
71. Ibid.

sults in an integration of personality which comes, not by growth or development, but rather by the eradication of the contrary principle of sin, with which every part of Adam's fallen race is afflicted."[72]

7. *H. Orton Wiley* understands that we receive initial sanctification at conversion. He writes, "Regeneration . . . is the impartation of a life that is holy in its nature; and concomitant with it, is an initial holiness or cleansing from guilt and acquired depravity."[73] Besides this initial sanctification, a believer may receive entire sanctification, but for Wiley there is no gradual sanctification. He says, "Now this holiness already begun [in initial sanctification] is to be perfected by the cleansing at a single stroke from inbred sin."[74]

8. *Richard S. Taylor* speaks of "progressive sanctification."[75] But this is only "the progressive establishment of one's Christian character."[76] He makes it clear that progressive sanctification is "not an increase of . . . essential holiness as far as purity . . . is concerned."[77] Elsewhere, speaking of the fact that Christians are to "grow in grace" (2 Pet. 3:18, KJV), he says, "This is intended to be a growth within holiness, not growth toward its attainment."[78] He explains that there is "a growth *in* holiness without such growth constituting a growth *of* holiness."[79] He says further, "In one sense only can we properly speak of developing in holiness. This relates to one's growth in love, when love is viewed as an element of holiness."[80]

9. *W. T. Purkiser* also sees the matter in this way. He says, "This puts the issue squarely before us. Entire sanctification, as understood by the holiness people, does not admit of degrees."[81]

---

72. White, *Eradication,* 74.

73. Wiley, *Christian Theology* 2:446.

74. Ibid.

75. Richard S. Taylor, *Preaching Holiness Today* (Kansas City: Beacon Hill Press of Kansas City, 1968), 55.

76. Ibid.

77. Ibid.

78. W. T. Purkiser, Richard S. Taylor, and Willard H. Taylor, *God, Man, and Salvation: A Biblical Theology* (Kansas City: Beacon Hill Press of Kansas City, 1977), 471. This volume's editor, J. Fred Parker, told the present writer that Richard S. Taylor wrote this part of the volume and that later editions would indicate who wrote what.

79. Ibid., 470.

80. Ibid., 472.

81. W. T. Purkiser, *Conflicting Concepts of Holiness* (Kansas City: Beacon Hill Press, 1953), 30-31.

He continues, "It is . . . perfect and complete in its kind."[82] "This does not mean," he explains, "that there is no growth in grace both before and after sanctification. What it does mean is that sanctification, as an act of God, is instantaneous, and is not produced by growth or self-discipline or a progressive control of the carnal nature."[83]

These treatments do not exhaust the significant Holiness Movement writers who have followed Clarke instead of Wesley in teaching that entire sanctification is instantaneous and not gradual. They are sufficient, though, to show that this occurred.

Receiving and Retaining the Experience

It is one thing to learn about entire sanctification—it is another to experience it.

God in His kindliness provides for this cleansing-empowerment, but He does not in overriding sovereignty bestow this, even as He does not unconditionally bestow the first work of grace. The main condition on our part for receiving both works of grace is faith. In the case of the first work of grace, it is faith preceded peculiarly by repentance; in the case of the second work, it is faith preceded peculiarly by consecration.

Palmer Method Flawed. Phoebe Palmer taught the Holiness Movement of the mid-19th century a three-step method of receiving entire sanctification that became widely accepted and is still used. The Palmer technique is (1) to put one's all on the altar, (2) to understand that Christ is the Altar, and (3) to understand that, since Scripture says that the altar sanctifies the gift, we are then sanctified wholly. Palmer based her method particularly on Matt. 23:19, KJV.

At least two important problems attach to this widely used Palmer technique.[84] For one thing, this approach tends toward urging faith in a Scripture passage instead of the personal and holy God who helped people write the Scriptures. With us Wesleyans, who believe in imparted righteousness, the important matter is that the "out there" of Scripture become the "in here" of

---

82. Ibid., 31.
83. Ibid.
84. See adverse appraisals in H. Ray Dunning, "Sanctification—Ceremony vs. Ethics," *The Preacher's Magazine,* Fall 1979, 10-12; Richard S. Taylor, *Exploring Christian Holiness,* vol. 3, 179-82; and Grider, *Entire Sanctification,* 116-17.

experience. We prayerfully guide believers toward the faith in God that occasions His bringing it about.

More important still, as an inadequacy of the Palmer method, is its misuse of Scripture. The passage she used is a quotation from Exod. 29:37; the KJV reads, "Seven days thou shalt make an atonement for the altar, and sanctify it; and it shall be an altar most holy: whatsoever toucheth the altar shall be holy." This obviously does not refer to believers being cleansed from sin; it refers to the setting apart for God's use of physical things and animals. Our RSV and NIV both show clearly that the New Testament quote from Exodus refers to that kind of sanctification, because they both say that it is "the altar that makes the gift sacred." If "sacred" is used, it is obvious that physical things or animals are referred to, for persons are never made "sacred."

"Steps" for Receiving Entire Sanctification. No technique can assure that we receive the experience. We receive entire sanctification when God bestows it, not when we have followed a prescribed technique for receiving it. However, methods or techniques that are biblically and theologically correct may still be applied usefully. Some steps for receiving entire sanctification will be given that might constitute in themselves a kind of technique.

1. *Understanding what is offered* is the earliest step. Since there are two types of sin, sin as committed act and sin as Adamic racial detriment, the economy of redemption includes two special stages in which the two types of sin are rectified: the acts are forgiven, and the state is cleansed away.

Although, in the Christian faith generally, the heart often precedes the mind, so that, as Augustine said, we "believe in order to know," considerable knowledge of the economy of God's grace is ideally a prerequisite of entire sanctification.

2. A second and somewhat similar step is to *prepare for receiving it.* For one thing, a person can read passages of Scripture that elucidate and urge the experience.[85]

Another way of preparing for entire sanctification is to read Holiness literature.[86]

---

85. See the section of this chapter titled "The Scriptural Basis," 381-85.

86. The writer's own book, *Entire Sanctification,* would naturally be advised. Others would include volumes 1 and 3 of *Exploring Christian Holiness*—the second volume, on the history of the doctrine, to be read perhaps later. Harry E. Jessop's *Foundations of Doctrine in Scripture and*

Still another important preparation is removal of hindrances to the experience. The writer's own special hindrance was an ambition to become a fiction author. It was only after that ambition was yielded to God that the experience was received by faith. Ambitions to do even what is entirely legitimate need to be yielded to God, because He might want to redirect the person slightly or greatly.

Another hindrance might have to do with economic matters. A person needs to be willing to live sacrificially, in self-denial.

Still another hindrance might be that one or more persons hold a too-sovereign place in the believer's life. God might expect us to break some personal ties and to strengthen other personal relationships.

A further hindrance might be the lack of felt need for the Adamic-sin purging. A believer in the glow of conversion may sense no need as yet for another special experience of redemptive grace. Many believers have found that only as time had passed, and life exigencies had arisen, was the need felt for cleansing from the state of Adamic depravity.

3. A third "step" in receiving entire sanctification is *consecration,* yielding ourselves to God to be used where, how, and with whom He wills. In consecration we make a "whole response" to God, donating ourselves as His children to His service. Paul urges such consecration in Rom. 12:1: "Therefore, I urge you, brothers, in view of God's mercy, to offer your bodies [selves] as living sacrifices, holy and pleasing to God—this is your spiritual act of worship." The Greek word for "offer," *paristēmi,* translated "present" in the KJV and RSV, is in the aorist tense. It refers to an all-at-once, completed presentation. We are thus to offer our "bodies," which probably means our total selves, including, for example, our talents and proficiencies, our ambitions, our possessions, our loved ones, our unknown future. The phrase "living sacrifices" means that we are to live out daily and yearly the sacrifice to God of all we are and all we might become.

Experience (Chicago: Chicago Evangelistic Institute, 1938) would also be useful, along with Samuel Logan Brengle's *Helps to Holiness* (London: Salvationist Publishing and Supplies, 1896), Charles Ewing Brown's *Meaning of Sanctification* (Anderson, Ind.: Warner Press, 1945), Stephen S. White's *Five Cardinal Elements in the Doctrine of Entire Sanctification,* and John Wesley's *Plain Account.*

4. *Faith* is the final and most crucial step in receiving entire sanctification. Actually, this is the one step that is always necessary, the others having only varying degrees of claim as steps in the receiving process.

That faith is what essentially occasions entire sanctification is suggested at least twice in Scripture. Peter, summing up Pentecost and Cornelius's Pentecost, says, "God, who knows the heart, showed that he accepted them by giving the Holy Spirit to them, just as he did to us. He made no distinction between us and them, for he purified their hearts by faith" (Acts 15:8-9). Later in Acts, Paul says that Christ called him to preach to the Gentiles "to open their eyes and turn them from darkness . . . so that they may receive forgiveness of sins and a place among those who are sanctified by faith in me" (26:18).[87]

The faith that procures entire sanctification is not instantaneous. It is true that many believers hear Holiness preaching, go forward to receive the second blessing, yield themselves to God, and by faith enter into entire sanctification—no trauma, no delay.

Others, however, pray but do not enter into the experience of entire sanctification. Sometimes they seek without fulfillment. They may be hindered by limited or incorrect understanding or incomplete consecration. They should not be urged to profess the experience, but to continue to seek until God effects it.

The faith that procures entire sanctification is durative. Faith is an expectant, plunging, obedient trust that, when God sees that we have met the conditions He sets, He will sanctify us wholly.

Exegesis supports the durative character of faith. Jesus said, "Truly . . . if you have faith, and do not doubt, you . . ." (Matt. 21:21, NASB). The word for "doubt" is in the aorist tense, meaning that one simply is not to doubt at all. The word for "faith" is a noun, which of course does not have tense. Yet its auxiliary, "have," does have tense, and its tense here is present. This is exegetical proof that faith can be durative—that faith is a state or condition that can last for an indefinite period of time.

The way in which "faith" is used in Scripture, in scores of passages, also suggests that it has duration. Jesus exhorted people

---

87. Manuscript evidence for another reference to faith as what procures the second work of grace is sufficient for it to be included in the NASB rendering of Rom. 5:2.

to "have faith in God" (Mark 11:22), which would have been continuous faith, because "have" is in the Greek present tense. Faith could "increase" (Luke 17:5). Stephen was "full of faith" (Acts 6:5). There is an "obedience that comes from faith" (Rom. 1:5). We can "walk in the footsteps of the faith" (4:12). It is something that can "remain" (*menei,* present tense), in a sustained way (1 Cor. 13:13).

This expectant, obedient trust, which might obtain for only an instant before entire sanctification, might also obtain for two minutes, or two days, or two weeks, or whatever. When God's conditions are met and He sanctifies us through and through, the faith that He will do this becomes transfigured into knowledge that He has. When it has happened, the Holy Spirit will confirm to us, probably then and there, that we have experienced what we have experienced.

The Witness of the Spirit

After we receive by faith the grace of entire sanctification, the Holy Spirit directly witnesses to us that the work has been accomplished. Some Holiness writers have suggested that this witness of the Spirit is often received at a later time. Beverly Carradine believed he received the witness three days following his entire sanctification. Samuel Logan Brengle believed that the witness of the Spirit was given to him two weeks after the time of his entire sanctification.

Since our experience needs to be interpreted, it is not necessarily presumptive to suggest that such persons might not be correct. Some type of direct witness of the Spirit is surely given at the time of our entire sanctification. How could something as significant as the baptism with the Holy Spirit and fire occur without our knowing about it? And why would the witness be withheld?

Acts 15:8-9 seems to suggest that, right on the heels of heart purification, the Holy Spirit bears witness to what has been accomplished. The RSV reads, "And God who knows the heart bore witness to them, giving them the Holy Spirit just as he did to us"—and the NASB and NIV also have "giving." The word for "giving" here is *dous,* an aorist participle from *didōmi,* and can be translated "having given." The use of an aorist participle, plus the way the passage reads, seems to suggest that this witness of the Spirit was received immediately after they had been given the Spirit in this way.

Such an immediate witness seems also to be implied when Paul says, "Now we have received, not the spirit of the world, but the Spirit who is from God, that we might know the things freely given to us by God" (1 Cor. 2:12, NASB). To have "received . . . the Spirit" might be a reference to Christ's Spirit baptism. And here, the Spirit helps us "know the things freely given to us by God," which would include entire sanctification. And it seems that He helps us know it just after it occurs—no delay being suggested.

The writer of Hebrews teaches the witness of the Spirit to entire sanctification—perhaps even to its immediacy. He writes, "For by one offering He has perfected for all time those who are sanctified. And the Holy Spirit also bears witness to us" (10:14-15, NASB).

The numerous "we knows" in 1 John are also significantly supportive, particularly where we read, "And we know by this that He abides in us, by the Spirit whom He has given us" (3:24, NASB). Again, nothing is said about any delay in this witness.

John Wesley emphasized the witness of the Spirit to both justification and entire sanctification. Wesley wrote sermons on it, and he treated it in his *Plain Account* and in letters and otherwise. He urged that believers expect the witness of the Spirit to follow entire sanctification immediately. In a letter in 1757 he wrote, "One fruit [of Christian perfection] given at the same instant (at least usually) is a direct, positive testimony of the Spirit that the work is done."[88]

Wesley taught that besides the direct witness of the Spirit to our hearts, there is an indirect witness from the "fruits" of our life. But the direct witness is primary. He said we should not "rest in any supposed fruit of the Spirit," but seek entire sanctification, and keep on seeking, until the Holy Spirit has witnessed of the grace in our hearts.[89]

Wesley also taught, as has been usual in the Holiness Movement, that the witness of the Spirit, as a direct impression upon our consciousness, might wax and wane. Yet he said that as we

---

88. John Wesley, *The Letters of the Rev. John Wesley,* ed. John Telford (London: Epworth Press, 1941), 3:213.
89. See Wesley, *Works* 5:133-34.

mature to where we are "fathers in Christ," we are likely to experience the consciousness with less fluctuation.

Retaining Entire Sanctification

Wesleyans believe that even those who are sanctified wholly can fall from God's redeeming grace through willful sin. Nevertheless, entire sanctification, as the "establishing grace," makes it much more likely that we will retain our spiritual condition. Original sin inclines one away from God, so a believer is better enabled to live the Christian life once Adamic depravity has been destroyed.

Establishment in grace through entire sanctification is taught in Scripture, a prime passage being 1 Thess. 3:10-13—as noted earlier. There Paul, writing to Christian believers, says: "Now may our God and Father . . . direct our way to you . . . so that He may establish your hearts unblamable in holiness before our God" (vv. 11, 13, NASB). "Establish" translates *stērixai*, aorist in tense, which suggests a completed, nongradual establishment. If a gradual establishment had been the intended meaning, the present tense would have been used.

Other verbs that surround this one, and that have to do with the same matter, are also aorist tense. The "complete" of NASB ("supply," RSV; "perfect," KJV) in 3:10 is aorist, as are "increase" and "abound" (KJV) in 3:11-12. Paul hopes for a special completed step-up in their love, not a gradual step-up in it.

Supportive of the establishing effect of holiness is Rom. 5:1-2—as also mentioned earlier: "Having been justified by faith, we have peace with God through our Lord Jesus Christ, through whom also we have obtained our introduction [admission] by faith into this grace in which we stand" (NASB). While the "also" and the second "by faith" are not in some of the oldest Greek manuscripts, their inclusion makes good sense context-wise; and they are found in some of the respected manuscripts. This passage seems to speak of a benefit beyond justification, in which one is established.

Peter's experience is also supportive of the baptism with the Holy Spirit as the establishing grace. Prior to his Pentecost, Peter denied Christ. The story of his failure is a familiar one (see John 18:17, 25-27).

After Pentecost had cleansed and empowered him (Acts 2:1-4; 15:8-9; 1:8), Peter is Christ's fearless disciple. Although jailed, beaten, and finally martyred (according to tradition), Peter stood straight up and spoke for Christ with holy boldness.

The leading writers of the Holiness Movement have given extensive treatment to the matter of this "establishing grace," for they have considered this to be one of the key results of entire sanctification in the life of the individual. For once original sin, the Adamic propensity to acts of sin, is expelled, a person is measurably helped toward becoming an established Christian. Thomas Cook said that while "absolute security does not belong to this world," still, "holiness secures the safest possible condition on earth."[90]

Asa Mahan declared that *"permanence and power* are the leading characteristics" of the baptism with the Holy Spirit.[91]

J. A. Wood, in his widely circulated *Perfect Love* (1880 edition), said: "In order to retain justification we have to live *obediently,* and that can be done more easily with a pure heart [through entire sanctification] than with an impure one. All things considered, the easiest religious life is the fullest and least obstructed religious life."[92]

Not long afterward, in 1905, C. W. Ruth wrote about Holiness experience that "while the possibility of backsliding is not removed, the liability of backsliding is reduced to a minimum."[93]

Although entire sanctification is properly understood as the establishing grace, it can be lost—and the first work of grace can be lost as well. Thus the need for taking advantage of the formal and informal means of grace—to assure a person's flowering and bearing fruit and thus being "saved" finally by standing "firm to the end" (Mark 13:13).

Carnality and Humanity

Distinguishing between carnality and humanity in attitudes and acts has been an important issue among Holiness people.

---

90. Cook, *New Testament Holiness,* 16.
91. Asa Mahan, *The Baptism of the Holy Ghost* (New York: W. C. Palmer, Publisher, 1882), 30.
92. Wood, *Perfect Love,* rev. ed., 130.
93. C. W. Ruth, *Bible Readings on the Second Blessing* (Salem, Mass.: Convention Book Store, 1905), 61.

While no one would presume to understand fully what carnality is, in distinction from what is essentially human and from the acquired aberrations of the human, some observations about what it does and does not consist of will be made.

Constituents of Carnality. Carnality is not necessarily evidenced by a hostility, or an anger, or nervousness, in which a person might become red-cheeked and lacking in interpersonal equilibrium. Such reaction might stem from natural temperament. It might stem from righteous anger, as when Jesus "looked around at them [compassionless men] with anger" (Mark 3:5, RSV). It might arise from resentment toward a parent or a fellow church member due to aberrating experiences in one's early life. It might arise from nervousness due to a physical or emotional problem. It is only the detriment due to Adam's bad representation of us that we are cleansed from when original sin is expelled at the time of our entire sanctification. Wesley felt, incorrectly, that the change at our entire sanctification is "immensely greater than that wrought when he [anyone] was justified."[94] As significant as cleansing from carnality is, it does not remove what is essentially human, such as temperament, the sex drive, and the deficiencies that we come by during this life (for example, prejudices).

Carnality is not in itself culpable. Because of an unconditional benefit of the Atonement, the "free gift" referred to in Rom. 5:15-17 (KJV), which was given to all, the guilt of Adam's sin has been waived—although the depravity itself, the bias to sin, is cleansed away only when believers are baptized with the Holy Spirit. In support of this view, H. Orton Wiley says, "Thus the condemnation which rested upon the race through Adam's sin is removed by the one oblation of Christ. By this we understand that no child of Adam is condemned eternally, either for the original offense, or its consequences. Thus . . . culpability does not attach to original sin."[95]

Carnality is being referred to here as the sin that remains in the believer after justification—the state of sin that inclines the believer

---

94. Wesley, *A Plain Account,* 61. I question Wesley at this point, because to be justified changes our eternal destiny, and because at this time we pass from death to life, and because we are then made children of God by adoption. Even the power over us of inbred sin, i.e., the enslavement to inbred sin, is broken at justification. In entire sanctification original sin is itself extirpated.

95. Wiley, *Christian Theology* 2:135.

to acts of sin (but does not cause them). It is not to be thought of as a physical substance, of course, but as a state that is relational—in which, being deprived of special helps of the Holy Spirit, we become estranged from God and biased toward acts of sin.

Although "carnality" might suggest to some that it is simply that aspect of the Adamic detriment that relates to the body, the word is used in Scripture to include the entire detriment we have received from the racial fall in Adam. Thus Paul termed "carnal" those Corinthian Christians who were filled with envy and strife and who were divided into factions (1 Cor. 3:3, KJV).

While the word for "carnal" is a cognate of *sarx,* and while *sarx* has many meanings, including the body, it is often used, particularly by Paul, in an ethical sense as the opposite of being in the Spirit. Thus we read in Kittel, "For Paul, orientation to the *pneuma* or the *sarx* is the total attitude which determines everything . . . Life is determined as a totality by *sarx* or *pneuma.*"[96] Those who are "in the flesh" cannot please God (Rom. 8:8); but those who are "in the Spirit" (v. 9) can, it is implied. One might live "according to the flesh" (v. 13); and yet, they that "belong to Christ," who are truly Christ's, "have crucified the flesh" (Gal. 5:24, all NASB).

John Wesley referred to carnality by many terms. He called it "pride, self-will, unbelief."[97] Particularly as it indwells believers, he called it a "bent to backsliding," "sin in a believer," "a proneness to depart from God."[98]

In the unbeliever, carnality is a total corruption of our nature—a total depravity, arising from being deprived through Adam's fall of certain ministries of the Holy Spirit.[99] Some Wesleyan theologians have taught that only the moral nature of man, and not the rational nature or the physical nature, suffered due to the Fall. Some have approached Pelagianism in ascribing the pos-

---

96. Schweizer, TDNT 7:135.

97. John Wesley, "On Sin in Believers," in *Four Sermons by Wesley* (London: Wesleyan Methodist Book Room, n.d.), 13.

98. Ibid.

99. Believers have the Holy Spirit indwelling them, according to Gal. 5:17, along with the *sarx;* but the unbeliever, apart from prevenient grace, is dead to God, due to carnality. Original sin is not even partly cleansed at regeneration, and yet its effects in a believer are not as great as in the unbeliever.

sibility of free choice and good deeds to us apart from grace.[100] In this they have departed from Paul, Arminius, and Wesley.[101]

The Human and Its Aberrations. One whole set of deficiencies we come by during this life, not nullified when the carnal mind is expelled at the time of our entire sanctification, is prejudices.

Take racial prejudice. It is not inherited from Adam; we do not enter the world with it. We acquire it from our environment.

The apostle Peter was prejudiced against Gentiles, and it obtained well after the time of his entire sanctification at Pentecost, as his initial reluctance to visit Cornelius demonstrated (see Acts 10). It required a special revelatory vision to convince him that he "should not call any man unholy or unclean" (Acts 10:28, NASB), and that "God is not one to show partiality, but in every nation the man who fears Him and does what is right, is welcome to Him" (vv. 34-35, NASB).

Even this special revelation did not assure that Peter would conduct his life consistently under social pressures. He was still subject to an intimidating desire simply to please people. That is why, more than 14 years after ministering to Cornelius, Paul needed to help him. Paul says, "But when Cephas came to Antioch I opposed him to his face, because he stood condemned. For before certain men came from James, he ate with the Gentiles; but when they came he drew back and separated himself, fearing the circumcision party" (Gal. 2:11-12, RSV). And Paul adds, "I said to Cephas before them all, 'If you, though a Jew, live like a Gentile and not like a Jew, how can you compel the Gentiles to live like Jews?'" (v. 14, RSV).

If Peter's Pentecost did not rout his prejudice against Gentiles, nor his too-great desire to please people, we may suppose that our Pentecost will not nullify such matters either. Prejudices against races, classes, and genders do not automatically vanish when one is sanctified wholly. They will be corrected under the continuing tutelage of the Holy Spirit.

Even homosexuality, as a tendency, will not always be extirpated when we are converted or when we are sanctified wholly. It might be a learned trait. Even if it is helped along by a congenital

---

100. For example, Hills, *Fundamental Christian Theology* 1:356-64; White, *Essential Christian Beliefs*, 27-32.
101. See the discussion of original sin in chapter 10.

trait, it obtains pronouncedly only in a small percentage of persons—a study released in 1993 suggesting a figure close to 2 percent, instead of about 10 percent, as an earlier study suggested.[102] It cannot be a characteristic of carnality, else all persons would experience it. When carnality is extirpated, therefore, homosexuality as a tendency might or might not be corrected. God might choose to work this special kind of miracle on behalf of a person even as He might extirpate the tendency toward drug use at the time of one's entire sanctification. But to be changed to a heterosexual, so that there would be no more propensity toward a same-gender person than a heterosexual person feels, does not necessarily happen at one's conversion or at one's entire sanctification. Again, the individual is enabled by the Holy Spirit's indwelling fullness to order life as God directs.

Among human aberrations that cannot be treated in detail here are the inclination toward tobacco, alcohol, and other drugs. They are acquired desires and are not necessarily extirpated when one is converted or when Adamic depravity is expelled. If such desires remain after initial sanctification, or even after entire sanctification, we are enabled not to implement the desires. We would be enabled not to use tobacco, alcohol, or other drugs, but they might not be revolting to a person who has had the habits in the way they are likely to be to others.

Entire sanctification is a sanctification, a cleansing, that is entire. No carnality, or original sin, remains to deprave our faculties, to incline us to acts of sin. Carnality has infected, as a fever does, our entire nature, including the body and the reason and the will and the emotions, and carnality is entirely extirpated. This state or condition of a bias, a leaning toward the life of sin, is crucified, destroyed, expelled (a term Wesley liked). Even so, entire sanctification is not a panacea; it does not necessarily right the derangements due to aberrating experiences that have happened during this life. Besides, there are numerous other psychological and physical and social problems that are not corrected when entire sanctification occurs—although we then have the help of the pervasive indwelling of the Holy Spirit in a growth in

---

102. Some authoritative opinion estimates it, however, as high as 10 to 15 percent. See Norman Pittenger, "A Theological Approach to Understanding Homosexuality," *Religion in Life* 43 (Winter 1974): 441.

grace through which there can be a gradual lessening of these problems. Only glorification will extirpate them completely; and even then, we will not be gods.

Concluding Observations. What ought Wesleyan-holiness people to believe, then, about carnality and humanity—including the acquired human aberrations such as prejudices? We ought to differentiate between carnality and humanity better than sometimes we have done. By carnality we ought to mean original sin, and we ought to understand that it consists of a depravity affecting all the aspects of human nature: reason, will, emotions, the body.

Further, we ought to place in the human area whatever is essential to human nature as such—for example, the sex drive, the desire to be appreciated, the desire for self-protection, the various kinds of temperament. The carnal infection of them is cleansed away at our entire sanctification, but they remain.

In entire sanctification we are cleansed from whatever spiritual detriment we enter the world with. But we are not necessarily cleansed from learned or otherwise acquired mental or emotional or physical aberrations. The Holy Spirit, after our entire sanctification, indwells us pervasively, that is, not hindered by indwelling sin (see Rom. 5:2-5). And He helps us not to disobey God willfully due to any of these aberrations, and more and more to become liberated from them—until glorification, when the liberation will become complete.

Entire Sanctification and Tongues

The Wesleyan-Holiness Movement spawned the modern tongues-speaking movement. Yet it is perhaps the least sympathetic to tongues-speaking of any of the major groupings of Christianity. There are several bases for this lack of sympathy.

It Twists the Emphasis. The main emphasis of the tongues people is the baptism in or with the Holy Spirit, but they twist that main emphasis. They do not teach that it occasions the cleansing away of original sin. To them it is a second work of grace, but not an entire sanctification. It is an empowerment evidenced by tongues-speaking.

The neo-Pentecostals, also called the charismatics, twist the emphasis similarly, denying that the baptism with the Holy Spirit cleanses away original sin. And with them, the various gifts of the Spirit are emphasized as resulting from this baptism—tongues being less important in relation to the other gifts than obtains in Pentecostalism as such.[103]

It Undermines the Bible's Significance. We already have a body of written-down revelation through prophets and apostles. It is authoritative, dependable, adequate, quite understandable. We can go to Holy Scripture and find encouragement, instruction, whatever. The messages given in tongues meetings, when the syllables are "interpreted," no doubt often by well-meaning Christians, are usually positive and beautiful and uplifting in themselves. But we can also find such messages in our Holy Bibles, and they are given to us through prophets and apostles who were authoritatively inspired in ways that no one today is or needs to be inspired. The Holy Spirit anoints Christ's spokespersons to elucidate Scripture; but there is no need for direct, postapostolic, word-for-word revelation—as to a gathered congregation. And if God were to elect to give that kind of revelation, it would undermine the place of and the authority of Scripture.

It Overstresses the Miraculous. In the tongues-speaking movement we also have an overemphasis on the miraculous. It teaches that a miracle occurs whereby we are given a divine and heavenly language; and another miracle in which the meaning of what is said in that heavenly language in interpreted.

But our faith is rooted in the soil of a particular history that the four Gospels and Acts narrate and the Epistles interpret. Jesus ridiculed the Pharisees who were constantly seeking a sign—that is, a miracle. Jesus said, "A wicked and adulterous generation asks ["craves," NASB] for a miraculous sign! But none will be given it except the sign of the prophet Jonah. For as Jonah was three days and three nights in the belly of a huge fish, so the Son of Man will be three days and three nights in the heart of the earth" (Matt. 12:39-40). Jesus is saying that the special miracle soon to occur is His resurrection from the dead. On that stupendous miracle we base our Christian faith.

---

103. Another rather important difference between the neo-Pentecostals and the Pentecostals is the matter of ecstasy. The Pentecostals traditionally praised God repeatedly until a state of ecstasy was reached, in which there was tongues-speaking. This is what has often been called ecstatic utterance. The neo-Pentecostals need no such ecstasy. They might come into a house, their hearts palpitating from playing a game, sit down at a table, and simply elect to say grace in tongues instead of in their regular language.

Miracles still happen. But mature Christians base their faith on the supernatural events by which Jesus Christ entered and exited this world. We who believe in the Incarnation and Resurrection do not require miracles ever and anon as somehow further substantiating our faith. Some of us suspect that such interest in the miraculous will detract from the miracles on which our faith is founded.

It Tends to Undermine Faith. If something as overt as speaking in unintelligible syllables were either the evidence of being baptized with the Spirit, or a gift of the Spirit, we could have overt, observable, audible evidence of our acceptance with God and of being baptized with the Spirit. We would not need obedient trust for our justification and our entire sanctification. We would have a kind of scientifically observable proof of being justified before God and of being Spirit baptized—very different from the inward witness of the Spirit. Give faith such legs to stand on, and it is hardly faith anymore.

It Satisfies People as a Substitute. One important reason why earnest Christians find tongues-speaking satisfying is because it serves the same psychologically satisfying purpose that the mantra serves in the oriental-type error of transcendental meditation. The mantra is a secret Sanskrit word that in itself does not mean anything to the devotee. When Christians allow themselves to say meaningless syllables, it helps them see that they are indeed willing, as Paul says he was, to be "fools for Christ's sake" (1 Cor. 4:10, NASB). That very willingness is no doubt why well-meaning Christians say that they find tongues-speaking to be satisfying. Many of us would rather do some other kind of unworldly thing, with inward satisfaction as a by-product—such as doing love deeds for which we are not remunerated or honored.

It Is Not in Agreement with Scripture. The main reason the Holiness Movement has never been sympathetic toward the tongues-speaking of the earlier Pentecostalism or of the more recent neo-Pentecostalism is because it is not in agreement with what the Bible teaches.

As a starter, it would seem strange that a curse for the pride of those "tower of Babel" builders (Gen. 11:1 ff.) was to confuse their languages if indeed God was going to own and use unintelligible syllables as a gift of the Holy Spirit in New Testament times. Actually, God seems to be interested in communicating His will, instead of disguising it—else why did the people at Pentecost from numerous language areas hear sermons in their own languages (see Acts 2)?

Insofar as tongues is a gift (1 Corinthians 12—14), several things suggest that this gift is God's help in the use of real languages. For one thing, the gift is to be exercised in the church only if someone who can interpret is present (see 1 Cor. 14:27-28). If it is some kind of miraculous, heavenly language, how could one be confident before speaking in a language of that sort that someone was present who could interpret its meaning? On the other hand, assuming that it is a real language, one could be confident ahead of time that an interpreter was present. Supposing, in a cosmopolitan center such as Corinth was, a person could not speak in the Greek that most of the congregation understood, but could speak Latin, and someone was present who could translate Latin into Greek. Both his speaking in that learned tongue, and a Greek-speaking person's ability to interpret it, could well be called "gifts," even though they were not miraculously given out of the blue.

In keeping with this, the Holy Spirit is often portrayed in Scripture as One who makes things plain, not as one who authors unintelligibilities. He guides us "into all truth" (John 16:13), especially as it is related to Christ (14:26; 16:13). He takes the difficult-to-understand things and makes them clear (John 16:14-29). He gives Christ's spokespersons clear and helpful things to say to people. He helps us interpret the meaning of Scripture (2 Pet. 1:19-21). Indeed, if tongues as a gift has to do with unintelligible syllables, the Holy Spirit would be opposing himself. He would be opposing the gifts He gives to other persons, or to the same persons, especially His help for prophesying and teaching.

Paul seems to consider "tongues" a problem; and it is only a problem at one church—his problem church at Corinth. And he speaks deprecatingly of it, saying, "I desire to speak five words with my mind, that I may instruct others also, rather than ten thousand words in a tongue" (1 Cor. 14:19, NASB).

When he says, "I thank God, I speak in tongues more than you all" (v. 18, NASB), he is simply speaking diplomatically (see 10:33). He was not saying he spoke more often in the unintelligible syllables that they resorted to. He was using tact, and saying that through his ability to speak several known languages he was speaking more often in these than they were in unintelligible syllables. His use of these other learned languages seems to have been outside the church, perhaps in talking with individuals in the cities he went to. He implies this when he says, "I speak in tongues more than you all; however, in the church I desire to speak five words with my mind [sensibly, using their language] . . . , rather than ten thousand words in a tongue" (14:18-19, NASB).

The Bible declares that love is far more important than even the best of spiritual gifts, and Scripture's emphasis is placed on Christian love (1 Cor. 12:31—13:13).

These, then, are several bases for the Holiness Movement's lack of sympathy for that admittedly interesting and divisive 20th-century phenomenon of both ecstatic and nonfrenzied (in neo-Pentecostalism) tongues-speaking.

In the main, surely, people who are part of that movement are well-meaning Christians. And they are often people whose faith is not simply a marginal matter, but meaningful to them. Their great growth is no doubt largely due to their desire to serve God utterly, to their appeal in great part to ordinary people, and to their encouragement of emotional, and even physical and audible, individual expression in worship services.

One aspect of the doctrine of entire sanctification, barely touched in this chapter, is the baptism with the Holy Spirit. We turn now to a study of this and devote to it an entire chapter, partly because this aspect of the doctrine has been a center of controversy in recent years.

16

The Second Work of Grace: Christ's Spirit Baptism

Denominations and parachurch organizations in the Wesleyan-Holiness Movement understand that entire sanctification is received through the baptism with the Holy Spirit.

The international Christian Holiness Association teaches: "Entire sanctification is a crisis experience subsequent to conversion which results in a heart cleansed from all sin and filled [a synonym of "baptized"] with the Holy Spirit." The Wesleyan Theological Society similarly teaches that besides "the new birth" there is "a subsequent work of God in the soul, a crisis, wrought by faith, whereby the heart is cleansed from all sin and filled [baptized, see Matt. 3:11; Acts 1:4-5; 2:4] with the Holy Spirit."[1]

That entire sanctification is effected by Christ's baptism with the Holy Spirit is the teaching of both the Eastern and the Western fathers of the early centuries of our Christian era. This is shown by the significant research of Paul M. Bassett.[2] The Bassett research shows more carefully than any previous work that the fathers in general, of both the Greek-writing East and the Latin-writing West, taught that entire sanctification is received through the baptism with the Holy Spirit.

The usual teaching in Calvinism is that the baptism with the Holy Spirit occurs at the time of our justification, and John Wesley's own teaching was of this type. James Dunn's position will now be treated as a typical Calvinistic one, followed by the simi-

---

1. See A. F. Harper, ed., *Holiness Teaching Today,* vol. 6 of *Great Holiness Classics* (Kansas City: Beacon Hill Press of Kansas City, 1987), 391-402, for a listing of the official teachings of these and 14 other English-speaking Holiness bodies.
2. *The Historical Development,* vol. 2 of *Exploring Christian Holiness,* 1-108.

lar view of Robert Lyon, a Wesleyan-holiness scholar. This will be followed by a treatment of John Wesley's view, then by the teaching of the American Holiness Movement. Finally it will be shown that the Holiness Movement teaching is the scriptural one.

The Calvinistic View of Dunn

Two rather recent books by Calvinist scholars take the view that Pentecost is initiatory—that it effects what Wesleyans would call the first work of grace. Frederick Dale Bruner's *Theology of the Holy Spirit* says: "The apostles considered Pentecost to be . . . the date of their conversion."[3] The other important book that argues for this view is James D. G. Dunn's *Baptism in the Holy Spirit.*[4] It argues for associating Pentecost with regeneration—not with a second work of grace.

Dunn's General Conclusions. Dunn says that John's Gospel is the area of Scripture most employed for the subsequent-to-regeneration view of Pentecost. He even says, "The author of the Fourth Gospel may have believed that the apostles' Spirit-baptism was distinct from and subsequent to their regeneration."[5]

While Dunn also admits that John 3:5, which has to do with water baptism, might support viewing Pentecost as a second work of grace,[6] he himself views Pentecost as occasioning conversion. He says that "it was only at Pentecost that the 120 became Christians."[7] He further says, "To become a Christian, in short, is to receive the Spirit of Christ, the Holy Spirit. What the Pentecostal [and the Holiness interpreter] attempts to separate into two works of God is in fact one single divine act."[8]

As Dunn views the matter, Pentecost, not the Incarnation nor the death and resurrection of Christ, begins the new dispensation. He writes:

---

3. Bruner, *A Theology of the Holy Spirit,* 195.
4. James D. G. Dunn, *Baptism in the Holy Spirit* (Louisville, Ky.: Westminster/John Knox Press and London: SCM Press, Ltd., 1970).
5. Ibid., 195. Reproduced from *Baptism in the Holy Spirit,* by James D. G. Dunn. Copyright 1970, SCM Press, published in the U.S.A. by The Westminster Press. Used by permission of Westminster/John Knox Press. In the same work Dunn writes, "For the Pentecostal [and the Holiness person] the Fourth Gospel is especially important since it shows him clearly that the disciples were regenerate before Pentecost and had received the Spirit before Pentecost."
6. Ibid., 204.
7. Ibid., 53.
8. Ibid., 96.

Certainly for the first Christians the gift of the Spirit was *the* decisive difference which marked off the old dispensation from the new (Mark 1:8; John 7:39; Acts 2:17, 33; 19:2; Romans 8:9; 2 Corinthians 3:3, 6-8; Hebrews 6:4f). The "last days" did not begin for the disciples till Pentecost (Acts 2:17). Only then did they enter into the distinctively Christian dispensation and into the distinctively Christian experience of the Spirit.[9]

Dunn's View as It Relates to Paul. While we of the Holiness Movement usually understand that Paul was converted on the Damascus road and filled or baptized with the Holy Spirit three days later in Damascus, Dunn understands that Paul's conversion was at the later time: "Paul's conversion was only completed when he called on Jesus as Lord, was filled with the Spirit and had his sins washed away; then, and only then, can he be called a Christian."[10]

Dunn feels, also, that Acts 22:16 shows that Paul was not converted on the Damascus road, but later, when Ananias visited him. Yet surely it means that Paul should be baptized to symbolize and dramatize and give testimony to the washing away of his sins that had occurred three days earlier. Dunn views it differently: "In Ananias' eyes Paul had yet to take that step which would clinch his committal and forgiveness. We have no record whatsoever of Paul taking the decisive step *prior* to his baptism; but we do have Ananias exhorting him to take that step—to have his sins washed away by calling on the name of the Lord Jesus (cf. 2:21; 9:14, 21, also Romans 10:13, 14)."[11]

Dunn on Cornelius. While I understand that Cornelius was already converted when Peter went to him, and before "the Holy Spirit fell upon all those who were listening to the message" (Acts 10:44, NASB), Dunn says that Cornelius was converted only when "the Holy Spirit had been poured out" (v. 45, NASB). Dunn writes, "Here at least, therefore, the baptism in the Spirit is God's act of acceptance, of forgiveness, cleansing and salvation, and not something separate from and beyond that which made Cornelius a Christian."[12]

---

9. Ibid., 46-47.
10. Ibid., 78.
11. Ibid.
12. Ibid., 82.

Dunn on the Samaritans. Since Dunn believes that "it is God's giving of the Spirit which makes a man a Christian, and, in the last analysis, nothing else,"[13] he has a special problem in interpreting what happened to the people at Samaria according to the Acts 8 record. Luke tells us that after Philip had proclaimed "Christ to them" (v. 5, all NASB), they "believed" and were "baptized" (v. 12). Word of this got back to Jerusalem, and "Peter and John" (v. 14) "came down and prayed for them, that they might receive the Holy Spirit" (v. 15). The apostles "began laying their hands on them, and they were receiving the Holy Spirit" (v. 17).

Dunn calls this a "riddle" but insists there were no conversions at Samaria before Peter and John got there and the people were baptized with the Spirit. He says, "The New Testament way is rather to say: Because the Spirit has not been given therefore the conditions have not been met [for conversion]. This is why Luke puts so much emphasis on the Samaritans' reception of the Spirit . . . (vv. 15-20)."[14]

Dunn struggles here and winds up suggesting, simply, that the Samaritans' "commitment was defective," and they were not converted until after the arrival of the apostles. He writes:

> Were the Samaritans Christians before Peter and John arrived? Philip's preaching seems to have been no different from that recorded elsewhere in Acts. The Samaritans' response seems to have been entirely satisfactory. And their baptism was fully Christian. However, there are a number of reasons for believing not only that their response and commitment was defective, but also that Luke intended his readers to know this.[15]

Dunn on the Ephesians. Again, whereas the "disciples" (Acts 19:1) at Ephesus, who had "believed" (v. 2), were surely Christians when Paul visited them, and that "the Holy Spirit came on them" (v. 6) then as a second work of grace—Dunn views it differently. He says, "The twelve Ephesians are therefore further examples of men who were not far short of Christianity, but were not yet Christians because they lacked the vital factor—the Holy Spirit."[16]

---

13. Ibid., 68.
14. Ibid.
15. Ibid.
16. Ibid., 88.

Dunn is forced to say: "It is true that in Acts *mathētai* usually equals 'Christians,' but the 19:1 usage is unique."[17] And according to Dunn, the aorist participle, *pisteusantes*, translated "since ye believed" (KJV) or "when you believed" (NASB, etc.), is not here used to express action that takes place prior in time to the action of the main verb. He calls it "a coincident aorist"[18]—expressing action that takes place at the same time as the action of the main verb, which is "receive." Why a coincident aorist? Because, for Dunn, "it is Paul's doctrine that a man receives the Spirit *when* he believes."[19] Here, obviously, theology determines exegesis.

The Wesley-Type View of Lyon

An article by Robert Lyon, titled "Baptism and Spirit Baptism in the New Testament,"[20] takes a position basically identical to that of James Dunn: that the Acts baptisms with the Holy Spirit occasion the first work of grace, and not the second. (Lyon believes in two works of grace as John Wesley did.)

Lyon on the Samaritan Experience. Lyon says that when the Samaritans "received" the Holy Spirit after Peter and John had gone to them, it was "the culmination of their conversion."[21] While he admits that this is "by all accounts the stickiest of all" the Acts narratives, he finally says, "One thing, however, is quite certain, viz., that when . . . they 'received' the Holy Spirit, it was their first experience of the Spirit and cannot be counted as a second experience."[22]

Lyon on Paul's Conversion. Again, Lyon says that "the visit of Ananias to Paul represents the culmination of the latter's conversion, at which time he is filled with the Spirit, that is, he received the Spirit."[23] On the time of Paul's conversion, Lyon is in agreement with James Dunn, and also with John Wesley.[24]

Lyon on Cornelius. Still further, Lyon understands that Cornelius was not converted until the Holy Spirit "fell" upon him

---

17. Ibid., 84.
18. Ibid., 87.
19. Ibid.
20. WTJ 14, no. 1 (Spring 1979): 14-26.
21. Ibid., 19.
22. Ibid.
23. Ibid.
24. See Wesley's *Explanatory Notes* on Acts 9:9.

and the others (Acts 11:15, NASB). He shows that the three verbs used to describe what happened to Cornelius, "fall upon," "pour out," and "receive," are equivalent expressions, and that the latter two of them "were used earlier of the Pentecost event."[25] Lyon goes on to say of this and other evidence: "This clearly equates the experience of Cornelius with what occurred at Pentecost. And it was most certainly the conversion of Cornelius and his incorporation into the body of Christ. . . . It is the account of a beginning, not a second blessing."[26]

Lyon on the Ephesians. Lyon understands, also, that the Ephesians were converted when, under Paul's help, "the Holy Spirit came on them" (Acts 19:6). There are "problems" here, he admits, for these men were already called "disciples" and had already "believed." He writes, "While certainly not free of ambiguities, what we seem to have here is an account of the conversion of disciples of John the Baptist (or of a similar 'preparation type movement') who had been prepared [earlier] for the gospel."[27]

John Wesley's View

John Wesley taught that the baptism with the Holy Spirit occurs at the time of our justification.[28]

Historian Timothy L. Smith, however, seeks to show that Wesley understood instead that the baptism with the Holy Spirit occasions entire sanctification. Smith's views appear in two articles: one in the *Wesleyan Theological Journal*, "How John Fletcher Became the Theologian of Wesleyan Perfectionism 1770-1776";[29] and the other in the *Preacher's Magazine*, "The Doctrine of the Sanctifying Spirit in John Wesley and John Fletcher."[30]

---

25. Lyon, WTJ, 20.
26. Ibid.
27. Ibid.
28. Leo Cox says, "This teaching of Wesley may appear strange to some who insist that the Holy Spirit is given subsequent to regeneration at the time of a 'second blessing,' but in this concept Wesley is at one with most Reformed teaching." *John Wesley's Concept of Perfection* (Kansas City: Beacon Hill Press, 1964), 122.
29. WTJ 15, no. 1 (Spring 1980): 68-87.
30. This *Preacher's Magazine* article disregards the negative evidence in Wesley's comments on Acts in his *Explanatory Notes upon the New Testament.* Smith writes, "That the language of Pentecost remained in the forefront of their [John and Charles Wesley's] thinking about sanctification, despite the interpretation of the passages concerning the outpouring of the Spirit in the Book of Acts that appeared on John Wesley's *Notes on the New Testament* in

Timothy Smith's Reinterpretation. Smith says that Wesley may have preceded Fletcher in understanding Pentecost as a second work of grace. He writes, "In his early writing and preaching, however, Fletcher may not have emphasized, as Wesley had after 1740, the second moment of sanctifying grace, nor held up the experience of the apostles at Pentecost as a model of it."[31]

According to Smith, Wesley agreed with Benson's and Fletcher's preaching that the 120 disciples of Christ experienced entire sanctification when they were "'filled with the Holy Spirit' on the morning of Pentecost Day."[32] To understand, instead, that Wesley viewed what happened that day to the 120 as justification "will not square at all with the long record of Wesley's teaching."[33] Smith says this in response to Wesley's quite apparent association of Pentecost with justification in a December 28, 1770, letter to Joseph Benson, in which Wesley wrote: "If they [the students at Trevecca College] like to call this 'receiving the Holy Ghost,' they may: only the phrase in that sense is not scriptural and not quite proper, for they all 'received the Holy Ghost' when they were justified."[34]

Smith disallows the obvious meaning of Wesley's statement because of another letter written to Benson seven days later. In that letter, Wesley, not discussing Pentecost, but another subject altogether, says, "I believe that one that is *perfected in love,* or *filled with the Holy Ghost,* may be properly termed a *father.*"[35] Since this is perhaps the only place in which Wesley seems to equate being "perfected in love" with being "filled with the Spirit," and since it is directly opposed to what he wrote to Benson seven days

---

1743, is clear from his response to the widespread testimonies to full salvation he reported in his Journal during the year 1762." That "response" is where Wesley wrote, "Many years ago my brother frequently said, 'Your day of Pentecost is not fully come, but I doubt not it will. And you will then hear of persons sanctified as frequently as you do now of persons justified.' And any unprejudiced reader may observe, that it was now fully come." Yet even a casual reading of this "response" of Wesley to the revival that was occurring does not in any way contradict the teaching in the *Notes* that Pentecost (even for the 120) and the later Pentecosts were instances of conversion. The "Pentecost" Wesley had hoped for was not solely the entire sanctification of believers. It was clearly a Pentecost in the sense of a revival outpouring, when various people would be both justified and sanctified wholly—and when, Charles Wesley says, you will "hear of persons sanctified as frequently as you do now of persons justified."

31. Smith, WTJ 15, no. 1, 70.
32. Ibid., 72.
33. Ibid.
34. Ibid., 71.
35. Ibid., 72.

earlier, and since it is directly opposed to Wesley's various comments on Acts passages in his *Explanatory Notes upon the New Testament*, I interpret *"perfected in love"* to be Wesley's own way of referring to entire sanctification; and I see the phrase *"or filled with the Holy Ghost"* to be a courteous way of referring to entire sanctification in wording that Benson (and Fletcher) would use. It is as though he might have added, for clarity, "or as you and Mr. Fletcher would say, *filled with the Holy Ghost.*"[36]

Wesley's Teaching in the "Notes." Smith scarcely refers to Wesley's comments in his *Explanatory Notes upon the New Testament*, and this is my special problem with Smith's study. He does not take into account the hard-and-fast contrary evidence contained in Wesley's comments on Acts passages in the *Notes*.[37]

In these *Notes* on the Acts text, Wesley simply misses what would be good opportunities to relate passages to his Christian perfection doctrine—if, indeed, he understood it this way as Smith says he did. Wesley comments on passages that the Holiness Movement has viewed as related to Christian perfection, but he relates them instead to the first work of grace.

At Acts 1:4-5 we read, "And . . . [Jesus] commanded them . . . to wait for the promise of the Father, which, saith he, ye have heard from me. For John indeed baptized with water; but ye shall be baptized with the Holy Ghost not many days hence."[38] Wesley does not comment at all about "the promise of the Father." His comment on "Ye shall be baptized with the Holy Ghost" connects it with justification: "And so are all true believers, to the end of the world." Smith says that, for Wesley, receiving the Holy Spirit

---

36. Smith uses Wesley's apparent equation of being "perfected in love" and being "filled with the Holy Ghost" as a special argument against the customary interpretation of "Mr. Fletcher's late discovery." Wesley had told Joseph Benson, in a letter of March 9, 1771, that Benson would be welcome as a preacher in the societies if he would "abstain from speaking of Universal Salvation and Mr. Fletcher's late discovery." While Smith interprets that "late discovery" as probably indicating "Wesley's continuing misimpression of Fletcher's view of regeneration" (*Preacher's Magazine*, September—November 1979, 56), I feel that it is probably a reference to Fletcher's recent espousal of Christian perfection as being wrought by the Spirit baptism.

37. It is Wesley's teaching in the other writings as well, as Herbert McGonigle shows in a superb article in WTJ 8 (Spring 1973): 61-72. McGonigle shows that in the *Notes*, in letters, in sermons, and in his *Plain Account*, Wesley says very little about the baptism with the Spirit, almost never using the term, but when using it, connecting it with justification and not with entire sanctification.

38. Wesley, *Notes*, Acts 1:4-5.

happens at conversion, but being baptized with or filled with the Holy Spirit occurs at the time of entire sanctification. This is not borne out in Wesley's comments on Acts 1:4-5.

It is interesting that Wesley makes no comment whatever on Acts 2:4: "And they [the 120, at Pentecost] were all filled with the Holy Ghost" (KJV). This would be a strange omission if he viewed being filled with the Spirit as receiving entire sanctification.

Commenting on Acts 2:38, where Peter said that after repenting, and after being baptized with water, his hearers would "receive the gift of the Holy Ghost" (KJV), Wesley says that the gift of the Holy Ghost means, not entire sanctification, but "the constant fruits of faith, even righteousness, and peace, and joy in the Holy Ghost."

Likewise, Wesley does not relate Acts 8:15 to the entire sanctification of the Samaritans. Instead, he comments vaguely on the phrase "the Holy Ghost": "In his miraculous gifts, or his sanctifying graces [note the plural]? Probably in both."

More significantly, Wesley implies that Paul was not converted on the Damascus road, but three days later when Ananias went to him and said, "Brother Saul, the Lord hath sent me, . . . that thou mayest recover thy sight, and be filled with the Holy Ghost."[39] Commenting on the "three days," Wesley exclaims, "An important season! So long he seems to have been in the pangs of the new birth." What the *Notes* only imply here, a letter written in 1758 to the Rev. Mr. Potter clearly states. Wesley writes, "It does not appear that his [Paul's] was a sudden conversion."[40] Wesley continues: "After he had seen this [the light], 'he was three days without sight . . .' And, probably, during the whole time, God was gradually working in his heart, till he 'arose, and, being baptized, washed away his sins, and was filled with the Holy Ghost.'"[41] This is a crystal-clear instance of Wesley's position—that being filled with the Holy Spirit happens at conversion.

Most significant are Wesley's comments in the *Notes* at Acts 10:44: "The Holy Ghost fell on all them that were hearing the word." Wesley says: "Thus were they consecrated to God, as the

---

39. Ibid., Acts 9:17.
40. Wesley, *Works* 9:93.
41. Ibid.

first-fruits of the Gentiles. And thus did God give a clear and satisfactory evidence that He had accepted them as well as the Jews." "Accepted" is another way of saying "received into favor," or "justified."

Wesley's notes on Acts 10:47 disprove Smith's contention that, for Wesley, receiving the Spirit refers to conversion, whereas to be baptized with or filled with the Spirit refers to entire sanctification, for in comments on that verse, Wesley twice uses interchangeably "baptism" with the Holy Spirit and "receiving" the Holy Spirit.

Wesley's Teaching Through Hymns. John Wesley clearly associated Christ's Spirit baptism with justification, not with entire sanctification, in his use of hymns, through which he fully intended to teach Christian doctrine. Only one of his brother Charles's 32 Pentecost hymns, from their widely used hymnal, *Hymns of Petition and Thanksgiving for the Promise of the Father,* or *Hymns for Whitsunday,* is included in the 78 hymns chosen by John as hymns on "full redemption," that is, holiness, or entire sanctification.[42] Moreover, the one hymn so selected contained eight stanzas; and the only three stanzas that are expressly on Pentecost were omitted from the hymn as John used it for the entire sanctification division of the 1780 hymnal. Several others of these 32 Pentecost hymns are used in the 1780 collection, but they are not included in the "Full Redemption" division on entire sanctification.

Ken Bible made a study of these two hymnals, along with others of the Wesley brothers, and reported his findings in "The Wesleys' Hymns on Full Redemption and Pentecost: a Brief Comparison."[43] Bible concludes that John Wesley did not understand that entire sanctification is received through the baptism with the Holy Spirit. Bible says, "It is obvious, however, that a careful examination of their [John's and Charles's] hymns casts grave

---

42. In 1780 John Wesley carefully selected 525 hymns from eight previous hymnals he and Charles had published for use in the Methodist societies—a hymnal that served the Methodists well into the next century. It was called *A Collection of Hymns for Use of the People Called Methodists.* It was representative of the thousands of hymns written mostly by Charles Wesley and afterward edited by John. In the preface to his hymnal, John Wesley states, "The hymns are not carelessly jumbled together, but carefully ranged under proper heads." And in it he says it "is, in effect, a little body of experimental and practical divinity."

43. WTJ, Fall 1982, 79-87.

doubts on any direct connection between Pentecost and full redemption in their thought."[44]

The American Holiness Movement View

Until the publication of Wynkoop's *Theology of Love* in 1971 and the *Wesleyan Theological Journal* of 1979, the American Holiness Movement, following the lead of the early fathers and John Fletcher, had taught almost universally that entire sanctification is received by the baptism with the Holy Spirit.

Anticipation in the Fathers. As mentioned earlier, Paul Bassett's research shows that the Eastern and Western fathers of the early centuries taught that entire sanctification is received by the baptism with the Holy Spirit. He shows that, according to Roman Catholic teaching, water baptism is a kind of first work of regenerating grace, and confirmation, when the Holy Spirit is received in a special way, is an instantaneously received cleansing from sin and an empowerment.

Bassett notes that, at first, confirmation (not then so named) occurred during the baptism service, but subsequent to baptism; later it was separated from baptism (usually infant) by several years (as at present, in Roman Catholicism). Receiving the Holy Spirit was a second experience, subsequent to regeneration, which was understood to occur at baptism.

Bassett quotes Tertullian to show that baptism was followed immediately by anointing with oil, laying on of hands, and invocation of the Spirit. "Then," said Tertullian, "down over the body thus cleansed and consecrated there comes, from the Father, the Holy Spirit."

Bassett comments, "What is clear here, and important to understanding the doctrine of entire sanctification, is the distinction between the actual act of baptizing and the actual act of receiving the Holy Spirit in His fullness."[45]

Our author then says that "Cyprian, writing a generation later . . . makes the same point even more clearly in several letters."[46] Then Bassett quotes Cyprian as saying, "Those who are baptized in the Church are brought before the bishops of the Church, then

---

44. Ibid., 86. My own view is that Charles did connect the two but that John did not.
45. Paul M. Bassett in Bassett and Greathouse, *Exploring Christian Holiness* 2:39.
46. Ibid.

by way of our prayers and the laying on of our hands they receive the Holy Spirit and are made perfect by the Lord's seal."[47]

Bassett asks, "How conscious was the early Church of the theological implications, and experiential implications, of its baptismal liturgy? Did it intend, by this two-part liturgy, to express two intimately related but theologically distinct 'works of grace'?" His answer: "Certainly their sensitivity to symbol, a sensitivity shared by the cultures around them, would seem to argue so."[48]

Tertullian and Cyprian are Western fathers, but the same kind of teaching developed in general in the East as well. Bassett writes, "Irenaeus, who was clearly a traditionalist in such matters, probably also understood baptism as expressing a 'secondness' and an 'instantaneity' with respect to the Spirit's coming upon the baptizand in fullness."[49] He quotes Irenaeus as saying, "By the effusion of the Spirit, man becomes spiritual and perfect. This is what brings him to the image and likeness of God."[50] Of Clement of Alexandria, Bassett writes, "It is clear that this perfection is instantaneously received, and it appears to be given subsequent to regeneration."[51] Of Origen he says that "it does not seem unfair to say that he did see sanctification as a distinct activity of divine grace—that is, distinct from justification."[52] Then Bassett adds, "And he did see it as being given to the believer in a moment distinct from the moment in which justification was given."[53]

Bassett feels that Gregory of Nyssa, who wrote *On Christian Perfection,* is closest to Wesley's doctrine of entire sanctification of any of the Eastern fathers.[54] However, writings attributed to Macarius the Egyptian (possibly written by Gregory of Nyssa) are even more similar to Wesley's teaching and even closer to the Holiness Movement understanding of entire sanctification than to Wesley's view. Those writings view entire sanctification as occurring through the fullness of the baptism with the Holy Spirit. Bassett says of Macarius that "this anointing [with oil, after baptism]

---

47. Ibid.
48. Ibid., 41.
49. Ibid., 47.
50. Ibid., 49.
51. Ibid., 57.
52. Ibid., 66.
53. Ibid.
54. Ibid., 108.

was apparently the point of the filling with the Holy Spirit, the moment of entire sanctification, liturgically expressed."[55] Bassett continues, "No matter how much growth in grace lay in the future, here was the Christian's essential purification, his perfection in righteousness."[56] Bassett reads him also as teaching that "beyond the sanctification and perfection liturgically signified, there is a deeper and more complete sanctifying and perfecting work of grace."[57] This "removes entire sanctification from the ritual,"[58] which is done, of course, in the Holiness Movement. It "rescues" a person "from indwelling sin, filling him with the Holy Ghost,"[59] as Macarius says and as the Holiness Movement teaches.

Anticipations in Britain. In Britain, the American Holiness Movement's emphasis on entire sanctification as received by the baptism with the Holy Spirit was already anticipated in John Wesley's time.

Only faint anticipation is found in Adam Clarke, the distinguished exegete of early Methodism. Clarke seems to have viewed the relationship between Pentecost and entire sanctification much as did Mr. Wesley, except for one or two isolated passages. Leo Cox writes, "Adam Clarke . . . emphasized the work of entire sanctification as a 'greater effusion of the Holy Ghost.'"[60] "Without question he associated the work of purifying from all sin with the Pentecostal outpouring of the Holy Spirit."[61] Yet Clarke does not place any emphasis at all on this understanding. His comments in his *Commentary* on Acts 2:1-8 and other passages in Acts never associate the baptism with the Holy Spirit with entire sanctification. In fact, Clarke clearly dissociates the Holy Spirit's falling upon the people at Samaria from "sanctification." He says it was "not for the sanctification of the souls of the people: this they had on believing in Christ Jesus."[62]

---

55. Ibid., 71.
56. Ibid.
57. Ibid.
58. Ibid.
59. Ibid.
60. Leo Cox, *John Wesley's Concept of Perfection,* 133. Cox here quotes John L. Peters, *Christian Perfection and American Methodism* (New York: Abingdon Press, 1956), 107.
61. Cox, *John Wesley's Concept of Perfection,* 133. As a reference Cox gives Adam Clarke, *The Holy Bible with a Commentary and Critical Notes* (New York: Abingdon Press), 5:682-83.
62. Clarke, *Commentary* 5:682-83.

In his *Entire Sanctification,* Clarke does not associate entire sanctification with the baptism with the Holy Spirit. In an essay, "The Holy Spirit," however, there is such isolated reference, which does not constitute an emphasis. Clarke writes, "God promised his Holy Spirit to sanctify and cleanse the heart, so as utterly to destroy all pride, anger, self-will, . . . and everything contrary to his own holiness. . . . He is also the sanctifying Spirit . . . and as such he condemns to utter destruction the whole of the carnal mind."[63]

John Fletcher, Wesley's close associate, in his lengthy treatment of "Christian Perfection" as the last of his *Checks to Antinomianism,* links the Spirit baptism with entire sanctification.

Fletcher corresponded with Wesley on this issue. He tried to prove to Wesley the validity of associating the baptism with the Holy Spirit with entire sanctification, but Wesley was unconvinced.[64]

It remained for the American Holiness Movement to elucidate the teaching.

Pre-Holiness Movement Teaching. A progenitor of Spirit-baptism teaching was Thomas Webb (1724-96), a captain of the British army who was converted through Mr. Wesley's preaching and became a local preacher. Sent to New York about 1766, he became "the first Apostle of Methodism in America."

The following excerpt from a Pentecost Day sermon by Webb contains a statement of his teaching: "The words of the text were written by the apostles after the act of justification had passed on them. But you see, my friends, this was not enough for them. They must receive the Holy Ghost *after* this. So must you. You must be sanctified. But you are not. You are only Christians in part. You have not received the Holy Ghost. I know it."[65]

British Methodist Hester Ann Rogers, whose *Memoirs and Letters* were circulated widely in American Methodism in the early 1800s, relates her struggle to receive entire sanctification as fol-

63. Clarke, *Christian Theology,* ed. Samuel Dunn (New York: T. Mason and G. Lane, 1840), 162-63.

64. See Donald W. Dayton, "The Doctrine of the Baptism of the Spirit: Its Emergence and Significance," WTJ 13 (Spring 1978): 116.

65. See John A. Knight, "John Fletcher's Influence on the Development of Wesleyan Theology in America," WTJ 13 (Spring 1978): 23. See also Coppedge, "Entire Sanctification in Early American Methodism, 1821-1835," WTJ, 1978.

lows: "Lord, cried I, make this the moment of my full salvation! Baptize me now with the Holy Ghost and the fire of pure love: Now 'make me a clean heart, and renew a right spirit within me.' Now enter thy temple, and cast out sin forever. Now cleanse the thoughts, desires and propensities of my heart, and let me perfectly love thee."[66]

After quoting this, Allan Coppedge says, "Quite clearly in her mind the experience of the baptism of the Spirit was identical with that of full salvation, and the widespread distribution of her story cannot but have made American Methodists more ready to see an intimate connection between the two concepts."[67]

Perhaps most important of all is the wide circulation in America, at this time, of John Fletcher's *Last Check*, in which he taught Spirit-baptism entire sanctification—but without extensive elucidation.

Significantly, at this time, some who were outside Methodism began to pick up this teaching, including the Cumberland Presbyterian Church, formed in 1810.

Merrill Gaddis says of them:

> Calvinistic predestination was never more completely set aside than by the evangelists of this denomination, nor can the present-day student detect any actual difference— from the standpoint of religious psychology and practical moral results—between the Cumberland "Paraclete baptism" and its empowerment on the one hand, and the Wesleyan second blessing or "entire sanctification" on the other.[68]

Besides the Cumberlands, the New Light Presbyterians, organized in the same area in 1803, taught in this way.

The Holiness Movement: Early Period. America's Holiness Movement began about the year 1835. That is the year Phoebe Palmer received entire sanctification and began a lay ministry that made her one of the promoters of Holiness teaching.

In 1835, also, Oberlin College began, educating men and women for Holiness ministry, including its social implementation. Asa Mahan became its first president, and Charles G. Finney its

---

66. See Thomas Coke, *The Experience and Spiritual Letters of Mrs. Hester Ann Rogers* (London: Milner and Somerby, n.d.), 14, quoted in Coppedge, WTJ, 1978, 46.

67. Coppedge, WTJ, 1978, 46.

68. Merrill E. Gaddis, "Christian Perfectionism in America" (Ph.D. diss., University of Chicago, 1929), 297-98.

first professor of systematic theology. Of special interest here is Finney's teaching.

1. *Finney's strategic contribution.* This appeared in articles and "letters" in the *Oberlin Evangelist* and, to some extent, in his *Systematic Theology.*

In his "Letters to Ministers of the Gospel," published in the *Oberlin Evangelist,* he writes clearly to the point we are discussing. In one such letter he says, "'The baptism of the Holy Ghost' is . . . universally promised . . . to Christians"; and "this blessing is to be sought and received after conversion." He says that new converts should be "baptized into the very death of Christ . . . and raised to a life of holiness in Christ." He also says, "I am fully concerned that pains enough are not taken, to lead one convert to seek earnestly the 'baptism of the Holy Ghost, after that he hath believed.'" And he confesses that his own "instruction to converts, in this respect, has been very defective."[69]

Finney does teach Pentecostal entire sanctification quite clearly in these "Letters," but there is very little teaching of this sort in his *Systematic Theology.* In that major work, he implies it but does not elucidate it. He teaches that the promises of "sanctification" were fulfilled by the baptism of the Holy Spirit at Pentecost. As he discusses the entire sanctification of believers, he says that "a promise of sanctification, to be of any avail to us, must be due at some certain time . . . to put us into the attitude of waiting for its fulfillment. . . . The promise of Christ to the Apostles concerning the outpouring of the Spirit on the day of Pentecost, may illustrate the meaning."[70]

In another area of *Systematic Theology,* still treating "sanctification," Finney implies, but does not say expressly, that receiving "the fullness of the Holy Spirit" is what makes us "perfect" in distinction from the Old Testament personages. He writes: "They [the patriarchs] did not receive the light and the glory of the Christian dispensation, nor the fullness of the Holy Spirit. And it is asserted in the Bible, that 'they without us,' that is without our privileges, 'could not be made perfect.'"[71]

---

69. *Oberlin Evangelist,* May 6, 1840.
70. Charles G. Finney, *Lectures on Systematic Theology* (Oberlin, Ohio: James M. Fitche, 1847), 210.
71. Ibid., 386.

2. *S. S. Smith's importance.* Stephen Sanford Smith (1797-1871) was not well known, yet he, on the teaching that entire sanctification is occasioned by the baptism with the Holy Spirit, was highly strategic.

S. S. Smith was a Congregational minister in Massachusetts. He published a strategic article in *Guide to Christian Perfection* (January 1841) titled "Power from on High," based on Luke 24:49: "Tarry ye in the city of Jerusalem, until ye be endued with power from on high" (KJV).

In this sermon Smith says, "The 120 who were baptized with the Holy Ghost on the day of Pentecost, had previously been 'born of God.'"[72] He goes on to say, "Evidently the gift of the Holy Ghost here alluded to [in John 7:39], is the power from on high referred to in the text, and as evidently it was not regeneration."[73]

Of this gift of power he says, "It was a measure and fullness of the divine influence as transformed the whole moral character of the recipients."[74]

In a footnote, Smith writes, "That the baptism with the Holy Ghost was thus a sanctifying power is evident from the words of Christ, John vii 38—'He that believeth on me, as the scripture hath said, from him shall flow rivers of living water.'" And in the same footnote: "Paul also assures us that this baptism was a sanctifying influence," and he adds that a person thus becomes "a sanctified vessel,"[75] with "every power and faculty of his soul brought into sweet subjection to the will of God."[76] He further says the baptism produces "perfect love."[77]

George Peck wrote considerably in the area of Christian perfection, but nowhere does he give a sustained treatment of entire sanctification through the baptism with the Holy Spirit. Within a 34-page article on "Christian Perfection," however, where he discusses how Christian perfection is to be "attained," he says something rather express on the matter of Spirit-baptism entire sanctification: "It is especially indicated as the work of the Holy Spirit

72. S. S. Smith, "Power from on High," in *Guide to Perfection*, ed. Timothy Merritt and D. S. King (Boston: T. Merritt and D. S. King, 1840-41), 147.
73. Ibid., 148.
74. Ibid., 150.
75. Ibid.
76. Ibid., 152.
77. Ibid.

by being denominated the *baptism of the Holy Ghost, sanctification of the Spirit*, etc. This view of our authors [he means Fletcher and other Methodists] is, that the work is *effected* and *sustained by the direct agency of the Spirit of God upon the Soul.*"[78]

Methodism's Bishop Hamline wrote an extended testimony titled "Baptism," first published in 1843 in the *Ladies' Repository* (of which he was editor), and republished in 1846 in *Guide to Holiness*—the new name for *Guide to Christian Perfection*. Couching his testimony in third-person language, the bishop devoted several pages to a careful recounting of his experience of entire sanctification, which he said occurred by the baptism of the Holy Spirit.

3. *Phoebe Palmer's contribution.* This lay Methodist evangelist and writer, by the mid-1850s, came to view entire sanctification as effected by the Spirit baptism. In a letter to her sister in 1859, she says she had taught "the endowment of power, the full baptism of the Holy Ghost, as the indispensable, ay, *absolute* necessity of all the disciples of Jesus." Mrs. Palmer's contribution to the doctrine and experience of entire sanctification in a general way is much more significant than is her contribution to the specific matter that the second work of grace happens by Spirit baptism.

4. *Asa Mahan's strategic significance.* Asa Mahan published in 1870 *The Baptism of the Holy Ghost*, a milestone book on this aspect of the doctrine of entire sanctification.

Mahan's main objective in his book was to show that the Spirit baptism is a second work of grace. He emphasized empowerment, but he did teach, though barely, that the baptism cleanses from sin.

Mahan believed, as most do today, that we do receive the Spirit at conversion, but not in His baptismal fullness. This is the way he interprets 1 Cor. 12:13, where we read, "By one Spirit we were all baptized into one body, whether Jews or Greeks, whether slaves or free, and we were all made to drink of one Spirit" (NASB). He says, "The Holy Ghost had given the disciples 'repentance unto life,' and 'was with them' as a sanctifying presence, had made their bodies His temple, and had 'baptized them into one body,' prior to Pentecost."[79]

---

78. George Peck, "Christian Perfection," *Methodist Quarterly Review*, ed. George Peck (New York: G. Lane and P. P. Sanford, 1841), vol. 23, 3rd ser., 1:151.

79. Mahan, *Baptism of the Holy Ghost*, 60.

5. *J. A. Wood on cleansing.* J. A. Wood taught that entire sanctification is wrought by the baptism with the Holy Spirit and that it is an empowerment. But more significantly, he affirmed that it is the time of our cleansing from sin.

Wood writes of the time "when the soul is baptized with the Holy Ghost, and sin is utterly destroyed, and love, pure, perfect love, fills the whole heart."[80]

There seemed to be at this time a groundswell toward viewing entire sanctification as being wrought by the baptism with the Holy Spirit. By 1885 it seems to have been almost universally agreed upon in the Holiness Movement. A. M. Hills wrote of the state of this teaching at that time:

> We are now prepared to give a formal definition of sanctification or Scriptural holiness, which would probably be accepted by the three hundred teachers and preachers in the National Holiness Association of America . . . : Entire Sanctification is a second definite work of grace wrought by the Baptism with the Holy Spirit in the heart of the believer subsequent to regeneration, received instantaneously by faith, by which the heart is cleansed from all corruption and filled with the perfect love of God.[81]

Of this, John Peters observes: "This definition had something of the force of an 'apostles' creed' within the Holiness movement. It was limited as was that first great formulary to the specific issues in controversy and was effective to expose the uncertain and to rout the disaffected. This was the phraseology in which the doctrine was presented, and its strength lay in its intensity."[82]

6. *Daniel Steele.* The most scholarly and respected of the Holiness Movement writers, Steele began in the early 1870s to urge the concept that the baptism with the Holy Spirit effects entire sanctification.

In *Love Enthroned,* he vigorously teaches that the baptism with the Holy Spirit effects a real, "Methodist-like" entire sanctification. He says, "The conclusion is inevitable, that the baptism of the Holy Ghost includes the extinction of sin in the believer's soul as its negative and minor part, and the fullness of love shed

---

80. Wood, *Perfect Love,* rev. ed., 4.
81. See A. M. Hills, *Scriptural Holiness and Keswick Teaching Compared* (Salem, Ohio: Schmul Publishing Co., 1983), 29.
82. Peters, *Christian Perfection and American Methodism,* 162.

abroad in the heart as its positive and greater part; in other words, it includes entire sanctification and Christian perfection."[83]

To Steele, one of the special "proofs" that the Spirit baptism is a "synonym for entire sanctification" is "Peter's incidental remark in Acts 15:9, that the Holy Ghost came to Cornelius and his house in his office as Sanctifier, 'purifying their hearts by faith.'"[84]

The Holiness Movement: Middle Period. The period from 1885 up to, but not including, Holiness exegetes and theologians now living or recently deceased can be considered the Holiness Movement's middle period.

1. *Its characteristics.* This middle period was a time when "Pentecostal" became widely used to describe the emphasis on entire sanctification. "Pentecostal" got into the names of many of the new denominations that were formed. The word "Pentecostal" was also used in the names of periodicals. Pentecostal meetings, Pentecostal testimonies, and Pentecostal groups within local churches were the common subjects in Holiness magazines.

2. *Its writers.* Phineas Bressee, founder of the Church of the Nazarene in America's West, taught that the Spirit baptism effects entire sanctification. As early as in 1894, Bresee contributed a chapter on "Baptism with the Holy Ghost" to a Holiness symposium edited by William Nast and titled *The Double Cure.*[85] In it, Bresee says, "It would not seem necessary to urge at length that these are the days of the Holy Ghost baptism."[86] He also says, "This baptism with the Holy Ghost imparts power to the soul,"[87] but he goes beyond the thought of empowerment to affirm that this is the time of heart purification. Bresee says:

> *It purified their hearts.* This, Peter clearly declares in the council at Jerusalem, telling them how God led him, and justified his going to Cornelius, a Gentile, by the fact that the Holy Ghost fell upon him and those gathered, as it did upon them in the beginning, and put no difference between them—"purifying their hearts by faith"—evidently declaring that the baptism of the Holy Ghost purifies the heart.[88]

---

83. Daniel Steele, *Love Enthroned* (Apollo, Tenn.: West Publishing Co., 1951), 66.

84. Ibid., 67.

85. Phineas Bresee, "Baptism with the Holy Ghost," in *The Double Cure,* ed. William Nast (Chicago: Christian Witness Co., 1894).

86. Ibid., 327.

87. Ibid., 335.

88. Ibid.

It was the following year that Bresee started the Church of the Nazarene—a denomination thus "born with the baptism with the Holy Spirit on its lips."[89]

Bresee's address to the 1903 Nazarene General Assembly shows how significant to him this aspect of holiness doctrine was:

> The fires of Pentecost in which this church was born have not grown dim. . . . The sanctification of believers through the baptism with the Holy Ghost by our risen Lord, giving power to witness for Him, has not ceased. . . . There prevails among us everywhere the deep conviction that the dispensational truth is that Jesus Christ baptizes with the Holy Ghost, cleansing, filling and empowering. . . . The result is that our people live, mostly, in the Pentecostal glory.[90]

Talking in these same terms, William McDonald says, "If the baptism of the Holy Spirit did purify the hearts of the first disciples from that depravity which lingered with and in them, even after they had been called, accepted, and commissioned of Jesus, then it may do the same thing for us. A Pentecost awaits us, as well as them."[91]

Dougan Clark, a Quaker, in his fine work, *The Theology of Holiness*, also teaches similarly:

> "God which knoweth the hearts, bare them witness, giving them the Holy Ghost, even as He did unto us, and put no difference between us and them, purifying their hearts by faith." Evidently here the chief of the apostles gives us to understand that the giving of the Holy Ghost, and the purifying of the heart by faith, are co-instantaneous and identical experiences. And if this be so, the Holy Ghost, who is a Divine person, and not a mere influence, must be the effective agent in purifying the heart, that is to say, it is He who by His Divine energy sanctifies us wholly.[92]

Also typically Holiness Movement in his understanding that entire sanctification occurs through the baptism with the Holy

---

89. Floyd T. Cunningham, in a term paper submitted for a Doctrine of Holiness class at Nazarene Theological Seminary, Kansas City.

90. See E. A. Girvin, *A Prince in Israel* (Kansas City: Pentecostal Nazarene Publishing House, 1916), 199.

91. William McDonald, *Another Comforter* (Boston: McDonald, Gill, 1890), 55.

92. Dougan Clark, *The Theology of Holiness* (Boston: McDonald and Gill Co., 1893), 165.

Spirit was A. M. Hills.[93] Along with teaching it in many positive ways, he laments its neglect in "the leading Protestant denominations in America" and adds: "The real cause of our leanness is: 'The Neglect of Pentecost.' The followers of Christ have ceased all too generally to repair to the sacred chamber and seek with importuning prayer for the BAPTISM WITH THE HOLY GHOST."[94] Hills deplored the Oberlin-Keswick neglect of a cleansing emphasis, writing, "There is a class of religious teachers who champion Pentecost, but belittle the experience. They commend the baptism with the Holy Ghost, but deny its efficacy to cleanse the heart from inbred sin."[95]

Also associating Pentecost with entire sanctification was E. P. Ellyson, who writes, "The atonement has provided a further experience wherein there is full cleansing from the state of sin. This cleansing is a part of the work of the baptism with the Holy Spirit."[96]

The major theologian of the Holiness Movement, H. Orton Wiley, explains, "The baptism with the Spirit . . . must be considered under a twofold aspect; *first*, as a death to the carnal nature; and *second*, as the fullness of life in the Spirit."[97] He goes on to say, "Since entire sanctification is effected by the baptism with the Spirit, it likewise has a twofold aspect—the cleansing from sin and full devotement to God."[98] In his 1,468-page *Systematic Theology*, Wiley devotes less than one page to "The Baptism with the Spirit," under that heading as such. Yet he frequently teaches entire sanctification by Spirit baptism elsewhere in this work. For example: "Nothing can be more evident than that the baptism with the Holy Ghost effects an internal and spiritual cleansing

---

93. Perhaps Finney and Hills and Wiley are the three most significant theologians of the Holiness Movement's history. Hills was a student of Finney at Oberlin and was long associated with Wiley in Nazarene work. Hills published his classic on Holiness in 1897 and his *Fundamental Christian Theology: A Systematic Theology*, in 1931. The first has perhaps been the most widely used work on Holiness by Nazarenes, having long been part of the home study course for ministers. His work on systematic theology replaced Miley's *Systematic Theology* in that course for the 1932 and 1936 quadrennia, until the first volume of H. Orton Wiley's three-volume *Christian Theology* appeared in 1941.

94. A. M. Hills, *Pentecost Rejected and the Effects on the Churches* (Cincinnati: Office of God's Revivalist, 1902), 5.

95. Ibid., 30.

96. E. P. Ellyson, *Bible Holiness* (Kansas City: Beacon Hill Press, 1952), 69.

97. Wiley, *Christian Theology* 2:323-24.

98. Ibid., 324.

which goes far deeper than John's baptism. One was for the remission of sins, the other for the removal of the sin principle."[99] He devoted many editorials to this subject in the early 1930s as editor of the *Herald of Holiness*.

S. S. White wrote rather extensively on the subject. He says that entire sanctification and the Spirit baptism "are simultaneous—identical in time but not necessarily in meaning."[100] And he writes, "The efficient cause [a reference to Aristotle, for White was as much a philosopher as a theologian] of entire sanctification is the baptism of Jesus with the Holy Spirit."[101]

White viewed Cornelius as "a saved man" (Acts 10:2, 22) who later "received the baptism with the Holy Spirit" (v. 44). And he associated that Caesarean Pentecost with cleansing from sin, explaining, "When the Holy Spirit fell upon Cornelius, his heart was purified or sanctified" (15:8-9).[102]

Concerning Christ's high-priestly prayer in John 17, he writes: "Pentecost as described in Acts 2 is the answer to the great high priestly prayer of Jesus for the sanctification of His disciples (John 17). If such were not the case, we would have no reason to believe that Christ's prayer was ever answered."[103]

Charles Ewing Brown, a Church of God (Anderson, Ind.) scholar, in *The Meaning of Sanctification*, devotes a chapter to the baptism with the Holy Spirit.

Speaking of the various "Pentecosts" in Acts, Brown says, "In every one of these instances there is reasonable evidence that the persons thus baptized with the Holy Ghost were seriously converted—were truly regenerated believers."[104]

Brown (in distinction from so many others) is aware that "the early Wesleyan theologians" viewed Pentecost differently. He writes, "Even the early Wesleyan theologians were so far misled . . . that they failed to put proper emphasis on the baptism of the Holy Spirit."[105] He adds, "They tended to interpret sanctification as a crisis experience, it is true, but found most of their texts in

---

99. Ibid., 444.
100. White, *Five Cardinal Elements in the Doctrine of Entire Sanctification*, 73.
101. Ibid., 75.
102. Ibid.
103. Ibid.
104. Brown, *The Meaning of Sanctification*, 104.
105. Ibid., 115.

other parts of the New Testament."[106] Brown himself says that "the scriptural description of that baptism with the Holy Spirit specifically describes it as a purification of the heart."[107] Here he is thinking especially of Acts 15:8-9.

The Holiness Movement: Recent Period. Several factors characterize the Holiness Movement's recent period. One is that we are enjoying better scholarship, and the literature is more substantial. The literature is not only more scholarly but also far more biblical—even exegetically biblical.

Some of the significant Wesleyan-holiness writers of the recent period have tended to prefer John Wesley to the Holiness Movement on the question of whether Christ's baptism with the Holy Spirit occasions entire sanctification. Mildred Wynkoop is one of these. In her thorough *Theology of Love* she never links the baptism with the Spirit with entire sanctification, and she even says some things that imply a deprecating of the linkage. Of Pentecost and the sanctification Jesus prayed for in John 17:17, she writes, "Though theology is inclined to relate them, it is of interest to note that *so far as any specific scripture* is concerned, the Pentecostal experience is not said to be an answer to Jesus' prayer in John 17."[108] She goes on to say, "In fact never is sanctification, as such, directly identified with the coming of the Spirit on that day."[109]

The usual recent Wesleyan-holiness teaching, however, has been that Christ's Spirit baptism occasions the second work of grace. This is the teaching, for example, of George A. Turner, W. T. Purkiser, Richard S. Taylor, and Donald Metz, whose views will be treated in turn.

George A. Turner aligns himself with the view of the Holiness Movement in general, that entire sanctification is effected by the Spirit baptism.[110]

Turner writes, "Pentecost is not presented as initiation into discipleship; rather it brings purifying (Acts 15:9) and empower-

---

106. Ibid.
107. Ibid.
108. Wynkoop, *A Theology of Love,* 321.
109. Ibid. Yet, surely, there is much in Scripture that connects cleansing with Pentecost (see Ezek. 36:25-27; Mal. 3:1-3; Matt. 3:11-12; John 7:37-39; Acts 15:8-9).
110. Turner, *The Vision Which Transforms,* 149 ff.

ing (Acts 1:8) to those already discipled or converted."[111] He argues for the need for the disciples, who were Christians, to be cleansed, when he writes: "In spite of the fact that their names were written in heaven and hence we would call them *converted* prior to Pentecost, still they had many evidences of "the old nature." They showed worldly attitudes such as intolerance, pride, selfishness, race prejudices, and fear. To all of these they present marked contrasts after Pentecost."[112]

One of the most significant of recent Holiness writers, the now late W. T. Purkiser, writes: "In a word, the baptism and consequent fullness of the Spirit are the means by which entire sanctification is wrought."[113]

Purkiser adds, "It is our conviction that the New Testament gives abundant warrant for assuming that the baptism with the Spirit and entire sanctification are two aspects of one and the same work of divine grace in Christian hearts."[114]

Richard S. Taylor has long taken this kind of view. In his "Doctrine of Holiness" section of the symposium *God, Man, and Salvation,* he treats it with some thoroughness.

In a summarizing way he says, "There is adequate basis in the New Testament for linking together entire sanctification and the baptism with the Holy Spirit. This baptism is distinct from and subsequent to the birth of the Spirit."[115] The Spirit baptism effects a deep-down cleansing, for, he says, "As fire is a deeper cleansing agent than water, so the fire of Pentecost speaks of inner purification beyond the expiation of water baptism (cf. Isa. 6:6-7 with Acts 15:8-9)."[116] He has no problems with the understanding that the disciples were Christian believers prior to Pentecost. He says, "Yet there is every evidence that Jesus considered His disciples to have already experienced what He urged upon Nicodemus (cf. John 14—17)."[117] He understands that the Spirit baptizes us into Christ in regeneration (1 Cor. 12:13) and that

111. George A. Turner, *Christian Holiness* (Kansas City: Beacon Hill Press of Kansas City, 1977), 73.
112. Ibid., 74.
113. Purkiser, *Sanctification and Its Synonyms,* 25.
114. Purkiser, *Conflicting Concepts of Holiness,* 64.
115. Richard S. Taylor, *God, Man, and Salvation,* 506.
116. Ibid., 490.
117. Ibid., 487.

Christ baptizes regenerated persons with the Holy Spirit as a second work of grace.[118]

Nothing could be plainer than his statement: "When men are sanctified wholly, they are baptized with the Holy Spirit, and when they are baptized with the Holy Spirit, they are sanctified wholly."[119]

Donald Metz, in his *Studies in Biblical Holiness*, does not go into this matter in depth, but he takes the same position that has dominated Holiness Movement teaching. Metz writes, "The baptism in or with the Holy Spirit brings a spiritual experience called entire sanctification."[120]

The Teaching of Scripture

With views of Dunn and Lyon and Wesley before us, along with the teaching of the fathers and of the American Holiness Movement, it is important to show that the Holiness Movement teaching is scriptural.

Scripture teaches that Pentecost itself, and the later Pentecosts of Acts, were not times of the conversion of these people, but times when Christian believers (already converted, already justified, regenerated) were sanctified wholly—cleansed from original sin and empowered for the holy life and for Christian service.

Pentecost for the 120 Was a Second Work. Robert Lyon, commenting on Acts 2:38, suggests that "Peter promised his hearers [at Pentecost] the very same experience which they had seen occur in the original outpouring." Yet Peter is surely talking in terms of what we in the Holiness Movement mean by two works of grace, one subsequent to the other. Following the NASB here, and including the theologically important words Lyon leaves out, Peter says, "Repent, and let each of you be baptized in the name of Jesus Christ for the forgiveness of your sins; and you shall receive the gift of the Holy Spirit." Here, they were to "repent." Later—it would have to be later, as thousands were involved—they were baptized with water, expressly said to be "for the forgiveness of your sins." This means that the water baptism, subsequent to

---

118. Ibid., 494.
119. Richard S. Taylor, *Life in the Spirit* (Kansas City: Beacon Hill Press of Kansas City, 1966), 82.
120. Metz, *Studies in Biblical Holiness,* 111.

their repentance, was to assert in symbol that their sins had been forgiven—the element of water itself being symbolical of the cleansing of regeneration (see Acts 22:16; Titus 3:5). Finally, after the NASB's semicolon, Peter says, "and you shall receive the gift of the Holy Spirit." This would be subsequent to their repentance, and also, in this case, subsequent to their water baptism. This passage might not be quite as clear as systematically theological language is capable of making it; yet it is quite clearly and emphatically what might be described as an exhortation to both works of grace, one subsequent to the other.

1. *The Romans 4 evidence.* Paul makes it clear in Romans 4 that justification could be experienced long before Pentecost. Thus the 120 "brothers" (Acts 1:15-16) could have been believers prior to Christ's death and resurrection. Paul says, "Abraham believed God, and it was credited to him as righteousness" (Rom. 4:3). Paul is here quoting Gen. 15:6, which also states that Abraham was justified or righteous. Paul does not seem to know anything about the dispensationalism that separates the pre-Pentecost people from justification by faith, because well after Christ's death and resurrection, he uses Abraham as an illustration of how one is still justified.

Paul knew, of course, when he was writing the Romans Epistle, that people were to "believe in him who raised Jesus our Lord from the dead" (4:24). But his point was that Abraham and Paul's readers were all justified by faith and not by works.

2. *Hebrews teaches this.* For all its contrasting of the two covenants, Hebrews shows that people were justified by faith under the old covenant. Hebrews 11 says that "by faith" one after another of the Old Testament personages, from Abel to Abraham to Moses and others, "gained what was promised" (v. 33) for those times and pleased God. It states that "the world was not worthy of them" (v. 38), and that many "were tortured and refused to be released, so that they might gain a better resurrection" (v. 35)—so that evidently they will be raptured along with post-Calvary Christians.

These people did not have the Christ revelation and knew only that a better day was promised. But they were justified, and they really did live by faith. The law itself was "only a shadow" and "not the realities" (10:1); yet that does not mean that their justified relationship to God was only a shadow and not a reality.

It was as real as our justification is, and they "were all commended for their faith" (11:39).

If they, including Abraham, were justified prior to Christ's death and resurrection, we may assume that the 120 "believers" (Acts 1:15) could be justified before Pentecost.

3. *John's Gospel teaches this.* Jesus urged upon Nicodemus the new birth, saying, "I say to you, unless one is born again, he cannot see the kingdom of God" (John 3:3, NASB). He adds, "Do not marvel that I said to you, 'You must be born again'" (v. 7, NASB). Jesus does not tell him that he must wait until Pentecost to be born anew. He even seems to chide Nicodemus for not being born again right then, because He says: "And you do not receive our witness" (v. 11, NASB).

It is well known, also, that this Gospel speaks much about eternal life, which is surely another name for conversion, or the first work of grace. People then already possessed eternal life. John the Baptist says, "He who believes in the Son has eternal life" (3:36, NASB). It is received when one "believes," which is precisely what one does in order to receive forgiveness or justification.

John the apostle speaks about persons who "believed." He says, "And from that city many of the Samaritans believed in Him" (4:39, NASB). They did so because a Samaritan woman, who had asked Christ for the water that would spring up to "eternal life" (vv. 14-15), had drunk of it and had witnessed to them. What are we talking about here if this is not regeneration, the new birth, conversion?

And how could regeneration be more clearly suggested than when Jesus later says, using the present tense, "For this is the will of My Father, that everyone who beholds the Son and believes in Him, may have eternal life; and I Myself will raise him up on the last day" (6:40, NASB). Then He adds, "Truly, truly, I say to you, he who believes has eternal life" (v. 47, NASB).

In chapter 15, the disciples are the branches of the Vine, and this, too, suggests their new birth, their first work of grace. Jesus' only special concern is that they "abide" in Him, the phrase "abide in me" appearing five times in verses 4-10 (KJV).

In chapter 17, we have Christ's extended prayer for His disciples, and again they seem to be persons in the first work of grace. He can say that they are "Mine" and that "I have been glorified in them" (v. 10, NASB). He prays the Father to "keep them" (v. 11, NASB), not to regenerate them. They are persons whom the Father has "given" to Christ (v. 9, NASB), and Christ had "guarded them" (v. 12, NASB). The "world has hated them, because they are not of the world" (v. 14, NASB). They had believed, for He says, "I do not ask in behalf of these alone, but for those also who believe in Me through their word" (v. 20, NASB). His prayer, "Sanctify them in the truth; Thy word is truth" (v. 17, NASB), is surely answered at Pentecost. The word for "sanctify" is in the aorist tense, suggesting the kind of completed and punctiliar event that Pentecost was when they received a "baptism" with the Holy Spirit.

The confession of Thomas, "My Lord and my God!" (20:28), suggests that regeneration occurred before Pentecost. Surely this is the confession of a believer in a full sense. It is even made after the Resurrection, and in part because of Christ's resurrection.

4. *The Synoptics are supportive.* Here people receive the forgiveness of sins; they repent and believe; their lives become different and commissioned.

The people who repented and were baptized under John the Baptist's preaching received the new birth. John called for repentance, a basic change of mind through which we begin to build our lives according to a different blueprint. "Repent, for the kingdom of heaven is at hand" (Matt. 3:2, NASB), he told all. He did not want lip service without their hearts in it, either, so he told them to "bring forth fruit in keeping with repentance" (v. 8, NASB). He made it clear, too, that it was Jesus he was proclaiming. Actually, in a sense, he told them he was offering a first step in redemption, baptizing them in water, and that Jesus himself, later, would offer a further stage in redemption, baptizing people with the Holy Spirit (v. 11).

Jesus demanded repentance also. "Repent, for the kingdom of heaven is at hand" (Matt. 4:17, NASB). People who repented are called "salt," and they are already "the light of the world" (5:13-14), glorifying the Father by "good works" (v. 16, NASB). Jesus gives them instructions as insiders who are to "love" their "enemies" (v. 44), as He says, "in order that you may be sons of your Father who is in heaven" (v. 45, NASB).

A person could receive God's forgiveness prior to Pentecost, one of the ways the New Testament has of talking about the first work of grace. Jesus says, "For if you forgive men for their transgressions, your heavenly Father will also forgive you. But if you do not forgive men, then your Father will not forgive your transgressions" (Matt. 6:14-15, NASB).

Abundant similar data is found in the Synoptics, including Mary Magdalene's transformation (Luke 8:2); but this will suffice to support the point being made that many people received the first work of grace prior to Pentecost.

Two Works of Grace at Samaria. The revival at Samaria, described in Acts 8:1-25, is a Gibraltar of two-works-of-grace teaching. Luke tells us that "Philip went down to the city of Samaria and began proclaiming Christ to them" (v. 5, NASB). Many who heard him preach believed on Christ and received water baptism (v. 12, a clear description of conversion). Luke tells us, further: "When the apostles in Jerusalem heard that Samaria had received the word of God, they sent them Peter and John, who came down and prayed for them, that they might receive the Holy Spirit. For He had not yet fallen upon any of them; they had simply been baptized in the name of the Lord Jesus. Then they began laying their hands on them, and they were receiving the Holy Spirit" (vv. 14-17, NASB).

As clearly as words can make it, then, they earlier believed and were baptized in the name of Christ; and quite later, after the apostles had arrived, they received the Holy Spirit—"for He had not yet fallen upon any of them."

Paul's Two Works of Grace. Something revolutionary happened to Paul on the road to Damascus. He made a complete turnaround—from Christianity's main persecutor to a commissioned representative of his former enemy, Christ.

Outward manifestations of this revolutionary change also occurred. The risen Christ appeared to him and conversed with him. Numerous commentators, whatever their own doctrinal stance, take the position that Paul's conversion did occur on the Damascus road.

Paul was then and there called to preach Christ. His call happened before Ananias visited him, for the Lord said to Ananias: "Go, for he is a chosen instrument of Mine, to bear My name before the Gentiles and kings and the sons of Israel" (Acts 9:15, NASB). The word for "chosen" is *eklogēs*, and it is pretty salvific. It is used of the remnant who enjoy God's grace in Rom. 11:5-7.

Paul twice calls Christ *kurie,* "Lord" (Acts 9:5; 22:8). In the second instance, if not both, the divine sovereignty of the Voice from heaven is recognized. Paul asks, "What shall I do, Lord?" (22:10). Significantly, the form of "Lord" that appears in both these places is identical to that used by the "full-fledged Christian," Ananias, who in 9:10, in full obedience, says: "Behold, here am I, Lord" (NASB).

Still more significant are the words of Ananias, "Brother Saul, the Lord Jesus . . . has sent me" (9:17, NASB). Dunn's suggestion that "brother" is used to suggest Jewish kinship is too much. Ananias is greeting Paul as a fellow Christian believer. Paul needed to hear those words of acceptance, because he had been the chief enemy of Christians.

If Ananias had gone to Paul in order to help him to be justified, to believe, to become a Christian, why do the accounts tell us nothing of that sort? They tell us the opposite, that Paul is called a brother, probably a Christian brother. Nothing in the accounts has conversion language in it. Ananias says that Christ "has sent me so that you may regain your sight, and be filled with the Holy Spirit" (9:17, NASB).

Ananias said to Paul, "And now why do you delay? Arise, and be baptized, and wash away your sins, calling on His name" (22:16, NASB). Water baptism does not wash away sins. This "brother" Christian was to receive baptism to symbolize and witness to the washing away of his sins that had already occurred.

Cornelius Is Already Converted. It must be admitted that Luke does not make it altogether clear that Cornelius is already a Christian when, upon him (and other Gentiles), "the gift of the Holy Spirit" was "poured out" (Acts 10:45); yet the evidence strongly suggests it.

For one thing, Cornelius is said in verse 2 to have been *eusebēs,* which means "reverent; pious, devout, religious."[121] Another way of translating this word is "godly." The same word is used in 2 Pet. 2:9 for "the godly" whom "the Lord knows how to rescue . . . from temptation." They are the opposite from "the unrighteous" (NASB). A cognate of this word, *eusebeia,* is used for the "godliness" of Paul and other Christians in 1 Tim. 2:2. An adverbial form, *eusebōs,* describes those who are decidedly "in

---

121. *The Analytical Greek Lexicon* (New York: Harper and Brothers, n.d.), 176.

452 ◁ A WESLEYAN-HOLINESS THEOLOGY

Christ Jesus," for Paul writes: "And indeed, all who desire to live godly in Christ Jesus will be persecuted" (2 Tim. 3:12, NASB). True, it can describe the worshipers of an "unknown god" (Acts 17:23, RSV), but the reference to Cornelius better suits its usage to designate Christian believers.

When Cornelius is called "righteous" in Acts 10:22, we have a much stronger suggestion that he is a Christian believer. It is a cognate of *dikaiosunē*, the regular word for justification in the New Testament. This very word, with the definite article *ho dikaios*, the Just One, is even one of the distinctive titles of Christ in Acts (3:14; 7:52; and 22:14, KJV). It is one of the New Testament's special words for what God himself is, "just," and for what He makes us into by "faith in Jesus" (Rom. 3:26). That his servants so designate Cornelius does not detract from our argument. It enhances it. The ancient Origen was probably correct in understanding that this is the centurion of Luke 7 whose servant Christ healed, who gave a synagogue to the Jews—which could be why the whole nation of the Jews held Cornelius in high esteem.

Cornelius "feared God with all his household" (Acts 10:2, NASB). This means that he reverenced God and saw to it that his family and helpers did also.

Besides, He "gave many alms to the Jewish people" (v. 2). This does not prove that he was a believer, but it is one quality of a believer's life.

He "prayed to God continually" (v. 2), and his prayers were answered—which does not happen in the absence of faith.

His stated willingness to hear and (by implication) obey the word of the Lord is characteristic of believers, not of the unsaved (v. 33).

God gives him a special "vision," and the visit and ministry of an "angel" (vv. 3-7).

Peter surely would be including Cornelius and giving him assurance of his acceptance with God when he says to him: "Of Him [Christ] all the prophets bear witness that through His name everyone who believes in Him receives forgiveness of sins" (v. 43).

And it is important to ask: If Cornelius is not already forgiven, what is wrong with our gracious God? If wayfaring people, though completely empty-headed, need not err in coming to God (Isa. 35:8, KJV), why has this "God-fearing" man erred so badly as not to be justified, with all his seeking of and openness toward God?

What is the minimum of intellectual understanding that is necessary before one can become a Christian? Is it one one-thousandth of what we might come to understand as mature Christians? If we are "righteous," as Scripture says Cornelius was, that is plenty, surely, for understanding that we are justified.

Dunn's translation of the aorist participle *pisteusasin* in Acts 11:17 makes Pentecost the time when Peter and others "believed," or were converted. That would argue for the conversion of Cornelius at the time of his baptism with the Spirit. The RSV reads, "If then God gave the same gift to them as he gave to us when we believed in the Lord Jesus Christ . . ." But the NASB, often more careful to follow the Greek, translates *pisteusasin* in the way aorist participles are normally rendered: "If God therefore gave to them the same gift as He gave to us also after believing in the Lord Jesus Christ, who was I that I could stand in God's way?" This usage indicates that their believing was prior to their being baptized with the Holy Spirit.

Dunn and others also get theological mileage for their Pentecost-is-conversion view from the next verse: "Well then, God has granted to the Gentiles also the repentance that leads to life" (v. 18, NASB). I see it differently. We are now back in Jerusalem, a long time later, and Peter is on the carpet for participating in gospel work among Gentiles. They are not speaking specifically about Cornelius's being baptized with the Spirit. They get after Peter because he shared Christ with the "uncircumcised" and "ate with them" (v. 3). They are not talking about Cornelius's baptism with the Spirit. They are questioning the extension of the gospel of God's forgiving grace to a Gentile.

Some Holiness writers understand that Cornelius was not a Christian until Peter visited him, but that he was justified immediately prior to the coming of the Holy Spirit upon him in baptismal fullness. Ralph Earle teaches that Cornelius became a Christian just before his Spirit baptism.[122] The word "saved" in Acts 11:14

---

122. See Ralph Earle, exegesis, "The Acts of the Apostles," in *The Evangelical Commentary* (Grand Rapids: Zondervan Publishing House, 1959), 136-37, 154; see also Earle's exegesis in the *Beacon Bible Commentary* (Kansas City: Beacon Hill Press of Kansas City, 1965), 7:382, where he refers to Adam Clarke in support; also Earle, *Meet the Early Church* (Kansas City: Nazarene Publishing House, 1959), 49-50: "Cornelius and his companions were so completely receptive to the message that when they heard about believing in Jesus they immediately did so and were

does not demand this interpretation. It is a much broader term than "justified," "forgiven," or "regenerated," as it is often used in Scripture (cf. Mark 16:16; Acts 2:21; 16:31; 1 Cor. 3:15).

Two Works of Grace at Ephesus. Acts 19:1-7 is not as incontestably "two works of grace" as in 8:1-25, but it is almost as clearly so. It tells how Paul found at Ephesus certain baptized disciples who had not yet "received"—or been filled with—the Holy Spirit, and they then received the Spirit.

On several bases, we understand that the Holy Spirit's coming upon them was subsequent to their conversion.

Paul calls them *mathētai,* disciples, a customary New Testament word for Christian believers. If it meant that they were disciples of anyone else, such as John the Baptist, and not of Christ, that specific would have been mentioned.

They had already believed. Paul asked them, "Did you receive the Holy Spirit when you believed?" (Acts 19:2). Again, we have an aorist participle, *pisteusantes,* "having believed" (or, "when you believed"). Customarily, the aorist participle expresses action that is prior to the action of the main verb of a sentence. The sense is, "Having believed, did you receive the Holy Spirit?" Familiar with John the Baptist's ministry, they had believed on the promised Christ, but they had not heard of the outpouring by Christ of the promised Spirit. Now they do—and they receive Him in His cleansing, empowering fullness as did the 120 at Pentecost.

These disciples at Ephesus are called "brethren" in Acts 18:27, where we read that "the brethren encouraged him [Apollos]" (NASB). It does not take much acquaintance with the New Testament to know that "brethren" is frequently its way of saying "Christians."

Luke tells us that "they were baptized in the name of the Lord Jesus" (v. 5, NASB).[123] And his next words are: "And when Paul had laid his hands upon them, the Holy Spirit came on them" (v. 6, NASB). To be candidates for baptism, they would have been believ-

---

saved. But their hearts were so hungry for all of God's will and so surrendered to Him that they were soon filled with the Holy Spirit in the same service."

123. Baptism in the name of the whole Trinity was not practiced in Acts. It is done only in "the name of the Lord Jesus." The Matthean Gospel, which in 28:19 gives the Trinitarian formula, had not as yet been written. After it was written and disseminated, baptisms were done with the Trinitarian formula—as has almost universally obtained in Christian history.

ers, as the account says they were. After believing, then, they were baptized; and after their baptism, the Holy Spirit "came on them."[124]

Surely, it is the teaching of Scripture that Christ's baptism with the Holy Spirit is not received in the first work of grace. It happens only to justified persons, so that it is properly referred to as the second work of grace.

---

124. This is the order in Acts 8: believing, baptism in water, then baptism with the Spirit. This is the usual order in the New Testament, although the order is not always altogether clear.

17

The Second Work of Grace: Touches of Error

Numerous errors or touches of error have been put forward within the Holiness Movement concerning the doctrine and experience of entire sanctification. Often, this has been due to a lay theology that has grown up like Topsy with the movement, although some of them have been promoted even by professional scholars.

Many of these errors and touches of error will be discussed here, keeping in mind that the present writer might also be in error in places and in need of correction. These matters need to be discussed as a means of further elucidating Holiness doctrine and experience.

A secondary purpose in adding this chapter is to demonstrate the importance of being theologically discriminating as one reads Holiness literature and participates in the life of the Holiness Movement—especially in its worship and its practice.

In Theological Constructs

In the area of theological understandings, several Holiness teachings have at least touches of error in them.

Purgatorial Entire Sanctification. It is an error to say that Roman Catholics teach that entire sanctification is received in purgatory. John Wesley himself suggested this in his widely used *Plain Account of Christian Perfection:* "Some say, 'This [Christian perfection] cannot be attained till we have been refined by the fire of purgatory.'"[1]

---

1. Wesley, *Plain Account,* 3.

Many people have repeated Wesley's error in books and magazines. As late as 1974, in *The Case for Entire Sanctification,* P. P. Belew wrote, "Another view, held by the Roman Catholic church, is that the believer is sanctified after death by the love-fires of purgatory."[2]

The Roman Catholics do not teach this. They teach that the guilt of original sin is cleansed away when a person receives water baptism. They teach that one is baptized or filled with or receives the Holy Spirit at confirmation, usually 10 years or so after infant baptism, which is similar to the Spirit baptism of Holiness doctrine. In purgatory, in their teaching, two kinds of cleansing take place—penal cleansing for the less serious venial sins, and temporary punishment for mortal sins.

Holiness or Hell. Some have taught or implied that if believers are not sanctified wholly, they will go into perdition after this life.

John Wesley wrote an extended treatise on original sin, and he taught, properly, there and elsewhere, that no one will ever go into eternal hell for Adam's sin alone.[3] This is because the guilt that had actually been ours due to Adam's sin was alleviated in all of us, because of Christ. Wesley says, "By the merits of Christ, all men are cleared from the guilt of Adam's actual sin."[4]

H. Orton Wiley was surely correct in saying that the free gift of Romans 5 was extended to all, removing the guilt—but not the depravity—due to Adam's sin. Because of this racial benefit of Christ's atonement, if we are justified at the time of our death, we would go into eternal bliss—original sin being cleansed away for such a person, who is walking in the light.

George D. Watson taught holiness or hell. He wrote, "Pardon and purity are both received by separate, specific acts of receptive faith . . . are both retained by constant submission . . . are both requisite to a happy, useful life, and both *absolutely essential* to admission to heaven."[5]

Some have understood the matter in this way in part because of Heb. 12:14: "Pursue peace with all men, and the sanctification

2. P. P. Belew, *The Case for Entire Sanctification* (Kansas City: Beacon Hill Press of Kansas City, 1974), 24.

3. See this extended treatise on the doctrine of original sin in Wesley, *Works* 9:196-464.

4. Ibid. 8:277.

5. George D. Watson, *A Holiness Manual* (Boston: Christian Witness Co., 1882), 51.

("holiness," KJV; "the holiness," RSV) without which no one will see the Lord" (NASB). Sanctification, here, might not be entire sanctification, but the kind of holiness that is begun in regeneration and that is maintained all through the Christian life.

The careful person will not teach holiness or hell. Such teaching implies that if we die in the justified state but are not sanctified wholly, we will enter into eternal hell. It is justification, not entire sanctification, that changes our eternal destiny. If we are justified and walking in the light, Christ's blood will cleanse us of original sin in an imputed way—as it does for infants, small children, and lifelong imbeciles.[6] Entire sanctification is imperative for our establishment in the Christian life. It is not a necessity in the way justification is.

A Mix-up on Motives. Entire sanctification does not make our motives pure, as has often been taught in the Holiness Movement. Carnality, original sin, is cleansed away in the second work of grace, which means that our motives are not sinful. Yet they are not necessarily pure—not necessarily good, acceptable, approved by God.

Motives are inward bases, springboards, for what we do. They can stem from the carnal nature; but they can also stem from the human nature. Insofar as they stem from the human nature, in those sanctified wholly, they might or might not be "pure" or appropriate.

Entire sanctification does not dehumanize us. This has always been taught in Holiness circles. This means that the various human desires, "instincts," are still basically what they previously were, only cleansed of their carnal infection.

The human in us, our "instinctive" desires, might inwardly motivate us in a direction that is not God's first choice for us. After entire sanctification, then, our motives are not carnal. They are pure in that sense, but only in that sense. In the wider sense of being pure—acceptable to God—they might not be pure. Growth in grace might need to take place before our humanity is brought more and more under the sovereignty of Christ.

---

6. If we, in accountable years, had refused Christ and then became altogether mentally ill for the remainder of our lives, we would probably go before God unjustified. But this would be exceedingly rare, for it does not take very much in the way of brains to turn to God and receive forgiveness. Even a rebel in a dying coma might have sufficient capacity to repent and believe.

Calling Entire Sanctification the Cleansing Experience. By calling entire sanctification the cleansing experience, we imply that there is no cleansing at the first work of grace. But an initial sanctification takes place at conversion, a cleansing from the propensity to acts of sin that builds up in us because of our acts of sin. When God forgives our past sins, He cleanses us of this acquired bias to them. This cleansing is the "washing of regeneration" (Titus 3:5, KJV).

Jesus Saves and the Spirit Sanctifies. "Jesus saves and the Holy Spirit sanctifies" has often been the form that testimonies have taken. This implies that Jesus accomplishes for us the first work of grace and that the Holy Spirit accomplishes the second.

To testify in this way is not a gross error, yet it is not quite correct. Each of the three Persons of the Trinity figures in a signal way in both works of God's grace.

Take the first work of grace. Jesus Christ provides for the forgiveness of our sins by His death and resurrection. The Holy Spirit convicts of sin and draws us to God through the proclaimed gospel. And the Father forgives us when we repent of our sins and believe in Christ.

In the second work of grace, Jesus Christ baptizes believers with the Holy Spirit, thus effecting entire sanctification. The Father wills our sanctification and cleanses His children.

Because the whole Trinity figures strategically in both works of grace, we tend to be incorrect when we say that Jesus saves and that the Holy Spirit sanctifies.

Of, Instead of with, the Spirit. A touch of theological error obtains when people speak of the baptism "of" instead of "with" the Holy Spirit. In the early history of the Holiness Movement, "of" instead of "with" was in widespread use. Jack Ford, in *What the Holiness People Believe,* issued as recently as 1954, uses this kind of wording, and it has also appeared in more recent writings of distinguished Holiness scholars.

If we use "of," we are saying that this is the Holy Spirit's baptism. If we use "with," we are saying that this is Christ's baptism.

"With" is how Scripture is worded (Matt. 3:11).

Errors in Sundry Terms. Several terms in wide use within the Holiness Movement have at least a touch of error in them.

1. *Self-will.* To call original sin "self-will" is not quite correct. The expression suggests that even after conversion our wills are

opposed to God's will. The term suggests an undermining of the first work of grace. Bertha Munro's term "self-willedness" is preferable because it implies a state, which is what original sin is.

2. *Rebellion.* Similar to self-will is the term "rebellion." The problem with the term "rebellion" is the very same as with self-will: it suggests an undercutting of what God does for us in the first work of grace. The Christian is not in a state of rebellion after repentance and justification.

Numerous generic, metaphoric, and concrete-act words for sin occur in the Hebrew and Greek of the Bible—and the most serious acts of all are the rebellious ones. Rebellion characterizes enemies of God, not children of God who have repented and are justified.

3. *Using "surrender" for "consecrate."* Widespread indeed is the use of surrender as a synonym of consecrate. Believers, who are already children of God, are exhorted to surrender themselves to God and let Him sanctify them wholly. This also tends to undermine repentance and regeneration. To surrender is what a rebel does. To consecrate is what a child of God does.

The word "yield" is an acceptable synonym of "consecrate," although it is closer in meaning to what a rebel might do than "consecrate" is.

4. *The self is crucified.* Holiness people have often been told that in entire sanctification the self is crucified. Gal. 2:20, 5:24, and 6:14 have been cited to support this notion, but these passages mean, surely, not that the self is crucified, but that the carnal infection of the self is crucified. The carnal mind, that has clung like a barnacle to the self (as Romans 7 suggests), is crucified, but the self is trued up—made a truer self than when it was infected.

In Scripture Interpretation

Eph. 5:18. This passage is a good text for urging people who have already been baptized and sealed with the Holy Spirit of promise (1:13-14) to continue in the Spirit-filled life. It is not a text for urging believers to become sanctified wholly, but it has been used often for that purpose.

Usually translated "Be filled with the Spirit," the present tense of "filled" is obscured. "Be being filled," a more accurate translation, is also much less literary.

Phil. 3:12. It is common knowledge that Paul disclaims being perfect in verse 12 and includes himself among the perfect ones in verse 15. In the earlier passage he says, "Not that I have already obtained it, or have already become perfect, but I press on in order that I may lay hold of that for which also I was laid hold of by Christ Jesus" (NASB). Then, in almost the same breath, he says, "Let us therefore, as many as are perfect, have this attitude" (NASB).

It has been wrongly assumed that Paul was disclaiming perfect conduct but implying a perfect heart. What Paul disclaims, however, is the resurrection perfection he speaks of in verse 11.

Rom. 6:6. Perhaps as widespread as any of the touches of error relating to inadequate interpretation of Scripture is the identification of what Paul calls the "old man" with original sin.

It no doubt refers to the old, unregenerate life, the kind of person that obtained before conversion, in contrast to the new "man," the person of the new birth, the regenerate person.

Holiness writers, in equating "old man" with original sin, are repeating an error as old as Adam Clarke and John Wesley. Clarke says, "We find that *palaios anthrōpos, the old man,* used here [in Rom. 6:6], and in Eph. 4:22, and Coloss. 3:9, is . . . the same which we mean by *indwelling sin,* or the *infection of our nature,* in consequence of the *fall.*"[7]

Even earlier, John Wesley took this same position. In his *Notes,* at Rom. 6:6, he says of "our old man": "Coeval with our being, and as old as the Fall; our evil nature; a strong and beautiful expression for that entire depravity and corruption which by nature spreads itself over the whole man, leaving no part uninfected."[8]

In Rom. 6:6, if the "old man" (KJV) is original sin, and if "the body of sin" is original sin, then Rom. 6:6 states that our original sin is crucified in order that original sin might be destroyed. If, however, our "old man" refers to the unregenerate life, in contrast to the new life in Christ (v. 4), then Paul is saying that we are regenerated in order that we might be sanctified wholly.

In verses 4 and 5 Paul talks about regeneration; and in verse 6 he speaks of both regeneration and entire sanctification. He says

---

7. Clarke, *Clarke's Commentary,* 6:77.
8. Wesley, *Notes,* 540.

in verse 4 that "we have been buried with Him through baptism into death" and raised to "walk in newness of life" (NASB). This gets us "planted" (v. 5, KJV) in Christ. Then, in verse 6, Paul says that God crucifies our former manner of life, regenerating us, in order to go ahead and destroy the state of original sin.

Eph. 4:19-25. Paul recounts here what had happened to his readers. They had "heard" Christ call, and they had been "taught in Him" the "truth" that "in reference to your former manner of life, you lay aside the old self . . . and put on the new self" (Eph. 4:21-24, NASB). Here the old self, or the old man, that had been put off is not original sin, but the unregenerate life.

The old man, or "old self," is connected integrally with their "former manner of life." The old man, then, is the unregenerate life, which is characterized both by original sin and acts of sin.

Furthermore, this old man is contrasted with the "new man" (KJV), and surely the new "man" is the "man" of the new birth. If so, the old man is the man, or self, that existed before the new birth and was characterized by sin.

The word "holiness" appears in Eph. 4:24 in many translations and has probably inclined some to connect the putting off of the old man with entire sanctification. But the word "holiness" is often used in Scripture without reference to entire sanctification. It is used of almost any part of the process of redemption.

Col. 3:9. Here both carnal affections and acts of sin are connected with the "old man" (KJV), which again suggests that the phrase refers to the unregenerate life instead of simply original sin. Paul speaks of putting off carnal affections such as "anger, wrath, malice" and also acts such as "abusive speech" (Col. 3:8, NASB). Then he says, "Do not lie to one another, since you laid aside the old self with its evil practices" (v. 9, NASB). If "old man," here, were a reference to original sin, Paul would be saying, "You may tell lies all you please while you are regenerate, but not after you are cleansed from original sin. Therefore, since original sin has now been put off, in a second work of grace, quit your lying to one another." If the "old man" refers to the unregenerate life, Paul is saying, "You people now have new hearts. Old things have passed away, and all things are new. Live therefore as regenerate persons, and 'Do not lie to one another,' seeing that you have put off the old life 'with its evil practices.'"

Extreme Interpretations of Scripture

Until around the century's turn and even later, the literature of the Holiness Movement occasionally reflected extreme interpretations of Scripture.

Extreme Interpretations on Healing. Some Holiness people began to teach extreme views about physical healing. While all God's graciousness to us is, broadly, due to Christ's atonement, it is extreme to say that one can expect to be healed the same way a sinner may expect to be saved or a believer sanctified through and through.

That the Sanctified Are the 144,000. Another extreme interpretation was Carradine's view that the 144,000 redeemed persons mentioned in the Book of Revelation refer to "those who were sanctified in this life." He wrote:

> Our own firm belief is that the 144,000 stand for those who were sanctified in this life, waiting not for the dying hour to receive a work of grace which Christ stands ready and willing and able to perform at the present moment. When we remember what it costs to obtain this blessing— what ridicule, opposition, persecution, and ecclesiastical rejection it invariably entails—we are not surprised that the suffering ones have a distinction accorded them that is not granted to all who are in heaven.[9]

Unscholarly Interpretations. Three of these will be noted here.

1. *Two covenants, so two works.* When Beverly Carradine based his teaching of two works of grace, in part, on the fact that there are two covenants, the Old Testament one and the New Testament one, he resorted to an extreme and unscholarly interpretation. Of these two covenants he wrote, "These two covenants embrace all that God does for the soul on earth, and accurately describe the two works of grace, regeneration and sanctification."[10]

There are two dispensations, and the Holy Spirit was poured out upon believers shortly after the second dispensation had begun. However, both works of grace could occur in the Old Testament dispensation—although entire sanctification was rare in Old Testament times. Isaiah, in chapter 6, might be an instance.

---

9. Beverly Carradine, *The Second Blessing in Symbol* (Louisville, Ky.: Pickett Publishing Co., 1896), 223-24.
10. Ibid., 87.

2. *That tongues are of Satan.* Some Holiness people taught that tongues-speaking is of Satan, including W. B. Godbey, who wrote, "The counterfeit Tongue Movement is the grandest rally Satan has made in our day to actually counterfeit the Holy Ghost, capture it and make capital of it."[11]

Godbey made little use of Scripture, history, or theology in opposing "unknown tongues." Chiefly he appeals to his own investigation and observation.

3. *Morrison, on Romans 7.* H. C. Morrison interpreted Romans 7 as depicting a regenerate person. He did not seem to know that James Arminius wrote over 250 pages on that chapter, taking an "awakened unregenerate" view of the person there described—and starting a long and stable and almost unanimous tradition of such interpretation in Arminian-Wesleyanism.

Morrison's eccentric scholarship is shown also in what he wrote on the "inward man" of Romans 7. According to the apostle Paul, everyone has an inward man, in distinction from the outer man of the body. Yet Morrison writes:

> Observe here that the inward man *delights in the law of God.* The sinner has no inward man except the "old man," and you may be sure that "old man" does not delight in the law of God. The inward man spoken of here is the regenerated man, the new man, imparted by the grace of God to the penitent sinner by regenerating grace, at the time of his justification. This *new "inward man,"* delights in the law of God, but the "old man" remaining in the nature makes war on the *new man,* and when the new man would do good, the "old man," (evil) is present with him, to hinder him in carrying out his good intentions.[12]

Extreme Claims for the Experience

The second work of grace, entire sanctification, is not a panacea. Sometimes Holiness people have made extreme claims about Holiness experience.

"Never Without Comfort." J. A. Wood was surely too extreme in saying that "the sanctified soul is never without comfort."[13]

---

11. W. B. Godbey, *Baptism of the Holy Ghost* (Greensboro, N.C.: Apostolic Messenger Office, n.d.), 19.

12. H. C. Morrison, *Baptism with the Holy Ghost* (Louisville, Ky.: Pentecostal Publishing Co., 1900), 24.

13. Wood, *Perfect Love,* rev. ed. (Chicago: S. K. J. Chesbro, 1880), 126.

While we would never be without the Comforter, we might at times be without comfort. Surely we might, in life's traumas, feel we are without "comfort." Right while we are living the life of entire sanctification, we might experience what the mystics have called the "dark night of the soul." To experience "comfort," we would need to avail ourselves of the various means of grace: Scripture reading, worship, the Lord's Supper, to specify only a few.

Impatience Is Conquered. The same writer includes "impatience" as one of the "fruits of inbred sin."[14] If so, when believers are cleansed from inbred sin, impatience should be gone. Such a claim is unrealistic.

Patience is listed with the "fruit of the Spirit" in Gal. 5:22, but impatience is not listed among the "acts of the sinful nature" in verses 19-21. Patience develops in the Spirit-filled life. Impatience can spring from human nature, even purified human nature, with its legitimate instincts and drives.

Their Quiet Is Untouched. Wood also says of the wholly sanctified that "the quiet of their spirit is untouched, and they are never destitute of peace."[15] Again, this is surely unrealistic. In justification we are at peace with God as Judge, and in entire sanctification the peace of God is given us. Yet we will not always and unvaryingly be aware of this peace.

When one is deserted by a spouse, when one is unfairly discharged from employment, when one's child is killed in an accident, when one is confronted by any savage tragedy, will the soul's quiet be untouched? If so, we would be robots—not humans. Scripture surely does not advertise any work of grace that effects such existential wonders as this.

One Has No Improper Desires. John Wesley contributed to incorrect understanding in affirming that the sanctified have no improper desires. R. T. Williams, in *Temptation: A Neglected Theme,*[16] taught correctly that improper desires are consistent with the devout Christian life. He taught that sin is committed only when one wills to implement a desire for what is sinful.

Desire for what is wrong, when the will does not agree with the desire, often occurs in the holy life. Some steps that could

---

14. Ibid.
15. Ibid.
16. R. T. Williams, *Temptation: A Neglected Theme* (Kansas City: Beacon Hill Press, 1920).

lead to sin are not themselves sinful. These steps include (1) the attention given to what is wrong; (2) the desire for what has attracted attention; (3) a prevolitional impulse toward what is desired; and (4) finally a person's judgment that turns on the red light of danger. If, at that point, we do not will to do what we have desired, we have not sinned.

All Prejudices Vanish. J. O. McClurkan taught extreme views on the vanishing of prejudices. He wrote, "The sanctified heart is absolutely cleansed of all . . . race prejudice. Holiness deepens and sweetens and broadens the nature until every man of all and every section and nationality and color or condition is loved as a brother. There is no North, no South, no Jew, nor Greek, no Barbarian to the sanctified."[17]

Yet since racial, educational, cultural and other prejudices are learned environmentally, they are not aspects of Adamic sin and are not necessarily routed in entire sanctification. Peter still had his prejudice against Gentiles well after his Pentecost and went to Gentile Cornelius only after being guided to do so by a triple vision. God helped the apostle from Capernaum, and He can help us on such matters. Although He is sovereign and might effect a miraculous deliverance, His race relations help will more likely be received through spiritual maturation.

It Gives Personality Integration. There is a profound integration that occurs when the dividedness of the regenerate, due to the carnal mind, is dissolved because that mind is expelled. The experience does help the believer to a special dimension of integrity. Frank Carver is correct at a profound depth when he says that "the biblical use of the word 'Holiness' can function as a synonym for integrity. There is a profound sense in which holiness is to God what integrity is to man."[18] Carver is correct when he talks of "exclusive allegiance to God,"[19] of "unadulterated grace,"[20] and of "a single trust."[21] Yet it is surely too much to say, as so many

---

17. J. O. McClurkan, *Zion's Outlook* 7 (February 1901): 8. See Timothy L. Smith, *Called unto Holiness*, vol. 1 (Kansas City: Beacon Hill Press, 1962), 183, for numerous other references to McClurkan's view at this point.

18. Frank Carver, "Biblical Foundations for the 'Secondness' of Entire Sanctification," *WTJ* 22, no. 2 (Fall 1987): 8.

19. Ibid.

20. Ibid., 16.

21. Ibid., 17.

have, that holiness is the integrating experience and then to give specific, extreme ways in which integration of experience results from entire sanctification. Donald Metz, in his *Studies in Biblical Holiness,* teaches more than is warranted in this regard. He says that entire sanctification will result in "a sense of self-respect and self-worth."[22] A poor self-image, however, does not arise from Adamic sin. That sin, we have usually said, is a source instead of pride. A bad self-image arises from demeaning experiences in childhood, and while entire sanctification might help a person to overcome this damage, it does not simply result in a straightening out of that kind of warp.

Metz also says that the integration results in "a consistent personality which is displayed in all relationships."[23] This is too much, surely.

Metz also said that there will be an "absence of inner spiritual conflicts."[24] If this means there will never be any spiritual doubts, this is different from the way many Holiness leaders have represented the Holiness experience. If there were an absence of all inner conflict, how could there be any temptations, or any falling from grace, or any dark night of the soul?

Even the matter of "selfless service"[25] is something that surely comes from an increasing sense of Christian responsibility through growth in grace, instead of being one of the "results"[26] of entire sanctification.

The Subconscious Is Cleansed. The late E. Stanley Jones, perhaps our century's most renowned Holiness preacher, taught erroneously at this point. Jones taught that in entire sanctification the subconscious—what we now often call the unconscious—is cleansed.

In requested testimony in a flyleaf for Charles Ewing Brown's thorough and superb study of entire sanctification, *The Meaning of Sanctification,* Jones wrote: "We live in two minds—the conscious and the subconscious. The subconscious is the residing place of the driving instincts: self, sex, and the herd . . . Into the

---

22. Metz, *Studies in Biblical Holiness,* 254.
23. Ibid.
24. Ibid.
25. Ibid.
26. Ibid.

conscious mind there is introduced at conversion a new life, a new loyalty, a new love. But the subconscious does not obey this new life . . . There ensues a clash."[27]

Jones goes on to say that "the area of the work of the Holy Spirit is largely, if not entirely, in the subconscious."[28] He says further, "I found that if I would surrender . . . He would cleanse at these depths . . . I surrendered and accepted the gift by faith."[29]

This all sounds beautiful, but it mines in the area of psychology and not in the area of Bible and theology; it suggests an equating of the subconscious with original sin. This cannot be. We come into the world with original sin but not with the subconscious. The subconscious, insofar as it still enjoys respect in the schools, has to do with what is packed into our inner minds during this life—often by aberrating experiences. From it our dreams arise. In it are a thousand thousand memories. It is why we often have unwilled hostility feelings toward authority figures. It is where racial prejudice resides when we volitionally intend not to be thus prejudiced.

Entire sanctification cleanses from original sin, but it does not necessarily right the derangements due to aberrating experiences that have happened during this life. These become corrected gradually as we grow in grace. They become fully corrected only when our mortality puts on immortality—only when the sanctified are glorified.

---

27. See Brown, *The Meaning of Sanctification*, ii.
28. Ibid.
29. Ibid.

18

The Church Itself

The Church of Jesus Christ, older than any university, dynasty, or government, is the most significant institution of society. Indeed, even as the Bible is more than the best of books, the Church is more than the best in any list of social institutions. Created by grace and headed by Christ, the Church is Spirit-led, worships God in Word and sacrament, engages itself with the Great Commission, and is uniquely significant.

This chapter will discuss a definition of the Church, its very necessity, its founding, its nature, and its unity. Following this, the Church and God's Word, the Church and the Spirit's ministry, the Church's ministry, and the Church's relation to the state will be discussed.

Definition of the Church

No definition of the Church can be found in the ancient fathers, Eastern or Western.[1] None was given by any of the ecumenical councils, nor by any of the three ancient creeds (Apostles', Nicene, Athanasian). Indeed, no single treatise was written on what the Church is until the 14th century, when John Wycliffe wrote his *De ecclesiae* (On the church).

The Greek New Testament word for "church" is *ekklēsia*, literally meaning "the called-out ones." In the Septuagint, Israel is referred to as an *ekklēsia*, meaning that it was called out from among the many nations of the world. In the New Testament, the word refers to believers who are called out from the world.

---

1. George Florovsky says, "The Fathers did not care so much for the *doctrine* of the Church precisely because the glorious *reality* of the church was open to their spiritual vision." *Bible, Church, Tradition: An Orthodox View* (Belmont, Mass.: Nordland Publishing Co., 1972), 57.

The word "church," therefore, originally referred to the people and only much later came to refer to the building where the people of God meet together in Christ's name.[2] The word is found 115 times in the New Testament. In 112 of these instances it refers to the church as people, either locally or universally. The other three instances, found in Acts 19:32, 39, and 41, are references simply to an assembly of opponents of the church who objected to Paul's ministry at Ephesus.

The Necessity of the Church

The church is not a rational necessity, but it is a practical necessity. This is because, although to be born again is intensely private, it is never a purely private matter.[3] When it happens, many other persons are affected by it.[4]

Born again, we enter into the community of believers known as the Church. We become members of the Body of Christ. And if we born-again persons are to continue in our new relationship with Christ, it is practically necessary for us to be part of a local church fellowship. In that "incendiary fellowship" called the church, a person will receive nourishment, instruction, hallowing worship experiences, and satisfying evangelism experiences.

The Founding of the Church

Three major views obtain on when the Church was founded. (1) The Church was founded when God called Abraham out and promised to bless all nations through him (see Gen. 12:1-3). (2) Jesus founded the Church and placed Peter as its earthly head— the Roman Catholic view. This is also basically the view of Wolfhart Pannenberg, who is interested in a loose church merger with a pope of a sort and a central governing body. Pannenberg

---

2. For the first three centuries, while Christianity was not the official religion of the Roman Empire, Christians were not permitted to build and own church structures. It was only after the divisiveness of Protestantism that the word "church" began to be used as a synonym for a given denomination.

3. See a discussion of all this in John S. Whale, "Life in the Spirit: The Christian Doctrine of the Church," in *Christian Doctrine* (New York: Macmillan Publishing Co., 1941).

4. Whale says that "according to physicists, the most distant star is disturbed every time my son throws his teddy-bear out of his pram" (ibid., 124). Whale also says that about the most private thing we can do is to die, but that we cannot do that without affecting other persons— and if, in our proud egocentricity, we try to unrelate ourselves from others, we relate ourselves to them badly.

has suggested that the Church was begun when Jesus instituted the Eucharist. (3) The Church was founded at Pentecost, a view generally held in Protestantism.

Here, the first two views will be treated as anticipations of the Church; and the last as when the Church was founded.

Anticipations in the Old Testament. William Robinson dates the founding of the Church to the call of Abraham: "At that moment the church of God—God's holy Israel—came into being."[5] While it might not be warranted to say with Robinson that the Church was founded then, that event was an important anticipation of it.

When Israel was called out from among the nations (2 Chron. 6:3), as the New Testament Church is called out from the world, that was also an anticipation of the Church.[6] We have, therefore, Israel in the Old Testament and the "Israel of God" (Gal. 6:16) in the New Testament. We have God's people Israel in the Old Testament and "God's elect" (1 Pet. 1:1) as the Church in the New Testament. Much is said about priests in the Old Testament, and we are all "priests" (Rev. 1:6) in the New Testament. The Church in Rom. 9:27 is the righteous remnant Isaiah had spoken of (10:22).

Even as the Church in the New Testament is Christ's Bride, Israel is Yahweh's Bride. Of her the Lord says, "In that day . . . you will call me 'my husband'" (Hos. 2:16); and He tells her, "I will betroth you to me forever" (v. 19). And even as Christ is the Vine and His disciples the branches in New Testament times (see John 15:1-8), so Israel is the vine of David. We read, "Israel was a spreading vine" (Hos. 10:1). And in an allegory, "the house of Israel" became "a vine and produced branches and put out leafy boughs" (Ezek. 17:6).

Old Testament anticipation of the New Testament Church is also found in numerous names and phrases referring to God's people that are similar to New Testament names and phrases denoting the church. We read of the house of Abraham, of Jacob

---

5. Robinson, *Biblical Doctrine of the Church*, 121.

6. "While the whole assembly of Israel was standing there, the king turned around and blessed them" (2 Chron. 6:3). Here the LXX uses the word *ekklēsia* for "assembly."

and/or of Israel (e.g., in Gen. 14:14; Exod. 19:3; Lev. 10:6; Ps. 114:1; Isa. 2:5). These are similar to New Testament passages. There we read of "the Son of the Most High" that "he will reign over the house of Jacob forever" (Luke 1:32-33).

In the Old Testament we read of the house of God or of the Lord (Gen. 28:17-22; Exod. 23:19, etc.). These passages are frequent in Kings and Chronicles and in Jeremiah. Similar passages occur in the New Testament (as in Matt. 12:4; 17:3, 15; Heb. 10:21). An interesting fact in this connection has to do with the naming of the Tabernacle, which literally meant "Tent of Meeting." Yahweh promised, "There I will meet you [the priests] and speak to you; there also I will meet with the Israelites, and the place will be consecrated by my glory. So I will consecrate the Tent of Meeting . . . They will know that I am the Lord their God . . . so that I might dwell among them" (Exod. 29:42-44, 46). This passage is similar to Christ's saying, "For where two or three come together in my name, there am I with them" (Matt. 18:20).

Old Testament anticipations of the Church are also contained in its looking for and longing for the Messiah—the Desire of all nations, a Light to enlighten both Jews and Gentiles; who dies on behalf of all in New Testament times, is raised from the dead, and becomes (especially for Paul) the great Head of the Church.

Anticipations in Jesus' Words and Actions. Roman Catholics have a special interest in Jesus' words, "And I tell you that you are Peter, and on this rock I will build my church" (Matt. 16:18). They hold that Peter—as the first bishop of Rome—was the rock upon which Christ builds the Church. Protestants usually understand that the rock on which Christ builds His Church is the confession Peter had just made—that Jesus was "the Christ, the Son of the living God" (v. 16). It is to be noted also that Jesus said, "I will build my church"—as though it was to be founded later, as at Pentecost. Clear anticipations of the Church do appear, however, during Jesus' incarnate years.

1. *In the kingdom of God/heaven.* Jesus referred to the church only twice (Matt. 16:16-18; 18:17), and it is surprising to find Him using the term at all in the era before Pentecost. Even some conservative scholars, such as Bernard Ramm, think Jesus actually used a different Aramaic word and that the inspired Matthew translated it into Greek as "church" because by then it meant

"church."[7] Jesus' characteristic way of referring to the people of God is to speak of the kingdom of God or the kingdom of heaven. In Matthew, which was written for Jews, who were reticent to use the term God, Jesus speaks of the kingdom of heaven, and not of the kingdom of God; but He strangely speaks also of the Church.[8]

The Kingdom was already realized; it was already "within" people (Luke 17:21), and yet it is what people were "waiting for" (Mark 15:43) and what people will be admitted to after the Judgment (Matt. 25:34). Sometimes it is used of what precedes the Church, sometimes of what obtains during the Church Age (Acts 28:23), and sometimes of heaven itself, where God sits on His "throne" and reigns (Revelation 22).

The point is that Jesus' characteristic way of referring to God's people is not to call them the Church, but to say that they are in the Kingdom—this usage anticipating the Church.

2. *In already being called out.* The Church is also anticipated when Jesus refers to His disciples as "not of the world" (John 17:14). To be "called out" from the world is what the Greek word for church, *ekklēsia*, means.

3. *In Jesus' expectation of unstinted service.* C. J. Cadeaux says, "No monarch with invincible armies at his beck and call could have asked of his subjects more unstinted sacrifice in his service."[9] Jesus expected His disciples to deny themselves and follow Him (Matt. 16:24), even as Paul later expected people in the Church to do (see Rom. 6:13; 12:1-2).

Pentecost as When the Church Was Founded. A number of factors support the understanding that the Church was founded at Pentecost.

1. *God's people are then called the Church.* The word "church" is only found twice in the Gospels, and in one of these references

---

7. This kind of development would probably not be inconsistent with either a verbal or a dynamic view of inspiration. The Holy Spirit would then be inspiring the writer to use "church," because that is what Jesus meant, even if He might have, in His Aramaic, used a looser term. Ramm says, "In general, 'church materials' are additions, interpretations, revisions of original materials, and unintentional accretions that came into the oral tradition and documents between the time of the apostles and the writing of the New Testament." This is from "Contemporary Theology and 'Church Material,'" *Christianity Today* 16, no. 22 (Aug. 11, 1972): 11.

8. This use of "heaven" in Matthew, instead of "God," is part and parcel of the matter discussed in the previous footnote. In the Aramaic, Jesus might have used "God," and Matthew might have used the word "heaven" instead of "God" as an inspired guidance of the Holy Spirit. In either case, the phrase means the same thing.

9. C. J. Cadeaux, *The Historic Mission of Jesus* (New York: Harper and Bros., 1941), 77.

Jesus says He will build it later (Matt. 16:18; 18:17). Prior to Pentecost, God's people are said to be in His kingdom (as noted earlier), to be disciples, to have believed or received eternal life, or whatever.

2. *Pentecost was "the beginning" of something.* According to Peter, "The Holy Spirit came on" the household of Cornelius "as he had come on us at the beginning" (Acts 11:15). This "beginning" is obviously Pentecost (vv. 16-17). The reference to a "beginning" could refer to the starting of the dispensation in which the Holy Spirit would be poured out on all sorts of people, as Joel (2:28) had prophesied. It might at the same time also refer to the beginning of the Church.

3. *Spirit fullness was now possessed.* Another basis for viewing the Church as founded on the Day of Pentecost is the fact that the Church now possessed the Holy Spirit in His baptismal fullness of heart purification (Acts 15:8-9) and power to witness (1:8). Before Pentecost, the Holy Spirit came upon believers only in isolated instances, for special reasons. He came thus upon the Old Testament prophets. And John the Baptist was "filled with the Holy Spirit even from birth" (Luke 1:15). Yet Joel had prophesied: "And afterward, I will pour out my Spirit on all people. Your sons and daughters will prophesy, your old men will dream dreams, your young men will see visions. Even on my servants, both men and women, I will pour out my Spirit in those days" (2:28-29).

Pentecost was the beginning of a dispensation in the economy of God's grace. And surely the Church could not have been what it was then, and now is, without being Spirit-filled.

4. *Evangelism now explodes.* We also understand that the Church was founded at Pentecost, because evangelism then burst all bounds.

On the morning of Pentecost Day, 3,000 were converted (Acts 2:41); soon other thousands became Christian believers (4:4). And from town to town, these early believers evangelized Gentiles as well as Jews and just about turned the then-known world right side up (17:6).

The 120 were empowered to witness, and they were immediately successful in evangelism. If to evangelize is a part of the Church's very essence, and if all and sundry of its workers need to be baptized with the Spirit and thus empowered to evangelize, then perhaps the Church was birthed at Pentecost.

5. *Christ's crucifixion and resurrection have now taken place.* The Church becomes composed of people who believed savingly in these events.

It is only after Christ's death and resurrection, and after Pentecost's empowerment, that the gospel could be presented to people in its gaunt reality and attractiveness. And from Pentecost onward, the Church was composed of people who believingly looked back to the Crucifixion and Resurrection. Thus Clarence Tucker Craig says, "Those who believed that God had raised Christ from the dead composed the Church."[10]

6. *The Lord's Supper is now begun.* While baptism in water occurred both before and after Pentecost, the Lord's Supper, instituted by Jesus, was observed by His followers only after Pentecost. And the Lord's Supper is integral to the very existence of the Church.[11] Through the Supper, believers participate in the Body of Christ—the Church. Thus Paul asks, "Is not the cup of thanksgiving for which we give thanks a participation in the blood of Christ? And is not the bread that we break a participation in the body of Christ?" (1 Cor. 10:16). His next words are, "Because there is one loaf, we, who are many, are one body, for we all partake of the one loaf" (v. 17). Partaking was a part of being in the one Body of Christ, the Church.

7. *Organization now occurs.* Prior to Pentecost, the institutional organization of believers did not exist. The 12 apostles had been chosen, and 3 of them (Peter, James, and John) were given special leadership within the group. Yet their leadership was largely spiritual, not institutional. After Pentecost, organization as an institution soon began. Right away, seven deacons were selected (Acts 6:1-6).

The church itself laid hands on Barnabas and Saul, sending them out for missionary evangelism. And on the missionary journeys, elders were appointed to be in charge of the local churches that were started. The word "elder" in Greek is *presbyteros,* from which we get the word "presbyter." These elders or presbyters were also called *episkopoi,* or bishops, meaning "overseers" (Acts

---

10. Clarence Tucker Craig, "The Church of the New Testament," in *Man's Disorder and God's Design* 1:34-35.

11. If it is said to be necessary to the Church's existence, the Salvation Army would not be a church—and the various Quaker denominations would not actually be, either.

20:17, 28). Further details of church organization are mentioned and implied in various New Testament writings, especially in the Pastoral Epistles.

On these bases, then, the Church seems to have begun at Pentecost. Before that, as George Ladd says, what obtains is "the circle of Jesus' disciples as the incipient church."[12] As Ladd also says, "The disciples before Pentecost should be considered only the embryo church," because, "strictly speaking, the *ekklesia* was born at Pentecost when the Holy Spirit was poured out upon the small circle of Jewish disciples of Jesus, constituting them the nucleus of Christ's body."[13]

The Nature of the Church

The Church is a divinely ordained organization-organism whose nature we can learn about in at least three ways: (1) by a study of the New Testament analogies, metaphors, or designations of the Church; (2) by reflecting on its nature through categories devised by theology itself, but based on Scripture; and (3) by noting its oneness.

Biblical Analogies of the Church. The New Testament contains in all about 80 minor analogies of the Church. Paul speaks of "the church of the living God, the pillar and ground of the truth" (1 Tim. 3:15, KJV). It is "God's field, God's building" (1 Cor. 3:9). Paul also calls the Church "bread" (5:7-8), a "loaf" of bread (10:16-17), a "vineyard" (9:7), an "olive tree" (Rom. 11:13-24), "members of God's household" (Eph. 2:19), and "the family of believers" (Gal. 6:10).[14]

Major biblical analogies of the Church include Christ's Bride, Christ's Body, and the new and true Israel.

1. *The Bride of Christ.* Scripture never actually defines the Church as the Bride of Christ but implies it in several places. Perhaps the clearest of these is in 2 Cor. 11:1 ff. Paul there says, "I promised you to one husband, to Christ, so that I might present

---

12. George Eldon Ladd, *A Theology of the New Testament* (Grand Rapids: William B. Eerdmans Publishing Co., 1974), 111.

13. Ibid., 347.

14. In the Gospels, before the Church as such comes into being (which probably happened at Pentecost), there are a number of pre-Church allusions to God's people that might be thought of as references to the Church. The faithful are "salt" (Matt. 5:13), a fishnet (Luke 5:1-11; John 21:1-14), etc.

you as a pure virgin to him" (v. 2). Here it is clear that Christ is the Husband; the Church, the virgin Bride.

Eph. 5:22-32 also implies that the Church is the Bride of Christ: "Now as the church submits to Christ, so also wives should submit to their husbands in everything" (v. 24). That Christ is like the Husband of the Church is further suggested as Paul admonishes, "Husbands, love your wives, just as Christ loved the church and gave himself up for her to make her holy" (vv. 25-26). Paul suggests that Christ, as a Husband, cares sacrificially for His Bride, the Church. He even likens the "one flesh" mystery of marriage to Christ's relationship to the Church: "'For this reason a man will leave his father and mother and be united to his wife, and the two will become one flesh.' This is a profound mystery— but I am talking about Christ and the church" (vv. 31-32).

A clear and significant New Testament implication that the Church is Christ's Bride is in Rev. 19:7-8. There John poetically exclaims: "Let us rejoice and be glad and give him glory! For the wedding of the Lamb has come, and his bride has made herself ready. Fine linen, bright and clean, was given her to wear."

Here Christ is the Lamb; the Church is the Bride. The Bride's "fine linen" clothing, "bright and clean," suggests the cleansing redemption the Church has received. The next verse reads: "Then the angel said to me, 'Write: Blessed are those who are invited to the wedding supper of the Lamb!'" Evidently, the Church is already Christ's Bride on this earth, but the "wedding supper" to celebrate the marriage is still an upcoming event.

2. *The Body of Christ.* Perhaps the most theologically significant of the New Testament analogies or metaphors of the Church is the Body of Christ. Appearing 19 times and only in Paul's Epistles, it is the most frequent such metaphor. Paul refers to the Church as "the body of Christ" 3 times (Rom. 12:5; 1 Cor. 12:27; Eph. 4:12). Three times he uses the phrase of Christ's body sacrificed on the Cross (Rom. 7:4, 1 Cor. 10:16; 11:24). In 13 other places he uses the word "body" to refer to the Church (1 Cor. 10:17; 12:12 [2 times], 13; Eph. 1:23; 3:6; 4:4, 16; 5:30; Col. 1:18, 24; 2:19; 3:15).[15] This usage prompts George Ladd to say,

---

15. Some books state that Paul used the "body" analogy for the Church 20 times. The writer's own count is 19.

"The most distinctive Pauline metaphor for the church is the body of Christ."[16]

Several theological truths are suggested by this Body of Christ analogy. One is unity amid diversity. Paul says, "Now the body is not made up of one part but of many" (1 Cor. 12:14). Moving from the physical body to the metaphorical, he says, "Now you are the body of Christ, and each one of you is a part of it" (v. 27). He goes on to say that "in the church God has . . . apostles . . . prophets . . . teachers," and others (v. 28); but in the diversity of offices and gifts, there is a unity—even as there is in our physical bodies.

The body metaphor also suggests that the Church is not merely an organization, but an organism. Admittedly, observably, and significantly, the Church is an organization. But the Church is also an organism. As such, you cannot add to it at its periphery as you do a mere organization, so that you have 30 churches in an area instead of 29. It grows by transformation from within—as a physical body does when food is ingested. This transformation from within is the new birth, and the Church is added to when this happens.

As the Body of Christ, the Church extends the Incarnation, Christ's enfleshment, into our present world. The faith-filled, love-filled, and hope-filled believers in Christ's Church constitute the kind of embodiment Christ now has in the world. The Church enfleshes His love for people. Christians are Christ's witnesses in His stead. They stand in for Christ until the time of the *parousia*.

Just as Christ now serves and speaks through His Body, the Church, so He now suffers in the Church. Did not Paul say, "For it has been granted to you on behalf of Christ not only to believe on him, but also to suffer for him" (Phil. 1:29)? And in Colossians, Paul says, "Now I rejoice in what was suffered for you, and I fill up in my flesh what is still lacking in regard to Christ's afflictions, for the sake of his body, which is the church" (1:24). What is lacking in Christ's suffering is in its distance from us in time and space—so that people tend to forget about it and disregard it. But when the Church, as Christ's present embodiment, stands right up in front of people and suffers for them, that claims their attention.

---

16. Ladd, *A Theology of the New Testament*, 545.

3. *The true Israel.* This analogy is exceedingly important theologically, because it meshes together the Old Testament and the New Testament, and Israel and the Church—meaning among other things that the Church is the new and true "Israel of God" (Gal. 6:16). From among the many people of Old Testament times, God chose one people, Israel, to be the recipients of His covenant love by calling, redeeming, sustaining, judging them. "Israel" as the inheritor of God's promises, however, is not the nation as a whole, but a believing, faithful remnant within the nation (Rom. 2:28-29; 9:6-8). True Israel is an olive tree into which both Jewish and Gentile branches are grafted (Romans 11)—the Church. John calls the Church the "chosen" or "elect lady" (2 John 1, KJV). Paul implies that Christians who were "Gentiles by birth" (Eph. 2:11) now held their "citizenship in Israel" (v. 12). Peter liked to tell Christians that they are God's people as Israel had been: "You are a chosen people ["race," RSV], a royal priesthood, a holy nation, a people belonging to God" (1 Pet. 2:9).

These, then, are a few of the numerous minor and major analogies or images or metaphors of the Church in the New Testament, all of which are theologically significant. From them we learn what the Church's nature is.

Theological Constructs of What the Church Is. Numerous theological statements of what the Church is, themselves based strategically on Scripture, need also to be considered in reflecting on the nature of the Church.

1. *The community of believers.* This is a peculiarly Protestant understanding: the priesthood of all believers is implied in this construct. It is essentially what Martin Luther understood the Church to be—and Karl Barth of our century.[17] "Believers," here, refers especially to people who believe in Christ's death and resurrection as the ground of their redemption and who have been justified by faith. The word "community" suggests the oneness that obtains in the Church, according to Scripture. The word "community" is in agreement, too, with the many biblical statements about the Church that suggest it is people—the *laos,* the laity.

2. *The saved and saving community.* This construct suggests, for one thing, that this community is "saved." Even the Society of

17. See Karl Barth, "The Living Congregation of the Living Lord Jesus Christ," in *Man's Disorder and God's Design,* 67-76.

Friends, among whom children are "enrolled as associate members," teach that "birthright" membership does not incorporate children into the Body of Christ. Only "by experiencing new birth" can one become a member of the Body of Christ.[18] It would not be a construct used by people who believe that one becomes a member of the Church through infant baptism, as in Roman Catholicism.[19] Liberal Protestants would not think of the Church as consisting of saved persons, for modernists do not usually believe in conversion.

The word "saved" is a Bible term used by Calvinists, Arminians, and other evangelicals. The word "saved," in this construct, means converted or born again. It means that only after we have personally repented and accepted Jesus Christ as our Savior are we members of the universal Church. It also means that only the saved should be accepted into membership in a local church.

The word "saving" would not be used in many denominations, but it would be appropriate for all evangelicals. The word "saving" implies that outside of Christ people are lost, and that the Church is the institution God uses to save them. Theological modernists among Protestants would not be comfortable with the term, unless it was understood loosely in that the Church is a sacrificial helper to people that saves them from such problems as emptiness and meaninglessness.

To evangelicals, though, "saving" means something quite special. It means that evangelism of the world belongs to the Church's very nature, its very being, its *esse*.

According to this definition of the Church, (1) the Church is composed of converted persons, and (2) the most important function of those converted persons, besides their own worship of God, is their evangelism, through which others are converted.

3. *An extension of the Incarnation.* The Church extends the Incarnation, in a sense, until the second coming of Christ.

This means that believers, today, in the Church as flesh-and-blood persons, are the way in which Christ now exists here con-

---

18. Cf. *Constitution and Discipline for the American Yearly Meetings* (New York: The Friends Book and Tract Committee, 1901), 2:2; *Discipline of Kansas Yearly Meeting of Friends* (Wichita, Kans.: Day's Print Shop, 1940), 2:2.

19. See F. X. Lawlor, "Membership in the Church," in *New Catholic Encyclopedia* (New York: McGraw-Hill Book Co., 1967), 9:637.

cretely. Living the kind of life urged by Christ, the Church extends the Incarnation into every present moment.

Strangely, George Eldon Ladd does not like this understanding of the Church. He writes, "It is too much to say that Paul thought of the church as an extension of the incarnation—that just as God was incarnate in Christ, Christ is incarnate in the church. Paul preserves clear distinction between Christ and the church."[20] Ladd seems to want to liberalize the equating, and then he cannot appreciate it. Perhaps, if he viewed it as theologians have meant it, he could agree with John S. Whale that "Christians everywhere confess that the church is the extension of the Incarnation."[21]

4. *Both human and divine.* The Church, like Christ, its Lord and Head, is both human and divine. As divine, the Church is constituted by Jesus Christ with Him as its Head. As divine, it often succeeds even when it is poorly managed, poorly nurtured, poorly financed. As divine, it is a mystery, and it takes theology to talk about what it is and what its mission is. As divine, it continues from age to age, undaunted in adversity—stomped on at times, but not stomped out. As divine, its members are partakers of the divine nature and are privileged to call upon divine resources as they seek to accomplish God's work and will.

But the Church is human also. As human, it is often less Christlike than it ought to be, less correct in its understandings, less effective in its witness than its divine resources would warrant. As human, its members are sometimes at odds with each other over how to promote its work. As human, it suffers. As human, sometimes its leadership fails—in strategy, in skills, in its teaching function, and sometimes, lamentably, in legal and moral dimensions.

5. *Unconquerable and conquering.* Another theological construct for understanding the nature of the Church is to view it as unconquerable and conquering.

The Church is unconquerable. Arrogant rulers may persecute and execute its members, but they cannot stamp out the Church.

Mao Tse-tung tried to rout the Church in China. The writer's medical doctor and friend was sent to prison for years, forced to

---

20. Ladd, *A Theology of the New Testament,* 545.
21. Whale, *Christian Doctrine* (Cambridge: Cambridge University Press, 1941), 19.

eat his food from the floor with his hands tied behind him, and he came through it as one of the most loving, sweet-spirited human beings to be found anywhere. Recent studies suggest that during the decades of severe persecution, and during the past few years of letup in the persecution, the number of Christians in China increased by several hundred percent. The writer's own recent trips there suggest that the Church in China is cautiously and prudently vigorous.[22]

The Church is also conquering. This is what Jesus told us would happen: "I will build my church, and the gates of Hades will not overcome it" (Matt. 16:18). This means, surely, that the Church is on the offensive, and the gates constructed by Satan and his kingdom will not prevail against the terrible offensive of the Church, as strong as an army with drums and slogans and right cause. The RSV changed the KJV "hell" to "death" but kept the KJV rendering: "shall not prevail against it." Whatever the translation, the passage means that the Church is unconquerable.

6. *A mystery.* This construct is deduced from where Paul speaks, particularly in Ephesians, of the Church as a mystery.

The Church is a mystery because of Christ's love for it. It is a mystery that Christ so loved the unlovable that He gave himself on the Cross for it. Paul speaks of "this love that surpasses knowledge" (3:19). Paul kneels "before the Father" (v. 14) and prays that the Church "may have power . . . to grasp how wide and long and high and deep is the love of Christ" (v. 18). Paul also says that "Christ loved us and gave himself up for us" (5:2) and urges: "Husbands, love your wives, just as Christ also loved the church and gave Himself up for her" (v. 25, NASB).

The Church is a mystery, also, because truths about it had to be revealed to Paul. He says that the mystery was "made known to me by revelation" (3:3). He speaks of "my insight into the mystery of Christ, which was not made known to men in other generations as it has now been revealed" (vv. 4-5). Important in what was revealed is that "the Gentiles are heirs together with Israel, members together of one body, and sharers together in the prom-

---

22. The writer visited with a pastor in a city of about 100,000 population in 1982 and found out that 1,100 persons had just attended service in the sanctuary where we were standing. The writer dumbly asked, "With what denomination are you affiliated?" and was told, "We're just Christians."

ise in Christ Jesus" (v. 6). To make this mystery "plain to every-one," Paul was graced to preach Christ to the Gentiles, unveiling what God had "kept hidden" during past ages (vv. 8-9).

The Church is also a mystery because of its ministry. Again, this is what Paul seems to say. After speaking of "the mystery of Christ" (3:4), he refers to "the gospel, of which I was made a min-ister" (vv. 6-7, NASB). Mystery obtains in God's calling Paul to ministry before the time of his birth (Gal. 1:15, NASB).

7. *Militant and triumphant.*[23] As militant, the Church is now in this world, fighting the good fight of faith against adversaries.

The most express reference concerning the Church militant is Eph. 6:13, 17, where Paul urges Christians to "put on the full armor of God" and lists various pieces of armor analogous to as-pects of the Christian faith. Some hymns also teach that the Church is militant, notably "Onward, Christian Soldiers."

As triumphant, the Church is composed of all who have died in the faith, finally victorious over all foes, including Satan and death itself.

The Church's Oneness. An aspect of the very nature of the Church is its oneness—its unity. In many ways the New Testa-ment teaches and implies the unity of the Church. Two of the New Testament's most important passages on the Church's one-ness will be discussed here.

Perhaps the most significant passage is Christ's prayer for His disciples in John 17. There Jesus prays, "Holy Father, protect them by the power of your name . . . so that they may be one as we are one" (v. 11). The oneness of Jesus and the Father is the theological basis Jesus gives for the oneness of His followers. And since Father, Son, and Holy Spirit are one, although distinct as Persons, this suggests that Christians can be one while they are distinct in many ways: for example, theologically, culturally, geo-graphically, denominationally.

Jesus also says, "My prayer is not for them alone. I pray also for those who will believe in me through their message, that all of

---

23. This is similar to the understanding that the Church is temporal and eternal, but it is the more preferable of these two kinds of distinction. Temporal is similar to the Church as mili-tant, but "eternal" is not similar to or equal to "triumphant." This is because what is eternal not only has an unending future but an unending past as well. But the Church as eternal has only an unending future. It does not have an unending past, so it is not strictly appropriate to say that the Church is eternal.

them may be one, Father, just as you are in me and I am in you" (vv. 20-21). Clearly, Jesus wants His followers in our era—and in every era—to be one. Again, they can be one and distinct at the same time—as are the Father and the Son.

The purpose of our oneness is evangelism. Jesus continues, "May they also be [one, KJV] in us so that the world may believe that you have sent me" (v. 21). He adds, "May they be brought to complete unity to let the world know that you sent me and have loved them even as you have loved me" (v. 23).

Another important unity passage is 1 Corinthians 12. Paul there says that there are "different kinds of gifts," but they are from "the same Spirit" (v. 4); and "different kinds of service," but they are all rendered for "the same Lord" (v. 5). He then adds, "Now to each one the manifestation of the Spirit is given for the common good" (v. 7). And after listing various gifts, He says, "All these are the work of one and the same Spirit" (v. 11). He uses the physical body as illustrative of all this, saying, "The body is a unit, though it is made up of many parts; and though all its parts are many, they form one body. So it is with Christ" (v. 12). He later says that we need each other in the Church even as the body's parts need each other (vv. 21, 26), and adds, "Now you are the body of Christ, and each one of you is a part of it" (v. 27).

Unity in the Ecumenical Movement. The 20th century's ecumenical movement led to the formation of the World Council of Churches in 1947. Ecumenicist C. C. Morrison began to talk about the sin of denominationalism. Visser't Hooft and others began to say that the greatest problem the Church faced was the existence of the churches. Denominational mergers were promoted, even when their official teachings were not very compatible.

Ecumenicism has had successes and failures. Three large Lutheran bodies have merged, even as many other bodies have done—such as the Methodist and the United Brethren denominations, and the large Northern and Southern U.S.A. Presbyterians. Yet the proposed merger of the Church of England and Methodism in England has been delayed almost indefinitely. The WCC, with over 300 member denominations, has alienated many people by its support of certain liberal political causes.

A monolithic denomination is not desirable. In Christian history, revival times have often occasioned a new order in Roman Catholicism or a new denomination in Protestantism—not mergers. A wide-scoped merger of denominations could result in scarcely more than a mutually agreed upon near-vacuity of belief. The Church can be one and apostolic and catholic right while it exists in denominational forms.

Four Important Church Matters

Before discussing the sacraments, we need to discuss four somewhat incohesive and yet important matters related to the Church: its relation (1) to God's Word, (2) to the Spirit's ministry, (3) to the ministry as a calling, and (4) to the state.

The Church and God's Word. Basic to the Church's function is its conveying the Word of God. The importance of this function is expressed by the ordination of ministers to "preach the Word" and to "administer the sacraments."

The Hebrew term for "word" is *dabar,* and T. F. Torrance says, "It looks as if the whole tabernacle or temple were constructed around the significance of *dabar.*"[24] This is because the word, the *torah,* the teaching, was deposited within the ark of the covenant, which was kept in the holy of holies. Torrance suggests that *dabar* is connected not only with proclamation but also with practice—a priest's or minister's lived-out life. And related to this, he says, "God's Word is Truth where His action corresponds to His Word."[25]

The significance of God's Word is also shown in the fact that the Old Testament word for "priest" "primarily denotes a truth sayer, or seer, that is, one who has to do with the Word of God"; and Torrance explains that "only in relation to this primary function [of mediating God's Word to people] does he have the other function of oblation."[26]

Liturgy, independent of God's Word, becomes idolatrous. Torrance says, "The more liturgical forms are turned into idols, the less men are disturbed by the speaking God."[27] An empty liturgicalism sent most of the prophets out of the priesthood itself, to protest its preoccupation with liturgical forms (see Amos 5:21 ff.).

If the Word of God is this important, then perhaps Emil Brunner was correct in observing that a study of theology is done

24. T. F. Torrance, *Royal Priesthood* (Edinburgh: Oliver and Boyd, 1955), 2.
25. Ibid., 1.
26. Ibid.
27. Ibid., 5.

significantly for the purpose of making preaching as difficult as it ought to be.

Preaching, Gerhard Ebeling has told us, is a time when the preacher mysteriously enters into the redemption events themselves by lifting them out of the past and presenting them to opened-up listeners.

The Church and the Spirit's Ministry. The Holy Spirit performs His own ministry through the heralded word and in various other ways. The Holy Spirit's ministry is wide scoped, makes extensive use of physicality, and is only somewhat predictable. These matters will be discussed.

1. *Its wide scope.* The Holy Spirit's ministry to the Church is exceedingly broad. He ministers through acts of kindness done by believers. He uses persons outside the Church to minister to Christ's people. He uses legislators and judges and heads of state more often than is realized to help Christ's people. He often prompts Christ's people toward safe driving procedures and in other ways helps in providences that Christians are often unaware of.

2. *Its use of physicality.* The Spirit uses physical things to administer God's grace to people. He uses nature generally: flowers, streams, mountains, stars, whatever. He uses church buildings with their furnishings. He uses olive oil for anointing the sick, and He uses the laying on of hands and the lifting up of hands. He uses the touch of a friend. He uses the words of people, their body language generally, their eyes specifically. Significantly, He uses the Holy Scriptures as we read them. Significantly also, He uses the water of baptism and the bread and grape juice or wine of Communion.

The Holy Spirit is certainly able to bypass all physicality and minister directly to us, Spirit to spirit, but this is not His usual way of getting messages to us. He usually works through physical or physical-like instrumentalities.

This means we should be on the lookout for what He might wish to reveal to us through such instrumentalities. And it means we should test impressions and impulses that seem to be from the Spirit by their agreement or non-agreement with His usual instrumentalities. The Holy Spirit's usual employment of physical or physical-like instrumentalities is a wide-ranging safeguard against foolish and damaging actions.

3. *Its predictability and unpredictability.* There is a certain predictability about the Holy Spirit's ministry to the Church. For example, if in corporate worship we sing joyfully, someone testifies, another person leads in prayer, and heaven bends low to bless these ways of worshiping, we may suppose that similar blessings will accrue if we worship in similar ways at a later time.

However, the Holy Spirit's particularity is only a prediction of His universality. In similar circumstances, He might minister quite differently. This keeps us from presumption, from supposing that we can simply press the right buttons and get the Spirit outpouring we desire. Also, at the later time, needy persons of a different ilk might be present who would be reticent to turn to Christ during a display of religious hilarity. Because of such matters as these, the Holy Spirit's particularity is only a prediction of His universality.

The Ministry as a Calling. The Church's ministry is a significant aspect of its being, and the theological structure that undergirds its ministry needs to be considered here.

1. *Its collegiality.* The church's ministry is characterized by collegiality. True collegiality is not achieved by aping others or by sacrificing truth to fellowship. Gregory Baum suggests that our collegiality ought to make our faith more pristine, more apostolic—not less. He writes, "Our dialogue and our ventures of collaboration must constantly lead us to great fidelity to the Gospel in our teaching, in our presentation of the truth, in our liturgical life, and in our way of holiness."[28]

Collegiality is a oneness with other ministers and Christians at the point of our faith's underpinnings. We are built upon the same foundation, and we drink from the same fountain—Christ Jesus.

Oneness obtains because we are all in the apostolic succession. Of this matter, Roman Catholic theologian Hans Kung writes, "Who succeeds the apostles? There can be only one basic answer: the Church! It is not a few individuals but the whole Church which enjoys apostolic succession."[29] We are in this succession if we have experienced Christ firsthand, as did the apos-

---

28. Gregory Baum, foreword in *Ecumenical Theology Today,* ed. Gregory Baum (New York: Paulist Press, 1964), 7.

29. *Die Kirche* (Freiburg-Basel-Vienna, 1967), 421, quoted in Johannes Remmers, *Apostolic Succession,* ed. Hans Kung (New York: Paulist Press, 1968), 41.

tles. We are in it, too, if we have been sent, as they were, to preach Christ to the ends of the world and to the end of the age.

We are in the apostolic succession also if we teach the doctrines taught by the apostles. The late Bishop James Pike was in an unbroken chain of consecrated to consecrator, as apostolic succession is usually understood. But Pike denied the plain teaching of the apostles, contained in the New Testament, in a number of instances. This is not the kind of succession that matters.

2. *Its authority*. Besides collegiality, the Church's ministry is characterized by authority. The minister's authority is such that he or she really does effect things. Due to the call, and to the office in Christ's Church, it might not be too churchly to admit that the minister really does dispense God's grace.

Evangelicals tend to slight the significance of the minister's authority. We even make jokes about the Roman Catholic belief that St. Peter was given the keys for opening the kingdom of heaven to people. The truth is, Peter was given those keys (Matt. 16:19; see Isa. 22:22)—and today's clergy are given them as well. What ministers do and say really will unlock the doors of heaven to people. Ministers unlock the doors of heaven for people when they offer them God's grace and it is accepted. What greater authority can there be than this?

The authority of the minister has its basis, in part, in the authenticity of the minister's experience of Jesus Christ as Redeemer and Lord. Such a minister has been sent out as an envoy, an ambassador, beseeching people in Christ's stead to be reconciled to God.

The minister's office differs in function, and not in kind, from that of laypersons. Even Anglican Charles Gore could say, "The difference between clergy and laity is not 'a difference of kind,' but of function."[30] The layperson's work is called "ministry" in the New Testament. For example, according to Eph. 4:11-12, "It was he [Christ] who gave some to be apostles, some to be prophets, some to be evangelists, and some to be pastors and teachers, to prepare God's people for works of service." The KJV and RSV translate the word for "service" as "ministry." It is from *diakonia*, the usual word for ministry. The point here is that whereas different functions are mentioned, all the people of God are in ministry.

---

30. Charles Gore, *The Church and the Ministry* (New York: Macmillan Publishing Co., 1886), 71.

The minister and the layperson are both priests, for the whole Church of God is a kingdom of priests (1 Pet. 2:5), even as they are all ministers; but the minister has a special office of bringing the entire *laos,* the entire laity, in all their needs, to God. The minister intercedes between estranged parties, God and rebels, and works toward their reconciliation—the world to God and God to the world.

The minister's prophetic office is even more distinct from the function of the layperson than is his priestly office. The minister must be close to the people to bring their needs to God, and close to God, entering His council chambers and hearing His proposals, in order to come forth with authority and proclaim the will of God to the people. God's will is determined chiefly from Scripture; and the minister possesses the authority of one who has been helped to interpret and apply Scripture.

3. *Its suffering.* The minister's suffering on behalf of others is redemptive. The suffering of Christ provides for redemption (1 Pet. 3:18), and the suffering of ministers helps to implement that redemption. Really, all Christians add in this way to Christ's sufferings, but the minister does it sort of full-time, as a professional.

The Church and the State. The relationship of the Church to the state is a matter of considerable importance. At least four types of relationship between the two have obtained in different eras. These will be discussed now, after which support will be given for the view that the church and the state should exist as separated but not antagonistic entities.

1. *The four relationships.* During the early Christian centuries the state was overlord to the Church. During that time, the state often persecuted the Church. The Church could not own property, and believers were harassed and martyred.

In the early fourth century the church gained legal status, and following this the church gradually became dominant over the state. The pope's crowning of Charlemagne as emperor of the Holy Roman Empire on Christmas Day in A.D. 800 demonstrated this kind of relationship. As the power of the papacy increased, Nicholas I (reigned 858-67) took the position that the popes are the real emperors and that princes as well as bishops are his subjects. Gregory VII (reigned 1073-85) argued that the pope had the power to give and take away empires, kingdoms, duchies, courtships, and the possessions of anyone at all. Innocent III (reigned 1198-1216) contended that the Lord left to Peter not only the government of the church but of the whole world. This notion is the basis of a papal message to the whole world each Christmas.

The third major relationship has been one in which the church and the state have been partners. This relationship has obtained in many countries under both Protestantism and Roman Catholicism. Luther and Calvin advocated it. Britain has promoted it through the last several centuries. Many South American countries have official connections with the Roman Catholic church.

The fourth major type of relationship is the one in which the two are separated, but not necessarily antagonists. This relationship between church and state has obtained in the United States of America almost from its inception as a nation to the present. The separation did not exist in the 13 colonies in America, 9 of which had official denominations. There the "partner" relationship obtained. But the Bill of Rights in 1790 erected a "wall of separation" between church and state. The First Amendment states that "Congress shall make no laws respecting an establishment of religion, or prohibiting the free exercise thereof." This allowed for the encouragement of all religious denominations and forbade the repression of any.

This separation allows the various denominations to promote their interest with equal freedom. No one of them is favored by law. It allows all of them nontaxation of property. It allows them to supply military chaplains to the nation and to the Senate in Washington, D.C. It allows the church, which is not directly supported by taxation, to be independently critical of the state.

Some have suggested that this separation of church and state was the most imaginative contribution to government accomplished by young America. Separation of the two had never previously obtained in any country. Indeed, hardly any country today has such official separation of church and state as obtains in the U.S.A.

2. *Separation argued for.* On a number of bases, the separation of church and state, as guaranteed by the United States Constitution, is the most satisfactory of the four relationships.

Basically, it is biblical. No doubt Scripture could be cited to support all four relationships. The Old Testament theocratic system, in which God chose kings and called prophets who guided the nation for Him, could be used to support the church being overlord to the state. Paul's teaching in Romans 13 about obeying the political authorities could be used to argue for the state being overlord to the church. The partner relationship might not be obviously scriptural, but Matt. 22:15-21 might be interpreted as supportive of the partner type. Here Jesus responds to a question of the legality of Jews paying taxes to Caesar. "Give to Caesar what is Caesar's," He said, "and to God what is God's." This sounds as if the state and the church are separated entities, both to be supported by Christ's followers.

Separation permits the church to sustain a prophetic role in relation to the state. Where any denomination has been "official" and supported by public taxation, church and clergy have not been sufficiently independent of the state to exercise a disturbingly prophetic role.

Separation of church and state also allows the church to enjoy a purifying role. Under separation, the various denominations flourish, partly through competition. If an official denomination needs purifying but is not competing in an open market of denominations, it might continue in impurity and even become corrupt. If an open market of religious freedom obtains, however, people will often turn from a corrupted denomination to embrace the teaching and life-style of a purer one. Business monopolies can become usurpative unless restricted by law, but an open market of business products and services assures that corrupt practices will not succeed. The church, likewise, tends to keep purified if no one denomination has a monopoly and if all must compete for the allegiance of their true-believer adherents.

On these bases at least—the biblical, the prophetic, and the purifying—the American separation of church and state is supportable.

19

The Church's Sacraments

The two sacraments, baptism and the Lord's Supper, are special means of receiving God's grace. They are more than rites or mere rituals.

The Need for the Sacraments

The two sacraments are needed on many bases. For one thing, words will not always suffice to express what we experience. Thus we need music and art. And thus we need both of the sacraments to express the core meanings of the Christian faith in extra-language, acted-out ways. As Goethe said, the highest cannot be spoken; it can only be acted.

The sacraments are also needed to focus our faith and to make it plain to people. Music will not do, because our Lord Christ did not institute that. For the same reason, art will not suffice.

The symbol of water was selected by Christ to help us focus on His death and resurrection. Baptism, by whatever mode, symbolizes our dying to our previous life and our rising to newness of life in Christ. That is why Paul said, "We were therefore buried with him through baptism into death in order that, just as Christ was raised from the dead through the glory of the Father, we too may live a new life" (Rom. 6:4).

When we receive the bread and wine of Communion, it symbolizes Christ's broken body and shed blood; and since we are to do this "until he comes" (1 Cor. 11:26), the act focuses our faith also upon the hope we have of Christ's second coming in power and glory.

Sacraments are needed, too, because they were instituted by Christ himself. Since our Christian faith is rooted in history, a particular history, we are not at liberty to decide the things that will bring special focus to our faith. Christ already did this, in a certain way at a certain time in history, as our Lord and Savior, the Head of the Church.

Thus we speak of baptism and the Supper as dominically instituted—instituted by our Lord himself. Even Roman Catholics, who finally came to have seven sacraments, say that only these two are dominically instituted.

For Protestants, who accept only Scripture as authoritative for doctrine and practice, only the sacraments instituted by Christ are considered valid.[1] Christ clearly instituted the Lord's Supper. He arranged for it to be observed, and He observed it with His disciples (Luke 22:7-20).

Christ did not overtly institute baptism. But Karl Barth is probably correct in observing that He instituted it (1) by being baptized himself (Matt. 3:13-17; Mark 1:9-11; Luke 3:21-22); and (2) by the Great Commission to baptize (Matt. 28:19).

So the two sacraments, baptism and the Lord's Supper, are needed because (1) our faith needs to be dramatized in ritual acts, (2) they bring focus to our faith, and (3) Christ himself instituted them, and we are not at liberty to replace them with other "focusers" of our faith.

Their Relation to Preaching

The sacraments are like poetry, whereas preaching is similar to prose. The sacraments are incandescent with meaning the way good poetry is, but the meaning is not spelled out as it is in preaching. The meaning of the sacraments might be missed, even as the meaning in poetry might be. What preaching declares, the sacraments dramatize. Preaching is the heralded word of God, whereas the sacraments constitute the visible word of God.

Their Relation to Symbols

Several important symbols are mentioned in the New Testament, but they are of less significance than the sacraments.

One of the symbols is foot washing.[2] Several Protestant denominations practice it and view it pretty much as a sacrament.

---

1. Roman Catholics accept both Scripture and tradition as authoritative.
2. For this presentation, the writer is borrowing from C. Ryder Smith, *The Sacramental Society* (London: Epworth Press, 1927).

Jesus washed His disciples' feet (John 13:1-17) and said, "Now that I, your Lord and Teacher, have washed your feet, you also should wash one another's feet. I have set you an example that you should do as I have done for you." He even added, "Now that you know these things, you will be blessed if you do them" (v. 17). Some have read this as the institution of an ordinance to be done as a continuing practice. But there is one gargantuan reason why the Church generally has not understood it in this way: the New Testament Church did not so understand it. Nowhere in Acts or the Epistles is foot washing urged. Nowhere is it practiced with regularity. Only once is it even referred to, and here it is an act of hospitality, not a religious ritual (1 Tim. 5:9-10). Baptism and the Lord's Supper are widely practiced and urged in Acts and the Epistles, but not foot washing.

At the other end of the spectrum from foot washing, in its relation to the sacraments, is the holy kiss. This was certainly a symbol practiced in New Testament times. Paul admonished the Romans (16:16), the Corinthians (1 Cor. 16:20; 2 Cor. 13:12), and the Thessalonians to "Greet one another with a holy kiss" (see 1 Thess. 5:26). And Peter says, "Greet one another with a kiss of love" (1 Pet. 5:14). Although urged by these apostles, it has been largely dropped in evangelical Protestantism. The kiss of peace, however, is still a part of certain Easter rites. Its being urged, but largely dropped, should serve to show that Christians today do not follow every single enjoinder of the New Testament Scriptures.[3]

Another New Testament symbol is the laying on of hands. It was done in order to bless children (Mark 10:15); in connection with healing (5:23; 6:5); as people received the Holy Spirit (Acts 8:17; 19:6); and to set people apart for Christian work (6:6; 13:3). It is a symbol widely practiced today in these ways.

The lifting up of hands is another of these symbols. It was done as a benediction. We read of Jesus, "When he had led them out to the vicinity of Bethany, he lifted up his hands and blessed them" (Luke 24:50).

---

3. Another of these is Paul's enjoinder to Timothy to "use a little wine because of your stomach and your frequent illnesses" (1 Tim. 5:23).

Ministers are given the office of pronouncing benedictions or blessings. Among evangelicals, though, some are too shy or too "low church" to receive and use this authority.

The lifting up of hands was also done in supplication, according to 1 Tim. 2:8: "I want men everywhere to lift up holy hands in prayer." To lift the hands is to do something physically, and when something is done physically, it is often an aid to faith.

Still another New Testament symbol is the right hand of fellowship. The leaders of the Jerusalem church, so Jewish in its interests, offered the right hand of fellowship to Paul and Barnabas, who had been taking the gospel to the Gentiles, and it was beautifully meaningful (Gal. 2:9). Today, pastors often offer the right hand of fellowship to persons being received into church membership.

Another New Testament symbol is anointing with oil (James 5:14), still widely and properly practiced, with the biblical precedent and authority for it usually cited.

All these symbols, and other New Testament symbols not discussed, are similar to sacraments in certain ways, and yet they are significantly different.

Symbols, like sacraments, are visible acts that aid faith. In both symbols and sacraments, a tangibility or a gesture means something more than itself, other than itself.

But the New Testament symbols and the two sacraments are also different, in several ways. The symbols are less obligatory than the sacraments are. For example, twice there was the laying on of hands for receiving the baptism with the Holy Spirit, but at other times the Spirit baptism occurred without mention of the laying on of hands. The symbol of laying on of hands was not necessarily obligatory.

Life teems with obligations of varying degrees of intensity. Compared with extra-New Testament symbols, and with those of the New Testament, the obligation to receive the two sacraments is highly intensified. It is like the obligation to save a friend's life, although it might involve some risk to one's own well-being or even to one's own life. It is like the obligation to maintain one's marriage vows.

Also, symbols are different from the sacraments, as C. Ryder Smith suggests, because the symbols only assume a relationship, but the sacraments assert it.[4] In receiving the sacraments, we assert to all and sundry that we are Christ's.

A third difference is that the sacraments are more essential to the Church's continuity than the symbols. Some of the symbols have been dropped or largely dropped, proof that the symbols are not viewed as essential to the Church's continuity. Drop the symbols, and you still have the Church you had before. Drop the sacraments, and it is questionable whether you do.

The sacraments, more than the symbols, are part of the Church's *esse,* its very being. Protestants might hesitate to say simply that the sacraments are of the Church's *esse,* for this would deny that noncommunicants, such as Quakers or Salvation Army members, are part of Christ's Church. It can surely be said that the sacraments belong to the Church's essence more surely than the symbols do.

The sacraments more readily, universally, and sovereignly convey grace to people than do the symbols. This is not to admit to sacerdotalism, the view that grace is automatically conveyed by the sacraments whatever the recipient's attitude. This is to say that when we receive a sacrament, we really do receive God's grace, and God really does covenant to extend to us the helps we need.

Yet another difference between the symbols and the sacraments should be mentioned: mere formalism is worse as regards the sacraments than as regards the symbols. Mere formalism obtains when the religious form observed does not express actual religious experience. It is bad when a symbol is used insincerely. Then Judas can kiss Jesus in a showy way and betray Him in the very symbol used. It is utterly bad, it is demonic, when sacraments are insincerely received. It would be utterly serious, for example, if a man and woman, in an adulterous affair with no intention of turning to God, would receive Communion in a local church with their spouses so as to continue to appear to be believers. This is why Paul tells the Corinthians that to eat and drink the Communion elements unworthily is to eat and drink "judgment" on themselves (1 Cor. 11:29).

---

4. See C. Ryder Smith, *The Sacramental Society,* 109 ff.

Baptism

Christian water baptism is initiatory. When administered to infants and other small children, it initiates them into a prevenient-grace covenant, and it advertises and asserts that they are members of the kingdom of God—the sphere where God reigns in frequent providential helps and in occasional miracles. When administered to believers, baptism asserts to the Church and to the world that the recipient has received Christ as Savior and Lord, having repented and believed the gospel.

People who do not believe in infant baptism tend to define baptism as an outward sign of an inward work of grace. For those who believe in it—as people do in most of the main Christian traditions—it is appropriate to define baptism as an outward sign of an inward state of grace. This is because infants have not received a work of grace, but they are in a state of prevenient grace and are in God's kingdom, as Jesus taught (Mark 10:13-16).

Since baptism is one of the two sacraments of the Church, it is better, actually, to put the word "sacrament" into the definition instead of "sign." Thus baptism might be defined as a sacrament that asserts outwardly that the recipient is in an inward state of grace.

Importance of Baptism. Paul said, "For Christ did not send me to baptize, but to preach the gospel" (1 Cor. 1:17). However, he said this to a church that was divided into quarreling factions, each claiming a different leader. Paul was glad he had not contributed fuel for their feuds by baptizing many of them (cf. vv. 14, 16). This passage does not suggest that to Paul baptism itself is unimportant. Paul himself was baptized and baptized others. John the Baptist attached great importance to water baptism. Those who repented he gladly baptized.

Baptism was widely practiced in New Testament times by John the Baptist, by Jesus' disciples, by Paul somewhat, and by various other persons, according to the Book of Acts. Besides this, we have a strict command from Christ himself to baptize. Jesus said, "Therefore go and make disciples of all nations, baptizing them in the name of the Father and of the Son and of the Holy Spirit" (Matt. 28:19).

One passage sounds as though baptism is necessary to salvation. Jesus said: "Truly, truly, I say to you, unless one is born of water and the Spirit, he cannot enter into the kingdom of God"

(John 3:5, NASB). This "born of water" is surely a reference to water baptism, being practiced and emphasized by John the Baptist right at that early period of Jesus' public ministry (see vv. 22ff.). However, this same chapter of John states several times that a person receives eternal life through believing, no mention being made of baptism. Jesus says, "Truly, truly, I say to you, unless one is born again, he cannot see the kingdom of God" (v. 3, NASB). Again: "Everyone who believes in him [the Son of Man, v. 14] may have eternal life" (v. 15). And in the most familiar of Bible verses, he says, "For God so loved the world that he gave his one and only Son, that whoever believes in him shall not perish but have eternal life" (v. 16).

1. *Its importance historically.* Baptism is important not only biblically but also historically. Through all the centuries, almost all Christian groups have believed in and practiced it. Baptism is emphasized in the *Didache,* also called *The Teaching of the Twelve,* which dates to sometime between the closing years of the first century and the middle of the second. The fathers, East and West, emphasized it also, as did the Reformers, John Wesley, and others, on to the present time. Only the Quakers and the Salvation Army, among groups of widely recognized standing in Christianity, do not baptize.

2. *Its importance theologically.* Besides scriptural and historical supports for baptism, there are, of course, theological supports for it. Baptism affirms the importance of physicality and of the concrete act—in distinction from what is merely conceptual. The employment of water in baptism is congruous with the Christian understanding that the whole universe and all that is in it has been created by God and is not to be debased nor deplored.

Baptism is supported theologically, further and similarly, because it occurs at a given time and place, and this is in keeping with our Christian faith, which is grounded upon events in history.

Baptism is supported theologically, also, because it is in keeping with the covenant emphasis of our Judeo-Christian faith. At baptism, infant or believer, the God who made covenants with Abraham and David and others in Old Testament times makes a covenant with the baptizands and extends His grace in special forms to them.

Also baptism is supported theologically because it is one of the means whereby we receive God's grace. As will be discussed in the next chapter, Scripture reading, prayer, worship, Christian fellowship, etc., are all means of our receiving God's grace; and baptism—a sacrament—is a most special means that God has ordained for extending His kindness to us.

The Matter of Mode. The mode of water baptism—whether it is to be administered by sprinkling, immersion, or pouring—has been a matter of debate among Christians for centuries.

1. *Sprinkling.* Of the three modes, this one probably carries the least support. One of the few passages of Scripture quoted in support of sprinkling is Luke 7:24, where Jesus asked, concerning the work of John the Baptist, "What did you go out into the desert to see? A reed swayed by the wind?" The "reed," here, is likely a reference to John himself, but some have taken the word literally and have suggested that John would dip a reed into the Jordan and spray or sprinkle water onto the people with it. The interpretation is farfetched.

According to some authorities, the practice of sprinkling can be traced back only as far as the 12th century. It is possible that sprinkling began as a slight variation in the practice of pouring.

2. *Immersion.* In this mode the baptizand is plunged beneath the water—usually once, although some groups submerge the baptizand three times, each time in the name of a different Person of the Trinity.

Numerous scriptural passages are given in support of immersion, none of which is unanswerably sound. Among the strongest of these is Rom. 6:4, where Paul says, "We were therefore buried with him through baptism into death in order that, just as Christ was raised from the dead through the glory of the Father, we too may live a new life."

Being "buried" with Christ might indicate being put completely under the water. Yet "buried" surely goes more naturally with death than with a momentary submersion into water. It is entirely possible that baptism by pouring indicates that the baptizand symbolically dies to his previous life and, through being born again, rises to newness of life in Christ.

Another passage used to support immersion is the reference to "plenty of water" in John 3:23, which speaks of John's baptizing. Yet "plenty of water" does not necessarily indicate water sufficient for immersion. If people stood waist-deep in water and had water poured over their heads, as they did according to Christian art that dates to as early as the third century of our era, a considerable amount of water would be needed.

According to Mark 1:10, Christ "was coming up out of the water" after His baptism, a favorite passage with immersionists. The words may indicate, however, that after being waist-deep in the water, Jesus "was coming up" out of the Jordan onto its bank—which would always be higher than the water level.

The literal meaning of the Greek word *baptidzō* has also been widely used to support immersion. The word means "to dip," and that might indicate submersion into water. Yet this does not necessarily mean submersion, as we shall see in our discussion of pouring.

3. *Pouring*. This mode has much warrant biblically, historically, and theologically. Biblically, it is strongly supportable. We are not sure that Scripture supports sprinkling or immersion as the mode, but we are certain that Spirit baptism is described as a pouring. And this might imply that water baptism was also by pouring. Joel (2:28) had prophesied that the Holy Spirit would be "poured out." Then John the Baptist said that Christ would "baptize" with the Holy Spirit (Matt. 3:11-12). And Jesus said, "Do not leave Jerusalem, but wait for the gift my Father promised [in Joel], which you have heard me speak about. For John baptized with water, but in a few days you will be baptized with the Holy Spirit" (Acts 1:4-5). Those promises by John and Jesus were fulfilled at Pentecost, when the Holy Spirit was "poured out." Thus Peter at Pentecost quoted Joel: "In the last days, God says, I will pour out my Spirit on all people. . . . I will pour out my Spirit in those days" (2:17-18).

An unquestionable linkage was made between the prophesied pouring and the promised baptism.

Possible indirect supports of baptism by pouring are to be found in certain other Scripture passages. One is the Acts 16:33 account of the conversion and baptism of the Philippian jailer and his entire household in the middle of the night. Baptism occurred right after his conversion to Christ—presumably in or near the jail itself. It would seem unlikely that sufficient water for immersion would have been available.

This is true also of the baptism of 3,000 on the Day of Pentecost. Some scholars question whether Jewish permission could have been secured to baptize in the Jerusalem reservoir at a time when the authorities were opposed to Christ's disciples. And it is questionable whether any other nearby body of water would have been large enough for baptizing so many persons by immersion.

Historically, baptism by pouring has considerable warrant. Roman Catholicism baptizes only by pouring, and its people understand that pouring has always been the mode used in that church. Because of its long use by the largest segment of Christendom, baptism by pouring has the greatest historical support of any of the three modes.

Theologically, pouring is also supportable. Our Christian water baptism somewhat grows out of Jewish practice. Yet the Jews, to purify with water, did not put the person or an object into the water, for that would have contaminated the water instead of cleansing the person or object. Instead, the Jews poured water over what was to be purified. Since the ceremony of baptism symbolizes cleansing, pouring seems to be theologically appropriate as a ceremony.

Whatever the mode of administration, baptism is valid. Matters on which Scripture does not give clear directives should not divide Christians.

Infant Baptism. Whether or not infants (and small children of unaccountable age) should receive Christian baptism has been widely and warmly disputed ever since Protestantism began. Long before that, it was opposed by Tertullian. Martin Luther left the refuge of Wartburg castle in early 1522, at the risk of his life, to contend with some in the Reformation movement who were opposing infant baptism. These people soon came to be known as Anabaptists, that is, rebaptizers (of persons baptized as infants). Historically, they are at the headstream of the Baptistic Protestant tradition—in which baptism is administered only to believers.

Arguments for and against infant baptism will here be presented. Again, this question, like that of the mode of baptism, should not divide Christians as decisively as it often has.

1. *Arguments against infant baptism.* Most important, it is argued that infant baptism is not expressly taught nor practiced in the New Testament. It is argued that the four entire households that were baptized (Acts 16:15, 33; 18:8; 1 Cor. 1:16) might not have included any infants or small children. It is also argued that repenting and believing is required in Scripture, prior to being baptized, and that this would preclude infants' receiving it.

Also, it is argued that the Great Commission calls for discipling prior to baptizing, which implies that candidates for baptism would have to be old enough to learn Christian doctrine. Infant baptizers, however, point out that this is a missionary type of command. It relates to new people who would become disciples and then receive baptism. It does not say that children should not be baptized.

Certain historical arguments against infant baptism are also given by its opposers. It is suggested that it is not at all certain that infant baptism was widely practiced in the early centuries of our era.

Many Anabaptists, during the Reformation, were martyred for their opposition to infant baptism.

Also, the Southern Baptist Convention, the largest Protestant denomination in the United States, and other Baptist and Baptistic groups do not believe in baptizing infants.

Theologically, infant baptism is opposed by some on several bases. Those baptized as infants or small children might assume that they do not need to be born again. Similarly, assuming themselves already to be Christians, they would not seek to become believers. Further, since Roman Catholics understand that the guilt of original sin is cleansed away in infant baptism, those who do not believe this should not practice such baptism. Yet, Pelagius, who did not believe in original sin at all, declared that he did not know of any heretic so impious as not to believe in baptizing infants.

2. *Arguments for infant baptism.* Pedobaptizers argue for it primarily on the basis of Scripture. The most singular scriptural supports for infant and small child baptism are the baptisms of four entire households recorded in the New Testament. Lydia "and the members of her household were baptized" (Acts 16:15). The Philippian jailer "and all his family were baptized" (v. 33). Also, "Crispus, the synagogue ruler, and his entire household believed in the Lord" and "were baptized" (18:8). And Paul says, "I also baptized the household of Stephanas" (1 Cor. 1:16).

Household baptisms, strengthened by such adjectives as *holos* (whole) and *pas* (all) and *hapartes* (entire, a strengthened form of *pas*), strongly imply that infants were baptized in these instances. Families were solidarities then, and the decisions of the father settled important matters for all other members of the family. This had long obtained in Judaism, and it obtained in the Gentile community of the first century.

The word *oikos*, for house, is even more inclusive than the Greek word for family, *genos*. It includes infants and other small children of slaves and servants. The households of persons such as Lydia and the Philippian jailer would likely have included slaves or servants or both. And Lydia and the jailer were employed and would likely have had, in their immediate natural family, children of unaccountable years.

There is a strong mathematical likelihood of small children in the four entire households whose baptisms are recorded in the New Testament. Family planning was impossible then; besides, children were understood to be blessings from God or the gods, and planning in the sense of avoiding pregnancy would have been unusual.

Somewhat supportive also of infant baptism are Jesus' words, "Let the little children come to me, and do not hinder them, for the kingdom of God belongs to such as these" (Mark 10:14). If they are of the Kingdom, why not assert this by baptizing them, since baptism's purpose—in part—is to assert identity with Christ's kingdom-Church.

Significant for this whole matter is the fact that the New Testament depicts the life of a missionary Church. A first generation of believers was entering the Church from pagan backgrounds and was being baptized. Not enough time had elapsed for a question to be raised about infants being baptized several years after the parents had been. Jeremias, who has worked through the early materials almost as carefully as anyone, is convinced that New Testament references to infant baptism are not more explicit because the Church at that time was in a missionary situation.

It is also to be noted that infant baptism is the New Testament counterpart of Old Testament circumcision. Even as God entered into a covenant with the male infant who was circumcised on his eighth day of life, God enters into a covenant to give special helps to an infant who is baptized.

This leads to the suggestion that infant baptism affirms the doctrine of prevenient grace—so important as a doctrine for Arminian-Wesleyanism.

It should be mentioned also that a high percentage of Christians in all the centuries have advocated infant baptism. It even

[^504]

argues for infant baptism that many of the relative few who do not believe in it feel the need to introduce infant dedication in lieu of it. And strangely, while saying they do not believe in infant baptism because they do not find it taught in Scripture, they teach and practice infant dedication—which, surely, no scholar in the world would say was taught or practiced by Christians in New Testament times.

The Lord's Supper

This sacrament will be treated from several standpoints: (1) the biblical teaching about it, (2) the history of the doctrine, (3) closed and open Communion, (4) Lord's Supper theories, and (5) observations on the Supper—including a statement about its significance.

The Biblical Teaching. There is considerable teaching in the New Testament and in the Old Testament on which the Lord's Supper doctrine and practice its based.

1. *The New Testament sources are the Synoptic Gospels, Acts, and 1 Corinthians.* In all the Synoptic Gospels we have mentions of the Lord's Supper, especially of its institution (Matt. 26:26-29; Mark 14:22-25; Luke 22:14-20).

Acts refers to the Lord's Supper a few times, somewhat vaguely, in its references to the "breaking of bread" (2:42, 46; 20:7, 11).

The only Epistle that mentions the Lord's Supper is 1 Corinthians, in which 10:15-17 refers to "the cup . . . which we bless" (v. 16, KJV), showing that Christ's example was followed in this respect (Mark 14:22, KJV). Because of this passage, also, we call the sacrament Communion. Paul asks, "Is it not the communion of the body of Christ?"

2. *Old Testament sources include its general teaching about sacrifices,* for in connection with the Supper the New Testament employs certain words that the Old Testament uses regarding sacrifices: for example, "body," "blood," "covenant," "poured out," "for you," "for many" (cf. Exod. 24:6-8; Lev. 2:2, 9, 16; 4:5-7, 34; 17:11, 14; 24:7; Num. 10:10; Heb. 9:11-28; 10:4-10, 19-20).

The specific Old Testament source for the Lord's Supper doctrine and practice is the Passover. It seems that the Lord's Supper was instituted just after the paschal meal (cf. Luke 22:7-18) and that the Supper interprets the importance of the true paschal lamb, Christ.

Historical Development. Several matters characterized the Lord's Supper doctrine and practice in the Church of the early centuries. It was a time of simple thanksgiving, which is why it is often called the Eucharist (from *eucharisteō,* meaning "I give thanks"). As early as the second century, water was mixed with wine as it was administered. This has long been practiced to symbolize the fact that water as well as blood flowed from Christ's riven side. During the early centuries the Supper, which might have been received each Lord's day as Christians met together (see Acts 20:7), was taken to the sick who could not be present at the house churches.

1. *Two differing early views.* Beginning in the second century (if not in the first or in the New Testament itself), two kinds of interpretation of the Supper began to appear. Some viewed the elements as undergoing some sort of undefined change: Irenaeus, Cyril of Jerusalem (ca. A.D. 315-86), Ambrose of the fourth century, and Gregory the Great of the sixth century. This tradition became enhanced until, in the ninth century, Paschasius Radbertus taught transubstantiation for the first time. He taught, that is, that the substance of the bread and wine is transformed into the actual body and blood of Christ while the appearance of the elements remains unchanged.

The view that the elements have symbolic meanings was promoted by some early fathers and early medieval theologians. Origen was one of them. Even Augustine, who viewed the elements as signs of something else—of Christ's death and resurrection—is also among these. Rabanus Maurus and John Scotus Erigena in the ninth century espoused the symbolic view, against the growing tendency in the church toward mystical change and even transubstantiation.

Certain refinements of the Supper's doctrine and practice occurred in time. Children, who in the early centuries had received Communion, were now denied it. It was feared they might spill or otherwise desecrate the elements, now considered to be Deity and worthy of worship. The wine was also withheld from the laity, due in part to its vulnerability to desecration. Shortly after Luther opposed these developments, the Council of Trent (1546-63) reaffirmed them for Roman Catholicism.

2. *Wycliffe's pre-Reformation doctrine.* John Wycliffe opposed transubstantiation in a treatise on the subject issued in 1380. He viewed it as idolatrous and as philosophically unacceptable because he felt it teaches the annihilation of matter. What he positively taught is not clear, but he more or less anticipated the consubstantiation view of Luther.

3. *Luther's view.* Martin Luther held to what was later called consubstantiation. He taught that Christ is literally present in, with, and under the elements, but that their substance is not transformed. Luther said that Christ is present in the elements of bread and wine the way heat is present in a red-hot poker. He felt that transubstantiation was an invention of the "coarse clowns" of medieval times who were basically following the "blind heathen master," Aristotle—who had distinguished between the substance of a thing and its appearance. "This is my body" (Luke 22:19) was taken literally by Luther; but not in the kind of literal sense taught by the Fourth Lateran Council (1215), which first made transubstantiation official for the Roman church. Luther urged that the cup be returned to the laity. He opposed private masses, saying that since Scripture calls it "communion" (1 Cor. 10:16), more than one person should be present for the fellowship of the sacrament. The communion referred to in Scripture, however, denotes our fellowship with Christ, not our fellowship with each other.

4. *Ulrich Zwingli's view.* At the opposite extreme from transubstantiation is the view of the Swiss reformer Zwingli (1484-1531). In his *Commentary on True and False Religion,* he argued against the view that "is," in "This is my body," should be taken literally. Incorrectly, from an exegetical standpoint, he believed that "this" does refer to the bread. But of importance was when he said that "is" should be taken metaphorically, based on the fact that, when Jesus said "I am the bread" (John 6:35), "I am the vine" (15:1), and other "I am" statements, He meant them to be taken metaphorically and not literally.

5. *John Calvin's view.* Calvin wrote extensively on the Lord's Supper, opposing the Catholic view, Luther's, and Zwingli's. He believed with Zwingli that the elements are symbolic, and with Luther that Christ really is present. But in disagreement with Luther, he believed that Christ, really present, is not literally but

spiritually present. What Calvin emphasized was the nourishment from this communion with the Christ who is thus present.

6. *John Wesley's view.* Wesley was an Anglican all his life and generally accepted their official eucharistic teaching. Anglicanism opposed the literalistic views of transubstantiation and consubstantiation and affirmed the Supper's memorial significance and Christ's spiritual presence. Wesley opposed the sacerdotal view that benefit is received even if the communicant is unreceptive to God's grace. He taught that the Supper is a "converting" ordinance when the unconverted person receives it obediently and with a receptive heart.

Wesley taught that it should be received frequently, and he supported this by reference to Paul's saying "as oft as ye drink it" (1 Cor. 11:25, KJV). Some studies of his journal and other sources have suggested that he received the Supper about every four or five days throughout his ministry.

Wesley interpreted Paul's caution about receiving Communion unworthily (1 Cor. 11:27) according to the context of the passage. Paul had reference to some who did not share their food with the needy, and some who were "drunk" while receiving Communion. An unconverted person whose heart is open to God would not eat and drink damnation in receiving the Supper. Instead, it would help the unconverted to be saved.

Wesley's Eucharist views, borrowed in basic ways from Anglicanism's Zwingli-Calvin type of view, became influential upon Methodism and numerous Holiness denominations. Yet many of them are different from Wesley in one special regard: it is not to them a "converting" ordinance or sacrament; only the converted are invited to partake.

Closed and Open Communion. In some denominations, Holy Communion is closed to nonmembers, while in others it is open to all Christians who are present.

1. *Closed Communion is defended* as the best way to safeguard against receiving the elements unworthily. Only members deemed active and in good standing are admitted to the Supper.

2. *Open Communion is practiced by many churches.* A number of scriptural supports may be cited in support of open Communion. One is John 10:16: "I have other sheep that are not of this sheep pen." Another is Luke 9:50: "Whoever is not against you is for you." Here, the person from a different group of believers is

not thereby pitted against Christ but is a worker on Christ's behalf.

Another scriptural support argues from the probability that church membership records were not kept in New Testament times.

Open Communion is also supported by the Bible's emphasis upon love for all others. If we love others, it may be assumed that we should not exclude them from the Lord's table if they profess to be Christians.

Open Communion also has supports that are more theological than biblical as such. One is the understanding that believers are members of the Body of Christ whether or not they are members of a given local church.

Another theological support is that since Christ instituted the Lord's Supper prior to the founding of the Church at Pentecost, to be a member of a given group, in the ecclesiastical sense of church membership, is not necessary in order to partake of Communion.

Another theological support is that regeneration makes one a Christian, not church membership (with or without good standing). Regeneration, therefore, should make one a proper recipient of Communion.

There are also historical and ecclesiastical supports for open Communion. Certain Christian traditions have practiced open Communion, and this becomes a kind of support for it.

There is also what might be called a practical support for open Communion. In a practical sense, it approaches the ridiculous to exclude fellow Christian believers from communion with Christ and other believers at the Lord's table. Christians who pray together, read Scripture together, and hear sermons together should be able to receive Communion together.

It is unfortunate if not ridiculous, in a local church setting, when a visiting Christian is prohibited from receiving Communion with the regular worshipers. In the same service where a universal gospel is preached, barriers to Communion are erected in Christ's name!

Lord's Supper Theories. A summary of the main Lord's Supper theories is now in order.

1. *Transubstantiation* is the official Roman Catholic teaching that, during the administration of the Eucharist, the substance

(but not the appearance) of the Communion bread and wine is transformed into the literal body and blood of Christ.

2. *Consubstantiation* is the view that Christ's body and blood are in, with, and under the bread and wine of the Supper. It views Christ's presence as literal. It is understood that Christ physically accompanies, or joins himself to, the elements. It is the view of Martin Luther.

3. *The memorial view* is that the chief purpose of the Supper is to commemorate, to recall, to bring again and again to focus in our minds, the long-past events of the Crucifixion and Resurrection. Its chief support is Christ's words "Do this . . . in remembrance of me" (1 Cor. 11:25). All Christians should see this as one of the correct understandings of the Supper. If we are to receive it in remembrance of Christ, it quite certainly has a memorial significance. Yet the Supper is not exclusively a memorial.

It takes little or no faith to memorialize an event. The "He is here" view, not the "We are there" theory, is the one that elicits faith from us. It takes God-given faith to believe that Christ is really and spiritually present with us and that we are communing with Him (1 Cor. 10:16).

4. *The spiritual presence view* is that, through faith, Christ is spiritually present with us in the Supper. The view certainly has scriptural sanction in 1 Cor. 10:16, where Paul says, "Is not the cup of thanksgiving for which we give thanks a participation ["communion," KJV] in the blood of Christ? And is not the bread that we break a participation ["communion," KJV] in the body of Christ?"

Observations on the Supper. Evangelicals should regard the Supper as a sacrament, and not as a mere rite or ordinance. We should not downplay the significance of this sacrament just because we believe in justification by faith.

The phrase "This is my body" (Luke 22:19), the most controverted text in Lord's Supper theology, should not be taken literally, but symbolically. Here the Greek New Testament word for "this" is neuter and therefore agrees in gender with the noun *sōma,* "body." The word therefore does not refer to the bread's being Christ's body, for the Greek word for bread, *artos,* is masculine. The Greek-writing people would be as unlikely to use a neuter pronoun in place of a masculine noun as we today would be to use "he" of a woman or "she" of a man. Evidently, Jesus was not saying that "this" bread is My body; but as Carlstadt of Luther's time said, He might have pointed to His own body and said, "This is my body," which is given for you. And if Christ is already physically present, why would we be told to observe the sacrament until He returns bodily?

We evangelical Wesleyans might make the Supper a "converting" sacrament in a somewhat different sense than Wesley did. Administering only to converted persons, we could urge the unconverted to confess their sins and accept God's forgiveness as the Supper is about to be served—and then they would be receiving it, appropriately, as believers.

To receive the Lord's Supper is a most important way by which a Christian believer grows in grace. This growth occurs because, in the Supper, we commune with Christ; because, in the Supper, we participate in a covenant; because, in the Supper, we receive God's strength, as the Holy Spirit ministers to us in our alert, obedient, and yearning openness. The growth occurs also because our attention is centered, in the Supper, on the Christ events through which we have received and will receive redemption. Our minds focus at this time on Christ's incarnation, crucifixion, and resurrection.

Our minds leap forward, too, in the Supper. We are to rehope at this time for the second coming of Christ to finalize our redemption.

The Supper helps us because we act out our faith in ritualistic drama, and ritualistic forms can be exceedingly beneficial if they really do express our beliefs and experience.

The Supper is beneficial, further and similarly, because it employs physicality to express our faith. We are people who believe that God himself created the whole world and that physicality is useful to our faith instead of a hindrance—as in idealistic Platonism. The Supper fits well into a faith that affirms the doctrines of creation, Incarnation, and Resurrection.

20

The Means of Grace

The various means of grace through which spiritual growth occurs are especially important to Wesleyan-holiness theology.

For one thing, in the understanding of this theological tradition, a believer may fall from grace. Taking steps to prevent this is therefore urgent. Also, this type of theology is interested in discipline toward holy living. Holiness of heart should issue in a holy life. This being so, the various means of receiving God's continued grace for living that type of life are emphasized.

Direct and indirect means of grace will be discussed, with the direct means receiving more of our attention.

Direct means of grace are the formal, appointed means: prayer, meditation, Bible reading, the Lord's Supper, worship (including hearing the Word of God through preaching), Christian conference, and fasting. Through them, God's grace is channeled to us immediately in distinction from mediately. They are, biblically and historically, the appointed and practiced ways in which God extends His many-faceted helps to us.

Indirect means of grace are the practices that, done by the help of the direct means of grace, are then themselves means of grace to us. Examples are Christian discipline, Christian service generally, and Christian suffering. Other practices could be included, but only these will be discussed.

The Direct Means

God's continued grace is needed if we are to maintain our redeemed status and if we are to live holy lives. The various direct means of grace will now engage our attention.

Prayer. This is a priority. To pray to God might be even a more deeply felt need than to read the Scriptures.

1. *The initiative is with God.* He bids us commune with Him. He offers audience with himself in all places, activities, and times. He creates in us the desire to commune with Him.

2. *Posture in prayer.* One widely practiced posture is kneeling. We thereby acknowledge God's greatness and our creatureliness. It is a posture often mentioned in Scripture accounts of prayer.

To stand while praying is also widely practiced. It, too, receives frequent mention in Scripture. Even as we stand to show respect for certain persons, we sometimes stand as we address God in prayer in order to show our respect for Him.

These are not, however, the only proper postures for prayer. In a friend-to-Friend fellowship with God, we may feel free to commune with Him while seated, lying down, fishing, jogging, or at any other time when communing with Him is natural to us.

3. *We address the Father.* Few people address the Holy Spirit. He can, of course, hear prayers addressed to Him, and in some liturgies, prayers are directed to Him.

Much more often, people address Jesus Christ in prayer. We may be prone to do this because He is so closely identified with us through the Incarnation.

Ideally, we are to address our prayers to God the Father. All of Jesus' prayers are addressed to the Father, and He taught us to pray to the Father in His name. The apostle Paul and other New Testament writers address all their actual prayers to the Father. A possible exception is Stephen's one-sentence prayer, which might be addressed to Christ (Acts 7:59). The only other possible exception is where we read in Rev. 22:20, the next to the last verse of the Bible, "Come, Lord Jesus."

Prayer to the Father is to be made in Jesus' name or for Jesus' sake. By this we admit that in ourselves we are unworthy of approaching the Father and undeserving of His help. This means also that Jesus is worthy, and that through His mediation we hold audience with God the Father.

The Holy Spirit's office is to prompt us to pray and guide us in what to say to the Father (Rom. 8:26).

4. *Praise precedes petition.* After addressing the Father, it is good to worship, adore, and praise Him for His past and present help before making any requests. As we mature, entire prayers may be devoted to praise and adoration of God, without any petitions.

When petitions are made, they will often be requests for help to more adequately glorify His holy name, instead of requests for a more pleasant life for ourselves. Friendship would shrivel and die if we requested favors from a friend just about every time we met. God is a person, with intellect, feeling, and will. And although He is infinite, His expectations in personal fellowship are not unlike ours in nature.

5. *We pray to a person.* As we pray, we need to think consciously of God as a person. He is not an abstract idea of the Good. If He were not a person, He could not hear and respond to our prayers.

6. *Prayer is like a gentle nudge.* Prayer does not bend God's will to our wills. Its purpose is the opposite—to bring ourselves into alignment with what He wants. And we are out of order, surely, if we try to pressure Him into acting on our behalf.

Many people say that God is obligated to do something because of what a Scripture passage states. The mature Christian will flee all such attempts to manipulate the Father, to control Him, to corner Him, to suggest that He has obligations toward us. In other words, prayer is not for pressuring God but is more like a gentle nudge.

7. *The question of fleeces.* Fleeces, in which we ask God to let something happen that will enable us to know His will, are at least questionable. Gideon used that method, but that was long before Bethlehem and Pentecost, and before we came to have the whole Bible as our guide. We are not impelled to put out a fleece just because a person did who lived long before God revealed himself through Christ and through the New Testament Scriptures.

We sometimes make "an open door" a kind of fleece. Christians often say that if "the door opens," they will take it as a sign that they are to walk through it. The "open door" might be a job offer. So what? The Holy Spirit, the Scriptures, the counsel of other Christians and even non-Christian professionals, our own best thoughts, and other factors all figure significantly in making decisions about job offers.

8. *Regularity in prayer.* Some kind of regularity in our praying is a significant factor. Most seasoned Christians have found regularity in prayer to be important. Daniel prayed with regularity: "Three times a day he got down on his knees and prayed, giving thanks to his God, just as he had done before" (6:10).

In regular prayer times, we might find ourselves praying in much the same way each time. If a given prayer is suited to our situation, it is not vainly repetitious to pray it daily for a while.

What we call the Lord's Prayer suggests the validity of this. Jesus taught His disciples a sort of prayer formula. Its repeated use has been beneficial to His people for centuries.

To pray early in the day in a regular way is also helpful. It has been the satisfying practice of many, on waking in the morning, to reach for their Bibles and prayer lists, then read, pray in a general way, and intercede for various persons and concerns.

9. *Our best words forward.* When praying, it is good to put our best words forward. God, of course, does not cock His ear to hear any small defect in the words we are using as we pray to Him. Yet since we respect God far more than we do any professional person, to speak a prayer as well as we are able might be a way of implementing our feeling of respect and honor toward Him. It helps us put into the prayer our whole being, including our intellect. And to pray articulately in private will help us lead in public prayer more meaningfully and more effectively.

10. *The place of intercession.* Intercession for others is profoundly important. References to intercession are numerous in the Old Testament. Abraham interceded for Sodom (Gen. 18:23-33). Jacob's blessing of Joseph's sons is of this nature (48:8-22). Moses was often a go-between for the idolatrous Israelites (Exod. 32:31-32). Samuel, grieved but tender, prayed all night for Saul (1 Sam. 15:11).

Intercession is often urged and practiced in the New Testament. Christ teaches us to pray for those who use us badly (Matt. 5:44). He said to Peter, "I have prayed for you, Simon, that your faith may not fail" (Luke 22:32). In John 17 we have a sustained prayer of Jesus for His disciples. In Acts, the young Church prayed for Peter (12:5-12) and for Barnabas and Saul (13:3).

Christians prayed for each other in New Testament times. Paul reminded his readers he was praying for them, and he often asked them to pray for him. As Daniel Steele said, he went forward for prayer in every Epistle he wrote.

11. *Why we pray so little.* Jesus, who presumably needed to pray so little, prayed so much; while we, who need to pray so much, pray so little. We deeply yearn for fellowship with God in prayer, and yet we often do not give prayer the attention it should receive.

Many Christians pray infrequently because they do not realize that praying is so crucial a means of grace. Some do not realize what a privilege it is. We might tend to pray too little, further, because we do not adequately conceptualize what is occurring when we pray: the two-way situation involved and the individual attention given us by God.

We might even tend to pray too little because, for lack of practice, we have not become very proficient at it. When we become proficient at prayer, understanding what is going on, realizing how strategic it is, and knowing how to speak our praise and our petitions, we will find praying more satisfying, and we will more readily engage in it.

Meditation. The other side of the coin of prayer is meditation. It, too, is a direct means of receiving God's grace.

It has become foreign to many of us to sit loose and quiet and contemplate Christ, the one way of access to God the Father. W. L. Walker, in an article on meditation in the old *International Standard Bible Encyclopedia,* wrote, "The lack of meditation is a great want in our modern life."

Long ago a psalm writer prayed, "May . . . the meditation of my heart be pleasing in your sight, O Lord" (19:14). In another psalm we read, "May my meditation be pleasing to him" (104:34). Well known to Christians is the passage in Psalm 1 where we read of the righteous person who "meditates day and night" on God's law (v. 2).

In meditation we are not looking for answers, as we might be in prayer; we are looking for God. In prayer, we speak and God listens; in meditation, *God* speaks and *we* listen.

In meditation, we are not as specific as we are in prayer. Unspecified yearnings for God are appropriate in meditation. They open up our souls on their heavenward side so broadly that the living, personal God above is able to reveal facets of himself to us.

The heart of the Christian who is practicing the art of meditation opens up to God so broadly that revelations from God are received that reason does not know how to process. Concepts might not all come from precepts; many of them might be direct revelations from the living God. Such revelations come only to opened-up persons who have receptacles for receiving God's disclosures that reason does not know anything about.

When these special disclosures are from God, they will be congruent with the special disclosures other opened-up Christians have received. Nor will they conflict with what Scripture tells us.

Just as it often helps to keep our mouths shut and our ears open when we are talking with friends, the same is true when we are talking with God. If prayer is a two-way street, and it is, we need to keep meditatively quiet, alert for what God will say back to us by impressing thoughts upon our inmost consciousness.

Scripture Reading. A third important means of grace is Scripture reading. We need to feed on Scripture all through life. As Bible moth John Wesley taught, a person is not given a stock of holiness but continues in the holy life only as that life is dynamically nurtured; and it is nurtured in part by Scripture.

1. *Applying its meaning.* If what the Bible says runs counter to the way we have understood things, we should ponder what it says, read it in another version, or see what a commentary says on a particular passage. When the meaning is determined, we should adapt it to our lives.

If the Bible seems to contradict itself, we need to read on, confident that it will finally explain itself. Passages that are clear in their meaning will help us understand those that are not clear.

The Spirit who indwells all believers will guide us into all truth (John 16:13). So we read the Bible prayerfully, asking the Holy Spirit to guide us in understanding it and in applying it to our lives.

We take into account that the Bible was written a long time ago and a long way off, by people some considered weird in their spiritual wisdom. We know it was written by people who had close-up revelations from God. For example, it was written long before we developed scientific medicines and surgeries, and sheer miracles were more often required then if cures were to occur at all.

Again, the Bible was written at a time when women were seldom well educated, seldom worked outside the home, and usually did not vote or hold property. We expect, therefore, to interpret the meaning of the Bible about the place of women according to those times and according to what God says in Scripture to people of all times. Its "all times" teaching, which determines the place of women today, is in such passages as Gal. 3:28: "There is neither Jew nor Greek, slave nor free, male nor female, for you are all one in Christ Jesus." This sounds like an equal rights state-ment written in the late 20th century.

2. *What version to read.* This is a matter of some importance. Almost any of them will be helpful, but some will suit us better than others.

If we feel that the language in which God speaks to us should be lofty, we might opt for the old standard—the King James Ver-sion. If we feel vividly that the God of Christmas is still close to us, we might want one of the up-to-date, down-to-earth, plain-talk versions. One of them is J. B. Phillips' translation. Another of these is *The Living Bible.* Its translator, Kenneth Taylor, often clar-ifies thoughts that are a bit obscure in other translations. Some-times, however, he and Phillips take too much liberty with the original text. Their "translations" are often paraphrastic.

A Bible version done by a large group is less likely to miss the meaning than a one-person translation or paraphrase. In a version, various translating committees must vote on each word and sentence. It is not as likely that the majority will agree on an incorrect meaning.

That is one reason why versions such as the *Revised Standard Version* and the *New English Bible* are good. The *New American Standard Bible* and more recently the *New International Version* were both done by scholars who would testify to being born again by God's grace. These versions read clearly, and one can pretty well depend on their being correct translations.

Whatever version we select, as we read it, we feel we hear God's voice and view His works.

3. *The Psalms are special.* The Psalms find us in the deepest parts of our existence, and they speak a kind of universal heart language. The Psalms contain perhaps the deepest, truest, most luminous insights ever expressed as to the way in which we ought to look upon our creaturely existence. They contain sus-tained, steady, in-depth looks at life lived under God's gracious sovereignty. John Calvin was referring to such matters as these when he called these bits of glory "an anatomy of all the parts of the soul." Doubts, fears, penitence, confidence, thanks, praise—all these are in this heart literature. Our souls coalesce with the souls of those psalm writers.

Their help has been important for some 3,000 years of Jewish and Christian history. The Psalms were used in ancient Temple worship for about 1,000 years, often being sung by a 150-voice choir, accompanied by numerous ram's horns and trumpets.

At the Last Supper, just before the departure to Gethsemane, Jesus received strength for His gathering storm by singing a psalm with the 11 apostles.

It is probable that these Hebrew songs helped Paul and Silas, jailed securely in Philippi. At midnight they broke out with "hymns of praise" (Acts 16:25, NASB), possibly based on the Psalms, and God broke in with release for them.

The early Christians, dauntless amid persecution, hid the Psalms away in their hearts. The people who wrote the New Testament quoted them frequently. Of the 287 quotations from the Old Testament appearing in the New Testament, 116 are from the Psalter.

Martyrs through the centuries were often bolstered by the Psalms during their last moments. John Huss, condemned to death in 1415 by the Council of Constance for "incorrect teachings," walked to his death reciting Psalm 31. A part of it reads: "Since you are my rock and my fortress, for the sake of your name lead and guide me. . . . Into your hands I commit my spirit; redeem me, O Lord, the God of truth" (vv. 3, 5).

In his trying times, Martin Luther, founder of Protestantism, turned to the Psalms and there found his strength "renewed like the eagle's."

Samuel Terrian wrote, "No other book of hymns and prayers has been used for so long a time and by so many diverse men and women."[1] And T. H. Robinson declared, "No other part of the Old Testament has exercised so wide, so deep, or so permanent an influence on the life of the human soul."[2]

English-speaking Protestants sang only the Psalms for a long time, convinced that in worship services all words sung should be from the Holy Scriptures. Later, paraphrases of the Psalms were sung. When other hymns were finally allowed, many of them were based on the Psalms.

1. Samuel Terrian, *The Psalms and Their Meaning for Today* (New York: Bobbs-Merrill Co., 1952), vii.

2. T. H. Robinson, *The Poetry of the Old Testament* (London: Gerald Duckworth and Co., 1947), 107.

The thoughts in the Psalms are as warm as sunshine, as human as a baby, as personal as our next-door neighbor's greeting. They are living experiences written out with incandescent words. People sensitive to God's marvelous works are stirred to their depths here, so that they think high thoughts about God as One who cares and is a refuge.

In the Psalms, surely, we have the heart of Old Testament religion. From the apostles onward we have rightly cherished this heart history of Israel as an integral part of our Christian heritage, for we find in them a language of tears and music and vision, of which hallelujahs and amens are born. We find in them a history of the Israelitish heart, which speaks with peculiar relevancy to the heart of the Christian who would grow and flower and bear fruit. In a special way, along with Scripture generally, they are a means of grace.

The Lord's Supper. A most select direct means of grace is the Lord's Supper, discussed at some length in the previous chapter. Our highest experiences can only be dramatized, and the Lord's Supper helps us to act out our faith.

A psychiatrist urges pastors whom he trains in a Lutheran seminary to see how long they can keep silent when they first visit a person who has lost a loved one. The sober expression, the handshake, the eyes holding for a moment the eyes of the bereaved person—this dramatizing of care is what the psychiatrist urges. At a time like that, the highest cannot be spoken.

When we Christians receive the Lord's Supper, the highest is acted out. We are prepared for the highest by a Communion meditation, by liturgy including audible prayer, and by Scripture reading. But when we come to the very highest, we do not say anything. We place the bread into our mouths and lift and drink the wine in silence, acting out our faith in the redemption from sin provided for by the death and resurrection of Jesus Christ.

In the Supper our Lord is present. The Christ of Calvary, risen and ascended, sits with us in the Supper. He companions us and strengthens us for life's struggles.

Growth in grace does not occur in the absence of faith. Nothing automatic is involved, but spiritual benefits accrue to the believing communicant. Christ has ordained the Supper to be a periodic means to the growth of the faith-filled and hope-filled Christian.

Worship. This is another important direct means of grace.

1. *The experience of wonder.* When we worship, we are recognizing "worthship" in a being far higher than ourselves. When we worship, we are in awestruck contemplation of the Trinity. When we worship, we express our religious instinct in penitence, praise, and holy joy before God our Creator-Redeemer. Worshiping is often, as someone has said, a "swift, resolute motion of the soul, intense as leaping flame."

The principal word for "worship" in the Old Testament denotes the idea of bowing down or prostrating oneself. This idea is found in at least 95 Old Testament passages. The main New Testament word for "worship," found numerous times, also carries the idea of bowing down or prostrating oneself upon the ground.

Our times tend to minimize the sphere of mystery and wonder. We need to take care lest we try to bring God down to our size and seek to find Him out completely. There is a sense in which the God of Bethlehem is no more than a heartbeat away from us who are Christ's. But God is still God. There is a barbed-wire area surrounding God's being, beyond which we creatures, in our contemplation, cannot pass. And without unfathomable mystery there is no high faith. That is why Paul asked, "Who hopes for what he already has?" (Rom. 8:24). With a deepening sense of wonder will come a deepening of rootage from which we will grow a little taller and become a little more steadfast in our faith.

2. *The promised Presence.* When we worship the God of unfathomable mystery, He really does meet with us as we go to the meeting place.

When Jesus came, He taught the importance of meeting God in spirit wherever the place of worship may be. To a Samaritan woman He said, "Yet a time is coming and has now come when the true worshipers will worship the Father in spirit and truth, for they are the kind of worshipers the Father seeks. God is spirit, and his worshipers must worship in spirit and in truth" (John 4:23-24).

According to Scripture, God has promised to meet with His people when they congregate for worship (Exod. 29:42-46; Matt. 18:20). Worship is a two-way street where the living and loving God, who is the kind of God the growing Christian needs, proves himself to be the kind of God the growing Christian has.

In a Roman Catholic worship service, usually called a mass, there might or might not be a sermon. In Protestantism generally, we would feel we had been shortchanged if we heard no sermon when we joined other growing Christians in a worship service.

3. *The sermon itself.* The sermon is an important means of grace. Preaching is "through and through an office of grace." It is this because the Holy Spirit designates certain people as God's spokespersons. It is this because the Holy Spirit guides such persons through years of preparation. It is this because the Spirit directs the church as it authorizes the prepared person. It is this because the Spirit charges God's spokesperson with a hidden fire. It is this because He indwells the worshiper's heart as he or she sits in the sanctuary and hears the Word of God declared—alert to God the whole time.

Usually the sermon is based on a passage from the Holy Scriptures, but it applies the age-old Word to the present age and to those of all ages who are present.

For many centuries, preaching has had a significant role in society as a whole. The Old Testament prophets were the earliest preachers, and several of them were more important in their time than were the kings. In New Testament times church people heard sermons in a more formal sense than people had in the Old Testament era. And in the post-New Testament centuries, the sermon has been heard and respected, based as it usually has been on the apostolic authority of New Testament writers.

Luther and others established the Reformation, significantly, by preaching to gathered groups of Christians. In the 18th century the preaching of John Wesley, George Whitefield, and others revived the church and probably averted revolution in England. Sermons figured prominently in the abolition of slavery in America.

The listener conceives of the preacher as called of God and the church at this particular time and place.

The public service, with the sermon at its center or close to its center, will help Christians to make growth strides that otherwise would be impossible.

Christian Conference. Our growth can also be augmented by conferring with other Christians.

We learn from Acts 15 that the early Christian got together at Jerusalem in a special conference to settle a disturbing issue. The question was whether people could be Christians without keeping Jewish regulations. They recognized justification by faith alone and imposed only a few regulations. Without that conference, Christianity might have become a sect of Judaism instead of a world-girdling faith.

Even Jesus found strength in conferring and having fellowship with small groups of friends. He had, of course, the 12 apostles, and 3 of the 12—Peter, James, and John—were His most special helpers. We are not to forget, either, the little house at Bethany where Jesus liked to relax and confer with Mary, Martha, and Lazarus.

The small classes into which Wesley divided his Methodist societies is a notable example of Christians seeking spiritual growth through small-group conferences.

The Christian who would grow in grace would do well to get together with other Christians and talk with them about Christian life and Christian service.

To confer with other Christians on important decisions is wise. Others can often view the whole matter with greater objectivity. For example, other persons might be able to see that someone we are inclining to as a marriage partner would be particularly unsuitable—or particularly suitable. This is true also of such important matters as career decisions or investments.

The Spirit has gifted certain Christians with discernment. It is wise to confer with them.

To seek advice from others is even a mark of Christian humility, the practice of which will help one grow in grace. By conferring, we admit that we are not self-sufficient and that we need the help of others.

Fasting. Unlike prayer and Scripture reading, fasting is a more take-it-or-leave-it means of grace. It is not enjoined for everyone in Scripture.

Some of God's people fast, while other do not. Paul often did (2 Cor. 6:5; 11:27, KJV), as did others (Acts 13:2; 14:23). We do not know whether some of the New Testament's honored characters fasted.

Jesus once fasted for 40 days (Matt. 4:2) but did not fast regularly. He was even accused of being a glutton (11:19). He did not expect His disciples to fast while He was with them in the flesh, but said they would fast later (Mark 2:20).

Martin Luther held that fasting is not a means of being justified, but a means by which the justified receive God's continued grace. Fasting, he insisted, should not be forced, but voluntary.

John and Charles Wesley included fasting or partial fasting as a general rule for the early Methodist societies. John Wesley said that God has "in all ages" appointed fasting as "a means of averting his wrath, and obtaining whatever blessings" are needed.[3]

1. *Purposes of fasting.* We fast, then, because Christ and others set us an example in this form of self-denial. We fast sometimes to express sorrow for the consequences of wrongdoing. During the Exile the Jews instituted four annual fast days to commemorate events connected with their subjugation to Babylon. When the world tumbled in on them, they fasted.

We fast when we need special guidance. After Cornelius had fasted (Acts 10:30, KJV), he was told to send for Peter—who helped him significantly. We fast as we pray for the effectiveness of those whom the church is sending forth into Kingdom work. The church at Antioch fasted and prayed before sending Paul and Barnabas into missionary work (13:2). We fast to dramatize the importance of the sacred over the secular. We fast, too, as an aid to prayer; John Wesley calls this a "weighty reason for fasting."[4]

Besides these so-called spiritual benefits of fasting, with their biblical and historical bases, the physical benefits must not be forgotten. Weight loss in overweight persons is an obvious advantage. Added to this benefit is the general rejuvenation of the body's functions, which many health authorities believe results from fasts of three or more days.

2. *Cautions in fasting.* This means of grace needs to be undertaken with cautions, especially with respect to motives. Fasting should not be done to display to others our devotion to Christ. When we fast, in fact, we are not to appear to be fasting (Matt. 6:16-18).

Fasting is futile if undertaken simply for the sake of suffering, for God is not interested in such.

---

3. Wesley, *Works* 5:351.
4. Ibid.

The Indirect Means

Having discussed these direct means of receiving God's grace, three indirect means will now be treated.

Discipline. In the Wesleyan tradition, influenced by Pietism and Mr. Wesley himself, discipline is an important indirect means of grace. Wesley is properly said to have wedded together the Roman Catholic interest in the disciplines of holy living with Luther's stress on justification by faith. The treatment of discipline here will be restricted to our bodies, our speech, our moods, and the things of this life.

1. *Our bodies.* The apostle Paul testified, "I beat my body and make it my slave" (1 Cor. 9:27). While the human body is a product of God's creative genius, it often occasions less-than-Christian actions. Its desires for sex and food, for example, require special discipline. A Christian who desires spiritual maturity should be concerned about maintaining a healthful weight level.

2. *Speech.* If we discipline our speech, we will not express every thought that crosses our minds. We will refrain from gossip. We will learn to be discriminating in our humor, not repeating stories or jokes that denigrate others. Curse words might come to mind in the moment of a sudden pain or disappointment, especially if we used such words habitually prior to becoming a Christian. The disciplined tongue will guard against using them.

3. *Moods.* Some Christians, by temperament itself, but also by a pattern set in earlier life through the influence of others, are prone to highs and lows on the emotional scales. They overact and overreact. Trifling matters can elate or depress them. Yet, as such Christians mature in God's grace, the discipline of moods can be an indirect means of grace.

4. *Material things.* The wise use and enjoyment of material things is crucial to spiritual growth. Keeping up with the Joneses is an obsession with too many. Luxuries become necessities for the Smiths when the Joneses get them.

While John Wesley's philosophy about money was "earn all you can, save all you can, and give all you can," the money philosophy of many today is (1) get all you can, (2) can all you get, and (3) keep all you can. Wesley had one of the highest incomes in all England, but he lived frugally and used nearly all his money for Christ's work. When his income enlarged, he still lived on just about the same amount he used as an Oxford student when his income was meager.

We read in James, "If a brother or sister is ill-clad and in lack of daily food, and one of you says to them, 'Go in peace, be warmed and filled,' without giving them the things needed for the body, what does it profit? So faith by itself, if it has no works, is dead" (2:15-17, RSV). With all due recognition that governmental programs (which are often by-products of the Christian faith) now help many of the needy, we Christians surely are not sufficiently caring.

A cult of affluence has emerged within the Church. It is affirmed that, if Jesus were here, He would wear the finest clothes and drive an expensive car—"a yellow Cadillac," one adherent said. This is a distortion of the biblical portrayal of the lowly Carpenter from insignificant Nazareth.

When millions are starving to death, and when the world has not been evangelized, we should reject the voices that advocate a cult of affluence and live by the sacrifice-demanding words of Jesus.

Of Mr. Average American after the two world wars, Henry Steele Commager wrote, "His culture was still predominantly material, his thinking quantitative, his genius inventive, experimental, and practical."[5]

High on the front of the art gallery in Kansas City the following words are chiseled in the stone: "The soul has greater need of the ideal than of the real." Those words are not chiseled deeply enough on the front side of our minds.

In his *In One Ear,* Eric Sevareid suggests that the real threat to humanity is not Communism or insects or even singing commercials—but things.

Nobody wants simply to decry the things that make for comfort—at least not many want to. What must be challenged is the place of priority given to things. When 800 were enrolled in business administration in a large American university and only 8 in the humanities, something is askew in the soul of the nation.

The Bible's answer to this sickness is the development of a vertical perspective. Paul stresses this vertical perspective when

---

5. Henry Steele Commager, *The American Mind* (New York: Yale University Press, 1950), 410.

he admonishes, "Since, then, you have been raised with Christ, set your hearts on things above . . . not on earthly things" (Col. 3:1-2). Such a discipline will free us from the tyranny of things. The simple, more sacrificial life-style, which will make other Christian services possible, will indirectly become a means of grace to us.

Service. A by-product of service to Christ is that we will grow in grace.

"When does the service begin?" A visitor whispered this to the person beside him when the Spirit did not seem to move anyone to break the silvery silence of a Quaker meeting.

Came the hushed answer, "The service begins when the meeting is over." Service to the least and the lost of this world should begin after we worshipers, with the sinews of our souls flexed by church attendance, leave the church and walk out into the busy ways of people.

Those who enter the chapel of Goshen Seminary in Indiana see the words, "Jesus is Lord." As they leave, they are faced at the back of the chapel with the command, "Go make disciples of all men."

One translation of Acts 8:4 has it that the early Christians went everywhere "gossiping the gospel"—making Christ the talk of every town. Why not? He is the captivating, compelling Savior who draws sinners to himself.

Many Christians have enough religion to make them decent, but not enough to make them dynamic. It is said that organizations, including churches, tend to pass through three stages: (1) when those connected with it work for a dream, (2) when they work for the organization itself, and (3) when they work to preserve their place in the organization. The continued growth of Christians in the Church is imperative if the dream stage is to be maintained. And the dream stage obtains when the church members see that the Church exists importantly for those not yet in it.

Thinking of my own need to grow in grace through service, I found myself praying like this:

Father, I am Your bread. Break me up and pass me around to the poor and needy of this world.

I am Your towel. Dampen me with tears and with me wash the feet of people who are weary with walking and with working.

I am Your light. Take me out to where the darkness is thick, there to shine and let Christ shine.

I am Your pen. Write with me whatever word You wish, and placard the word where the least and the lost of the world will see it and read it and be helped by it.

I am Your salt. Sprinkle me on all the things that You want for people, so that my faith and love and hope will flavor their experiences.

I am Your water. Pour me into people who thirst for You but do not even know that it is You for whom they thirst. Pour into them the trust that You have helped me to place in You. Pour into them the inward witness that is in me. Pour into them the promise that soon the summer drought will pass and refreshing rivers of water will gush down over them.

I am Yours, Lord God. Use me up in what You will, when You will, where You will, for whom You will, even if it means that I am given responsibilities that are considerable and costly.

Suffering. To inch taller in character and in accomplishments through suffering or in spite of suffering has often happened. Suffering, when responded to triumphantly and creatively, can occasion a Christian's growth in grace.

Jesus Christ "learned obedience through what he suffered" (Heb. 5:8, RSV) and ultimately suffered for the redemption of the human race.

Paul told the Colossian church that when we Christians suffer, we make up what is lacking in Christ's suffering (1:24). God does not directly will every illness, but He has a will in every illness. His will, surely, is that we react creatively to trying times.

These, then, are important means of grace: direct ones such as prayer, meditation, Scripture reading, the Lord's Supper, worship, Christian conference, and fasting; and indirect ones such as discipline, service, and suffering.

If we enter into these means of grace, open and alert to God, we will receive grace, and we will grow in measurable ways.

1. The means of grace are proven effective when our interests and concerns become broad in scope. As we mature in grace, we will become more interested in people who are not immediately and significantly related to us by family or work. We will become

more interested in the spread of the gospel outside our local church, without losing interest there.

2. Further, as we receive the means of grace, we will be less satisfied with the quality of the services we are rendering to Christ in His Church and will earnestly desire to serve more effectively. We will become more responsive to and less threatened by criticisms of our performance.

3. Effectiveness of the means of grace is shown in a growing ability to control our emotions. When we are hurt, we will patiently and forgivingly try to understand the actions and reactions of others. Service to them will become more important than defense of ourselves. Our hurts will be real, but they will not control our responses.

4. Further, the means of grace will install in us some backup gears ready for us at any time. We will more readily admit our mistakes and more quickly apologize for hurting others.

5. Still further, our understanding of the ideal Christian life will probably change. The definition and expression of Christian faith will become less negative, more positive.

6. Also, our knowledge of God and His Word will increase and change. The folk theology we have learned, perhaps from persons who had odd ideas, will tend to slough off. We will discover additional bases for believing time-honored Christian teachings.

In a sermon on the means of grace, Wesley includes some cautions that are still apt. He reminds us that means are not ends. There is no power resident in the means to automatically produce grace and growth in us, regardless of where our hearts are. He writes, "In using all means, seek God alone. In and through every outward thing, look singly to the *power* of his Spirit, and the *merits* of his Son."[6]

---

6. Wesley, *Works* 5:201, see 185-201.

21

Last Things as Last Word

Prophecy concerning the order of events in the very last days has not been a matter of keen interest to the Wesleyan-holiness tradition for two major reasons. (1) The Bible is not altogether clear on many of these matters. It is clear that Christ is to return, for example, but the relation of the Second Coming to other events is somewhat unclear. (2) Wesleyan-holiness people are much more interested in redeeming grace and holy living. God's design for the close of history will be filled with blessings for His people, whenever and however it unfolds.

A number of matters relating to eschatology will nevertheless be discussed as this volume of Christian theology is concluded. These are (1) death as the last enemy, (2) Armageddon, (3) the Tribulation, (4) the Antichrist; (5) the millennium, (6) the Second Coming, (7) destiny, and (8) last things as last word.

Death as the Last Enemy

Scripture views death as "the last enemy" (1 Cor. 15:26). It is a result of human sin: "in Adam all die" (v. 22); "sin entered the world through one man, and death through sin" (Rom. 5:12). Evidently, if our representative, Adam, had not sinned, we would not have died physically. The usual teaching in Christian theology is that, except for sin, we would have been translated to the next life (without death), as seems to have happened in the case of Enoch (Gen. 5:24) and Elijah (2 Kings 2:11). Because death is undesirable, Jesus struggled in the Garden of Gethsemane the night before His crucifixion (Matt. 26:38-39; Mark 14:34-36; Luke 22:41-44).

Oscar Cullmann graphically contrasts the deaths of Socrates and Jesus to show that the Christian view of death is the opposite of the Greek view. Cullmann writes, "Plato shows us how Socrates goes to his death in complete peace and composure. . . . Socrates cannot fear death, since indeed it frees him from the body. . . . Death is the soul's great friend."[1] Jesus approached His death, however, with deep distress (Mark 14:33). Cullmann says, "Death for Him is not something divine; it is something dreadful."[2]

Even for Christians, from the human perspective, death is indeed dreadful. It is a result of sin and is our last enemy. Even so, the Father helped Jesus face it, and God has helped Christians in all ages face it. Our Best Friend has the power over our worst foe, as Christ's resurrection assures us.

Armageddon

A widely misunderstood matter is Armageddon, a word used only once in the Bible (Rev. 16:16). No one knows whether the reference is to a locality (Jerusalem itself, or the mountain of Megiddo nearby), an event (a battle), or to the stretched-out opposition to God's people during all time. Revelation says, "They [three evil spirits] are spirits of demons performing miraculous signs, and they go out to the kings of the whole world, to gather them for the battle on the great day of God Almighty" (v. 14). So the evil "kings of the whole world" will be arrayed against Israel, and this is Armageddon.

It is probable that, without naming it "Armageddon," in Ezekiel and Zechariah, refer to this "battle." Ezekiel says, "You [Gog, of the land of Magog] will come from your place in the far north, you and many nations with you, all of them riding on horses, a great horde, a mighty army. You will advance against my people Israel" (38:2, 15-16). Zechariah says, "I will gather all the nations to Jerusalem to fight against it" (14:2).

Although many popular writers are confident that a literal Battle of Armageddon will take place, these references are no doubt to the stretched-out opposition to Israel and the Church. We know that much material in Ezekiel, Zechariah, and Revelation is to be understood symbolically. In the immediate context of the Zechariah reference, for example, we are required to interpret

---

1. Oscar Cullmann, *Immortality,* ed. T. Penelhum (Belmont, Calif.: Wadsworth Publishing Co., 1973), 60.
2. Ibid., 62.

LAST THINGS AS LAST WORD ▷ 531

the meaning as symbolical. There we read, "On that day [of the battle] . . . the Mount of Olives will be split in two from east to west, forming a great valley, with half of the mountain moving north and half moving south" (14:4). If some references to this battle must be interpreted symbolically, perhaps the battle itself is to be understood in that way.

The Tribulation

Premillennialists understand that the Bible's references to tribulation, or to the Tribulation, refer especially to a seven-year period of opposition to God's people. They divide over whether the Rapture of the Church will happen just before it starts (the pretribulation view), at its middle (the midtribulation view), or after the seven years (the posttribulation view; see Matt. 24:21; Rev. 2:22; 3:10; 7:14).

The present writer understands that the tribulation referred to in Scripture usually refers to the opposition earlier to the Jews and later to the Church, and that there seems to be an intensification of this opposition just before Christ's return—but not so definite an intensification that we would not look for Christ's return to occur at any time.

The Antichrist

This refers to one or more opposition figures rising up against Christ. Christians, for many centuries, have said this person or that person is evidently the Antichrist—and they were all proven wrong. Martin Luther, in *The Papacy at Rome,* said that the pope was Antichrist, who was Pope Leo X when that tract was written in 1520. Hitler, Mussolini, Stalin, and even Saddam Hussein, of our century, have been designated as possibly the Antichrist, and those designations have proved to be incorrect (see 2 Thess. 2:1-12; 1 John 2:18; 4:3; 2 John 7; Matt. 24:5, 24; Mark 13:22; Luke 21:8).

Only John uses the actual term (1 John 2:18, 22; 4:3; and 2 John 7). Clearly, John, by using the plural "antichrists," sometimes means anyone who opposes Christ overtly. He says, "Dear children . . . as you have heard that the antichrist is coming, even now many antichrists have come" (1 John 2:18). John also identifies as "the deceiver and the antichrist" any person who denies "Jesus Christ as coming in the flesh" (2 John 7). Paul's "man of lawlessness" (2 Thess. 2:3) seems, perhaps, to be a particular opposition figure who "will exalt himself . . . proclaiming himself to be God" (v. 4). It might be that all opposition figures are antichrists and that a particular such figure is to arise before Christ's return.

The Millennium

Millennialism is one of the most controverted issues within recent evangelicalism.[3] The controversy revolves around (1) whether Christ will reign on earth literally for 1,000 years; (2) the relation between Christ's second coming and this millennium; (3) whether the return of Christ will be divided into the Rapture and the Revelation, with the Tribulation between them; (4) whether there are to be two resurrections, the first of the righteous dead before the millennium and the second of the wicked dead after the millennium; (5) whether there will be redemption after the Rapture for Israel; (6) whether there will be two kingly reigns, one over Israel and the other over the Church; and (7) whether, as dispensationalists teach, the Temple will be rebuilt and sacrifices again offered for sin, although Hebrews 8—10 surely teaches that Christ became the once-for-all-time Sacrifice for sin.

Millennial Theories. Three principal millennial theories have been held: premillennialism, amillennialism, and postmillennialism. They are based on interpretations of various scriptures, but most particularly Rev. 20:1-7:

> And I saw an angel coming down out of heaven . . . He seized the dragon, that ancient serpent, who is the devil, or Satan, and bound him for a thousand years. He threw him into the Abyss, and locked and sealed it over him, to keep him from deceiving the nations anymore until the thousand years were ended. After that, he must be set free for a short time.
>
> I saw thrones on which were seated those who had been given authority to judge. And I saw the souls of those who had been beheaded because of their testimony for Jesus and becasue of the word of God. They had not worshiped the beast or his image and had not received his mark on their foreheads or their hands. They came to life

---

3. Donald Bloesch wrote, "Apart from biblical inerrancy no doctrine has caused greater division in evangelical Christianity in the present day than the millennium." *Essentials of Evangelical Theology* (New York: Harper and Row, 1979), 1:189.

and reigned with Christ a thousand years. (The rest of the dead did not come to life until the thousand years were ended.) This is the first resurrection. Blessed and holy are those who have part in the first resurrection. The second death has no power over them, but they will . . . reign with him [Christ] for a thousand years.

When the thousand years are over, Satan will be released from his prison.

With this special passage in mind, along with numerous other related passages, the three principal millennial theories will be discussed, and numerous supports will be given for a type of amillennialism or postmillennialism, herein called realized millennialism.

1. *Premillennialism.* This is the view that Christ's second coming will occur prior to a literal 1,000-year earthly reign of Christ with His resurrected and glorified people. Early it was called chiliasm and was believed by many church fathers and by the Montanists. But it fell into disrepute because (1) the anticipated Second Coming did not happen; (2) Origen and others spiritualized the matter of the millennium; and (3) Augustine influenced the church (until after the Reformation) toward an amillennial view.

It was revived, however, after the Reformation (16th century), among some of the Anabaptists, and has many adherents as the 20th century closes.

A problem with premillennialism is its tendency to pessimism: that things will get worse and worse until Christ returns. This view tends to discourage implementation of Christ's kingly rule in the world by evangelism and social improvement programs.

The one millennial view to which Scripture stands most clearly opposed is dispensational premillennialism, begun by J. N. Darby in England in the 1830s and popularized by C. I. Scofield in the *Scofield Reference Bible* of 1909. This view bifurcates between Jews and Gentiles, maintaining that God still has different redemption scenarios for the two groups. Its adherents do not understand that the Church is the new and true Israel. Instead, they view the Church as an interim scheme of God, devised only after Israel rejected Christ as its Messiah. It expects another Temple to be built when the millennium begins, with sacrifices for sin again offered in it and the Old Testament priesthood reinstituted. At the Rapture, the Church will be taken away, and seven years of tribulation are to begin, the latter half of which will be extremely severe. Yet during this time many Jews will turn to Christ and will go forth preaching Christ their Messiah, and multitudes of people not taken away in the Rapture, given this second chance, will accept Christ—so many, in fact, that it will be a revival such as the Church never did see in all its history. And this, after the Holy Spirit is largely withdrawn since He had been with the Church and had gone away with the Church at the Rapture. Also, this is to occur at a time when Antichrist is raging in power.

Another problem with dispensational premillennialism is its teaching of two comings of Christ: one, the Rapture, to catch away the saints; another, seven years later, the Revelation, when He will return with the saints to set up His 1,000-year reign on the earth. This exempts the Church from the Tribulation period; yet surely God does not exempt Christians from such; He instead sustains us in our trying times.

2. *Amillennialism.* This is the theory that we are not to expect a literal 1,000-year earthly reign of Christ after the Second Coming.

Basically, this position is taken because the references to the millennium are interpreted symbolically and not literally. Amillennialists differ somewhat on just what the millennium does mean symbolically. Most of them say that it refers to Christ's present rule in the world, during the Church Age—between Christ's first advent and His second coming. It is understood that Christ's resurrection is especially what binds Satan. Amillennialists also teach that for the dead in Christ, and especially for the martyred dead referred to in Rev. 20:1-7, Satan is altogether bound, because they have made it from the Church militant to the Church triumphant. All amillennialists teach, along with all postmillennialists, that the Judgment and the final destiny—determinations of heaven and hell—will take place immediately after Christ's second coming.

3. *Postmillennialism.* This is the view that, after a historical millennium of indefinite duration, Christ will return to subdue Antichrist and Satan and to judge all humans—who will then, immediately, enter into their eternal heaven or hell destinies. Some postmillennialists believe we are already in the millennium; but many, including most scholars in America's mid-19th-century Holiness Movement and the rather-recent Loraine Boettner (who wrote *The Millennium* in 1958) have said that, although the gospel is succeeding more and more, we are not yet into this historical

reign of Christ referred to as the millennium. Again, while some postmillennialists are not reckless in believing that the gospel will succeed in getting almost everyone in the whole world converted, their usual view (including again that of Loraine Boettner) is that just such success will indeed happen.

Scripture support of this confident view of the Christianizing of the world is taken from both the Old Testament and the New Testament. They find convincing such passages as Ps. 47:2—"How awesome is the Lord Most High, the great King over all the earth!" and Ps. 72:7-8, 11: "In his days the righteous will flourish . . . He will rule from sea to sea . . . All kings will bow down to him and all nations will serve him."

It is interesting that they are not able to give as much support from the New Testament as from the Old Testament. They use Acts 15:16-18, which refers to the Old Testament; but here it is only that God will work so that "the remnant of men may seek the Lord." The principal New Testament support is Christ's death as the propitiation for the sins of the whole world (John 3:16; 8:12; 2 Cor. 5:19; 1 John 2:2; 4:10, NASB).

4. *Realized millennialism argued for.* After much study, the present writer supports a postmillennial-amillennial type of view, which he would call realized millennialism. This views the millennium as the whole Church-Age time between Christ's two advents, during which Christ truly reigns over the dead in Christ now in the intermediate state and especially over the martyred dead (see Rev. 20:1-7), and more or less over the whole world, because Satan is only a limping sovereign due to Christ's resurrection and the descent of the Holy Spirit at Pentecost. The word "realized" is used with "millennium" to affirm that we are in a real millennium, a real reign of Christ over a kingdom. Postmillennialism might be the most appropriate of all the terms to express this writer's view, because it indicates that the millennium is real and historical and that Christ's second advent will occur at the close of this reign of Christ, this millennium. Yet the term "postmillennialism" has been preempted by many persons who teach incorrectly at two important points: that the millennium has not as yet begun, and that, when it does begin and as it continues, the whole world will become Christianized.

Many postmillennialists have understood that the millennium has not begun as yet. Henry Cowles, a professor at Oberlin

College in Ohio and editor of the *Oberlin Evangelist*,[4] wrote 23 essays on the millennium for that magazine beginning in 1841, urging implementation of Jesus' teachings. This would launch the millennium—after which the Second Coming, the resurrection, the Judgment, and the eternal separation of persons into the tormented and the blissful would occur. This Cowles-type scenario was the usual teaching of the American Holiness Movement of the 19th century. The present writer understands that the millennium, of indefinite duration, began with the Christ event, and particularly with the resurrection of Jesus and with Pentecost as the hilarious early implementation of God's reign.

Also, many postmillennialists unrealistically teach that, almost to a person, the whole world will accept Christ as Lord and Savior before the Second Coming occurs. Loraine Boettner, for example, who, like Cowles, does not understand that the millennium has begun as yet, says:

> This process ultimately shall be completed, and before Christ comes again we shall see a Christianized world. This does not mean that all sin ever will be eradicated. There always will become tares among the wheat until the time of harvest—and the harvest, the Lord tells us, is the end of the world. . . . But it does mean that Christian principles of life and conduct are to become the accepted standards in public and private life.[5]

a. One support of realized millennialism is that it views Christ as already reigning over a kingdom, so that we are not awaiting a future earthly kingdom—and this is surely biblical. The kingdom of God did not cease after the Church was begun at Pentecost; it continued. The last verse of Acts, for example, states of Paul, "Boldly and without hindrance he preached the kingdom of God and taught about the Lord Jesus Christ" (28:31).

b. Another support of realized millennialism is that a view similar to it was almost universally held by Christians from

---

4. For the views held by significant figures in the Methodist tradition, especially in the American Holiness Movement of the 19th century, see Donald W. Dayton, *Theological Roots of Pentecostalism* (Grand Rapids: Francis Asbury Press of Zondervan Publishing House, 1987), 143 ff.

5. Loraine Boettner, *The Millennium* (Philadelphia: Presbyterian and Reformed Publishing Co., 1958), 38.

the time of Augustine in the 5th century until after the Reformation in the 16th century.

c. The view also accounts for what is said about the reign of Christ over the martyred dead in Rev. 20:1-7. There, not all the redeemed dead, but only the martyred dead, are spoken of: "And I saw the souls of those who had been beheaded because of their testimony for Jesus and because of the word of God" (v. 4). "They came to life," John says, which might refer to a blissful alerting in paradise, and they "reigned with Christ a thousand years" (v. 4). When they made it triumphantly into the next world, they "came to life" with thankfulness and began to "reign with Christ" as redeemed persons. For them, Satan was entirely bound, unable to do them any hurt whatever. Their reigning with Christ 1,000 years seems to refer to their victorious reign as the martyred dead during the entire millennial age—when, on earth, the resurrected Christ continues to reign and to suppress Satan.[6]

The proposed view here is similar to amillennialism in understanding that the millennium is much more than a thousand years in duration (2 Pet. 3:8).

d. This understanding also encourages Christian social action, as did Jesus and James and Paul. This is preferable to premillennialism's neglect of social action programs, based upon its assumption that things are supposed to worsen until the Second Coming.

e. The type of millennialism being discussed here is also consistent with the hope that the Second Coming might occur at any time. If Christ's kingly reign began with His resurrection, the millennium can be completed at any time—allowing for the possibility of the Second Coming at any time.

f. Further support for this scenario is that it views the Church as the true Israel and as the inheritor of the promises made to Israel. It does not understand that Israel will be treated in one way and Gentiles in another, but that all must accept Christ before the Second Coming as the one way to salvation.

---

6. On the view that this does not refer to the martyred dead, but to all the deceased believers and to their physical resurrection, you have two resurrections. An interpretation of this type would be possibly valid, based solely on the Rev. 20:1-7 passage. Then, however, the interpreter will have trouble with all the remainder of the Bible passages referring to our physical resurrection—which make no time distinction between the resurrection of the righteous and that of the wicked.

    g. A strong point in favor of realized millennialism is that it encourages the proclamation of the gospel. If the gospel is to flourish more and more, instead of less and less as in premillennialism, this encourages an all-out endeavor to proclaim Christ "where'er the sun / Does his successive journeys run" (Isaac Watts).

    h. This scenario also allows for the biblical teaching that there will be tribulation; antichrist's opposition to the gospel; and a falling away of many just before the Second Coming (Matt. 24:12; 2 Thess. 2:3-4, KJV; Rev. 7:14).

    In American and other cultures as the 20th century closes, the flourishing of the gospel along with widespread opposition can be seen. Evangelical faith is succeeding as never before, but drug dependency, pornography, and public vulgarity are also in play as never before. All this is within the purview of realized millennialism, which recognizes that Scripture teaches both the increasing effectiveness of the gospel and a worsening of society before Christ's return.

    i. This scenario, also, views probation as over when the Second Coming occurs, whereas some premillennialists of the dispensational ilk understand that the redemption of many persons will happen after what we call the Second Coming.

    j. A most important advantage of this vision is its compacting together within a brief span of time the Second Coming, the subduing of all alien power, the Judgment, and the final heaven-hell parting of persons. While only one passage of Scripture can be interpreted as teaching that there will be a resurrection of the righteous and a later resurrection of the wicked (Rev. 20:6), numerous passages teach clearly that there will be only one resurrection of both, at Christ's second coming, and that the Judgment will take place immediately. Dan. 12:2 speaks of only one general resurrection, and no millennium is there mentioned as then preceding the Judgment. We read, "Multitudes who sleep in the dust of the earth will awake: some to everlasting life, others to shame and everlasting contempt." Likewise, Jesus' parable of the net has in it no separate resurrections and no millennial space between the end of the Kingdom work and the Judgment. There we read,

    Once again, the kingdom of heaven is like a net that was let down into the lake and caught all kinds of fish. When it was full, the fishermen pulled it up on the shore. Then they sat down and collected the good fish in baskets, but threw the bad away. This is how it will be at the end of the age. The angels will come and separate the wicked from the righteous and throw them into the fiery furnace, where there will be weeping and gnashing of teeth *(Matt. 13:47-50)*.

One general resurrection and immediate Judgment are clearly taught in John 5:28-29, where Jesus says, "Do not be amazed at this, for a time is coming [one time!] when all who are in their graves will hear his voice and come out—those who have done good will rise to live, and those who have done evil will rise to be condemned."

Jesus also says, "When the Son of Man comes . . . All the nations will be gathered before him, and he will separate the people one from another" (Matt. 25:31-32). To some He will say, "Take your inheritance," and to the others, "Depart from me . . . into the eternal fire" (vv. 34, 41). And Paul says that "there will be a resurrection of both the righteous and the wicked" (Acts 24:15).

Paul also says that the Judgment will occur when Christ returns—not a 1,000-year earthly reign. In 1 Cor. 15:23 ff., referring to the time "when he [Christ] comes," Paul says: "Then the end will come, when he hands over the kingdom to God the Father after he has destroyed all dominion, authority and power. For he must reign until he has put all his enemies under his feet."

k. This vision agrees also with the Apostles' Creed writers. This oldest of the ecumenical creeds supplies no hint of a millennium between the Second Coming and the Judgment. In this creed we simply affirm that Christ "will come to judge the quick and the dead"—not to set up a 1,000-year reign and then judge us.

l. This vision is also in keeping with the usual teachings in John Wesley and the Holiness Movement—who might have been a bit more postmillennial than amillennial (the terms were invented only a few generations ago), but whose views, in general, were in keeping with realized millennialism. In John Wesley's sermon on Christians as salt, from Matthew 5, he outlines a strategy for gradual social change that is in keeping with either postmillennialism or realized millennialism.[7] Wesley believed that the

7. Ralph Thompson says, "While John Wesley did not emphasize postmillennialism, his writings reveal that he tended to think in keeping with that frame of reference." ("Eschatology," in *A Contemporary Wesleyan Theology*, ed. Charles W. Carter [Grand Rapids: Francis Asbury Press, 1983], 2:1119.)

church should establish holiness in society, including the abolition of slavery and poverty.[8] He was what Reinhold Niebuhr would call a "transformationist." He lived simply and worked assiduously for social change.[9]

Adam Clarke was also of this persuasion. Commenting on Rev. 20:2, he says: "Yet there is no doubt that the earth is in a state of progressive moral improvement; and that the light of true religion is shining more copiously everywhere, and will shine more and more to the perfect day."[10]

The Second Coming

Although there is room for debate about the relation of Christ's second coming to such matters as the Tribulation and the millennium, almost all Christians in all eras have understood that Christ will return to this earth. This near unanimity has obtained because Scripture is replete with teaching on the subject.

Its Promise. Numerous passages of Scripture contain the promise of Christ's second coming. Jesus said, "I am going there to prepare a place for you. And if I go and prepare a place for you, I will come back and take you to be with me" (John 14:2-3). At the Ascension, angels said, "This same Jesus, who has been taken from you into heaven, will come back in the same way you have seen him go into heaven" (Acts 1:10-11). The writer of Hebrews says, "So Christ was sacrificed once to take away the sins of many people; and he will appear a second time" (9:28). Paul says that "we wait for the blessed hope—the glorious appearing of our great God and Savior, Jesus Christ" (Titus 2:13).

Its Manner. Paul gives one of Scripture's most detailed predictions of the manner of Christ's second coming in 1 Thess. 4:16-17: "For the Lord himself will come down from heaven, with a loud command, with the voice of the archangel and with the

---

8. For a treatment of Wesley's type of view, see Leon Hynson, "The Kingdom of God in the Theology of John Wesley," WTJ 23, nos. 1-2 (Spring-Fall 1988): 46.

9. Arias, who suggests that Wesley did not believe with Augustine that the Kingdom became the Church, entertains the idea that Wesley's doctrine of prevenient grace might be his kingdom of God—that type of grace being broader than the Church, even as the kingdom of God is. See Mortimer Arias, "The Kingdom of God," WTJ 23, nos. 1-2 (Spring-Fall 1988): 33.

10. Adam Clarke, *Clarke's Commentary* (Nashville: Abingdon-Cokesbury Press), 6:1054.

trumpet call of God, and the dead in Christ will rise first. After that, we who are still alive and are left will be caught up together with them in the clouds to meet the Lord in the air. And so we will be with the Lord forever."

The return of Christ will evidently be literal and physical. Christ will return "in like manner" as He was seen going into heaven (Acts 1:11, KJV), and He ascended in a resurrected physical body. We also read, "Look, he is coming with the clouds, and every eye will see him, even those who pierced him" (Rev. 1:7). Surely, not every eye of believers all over our round earth will see a physical return. This might mean that every eye in the vicinity will, and that everyone who would be in the vicinity could.

Its Purpose. The Second Coming will have two principal purposes. One is our glorification. Hebrews says that "he will appear a second time, not to bear sin [as at His first coming], but to bring salvation to those who are waiting for him" (9:28). The people awaiting him are believers, already saved from sin. The salvation He brings them is glorification; we will all receive immortality, "the redemption of our bodies" (Rom. 8:23). Indeed, the entire created world is to be redeemed at this time (vv. 19-21). This seems to mean that the polluted air and soil and water will be cleansed. Peter might refer to this when he says, "But the day of the Lord will come like a thief. The heavens will disappear with a roar; the elements will be destroyed by fire, and the earth and everything in it will be laid bare" (2 Pet. 3:10). And this might be why John says, "Then I saw a new heaven and a new earth, for the first heaven and the first earth had passed away" (Rev. 21:1).

The other special purpose of the Second Coming is judgment. When the Second Coming happens, the Judgment will take place right away. As noted in the above study of millennialism, Jesus knows nothing of a millennial reign that will begin only after the Second Coming. The Kingdom began with the preaching of John the Baptist and himself, and it is both present and future. So Jesus says, "For the Son of Man is going to come in his Father's glory with his angels, and then [not 1,000 years later!] he will reward each person according to what he has done" (Matt. 16:27; see also 25:33-41).

As with Jesus, so with Paul. Paul knows nothing of a 1,000-year reign with Christ between the Second Coming and the Judgment. Paul says, "Therefore judge nothing before the appointed time; wait till the Lord comes. He will bring to light what is hidden in darkness and will expose the motives of men's hearts. At that time each will receive his praise from God" (1 Cor. 4:5). When "the Lord comes," the Judgment will take place. Paul implies the same when he says, "In the presence of God and of Christ Jesus, who will judge the living and the dead, and in view of his appearing and his kingdom, I give you this charge" (2 Tim. 4:1). To "judge the living and the dead" seems to be the reason for His "appearing." But there will be no kingly rule of 1,000 years between the appearing and the Judgment, as all premillennialists teach.

Jude, quoting Enoch, also teaches that Christ will judge the world and that the Judgment will immediately follow the Second Coming: "See, the Lord is coming with thousands upon thousands of his holy ones to judge everyone" (14-15). As clearly as words can say it, Christ will return to judge everyone—not to reign 1,000 years and then judge everyone.

Its Time Unknown. The ancient Montanists were convinced that the Second Coming would happen so soon that they discouraged marriage and forbade remarriage for the widowed. Other groups and individuals, across the centuries, have also set dates for the Second Coming and have been proven wrong. Martin Luther believed that the Second Coming would happen within a hundred years—a type of date setting.[11] William Miller, who started the Adventists, said it would happen in 1844—and was proven wrong. The Jehovah's Witnesses said it would happen in 1914, and they still say, strangely, that it did happen in that year. Even Billy Graham stated many years ago that he believed the Second Coming would happen within 10 years—and he was proven wrong.

All this date setting, including the setting of a date within a given number of years, is surely unbiblical. According to Jesus, "No one knows about that day or hour, not even the angels in heaven, nor the Son, but only the Father. As it was in the days of Noah, so it will be at the coming of the Son of Man" (Matt. 24:36-37).[12]

---

11. "The last day is at the door, and I believe that the world will not endure a hundred years." Quoted in Hugh Thompson Kerr, Jr., ed., *A Compend of Luther's Theology* (Philadelphia: Westminster Press, 1943), 245.

12. A strange thing occurs in the context of this passage. The passage might refer to the fall of Jerusalem, which took place in A.D. 70, since Jesus says that "this generation will certainly not pass away until all these things have happened" (Matt. 24:34). That event was indeed "the

We cannot date the Second Coming from the signs of its nearness that Scripture mentions—if we assume that the signs of Matthew 24 refer to the Second Coming and not to the fall of Jerusalem. It will occur after the gospel has been preached to all nations (Mark 13:10), but we cannot tell when that has happened or when it has happened to the extent needed. Besides, Scripture often speaks loosely about gospel success. In Mark 16:20, not in any of our early manuscripts, we read that "the disciples went out and preached everywhere." And in Acts 2:5 it is said that "there were staying in Jerusalem God-fearing Jews from every nation under heaven," and not nearly every nation is included when they are enumerated in verses 8-11.

We do not know when the second coming of Christ will occur. Signs of its approach are not very definite, and many of the signs of Matthew 24 are probably signs of the A.D. 70 fall of Jerusalem. In the Father's intention, only He knows. It is ours to be ready, to wait expectantly, to help Christ build His kingdom in the hearts of people in the meantime.

Destiny

Destiny has to do with where we go after our life on earth is over, and what our existence there is to be like. The two places of eternal destiny, for Protestants, are heaven and hell. Roman Catholics generally teach a third destiny, limbo, where unbaptized persons who die in their unaccountable years go. Roman Catholics believe also in purgatory, a temporary place of punishment. Protestants in general believe in the intermediate state, where both the justified and the finally impenitent will await the Judgment (following which, they will enter into either heaven or hell).

Intermediate State. This is the status of everyone, between death and judgment. Jesus said to the thief being crucified with Him, "Today you will be with me in paradise" (Luke 23:43). Paradise, a place where Christ is present, is one biblical name for the place where the righteous go immediately upon their death (see

---

end of the age" (v. 3), for the Temple was then destroyed, and it was the end of hundreds of years of Temple ceremonialism. Indeed, Jesus' "not one stone here will be left on another" (v. 2) seems to refer to the fall of Jerusalem—described by Josephus, who was present during the Roman siege, as an utter destruction.

also 2 Cor. 12:4; Rev. 2:7). The righteous, there, are already in bliss, according to Luke 16:19-31; and for the wicked man in *hadēs* (Hades), not *gehenna* (Gehenna), punishment for sin has already begun.

Purgatory. Roman Catholics believe in this as a place for temporary punishment prior to a person's entrance into heaven. Jerome, in the Latin Vulgate, translated *metanoeite* as "do penance," instead of "repent ye" (Matt. 3:2; Mark 1:15, KJV). This occasioned among Roman Catholics the understanding that doing good works is the gist of repentance. Not believing, therefore, in being justified by faith alone, they teach that people will be punished for lesser sins in the fires of purgatory, and for mortal sins in hell.

Numerous "abuses," as Luther called them, arose in connection with purgatory doctrine. The purchase of indulgences would shorten a person's stay in purgatory, and the purchasers were not required to truly repent.

Annihilationism. This is the belief that the wicked will be punished by extinction. The fourth-century Arnobius is the only father of significance to take this view—saying that the wicked will be punished according to the degree of their wickedness and then annihilated.

A type of annihilationism has been taught in recent times by some of the modernistic personalists such as E. S. Brightman. They taught that some people do not rise, in this life, to the status of persons, and that such people will not continue to exist after this life is over.

Universalism. This is the view that everyone will be redeemed to a state of bliss in the next life. Historically, there have been at least three major kinds of universalism. One is based on the cyclical metaphysical view that everything that comes forth from God will finally return to Him. Plato had taught a cyclical view that influenced even Christian thinkers. What flows out from God must always return to Him. Origen said that the end is always like the beginning, which is to say about the same thing. This form of universalism was taught by John Scotus Erigena, who taught that all of nature (all reality) is divided into four aspects. They are (1) nature that creates and is not created (God as *alpha*); (2) nature that is created and creates (humans); (3) nature that is created and does not create (the physical world); and (4) nature that is uncreated (God as *omega*).[13] In this view, all existence is unified. It is a type of pantheism; and in such views, eternal hell is excluded, all persons becoming redeemed.

Another type of universalism is the Abelardian kind, in which all will be saved because God's love will not allow anything otherwise. As universalist Nels F. S. Ferré liked to say, God has "no permanent problem children."

A third type of universalism is that of Karl Barth (who denied being a universalist). He taught that, because of Christ, God has a "yes" to say to everyone.

The Judgment. With the second coming of Christ, the Judgment will occur—as noted earlier. Then the righteous will be rewarded and the wicked will be punished. It is sometimes called the Great White Throne Judgment because of its description in Rev. 20:12-13:

> And I saw the dead, great and small, standing before the throne, and books were opened. Another book was opened, which is the book of life. The dead were judged according to what they had done as recorded in the books. The sea gave up the dead that were in it, and death and Hades gave up the dead that were in them, and each person was judged according to what he had done.

Both the righteous and the wicked will be there, which is also indicated in Jesus' description of the Judgment in Matt. 25:32-33. Paul implies that all will be there, when he says, "For we must all appear before the judgment seat of Christ, that each one may receive what is due him for the things done while in the body, whether good or bad" (2 Cor. 5:10; see also Isa. 66:16; Jer. 25:31; Joel 3:12; John 12:48; Acts 17:31; Rom. 2:16; Heb. 9:27).

An important function of the Judgment will be to decide degrees of reward and punishment. Another important function will be the transfer of the righteous and the wicked from their respective intermediate states of bliss and torment to the eternal states of heaven and hell.

Hell. The finally impenitent, with degrees of punishment meted out to them at the Judgment according to the gravity of their sins, will be dispatched into the eternal punishment of hell.

---

13. Frederick Copleston, S.J., *Augustine to Scotus*, vol. 2 of *A History of Philosophy* (London: Search Press, 1976), 116.

1. *The clear teaching of Scripture.* The Old Testament is not very clear on this. There the wicked are punished during this life; upon death they go to a lower and more shadowy *sheol* than do the righteous. Perhaps only Daniel, among Old Testament writers, teaches eternal punishment. He says, "Multitudes who sleep in the dust of the earth will awake: some to everlasting life, others to shame and everlasting contempt" (12:2).

But the New Testament speaks clearly about eternal punishment for the wicked dead, and no one teaches it more clearly than Jesus. Except for James (3:6), Jesus is the only one who uses the term *gehenna*—the word for hell that always refers to eternal punishment (see Matt. 5:22, 29, 30; 10:28; 18:9; 23:15, 33; Mark 9:43, 45, 47; Luke 12:5). Jesus also uses other expressions that indicate eternal punishment. In describing the Judgment, He says "the King" will say to the wicked, "Depart from me, you who are cursed, into the eternal fire prepared for the devil and his angels" (Matt. 25:41). He adds, "Then they will go away to eternal punishment, but the righteous to eternal life" (v. 46; see also 8:12; 10:28; 13:41-42; 24:51).

Paul also teaches eternal punishment. Referring to "God's judgment" that immediately follows Christ's return, he says: "He will punish those who do not know God and do not obey the gospel of our Lord Jesus. They will be punished with everlasting destruction and shut out from the presence of the Lord" (2 Thess. 1:5, 8-9; cf. Rom. 2:1-16). And according to John, the wicked enter into the "second death," which is evidently the same as *gehenna,* for it is described as "the lake of fire" (Rev. 20:14). "The second death" implies the irrevocableness of the punishment, although the word "eternal" is not found here.

2. *Arguments against hell and responses.* It is widely argued that the God of love would neither provide nor allow a place of eternal punishment for those who refuse to submit to Him during this life. This, however, sacrifices God's holiness to His love, which Scripture never does. Love does not put the criminal to death, but justice does. To say, therefore, that there is no eternal hell because God is a God of love is to forget two things at least: that He is more basically a God of holiness; and that the holy God is just as well as loving. When infinite holiness is sinned against and grace is refused, justice decrees punishment that is eternal.

Another theological argument often posed against eternal hell is that it is irrational or illogical. That is, it is not reasonable to impose eternal punishment for temporal sin. Yet what is reasonable is not a special interest of Scripture. That one can disobey God for decades and be forgiven in an instant is not reasonable. Buddhism's law of karma is reasonable: all deeds, good and bad, work themselves out to their just moral recompense. Forgiveness of sins is not reasonable, as many other Christian understandings are not: answers to prayer, the efficacy of the sacraments, the virgin conception of Christ, His incarnation, His physical resurrection, our hoped-for resurrection, angels and demons, etc.

Heaven. Those who have died in a redeemed state and those who are living a redeemed life at the time of the Second Coming will enjoy bliss eternally in heaven.

1. *What it will be like.* Except for Revelation, Scripture tells us little about heaven, and much of its description is to be understood symbolically. In Rev. 21:10-27, the "twelve gates," "with twelve angels at the gates" (v. 12), might mean that people will enter it from many directions and backgrounds; the "wall" (v. 14) might mean that not all will be admitted. Its being a "city of pure gold" (v. 18) might mean that it will be a place of rare beauty. It will not have a temple, "because the Lord God Almighty and the Lamb are its temple" (v. 22); and it will not have or need a "sun" or "moon," and "there will be no night," for "the glory of God gives it light" (vv. 23-25). Its being cube-shaped (v. 16) might be a symbolic way of saying that it will be a perfect place.

2. *Activities in heaven.* Scripture teaches clearly that in heaven we will enter into numerous activities—activities that will engage our highest faculties in increasingly enlarged ways, no doubt. For one thing, there will be governmental ministries. The "spirits of righteous men made perfect" (Heb. 12:23) will occupy the "city of the living God" (v. 22), and people are to assist in governing the whole. As Jesus taught, the good servant, who had been "trustworthy in a very small matter" on earth, is to "take charge of ten cities" in heaven (Luke 19:17). The servant who had been given five talents and who had "gained five more" is told: "Well done, good and faithful servant! You have been faithful with a few things; I will put you in charge of many things. Come and share your master's happiness!" (Matt. 25:20-21). Perhaps new songs are to be written and sung in heaven (Rev. 5:9). The "redeemed

from the earth," too, are to learn a "new song" (14:3). So while the redeemed will continually worship God in heaven, perhaps they will worship in part by such activities as these.

3. *Degrees of reward.* While justification is by faith and not by good works, there will be degrees of reward in heaven based on our service record. This is the clear teaching of Scripture. All, on that day, will be judged "according to what they had done as recorded in the books" (Rev. 20:12). Jesus said, "Behold, I am coming soon! My reward is with me, and I will give to everyone according to what he has done" (22:12).

About these rewards, a few observations need to be made. One is that we will no doubt be elated with whatever reward we receive, and the reward will be peculiarly suited to us, adapted for our most intense happiness. Another is that the rewards might not conform to our expectations. For instance, those two women who prayed so that D. L. Moody would come to Britain to evangelize might receive as much reward for the work of that campaign as Moody will. Again, the rewards might be based in part on our capacity for receiving them, and also on what we did in light of our opportunities.

Our redemption will be so complete, and heaven so much filled with love, that the degrees of reward will not be an occasion for envy.

The adage "You can't take it with you" is correct as relates to earthly possessions. Evidently, because of the clear provision for rewards in heaven, and because kings—and presumably others— bring their honor into it, we will be able to take with us varying types of service records.

Last Things as Last Word

On a number of eschatological matters, believers are required to walk by faith, there being no clear teaching in Scripture on them. Yet Scripture is clear on the matter of the last word. It is clear in teaching that the *eschaton* has appeared and that the *eschaton*, the last thing, is in the main Christ, who himself is both the last thing and the last word to be spoken to us by the creating, redeeming, speaking God.

In Old Testament times the not-yet was always in the air. The seers of those times lifted people's wearied eyes to the dawning of a special day, when an ever-widening and deepening river of redemption would flow out from the Temple (see Ezekiel 47) to refresh, replenish, and redeem the responsive in all nations.

Finally, then, in the fullness of time, at our "finest hour," it happened—something that divided all of our remembered past into B.C. and A.D. The *eschaton*, the last thing as the last word, had appeared and had spoken, and we call Him Christ—Jesus Christ.

At present we anticipate Christ's second coming, and we anticipate whatever our good God in His all-power and loving-kindness might wish to lavish upon those made righteous through Christ. But on this side of Bethlehem and Calvary and the emptied tomb and the Ascension, and in the time of His intercession for us at the Father's right hand, the Church does not look for any new word from God. The last word was spoken by Christ—and through the Gospels that narrate the salvific Christ events, through Acts that tells of the early preaching of Christ, and through the Epistles that interpret the meaning of all these things. Aberrant cults may claim new revelations, but Christians know that the last word was spoken when the Word was made flesh and lived among us and died for us and was raised by the Father's mighty power—and when apostles and other eyewitnesses to those events were inspired by the Spirit to write the New Testament Scriptures, adding them to the word of God in the Old Testament. Last things? Yes, with their certainties and their uncertainties. Last word? Yes. By all means, yes. And that is all.

Bibliography
and
Indexes

Bibliography

BOOKS CITED

Aquinas, Thomas. *The Trinity and the Unicity of the Intellect.* Translated by Sister Rose Emmanuell Brennan. St. Louis: Herder, 1946.

Arminius, James. *Works of Arminius.* London: Longman, Green, 1828.

————. *Writings.* Edited and translated by James Nichols and W. R. Bagnall. Reprint, Grand Rapids: Baker Book House, 1956.

Arndt, William, and F. Wilbur Gingrich. *A Greek-English Lexicon of the New Testament.* Chicago: University of Chicago Press, 1957, 1979.

Augustine. *On Christian Doctrine.* Edinburgh: T. and T. Clark, 1892.

Aulén, Gustav. *The Faith of the Christian Church.* Philadelphia: Muhlenberg Press, 1948.

Baab, Otto. *Theology of the Old Testament.* New York: Abingdon-Cokesbury, 1949.

Baillie, John. *The Place of Jesus Christ in Modern Christianity.* New York: Charles Scribner's Sons, 1929.

Barclay, Robert. *An Apology for the True Christian Divinity.* Philadelphia: Friends Society, 1872.

Barclay, William. *Crucified and Crowned.* London: SCM Press, 1961.

Barnette, Henlee. *The Church and the Ecological Crisis.* Grand Rapids: William B. Eerdmans Publishing Co., 1972.

Barr, James. *Biblical Words for Time.* London: SCM Press, 1962.

————. *Fundamentalism.* Philadelphia: Westminster Press, 1977.

Barth, Karl. *Church Dogmatics.* Edited by G. C. Bromiley and T. F. Torrance. Edinburgh: T. and T. Clark, 1936-69.

————. *Church Dogmatics.* Translated by G. T. Thomson. New York: Charles Scribner's Sons, 1955.

————. *Credo.* New York: Charles Scribner's Sons, 1936.

————. *The Resurrection of the Dead.* Translated by H. J. Stenning. London: Hodder and Stoughton, 1933.

Bassett, Paul M., and William M. Greathouse. *The Historical Development.* Vol. 2 of *Exploring Christian Holiness.* Kansas City: Beacon Hill Press of Kansas City, 1984.

Baum, Gregory, ed. *Ecumenical Theology Today.* New York: Paulist Press, 1964.

Bavinck, Herman. *The Doctrine of God.* Translated by William Hendricksen. 1895-99. Reprint, Grand Rapids: Baker Book House, 1951.

————. *Our Reasonable Faith.* Reprint, Grand Rapids: William B. Eerdmans Publishing Co., 1956.

Beckwith, Clarence. *The Idea of God.* New York: Macmillan Publishing Co., 1922.

Belew, P. P. *The Case of Entire Sanctification.* Kansas City: Beacon Hill Press of Kansas City, 1974.

Berkhof, Hendrikus. *Christian Faith.* Grand Rapids: William B. Eerdmans Publishing Co., 1979.

Berkhof, Louis. *Manual of Christian Doctrine.* Grand Rapids: William B. Eerdmans Publishing Co., 1933.

————. *Systematic Theology.* Grand Rapids: William B. Eerdmans Publishing Co., 1930, 1938.

Blackwood, Andrew. *The Prophets: Elijah to Christ.* New York: Fleming H. Revell Co., 1917.

Bloesch, Donald. *Essentials of Evangelical Theology.* New York: Harper and Row, 1979.

————. *A Theology of Word and Spirit.* Downers Grove, Ill.: InterVarsity Press, 1992.

Boardman, W. E. *The Higher Christian Life.* Boston: Henry Hoyt, 1871.

Boettner, Loraine. *The Millennium.* Philadelphia: Presbyterian and Reformed Publishing Co., 1958.

Brandt, Caspar. *The Life of James Arminius.* Translated by John Guthrie. London: Ward and Co., 1858.

Bready, J. Wesley. *This Freedom Whence?* New York: American Tract Society, 1942.

Brightman, Edgar Sheffield. *The Finding of God.* New York: Abingdon Press, 1931.

————. *A Philosophy of Religion.* New York: Prentice-Hall, 1940.

Brockett, Henry. *Scriptural Freedom from Sin.* Kansas City: Nazarene Publishing House, 1941.

Brown, Charles Ewing. *The Meaning of Sanctification.* Anderson, Ind.: Warner Press, 1945.

Brown, William Adams. *Christian Theology in Outline.* New York: Charles Scribner's Sons, 1907.

Browning, Robert A. *Pippa Passes By and Other Poems.* In *The Temple Classics.* London: Dent and Co., 1846.

Bruner, Frederick Dale. *A Theology of the Holy Spirit.* Grand Rapids: William B. Eerdmans Publishing Co., 1970.

Brunner, Emil. *The Divine-Human Encounter.* Philadelphia: Westminster Press, 1943.

————. *The Mediator: A Study of the Central Doctrine of the Christian Faith.* Translated by Olive Wyon. Philadelphia: Westminster Press, 1947.

————. *Reason and Revelation.* Philadelphia: Westminster Press, 1951.

————. *The Theology of Crisis.* New York: Charles Scribner's Sons, 1929.

Bryden, James Davenport. *Letters to Mark.* New York: Harper and Brothers Publishers, 1953.

Bulgakov, Sergius. *The Orthodox Church.* Translated by Elizabeth S. Cram. Edited by Donald A. Lowrie. London: Century Press, 1953.

————. *The Wisdom of God.* London: William and Norgate, 1937.

Bultmann, Rudolf. *Theology of the New Testament.* New York: Charles Scribner's Sons, 1951, 1954.

————. *Theology of the New Testament.* London: SCM Press, 1955.

Buswell, J. Oliver, Jr. *A Systematic Theology of the Christian Religion.* Grand Rapids: Zondervan Publishing House, 1962.

Cadeaux, C. J. *The Historic Mission of Jesus.* New York: Harper and Brothers, 1941.

Caird, C. B. *The Apostolic Age.* London: Gerald Duckworth and Co., 1955.

Calvin, John. *The Institutes of the Christian Religion.* Translated by John Allen. Philadelphia: Presbyterian Board of Publication and Sabbath-School Work, 1813.

———. *The Institutes of the Christian Religion.* Eighth edition. Translated by Henry Beveridge. Grand Rapids: William B. Eerdmans Publishing Co., 1954.

Carlyle, Thomas. *The French Revolution.* New York: Random House, 1934.

Carradine, Beverly. *The Second Blessing in Symbol.* Louisville, Ky.: Picket Publishing Co., 1896.

Cell, George Croft. *A Rediscovery of Wesley.* New York: Henry Holt and Co., 1935.

Chafer, Lewis Sperry. *Systematic Theology.* Dallas: Dallas Theological Seminary, 1947.

Childs, Brevard. *Introduction to the Old Testament as Scripture.* Philadelphia: Fortress Press, 1979.

Clark, Dougan. *The Theology of Holiness.* Boston: McDonald and Gill Co., 1893.

Clarke, Adam. *Christian Theology.* Edited by Samuel Dunn. New York: T. Mason and G. Lane, 1840.

———. *Entire Sanctification.* Louisville, Ky.: Pentecostal Publishing Co., n.d.

———. *Miscellaneous Works.* 13 vols. London: T. Tegg, 1839-45.

———. *The New Testament . . . with Commentary and Critical Notes.* New York: Abingdon-Cokesbury, 1836.

Clarke, J. B. B., ed. *An Account of the Infancy, Religious and Literary Life of Adam Clarke.* 3 vols. London: T. S. Clarke, 1833.

Cobb, John B., Jr. *God and the World.* Philadelphia: Westminster Press, 1969.

Coder, S. Maxwell, and G. Howe. *The Bible, Science, and Creation.* Chicago: Moody Press, 1965.

Coke, Thomas. *The Experience and Spiritual Letters of Mrs. Hester Ann Rogers.* London: Milner and Somerby, n.d.

Commager, Henry Steele. *The American Mind.* New York: Yale University Press, 1950.

Constitution and Discipline for The American Yearly Meetings. New York: The Friend's Book and Tract Committee, 1901.

Cook, Thomas. *New Testament Holiness.* Salem, Ohio: Schmul Publishers, 1978.

Copleston, Frederick, S. J. *Augustine to Scotus.* Vol. 2 of *A History of Philosophy.* London: Search Press, 1976.

Cornhill, Carl Heinrich. *The Prophets of Israel.* Translated by S. F. Corkran. Chicago: Open Court Publishing Co., 1895.

Cox, Leo. *John Wesley's Concept of Perfection.* Kansas City: Beacon Hill Press, 1964.

Cozzens, James. *By Love Possessed.* New York: Harcourt, Brace and Co., 1957.

Cullmann, Oscar. *Christ and Time.* Philadelphia: Westminster Press, 1950.

———. *Immortality.* Edited by T. Penelhum. Belmont, Calif.: Wadsworth Publishing Co., 1973.

Curtis, Olin A. *The Christian Faith.* New York: Eaton and Mains, 1905.

Dayton, Donald W. *Discovering an Evangelical Heritage.* New York: Harper and Row, 1976.

———. *Theological Roots of Pentecostalism.* Grand Rapids: Francis Asbury Press of Zondervan Publishing House, 1987.

Delitzsch, Franz. *A New Commentary on Genesis.* Edinburgh: T. and T. Clark, 1899.

Denney, James. *The Christian Doctrine of Reconciliation.* New York: Hodder and Stoughton, 1917.

————. *Studies in Theology*. Grand Rapids: Baker Book House, 1976.

Dieter, Melvin, et al. *Five Views on Sanctification*. Grand Rapids: Zondervan Publishing House, 1987.

Discipline of Kansas Yearly Meeting of Friends. Wichita, Kans.: Day's Print Shop, 1940.

Dods, Marcus. *Mohammed, Buddha, and Christ*. London: Hodder and Stoughton, 1877.

Drummond, James. *Philo Judeas*. London: Williams and Norgate, 1888.

Dunn, James D. G. *Baptism in the Holy Spirit*. Louisville, Ky.: Westminster/John Knox Press; London: SCM Press, 1970.

Dunning, H. Ray. *Grace, Faith, and Holiness*. Kansas City: Beacon Hill Press of Kansas City, 1988.

Earle, Ralph. *Beacon Bible Commentary*. Kansas City: Beacon Hill Press of Kansas City, 1965.

————. *Meet the Early Church*. Kansas City: Nazarene Publishing House, 1959.

————. *Romans*. Vol. 3 of *Word Meanings in the New Testament*. Kansas City: Beacon Hill Press of Kansas City, 1974.

Eddy, Mary Baker. *Science and Health with Key to the Scriptures*. Boston: Joseph Armstrong, 1934.

Ellyson, E. P. *Bible Holiness*. Kansas City: Beacon Hill Press, 1952.

Farrar, Frederic. *History of Interpretations*. New York: Dutton, 1886.

The Fathers of the Church. New York: Cima Publishing Co., 1947.

Ferré, Nels F. S. *The Christian Faith*. New York: Harper and Brothers, 1942.

————. *The Christian Understanding of God*. New York: Harper and Brothers, 1951.

Filson, Floyd. *Jesus Christ, the Risen Lord*. New York: Abingdon Press, 1956.

Finney, Charles G. *Finney's Systematic Theology*. Edited by J. H. Fairchild. 1846. Reprint, Minneapolis: Bethany Fellowship, 1976.

————. *Lectures on Systematic Theology*. Oberlin, Ohio: James M. Fitche, 1847.

Fisher, George P. *History of the Christian Church*. New York: Charles Scribner's Sons, 1920.

Fiske, John. *Through Nature to God*. Boston: Houghton Mifflin and Co., 1990.

Fletcher, Joseph. *Situation Ethics*. Philadelphia: Westminster Press, 1966.

Florovsky, George. *Bible, Church, Tradition: An Orthodox View*. Belmont, Mass.: Nordland Publishing Co., 1972.

Forsyth, P. T. *The Work of Christ*. London: Independence Press, 1910.

Fuhrmann, Paul T. *An Introduction to the Great Creeds of the Church*. Philadelphia: Westminster Press, 1966.

Galloway, Allan D. *The Cosmic Christ*. New York: Harper and Brothers, 1951.

Geisler, Norman. *Philosophy of Religion*. Grand Rapids: Zondervan Publishing House, 1974.

Godbey, W. B. *Baptism of the Holy Ghost*. Greensboro, N.C.: Apostolic Messenger Office, n.d.

Gordon, George A. *Immortality and the New Theodicy*. New York: Funk and Wagnalls Co., 1899.

Gore, Charles. *The Church and the Ministry*. New York: Macmillan Publishing Co., 1886.

Gould, J. Glenn. *The Whole Counsel of God*. Kansas City: Beacon Hill Press, 1945.

Green, Richard. *John Wesley, Evangelist*. London: Religious Tract Society, 1905.

Grider, J. Kenneth. *Entire Sanctification: The Distinctive Doctrine of Wesleyanism.* Kansas City: Beacon Hill Press of Kansas City, 1980.

Harper, A. F., ed. *Holiness Teaching Today.* Vol. 6 of *Great Holiness Classics.* Kansas City: Beacon Hill Press of Kansas City, 1987.

Hazelton, Roger. *God's Way with Man.* New York: Abingdon Press, 1956.

Hick, John. *Evil and the God of Love.* New York: Harper and Row, 1966.

Hills, A. M. *Fundamental Christian Theology: A Systematic Theology.* 2 vols. Pasadena, Calif.: C. J. Kinne, 1931.

————. *Pentecost Rejected and the Effects on the Churches.* Cincinnati: Office of God's Revivalist, 1902.

————. *Scriptural Holiness and Keswick Teaching Compared.* Salem, Ohio: Schmul Publishing Co., 1983.

Hocking, William Ernest. *The Meaning of God in Human Experience.* New Haven, Conn.: Yale University Press, 1912.

Hodge, Charles. *Systematic Theology.* Grand Rapids: William B. Eerdmans Publishing Co., n.d.

Hoernle, R. F. Alfred. *Matters, Life, Mind, and God.* New York: Harcourt, Brace and Co., 1922.

Howard, Richard E. *Newness of Life: A Study in the Thought of Paul.* Kansas City: Beacon Hill Press of Kansas City, 1975.

Inge, W. R., et al. *Contentio Veritatis.* London: J. Murray, 1902.

Irenaeus. *Against Heresies.* Vols.1-5. Translated by Alexander Roberts and W. H. Rambaut. Edinburgh: T. and T. Clark, 1919.

James, William. *A Pluralistic Universe.* London: Longmans, Green and Co., 1909.

————. *Some Problems of Philosophy.* London: Longmans, Green and Co., 1924.

Joad, C. E. M. *God and Evil.* New York: Harpers, 1943.

Jones, E. Stanley. *Christ and Human Suffering.* New York: Abingdon Press, 1933.

Kendall, R. T. *Calvin and English Calvinism to 1649.* London: Oxford University Press, 1979.

Kierkegaard, Søren. *The Concept of Dread.* Translated by Walter Lowrie. Princeton, N.J.: Princeton University Press, 1944.

————. *Either/Or: A Fragment of Life.* Translated by David F. Swenson and Lillian Marvin Swenson. Princeton, N.J.: Princeton University Press; London: Oxford University Press, 1944.

————. *Fear and Trembling.* Translated by Walter Lowrie. Princeton, N.J.: Princeton University Press, 1941.

————. *Purity of Heart Is to Will One Thing: Spiritual Preparation for the Feast of Confession.* Translated by Douglas V. Steer. New York: Harper and Brothers, 1958.

Kirkpatrick, A. F. *The Doctrine of Israel.* Translated by S. F. Corkran. Chicago: Open Court Publishing Co., 1895.

————. *The Doctrine of the Prophets.* New York: Macmillan Publishing Co., 1907.

Knight, G. A. F. *A Biblical Approach to the Doctrine of the Trinity.* Edinburgh: Oliver and Boyd, 1953.

Knudson, A. C. *The Beacon Lights of Prophecy.* New York: Eaton and Mains, 1914.

————. *Principles of Christian Ethics.* New York: Abingdon-Cokesbury, 1943.

————. *Religious Ideas for the Old Testament.* New York: Abingdon Press, 1918

————. *The Religous Teaching of the Old Testament.* New York: Abingdon Press, 1918.

Krutch, Joseph Wood. *The Modern Temper.* New York: Harcourt, Brace and Co., 1929.

Kung, Hans. *The Church.* New York: Sheed and Ward, 1967.

Ladd, George Eldon. *A Theology of the New Testament.* Grand Rapids: William B. Eerdmans Publishing Co., 1974.

Lange, John Peter. *Commentary on Holy Scripture: Genesis, Exodus, Leviticus, and Numbers.* Grand Rapids: Zondervan Publishing House, n.d.

Lawson, John. *Introduction to Christian Doctrine.* Wilmore, Ky.: Asbury Press, 1980.

Leith, John. *Creeds of the Churches.* Richmond, Va.: John Knox Press, 1973.

Lewis, C. S. *Miracles.* New York: Macmillan Publishing Co., 1947.

———. *The Problem of Pain.* New York: Macmillan Publishing Co., 1945.

Lewis, Edwin. *The Creator and the Adversary.* New York: Abingdon-Cokesbury Press, 1948.

———. *Jesus Christ and the Human Quest.* New York: Abingdon Press, 1924.

———. *A Philosophy of the Christian Revelation.* New York: Harper and Row, 1940.

A Library of Fathers of the Holy Catholic Church. 41 vols. London: Rivingtons, 1844.

Lindsay, A. D. *Socrates' Discourses.* New York: E. P. Dutton, 1933.

Lindsell, Harold. *The Battle for the Bible.* Grand Rapids: Zondervan Publishing House, 1976.

Lindsey, Hal. *Satan Is Alive and Well on Planet Earth.* New York: Bantam Books, 1974.

Lindström, Harald. *Wesley and Sanctification.* London: Epworth Press, 1946.

Little, Paul E. *Know Why You Believe.* Downers Grove, Ill.: InterVarsity Press, 1973.

Lowry, Charles W. *The Trinity and Christian Devotion.* New York: Harper and Brothers, 1946.

Machen, J. Gresham. *The Virgin Birth of Christ.* London: J. Clarke, 1958.

Mackintosh, H. R. *The Doctrine of the Person of Jesus Christ.* New York: Charles Scribner's Sons, 1912.

MacLaren, Alexander. *Exposition of Holy Scripture: Genesis et al.* Grand Rapids: William B. Eerdmans Publishing Co., 1944.

MacLeish, Archibald. *J. B.* Boston: Houghton Mifflin Co., 1946.

Mahan, Asa. *The Baptism of the Holy Ghost.* New York: W. C. Palmer, Publisher, 1882.

Manual of the Church of the Nazarene. Kansas City: Nazarene Publishing House, 1980.

Marney, Carlyle. *Faith in Conflict.* New York: Abingdon Press, 1957.

Marshall, I. Howard. *Grace Unlimited.* Edited by Clark H. Pinnock. Minneapolis: Bethany Fellowship, 1975.

Martin, Alfred W. *Great Religious Teachers of the East.* New York: Macmillan Publishing Co., 1911.

McCown, Wayne, and James Massey, ed. *God's Word for Today.* Anderson, Ind.: Warner Press, 1982.

McDonald, William. *Another Comforter.* Boston: McDonald, Gill, 1890.

McKenzie, John L. *Second Isaiah.* In *The Anchor Bible.* Garden City, N.Y.: Doubleday and Co., 1968.

Metz, Donald S. *Studies in Biblical Holiness.* Kansas City: Beacon Hill Press of Kansas City, 1971.

Miley, John. *The Atonement in Christ.* New York: Hunt and Eaton, 1889.

———. *Systematic Theology.* New York: Eaton and Mains, 1892.

Moltmann, Jürgen. *The Theology of Hope*. Translated by James Leitch. New York: Harper and Row, 1967.

Moore, John M. *Methodism in Belief and Action*. New York: Abingdon-Cokesbury Press, 1946.

Morrison, H. C. *Baptism with the Holy Ghost*. Louisville, Ky.: Pentecostal Publishing Co., 1900.

Moulton, J. H. *Prolegomena*. Vol. 1 of *A Grammar of the New Testament Greek*. Edinburgh: T. and T. Clark, 1906.

Muller, J. A. *Apostle of China: Samuel Issac Joseph Schereschewsky*. New York: Morehouse Publishing Co., 1937.

Muller, Julius. *The Christian Doctrine of Sin*. Edinburgh: T. and T. Clark, 1885.

Niebuhr, Reinhold. *The Nature and Destiny of Man*. New York: Charles Scribner's Sons, 1941-43.

Niebuhr, Richard. *The Meaning of Revelation*. New York: Macmillan Co., 1941.

North, Eric. *The Book of a Thousand Tongues*. New York: Harper, 1938.

Orchard, William Edwin. *Foundations of Faith*. New York: George H. Doran Co., 1924.

Orr, James. *The Bible Under Trial*. London: Marshall, 1907.

————. *The Progress of Dogma*. London: Hodder and Stoughton, 1897.

————. *The Virgin Birth of Christ*. New York: Charles Scribner's Sons, 1907.

Otto, Rudolph. *The Idea of the Holy*. London: Oxford University Press, 1923.

Pannenberg, Wolfhart. *Jesus—God and Man*. Translated by Lewis L. Wilkins and Duane A. Priebe. London: SCM Press, 1968.

Parker, Dewitt H., ed. *Schopenhauer Selections*. New York: Charles Scribner's Sons, 1928.

Paterson, John. *The Godly Fellowship of the Prophets*. New York: Charles Scribner's Sons, 1948.

Pelikan, Jaroslav, ed. *Luther's Works*. St. Louis: Concordia Publishing House, 1958.

Plato. *The Republic*. Translated by F. M. Cornford. New York: University Press, 1945.

Pope, Alexander. *Essay on Man*. Edited by Mark Pattison. Oxford: Clarendon Press, 1904.

Pringle-Pattison, Andrew Seth. *The Idea of God in the Light of Recent Philosophy*. Revised edition. Millwood, N.Y.: Kraus, 1920.

Pun, Pattle P. T. *Evolution: Nature and Scripture in Conflict?* Grand Rapids: Zondervan Publishing House, 1982.

Purkiser, W. T. *The Biblical Foundations*. Vol. 1 of *Exploring Christian Holiness*. Kansas City: Beacon Hill Press of Kansas City, 1983.

————. *Conflicting Concepts of Holiness*. Kansas City: Beacon Hill Press, 1953.

————. *Exploring Our Christian Faith*. Kansas City: Beacon Hill Press, 1960.

————. *Sanctification and Its Synonyms: Studies in the Biblical Theology of Holiness*. Kansas City: Beacon Hill Press, 1961.

Purkiser, W. T., Richard S. Taylor, and Willard H. Taylor. *God, Man, and Salvation: A Biblical Theology*. Kansas City: Beacon Hill Press of Kansas City, 1977.

Rahner, Karl. *The Trinity*. New York: Seabury, 1974.

Rall, Harris Franklin. *Christianity*. New York: Charles Scribner's Sons, 1944.

Ramm, Bernard. *The Christian View of Science and Scripture*. Grand Rapids: William B. Eerdmans Publishing Co., 1955.

560 ◁ A WESLEYAN-HOLINESS THEOLOGY

Rauschenbusch, Walter. *Christianity and the Social Order.* New York: Macmillan Publishing Co., 1907.

Reid, W. Stanford, ed. *John Calvin: His Influence in the Western World.* Grand Rapids: Zondervan Publishing House, 1982.

Richardson, Alan. *An Introduction to the Theology of the New Testament.* New York: Harper and Row, 1958.

Richardson, Cyril C. *The Doctrine of the Trinity.* New York: Abingdon Press, 1958.

Robertson, A. T., and W. H. Davis. *A New Short Grammar of the Greek New Testament.* New York: Richard S. Smith, 1931.

Robinson, H. Wheeler. *The Christian Doctrine of Man.* Edinburgh: T. and T. Clark, 1911.

————. *Suffering: Human and Divine.* New York: Macmillan Publishing Co., 1939.

Robinson, J. A. T. *In the End, God.* New York: Harper and Row, 1950.

————. *Redating the New Testament.* Philadelphia: Westminster Press, 1976.

Robinson, T. H. *The Poetry of the Old Testament.* London: Gerald Duckworth and Co., 1947.

Robinson, William. *The Biblical Doctrine of the Church.* St. Louis: Bethany Press, 1948.

Rogers, Jack. *Confessions of a Conservative Evangelical.* Philadelphia: Westminster Press, 1974.

Rowley, H. H. *Submission in Suffering.* Cardiff, Wales: University of Wales Press, 1951.

Rust, E. C. *Nature and Man in Biblical Thought.* London: Lutterworth Press, 1953.

Ruth, C. W. *Bible Readings on the Second Blessing.* Salem, Mass.: Convention Book Store, 1905.

————. *Entire Sanctification.* Kansas City: Nazarene Publishing House, 1939.

Sanders, James A. *Torah and Canon.* Philadelphia: Fortress Press, 1972.

Schaff, Philip. *Creeds of Christendom.* 3 vols. Reprint, Grand Rapids: Baker Book House, 1977.

————. *Creeds of the Churches.* Richmond, Va.: John Knox Press, 1973.

————. *History of the Christian Church.* Grand Rapids: William B. Eerdmans Publishing Co., 1949.

Schleiermacher, Friedrich. *The Christian Faith.* Translated by H. R. Mackintosh and J. S. Stewart. Philadelphia: Fortress Press, 1928.

Schweizer, Eduard. *Theological Dictionary of the New Testament.* Edited by Gerhard Friedrich Kittel. Translated by Geoffrey W. Bromiley. Grand Rapids: William B. Eerdmans Publishing Co., 1971.

Shedd, W. G. T. *Dogmatic Theology.* 3 vols. Second edition, New York: Charles Scribner's Sons, 1899.

Smith, C. Ryder. *The Bible Doctrine of Sin and the Ways of God with Sinners.* London: Epworth Press, 1953.

————. *The Sacramental Society.* London: Epworth Press, 1927.

Smith, Hannah Whitall. *The Christian's Secret of a Happy Life.* Westwood, N.J.: Fleming H. Revell Co., n.d.

Smith, Timothy L. *Called unto Holiness.* Vol. 1. Kansas City: Beacon Hill Press, 1962.

————. *Revivalism and Social Reform in Mid-Nineteenth Century America.* New York: Abingdon Press, 1957.

Snaith, Norman H. *The Distinctive Ideas of the Old Testament.* New York: Schocken Books, 1964.

Spinoza, Benedict de. *Philosophy of Benedict de Spinoza.* Translated by R. H. M. Elwes. New York: Tudor Publishing Co., 1933.

Stauffer, Ethelbert. *New Testament Theology.* New York: Macmillan Publishing Co., 1955.

Steele, Daniel. *Love Enthroned.* Apollo, Tenn.: West Publishing Co., 1951.

———. *Milestone Papers.* New York: Eaton and Mains, 1878.

Strong, Augustus H. *Systematic Theology.* Philadelphia: Griffith and Rowland Press, 1907.

Stroup, N. W. *The Fact of Sin.* New York: Eaton and Mains, 1908.

Taylor, Richard S. *Biblical Authority and Christian Faith.* Kansas City: Beacon Hill Press of Kansas City, 1980.

———. *Life in the Spirit.* Kansas City: Beacon Hill Press of Kansas City, 1966.

———. *A Right Conception of Sin.* Kansas City: Beacon Hill Press, 1939.

———. *The Theological Formulation.* Vol. 3 of *Exploring Christian Holiness.* Kansas City: Beacon Hill Press of Kansas City, 1985.

Taylor, Vincent. *The Historical Evidence for the Virgin Birth.* Oxford: Clarendon Press, 1920.

Temple, William. *Nature, Man, and God.* New York: AMS Press, 1979.

Tennant, F. R. *The Sources of the Doctrines of the Fall and Original Sin.* New York: Schocken Books, 1968.

Terrian, Samuel. *The Psalms and Their Meaning for Today.* New York: Bobbs-Merrill Co., 1952.

Terry, Milton Spenser. *Biblical Dogmatics.* New York: Eaton and Mains; Cincinnati: Jennings and Graham, 1907.

Tertullian. *Against Praxeas.* Translated by A. Souter. New York: Macmillan Publishing Co., 1920.

Thayer, Joseph H., trans. *Greek-English Lexicon of the New Testament.* Grand Rapids: Zondervan Publishing House, n.d.

Thiessen, Henry C. *Lectures in Systematic Theology.* Grand Rapids: William B. Eerdmans Publishing Co., 1979.

Thompson, Archibald, ed. *Select Writings and Letters of Athanasius.* In *A Select Library of Nicene and Post-Nicene Fathers of the Christian Church.* Oxford: Parker and Co., 1892.

Thompson, Ralph. *A Contemporary Wesleyan Theology.* Edited by Charles W. Carter. Grand Rapids: Francis Asbury Press of Zondervan Publishing House, 1983.

Thornton, Lionel S. *The Common Life in the Body of Christ.* London: Dacre Press, 1942.

———. *Revelation and the Modern World.* London: Dacre Press, 1950.

Tillich, Paul. *Biblical Religion and the Search for Ultimate Reality.* Chicago: University of Chicago Press, 1955.

———. *The New Being.* New York: Charles Scribner's Sons, 1955.

———. *The Protestant Era.* Translated by James Luther Adams. Chicago: University of Chicago Press, 1948.

———. *Systematic Theology.* 3 vols. Chicago: University of Chicago Press, 1951-63.

Toland, John. *Christianity Not Mysterious.* 1696. Reprint, New York: Garland Publishing, 1978.

Torrance, T. F. *Royal Priesthood.* Edinburgh: Oliver and Boyd, 1955.

Tsanoff, Radoslav A. *The Nature of Evil.* New York: Macmillan Publishing Co., 1931.

Turner, George Allen. *Christian Holiness.* Kansas City: Beacon Hill Press of Kansas City, 1977.

————. *The Vision Which Transforms.* Kansas City: Beacon Hill Press, 1964.

Van Dyke, Henry. *The Gospel for a World of Sin.* New York: Macmillan Publishing Co., 1899.

Vine, W. E. *Vine's Expository Dictionary of Old and New Testament Words.* Old Tappan, N.J.: Fleming H. Revell Co., 1981.

Walker, Alan. *The Many-Sided Cross of Jesus.* New York: Abingdon Press, 1962.

Walker, Edward F. *Sanctify Them.* Revised by J. Kenneth Grider. Kansas City: Beacon Hill Press of Kansas City, 1968.

Watson, George D. *A Holiness Manual.* Boston: Christian Witness Co., 1882.

Wesley, John. *The Doctrine of Original Sin.* New York: J. Soule and T. Mason, 1817.

————. *Explanatory Notes upon the New Testament.* London: Epworth Press, 1941.

————. *The Journal of the Rev. John Wesley, A.M.* Edited by Nehemiah Curnock. 8 vols. London: Epworth Press, 1938.

————. *The Letters of the Rev. John Wesley.* Edited by John Telford. London: Epworth Press, 1941.

————. *A Plain Account of Christian Perfection.* Kansas City: Beacon Hill Press, 1950.

Whale, John S. *The Christian Answer to the Problem of Evil.* London: Student Christian Movement Press, 1936.

————. *Christian Doctrine.* Cambridge: Cambridge University Press; New York: Macmillan Publishing Co., 1941.

White, Stephen S. *Eradication Defined, Explained, Authenticated.* Kansas City: Beacon Hill Press, 1954.

————. *Essential Christian Beliefs.* Kansas City: Nazarene Publishing House, 1940.

————. *Five Cardinal Elements in the Doctrine of Entire Sanctification.* Kansas City: Beacon Hill Press, 1948.

Wiley, H. Orton. *Christian Theology.* 3 vols. Kansas City: Beacon Hill Press, 1940-43.

————. *The Epistle to the Hebrews.* Kansas City: Beacon Hill Press, 1959.

Williams, R. T. *Temptation: A Neglected Theme.* Kansas City: Beacon Hill Press, 1920.

Wood, J. A. *Perfect Love.* New York: Office of the Methodist Home Journal, 1861. Revised editions, Pasadena, Calif.: John A. Wood; Chicago: S. K. J. Chesbro, 1880.

Wright, George Ernest. *God Who Acts.* Chicago: H. Regnery, 1952.

Wynkoop, Mildred. *A Theology of Love: The Dynamic of Wesleyanism.* Kansas City: Beacon Hill Press of Kansas City, 1972.

Young, Davis A. *Christianity and the Age of the Earth.* Grand Rapids: Zondervan Publishing House, 1982.

Young, E. J. *Studies in Genesis.* Philadelphia: Presbyterian and Reformed Publishing Co., 1964.

ARTICLES CITED

Arnett, William. "Predestination." In *Beacon Dictionary of Theology.* Edited by Richard S. Taylor. Kansas City: Beacon Hill Press of Kansas City, 1984.

Bangs, Carl. "James Arminius: Christian Scholar. Three Basic Principles of Arminius." *Herald of Holiness,* Oct. 5, 1960.

Barth, Karl. "The Living Congregation of the Living Lord Jesus Christ." In *Man's Disorder and God's Design: The Amsterdam Assembly Series*. New York: Harper and Row, 1948.

Bresee, Phineas. "Baptism with the Holy Ghost." In *The Double Cure*. Edited by William Nast. Chicago: Christian Witness Co., 1894.

Brunner, Emil. "Christian Doctrine of God." In *Dogmatics*. Translated by Olive Wyon. Philadelphia: Westminster Press, 1950.

Bultmann, Rudolf. "New Testament and Mythology." In *Kerygma and Myth*. Edited by Hans Bartsch. Translated by R. F. Fuller. London: Society for Promoting Christian Knowledge, 1953.

Carver, Frank. "Biblical Foundations for the 'Secondness' of the Entire Sanctification." *Wesleyan Theological Journal* 22:2 (Fall 1987).

Craig, Clarence Tucker. "The Church of the New Testament." In *Man's Disorder and God's Design: The Amsterdam Assembly Series*. New York: Harper and Row, 1948.

————. "The First Epistle to the Corinthians: Introduction and Exegesis." In *Interpreter's Bible*. Edited by George A. Buttrick. Nashville: Abingdon Press, 1953.

Dayton, Donald W. "The Doctrine of the Baptism of the Spirit: Its Emergence and Significance." *Wesleyan Theological Journal* 13 (Spring 1978).

Dayton, Wilbur T. "Initial Sanctification and Its Concomitants." In *The Word and the Doctrine*. Compiled by Kenneth E. Geiger. Kansas City: Beacon Hill Press, 1965.

DeMent, Byron H. "Repentance." In *International Standard Bible Encyclopedia*. Edited by James Orr. Grand Rapids: William B. Eerdmans Publishing Co., 1955.

Dunning, H. Ray. "Santification—Ceremony vs. Ethics." *The Preacher's Magazine*, Fall 1979.

Eager, George B. "Harlot." In *International Standard Bible Encyclopedia*. Chicago: Howard-Severance Co., 1915.

Earle, Ralph. "The Acts of the Apostles." In *The Evangelical Commentary*. Grand Rapids: Zondervan Publishing House, 1959.

————. "Mark." In *Evangelical Commentary*. Grand Rapids: Zondervan Publishing House, 1957.

Geden, A. S. "Buddha." In Vol. 2 of *Encyclopaedia of Religion and Ethics*. Edited by James Hastings. Edinburgh: T. and T. Clark, 1909.

Grider, J. Kenneth. "Ezekiel." In *Beacon Bible Commentary*. Kansas City: Beacon Hill Press of Kansas City, 1966.

Grosheide, F. W. "Commentary on the First Epistle to the Corinthians." In *New International Commentary on the New Testament*. Grand Rapids: William B. Eerdmans Publishing Co., 1953.

Hellengers, Andre E. "Fetal Development." *Theological Studies* 31 (March 1970).

Hitching, Francis. "Where Darwin Went Wrong." *Reader's Digest*, Far East Edition, Oct. 1982.

Hynson, Leon. "The Kingdom of God in the Theology of John Wesley." *Wesleyan Theological Journal* 23:1-2 (Spring-Fall 1988).

Kantzer, Kenneth S. "Stoics." In *Baker's Dictionary of Theology*. Edited by E. F. Harrison. Grand Rapids: Baker Book House, 1960.

Knight, John A. "John Fletcher's Influence on the Development of Wesleyan Theology in America." *Wesleyan Theological Journal* 13 (Spring 1978).

Maddox, Randy. "The Use of the Aorist Tense in Holiness Exegesis." *Wesleyan Theological Journal* 16 (Fall 1981).

Mannes, Marya. "A Woman Views Abortion." In *The Case for Legalized Abortion Now.* Edited by Allan F. Guttmacher. Berkeley, Calif.: Diablo Press, 1967.

McClurkan, J. O. *Zion's Outlook* 7 (Feb. 1901).

McGonigle, Herbert. *Wesleyan Theological Journal* 8 (Spring 1973).

Moody, Howard. "Abortion: Woman's Right and Legal Problems." *Christianity and Crisis* 31 (Mar. 8, 1971): 27.

Mullen, Wilbur H. "John Wesley and Liberal Religion." *Religion in Life,* Autumn 1966.

Napier, Davie. "The Problem of the Dark." *The Pulpit,* Nov. 1958.

Pannenberg, Wolfhart. "Appearance as the Arrival of the Future." In *New Theology No. 5.* Edited by Martin Marty and Dean Peerman. New York: Macmillan Publishing Co., 1968.

Peck, George. "Christian Perfection." *Methodist Quarterly Review.* New York: G. Lane and P. P. Sanford, 1841.

Pittenger, Norman. "A Theological Approach to Understanding Homosexuality." *Religion in Life* 43 (Winter 1974).

Ramm, Bernard. "Contemporary Theology and 'Church Material.'" *Christianity Today* 16 (Aug. 11, 1972).

Schopenhauer, Arthur. "On Suicide." In *The Works of Schopenhauer.* Edited by Will Durant. New York: Simon and Schuster, 1928.

Smith, S. S. "Power from on High." *Guide to Perfection.* Edited by Timothy Meritt and D. S. King. Boston: T. Meritt and D. S. King, 1840-41.

Taylor, Willard. "The Baptism with the Holy Spirit: Promise of Grace or Judgment?" *Wesleyan Theological Journal* 12 (Spring 1977).

Warfield, B. B. "On the Antiquity and the Unity of the Human Race." In *Biblical and Theological Studies.* Philadelphia: Presbyterian and Reformed Publishing Co., reprinted 1952.

Wesley, John. "On Predestination." In *The Works of the Rev. John Wesley.* Grand Rapids: Baker Book House, 1979.

———. "On Sin in Believers." In *Four Sermons by Wesley.* London: Wesleyan Methodist Book Room, n.d.

Wright, G. Ernest. "The Faith of Israel." In *The Interpreter's Bible.* Vol. 1. Edited by George A. Buttrick. Nashville: Abingdon Press, 1952-53.

UNPUBLISHED WORKS CITED

Gaddis, Merill E. "Christian Perfectionism in America." Ph.D. dissertation. University of Chicago, 1929.

Johnson, Andy. "The Instantaneousness of Entire Sanctification." A term paper not in any library. June 1988.

Strickland, William. "John Goodwin." Ph.D. dissertation. Vanderbilt University, 1967.

Taylor, Willard H. Ph.D. dissertation for Northwestern University on flesh and Spirit, lodged in Nazarene Theological Seminary Library.

Winget, Wilfred. "The Significance of Blood in Atonenment." Thesis. Nazarene Theological Seminary, 1955.

Subject Index

Persons Index

575

Scripture References Index